Lecture Notes
in Business Information Processing

358

Rim Jallouli · Mohamed Anis Bach Tobji ·
Deny Bélisle · Sehl Mellouli ·
Farid Abdallah · Ibrahim Osman (Eds.)

Digital Economy

Emerging Technologies and Business Innovation

4th International Conference, ICDEc 2019
Beirut, Lebanon, April 15–18, 2019
Proceedings

Springer

Editors
Rim Jallouli ⓘ
ESEN, University of Manouba
Manouba, Tunisia

Mohamed Anis Bach Tobji ⓘ
ESEN, University of Manouba
Manouba, Tunisia

Deny Bélisle
Université de Sherbrooke
Sherbrooke, QC, Canada

Sehl Mellouli
Université Laval
Quebec, QC, Canada

Farid Abdallah
International University of Beirut
Mazraa, Lebanon

Ibrahim Osman
American University of Beirut
Beirut, Lebanon

ISSN 1865-1348   ISSN 1865-1356   (electronic)
Lecture Notes in Business Information Processing
ISBN 978-3-030-30873-5   ISBN 978-3-030-30874-2   (eBook)
https://doi.org/10.1007/978-3-030-30874-2

This Springer imprint is published by the registered company Springer Nature Switzerland AG
The registered company address is: Gewerbestrasse 11, 6330 Cham, Switzerland

Preface

The telecommunication and the computer engineering fields offer new opportunities with the ease of connectivity, the relative low cost of connecting devices, the communication infrastructure, and also data analysis and approaches of processing data. Therefore, many reports and scientific papers published in the last decade aim to define the boundaries of the digital economy, and highlight its role in creating value for individuals, organizations, and business. The emerging technologies have drawn a lot of attention from the business community as there are numerous and increasing innovative tools that guide managers and orient the firm's strategic decisions.

The International Conference on Digital Economy (ICDEc) was founded in 2016 to discuss innovative research and projects related to the supporting role of information system technologies in the digital transformation process, business innovation, and e-commerce.

The fourth edition took place at the International University of Beirut, Lebanon during April, 15–18, 2019. The theme of ICDEc 2019 was "Digital Economy: Emerging Technologies and Business Innovation." ICDEc 2019 offered a number of sessions discussing the digital transformation and empowerment, digital business models, innovative research in data science and intelligent systems, e-commerce, e-learning, e-finance, data protection, social media communication, and digital marketing.

The papers submitted to the ICDEc 2019 competitive sessions were reviewed using a double-blind peer-review process. Each paper received between two and six reviews; the average was 3.38 reviews per paper. 31 papers were selected with the help of PhD researches and distinguished professors in the fields of computer science and business innovation. The Program Committee members were from about 30 universities around the world. We express our appreciation for their contribution to the reviewing process.

All participants to ICDEc 2019 were invited to benefit of the insightful keynote speeches on "The Fake News Mechanisms: When the Web Goes Wrong," "Digital Business Models," and "General Data Protection Regulation," given respectively by Dr. Stefan B. Bazan, Dr. Nizar Abdelkafi, and Dr. Mona Al Achkar Jabbour, to whom we express our gratitude. In addition, the participants enjoyed the cultural journey inside Geita Grotto (Lebanon's natural wonder), the social events (the welcoming reception and the Gala Dinner), as well as the regular scientific sessions where authors presented and debated their contributions.

We express our deepest gratitude to the country chairs, the Organization and Finance Committees, as well as the Scientific and Program Committees for their support in making this conference successful. Special thanks go to the sponsors and scientific partners of the conference, mainly the International University of Beirut BIU for hosting ICDEc 2019.

The intended audience of this book will mainly consist of researchers and practitioners in the following domains: information system technologies, computer science, data science, intelligent systems, digital business models, digital marketing, and e-learning.

May 2019

Rim Jallouli
Mohamed Anis Bach Tobji
Deny Bélisle
Sehl Mellouli
Farid Abdallah
Ibrahim Osman

Organization

General Co-chairs

Farid Abdallah   International University of Beirut, Lebanon
Ibrahim Osman   American University of Beirut, Lebanon

Program Committee Co-chairs

Deny Bélisle   Université de Sherbrooke, Canada
Sehl Mellouli   Université Laval, Canada

Advisory Board

Olfa Nasraoui   University of Louisville, USA
Anton Nijholt   University of Twente, The Netherlands
Yamen Koubaa   France Business School, France
Rhouma Rhouma   College of Applied Sciences, Oman

Steering Committee

Mohamed Anis Bach Tobji   University of Tunis, Tunisia
Rim Jallouli   University of Manouba, Tunisia

Organization Committee Chair

Mohammad Makki   International University of Beirut, Lebanon

Organization Committee

Rania Baltagi   International University of Beirut, Lebanon
Jaafar Berro   International University of Beirut, Lebanon
Zeina Haidar   International University of Beirut, Lebanon
Chayma Maatougui   Tunisian Association of Digital Economy, Tunisia
Laila Manasfi   International University of Beirut, Lebanon
Assala Ollaik   International University of Beirut, Lebanon
Wael Salloum   International University of Beirut, Lebanon
Lina Shouman   International University of Beirut, Lebanon
Abeer Tabet   International University of Beirut, Lebanon

Publication Chair

Meriam Belkhir   University of Sfax, Tunisia

IT Chair

Nassim Bahri   One Way IT, Tunisia

Junior Committee

Ons Aouedi   University of Manouba, Tunisia
Rihab Melki   TANIT WEB, Tunisia
Salma Mzoughi   University of Manouba, Tunisia

Program Committee

Ajith Abraham   Machine Intelligence Research Labs, USA
Loubna Al-Saghir Oueidat   Saint Joseph University of Beirut, Lebanon
Zeyad Alfawaer   University of Damman, Saudi Arabia
Raouia Ayachi   University of Tunis, Tunisia
Wadiaa Bahrini   University of Manouba, Tunisia
Stuart Barnes   King's College London, UK
Stéphane Bazan   Saint-Joseph University of Beirut, Lebanon
Adel Ben Taziri   The Virtual University of Tunis, Tunisia
Rami Belkaroui   University of Tunis, Tunisia
Sarra Ben Abbès   University Paris 13, France
Alexandre Benoit   Université de Savoie, France
Bastien Bodenstein   Fraunhofer IMW, Germany
Rim Boudali Methamem   University of Carthage, Tunisia
Amani Boussaada   University of Tunis El Manar, Tunisia
Altan Cakir   Istanbul Technical University, Turkey
Qiushi Cao   INSA Rouen, France
Yousra Chabchoub   ISEP, France
Ismahene Chahbi   University of Manouba, Tunisia
Mouna Chebbah   University of Manouba, Tunisia
Lilia Cheniti   University of Sousse, Tunisia
Soumaya Cheikhrouhou   Université de Sherbrooke, Canada
Juan Manuel Corchado   University of Salamanca, Spain
Mouna Dammak   University of Sfax, Tunisia
Faiza Djidjekh   University of Biskra, Algeria
Olfa Dridi Mekni   University of Bizerte, Tunisia
Mariem El Ghali   University of Manouba, Tunisia
Nabila El Jed   University of Manouba, Tunisia
Jihene El Ouakdi   University of Manouba, Tunisia
Frank Emmert-Streib   Tampere University of Technology, Finland
Yamna Ettarres   University of Manouba, Tunisia
Imen Fourati   University of Tunis El Manar, Tunisia
Zied Ftiti   EDC Business School, France
Cherif Ghazel   University of Manouba, Tunisia
Dorra Guermazi   University of Manouba, Tunisia

Hassène Gritli	University Tunis El Manar, Tunisia
Safa Kaabi	University of Manouba, Tunisia
Benjamin Klement	Fraunhofer IMW, Germany
Aymen Haj Kacem	University of Tunis, Tunisia
Payam Hanafizadeh	Allameh Tabataba'i University, Iran
Abdallah Handoura	College of Telecom & Information, Saudi Arabia
Nizar Hariri	Université Saint-Joseph de Beyrouth, Lebanon
Sarah Hariri Haykal	Saint Joseph University of Beirut, Lebanon
Reaan Immelman	ABSA Group Limited, South Africa
Dyah Ismoyowati	Universitas Gadjah Mada, Indonesia
Hela Khemakhem	University of Sfax, Tunisia
Maher Kooli	Université du Québec, Canada
Hasna Koubaa	University of Manouba, Tunisia
Nadia Labidi	Sup'Com, Tunisia
Stéphane Legendre	Université de Sherbrooke, Canada
Dhouha Maater	University of Manouba, Tunisia
Vincenzo Maltese	University of Trento, Italy
Thouraya Mellah	University of Manouba, Tunisia
Yosra Miaoui	University of Carthage, Tunisia
Elaine Mosconi	Université de Sherbrooke, Canada
Ines Moussa	Sup'Com, Tunisia
Anis Naanaa	University Tunis El Manar, Tunisia
Hayfa Nakouri	University of Manouba, Tunisia
Klimis Ntalianis	University of West Attica, Greece
Nessrine Omrani	Paris School of Business, France
Omar Oueslati	University of Manouba, Tunisia
Malgorzata Pankowska	University of Economics in Katowice, Poland
Angela Pereira	Instituto Politécnico de Leiria, Portugal
Anna Pohle	Fraunhofer IMW, Germany
Joachim Posegga	University of Passau, Germany
Antoun Nakhle Racquel	Saint Joseph University of Beirut, Lebanon
Ines Rekhis	Manouba University, Tunisia
Mornay Roberts-Lombard	University of Johannesburg, South Africa
Ahmed Samet	INSA Strasbourg, France
Sudarshan Seshanna	CMS Business School and Jain University, India
Fatma Siala	University of Tunis El Manar, Tunisia
Layth Sliman	EFREI Paris, France
Abir Smiti	University of Tunis, Tunisia
Lamia Soltani	University of Manouba, Tunisia
Gerald Thaver	ABSA, South Africa
Mouna Sebri	Université de Sherbrooke, Canada
Lilia Sfaxi	University of Carthage, Tunisia
Nadine Sinno	Lebanese International University, Lebanon
Ines Thabet	University of Manouba, Tunisia
Mourad Touzani	NEOMA Business School, France
Narjes Touzani	ISIT'Com, Tunisia

Karl Trela	Fraunhofer IMW, Germany
Imene Trigui	University Tunis El Manar, Tunisia
Chau Yuen	SUTD, Singapore
Nadia Yacoubi Ayadi	University of Tunis, Tunisia
David Ziegler	Fraunhofer IMW, Germany
Fang Zhao	Edith Cowan University, Australia

Organizers

Association Tunisienne D'économie Numérique

The International University of Beirut

Scientific and Organizing Partners

École Supérieure D'économie Numérique

Université de la manouba

American University of Beirut

Beirut Economics Congress

Faculté De Sciences Économiques

Université Saint-Joseph De Beyrouth

Observatoire Universitaire De La Réalité Socio-Économique

Sponsors

Bureau Des Études Techniques D'assistance Et De Pilotage

WESS E-COMMERCE
Just doing E-business

Wess E-Commerce

Contents

Digital Transformation

Assessment the Company's Readiness for Digital Transformation:
Clarifying the Issue... 3
    Tatiana Lezina, Olga Stoianova, Victoriia Ivanova,
    and Lyudmila Gadasina

The Impact of Management by Objectives (MBO) on Organizational
Outcome in a Digital World: A Case Study in the Aviation Industry.......... 15
    Farid Abdallah and Walid Elhoss

The Effect of Digital Transformation on Innovation and Entrepreneurship
in the Tourism Sector: The Case of Lebanese Tourism Services Providers ... 29
    Nadine Sinno

E-Finance

Testing the Significance of Artificial Intelligence Investment
in Determining Stock Prices................................... 43
    Mohammad Makki and Mira Abdallah

The Interest Rate Behaviour of Bitcoin as a Digital Asset 53
    Thabo J. Gopane

Limitations of Digitizing Trade Finance Services in Yemeni
Banking Sector...................................... 66
    Rami Al-Sabri

Social Media Communication

Social Networks and Societal Strategic Orientation in the Hotel Sector:
Netnographic Study....................................... 87
    Hasna Koubaa and Rim Jallouli

Luxury and Mass Media: How Can Brands Manage the Paradox Between
Luxury Inaccessibility and Social Media Communication Tools?.......... 110
    Wafa Hamzaoui, Nadine Tournois, and Enes Hamzagic

The Return on Investment of Professional Social Networks 120
    Yamen Koubaa and Fares Medjani

Intelligent Systems

A Trusted Group-Based Revocation Process for Intelligent
Transportation System   133
   Hamssa Hasrouny, Abed Ellatif Samhat, Carole Bassil, and Anis Laouiti

On the Verification of Data Encryption Requirements in Internet
of Things Using Event-B   147
   Imed Abbassi, Layth Sliman, Mohamed Graiet, and Walid Gaaloul

CaRT: Framework for Semantic Query Correction and Relaxation.   157
   Oumaima Mbazaia and Karim Kamoun

E-commerce and Business Analytics

E-commerce and Business Analytics: A Literature Review   173
   Emrah Bilgic and Yanqing Duan

Overview of E-commerce Technologies, Data Analysis Capabilities
and Marketing Knowledge   183
   Safa Kaabi and Rim Jallouli

E-commerce and Commodity Fetishism Violence in New Media Marketing . . .   194
   Hassan Choubassi, Sahar Sharara, and Sarah Khayat

E-Learning and Cloud Education

Toward Information Overload: Measuring Visual Activity in Teaching
Materials Production   203
   Kristian Dokic, Tomislava Lauc, and Bojan Radisic

A Reflection on E-learning Effectiveness in Tunisia   215
   Rabeb Mbarek

Deeper Learning Versus Surface Learning: The SAMR Model to Assess
E-Learning Pedagogy   230
   Dina Shouman and Levon Momdjian

Personal Effectiveness, Commitment and Organizational Trust Impact
on e-Learning Effectiveness   239
   Arem Say, Ibticem Ben Zammel, and Tharwa Najar

E-Commerce and Digital Economy

Transparency in the E-Journals Market: Controlled Preferences and Altered
Rational Choices.   253
   Rim Haidar, Nizar Hariri, and Racquel Antoun

Going Viral: Elements that Lead Videos to Become Viral   266
Rania Abouyounes

A Quantitative Model for Replacement of Medical Equipment Based
on Technical and Economic Factors   278
Yasmine Jarikji, Bassam Hussein, and Mohamad Hajj-Hassan

Data Science

A New Spark Based K-Means Clustering with Data Removing Strategy   289
Kenza Rziga, Mohamed Aymen Ben HajKacem, and Nadia Essoussi

Reinforcement Learning for New Adaptive Gamified LMS.   305
Eya Chtouka, Wided Guezguez, and Nahla Ben Amor

A Framework for Facial Image Analytics Using Deep Learning
in Social Sciences Research   315
Stuart J. Barnes and Richard Rutter

Digital Marketing

Motivations and Inhibitions Behind the Adoption and Continuous Use of
IoT Wearable Devices: Exploring and Comparing Three Major Frameworks. . .   323
Mourad Touzani and Ahmed Anis Charfi

Marketing Strategies in the Age of Technology.   342
Caroline Kassabli Al Fakhry

Smart Packaging: Consumer's Perception and Diagnostic
of Traceability Information.   352
Mouna Karoui Daoud and Imene Trabelsi Trigui

Digital Business Models

Multi-sided Platforms in the Sharing Economy – A Case Study Analysis
for the Development of a Generic Platform   373
Claudia Vienken, Nizar Abdelkafi, and Cyrine Tangour

So You Want to Be a Platform: Where to Start?.   387
Lino Markfort, Sebastian Haugk, and Cyrine Tangour

Digital Business Model Patterns of Big Pharmaceutical Companies -
A Cluster Analysis   397
Cyrine Tangour, Marc Gebauer, Luise Fischer, and Herwig Winkler

Correction to: Digital Business Model Patterns of Big Pharmaceutical
Companies - A Cluster Analysis C1
Cyrine Tangour, Marc Gebauer, Luise Fischer, and Herwig Winkler

Author Index   413

Digital Transformation

Assessment the Company's Readiness for Digital Transformation: Clarifying the Issue

Tatiana Lezina^(✉), Olga Stoianova, Victoriia Ivanova, and Lyudmila Gadasina

Saint Petersburg State University, 7/9 Universitetskaya nab.,
Saint Petersburg 199034, Russian Federation
{t.lezina, o.stoyanova, v.ivanova, l.gadasina}@spbu.ru

Abstract. Surveys show that only every third company in Russia has chosen a digital transformation strategy and has implemented it. What slows down the development of these kinds of strategies in companies? The choice of the strategy is partly defined by the level of readiness of the company's management system, business processes, architecture, etc. Existing tools of evaluating companies' readiness for digital transformation lack of universality, formalization and often use highly professional terminology. The study is aimed at answering the questions of whether the key terms concerned with digitalization are understandable by Russian companies and whether it is possible to use existing criteria systems to assess companies' readiness for digital transformation. The article presents the results of a survey of Russian companies' representatives conducted using a questionnaire developed on the basis of the proposed approach for evaluating readiness. The approach involves the sequential decomposition of the objects of estimation and the grouping of their characteristics and sub-characteristics into the following domains: system management, maturity of the company's architecture, readiness of business processes, maturity of data management, and personnel readiness.

Keywords: Digital transformation · The company's readiness ·
Domains of indicators · Readiness assessment

1 Introduction

IT development and, particularly, the trend of developing the digital economy in Russia motivate companies for digital transformation (DT). However, a key problem for any company is choosing an appropriate strategy. In 2018, only 35% of the surveyed 300 Russian companies from different industries chose a digital transformation strategy and implemented it and 26% of those companies are going to develop a corresponding digital strategy [1]. It begs the question, what hinders the development of digital transformation strategies in companies?

The authors' experience in consulting the companies of different size and different industries demonstrates that an understanding of goals of digital transformation and its content varies widely. A company's management, responsible for the choice of a digital transformation strategy, often does not have neither experience nor tools of such choice.

R. Jallouli et al. (Eds.): ICDEc 2019, LNBIP 358, pp. 3–14, 2019.
https://doi.org/10.1007/978-3-030-30874-2_1

Several studies and descriptions of successful cases of digital transformation does not provide companies with a tool of choosing a strategy considering company's readiness for digital transformation. The proposed solutions lack of universality and the formalization. Moreover, some of existing tools for evaluating companies' digital maturity/readiness use highly professional terminology understandable to IT professionals and are not familiar to company managers. A wrong interpretation of concepts leads to incorrect readiness assessments and limits the variants of strategies.

To identify the level of understanding of basic terms concerned with digitalization and digital transformation in Russian companies, the following research questions were posed:

RQ1: Are the key terms concerned with digitalization understandable by Russian companies?
RQ2: Is it possible to use existing criteria systems for assessing companies' readiness for digital transformation?

2   Related Work

The topic of digital business transformation is actively discussed both in academic and business communities, but interpretations of "digital transformation" concept varies widely [2–4]. For example, according to [2] digital transformation is "the process of re-inventing a business to digitize operations and formulate expanded relationships in the supply chain" and according to [4] "digital transformation—the use of technology to radically improve the performance or reach of enterprises". In [5] "digital transformation is a focused and continuous digital evolution of a company, business model, idea or methodology, both strategically and tactically". The given examples of definitions confirm the problem of consistency in understanding and interpreting the concept of digital transformation and related key terms. It allows to formulate the following research hypothesis:

H1: The concept of digital transformation needs further clarifying.

Urgent issues of digital transformation are adaptation of existing business models, new corporate business processes and roles that need to be developed at the stage of transition from products to digital services, and the creation of a new technological ecosystem [6–8]. The descriptions of options for a digital transformation strategy are most often given in studies on the strategic management of companies' digital transformation [9, 10]. However, there are no formal models for choosing the form and strategy of transformation.

Research in the field of digital transformation is actively conducted not only by the scientific community but also by consulting agencies. However, the theoretical and methodological basis for the choice of strategy is rather fuzzy. Theoretical bases of digital transformation strategy selection are considered, as a rule, for specific areas. Larger companies have made more progress toward digital transformation than their smaller counterparts. In Russia, the leaders of digital transformation are banks and big corporations. Their experience is of great interest, but the description of the corresponding cases is presented in literature only in a fragmented way and is not universal.

The existing and described solutions for assessing the company's readiness for digital transformation are based on the following approaches: value chain analysis [11], balanced scorecard [12], Porter's five forces analysis [11], life cycle analysis [13], etc. Among the problems of digital transformation, many authors highlight the problem of assessing the level of the company's digitalization [14, 15]. Many authors do not distinguish between the terms "level of digitalization" and "readiness" for transformation. In this study, we distinguish these concepts and consider only the concept of readiness.

Table 1 presents different approaches to assessing companies' readiness for digital transformation.

Table 1. Existing frameworks/models of readiness for digital transformation

Framework/Model name	Institution/Source	Assessment approach
The five digital business aptitude domains	KPMG [16]	Suggested domains: vision & strategy, digital talent, digital first processes, sourcing and infrastructure, governance
The Digital Maturity Model 4.0.	Forrester/Gill and VanBoskirk [17]	Four dimensions determine digital maturity: culture, organization, technology, insights
Digital Acceleration Index	BCG [18]	The 4 building blocks evaluated: business strategy driven by digital, digitize the core, new digital growth, enablers
Industry 4.0 Maturity Model	Schumacher, Eril, Sihn [19]	62 maturity items which are grouped into nine dimensions: strategy, leadership, customers, products, operation, culture, people, governance, technology
Digital REadiness Assessment MaturitY model	De Carolis, etc. [13]	Evaluation the maturity indexes of company's process area: design and engineering; production management; quality management; maintenance management; logistics management
Digital Services Capability Model	Wulf, Mettler, Brenner [12]	17 capabilities of digital transformation in eight classes: consumers, services, processes and activities, organization, information, technologies and infrastructure, strategies, environment

(continued)

Table 1. (*continued*)

Framework/Model name	Institution/Source	Assessment approach
Organizations digital readiness framework	Sánchez, Zuntini [11]	External and internal analysis including: ecosystem collaboration, five forces analysis, resources and capabilities, value chain analysis, initial conditions, barriers
Interrelationship between the digital transformation, strategy and organizational capability	Schumann, Tittmann [20]	Assessment in three dimensions: digital transformation, digital business strategy, organizational capability
Digital transformation framework	Matt, Hess, Benlian [21]	The four different dimensions: use of technologies, changes in value creation, structural changes, financial aspects

The analysis shows that approaches to evaluating companies' readiness for digital transformation are very different. Moreover, in the presented studies, there is no justification for choosing the estimated parameters or the factors of readiness. It allows to create the second research hypothesis:

H2: The existing criteria systems for assessing companies' readiness for digital transformation need clarification and adaptation for practical use.

3   Conceptual Framework for Assessing the Companies' Readiness for Digital Transformation

3.1   An Approach to Evaluating the Companies' Readiness for Digital Transformation

The authors' approach to evaluating the companies' readiness for digital transformation proposes the sequential decomposition of the objects of estimation and the grouping of their characteristics and sub-characteristics into domains. Decomposition is carried out from the level of the control system to the architectural level and its elements. The authors distinguish the following set of domains: systematic management, maturity of the company's architecture, readiness of business processes, maturity of data management, and personnel readiness. The authors do not consider such domain as technologies. Russian practice shows that a high level of technological readiness is not sufficient for successful digital transformation. Moreover, many companies are ready to "invest" in technology, in case the future digital transformation effects are clear.

The mentioned domains are allocated in the paper in accordance with the architectural approach based on the following interpretation of the concept of digital transformation. Transformation (from lat.) means change. Digital transformation includes successive interrelated changes in the elements of a company's system. Any company is a highly connected system. In such a system, it is necessary to consider not only the consequences of direct control actions but also their effects transmitted through system relationships. Therefore, systematic management is the first and key domain.

Consistency is an approach to company management, and enterprise architecture is one of the methodologies based on this approach. Enterprise architecture is the methodology of proactive and holistic management of the company's response to environmental impacts by identifying and analyzing changes in business vision and outcomes. [22]. In accordance with this methodology, enterprise architecture is created as a mechanism of systematic management. This mechanism determines the opportunities and limitations for the company's digital transformation. It explains the presence of the maturity architecture domain in the criteria for assessing the company's readiness for digital transformation.

Enterprise Architecture is implemented in companies at the level of business processes. However, even a well-built methodology does not guarantee the success of any business idea if the company's business processes are not optimized for it. Accordingly, as the next domain, the authors highlighted the readiness of business processes domain.

In modern companies, data is generated by business processes and is used for evaluation and management. Data quality is a critical factor for management. A high level of data quality in a company of any size in any industry is ensured by an effective data management system. Therefore, the authors identified the data management maturity domain.

It is generally recognized that any changes are impossible without the involvement and professionalism of a company's staff. This has led to the emergence of the personnel readiness domain.

3.2 Criteria for Assessing the Company's Readiness for Digital Transformation

Within the framework of the study, the authors formulated the criteria of readiness for digital transformation for each domain (Table 2) and characteristics specifying them (a fragment of which is presented in Table 3). The presented criteria and characteristics were verified by experts—representatives of large, successful companies from the following industries: fuel and energy (3), light industry (1), public service (2), construction (1), R&D (2), and the woodworking industry (1).

To obtain estimates of the presented characteristics, a questionnaire was created. An example of questions for the systematic management domain is given in Table 4.

Table 2. Criteria of company's readiness for digital transformation

Domain	Criteria
Systematic management	Consistency of goals, objectives and plans Quality and effectiveness of change management Quality of internal and external feedback in the management system
Maturity of the company's architecture	Involvement of IT in management and understanding of the business' needs Correspondence between IT and business strategies Efficiency of IT
Readiness of business process	Business processes standardization Business processes integration Automation of business processes
Maturity of data management	Management's involvement in data management Organization of data structures Data quality
Personnel readiness	Motivation for change Digital competence of personnel

Table 3. Characteristics specifying criteria

Criteria	Characteristic
Consistency of goals, objectives, and plans	- Vertical consistency of goals, objectives, and plans (from strategic to operational level) - Horizontal consistency of goals, objectives, and plans (between functional areas, departments)
Quality and effectiveness of change management	- The speed of implementation of various (not necessarily digital) changes in the company - Completeness of changes
Quality of internal and external feedback in the management system	- Quality of feedback in the management system within the company - Quality of feedback between the company and contractors

3.3 General Characteristics of the Questionnaire and Question Samples

The questionnaire contained six groups of questions.

The questions of the first group aimed at identifying the profile of respondents (position in the company and belonging to IT) and assessing the characteristics of the company (size and scope of activity) in which they work.

The respondents were also asked:

– whether their company needed digital transformation,
– how they assess the level of the company's readiness for digital transformation,
– how they assess the current use of information technologies.

Table 4. Examples of questions for the systematic management domain

Questions	Answer options
How the company' goals and objectives are fixed	- Are formally described (in the form of strategic maps, goal trees, etc.) - Are described in detail in the text documents - Only strategic goals are fixed - Are not documented anywhere
Do you use goals and objectives cascading	- Yes, we use - We don't use, because we don't understand the concept - We don't use, because don't have time and resources - We don't understand the concept
Does the company use KPIs	- Yes - Only in some departments - No, we don't need KPIs - We don't understand the concept
How the company analyses the external environment	- Modern technologies and tools of data analysis are used - Only spreadsheets are used - The analysis is carried out without the use of specialized tools - The corresponding analysis is not carried out
How the company has established feedback	- The company regularly conducts electronic surveys to identify problems and analyze proposals - Employees' feedback is organized in the form of e-mails or paper letters - Regular meetings are held to discuss problems and suggestions - Problems and suggestions are discussed individually - The feedback analysis is rather formal

The remaining five groups of questions corresponded to the distinguished domains. The questions presented in each group reveal the criteria of companies' readiness for digital transformation (criteria questions) formulated by the authors. Meanwhile, the wording of the questions deliberately did not contain a narrow professional terminology of the field of knowledge corresponding to each of the domains. This is justified by the fact that the survey was aimed at a wide audience of respondents from different professional fields and industries.

Example criteria issues for the systematic management are shown in Table 4.

In each group of questions, the authors added a diagnostic question, the purpose of which was to analyze the comprehensive assessments of companies' readiness for digital transformation in the context of each domain and the respondents" understanding of the assessed domains.

An example of a diagnostic question for the systematic management domain is the question "Do you think management in a company is systematic?" with options of answers: "Yes", "No", "The concept of systematic management requires additional explanation", and "I find it difficult to estimate". Each question offered the response option "Other" for analysis additional comments of the respondents.

4 Results and Discussion

4.1 General Characteristics of Responses

The total number of respondents was 112.

The company's activities were distributed as above (see Fig. 1). The most part of respondents (41%) were from manufacturing companies. The second big part of respondents (20.45%) represented the service sector. In third place (17%) was employees of the fuel and energy industry, which is specific for Russia.

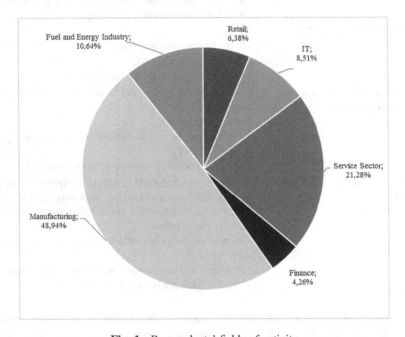

Fig. 1. Respondents' fields of activity

Among the respondents there were 23.5% representatives of large companies (more than 10 thousand employees), 23.3% - representatives of companies of medium size (from 1000 to 10000 employees), and 51.2% - from small companies.

11.6% of the respondents were CEOs, 34.9% were heads of departments, and 53.5% were specialists.

41.9% of all the respondents were specialists in IT, and 58.1% did not belong to IT departments. 72.7% of the respondents answered positively to the question whether the company needed digital transformation: 34.1% of which answered that their companies couldn't develop without digital transformation while 38.6% answered that their companies needed it, but that it was not the company's priority. 22.7% of respondents answered that they didn't fully understand what digital transformation was.

4.5% of respondents admitted that digital transformation was not needed in their company, as the current state of the company suited CEOs. None of the respondents chose the option associated with the fact that the company's activities didn't involve the use of information technology. At the same time, according to the questionnaire, 14% of the answers confirmed that the level of companies' readiness for digital transformation is high, 41.9% that it is medium, and 27.9% that it is low. 11.6% of the respondents answered that it was difficult to answer and 4.7% declared that their companies were not interested in digital transformation.

When asked about the current level of use of information technologies in the company, 40.9% of respondents said that most of the processes were implemented with the support of IT and 54.6% noted the use of IT only for some tasks. 4.5% of respondents did not understand the question. It's interesting that 95.5% of the respondents work in companies that actively use IT, but 72.7% of them believe their company needs digital transformation. This confirms the insufficient IT efficiency.

4.2 Answers to Diagnostic Questions

Figure 2 shows the respondents' answers to diagnostic questions.

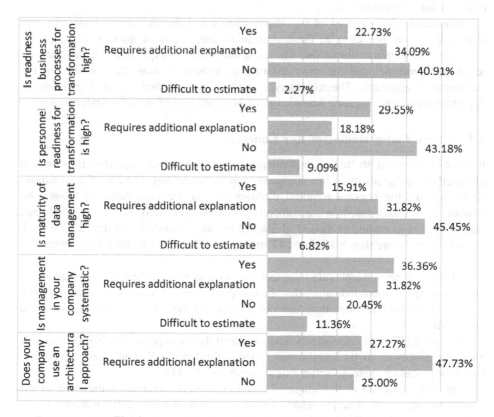

Fig. 2. Respondents' answers to diagnostic questions

When asked whether management in the company was systematic, 31.82% of the respondents answered that this concept required clarification while 11.36% found that it was difficult to assess the level of consistency.

When asked about the readiness of the company's business processes for transformation, 34.09% of the respondents stated that the concept required additional explanation and 2.27% found it difficult to estimate.

Note that respondents belonging to different levels of management showed different levels of comprehension regarding key concepts. For example, the share of those who do not know about the architectural approach among the heads of departments is 73.3% against 40% among the surveyed CEOs.

When asked about the maturity of data management in the company, 31.82% of respondents said they did not understand the question. The highest percentage of respondents that did not understand the question included specialists and most of the CEOs and departments have tried to assess the level of maturity of data management in their companies.

The issue of assessing the readiness of the personnel to digital transformation was the clearest. Only 18.18% of respondents said the concept of readiness of the personnel required further explanation.

In general, about a third of the respondents stated that the digital transformation terminology was not clear to them despite having a general understanding of the necessity of digital transformation. The most understandable question was the question regarding personnel and the most difficult to understand was the question on the architectural approach. The company's executives were better than the heads of departments concerning their knowledge of key concepts of digital transformation.

4.3   Check Understanding of Key Concepts

It is noteworthy that 36.36% of respondents answered positively regarding the question of whether management in the company was systemic and 31.82% of respondents answered that the concept required clarification. At the same time, of those who answered that management in the company was systematic, only 37.5% of respondents said they used cascading goals and 31.3% did not have knowledge of this. 23.5% of IT specialists and more than half of non-IT managers did not understand what a cascading goal is.

14% of the respondents rated the maturity of data management in the company as high, with half of them indicating that the company does not have data architecture and a third of respondents said they did not understand the question about master data uniformity.

Among 22.73% of respondents who indicated their companies are highly ready for business processes to be transformed, only a third noted that all their company's business processes were, to some extent, supported by IT.

The data obtained at this stage of research showed there are differences in the interpretation of key concepts related to the readiness of companies for digital transformation, namely in the interpretation of terms "the system of management", "the maturity of data management", and "readiness of business processes".

5 Conclusion

The study shows that regarding a common understanding of the need for digital transformation by most respondents, a significant number of respondents demonstrate a lack of understanding of corresponding terminology. Moreover, the data obtained at this stage of the study indicate the diversity in interpreting and defining the links between the key concepts related to the readiness of companies for digital transformation. Therefore, it is highly important to develop (clarify) the digital transformation glossaries and, in the next stages, to create ontologies for the uniformity of interpretations and relationships between the key concepts of digital transformation.

The further direction of the research is developing an updated detailed questionnaire to diagnose the level of readiness of companies for digital transformation and identify barriers to digitalization. The questionnaire's refinement is planned in the direction of detailing the criteria to the level of characteristics, sub-characteristics, and metrics.

According to the authors' experience, only representatives of companies for whom the practical use of the survey results is important are ready to answer the detailed questionnaires. The study shows, that in several cases, an understanding of the practical importance of digital transformation is formed in the process of answering the questionnaire. That is why the self-diagnostic tools in the form of a simplified version of a questionnaire assessing the readiness of companies for digital transformation are needed.

The discussion is limited to analyses of the current attitude and understanding of key aspects of digital transformation by Russian companies and does not include deep theoretical analysis of this concept. This paper is one of the steps towards our research goal to create a model for assessing companies' readiness for digital transformation, including criteria, characteristics, metrics, and evaluating algorithms.

References

1. Analytical report: Digital Transformation in Russia. KMDA (2018). https://komanda-a.pro/blog/dtr_2018
2. Bowersox, D.J., Closs, D.J., Drayer, R.W.: The digital transformation: technology and beyond. Supply Chain Manag. Rev. 9(1), 22–29 (2005)
3. Schallmo, D., Williams, C.A., Boardman, L.: Digital transformation of business models-best practice, enablers, and roadmap. Int. J. Innov. Manag. 21(8), 1740014 (2017). (17 p.). https://doi.org/10.1007/978-3-319-72844-5_3
4. Westerman, G., Calméjane, C., Bonnet, D., Ferraris, P., McAfee, A.: Digital Transformation: A Roadmap for Billion-Dollar Organizations, pp. 1–68. MIT Sloan Management, MIT Center for Digital Business and Capgemini Consulting (2011)
5. Mazzone, M.: Digital or death: digital transformation is the only choice for a business to survive, smash and conquer, 1st edn. Smashbox Consulting Inc. (2014)
6. Andersson, P., Movin, S., Mähring, M., Teigland, R., Wennberg, K.: Managing Digital Transformation. Stockholm School of Economics Institute for Research, Stockholm (2018)
7. Andriole, S.J.: Five myths about digital transformation. MIT Sloan Manag. Rev. (Spring) 58 (3), 20–22 (2017)

8. Kotarba, M.: Digital transformation of business models. Found. Manag. **10**, 123–142 (2018). https://doi.org/10.2478/fman-2018-0011
9. Kane, G.C., Palmer, D., Phillips, A.N., Kiron, D., Buckley, N.: Aligning the organization for its digital future. MIT Sloan Manag. Rev. (Winter) **58**(1), 1–28 (2016)
10. Ross, J.W., Sebastian, I.M., Beath, C.M.: Beath how to develop a great digital strategy. MIT Sloan Manag. Rev. (Winter) **58**(3), 7–9 (2017)
11. Sánchez, M., Zuntini, J.: Organizational readiness for the digital transformation: a case study research. Revista Gestão Tecnologia **18**(2), 70–99 (2018). https://doi.org/10.20397/2177-6652/2018.v18i2.1316
12. Wulf, J., Mettler, T., Brenner, W.: Using a digital services capability model to assess readiness for the digital consumer. MIS Q. Executive **16**(3), 171–195 (2017)
13. De Carolis, A., Macchi, M., Negri, E., Terzi, S.: Guiding manufacturing companies towards digitalization a methodology for supporting manufacturing companies in defining their digitalization roadmap. In: 2017 International Conference on Engineering Technology and Innovation (ICE/ITMC), pp. 487–495 (2017). https://doi.org/10.1109/ice.2017.8279925
14. Gottlieb, J., Willmott, P.: The digital tipping point: McKinsey Global Survey results. McKinsey Quarterly (2014). McKinsey & Company. https://www.mckinsey.com/business-functions/digital-mckinsey/our-insights/the-digital-tipping-point-mckinsey-global-survey-results
15. Kotarba, M.: Measuring digitalization key metrics. Found. Manag. **9**, 123–138 (2017). https://doi.org/10.1515/fman-2017-0010
16. Are you ready for digital transformation? Measuring your digital business aptitude. KPMG (2016). https://assets.kpmg.com/content/dam/kpmg/pdf/2016/04/measuring-digital-business-aptitude.pdf
17. Gill, M., VanBoskirk, S.: The Digital Maturity Model 4.0. Benchmarks: Digital business transformation playbook (2016). https://forrester.nitro-digital.com/pdf/Forrester-s%20Digital%20Maturity%20Model%204.0.pdf
18. Digital Acceleration Index. BCG (2016). https://www.bcg.com/ru-ru/capabilities/technology-digital/digital-acceleration-index.aspx
19. Schumacher, A., Erol, S., Sihn, W.: A maturity model for assessing industry 4.0 readiness and maturity of manufacturing enterprises. Procedia CIRP **52**, 161–166 (2016). https://doi.org/10.1016/j.procir.2016.07.040
20. Schumann, C.A., Tittmann, C.: Digital transformation in context of knowledge management. In: Proceedings of the 16th European Conference on Knowledge Management, vol. 1, pp. 671–676 (2015)
21. Matt, C., Hess, T., Benlian, A.: Digital transformation strategies. Bus. Inf. Syst. Eng. **57**(5), 339–343 (2015). https://doi.org/10.1007/s12599-015-0401-5
22. Gartner IT Glossary (2018). https://www.gartner.com/it-glossary/enterprise-architecture-ea/

The Impact of Management by Objectives (MBO) on Organizational Outcome in a Digital World: A Case Study in the Aviation Industry

Farid Abdallah[✉] and Walid Elhoss

Lebanese International University – LIU, Beirut, Lebanon
farid.abdallah@liu.edu.lb, walidhoss@gmail.com

Abstract. Adopting new management techniques has allowed organizations to cope with changes and deliver better results. One of those techniques is Management by Objectives (hereinafter mentioned as MBO). MBO is a simple need-to-achieve principle that allows managers and subordinates to jointly identify organizational goals. This paper examines the impact of applying MBO on organizational outcome in terms of productivity and efficiency in the aviation industry. A survey was distributed to a population of 200 targeted participants. Out of 130 respondents, a sample of 106 participants from the aviation industry was selected based on purposive sampling. Additionally, three field interviews were conducted with senior officers in the aviation sector. Survey results were analyzed using Microsoft Excel Statistical Package, while field interviews were analyzed through coding. The findings indicated that applying MBO in the aviation industry delivered better results in terms of productivity and efficiency, especially when supported by investing in technology.

Keywords: Management techniques · MBO · Productivity · Technology · Aviation · Coding · Statistics

1 Introduction

A plethora of management studies has discussed performance and goal setting since 1911 until today. Drucker (1954) was a pioneer in introducing a combination of a three-process management philosophy that reshaped the manager-subordinate relationship from dictating objectives to a flexible approach involving all organizational layers; this approach was tagged as MBO. Drucker (1954) defined management by objectives as *"[a] management model that aims to improve the performance of an organization by clearly defining objectives that are agreed by both management and employees."*

Recently Al Noah (2011) and Hollmann (2013) cited that whenever MBO is applied, it increases productivity and boosts organizational output. Additionally, Antoni (2005) revealed that MBO stimulates group efficiency, productivity, and job satisfaction. Thomson (1998) stated that MBO triggers better performance in employees. This encouraged organizations to adopt MBO as a modern approach to management.

R. Jallouli et al. (Eds.): ICDEc 2019, LNBIP 358, pp. 15–28, 2019.
https://doi.org/10.1007/978-3-030-30874-2_2

According to Kyriakopoulos (2012); Locke and Latham (1991); Rose (1977); Odiorne (1965); and Drucker (1954), MBO triggers self-control, improves organizational culture, and drives employee motivation.

On the other hand, skeptics of the MBO philosophy state that it is time-consuming, costly, useless, triggers conflicts, and requires structural changes (Al Qwareen 2010), (Kumar 2012), and (Jamieson 1973).

Critics further argued that applying MBO is associated with behavioral problems. Hence, King and King (1990) and Kahn et al. (1964) argue that MBO creates role ambiguity amongst employees. When individuals experience multiple roles, they experience role stress (Kahn et al. 1964). Both role stress and role ambiguity hamper the successful implementation of MBO.

Moreover, Bandura (1977) and Gilboa et al. (2008) cited that self-efficacy of employees is a significant challenge in applying MBO. The higher the employees' self-efficacy, the more they can achieve goals. It is the role of the top management to train their employees how to raise their self-efficacy in order to be part of the goal-setting process.

The aim of this paper is to evaluate the effect of applying MBO on the organizational output in the aviation industry in terms productivity and efficiency (which constitutes the research question of the paper). The latter shall be achieved through analyzing data retrieved from survey responses and field interviews. The authors will provide an overview of MBO advantages and limitations to assess multiple scenarios of output.

1.1 Overview of the Aviation Industry

The aviation industry is one of the fastest growing sectors around the world. Passenger demand grew by 65% in 2017 compared to 2007; it transported around 4.1 billion passengers in 2017 which is more than half the world's population (IATA 2018). The success of the aviation industry is not only related to being the fastest and safest mode of transport but also to its continuous development on both the operational and business sides (IATA 2018).

Aviation firms vary in their business nature between airlines, organizations, and service providers; some are private companies while others are state-owned or have a heterogeneous business model. Therefore, each has a different organizational structure and management methods that are tailored to fit the organization's specific environment and contingencies. Many aviation organizations have undergone critical restructuring activities during the past years in order to boost productivity and cut costs. This has primarily taken place due to the increase in the level of competition and operating expenses, which has obliged firms to operate on very thin margins to compete (IATA 2018).

2 Literature Review

In 1922, James O. McKinsey first recognized the concept of MBO, which was studied later by several scholars like John Humble, Dale McConkey, George Odiorne, Edward Schleh, and Douglas Mcgregor. General Motors was the first company to adopt MBO in 1954 to support manufacturing activities by increasing productivity and reducing cost (Odiorne 1965).

Carroll and Tosi (1973) stated that MBO is a management style dedicated to motivating managers and materializing their suggestions as goals for the organization. Ramosaj (2007) mentioned that MBO is a process that identifies synergies between managers' individual objectives to create broader organizational aims. Similarly, Weihrich (2000) said that the focus should be on individual contributions to create organizational objectives.

Recently, Hollmann (2013) defined MBO as *"a process whereby each manager establishes and works toward achieving specific objectives in key areas of his job responsibility during a specified time period."*

Under MBO, organizations have witnessed better output, greater satisfaction and fewer conflicts between managers and subordinates. McConkey (1967) favored the term "management by results" over that of "management by objectives" and defined it as an approach to manage, plan, and evaluate objectives over a certain period, where achieved results are compared to the expected results.

Additionally, management by objectives helps in group formulation and direction. According to Fulk et al. (2011), there is a substantial connection between MBO and group development especially the model developed by Tuckman and Jensen (1986).

2.1 Advantages of MBO

MBO sets clear goals and objectives that are measurable and achievable. Joint goal setting enhances intragroup communication and lifts team spirit. Also, it increases commitment towards achieving those goals. According to Antoni (2005), when employees have a better understanding of what is required from them their productivity increases to the maximum level.

Moreover, MBO allows managers to monitor and control their subordinates' performance frequently, as highlighted by several researchers. For instance, Akrani (2010) stated that MBO's focus is on developing action plans, roadmaps, mobilizing resources and how to match those resources with the organizational objectives.

A critical success factor of MBO is continuous feedback and evaluation, which leads to more coordination between managers and their subordinates leading to a better employee-management relationship. Accordingly, MBO improves communication and coordination between managers and subordinates (Kumar 2012).

Training and development are principles of implementing MBO. Abdullah (2010) stated that continuous training is required primarily for individuals participating in goal setting. Under MBO employees are trained to develop self-control, which- in turn- leads to better leadership skills (Al Noah 2011). Training allows employees to gain better acceptance of their managers, leading to more development within the organization hierarchy, ultimately resulting in the improvement of workforce skills.

2.2   Limitations of MBO

Management by objectives is easier discussed in theory than implemented in practice. MBO requires the involvement of all layers of the organization, which consumes a substantial sum of time and resources (Kumar 2012).

Also, applying MBO requires financial investment on a large scale since it involves the entire organization. Sah (2012) expressed his concerns about applying MBO because the program overemphasizes goal-setting in order to drive outcomes.

Another drawback cited by Al Qwareen (2010) was that MBO is mostly applicable in the private sector and not in the public sector. The latter stated that the public sector is not profit oriented and it has many organizational layers that make the implementation of MBO hard to achieve.

A further disadvantage indicated by Thomson (1998) was the difficulty of setting quantitative goals. The core of MBO is to measure the results achieved from assigned objectives; but what if the objectives are intangible or quantitative? How can they be measured? Is it by observation? Thomson (1998) also criticized MBO for focusing on short-term goals.

Kumar (2012) stated that MBO also has limited application, in the sense that it is not suitable for everyone. Kumar argued that MBO is only applicable if the joint consent of the manager and the subordinate is obtained.

Jamieson (1973) argued that implementing MBO sometimes requires an unnecessary change in the organizational structure, which is costly, time-consuming, and may cause internal conflicts. Moreover, Jamieson (1973) cited that most organizations expect that MBO will solve all managerial problems.

On the other hand, MBO has some behavioral implications. As stated by Jamieson (1973) during MBO management-subordinate interviews to set corporate objectives, managers may lack interpersonal skills to conduct this social interaction, where they need to integrate objectives and find solutions for conflicts. Problems may arise from manager-subordinate incompatibility, relating salary to performance, employees not willing to change status-quo and a lot more to mention (Levinson 2003). In an article published at the Harvard Business Review by, he states that MBO ignores subordinates' objectives in an attempt to achieve only organizational goals. The title of the article was "*Management by whose objectives?*" and that precisely what Levinson (2003) wanted to imply.

Jamieson (1973) added that changes in authority and control could initiate conflicts between managers and subordinates, since as we have outlined earlier, MBO programs may require a change in the organizational structure.

King and King (1990) relates the failure of MBO programs to role ambiguity, when the role of an individual in the overall objectives of an organization is ambiguous or not identified properly.

3   Methodology

In order to achieve the aim of this research paper, the authors used a qualitative approach to assess the benefits of applying MBO in the aviation sector. Primary data collection methods included a survey and three structured interviews, while the secondary data collection method was based on a literature review.

The survey consists of open and close-ended questions, including a blank space for the opinion of the participant. It includes two sections; section one is designated to collect demographic information about the participants (including age, sex, position, and working experience), while the second part recognizes their input regarding the applicability of MBO and its effect on the overall organizational outcome.

In the first section of the survey, age sectors were distributed from a minimum of 25 years. Positions were distributed from top management to front liners, with an extra field to mention to which department every post is related. The reason behind adding this field is to identify which departments are more involved in applying management by objectives. A minimum of at least two year's work experience has been deemed adequate as experience which affords the employee sufficient time to get involved in defining his/her objectives after gaining a better understanding of the business nature.

As for section two, it consists of two direct questions to determine whether the participant has experienced management by objectives at his/her workplace and if so, he/she must be able to identify the critical success factors of MBO that the management should focus on to yield better results in terms of productivity and efficiency. The critical success factors are given a rank from one to five, where five is most significant and one is least significant.

This is succeeded by thirteen questions based on a Likert scale from 5 – 1 described as follows: 5 = Strongly Agree (SA), 4 = Agree (A), 3 = Neutral (N), 2 = Disagree (D), and 1 = Strongly Disagree (SD). By answering those questions respondents will provide the authors with a clear understanding of how MBO improved the overall output of their respective organizations in terms of productivity and efficiency. Questions number fourteen and fifteen are intentionally left open-ended.

4   Results and Discussions

This paper has adopted the content analysis method to analyze qualitative data collected. According to McNabb (2009) content analysis is a quantitative data analysis method used to interpret and analyze all types of written documentation, videos, and speeches.

On the other hand, this research collected quantitative data through a survey which was distributed to a population of 200 target respondents. The quantitative data was aggregated and analyzed using Microsoft Excel Statistical Package.

4.1   Survey Results

Data retrieved from the survey results were clustered into two main parts based on the management level. The first part comprised top management and the second part middle and front-line management. In addition, in order to provide accurate results concerning question number two under section two of the survey "What is the most important factor that needs to be considered under MBO to yield better productivity (rank 5 best − 1 least)" ranking the determinants of MBO, the researchers assigned numerical values to the evaluation dimensions as follows:

The following formula was used to identify the precise ranking of each determinant based on the survey results (Table 1):

Table 1. Numerical values assigned for ranking MBO determinants

Rank (1-least: 5-best)	Numerical value
1	1.000
2	2.000
3	3.000
4	4.000
5	5.000

Determinant Rank = DR, Numerical Value for each corresponding rank = NV, Frequency of Selection for each rank = FR

$$DR = \sum FR_1 x NV_1 + FR_2 x NV_2 + FR_3 x NV_3 + FR_n x NV_n$$

A sample of 106 participants was selected including front, middle, and top management from the aviation industry (Table 2).

Table 2. Distribution of participants based on their management level

Management level	Frequency	Share of total
Top management	19	17.9%
Middle management	45	42.5%
Front-line management	42	39.6%

Table 3 shows the age distribution of the respondents, most of the sample (66%) was between 26–36 years. The smallest group (3.8%) represents the age category of 48 years and over. Middle management had the biggest share of the largest age category of respondents recording 32 participants, while 26 were from front line management and only 12 from top management.

Table 3. Distribution of participants based on their age

Age category	Frequency	Share of total
Between 26–36 years	70	66.0%
Between 37–47 years	19	17.9%
25 years and less	13	12.3%
48 years and more	4	3.8%

Most of the respondents were females 52.8%, while males represented 47.2% of total respondents. Majority of the respondents have been working within the same organization for a period of 6–10 years (34.9%), while the lowest percentage of respondents represented people working within the same organization for a period of two or less years (13.2%). This shows that most of the respondents have a good understanding of their organizational culture and nature of the business (Table 4).

Table 4. Distribution of participants based on their working experience

Working experience	Frequency	Share of total
Between 6–10 years	37	34.9%
11 years and more	31	29.2%
Between 3–5 years	24	22.6%
2 years or less	14	13.2%

After illustrating the demographic data of the participants, this part will analyze and interpret the effect of applying MBO on the organizational outcome. Before starting the analysis, it is worth mentioning that 66% of the survey respondents (70 responses) experienced MBO at their workplace which allows this research to build conclusions on reasonable grounds. The first question addressed the participants to rank the most critical factors that needs to be considered under MBO to yield better productivity (Fig. 1).

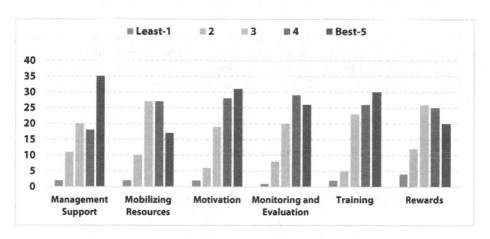

Fig. 1. Ranking of the most important factors under applying MBO

Based on the results illustrated in the above chart, the reader can conclude that management support is considered the most important factor that should be considered while applying MBO, recording 35 records as the "best" factor to be considered, followed by motivation, then training, then, monitoring and evaluation, then rewards, and finally mobilizing resources.

However, after applying the developed formula, the researchers noted different patterns. "Motivation" ranked first with a score of 338 points, followed by "Training" 335 points, then "Management Support" 331, then "Monitoring and Evaluation" 323, then "Rewards" 306, and finally "Mobilizing Resources" 296. It is worth mentioning that the differences are not significant, as the difference between the first and last ranked determinants is only 42 points (Fig. 2).

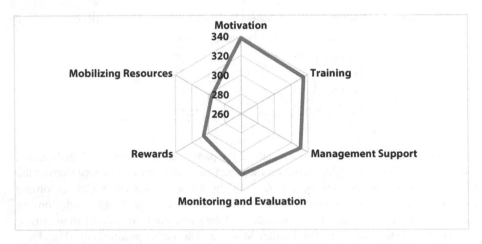

Fig. 2. Rank of MBO determinants obtained after applying the developed formula

On the other hand, after analyzing the responses aggregated from top management the researchers noted different results. "Management Support" ranked first with a score of 58 points, followed by "Motivation" 57 points, then "Monitoring and Evaluation" 57, then "Training" 54, then "Rewards" 51, and finally "Mobilizing Resources" 296 (Fig. 3).

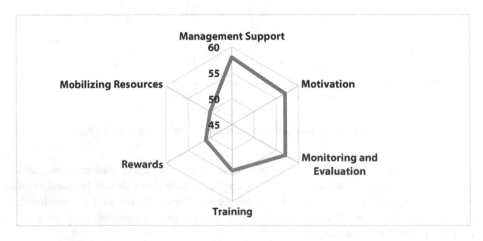

Fig. 3. Rank of MBO determinants based on top management responses

After clustering responses, the rank of MBO determinants changed, yet the last two factors "Rewards" and "Mobilizing Resources" remained at the same rank.

Analyzing questions 3 to 13 which addressed the participants to express their opinion by stating whether applying MBO helped in improving the overall output of the organization in terms of productivity and efficiency. Participants had to base their answers on a Likert Scale defined as below:

5 = Strongly Agree (SA), 4 = Agree (A), 3 = Neutral (N), 2 = Disagree (D), and 1 = Strongly Disagree (SD).

Average responses for all answers came positive on all statements recording an average of 75.4% respondents "strongly agree" and "agree" with what the survey questions imply. On Average 17.5% of the respondents submitted "Neutral" as an answer, while only an average of 7.1% submitted answers which "disagree" and "strongly disagree" with the survey questions.

Looking at Question 6: "Fixed employee roles yields better performance" neutral results outpaced responses recorded for respondents who "strongly agree" and "agree". Also, respondents who "disagreed" with this question recorded 18.9% of total responses recorded.

Similarly, Question 11: "Individual objectives are better achieved under MBO" "neutral" results recorded 23.6% almost leveling with respondents who "strongly agree". Respondents who "disagreed" with this statement recorded 13.2% of total responses recorded.

4.2 Interviews Results

The formal interviews were conducted with three high ranking officers from three different organizations in the aviation industry namely, the International Air Transport Association (hereinafter mentioned as IATA), the Arab Air Carriers Organization (hereinafter mentioned as AACO), and Royal Jordanian Airline (hereinafter mentioned as RJ).

All participants agreed that MBO is the right management style to follow. Emphasizing the role of employees to assign and identify their objectives will enhance their focus and will lead to better results. In addition, Interviewees stated that the program allows employees to know how their objectives will contribute to the organization when achieved. Though interviewees did not provide the researchers with concrete numbers due to confidentiality issues (except for AACO), but all interviewees confirmed that it reduced incurred costs by a significant margin.

Interviewees identified four major determinants of the program, namely, mobilizing resources, management support, training and development, and monitoring and evaluation. Based on the aggregated responses, the interviewees also stated secondary factors such as rewards, human relations, and focus on groups.

As for MBO application, two organizations applied MBO using the managers' letter approach (IATA and AACO). While RJ applied MBO using an integrated solution allowing every department to post its aggregated objectives on an internal system which is visible to other departments having interrelated tasks and then approved by the Chief Executive Officer (CEO) and Chief Operating Officer (COO). All interviewees agreed that they had witnessed better output by identifying synergies between departments, which led them to minimize overlapping tasks, therefore reducing working hours.

Interviewees stated that most of the implications were mentioned by the interviewer. However, AACO's Secretary General stated that the major implication the organization faced while applying MBO was when individuals overestimate their abilities. The challenge was to channel this energy in line with organizational objectives.

Interviewees agreed that MBO will continue to spread aided by the technological development where such tasks could be done momentarily. Also, they emphasized that MBO fosters group development which is the key to success nowadays. RJ interviewee stated:

> *"Perhaps it was the best thing we have done through years, especially on the level of the maintenance department, when the team noticed that their ideas are under tasks to be achieved, they were self-motivated, and we noticed several initiatives to perform some tasks in an efficient way, in other words we noticed innovative behavior."*

5   Conclusion

Based on the findings of the survey and field work, the authors concluded that applying MBO in the aviation industry delivered better results in terms of productivity and efficiency. MBO serves as a catalyst to enhance organizational performance by focusing on objectives and creating synergies between employees. Additionally, the spread of such management styles is highly recommended to be supported by technological investment.

Additionally, this study is considered novel as none of the cited papers in the literature review argued the effect of applying MBO in terms of productivity and efficiency in the aviation industry.

The authors also concluded that prior to applying an MBO program in the aviation industry, the top management must evaluate the current status of the employees and their subordinates to determine whether they are ready to engage in such a complex activity in order to minimize future deficiencies. In addition, interviews between management and subordinates must be done in order to determine the latter's aim from the program and their willingness to be part of it to avoid any future implications.

Appendix A

Survey
   Section 1: general information, please tick the checkbox when applicable

Age*
25 years and less   ☐
Between 26-36 years   ☐
Between 37-47 years   ☐
48 years and more   ☐

Position*
Top Management   ☐
Middle Management   ☐
Front line Management   ☐
Department
....
Sex*
Male   ☐
Female   ☐
Working Experience*

2 years or less   ☐
Between 3-5 years   ☐
Between 6-10 years   ☐
11 years and more   ☐
      *Required

Section 2: Effect of MBO on Organizational Outcome*
   Guidance: please express your opinion by stating whether applying MBO has helped in increasing overall output of the organization
   Key: 5 = Strongly Agree (SA), 4 = Agree (A), 3 = Neutral (N), 2 = Disagree (D), and 1 = Strongly Disagree (SD).

3. Is Management by Objectives (MBO) applied at your organization: Yes ☐ No ☐ **(if no please proceed to question number three)**
4. What is the most important factor that needs to be considered under MBO to yield better productivity: (rank 5 best – 1 least)

Management support	
Mobilizing resources	
Motivation	
Monitoring and evaluation	
Training	
Rewards	

	SA, 5	A, 4	N, 3	D, 2	SD, 1
Employee engagement in goal-setting yields better productivity*	☐	☐	☐	☐	☐
Defining accurate timelines in terms of achieving objectives has a positive impact on productivity*	☐	☐	☐	☐	☐
Managing by flexible goals yields better productivity*	☐	☐	☐	☐	☐
Fixed employee roles yields better performance*	☐	☐	☐	☐	☐
MBO has a positive effect on organizational effectiveness*	☐	☐	☐	☐	☐
Applying MBO assists organizations in adapting to market changes, leading to better productivity*	☐	☐	☐	☐	☐
Continuous monitoring and evaluation of objectives is necessary for achieving better results*	☐	☐	☐	☐	☐
Regular meetings between management and employees yields better performance*	☐	☐	☐	☐	☐
Individual objectives are better achieved under MBO*	☐	☐	☐	☐	☐
Performance evaluation should be linked to task accomplishment*	☐	☐	☐	☐	☐
Rewards and remunerations under MBO are essential to accomplish goals*	☐	☐	☐	☐	☐

*Required

Appendix B

Interview Questionnaire

1. Management by Objectives (MBO) is a management technique that allows organizations to set their objectives by molding employees' goals and objectives. What do you think about this approach?
2. Do you think MBO is an effective tool to increase organizational output? What do you think are the determinants of MBO?
3. How did you apply MBO at your organization? And did you witness better output?
4. What implications was associated with MBO application? Is it behavioral? Lack of knowledge? Role stress and work overload? Please specify.
5. Do you think MBO will continue to spread in the presence of more flat organizational structures?

References

Abdullah, A.: The impact of the application of Management by Objectives on the performance of Industrial Organisations (2010). http://e-thesis.mutah.edu.jo/index.php/faculty-of-business-administration/53-department-of-public-administration/804-2012-05-08-19-02-48.html

Akrani, G.: Management by objectives (MBO), Education, Management, Study Notes (2010). http://kalyan-city.blogspot.co.uk/2010/06/management-by-objectives-mbo-peter.html

Al Noah, A.: The reality and the importance of applying the principals of the method of management by objectives in the city of Riyadh. Saudi Soc. Educ. Psychol. Sci. J. Educ. Psychol. 37, 83–112 (2011)

Al Qwareen, E.: The management model with aims in the sport federations for the groups games in Jordan and how can be applied. Al Najah Univ. J. Res. Humanit. 24(4), 1102–1128 (2010)

Antoni, C.: Management by objectives – an effective. Int. J. Hum. Resource Manag. 16(2), 174–184 (2005)

Bandura, A.: Self-efficacy: toward a unifying theory of behavioral change. Psychol. Rev. 84, 191–215 (1977)

Carroll, S., Tosi, H.: Management by Objectives. Macmillan, New York (1973)

Drucker, P.F.: The Practice of Management. Harper & Row, New York (1954)

Fulk, H.K., Bell, R.L., Bodie, N.: Team management by objectives: enhancing developing: teams' performance. J. Manag. Policy Pract. 12(3), 17–26 (2011)

Gilboa, S., Shirom, A., Cooper, C.: A meta-analysis of work demand stressors and job performance examining main and moderating effects. Pers. Psychol. 61(2), 227–271 (2008)

Hollmann, R.: Supportive organizational climate and managerial assessment of MBO effectiveness. Acad. Manag. J. 19(4), 560–576 (2013)

IATA. IATA Anuual Report. IATA, Monteral (2018)

Jamieson, B.D.: Behavioral problems with management by objectives. Acad. Manag. J. 16(3), 496–505 (1973)

Kahn, R.L., Wolfe, D.M., Quinn, R.P., Snoek, J.D., Rosenthal, R.A.: Organizational stress: studies in role conflict and ambiguity. Oxford J. 30 (1964)

King, L.A., King, D.W.: Role conflict and role ambiguity: a critical assessment of construct validity. Psychol. Bull. 107(1), 48–64 (1990)

Kumar, S.: Management by objectives (MBO): a tool of performance appraisal. Indian J. Public Adm. **3**(4), 749–756 (2012)

Kyriakopoulos, G.: Half a century of management by objectives (MBO): a review. Afr. J. Bus. Manag. **6**(5), 1772–1786 (2012)

Levinson, H.: Management by whose objectives? Harvard Bus. Rev. **1** (2003)

Locke, E.A., Latham, G.P.: A theory of goal setting and task performance. Acad. Manag. Rev. **16** (2), 480–483 (1991)

McConkey, D.D.: How to Manage by Results, p. 15. American Management Association, New York (1967)

McNabb, D.E.: Qualitative research approaches and methods. In: Research Methods For Political Science: Quantitative and Qualitative Approaches, pp. 225–263. Routledge, London and New York (2009)

Odiorne, G.S.: Management by objectives. In: Management by Objectives, p. 26. Pitman, New York (1965)

Ramosaj, B.: Menagement. Botimi i pestë. Universiteti i Prishtinës "Hasan Prishtina", Prishtina (2007)

Rose, R.: Implementation and evaporation: the record of MBO. Public Adm. Rev. **37**(1), 64–71 (1977)

Sah, D.P.: Management by objectives, 15 June 2012. http://durgaprasadsah.hubpages.com/hub/mbo. Accessed 2018

Thomson, T.M.: Management by objectives. In: The Pfeiffer Library Volume, vol. 20, no. 2, pp. 1–25 (1998)

Tuckman, B., Jensen, M.A.: Stages of small-group development revisited. Group Organ. Stud. **2** (4), 419 (1986)

Weihrich, H.: A new approach to MBO: updating a time-honored technique. Weihrich, Heinz (2000)

The Effect of Digital Transformation on Innovation and Entrepreneurship in the Tourism Sector: The Case of Lebanese Tourism Services Providers

Nadine Sinno[(✉)]

The International University of Beirut, Beirut, Lebanon
Nadine.sinno@liu.edu.lb

Abstract. The service industry is one of the early adopters of digitalization which included airlines, travel agencies and hotels. This digitization has created a new sector in the Tourism Industry named: Electronic tourism (hereinafter mentioned as E-Tourism). E-tourism pertains to all tourism services using a single platform. The evolution of E-Tourism has reshaped business practices and strategies and directly affected suppliers approaches and client's consumptions behavior. Major online platforms were introduced to endorse E-tourism and to modernize traditional distribution systems to become E-distribution processes. The adoption of digital platforms has made the tourism services available to all market segments, therefore, a higher consumption of the tourism services has been recorded.

In fact, the number of the international tourist's activity accelerated during the past 10 years recording nearly double the number recorded in 2007.

This paper discusses the effect of the digital transformation in tourism by boosting the entrepreneurial traits of the suppliers from one hand and affecting the tourists/traveler's culture of consumption from the other hand.

A qualitative approach has been adopted by conducting in depth interviews with executives in the tourism sector to link e-tourism to entrepreneurship. Moreover, a questionnaire has been distributed to E-tourism consumers to understand their consumption patterns and culture.

The purpose of this paper is to acknowledge the importance of tourism digitization in boosting innovation and entrepreneurship in the tourism industry.

Keywords: E-Tourism · Digital · Transformation · Entrepreneurship · Innovation

1 Introduction

1.1 Definitions and Overview

Tourism was first defined in 1905 by Guyer Feuler as the set of activities done by individuals traveling and staying outside their environment for more than one night for business, leisure, and other purposes. The first governing body for international tourism was found In January 2nd of the year 1975, as the "United Nations World Tourism

© Springer Nature Switzerland AG 2019
R. Jallouli et al. (Eds.): ICDEc 2019, LNBIP 358, pp. 29–39, 2019.
https://doi.org/10.1007/978-3-030-30874-2_3

Organization" (hereinafter mentioned as UNWTO) with its headquarters in Madrid, Spain. According to the UNWTO (2007), a tourist/traveler is a visitor either domestic, inbound, or outbound that his trip includes a layover for one night that is conducted for business or leisure.

The Tourism sector is defined by the UNWTO (2007) as a subcategory of travel. "The tourism sector is the cluster of production units in different industries that provide consumption goods and services demanded by visitors. Such industries are called tourism industries because visitor acquisition represents such a significant share of their supply that, in the absence of visitors their production of these would cease to exist in meaningful quantity (2018)".

Similarly, the UK Essays (2016) stated that tourism comprises multiple activities conducted by travelers staying in a place outside their living area for leisure or business. Many people have witnessed the act of "tourism" but yet many failed to describe it in real terms (go2HR 2018).

Travel was historically perceived as a dangerous voyage or expedition and a daunting job for the employees. In contrast, today, travel is a part of stress release, relaxation, out of the box business meetings and an enjoyable industry. The shift of the perception of the tourism activity from overwhelming to pleasurable is highly dependable on the digital transformation and innovation. This is perfectly revealed in the acceleration of the number of international tourists during the past 10 years recording nearly double the number recorded in 2007. In 2017, international tourist arrivals reached around 1,326 million worldwide. The leap in tourist numbers was mainly affected by two factors, the breakthrough of the holistic online travel platforms and the drastic drop in air fares.

1.2 Benefits of Tourism

The tourism sector is an essential component of the world's economy. Travel & tourism generated USD 2,570.1 billion in 2017 to the global economy (which is equivalent to 10.4% of the global GDP) (WTTC 2018). In addition, travel & tourism sector employed in total around 313.2 million people (which is equivalent to 9.9% of the world's employment) (WTTC 2018).

Looking on the cash flow side, in 2017, international tourism receipts reached USD 1,494.2 billion (an average of 1,100 USD spent by each tourist including but not limited to airline ticket, hotel accommodation, and daily spending) (WTTC 2018). In addition, travel & tourism generated USD 884.2 billion of investments in 2017 (which is equivalent to 4.5% of total worldwide investments) (WTTC 2018).

On the other hand, travel and tourism has social and cultural benefits. A significant number of tourists are motivated to travel by the influence of their friends and families (Backer 2008). According to the annual report of the UNWTO in 2016, visiting friends and relatives (hereinafter mentioned as VFR) tourists accounted for 33% of total international tourist arrivals worldwide. In addition, tourism allows people to explore new cultures and traditions. However, this encouragement and motivation for travel was not possible to grow in real numbers until the evolution of E-Tourism. Electronic platforms are the main instruments for this exponential expansion of the tourism industry.

2 E – Tourism

2.1 Definitions and Overview

The service industry was one of the early adopters of digitalization which included banks, airlines, hotels and many others. Electronic tourism (hereinafter mentioned as E-Tourism) pertains to all tourism branches on one platform. The evolution of E-Tourism has reshaped business practices and strategies, leading to the globalization of tourism (Cezar et al. 2002).

Tourists have become more sophisticated and experienced, especially frequent travelers. To cope with this evolvement in behavior, E-Tourism allowed tourists to have timely and easy access to information that is available at a click of a button. This progress has connected tour operators, service providers, and customers without the need for intermediaries. E-Tourism platforms offered customers a holistic approach to plan a vacation meaning to plan a full package. The E - services vary from booking hotel accommodations, airline tickets, tour operators, rent a car, finding touristic attractions, etc. In addition, the marketing approach offered through E-Tourism platform acts as an eyeopener to new destinations that maybe out of the customers' scope of interest (Cezar et al. 2002). The traveler, now, explores a bundle of services, easily, modestly inexpensive and controllable at any moment. This flexibility in the supply, encouraged a higher demand and increased awareness about the benefits of travel. Who wouldn't prefer flexibility over strictness? Who wouldn't choose to be in control instead of being controlled? This whole e-tourism platform reformed the perspective of the traveler. Travel and tourism is now under the control of the clients' wants. Everybody has to adapt to the new technological development, from suppliers to intermediaries to finally clients' perspectives and reactions.

2.2 E-Tourism and Consumers' Perspectives

E-Tourism represented by online travel agents (hereinafter mentioned as OTAs) are a perfect example of customers empowerment. In fact, OTAs have authorized tourists and allowed them to gain access to a wider based discounted, tailored, and up to date travel information. E-Tourism allows consumers to have timely and accurate access to information. E-Tourism provides diversified products, allowing the consumer to have a one-stop online shop. Furthermore, E-Tourism works on an economies of scale strategy i.e. it reduces transactional costs on consumers as more inventory are reserved through online platforms. E-tourism draws the consumers' attention with tailored offers upon his predetermined preferences, which saves more time in thinking about what places to visit or at which restaurants to dine in. Moreover, mobile integration has aided the move of tourism into the digital age. Today, many smartphone users prefer travel apps to plan their trips. In addition, E-Tourism allowed customers to monitor multiple variables to conduct a travel plan, including automatic notifications on air fares, hotel bookings, price comparison, availability, and so on.

On the other hand, advanced marketing strategies gathering consumers' data from social media platforms (data exhaust) can be used to pop-up tailored adds based on customers' preferences of travel. Again, easing the burden on the customer to surf the internet and reidentify his/her set of preferences. This digital transformation in tourism has led the customer to feel as if he/she is in command while actually he/she being driven by online marketing strategies manipulated by the suppliers. This is where globalization and information technology has opened a new door for entrepreneurship through E-Tourism.

3 Innovation, Entrepreneurship and E-Tourism

3.1 Entrepreneurship

Entrepreneurship has often become a "buzz" word in the public debate. There is no universal rule or book of guidance for entrepreneurship, yet there are characteristics which can be discussed. Entrepreneurship can be observed in the fields of technology, economics, finance, management, and social serving. Entrepreneurship can be simply associated with setting a foundation of a business.

In the new millennia, governments, practitioners and academics around the world are seeking ways to foster entrepreneurship as a means of achieving economic development (Chell et al. 2010). Entrepreneurship and innovations are desirable as they create employment opportunities, develop new industries and introduce new business models that address economic and social needs. It is widely known that the rapid growth of Western economies in the past two decades has been attributed to the Information Technology (IT) revolution spurred by the emergence of innovative, entrepreneurial ventures. This is where e-tourism is involved.

Entrepreneurs are innovative people, willing to take the risk in the sake of accomplishment, whether social, financial, or academic.

As for the innovation and entrepreneurship in the tourism industry, UNWTO defines innovation in tourism as: "the introduction of a new or improved component which intends to bring tangible and intangible benefits to tourism stakeholders and the local community, improves the value of the tourism experience and the core competencies of the tourism sector and hence enhance tourism competitiveness and/or sustainability. Innovation in tourism may cover potential areas, such as tourism destinations, tourism products, technology, processes, organizations and business models, skills, architecture, services, tools and/or practices for management, marketing, communication, operation, quality assurance and pricing" (UNWTO 2018). Therefore, OTA's are major entrepreneurs in the history. In fact, Trivago, Airbnb, hopper, skyscanner, expedia, and booking.com are all holistic approaches for tourism, each platform has its own characteristics and provides a differentiated service. Hopper, for example, provides forecast for air fares, while Airbnb supply its users with apartments that can be rented and cheaper than hotels. Whereas skyscanner, provides its users with a matrix of what are the cheapest airfares, hotels, and car rental agencies during a period of time. All of these innovations reshaped the tourism industry from one side and the consumers culture of consumption from the other side.

3.2   E - Services Providers as Entrepreneurs

E-Tourism through OTAs and service providers platforms, have gained access to a wider consumer database. Today, is the Era of data, the internet of things, artificial intelligence, and data analysis. Tourism today speaks the social platforms' language. Providers have access to consumer data, their number of clicks, previous transactions, demographics, travel preferences, and even their targeted countries to visit. Using this data, service providers are being able to tailor their products based on customers' needs. For example, if a traveler surfs booking.com for a hotel booking in Amman – Jordan, he/she will continue to receive adds on all connected social media platforms associated with his google accounts on deals arising for Amman – Jordan. Indeed, this is not a free service, and service providers are paying a lot of money to gain access to the consumers' social activities, yet benefits outpace the costs incurred. OTAs have unchained customers from the past 50 years of global distribution systems domination and the bilateral agreements conducted between airlines that agreed on pricing, legroom, schedules and services.

The travel & tourism is a USD 1.2$ billion worth industry, and companies will continue to invest in creating more solutions to better cope with tech-savvy customers to satisfy their needs, meet their expectations, and serve them in the best possible way (Newman 2018). However, who is in control today? The supplier or the consumer?

4   The Effect of E-Tourism on Consumer's Culture and Consumption

4.1   Culture and Consumption

According to Cohen (1974), tourists travel to escape their daily environment, and when they travel they take with them all their environment. As a result, they travel within an "environmental bubble" that represents the cultural, behavioral and the value system that characterizes a consumer, even on vacation.

From this observation, Cohen identified four typologies of tourists:

Institutionalized Tourists
Tourists organize their trips through a tourism agent (tour operators, travel agencies). The environment of their vacation in the chosen destination must be similar to their daily environment.

In this case, there are two kinds of tourists: organized mass tourists and individual mass tourists:

Organized Mass Tourist
The package purchased is composed of a complete itinerary, with all activities decided and organized by the tourist actor. The hotel must be similar to its usual surroundings,

for example: an international chain that the tourist knows in advance and contacts with the local culture are rare.

The tourist seeks to eat the same dishes and speak the same language as in his/her home country. The tourism experience is planned, controlled and managed by the tourism industry. The package is a tourist service that sells for mass tourists, nothing is personalized but everything is planned in a way that the tourist is satisfied when he/she is in a comfortable environment, reducing the notion of novelty (meeting with locals).

The Individual Mass Tourist

This tourist buys a package pre-organized but adds elements, sites, activities of his/her choice to add a dimension of novelty and get a little out of its environmental bubble. For example, he/she may add a short excursion personally organized.

Non-institutionalized Tourists

Prefer to travel individually and without contacting tourist service providers. Their travel goals are to meet new cultures and try different experiences than the ones they are accustomed to in their daily lives.

The Explorer

This tourist travels to experience the lives of others. He/she tries to speak the local language of the destinations, to eat the traditional dishes, and to dress like the locals. However, this tourist prefers to make sure that the facilities provided by the tourist industry are available if needed.

Thus, a minimum level of comfort must be present and the notion of safety is also paramount (easy access to care, contact with banking institutions, underwriting insurance, etc.). This tourist travels most often to exotic destinations not explored by mass tourism.

The Sailor

This category, the least common, includes individuals who want to dissociate themselves completely from mass tourists. The first goal of the trip is to live as one of the locals. Therefore, trying to escape completely from the environmental bubble.

Consequently, there are several forms of consumption's culture by the tourists. How would the service provider adapt? Could E-tourism be the solution? In this case, the tourism services providers must analyze which tourists can be targeted by e-platforms and how.

4.2   E-Tourism and Culture of Tourism Consumption

E-tourism is a win-win deal for consumers and suppliers. Nevertheless, there are some hidden remunerations which should be uncovered while discussing the effect on consumers culture of consumption. In fact, the data exhaust of tourists/travelers' preferences can be a great way to influence consumers choices of destinations, hotels, sightseeing, attractions and entertainment.

Linking the above-mentioned to the aspects of E-Tourism, it can be stated that E-Tourism indirectly acts as an eyeopener on different services and a way to invent new services/products and markets which falls directly into the definition of innovation in tourism. For instance, adds from OTAs are not always targeted towards consumer preferences, these adds sometimes provide the consumer with suggestions based on likes, clicks, comments, and even random search categories. For example, service providers are now focused on promoting southeastern Europe as convenient places to visit with low budgets and interesting attractions. By this, the service providers are targeting both consumers willing to spend less and the ones interested in site seeing and cultural exploration. Through this process, E-Tourism is contributing to multiple aspects. Mainly, this approach is creating a new product/service, promoting cross-cultural knowledge of tourists and at the same time satisfying their needs. This approach is a pure illustration of how e-tourism and digital transformation is promoting innovation and entrepreneurship in the tourism sector. Moreover, the new markets, such as Southeastern Europe, now have the opportunity to develop the services provided in the destinations leading to new products and more innovation and entrepreneurship.

The below table statistically summarizes the impact of E-Tourism on Southeastern European countries in specific, illustrating how the number of tourist arrivals have evolved comparing 2007 to 2017 (Table 1):

Table 1. International tourist arrival - Source: UNWTO (E-Library – Tourism Statistics 2019).

Country	2007	2017	Growth
Armenia	319,000	1,495,000	368.7%
Georgia	1,067,000	4,069,000	281.3%
Bosnia & Herzg	306,000	922,000	201.3%
Azerbaijan	1,011,000	2,454,000	142.7%
Serbia	696,000	1,497,000	115.1%
Czech Rep.	6,680,000	12,808,000	91.7%
Montenegro	984,000	1,877,000	90.8%
Romania	1,551,000	2,760,000	77.9%
Hungary	8,638,000	15,256,000	76.6%
Bulgaria	5,151,000	8,883,000	72.5%
Turkey	22,248,000	37,601,000	69.0%
Croatia	9,307,000	15,593,000	67.5%
Poland	14,975,000	18,258,000	21.9%

In result, the western world is evidently putting an enormous effort in using technology as a tool for innovation, entrepreneurship, competitiveness, cultural and market influence. However, the Lebanese tourism providers seem to be very far from this technological approach leaning towards the traditional strategies. In an attempt to understand the Lebanese E-tourism market, a qualitative study has been conducted through in-depth interviews with executives in the tourism industry. Moreover, a questionnaire has been distributed to tourism consumers to understand their consumption patterns and culture.

5 Empirical Study – The Case of Lebanese Tourism Services Providers

5.1 Methodology

A qualitative approach has been adopted by conducting in depth interviews with executives in the tourism sector to link e-tourism to entrepreneurship. Additionally, a questionnaire has been distributed to E-tourism consumers to understand their consumption patterns and culture.

The in-depth interviews were conducted with ten executives from the Lebanese Travel and Tourism Industry. The interviews' main purposes are, on one hand, to identify the use of digital platforms by the tourism services providers and, on the other hand, to determine if the tourism services providers adapt their offerings according to digital innovations and e-consumers' preferences.

As for the consumer's questionnaire, it was circulated through google docs, shared on social media platforms namely Facebook and Twitter. The study was able to collect around sixty respondents. The questions revealed how often E-consumers use the internet to search for travel services and if they book their travel services online, which applications or platforms appeals to them the most?

The purpose of this study is to recognize the importance of tourism digitization in boosting innovation and entrepreneurship in the Lebanese tourism industry taking into consideration e-tourists consumption patterns and preferences.

5.2 Overview of the Lebanese Tourism Services Providers

A substantial effort has been made by the private and the public sector to promote Lebanon as a tourist destination. The tourist potential is, however, far from being fully exploited and one can reasonably think that Lebanon will return to its pre-war tourist level.

According to the Association of Travel Agents in Lebanon (ATTAL), there are 243 travel agencies in Lebanon of which 23 dominate the market and the others are distributors of their tourist services.

5.3 E-Tourism and Entrepreneurship by the Lebanese Tourism Service Providers

The political context in Lebanon influences the country's work and economy. In fact, the directors of companies do not follow a rational economic approach. Political, family or even community situations greatly influence managers' decisions (recruitment decisions, managerial decisions, target clients).

Lebanese businesses are still mostly in the hands of family groups that hold important traditional contacts with the countries of the region. However, with the current context of uncertainty and open markets, this is not enough. One of the major challenges is to improve the quality of production while remaining competitive. Few of the tourism services providers have emerged into the digital era of services. Therefore, it is mainly observed that their full effort is put into providing competitive prices.

5.4   E-Tourism and the Lebanese Culture of Consumption

Lebanese tourists are considered to be somehow psychocentrics, meaning that they are non-adventurous, they prefer to visit known areas where the destination is at its mature lifecycle phase. In fact, most of the Lebanese tourists prefer to inquire multiple times before booking any destination, and they do not confirm the booking until they are totally acquainted with every single detail about the destination. The details enquired for may include: shopping areas, prices, taxi tariffs, culture of the destination, maps, street names, hotels. etc. Therefore, and according to the questionnaire's responses, around the majority of the Lebanese tourism consumers use the internet to search for travel services and destination information. However, only half of these respondents confirmed using the digital application to book these services.

Consequently, the Lebanese tourists' still book through the current intermediaries to ensure the provision of safety, security, the best value and quality of service. This implies that the Lebanese culture of consumption is still dependent on the traditional booking methods via travel agents and tour operators and they still believe in visiting physical/tangible tourism offices.

The Lebanese customers are looking for high quality of service and liability offered by the tourism services intermediaries or suppliers. Their perception of the level of quality of service is influenced by how the service is delivered and the final result of the service (the experience at the time of the trip) which is named "subjective culture". According to Triandis (2002), Subjective culture occurs when cultural characteristics reflect the perception of the quality of service and therefore the consumer behavior.

In conclusion, the Lebanese tourism service providers are not adapting to the world's digital development due to the remaining existence of traditional cultural consumption. Nonetheless, this traditional consumption will not last forever, as the new generation will definitely shift towards the digital consumption. Therefore, sooner or later the tourism services providers will have to adapt to the new global market and become more innovators.

5.5   Conclusion and Recommendations

As noticed by the field study, the Lebanese enterprises usually work with previous data where forecasts are based on data from the previous year and the figures from the prior years are the budgeted figures for the following year.

When the company matches the results of the previous year, it considers that it has achieved a good performance. Budgets are used for pricing, sales forecasting and not for investment decisions, entrepreneurship or innovation.

The forecasts are made for the short term, which is less than a year. Medium-term and long-term forecasts are non-existent. In fact, an interviewee mentioned that long-term forecasting attempt, in a context of uncertainty, fails. Thus, Lebanese tourism businesses seek profits in the short term, which means that they do not enter into long-term investments.

Therefore, instead of providing a list of recommendations, a very imperative concept should be introduced: Innovation.

Innovation, should be a basic policy in the tourism companies where managers and executives should include design thinking as a tool for offering the best innovative services, whether in e-tourism or not.

Innovation is the key to the success of multiple startups, which means, it is the mean to stretch the services offered to an international basis reaching a significant growth of market.

As a result, in order to keep a competitive advantage, the tourism services providers are in an excessive need to have innovation solutions, otherwise, their business will eventually be diluted in a big pool of replicated provision of services.

The first step for the Lebanese tourism services providers is to enter this huge digital market, yet, innovatively without facing abundant competition.

The problem that is very possible to arise in the near future is: what if, soon, the market faces a flood of an oversupply of digital tourism services? Would that leave a space for innovations? Or would it just mean that the world would have to live with the saturation of supply in the favor of the consumers?

References

Backer, E.: Participants' characteristics and economic benefits of visiting friends and relatives (VFR) tourism—an international survey of the literature with implications for Ghana. Int. J. Tourism Res. **10**(6), 609–621 (2008)

Cezar, M., Beatrice, S., Alexandra, M.: The development, success, and impact of electronic tourism in the digital age. J. Inf. Syst. Oper. Manag. **10**(2), 416–424 (2002)

Chell, E., Nicolopoulou, K., Karataş-Özkan, M.: Social entrepreneurship and enterprise: international and innovation perspectives. Entrepreneurship Reg. Dev. **22**(6), 485–493 (2010). https://doi.org/10.1080/08985626.2010.488396

Cohen, E.: Who is a tourist'? A conceptual clarification. Sociol. Rev. **22**(4), 527–555 (1974)

Newman, D.: Forbes (2018). https://www.forbes.com/sites/danielnewman/2018/01/02/top-6-digital-transformation-trends-in-hospitality-and-tourism/#2e0a56fe67df. Accessed 21 Dec 2018

go2HR, T.S.: go2HR (2018). https://www.go2hr.ca/getting-know-bcs-tourism-industry/what-is-tourism. Accessed 21 Dec 2018

Khadige, C.: Intelligence, entrepreneuriat et résilience d'entreprise- tiré de. http://www.fgm.usj.edu.lb/files/a122009.pdf

UKEssays, U.: ukessays (2016). https://www.ukessays.com/essays/tourism/definition-of-tourism.php#citethis. Accessed 21 Dec 2018

UNWTO: Understanding Tourism: Basic Glossary, s.l.: UNWTO (2007)

UNWTO: UNWTO (2018). http://publications.unwto.org/publication/UNWTO-Tourism-definitions. Accessed 21 Dec 2018

UNWTO: E-Library: Tourism Statistics (2019). https://www.e-unwto.org/toc/unwtotfb/current. Accessed 24 Feb 2019

WTTC: Travel & tourism, Economic Impact (World). WTTC, London (2018)

E-Finance

Testing the Significance of Artificial Intelligence Investment in Determining Stock Prices

Mohammad Makki[1] and Mira Abdallah[2(✉)]

[1] International University of Beirut – BIU, Beirut, Lebanon
Mohammad.makki@liu.edu.lb
[2] International University of Beirut – BIU, Kousba, El-Koura, Lebanon
Mira.abdallah@liu.edu.lb

Abstract. Artificial Intelligence (AI) is a machine or computer framework that involves several algorithms including machine adapting, profound learning and natural language processing. It has the ability to learn on its own from historical data to facilitate the work and interactions of employees, customers and advance operations. This paper investigates the significance of artificial intelligence investment in determining stock prices. A sample of 12 companies, operating in different industries, were randomly selected and a total of 540 observations on Stock Prices, Book Value per Share, Book to Market ratio, Free Cash Flow Yield, Return on Assets and Artificial Intelligence Investment were recorded. The regression results, using E-Views software, indicated that artificial intelligence investment significantly and directly affects stock prices.

Keywords: Artificial Intelligence · Stock prices · Fundamental analysis · Investment · Research and development · Regression

1 Introduction

Artificial Intelligence (AI) is the science of designing smart machines, particularly smart computer programs (Swarup 2012). This science advances continuously to enable smart machines to expand human capacities by detecting, grasping, acting and adapting—thereby enabling individuals to accomplish significantly more. Companies in different industries are investing resources in AI since it is enhancing industry procedures and making machines "SMART"; it is considered as a way to cultivate advancement, streamline business expertise and enhance profitability (PwC Governance Insight Center 2017).

When AI advancements are incorporated by businesses, they can make an exceedingly versatile business capacity, allowing companies to grow faster and expand. Greenman (2018) conducted a research to find out who will generate money in Artificial Intelligence AI; he concluded that AI will help big companies become bigger while having control over technology, data, customers and capital. As reported by McKinsey Global Institute (2017), artificial intelligence deals signed by technology companies, in 2015, expanded four times more than in 2010, achieving 8.5 billion dollars. Tech giants like Google, Facebook, Amazon and Microsoft are in race for

© Springer Nature Switzerland AG 2019
R. Jallouli et al. (Eds.): ICDEc 2019, LNBIP 358, pp. 43–52, 2019.
https://doi.org/10.1007/978-3-030-30874-2_4

employing the best AI rare talents, and spending huge amounts on research and development. International Data Corporation (IDC) speculates that expenditures on AI and machine learning (ML) will grow from $12 billion in 2017 to $57.6 billion by 2021 (Framingham 2017).

McKinsey Global Institute (2017) estimates that the total external investment in AI was between eight to twelve billion dollars in 2016, with machine learning attracting about 60% of that investment. Machine learning patents expanded thirty-four percent from 2013 to 2017; ranking number three in the quickest developing licenses conceded classification. Given the mentioned facts, new dimensions of business potential outcomes are developed leading to higher productivity. Artificial intelligence is winding up increasingly worldwide at a gigantic pace and will significantly affect how businesses operate and how we perform out our daily routine (Gupta 2018).

In this paper we aim at exploring the significance of artificial intelligence investment (AII) in determining stock prices, while hypothesizing a positive relationship between the two variables. In the following sections, we will summarize the available literature in the field of determining stock prices, present the adopted research methodology, discuss the regression results and highlight the conclusions.

2 Literature Review

Trading stocks is a challenging task that requires time and market expertise especially that stock prices are driven by several microeconomic and macroeconomic factors (Pilinkus 2010). For any investor willing to buy stocks, the company's profile, its future agenda, the stock price, and the local and international economic conditions are crucial in determining her/his decisions. Many studies in the field investigated major microeconomic factors affecting investor's decisions and provided solid evidence on the importance of considering fundamental analysis; the analysis of company' stock price based on financial ratios found in the company's quarterly issued reports. No studies examined artificial intelligence investment as an exogenous variable determining stock prices. The available literature focused on the importance of using AI for stock price prediction.

Santos et al. (1993) showed that innovative investment in technology positively impact stock returns and increase the value of the firm. After studying the automation process of Artificial Intelligence and their impact on different sectors and fields, Cockburn et al. (2017) confirmed that AI is an innovative technology.

Samuel et al. (1996) tested the relationship between spending on research and development (R&D) - basically spending on innovative technology - on stock returns. They also considered in their model the size of the firm, leverage, dividends, industry and structure. The results revealed that spending on R&D, debt ratio and institutional ownership were positively affecting stock returns. Chan et al. (2002) examined the effects of spending on research and development (R&D) on stock prices, and they discovered that firms with high spending on R&D, relative to their market value, generate high excess returns in the future although they tend to have poor past returns. They concluded that spending on R&D has a positive significant relationship with stock prices.

Financial ratios are vital indicators of company's performance; it is deemed essential to consider them while taking investment decisions. Among the most utilized ratios are debt ratio, current ratio, price to earnings ratio, book value, and book to market, return on investment, free cash flow yield and return on assets. While analyzing 55 companies, listed on the Karachi Stock Exchange, between years 2001 and 2010, Khan et al. (2011) discovered that dividends, earnings per stock, return on equity and net profit directly affect stock prices, whereas retention ratio inversely affects them.

Şerife (2014) investigated the significance of several financial ratios on stock prices, by considering many sectors; electricity, food, communication, paper, chemistry, metal product, metal main, stone, textile, commerce and transportation. He figured out that Book Value is the most significant ratio among all selected sectors. In their study analyzing the fundamentals of the banking sector, Pradhan et al. (2017), found that return on assets, earnings per share and dividends per share are positively related to stock prices. Arkan (2016) studied the importance of financial ratios in three different sectors: industry, service and investment. He concluded that return on assets and return on equity are significant with positive impact on stock prices.

Hagel III et al. (2010) revealed that although return on equity is usually used by Wall Street traders and is considered as an accurate index for measuring companies' performance, it can be manipulated, and hides some deficiencies of company's financials. Their study concluded that return on assets highlights precisely the firm's capacity and is considered as an important ratio while predicting long term investment opportunities.

KLam (2002) investigated the impact of beta, company size, book leverage, book-to-market ratio and price earnings ratio on stock prices. The study revealed that beta has no impact on stock prices whereas all other variables do. However, company's size, book-to-market ratio and price to earnings ratio dominated other variables and were considered to be the most significant ones.

Saeidi and Okhli (2012) evaluated the impact of the return on asset ratio on the stock price in the Tehran stock exchange. They further considered several variables as firm's size, age and beta. Their research revealed that return on asset ratio has a strong positive impact on the stock prices. Khan et al. (2012) reported that the aim of their research is to investigate the ability of earning yield, dividend yield and book-to-market ratio, in predicting stock returns. The results showed that dividend yield and earning yield ratios have direct positive association with stock returns, whereas book-to-market ratio has significant negative relationship with stock returns. On the other side Chen et al. (2013) concluded that free cash flow yield is an important variable in determining stock prices. Mack (2016) studied the effect of free cash flow yield on the stock prices and found that if a trader is investing in a company using the mentioned ratio, she/he will receive higher returns.

3 Methodology

The main purpose of this paper is to examine the significance of AII in determining stock prices. To achieve our purpose we considered data of twelve companies selected randomly from several industries. The choice of companies was made based data availability and since the purpose is to investigate the significance of AII on stock prices, the industries that the companies operate in are not important for the study. The companies and the stock names in brackets are: Apple (AAPL), Google (GOOG); Amazon (AMZN); Microsoft (MSFT); International Business Machines (IBM); Salesforce.inc (CRM); Schweitzer-Mauduit International, Inc. (SWM); Miller Industries, Inc. (MLR); Ultra Petroleum Corp (UPL); Nutritional High International, Inc. (EAT), Penns Woods Bancorp, Inc. (PWOD) and Ashford Hospitality Trust (AHT). The observations were selected between the third quarter of 2004 and the fourth quarter of 2015, where we reported the values at the end of each quarter.

The first six mentioned companies invest in AI while the remaining six companies do not invest in AI. To better handle the topic, we included several financial ratios in the multiple regressions since AII is not the only exogenous variable determining stock prices. Quarterly Data on stock prices and some major corporate fundamentals were collected from Quandl; an online platform that provides financial, economic, and alternative data. We faced major difficulty in determining the starting date of the observations, thus we considered the third quarter of 2004 as all needed fundamentals of the mentioned companies were available and publically reported.

The panel data sample included 540 observations and the variables used in the regressions were: Stock Prices, Book Value per Share, Book to Market ratio, Free Cash Flow Yield, Return on Assets and Artificial Intelligence Investment. E-Views software was utilized to generate the results.

Multiple linear regressions with fixed and random effects were performed. Descriptive statistics and residual normality, Unit root, multi-collinearity and Hausman tests were conducted. Below is a brief description of the considered variables:

3.1   Artificial Intelligence Investment AII

We were unable to find the exact dollar amount spent by each company on research and development; mainly on artificial intelligence investment. Thus we considered AII as a dummy variable. AII took the following values:

AII = 0 when the company doesn't invest in artificial intelligence in a specific quarter
AII = 1 when the company invests in artificial intelligence in a specific quarter

3.2   Financial Ratios

Book Value per Share (BVPS); is usually used by traders when evaluating company' stock price by comparing the BVPS to the market value. It is calculated using the formula: (Total Assets − Intangible assets − Total Liabilities) ÷ number of shares outstanding. Book Value per Share is expected to directly affect stock prices.

Book to Market ratio (BMR) helps in comparing the Book value to the market value. Usually, market value should be higher than the book value since it takes into consideration the intangible assets of a company. Therefore, when this ratio is higher than one, it is a good indicator that the stock is undervalued and hence its price will increase. It is calculated using the formula: Book value ÷ market value. Book to Market ratio is expected to inversely affect stock prices.

Free Cash Flow Yield (FCFY) represents the yearly percentage of the stock price generated by the company. It is calculated using the formula: (cash from operations − capital expenditures) ÷ Market cap. Free Cash Flow Yield is expected to directly affect stock prices.

Return on Assets (ROA) measures the efficiency of a company in converting its assets into net income or profits. Thus the higher the value of this ratio, the more profitable the company is. It is calculated using the formula: Net income ÷ Total Assets. Return on Assets is expected to directly affect stock prices.

4   Results and Discussion

Natural logs were applied to stock price to remove trends, and the unit root test was performed for each variable to ensure stationarity. Taking into consideration that the null hypothesis is "there is unit root", the resulted P-value was compared with 5% level of significance and first differencing was applied for correction. The variables considered in the models were: Ln stock price (−1), BMR (−1), BVPS (−1), FCFY, ROA and AII. Note that (−1) refers to applying first differencing. The correlation matrix was generated to test for multi-collinearity between variables and the results, shown in Table 1 didn't record any values exceeding 0.5. There is no multi-collinearity between the selected variables.

Table 1. Correlation matrix

Matrix	BMR	BVPS	FCFY	ROA	AI
BMR	1	−0.023	0.401	−0.139	−0.192
BVPS	−0.02	1	0.008	0.067	0.406
FCFY	0.401	0.008	1	0.045	0.023
ROA	−0.139	0.067	0.045	1	0.289
AI	−0.192	0.406	0.023	0.289	1

The regression function stated in Eq. 1 was regressed with fixed effect and then again with random effect. The results are presented below:

$$LN(Price) = \beta_1 + \beta_2 BVPS + \beta_3 BMR + \beta_4 FCFY + \beta_5 ROA + \beta_6 AII + ui \quad (1)$$

Where β_1 = the model intercept, β_2 to β_6 = partial slope coefficients and ui = stochastic disturbance term. The error term should be normally distributed.

The regression results using the fixed effect model are presented in Table 2. When we consider fixed effect model, we know that unobserved variables are allowed to have any association with the observed variables. Fixed effect model controls the effects of time-invariant variables with time-invariant effects. This applies to all variables whether explicitly measured or not (Williams 2018).

Table 2. Fixed effect model regression results

Dependent Variable: LNPRICE(-1)				
Method: Panel Least Squares				
Sample (adjusted): 2004Q4 2015Q4				
Periods included: 45				
Cross-sections included: 12				
Total panel (balanced) observations: 540				
Variable	Coefficient	Std. Error	t-Statistic	Prob.
C	2.935	0.041	71.667	0.000
BMR(-1)	−0.149	0.016	−9.064	0.000
BVPS(-1)	0.009	0.002	5.563	0.000
FCFY	0.020	0.039	0.527	0.598
ROA	1.840	0.674	2.731	0.006
AII	1.231	0.096	12.807	0.000
Effects specification				
Cross-section fixed (dummy variables)				
R-squared	0.866	Mean dependent var		3.380
Adjusted R-squared	0.862	S.D. dependent var		1.285
S.E. of regression	0.477	Akaike info criterion		1.389
Sum squared resid	119.135	Schwarz criterion		1.5246
Log likelihood	-358.174	Hannan-Quinn criter.		1.442
F-statistic	211.550	Durbin-Watson stat		0.229
Prob (F-statistic)	0.000			

Since the P-value of F-statistic is lower than 5% level of significance, we conclude that the overall model is significant. Free cash flow yield (FCFY) indicated a P-value higher than 5%, thus it is insignificant, leaving us with the regression results of Eq. 2.

$$LN(Price) = 2.9 - 0.15BMR + 0.009BVPS + 0.02FCFY + 1.8ROA + 1.2AII \quad (2)$$

We also tested for residual normality and the results in Fig. 1 indicated that the Jarque-Bera P-value is higher than the 0.01 level of significance, thus we didn't reject the null hypothesis and we concluded that residuals are normally distributed.

The regression results using the random effect model are presented in Table 3. Random effect model assumes that the unobserved variables are uncorrelated with all the observed variables. Although the assumption might be wrong since standard errors may be very high with fixed effects, random effects allows the estimation with time-invariant variables' effects. The model is usually considered in some specific circumstances and can be estimated with Generalized Least Squares (Williams 2018).

Since the P-value of F-statistic is lower than 5% level of significance, we conclude that the overall model is significant. Free cash flow yield (FCFY) indicated a P-value higher than 0.05, thus it is insignificant, leaving us with the regression in Eq. 3:

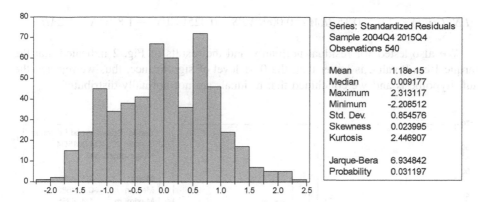

Fig. 1. Residuals descriptive statistics and histogram (Fixed effect)

Table 3. Random effect model regression results

Dependent Variable: LNPRICE(-1)				
Method: Panel EGLS (Cross-section random effects)				
Sample (adjusted): 2004Q4 2015Q4				
Periods included: 45				
Cross-sections included: 12				
Total panel (balanced) observations: 540				
Swamy and Arora estimator of component variances				
Variable	Coefficient	Std. Error	t-Statistic	Prob.
C	2.934	0.140	20.894	0.000
BMR(-1)	−0.157	0.016	9.631	0.000
BVPS(-1)	0.010	0.001	6.0621	0.000
FCFY	0.025	0.038	0.668	0.504
ROA	1.842	0.672	2.742	0.006
AII	1.222	0.093	13.128	0.000
Effects specification				
			S.D.	Rho
Cross-section random			0.466	0.488
Idiosyncratic random			0.477	0.512
Weighted statistics				
R-squared	0.441	Mean dependent var	0.510	
Adjusted R-squared	0.436	S.D. dependent var	0.645	
S.E. of regression	0.485	Sum squared resid	125.471	
F-statistic	84.377	Durbin-Watson stat	0.225	
Prob(F-statistic)	0.000			
Un weighted statistics				
R-squared	0.558	Mean dependent var	3.380	
Sum squared resid	393.632	Durbin-Watson stat	0.071	

$$LN(Price) = 2.9 - 0.15BRM + 0.009BVPS + 0.025FCFY + 1.8ROA + 1.2AII \quad (3)$$

We also tested for residual normality and the results of Fig. 2 indicated that the Jarque-Bera P-value is lower than the 0.01 level of significance, thus we rejected the null hypothesis and we concluded that residuals are not normally distributed.

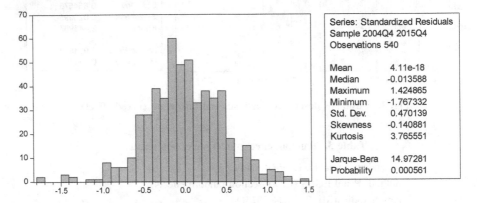

Fig. 2. Residuals descriptive statistics and histogram (Random effect)

To select the appropriate model we performed the Hausman test noting that the null hypothesis is that "Random effect Model is appropriate" while the alternative hypothesis is that "Fixed effect Model is appropriate". The results of the test indicated a P-value of 0.0006, which came to be lower than 5% level of significance and entitled us to reject the null hypothesis and retain the alternative one. The selected model is the Fixed Effect Model with Eq. 2 mentioned below.

$$LN(Price) = 2.9 - 0.15BMR + 0.009BVPS + 0.02FCFY + 1.8ROA + 1.2AII$$

The regression results showed that all variables are significant in determining stock prices except for FCFY. Based on the selected sample, the claim that AII determines stock prices and directly affects them was satisfied. Based on the equation, investing in AI leads to 4.1 percent increase in stock prices since natural logs were applied to stock prices; a move from 'D = 0' to 'D = 1'will increase the change in stock prices by 4.1%. When companies do not invest in artificial intelligence, the effect of the slope coefficient of AII is diluted and the intercept coefficient is held constant. Furthermore all other selected fundamental ratios except Free Cash Flow Yield were significant and the results came in line with the literature findings. Book value per share and returns on assets were directly affecting stock prices while book-to-market ratio inversely affects them.

5   Conclusion

Artificial intelligence is an emerging technological innovation that is paving the future of businesses and granting them better opportunities. Many companies are investing huge amounts on research and development especially in the field of artificial intelligence, since they are producing with faster and efficient techniques and business procedures. In this paper, artificial intelligence investment AII, among other fundamental ratios, was claimed to be a significant exogenous variable in determining stock prices. A sample of 540 observations was selected and the regression results indicated that AII is a significant variable that can be used to determine stock prices and in line with the available literature. On the other hand, the fundamental ratios considered were significant except for FCFY and the regression coefficients indicated the right signs as per literature. Although AII was treated as a dummy variable used to answer our claim, the paper opens the door for future research in the field of AI, where specific dollar amounts spent on artificial intelligence investment by companies can be considered to determine if more is better.

References

Arkan, T.: The importance of financial ratios in predicting stock price trends: a case study in emerging markets. Finanse Rynki Finansowe Ubezpieczenia nr 1(79), 13–26 (2016)

Chan, L., Lakonishok, J., Sougiannis, T.: The Stock Market Valuation of Research and Development Expenditures. The American Finance Association (2002)

Chen, L., Da, Z., Zhao, X.: What drives stock price movements? Rev. Finan. Stud. 26(4), 841–876 (2013)

Cockburn, I., Henderson, R., Stern, S.: The impact of artificial intelligence on innovation. Paper prepared for the NBER Conference on Research Issues in Artificial Intelligence – Toronto (2017)

Framingham, Massachusetts. IDC Spending Guide Forecasts Worldwide Spending on Cognitive and Artificial Intelligence Systems to Reach $57.6 Billion in 2021 (2017)

Greenman, S.: Towards data science. Who is going to make money in AI? (2018)

Gupta, J.: Customer think. How AI will transform the future of business (2018)

Hagel III, J., Brown, J., Davison, L.: The best way to measure company performance. Harvard Bus. Rev. (2010)

Khan, K.I., Aamir, M., Qayyum, A., Nasir, A., Khan, M.I.: Can dividend decisions affect the stock prices: a case of dividend paying companies of KSE. Int. Res. J. Finan. Econ. 76(68), 69–74 (2011)

Khan, M., Gul, S., Rehman, S., Razzaq, N., Kamran, A.: Financial ratios and stock return predictability (Evidence from Pakistan). Res. J. Finan. Account. 3(10), 1–6 (2012)

KLam, K.: The relationship between size, book-to-market equity ratio, earnings–price ratio, and return for the Hong Kong stock market. Glob. Finan. J. 13(2), 163–179 (2002)

Mack, M.: Portfolio Manager. The Power of Free Cash Flow Yield (2016). https://www.paceretfs.com/media/pacer_perspective_may2016.pdf

McKinsey Global Institute: Artificial Intelligence, the next digital frontier (2017)

Pilinkus, D.: Macroeconomic indicators and their impact on stock market performance in the short and long run: the case of the baltic states. Technol. Econ. Dev. Econ. 16(2), 291–304 (2010)

Pradhan, R., Paudel, L.: Impact of fundamental factors on stock price: a case of nepalese commercial banks. Nepalese J. Eng. Nepalese J. Manag. 1–13 (2017). https://doi.org/10.2139/ssrn.3044108

PwC Governance Insights Center: The Essential Eight technologies Board byte: artificial intelligence (2017)

Quandl data. https://www.quandl.com/databases/SF1

Saeidi, P., Okhli, A.: Studying the effect of assets return rate on stock price of the companies accepted in Tehran stock exchange. Bus. Econ. Horiz. 8(2), 12–22 (2012)

Samuel, S., George, T., Zaher, Z.: The valuation of corporate R&D expenditures: evidence from investment opportunities and free cash flow. Financ. Manage. 25(1), 105–110 (1996)

Santos, B., Peffers, K., Mauer, D.: The impact of information technology investment announcements on the market value of the firm. Inf. Syst. Res. 4(1) (1993). https://doi.org/10.1287/isre.4.1.1

Şerife, Ö.: The Effect of Company Fundamentals (Microeconomic Factors) on Stock Values. European Researcher (2014)

Swarup, P.: Artificial intelligence. Int. J. Comput. Corporate Res. 2(4), 1–12 (2012)

Williams, R.: Fixed effects vs Random effects (2018). https://www3.nd.edu/∼rwilliam/stats3/panel04-fixedvsrandom.pdf

The Interest Rate Behaviour of Bitcoin as a Digital Asset

Thabo J. Gopane$^{(\boxtimes)}$ (iD)

Department of Finance and Investment Management,
University of Johannesburg, Kingsway Road, Auckland Park,
Johannesburg, South Africa
tjgopane@uj.ac.za

Abstract. The objective of this study is to assess interest rate behaviour of bitcoin as a digital asset in relation to market rates. The implied bitcoin interest rate is quantified through the assumptions of *uncovered interest parity* theory, and implied bitcoin exchange rate determined from the triangular of USD/BTC, and EUR/BTC. The Vector Autoregressive model is regressed on implied bitcoin interest rate along with four maturity classes of LIBOR interest rates for US and Euro markets respectively. The results show that there is a uni–directional impact with bitcoin interest rate responding to shocks from market rates, while shocks emanating from bitcoin to market rates are non-existent, or not statistically significant. The findings of this study have potential value towards monetary policy and capital market investors.

Keywords: Bitcoin · Cryptocurrency · Digital asset · Exchange rate · Interest rate

1 Introduction

The monetary system of cryptocurrency was introduced through its first-born, Bitcoin, on 3 January 2009 by a pseudonymous developer code-named Satoshi Nakamoto through a nine-page article published in the internet [1]. Cryptocurrency was conceived as decentralized digital currency where transactions are validated via cryptography without the need of central party (like bank) to usher-in trust among parties. Therefore, the system is said to be characterized by a combination of three elements namely, pseudo-anonymity, independence, and double-spending protection [2]. The predecessor technologies used in cryptocurrency like cryptography, blockchain, along with proof-of-work, were pioneered by Chaum [3], and Haber and Stornetta [4]; among others. The history of cryptocurrency is discussed elsewhere [5].

Notwithstanding the potential benefit of Bitcoin's innovative technology, blockchain, the continued expansion in virtual currency market has caused authorities to ponder the risk implications on financial stability, tax policy, and other governance issues. Consequently, governments around the world have varied levels of concern which lead them to either ignore, intervene, regulate, or declare a down right ban on some or all cryptocurrency activities [2].

© Springer Nature Switzerland AG 2019
R. Jallouli et al. (Eds.): ICDEc 2019, LNBIP 358, pp. 53–65, 2019.
https://doi.org/10.1007/978-3-030-30874-2_5

Since the launch of Bitcoin, the market continues to experience exponential growth in alternative cryptocurrencies (classified as Altcoins), and at the time of writing they are numbered 2 104. Nevertheless, Bitcoin still maintains a dominant market share of approximately thirty-eight percent. It is partly for this reason that this paper focus on Bitcoin. Further, since Bitcoin is the oldest in the market, it has a first-mover advantage on longest and possibly more consistent time series. The results of the paper may be applicable to comparable markets. This paper is particularly focusing on a financial product traded in the Bitcoin financial system, bitcoin.

An increasing number of studies have shown interest to explore the interaction of bitcoin as a digital asset within the economy [6, 7]; as well as bitcoin exchange rate dynamics [8–10]. Most studies tend to accept bitcoin price denominated in fiat currency (like US Dollar) as a bitcoin exchange rate. On the contrary, Smith [11] posits that bitcoin is not a currency, and therefore it is untenable to view its price as exchange rate. Smith assessed the behaviour of bitcoin as a commodity by comparing the market against implied bitcoin exchange rates. The current study follows the same analytical perspective. In particular, this paper contextualises Smith [11]'s empirical analysis within the well-known *Uncovered Interest Parity* (UIP) theory, and show that Smith explored part of the UIP (exchange rates), and as such, this paper evaluates the remainder (interest rates).

The rest of the paper is organised as follows: section two introduces UIP theory, and then uses it to derive implied bitcoin interest rate. Section three outlines the econometric methodology, which is implemented in section four to give empirical results and discussion, while section five concludes.

2 Theoretical Framework

Studies in finance have explored different aspect of bitcoin as digital asset including risk-return characteristic [12], return volatility [13], and transaction activity [14]. As an asset, bitcoin is expected to be affected by the knock-on effects among other assets [10] and transmissions from global economy [7]. One variable that have received little to no attention in the empirical studies of bitcoin and financial markets is interest rate. The reason for this could be that the sources of bitcoin historical data have only started accumulating this time series.

It is the desire of this paper to study the behaviour of bitcoin towards market interest rates. To circumvent the challenge of lack of time series data for bitcoin, we use the theory of UIP to derive and compute bitcoin implied interest rate. The theory of UIP says that in a globally integrated economy, where markets are competitive, and costs are insignificant, then the log ratio of spot and forward exchange rates will equal the interest differentials between the two countries, for the currencies under consideration:

$$f_{t+k} - s_t = i_t - i_t^*$$

(1)

The variable s_t is the domestic spot exchange rate (price of foreign in terms of domestic currency), and f_{t+k}, is the forward exchange rate k periods away from current period, t. The domestic interest rate (i_t) and foreign rate (i_t^*) are both spot rates. Further discussion of UIP is elaborated in important reviews by Froot and Thaler [15], Engel [16], and Chinn [17]. The forward exchange rate may be estimated with spot exchange rate that is expected k periods away (S_{t+k}^e), plus adjustment for risk premium (η_{t+k}), as shown in Eq. 2:

$$f_{t+k} = S_{t+k}^e + \eta_{t+k} \tag{2}$$

If we substitute Eq. 2 into 1, and incorporate the conditions of risk-neutrality $(\eta_{t+k} = 0)$ as well as rational expectation, we obtain Eq. 3, after re-arrangement. Equation 3 says that the expected change in the log of spot exchange rate $(S_{t+k}^e - s_t)$, is a function of current period interest rate differential, which is the key equation of UIP.

$$S_{t+k}^e - s_t = \left(i_t - i_t^*\right) \tag{3}$$

In order to reflect the intuition of comparison for returns or interest rates between two assets, Eq. 3 may be re-stated as:

$$i_t = i_t^* + S_{t+k}^e - s_t \tag{4}$$

Equation 4 says the return on domestic investment (i_t) equals return from foreign investment (i_t^*) plus depreciation $(S_{t+k}^e - s_t)$. Suppose one contemplates investing in either bitcoin or another asset. In order to implement this investment decision, the investor needs to compare the relevant rates of return. The question to ask is: Does a return in, say domestic US asset or USD denominated $(r_\$)$ out-perform a return on an alternative bitcoin asset $(r_\text{Ƀ})$ after adjusting for currency depreciation (or appreciation) between US dollar ($) and bitcoin (Ƀ) given current $(S_{\$/Ƀ})$, and expected $(S_{\$/Ƀ}^e)$ exchange rates, respectively? This statement is presented as Eq. 5 which is the same as Eq. 4 in levels (or before logs), where we let $r_\$ = i_t$, and $r_\text{Ƀ} = i_t^*$:

$$r_\$ = r_\text{Ƀ} + \frac{S_{\$/Ƀ}^e - S_{\$/Ƀ}}{S_{\$/Ƀ}} \tag{5}$$

To compute bitcoin rate, $r_\text{Ƀ}$: First we follow Smith [11]'s persuasive argument that if bitcoin is an asset then its listed value is not exchange rate but its price (just like gold price). So, to determine the implied bitcoin exchange rate, we divide its US dollar price, $\$/Ƀ$ by its Euro price €/Ƀ, to choose the reasonably stable exchange rates in the global economy. The resulting implied bitcoin exchange rate is, $/€. We use different symbols to reflect *implied* (Z) as opposed to *market* (S) exchange rates. So we substitute $Z_{\$/€}$ in Eq. 5 and re-arrange to obtain:

$$r_\beta = r_\$ - \frac{Z^e_{\$/\euro} - Z_{\$/\euro}}{Z_{\$/\euro}} \tag{6}$$

A similar relationship between actual market exchange rates for USD and Euro may be represented as:

$$r_\euro = r_\$ - \frac{S^e_{\$/\euro} - S_{\$/\euro}}{S_{\$/\euro}} \tag{7}$$

Algebraically and empirically the right hand side (RHS) of 6 and 7 are supposed to be equal. This was precisely the empirical study of Smith [11] to study the relationship of implied bitcoin exchange rates among three countries USA, Australia, and UK.

3 Methodology

3.1 Econometric Model

The previous section used the theory of UIP to derive a formula for implied bitcoin interest rate (Eq. 6). A log transformation of Eq. 6 gives 8, which will be a variable of focus henceforth in econometric modelling. Equation 8 is derived in the context of US market. If we replace the US based rate $(r_{\$,t})$ with the Euro based interest rate $(r_{\euro,t})$, and then take the inverse of the USD/EUR exchange rate, and take the logs in 6, we get the counter-part, Euro based implied bitcoin interest rate in 9.

$$[US\ implied\ r_{btc}]_t = r_{\$,t} - (z_{t+1} - z_t) \tag{8}$$

$$[Euro\ implied\ r_{btc}]_t = r_{\euro,t} - (\tilde{z}_{t+1} - \tilde{z}_t) \tag{9}$$

Equations 8 and 9 are consistent with Lothian [18]'s UIP test equation number 4. The study proceeds to model the relationship of bitcoin interest rate in relation to market interest rates. Econometrically, we consider a set of k time series variables, $y_t \in \{y_{1t}; y_{2t}; \ldots; y_{kt}\}$ within a Vector Autoregressive system of p lags, VAR (p):

$$y_t = A_1 y_{t-1} + A_2 y_{t-2} + \ldots + A_p y_{t-p} + \varepsilon_t, \ \varepsilon_t \sim \left(0, \sum_\varepsilon\right) \tag{10}$$

Where the A's are $k \times k$ coefficient matrices, and ε are white noise error terms. For the current study, the vector of y_t consists of a set of daily interest rates on London Inter–Bank Rates (LIBOR) for USA, and Euro markets in four maturity classes, 1–month, 3–month, 6–month, and 12–month. These four rates coupled with implied bitcoin (from 8, or 9), are estimated within a VAR system in 10. The regression is run twice, first for USA market, and then for the Euro market.

3.2 Data Description

The current study uses data on London Inter-Bank Offered Rates (LIBOR), as well as USD/EUR exchange rates from the Federal Reserve Bank of St. Louis, USA. Both the US, and Euro denominated bitcoin prices are obtained from Bitcoinity.com. The important preparation of the data set entailed matching the 5–day week for LIBOR rates with the 7–day week for bitcoin prices. After a successful date matching of the two data sets, and the necessary cleaning, the final sample size is 1 798 data points, for the period, 26 August 2011 to 4 January 2019) for both USA, and Euro. The overall sample descriptive statistics are summarized in Table 1. Judging by the magnitude of the means, the US rates are generally higher than the Euro's but both market tend to have stable standard deviations. All time series have a positive skewness which is to be expected for interest rate. The peakedness or flatness of the series are within the normal statistic of 3, but less so is the implied interest rate within the US market. These levels interest rates along with bitcoin prices, and exchange rates are further summarized in Figs. 1, and 2.

Table 1. Summary of descriptive statistics for Euro and US based LIBOR markets

Details	EURO based LIBOR markets				USA LIBOR Markets				Euro implied	US implied
	12-month	6-month	3-month	1-month	12-month	6-month	3-month	1-month	btc rate	btc rate
Mean	0.1988	0.0636	-0.0380	-0.1157	1.2638	0.9712	0.7755	0.6105	-0.2167	-0.5744
Median	0.1628	0.0569	-0.0075	-0.0558	1.0484	0.7284	0.4606	0.2418	-0.2182	-0.9126
Maximum	1.1261	1.0068	0.9270	0.8362	3.1441	2.9079	2.8238	2.5224	0.1453	1.2027
Minimum	-0.3058	-0.4134	-0.4931	-0.5442	0.5335	0.3194	0.2229	0.1478	-0.4278	-1.6438
Std. Dev.	0.3847	0.3801	0.3758	0.3575	0.7193	0.7172	0.7020	0.6499	0.1163	0.8433
Skewness	0.6799	0.7063	0.6593	0.5826	1.1182	1.2221	1.4097	1.4586	0.6389	0.8601
Kurtosis	2.8107	2.9212	2.9004	2.8598	3.2160	3.4151	3.7891	3.7955	3.3896	2.3615
Observations	1798	1798	1798	1798	1798	1798	1798	1798	1798	1798

Figure 1 shows distinct difference in patterns for bitcoin prices, and implied exchange rate. Both price denominations of bitcoin (USD and Euro) move on top of each other from 2011 before experiencing a small misalignment around the highest peak of bitcoin trading activity towards the end of 2017.

In Fig. 2, there is a distinct pattern of inverse co-movement between the US and Euro LIBOR markets, which are more evident from the end of 2015 onwards. The set of US rates tend bunch together in upward-slope while the Euro rates are downward-sloping, for the period under consideration, August 2011 to January 2019. After stationarity test, all interest rate variables revealed integration of order one, I(1). Consequently, the variables were differenced once before running the VAR system for the usual asymptotic and econometric regularities.

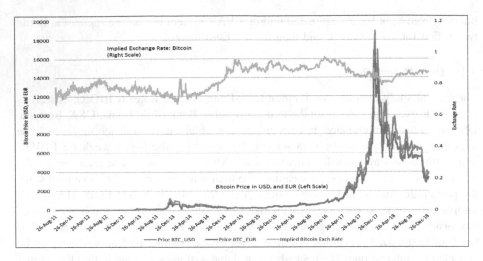

Fig. 1. Diagram of bitcoin price and implied bitcoin exchange rate

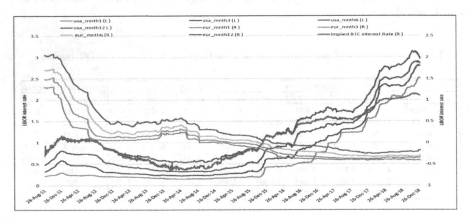

Fig. 2. A LIBOR market rates for USA, and Euro area

4 Empirical Results and Interpretation

The focus and interest of the current study is to examine the behaviour of bitcoin interest rate in relation to market rates. The VAR system was regressed twice: First for Euro, and then the US based LIBOR markets. In each run, the VAR system was regressed with 5 variables, 1–month, 3–month, 6–month, and 12–month, along with the respective bitcoin implied interest rate for Euro, or US markets. The implied bitcoin interest rates are quantified in Eqs. 8, and 9, respectively. The key results of the study are summarized in

Fig. 3 (for USA), and Fig. 4 (for Euro). Both diagrams report impulse response functions (IRF) for Cholesky's one standard deviation accumulated shock dynamics observed over a period of 120 days. The innovations are reported within the bands of confidence intervals. Panel A (Fig. 3) shows (from top to bottom) responses of implied bitcoin rate to 12–month; 6–month; 3–month, and 1–month LIBOR rates, respectively. A one standard deviation shock to US based interest rate is associated with a positive response from implied bitcoin rates which (in accumulated measure) dissipates in approximately 30 days. The bitcoin rate's response to all four LIBOR maturities has approximate comparable response. Panel B shows the US market responses to shocks emanating from bitcoin. In all instances (12–month; 6–month; 3–month; and 1–month), there is no statistically significant shock moving from bitcoin rates to US LIBOR market. The regression was replicated on Euro based LIBOR market against the implied Euro bitcoin rate, and the results are reported in Fig. 4.

Panel D of Fig. 4, shows statistically significant response of the implied bitcoin rate to shocks emanating from the Euro based LIBOR market. In contrast Panel E shows that none of the Euro based LIBOR interest rates (12–month; 6–month; 3–month; and 1–month) respond to shocks from bitcoin rate. To be more precise, the shocks are not big enough to be statistically significant. When we take into consideration that both Figs. 3 and 4 report accumulated responses to shocks, this shows that the bitcoin shocks are generally too small to have significant impact on the market under consideration. The supportive VAR regression outputs for Euro, and USA are appended in Tables 2, and 3. The numbers in brackets are t-statistic. Statistical significance for absolute magnitudes for the given t-statistics correspond to critical values of 2.58, 1.96, and 1.645 at one percent, five percent, and ten percent levels of test, respectively. The VAR model stability was satisfied as all the characteristic polynomial roots lie within a unit circle.

4.1 Discussion of Results

It appears that Bitcoin was designed to function as "... an electronic payment system..." [1:1]. However, for purposes of tax laws, financial stability regulatory codes, as well as investment analysis, debate continue to ponder the classification of bitcoin whether: currency, or asset. Some maintains that bitcoin is a digital currency [19], while others insist it is a digital asset [20]. The distinction is useful for interpretation purposes but this is not a major problem for this paper since the theory driving our empirical analysis does accommodate currency as an asset (in the form of deposit) from which one may receive return in the form of interest. Nevertheless, the digital asset identity of bitcoin is more persuasive, and this is the angle supported by the current study.

The objective of this paper was to study the Behaviour of implied bitcoin interest derived from UIP theory. That is, whether there is a relationship, or dynamic interactions between bitcoin interest rate, and financial market interest rate. The results show that there is statistically significant shocks emanating from LIBOR interest rate market towards bitcoin implied interest rate. The shocks from the bitcoin interest rate towards LIBOR market rates are either non-existent or not statistically significant. These results are consistent with Smith [11], which is the closest paper to the current study. Smith used triangular concept of exchange rates to derive implied exchange rate for bitcoin, and then used the same along with market exchange rates from USA, Australia, and UK. Smith found that implied bitcoin exchange rates respond to shocks from market exchange rates but not conversely, which is a similar result from the current study. This type of finding is consistent with the broader policy reviews by international financial institutions [21] which observe that, cryptocurrency as a sub-sector in financial market is still very small to bring about meaningful economic disturbance. Further, though not tested in this paper, it is also possible that the limited interaction between conventional markets and bitcoin is due in part to its reported uniqueness [12, 22] as an asset class.

5 Conclusion

The study investigated the dynamic behaviour of implied bitcoin interest rate against market interest rates for USA, and Euro based LIBOR in four maturity classes (12–month; 6–month; 3–month; and 1–month) using Vector Autoregressive model. The implied bitcoin interest rate was quantified through uncovered interest parity model. The results show that bitcoin responds to market rates for both USA, and Euro but the shocks emanating from bitcoin interest rate are not statistically significant. These findings are consistent with comparable studies that assessed implied bitcoin exchange rates against market exchange rates but inconsistent with studies that find bitcoin does not respond to economic fundamentals. The results of this study will be useful to monetary policy makers and investors.

Appendix

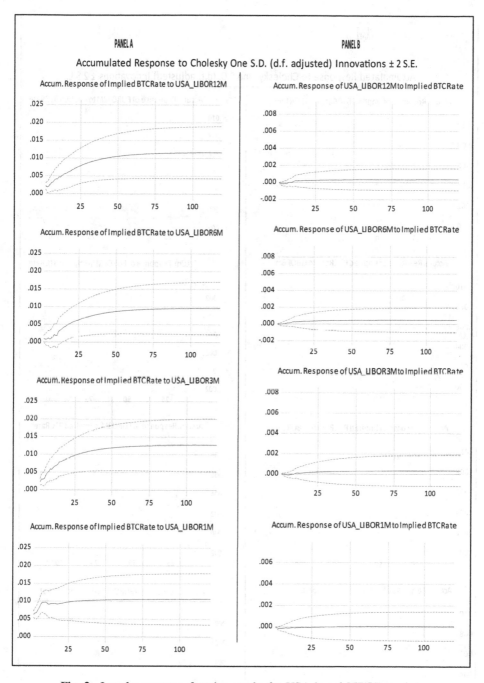

Fig. 3. Impulse response function graphs for USA based LIBOR market

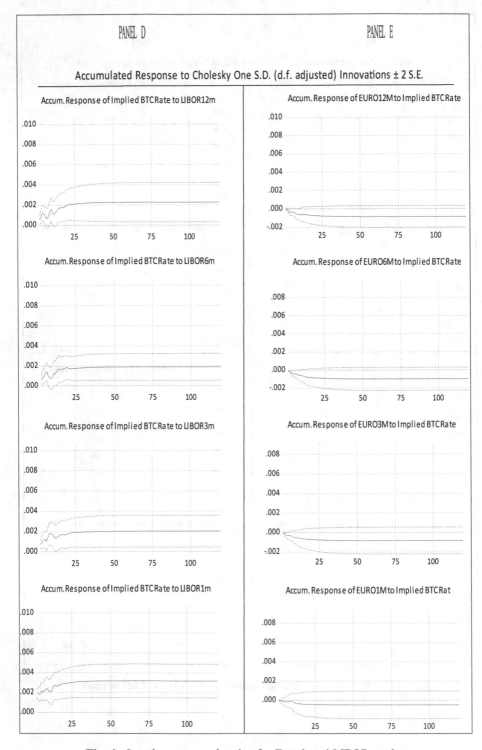

Fig. 4. Impulse response function for Euro based LIBOR market

Table 2. VAR results for US based LIBOR markets and Implied btc rate.

Variable	LIBOR_12m	LIBOR_6m	LIBOR_3m	LIBOR_1m	Impld btc rate
US LIBOR 12m(t-1)	-0.058	-0.016	-0.082	-0.031	-0.341
	(-1.338)	(-0.497)	(-2.859)	(-1.052)	(-1.242)
US LIBOR 12m(t-2)	-0.017	-0.083	-0.069	-0.036	-0.071
	(-0.409)	(-2.569)	(-2.437)	(-1.233)	(-0.259)
US LIBOR 6m(t-1)	0.076	0.048	0.127	-0.037	-0.261
	(1.177)	(0.984)	(2.92)	(-0.829)	(-0.629)
US LIBOR 6m(t-2)	0.113	0.188	0.122	-0.020	0.267
	(1.761)	(3.898)	(2.859)	(-0.459)	(0.653)
US LIBOR 3m(t-1)	0.283	0.323	0.212	0.161	0.697
	(5.191)	(7.859)	(5.827)	(4.278)	(2.003)
US LIBOR 3m(t-2)	0.100	0.093	0.140	0.183	0.786
	(1.978)	(2.436)	(4.15)	(5.25)	(2.43)
US LIBOR 1m(t-1)	-0.082	-0.057	0.068	1.243	-0.376
	(-2.023)	(-1.859)	(2.498)	(44.435)	(-1.452)
US LIBOR 1m(t-2)	0.082	0.057	-0.067	-0.242	0.376
	(2.029)	(1.871)	(-2.472)	(-8.643)	(1.451)
Impld btc rate(t-1)	-0.007	-0.001	-0.001	-0.007	0.267
	(-1.784)	(-0.53)	(-0.253)	(-2.63)	(11.205)
Impld btc rate(t-2)	0.000	0.001	0.000	0.005	-0.249
	(-0.089)	(0.225)	(-0.098)	(2.013)	(-10.883)
Intercept	0.000	0.000	0.000	0.000	0.000
	(0.775)	(0.801)	(-0.038)	(-0.365)	(0.103)

Table 3. VAR results for Euro based LIBOR markets and Implied btc rate.

Variable	LIBOR_12m	LIBOR_6m	LIBOR_3m	LIBOR_1m	Impld btc rate
Euro LIBOR 12m(t-1)	0.073731	0.092235	0.055846	-0.035631	0.04158
	(2.51)	(3.023)	(1.373)	(-0.783)	(0.548)
Euro LIBOR 12m(t-2)	0.039206	0.006863	0.030162	0.086218	0.062308
	(1.333)	(0.225)	(0.74)	(1.892)	(0.819)
Euro LIBOR 6m(t-1)	0.014747	0.005958	0.107998	0.017982	0.062786
	(0.5)	(0.195)	(2.644)	(0.394)	(0.824)
Euro LIBOR 6m(t-2)	0.043385	-0.010614	-0.010323	-0.10633	-0.018331
	(1.477)	(-0.348)	(-0.254)	(-2.337)	(-0.241)
Euro LIBOR 3m(t-1)	0.043407	0.081918	-0.077023	0.127904	0.042766
	(2.255)	(4.097)	(-2.889)	(4.291)	(0.859)
Euro LIBOR 3m(t-2)	0.010728	0.065578	0.012403	0.142504	0.07784
	(0.545)	(3.205)	(0.455)	(4.671)	(1.529)
Euro LIBOR 1m(t-1)	-0.046789	-0.014445	0.024493	0.048793	-0.079624
	(-2.834)	(-0.842)	(1.071)	(1.908)	(-1.865)
Euro LIBOR 1m(t-2)	0.030144	0.031386	0.083425	-0.015223	0.084616
	(1.82)	(1.824)	(3.636)	(-0.593)	(1.976)
Impld btc rate(t-1)	0.000828	-0.007881	-0.000555	-0.000848	0.137106
	(0.092)	(-0.843)	(-0.045)	(-0.061)	(5.891)
Impld btc rate(t-2)	-0.018323	-0.00496	-0.020833	0.016689	-0.256282
	(-2.044)	(-0.533)	(-1.678)	(1.202)	(-11.061)
Intercept	-0.000424	-0.000473	-0.000527	-0.000583	-0.000147
	-8.40E-05	-8.70E-05	-0.00012	-0.00013	-0.00022
	(-5.067)	(-5.448)	(-4.545)	(-4.499)	(-0.682)

References

1. Nakamoto, S.: Bitcoin: A Peer-to-Peer Electronic Cash System (2008). https://bitcoin.org/bitcoin.pdf
2. Lansky: Possible state approaches to cryptocurrencies. J. Syst. Integr. **9**(1), 19–31 (2018). https://doi.org/10.20470/jsi.v9i1.335
3. Chaum, D.: Blind signatures for untraceable payments. In: Chaum, D., Rivest, R.L., Sherman, A.T. (eds.) Advances in Cryptology, pp. 199–203. Springer, Boston, MA (1983). https://doi.org/10.1007/978-1-4757-0602-4_18
4. Haber, S., Stornetta, W.S.: Secure names for bitstrings. In: Proceedings of the 4th ACM Conference on Computer and Communication Security (1997). https://doi.org/10.1145/266420.266430
5. Wolfson, S.N.: Bitcoin: the early market. J. Bus. Econ. Res. **13**(4), 201–214 (2015). https://doi.org/10.19030/jber.v13i4.9452
6. Zhou, S.: Exploring the driving forces of the bitcoin exchange rate dynamics: an EGARCH Approach. MPRA Working Paper, No. 89445 (2018). https://doi.org/10.1007/s40822-018-0108-2
7. Corbet, S., Meegan, A., Larkin, C., Lucey, B., Yarovaya, L.: Exploring the dynamic relationships between cryptocurrencies and other financial assets. Econ. Lett. **165**, 28–34 (2018). https://doi.org/10.1016/j.econlet.2018.01.004
8. Hencic, A., Gouriéroux, C.: Noncausal autoregressive model in application to bitcoin/USD exchange rates. In: Huynh, V.-N., Kreinovich, V., Sriboonchitta, S., Suriya, K. (eds.) Econometrics of Risk. SCI, vol. 583, pp. 17–40. Springer, Cham (2015). https://doi.org/10.1007/978-3-319-13449-9_2
9. Briere, M., Oosterlinck, K., Szafarz, A.: Virtual currency, tangible return: portfolio diversification with Bitcoins. J. Asset Manag. **16**, 365–373 (2015). https://doi.org/10.1057/jam.2015.5
10. Dyhrberg, A.H.: Bitcoin, gold and the dollar–a GARCH volatility analysis. Finan. Res. Lett. **16**, 85–92 (2016). https://doi.org/10.1016/j.frl.2015.10.008
11. Smith, J.: An analysis of bitcoin exchange rates. SSRN Working Paper, No. 2493797, May (2016). https://doi.org/10.2139/ssrn.2493797
12. Ankenbrand, T., Bieri, D.: Assessment of cryptocurrencies as an asset class by their characteristics. Invest. Manag. Finan. Innov. **15**, 169–181 (2018). https://doi.org/10.21511/imfi.15(3).2018.14
13. Katsiampa, P.: Volatility estimation for bitcoin: a comparison of GARCH models. Econ. Lett. **158**, 3–6 (2017). https://doi.org/10.1016/j.econlet.2017.06.023
14. Koutmos, D.: Bitcoin returns and transaction activity. Econ. Lett. **167**, 81–85 (2018). https://doi.org/10.1016/j.econlet.2018.03.021
15. Froot, K.A., Thaler, R.H.: Anomalies: foreign exchange. J. Econ. Perspect. **4**, 179–192 (1990). https://doi.org/10.1257/jep.4.3.179
16. Engel, C.: The forward discount anomaly and the risk premium: a survey of recent evidence. J. Empirical Finan. **3**, 123–192 (1996). https://doi.org/10.3386/w5312
17. Chinn, M.: The (partial) rehabilitation of interest rate parity in floating rate era: longer horizons, alternative expectations and emerging markets. J. Int. Money Finan. **25**, 7–21 (2006). https://doi.org/10.1016/j.jimonfin.2005.10.003
18. Lothian, J.R.: Uncovered interest parity: the long and the short of it. J. Empirical Finan. **36**, 1–7 (2016). https://doi.org/10.1016/j.jempfin.2015.12.001
19. Brito, J., Castillo, A.: Bitcoin: A primer for policymakers. Mercatus Center, George Mason University (2013)

20. Bank of International Settlement: Digital currencies. Committee on Payments and Market Infrastructures. BIS, November 2015
21. Claeys, G., Demertzis, M., Efstathiou, K.: Cryptocurrencies and monetary policy. Monetary Dialogue, European Parliament, July 2018. https://doi.org/10.2861/963879
22. Liu, Y., Tsyvinski, A.: Risks and returns of cryptocurrency. NBER Working Paper, No. 24877, August 2018

Limitations of Digitizing Trade Finance Services in Yemeni Banking Sector

Rami Al-Sabri[✉]

School of Business, Lebanese International University, Sana'a, Yemen
alsabrirami@gmail.com

Abstract. This exploratory research paper aimed to figure out the limitations of adopting technological innovation to digitize trade finance services in Yemeni banking sector using paper-less trade finance instruments instead of paper-based ones. For the purpose of this study, a qualitative study using thematic analysis approach was applied through face-to-face interviews. The analysis of the interviews showed out the limitations of digitizing trade finance services in Yemeni banking sector within three categories, firstly *organizational limitations* which summarized by resistance to change and legal deficiencies. Secondly, *Technical Limitations* which consist of IT management, IT skills and training and IT infrastructure. Finally, *Adoption Limitations* which summarized by awareness, online transaction trust and culture. A number of recommendations have been made to governmental authorities and banks as well, which include updating the articles related to trade finance in the current commercial law, creating new law for electronic transactions, upgrade the communication infrastructure.

Keywords: Trade finance digitizing · Limitations · Technology · Yemeni banking sector

1 Introduction

International Trade in products and services had grown quickly through years. Therefore, the world's trading countries had turned out to be more integrated. Yemen had joined World Trade Organization (WTO) on June 2014 to be the 160th member and the 7th Least Development Country (LDC) enrolled this organization since its establishment in 1995. As a result, it is vital to determine the elements and factors shaping and influencing the creation and the intensity of international trade between Yemen and other countries [1].

One of factors influencing International Trade is financing the transactions which it is fundamental for turning the wheels of global commerce. However, challenges still remain in mitigating risks and improving operational efficiency. The greatest challenge in trade finance is the significant operational cost and risk involved in the paper-based transactions with instruments such as Documentary Letters of Credit and Documentary Collection [2]. Efforts to digitize manual solutions started decades ago, and there had been attempts by both industry players and banks to deliver new solutions to digitize various parts of the trade finance value chain, five potentially disruptive technologies

© Springer Nature Switzerland AG 2019
R. Jallouli et al. (Eds.): ICDEc 2019, LNBIP 358, pp. 66–84, 2019.
https://doi.org/10.1007/978-3-030-30874-2_6

had emerged in trade finance over recent years: Electronic Letter of Credit (e-LC), MT798, Bank Payment Obligation (BPO), Electronic Bill of Lading (e-BL) and Blockchain technology [2].

Financing trade transactions using traditional instruments is conditional with complied paper-based documents presented by sellers to buyers via banks. This traditional mechanism causes delay in payment as the physical transferring of documents from country to another takes time in addition to the time of checking these documents by involved banks [3]. The consumed time in this mechanism and the fact of documents fraud possibility is increasing the operational risk, cost and reduce the payment efficiency. Therefore, there were many attempts to replace the paper-based documents by "data" in order to avoid the negative side effects resulted by utilizing paper-based documents. The digitizing processes had started in many leader banks around the world, and because this new technology didn't be adopted yet by Yemeni banking sector, this study aimed to answer the research question, *What are the limitations which prevent adopting digitized trade finance instruments in Yemeni banking sector?*

This study will contribute to determine the limitations and restrictions of adopting paper-less trade services in Yemeni banking sector in order to be dominated by using the findings and recommendations of the study as a guideline to adopt such modern instruments of trade finance by Yemeni banks. On other hand, this study will be a good contributor to spread up the culture of paper-less trade finance and digitizing technologies among banks operating in Yemeni banking sector in order to be prepared to enter the digital era successfully.

1.1 Scope of the Study

The main provider for trade finance services in Yemen are the banks. Therefore, the scope of the study was the banking sector in Yemen. The researcher had collected primary data from the headquarters of analyzed banks in Sana'a city because trade finance operations of Yemeni banks are centralized in their headquarters.

2 Literature Review

Financing trade transactions is one of the core services conducted by banks operating in Yemen and it represents a major source for commissions to them, for instance, the commission of trade finance services in Yemen Commercial Bank was representing 75% and 74% of total commission of banking services offered in 2012 and 2013 respectively [4] and the same case in Tadhamon International Islamic Bank, the commission of trade finance services was representing 75% and 71% of total commission of banking services offered in 2013 and 2014 respectively [5].

All trade finance instruments used in Yemeni banking sector are considering under paper-based category which means that payment is correlating directly to complied documents in order to be proceeded, such as documentary letters of credit, documentary collections and letters of guarantees [6]. Earlier studies defined that Paper-based trade finance instruments are facing some problems in terms of cost efficiency, fraud and security and despite the enlargement of hardware and software technology that had created electronic substitutes to paper documents, many banks around the world still using traditional paper-based documents in their trade services [7].

Banks are facing a strong competitive coerce caused from demand-oriented market. This trend goes in line with the increasing usage of internet-based financial services. As a result, corporate clients are expecting lower prices and faster service processing in trade finance transactions. However, a major problem is the reliance of most banks on paper documents due to legal limitations. Consequently, many of papers are used in banks and in order to facilitate enhancing efficiency, a major opportunity was seen in digitizing these documents [8].

In order to be able to carry out trade with electronic documents, the existing trade payment methods should also be simplified and modified to the electronic environment. Electronic environment permits eliminating the complexities of paper-based procedures and it will be suitable to be used in a single platform to replace traditional payment methods if possible [9].

2.1   Traditional Paper-Based Payment Methods

Payment methods are fundamental of the trade transaction in which banks often play the role of financial intermediation between the parties of the transaction. The risk of these payment methods varies from one method to another, either from the perspective of the exporter or buyer [10]. The payment method is chosen based on the commercial status between the two parties, If the exporter is in a better commercial position than the importer, he will impose the less risky means of payment for him to ensure. Conversely, if the importer is in a better commercial position than the exporter, he will impose the least risky means of payment for him, and there are balanced methods of payment that protect the rights of both parties to the trade process in varying proportions [11]. Generally, there are four main methods of payment in trade; each of them implies a little different balance of risk between importer and exporter.

Cash in Advance. Cash in advance is the safest payment method for exporter as the latter arrange to receive funds from importer before shipping the goods, leaving the importer at big risk that the exporter will not comply with all the contract terms and conditions, however, this method is infrequent in competitive market which make the exporter resort to use this method partially (e.g., 10–30% Advance Payment) which considered more acceptable to the importer than full advance payment method [12]. Advance payment terms can be proceeded as a particular payment method and can be integrated into a letter of credit, which allow the exporter to receive an advance a percentage of LC value against presentation a certain documents to the issuing bank [10].

Letters of Credit. Letter of Credit had been described as 'the lifeblood of international commerce' after World War I, and it was considered to be the most accepted trade finance instruments of payment guaranteed by third party, usually a bank, and it is a document issued by the importer's bank to undertake paying the exporter against presentation complied documents with the terms and conditions of the LC [13]. These documents (e.g., Commercial invoice, bill of lading, inspection certificate) are providing an essential proof that the goods had been accurately shipped to the importer [14].

Documentary Collection. Documentary Collection is an international payment method, but it is not as safe as a letter of credit for the exporter. Under this method of payment, the exporter ships the goods and sends the shipping documents to the importer's bank with preparing to take the risk that the importer will not accept the documents and accordingly will not pay the documents value [15].

Open Account. In contrary to Cash in Advance method, Open account represents the safest payment method for importer. Open account is typically used in long-established relationships, as the exporter has a risk exposure to payment delays and/or payment defaults. The exporter ships the goods along with related documents to importer and the latter pays as agreed with the exporter whether at the sight of the documents or after period of time [16].

2.2 Digitized Instruments of Trade Finance

Technology and banking services had a long and close association. Both of them had been benefitting significantly by this association. In 1974, most of LCs were transmitted by telex, cable or mail. Article 4 of the UCP[1] (1974 revised version) reflected this practice by listing "cable, telegram or telex" as the means to advise LCs [17]. However, the 1983 revised version of UCP had replaced these means with the term "teletransmission," which made a remarkable move in banking practice. In less than a decade, the interbank LC messages changed from paper communications to teletransmissions. A closer look at the evolution of LC format expose that the move to an electronic format started many years earlier with the introduction of cabled and telexed LCs [17].

Society of Worldwide Interbank Financial Telecommunication (SWIFT) established in 1973 as a bank-owned, Belgian, not-for-profit cooperative organization. Its intention was to facilitate the communication of bank-to-bank financial transaction messages. This new method of telecommunication between banks had saved many costs in comparing with using telex in the early 1980s which encourage adopting a method of electronic communication recognized as Electronic Data Interchange (EDI) [17].

According to the 10th edition of the ICC[2] Banking Commission annual global survey on trade finance for 2018 which covered 251 respondents from banks in 91 countries, 12% of respondents confirmed that they had implemented technology solutions successfully, 49% of the respondents confirmed that they are in developing level and the technological solutions are under progress, 37% of respondents said implementing some form of technology solutions is not in their agenda currently, however 30% are planning to implement such solutions in the next one or two years [18].

---

[1] Uniform Customs and Practice for Documentary Credits which issued by International Chamber of Commerce, Paris.

[2] International Chamber of Commerce, Paris.

Digital innovations in the customer edge can generate more valuable relationships, and by automating many difficult paper-based procedures, digitizing technology can decrease operational costs and increase a bank's operational path without needing more staff. The next generation of trade finance technologies such as e-LCs, SWIFT for corporate (MT798), BPOs, e-BLs and Blockchain technology may push trade toward the paper-less business long envisaged [18, 19].

Electronic Letter of Credit (e-LC). Like paper-based letter of credit, e-LC developed as one of the improvements to meet the demand of international trade. The effects of technology innovations on trade practices sharpened the appetite for excessive trade and competitiveness in the trade industry [20]. As an approach to ease some of the international trade transactions payment difficulties, some traders started to use of an electronic letters of credit, where all related documents are in a digital form, with better transactions speed and more efficiency at lower costs. However, this method demanded some legal construction to govern its operation. The main legal limitation is the lack of legal acknowledgment by the courts because of their nature, being data messages, and lack of acknowledgment in digital signatures and digital contracts, especially in developing countries and least developing countries [3].

SWIFT for Corporate (MT798). MT798, which known as "trade envelope", is an authenticated SWIFT message that permits exchange of trade data under category 7 of SWIFT messages such as MT700 and MT760 between corporations and member Banks of the SWIFT system in order to reduce process complication and allows corporations to deal from multiple banks easily [21–23].

Bank Payment Obligation (BPO). ICC had defined BPO as "an irrevocable and independent undertaking of an Obligor Bank to pay or incur a deferred payment obligation and pay at maturity a specified amount to a Recipient Bank following Submission of all data sets required by an Established Baseline and resulting in a Data Match or an acceptance of a Data Mismatch" [24].

Instead of physical documents being presented to banks as is the case with traditional LCs, trade data is electronically submitted by both buyer and seller to their banks to be matched automatically on a special platform called a Transaction Matching Application (TMA) via the standard format ISO20022 TSMT (Trade Services Management). This is an XML standard intended completely for exchanging data among involved banks and the Transaction Matching Application. The matching takes place via the latter application against an established 'baseline'. Only regulated banks have access to Transaction Matching Application to undertake these transactions [25, 26].

Electronic Bill of Lading (e-BL). Bill of Lading can be considered as the most essential documents in trade because of its function as evidence that goods shipped to importer's country and it indicates the ownership of the goods. Consequently, the attempts to digitize such vital documents started since around the eighties of last century, but only in recent years we had practical solutions from Bolero and essDOCS as a digital document platforms seek to lead the industry toward paper-less trade by transmitting shipping documents immediately and electronically among commercial parties [27] in order to shorten the payment settlement process and improve the position of exporters' working capital [28].

Blockchain Technology. From a technical perspective, the Blockchain is defined as a distributed simulated database that permits secure transactions without a central authority. From a functional perspective, the Blockchain key element is the absence of a central authority for transaction validation, which is performed by a peer-to-peer network throughout a consensus process. A Blockchain system is composed by two types of entities [29]:

- Participants, who execute operations secured by means of cryptographic signatures.
- A peer-to-peer network of nodes, selected to certify transactions and to contribute in the consensus process.

To avoid the complexity of traditional paper-based trade finance, a Blockchain technology had outlined a solution using smart contracts which can speed up and automate this process of trade finance [29, 30].

2.3 Digitizing Readiness and Limitation in Yemen

According to the Ministry of Telecommunication's proposal to adopt an ICT strategy, the name of the Ministry was modified to the Ministry of Telecommunications and IT in 2003. As part of the national strategy to support integrated development plans for the years 2001–2005, the plan to deliver and facilitate ICT services met government approval. This is supported by the Ministry's announcement of the commencing a national program for IT (E-government) in 2002 [31, 32].

Internet Connectivity. Since 1995, the Republic of Yemen's connection to the external world was enabled via fiber optic network through a sea cable extending 226 km to Djibouti and to other Arab countries, South-East Asia and Europe. However, the internet service was launched the following year by a sole provider "Tele-Yemen", a company possessed by the British Cable and Wireless Company and the Yemeni government with a 51% and 49% division respectively and at the end of 2003 the ownership of the company transferred to the government to become the Public Telecommunication Corporation. Moreover, since its launching in 1996, the dial-up continued the means for Internet access. The number of subscribers in 2012 was 857,970 showing a significant increase from 455,429 in 2009. This was followed by the introduction of the ISDN in 2001 at a speed of 64 Kb/s and then at 128 Kb/s [33].

Legal and Regulation Environment. The legal and regulatory environment in Yemen is unsatisfactory for the activation of ICT sector's role. The Law of Telecommunications and IT Bill which was concurred by the Yemeni government under resolution 393 for year 2008 and transferring it to the parliament in preparation for its concurrence. The parliament in its turn transferred the bill to a committee since 2009 and it had not been concurred yet. Law No. 13 for the year 2012 regarding the right access information had already been discussed [33].

3 Methodology

A Qualitative research method had been chosen to conduct the research due to the exploratory nature of the study to investigate the limitations of adopting new technologies to digitize trade finance services in Yemeni banking sector which consists of 13 banks representing the population of the study. Only eight banks will be analyzed as a sample of the study for the following reasons: imprecise

- The selected banks represent sixty two percent of the study's population.
- The selected banks are mix of all banking categories in Yemeni banking sector (two Foreign banks, two Islamic banks and four Commercial banks).
- The selected banks are the top eight banks in terms of trade finance transactions according to the extracted data from their Financial Statements of the years (2010–2015) which compared the outstanding liabilities of trade finance products as at end of each year and the related commissions gained under these products (*Please see Appendices No. 1 & 2*).

Table 1. Population and sample of the study

Population	Sample
1. Arab Bank PLC (AB)	1. Arab Bank PLC
2. Cooperative Agriculture Credit Bank (CAC)	2. Cooperative Agriculture Credit Bank
3. International Bank of Yemen (IBY)	3. International Bank of Yemen
4. Islamic Bank for Finance & Invest. (IBFI)	4. Saba Islamic Bank
5. National Bank of Yemen (NBY)	5. Tadhamon International Islamic Bank
6. Qatar National Bank (QNB)	6. United Bank Limited
7. Saba Islamic Bank (SIB)	7. Yemen Bank for Recon. and Develop.
8. Shamil Bank of Yemen & Bahrain (SBYB)	8. Yemen Commercial Bank
9. Tadhamon International Islamic Bank (TIIB)	
10. United Bank Limited (UBL)	
11. Yemen Bank for Recon. and Develop. (YBRD)	
12. Yemen Commercial Bank (YCB)	
13. Yemen Kuwait Bank for Trade and Invest. (YKB)	

A face to face semi-structured interview had been conducted with eleven of the examined banks' trade finance senior managers. In spite of the fact that a structured interview had a formalized and restricted set of questions, a semi-structured interview is flexible, permitting new questions to be brought up during the interview as a result of what the interviewee says. This was necessary since the experiences of the interviewees add more value to the research; however, the semi-structured interview was based on a framework of themes to be investigated, which driven the interview to discover the most critical perspectives (*please see Appendices No. 3 & 4*). According to Fusch and Ness [34], data saturation is reached when there is sufficient data to imitate the study, when the ability to obtain additional new information has been accomplished, and when further coding is no longer viable. The researcher had noticed, during the eighth interview, that the data gathered from interviews were repeated and no new information can be added. However, he continued conducting interviews up to eleven interviews to ensure that no new data could be added enriching the study.

3.1 Data Analysis

The researcher had depended on the Thematic Analysis approach to analyze the primary data gathered from the conducted interviews and followed the six phases developed by Braun and Clarke [35] under this approach of analysis as per the following:

Familiarization with Data. After finishing the interview sessions, the researcher had transcribed the data into written form and before reading these transcripts; the researcher had created a "start list" of possible codes with a description of representations of each code.

Generating Initial Codes. When the data got familiar, the researcher had generated an initial list of items from the data set that had a reoccurring pattern and started the coding process attempting to go beyond surface meaning of the data to make sense of the data and express accurate information of what the data means. The researcher had used the software ATLAS.ti for coding process and strived to improve these codes by adding, subtracting, combining or splitting possible codes.

Searching for Themes. Themes are sentences or phrases that recognize what the data means; they label an outcome of coding for analytic consideration. In this phase, the researcher had begun examining how codes combine to form over-reaching themes in the data. The researcher had prepared a list of themes and began to focus on broader patterns in the data, merging coded data with proposed themes in order to consider how relationships are formed between codes and themes.

Reviewing Themes. In this phase, the researcher had reviewed coded data extracted in order to identify if themes form had logical patterns, then started assessing if the possible thematic map accurately reflects the meanings in the data set in order to provide an accurate representation of interviewees' experiences. By the end of this phase, the researcher had an idea of what themes are and how they fit together so that they convey consistent information of gathered data.

Defining and Naming Themes. The researcher had considered themes within the whole depiction and also as independent themes in order to identify whether current themes contain sub-themes and to discover further depth of themes. The researcher had conducted and noted a detailed analysis to identify the story of each theme and its importance.

Producing the Report. Finally, the researcher began the process of writing the final report and accordingly deciding on themes that make significant contributions to answer research questions. The aim of this phase is to write the thematic analysis to convey the complicated gathered data in a way that persuades the reader of the validity and merit of the analysis.

4 Findings

As a result of data analysis, a final thematic map had been illustrated in order to be the base of finalizing the findings of the study accordingly.

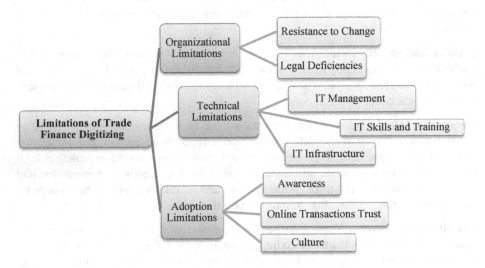

Fig. 1. Final thematic map

4.1 Organizational Limitations

According to the response of interviewees there are many organizational limitations for digitizing trade finance services, can be summarized by the following:

1. **Resistance to change**: This limitation has been shown in the respondents answers from two different perspectives, the first one was focusing on the resistance of changes from the customer side as all interviewees had confirmed that the most of their corporate customers are avoiding the electronic presentation of documents under trade finance transactions as they are not capable to use the same, in addition that a number of corporate customers are not educated well which make them afraid to utilize such technology in their business. The other perspective of changes resistance was focusing on the banks' employees who fear losing their jobs as some

interviewees had a point of view that adoption such technology will cause decrease of the staff numbers especially those whom work in examination of documents and archiving process.

2. **Legal Deficiencies**: According to interviewees, the local laws and regulations have a huge lack in terms of paper-based trade finance transactions if compared with international laws or rules issued by ICC in this regard. For this weak legal environment, adoption digitizing technology will create a big challenge to the concerned governmental authorities to update the current law and to create new laws for the electronic documents in order to have a legal back for the digitizing transactions and protect the rights of involved parties whether banks, exporters or importers.

4.2 Technical Limitations

The interviewees had mentioned the following technical limitations:

1. **IT Management**: Some interviewees had complained that their IT managements have some negligence from the top management in terms of budget and providing the latest updated software to the users. Top managements in those banks are trying to decrease the general expenses on the account of IT division which cause many technical issue and inability to adopt new technologies.
2. **IT Skills and Training**: According to the information collected by interviewees, the IT skills of the staff represents an obstacle to use new systems or adopt new technologies as most of staff has the basic IT knowledges to run their ordinary duties and the percentage of IT training courses are too small comparing with other banking aspects training courses.
3. **IT Infrastructure**: The current telecommunications infrastructure is not effective enough to deliver digitized trade finance services as shown in all answers of interviewees due to the continuous failure of the service.

4.3 Adoption Limitations

Adoption limitations can be summarized by the following:

1. **Awareness**: The awareness of the importance of digitized trade finance services is very low in banks and corporate customers as well. The corporate customers are not aware because the available paper-based instruments are enough for them to run their business and the banks are not aware because there is no demand from their customers to affect such technology in their trade finance services.
2. **Online Transaction Trust**: Most of corporate customers do not trust the banking transactions via online platforms and prefer the paper-based procedures. The reasons of this distrust, according to the interviewees, are the lack of awareness as

explained in previous point, lack of effective IT solving problems support from the banks provide the e-banking services and the culture of the society which will be explained in next point.

3. **Culture**: Subject to interviewees examples, the Yemeni culture is correlated with paper-based documents since long time. This appears with the preference of using banknotes instead of ATM cards, the property ownership documents, contracts and governmental transactions. The paper-based documents give the impression that all rights are preserved in papers which make this limitation a big challenge to enter digital era effectively.

5   Recommendations

Based on findings of the study a number of recommendations have been made to the governmental authorities and to banks operating in Yemen as well.

5.1   Recommendations to Governmental Authorities

The below recommendations are approaching the legal authorities, Central bank of Yemen, Chamber of commerce and Industry and Ministry of communications and IT.

1. The concerned legal authorities should work on updating the articles related to trade finance transactions in the current commercial law and create new law for electronic transactions and documents.
2. Chamber of commerce and Industry should promote for the digitization solutions in this field among its member from exporters and importers in order to create the awareness to them which consequently create the required demand to these digitized instruments.
3. Central Bank of Yemen has an effective role in banking sector and it can encourage banks to use this new trend as the first stage, then start to create a mechanism to manage the process of digitizing trade finance services and circular it to all banks.
4. Ministry of Communications and IT should upgrade the current infrastructure in order to be capable for the digitized trade finance instruments as the IT infrastructure is an essential asset for this project.

5.2   Recommendations to Banks Operating in Yemen

In addition to the above recommendation which approached the governmental authorities, the below recommendations are approaching the banks operating in Yemeni banking sector.

1. The banks should carry out awareness campaigns among their staff that the adoption of digital services does not mean abandoning traditional ones. Therefore, the

chances of losing jobs are small and they have to clarify that increasing the quality and variety of services means creating new job opportunity and increasing the profitability of the bank and thus reducing the chances of jobs losing. This procedure is important for reducing staff resistance to change. On the other hand, the banks should market ideas and digital solutions among its customers to support the promotional role that is supposed to be carried out by the Chamber of Commerce and Industry under the recommendation No. 2 addressed to governmental authorities and thus helps to reduce the resistance to change among banks' customers.

2. Banks should increase their investment in IT managements and increasing their budgets to increase their efficiency to be appropriate for adopting digital technology solutions. Investment in the technological aspect is a well-worthy investment for any business nowadays as the global trend indicates that the technological solutions will be the dominant business in the near future.

3. Banks should pay attention to train their staff on the technological aspect. Training should not be limited to IT staff only, but must include all employees, especially those working in the trade finance division, to be qualified for the requirements of the new technologies.

4. The role of banks is not limited to the activation of electronic services, but they must promote them and provide appropriate offers that encourage customers to use them, such as reducing service fees and providing effective support services for the purpose of reducing customer complaints for this type of services and accordingly increasing the trust to such services.

5. Increasing trust in e-services will contribute, albeit slightly, to change the dominant paper-based culture of bank' customers gradually and banks play an effective role to increase the awareness to their customers about the importance and effectiveness of e-services compared to paper-based ones. It's recommended also that all banks operating in Yemen agree to impose additional fees on traditional services and exempt electronic services from fees for the purpose of encouraging customers to run their business through the electronic channels and thus contribute to changing the dominant paper-based culture.

6 Limitations of the Study

1. **The current situation in Yemen.** As a result of the ongoing conflict in Yemen during the time of conducting this study and freezing of the main air and sea ports in Yemen, the trade statistics has been dropped down in terms of importing and exporting as well and this collapse reflected negatively to the activities of trade finance in banks and accordingly to their desire to improve their quality of services. Furthermore, most of Yemeni banks didn't publish their financial statements for 2016 upfront which limit this study to the financial figures from 2010 to 2015 only.

2. **The scope of the study.** Yemeni banking sector is the scope of this study, which means that the findings and recommendations which will be associated with this research cannot, necessarily, be applied to other banking sectors in other least developing countries.

3. **Other commercial parties than banks.** This study focused on digitizing trade finance services in banks without any direct consideration to the opinions of other trade business parties i.e. exporters and importers in Yemen which can contribute to the outcomes of this study.

7 Future Research

Given the limitations of the study, there can be suggested future research in the following points:

1. Expand the sample of the study population including Central Bank of Yemen upon finishing the ongoing conflict in Yemen to get more experience in order to determine more limitations.
2. This study can be an applicable base for other researchers whom need to investigate the limitations of trade finance digitizing in any other banking sector outside Yemen especially for least development countries.
3. Future studies can approach other commercial parties such as exporters, importers, custom authority, insurance companies and others (if applicable) to investigate the limitations from their perspectives.
4. Other researchers can go deeper and analyze each limitation in a separate study such as the legal limitations and technical limitation which can be a field for valued future researches.

8 Conclusion

The study aimed to investigate the limitations of digitizing trade finance services in Yemeni banking sector. For this purpose, a research question had been framed to interrogate the limitations of digitizing trade finance services in Yemeni banks. In order to answer this question, a qualitative methodology had been approached via face-to-face interviews conducted with trade finance senior managers of examined banks. The primary data gathered from these interviews had been analyzed using thematic approach with supporting of ATLAS.ti software. Consequently, the findings divided the limitations into three categories, organizational limitations, technical limitations and adoption limitations. After reviewing the literature and the analyzing the primary data through face-to-face interviews conducted, the research question had been answered. The findings showed that the limitations of trade finance digitizing had been categorized into three categories, organizational *limitations* which summarized by resistance to change, legal deficiencies and IT management. *Technical Limitations* which consist of IT skills and training and IT infrastructure. Finally, *Adoption Limitations* which summarized by awareness, online transaction trust and culture.

Acknowledgement. The author gratefully thanks his MBA supervisor Emad Al-Ramada.

Appendix 1. Trade Finance Outstanding Liabilities of Yemeni Banks as at End of the Year (in Thousand YER)

Bank	2010	Bank	2011	Bank	2012	Bank	2013	Bank	2014	Bank	2015
TIIB	74,652,252	AB	66,248,248	CAC	52,327,567	CAC	52,430,993	CAC	77,405,590	CAC	44,838,045
CAC	69,392,438	CAC	49,505,878	AB	52,236,097	TIIB	51,316,956	TIIB	53,373,597	IBY	29,038,339
AB	48,200,562	YBRD	46,193,831	TIIB	44,236,517	YBRD	51,239,025	YBRD	51,838,501	TIIB	27,440,590
IBY	44,983,446	TIIB	36,316,525	YBRD	41,489,909	IBY	46,209,948	IBY	48,258,819	UBL	25,620,557
SIB	34,762,197	IBY	34,269,252	IBY	36,643,727	AB	45,737,525	AB	43,510,865	YBRD	25,047,265
YCB	30,487,931	YCB	30,594,766	SIB	34,333,412	SIB	41,788,039	YCB	43,432,419	QNB	24,807,507
YBRD	29,478,128	UBL	25,609,807	YCB	31,932,510	YCB	38,596,148	SIB	39,365,860	SIB	24,772,142
NBY	25,990,856	NBY	18,015,388	UBL	29,068,190	UBL	35,208,586	UBL	36,087,426	YCB	24,021,475
SBYB	22,842,094	SBYB	17,381,643	NBY	27,307,388	QNB	22,235,378	QNB	31,398,638	AB	19,793,821
UBL	22,290,780	SIB	17,277,360	YKB	19,123,702	YKB	17,416,667	YKB	21,335,620	NBY	14,737,005
YKB	12,543,835	YKB	8,684,412	SBYB	14,907,384	NBY	17,028,165	NBY	21,000,606	YKB	13,841,729
IBFI	7,401,758	IBFI	6,993,452	IBFI	6,473,286	SBYB	6,351,254	SBYB	13,758,936	SBYB	6,486,954
QNB	2,978,530	QNB	1,598,191	QNB	3,039,893	IBFI	5,633,911	IBFI	7,527,835	IBFI	2,760,568

Source: Financial Statements of subject banks [4, 5, 36–46]

Appendix 2. Trade Finance Commission of Yemeni Banks as at End of the Year (in Thousand YER)

Bank	2010	Bank	2011	Bank	2012	Bank	2013	Bank	2014	Bank	2015
TIIB	1,202,932	TIIB	990,059	TIIB	1,217,072	TIIB	1,734,935	TIIB	1,211,676	CAC	1,039,153
CAC	1,041,474	CAC	772,971	SIB	646,292	CAC	862,209	CAC	1,083,778	TIIB	826,878
YCB	768,399	AB	608,286	CAC	590,845	SIB	786,854	SIB	771,718	YBRD	374,210
AB	743,322	YCB	454,588	AB	552,037	AB	747,433	YBRD	713,559	AB	333,440
SIB	641,370	YBRD	383,353	YBRD	514,909	YBRD	641,803	AB	677,462	SIB	299,252
IBY	551,753	IBY	360,276	YCB	467,382	YCB	532,343	YCB	585,759	YCB	256,136
YBRD	511,396	SIB	296,467	IBY	352,087	IBY	469,819	IBY	354,352	IBY	210,053
NBY	378,804	UBL	250,129	UBL	330,359	UBL	354,356	UBL	343,259	QNB	199,877
SBYB	362,529	NBY	212,640	YKB	310,406	NBY	286,519	NBY	311,672	UBL	180,700
YKB	253,963	SBYB	194,734	NBY	243,408	YKB	283,063	YKB	284,384	NBY	173,494
UBL	199,451	YKB	174,811	SBYB	235,114	SBYB	213,641	SBYB	207,253	YKB	140,431
IBFI	115,658	IBFI	109,604	IBFI	166,830	IBFI	155,384	IBFI	139,382	SBYB	114,314
QNB	31,745	QNB	49,893	QNB	39,770	QNB	120,359	QNB	132,262	IBFI	88,773

Source: Financial Statements of subject banks [4, 5, 36—46]

Appendix 3. Interview Guidelines

The interviewer had conducted the interviews basing on the following table as a guideline. The questions provided in the interview were what mentioned in the table under the category "*Main Questions*". In addition to the questions of this category and depending if the respondent had much to say about the subject, additional questions were added under another category i.e. "*Additional Questions*" to get more information and understand better their experiences. For ethical purpose, the study had guaranteed the confidentiality and privacy of interviewees by avoiding of collecting any personal information that may identify them and the recording of the interviews had been conducted only after the verbal approval of interviewees that allows the researcher to record the interview session. Following table summarizes the guidelines of the interview.

Main questions	Additional questions
What is the current readiness status of your bank to adopt digitizing technologies to your trade finance services in your bank and what are the limitations which will prevent this adopting?	Could you please classify the limitations into categories?
What are the requirements of adopting digitization technologies to trade finance services in your bank?	Do you apply, currently, any type of paper-less technologies to facilitate your trade finance services

Appendix 4. Details of Sample Analyzed and Interviewees

The bank	Region	Ownership of capital	Interviewees no.	Males	Female
Arab Bank PLC	Sana'a	Foreign	1	1	0
Cooperative Agriculture Credit Bank	Sana'a	Government	3	2	1
International Bank of Yemen	Sana'a	Private Sector 85%	1	0	1
		Foreign 15%			
Saba Islamic Bank	Sana'a	Private Sector 85%	1	1	0
		Foreign 15%			
Tadhamon International Islamic Bank	Sana'a	Private Sector 96.7%	1	1	0
		Foreign 3.3%			
United Bank Limited	Sana'a	Foreign	1	1	0

(*continued*)

(*continued*)

The bank	Region	Ownership of capital	Interviewees no.	Males	Female
Yemen Bank for Recon. and Develop.	Sana'a	Government 51%	1	1	0
		Private Sector 49%			
Yemen Commercial Bank	Sana'a	Private Sector 90%	2	2	0
		Government 10%			
Total			**11**	**9**	**2**

References

1. WTO: Yemen to become 160th WTO member, 27 May 2014. World Trade Organization. https://www.wto.org/english/news_e/news14_e/acc_yem_27may14_e.htm
2. Dab, S., Ramachandran, S., Chandna, R., Ravi, H., Grealish, A., Maarten, P.: Digital Revolution in Trade Finance, 30 August 2016. Boston Consulting Group. https://www.bcg.com/publications/2016/digital-revolution-trade-finance.aspx
3. Basimanyane, D.K.: The legal implications of electronic letter of credit as a cross border trade payment mechanism. Master thesis, University of Pretoria (2016)
4. YCB: Financial Statements. Yemen Commercial Bank, Sana'a (2010, 2011, 2012, 2013, 2014 and 2015)
5. TIIB: Financial Statements. Tadhamon International Islamic Bank, Sana'a (2010, 2011, 2012, 2013, 2014 and 2015)
6. Al-Zubairi, A.: YBRD history in serving the community and the Economy. Yemen Bank for Reconstruction and Development, Sana'a (2012)
7. Jervis, M., Masoodian, M.: How do people attempt to integrate the management of their paper and electronic documents? Aslib J. Inf. **66**(2), 134–155 (2014). https://doi.org/10.1108/AJIM-01-2013-0007
8. Leyer, M., Hollmann, M.: Introduction of electronic documents: how business process simulation can help? Bus. Process Manag. **20**(6), 950–970 (2014). https://doi.org/10.1108/BPMJ-05-2013-0062
9. Civelek, M.E., Uca, N., Çemberci, M.: eUCP and electronic commerce investments: e-signature and paperless foreign trade. Eurasian Acad. Sci. Eurasian Bus. Econ. J. **3**(1), 60–70 (2015). http://dx.doi.org/10.17740/eas.econ.2015
10. ACT & WWCP: The Treasurer's Guide to Trade Finance. The Association of Corporate Treasurers & WWCP Ltd, Second Edition (2013)
11. Grath, A.: The handbook of international trade and finance: the complete guide to risk management, international payments and currency management, bonds and guarantees, credit insurance and trade finance. Kogan Page Publishers (2011)
12. Jimenez, G.C.: ICC Guide to Export/Import, Global Standards for International Trade. International Chamber of Commerce Publishing, S.A., Paris, France (2012)
13. Bergami, R.: Risk Management in Australian Manufacturing Exports: the Case of Letters of Credit to ASEAN. Ph.D. thesis, Victoria University, Australia (2011)

14. Cronican, W.P.: Buyer beware: electronic letters of credit and the need for default rules. Mcgeorge Law Rev. **45**(2), 383–405 (2013)
15. Dorsey, T.: Trade finance stumbles. Finan. Dev. **46**(1), 18–19 (2009)
16. Hinkelman, E.G.: A Short Course in International Payments, 2nd edn. World Trade Press (2003)
17. Kozolchyk, B.: The paperless letter of credit and related documents of title. Law Contemp. Probl. **55**(3), 39–101 (1992)
18. ICC Banking Commission: Global Trade - Securing Future Growth, ICC Global Survey on Trade Finance. ICC (2018)
19. SWIFT's Corporate and Supply Chain Market Management team.: Digitising Trade Finance, Facilitating trade finance digitisation through technology-based messaging and legal industry standards. SWIFT (2016)
20. Galland, M.W.: Paperless letters of credit and EDI on the internet. Electron. Markets **5**(3), 13–14 (1995). https://doi.org/10.1080/10196789500000032
21. Citibank: Citi's Capability for SWIFT MT798: Frequently Asked Questions. Citibank Treasury and Trade Solutions (2015)
22. SWIFT's Corporate and Supply Chain Market Management team: Digitising Trade Finance using MT 798, Facilitating multi-banking in documentary trade finance. SWIFT (2016)
23. Hänninen, J.: Trade Finance: The future is digital - recent developments in Nokia Corporation. Danske Bank Annual Conference 2017. Helsinki (2017)
24. ICC: Uniform Rules for Bank Payment Obligation, ICC Publication Number 750. International Chamber of Commerce Publishing, S.A., Paris, France (2013)
25. Hennah, D.J.: The ICC Guide to the Uniform Rules for Bank Payment Obligations, ICC Publication Number 751E. International Chamber of Commerce Publishing, S.A., Paris, France (2013)
26. Susmus, T., Baslangic, S.: The new payment term BPO and its effects on turkish international business. Procedia Econ. Finan. **33**, 321–330 (2015)
27. Ugwuokpe, K.S.: The bill of lading in an era of electronic commerce: legal developments and the reform options for Nigeria. Master thesis, Dalhousie University, Halifax, Nova Scotia (2016)
28. Dubovec, M.: The problems and possibilities for using electronic bills of lading as collateral. Arizona J. Int. Comp. Law **23**(2), 437 (2006)
29. Biella, M., Zinetti, V.: Blockchain Technology and Applications from a Financial Perspective. UniCredit Bank (2016)
30. Parker, L.: New World Economic Forum report examines nine financial use cases for blockchains, 14 August 2016. Brave new coin. https://bravenewcoin.com/news/new-world-economic-forum-report-examines-nine-financial-use-cases-for-blockchains
31. Al-Aghbari, A., Abu-ulbeh, W., Ibrahim, O., Saeed, F.: The readiness and limitations of e-government in yemen. Jurnal Teknologi (Sci. Eng.) **73**, 107–115 (2015)
32. ESCWA: Trade Facilitation and Paperless Trade Implementation Survey 2015 conducted by Joint United Nations Regional Commissions UNRCs, West Asia Report. United Nations Economic and Social Commission for Western Asia (2015)
33. ESCWA: National Profile of the Information Society in Yemen. United Nation (2013)
34. Fusch, P., Ness, L.: Are we there yet? Data saturation in qualitative research. Qual. Rep. **20**(9), 1408–1416 (2015)
35. Braun, V., Clarke, V.: Using thematic analysis in psychology. Qual. Res. Psychol. **3**(2), 77–101 (2006). https://doi.org/10.1191/1478088706qp063oa
36. Arab Bank PLC: Financial Statements. Arab Bank PLC, Sana'a (2010, 2011, 2012, 2013, 2014 and 2015)

37. Cac Bank: Financial Statements. Cooperative Agriculture Credit Bank, Sana'a (2010, 2011, 2012, 2013, 2014 and 2015)
38. IBFI: Financial Statements. Islamic Bank for Finance & Investment, Sana'a (2010, 2011, 2012, 2013, 2014 and 2015)
39. IBY: Financial Statements. International Bank of Yemen, Sana'a (2010, 2011, 2012, 2013, 2014 and 2015)
40. NBY: Financial Statements. National Bank of Yemen, Aden (2010, 2011, 2012, 2013, 2014 and 2015)
41. QNB: Financial Statements. Qatar National Bank, Sana'a (2010, 2011, 2012, 2013, 2014 and 2015)
42. SBYB: Financial Statements. Shamil Bank of Yemen & Bahrain, Sana'a (2010, 2011, 2012, 2013, 2014 and 2015)
43. SIB: Financial Statements. Saba Islamic Bank, Sana'a (2010, 2011, 2012, 2013, 2014 and 2015)
44. UBL: Financial Statements. United Bank Limited, Sana'a (2010, 2011, 2012, 2013, 2014 and 2015)
45. YBRD: Financial Statements. Yemen Bank for Reconstruction and Development, Sana'a (2010, 2011, 2012, 2013, 2014 and 2015)
46. YKB: Financial Statements. Yemen Kuwait Bank for Trade and Investment, Sana'a (2010, 2011, 2012, 2013, 2014 and 2015)

Social Media Communication

Social Networks and Societal Strategic Orientation in the Hotel Sector: Netnographic Study

Hasna Koubaa and Rim Jallouli[✉]

University of Manouba, Manouba, Tunisia
hasnaelleuch@yahoo.fr, rimjallouli@esen-manouba.org

Abstract. In the marketing literature of sustainable tourism, a debate is emerging around the perception of guests and their behavior regarding the sustainable aspects of a hotel. Clients leave electronic traces in all travel-related activities, providing comments on community websites or through online surveys. Hence, social networks offer a valuable database of feedback about guest stays in hotels. Since the studied context is still emerging and needs to be explored, we have initiated a Netnographic study as a method of data collection. Our research proposes to study the comments on the travel website "HolidayCheck" of guests who have had a recent experience in a Tunisian hotel of the international channel MagicLife (ML). The aim is to explore the main facets of a hotel's societal strategic orientation in their verbatim namely: physical well-being, psychological well-being, environmental orientation, social relations and economic contribution. The results indicate the presence of the societal dimensions in the online evaluations of the guests but in a disproportionate way. Positive and negative connotations are also present in the feedbacks of these guests.

The major implications for hoteliers highlight the need to understand how potential consumers perceive societal dimensions and possibly how this affects their reservation interests. Also, this study allows optimizing the hotels' decision-making and investments in societal strategic orientation.

Keywords: Societal strategic orientation · Hospitality · Social networks · Content analysis · Netnographic study

1 Introduction

The tourism industry is known as the world's leading industry. Lozato-Giotart et al. (2012) described it as a planetary power with regard to the different types of flows generated. According to the UNWTO (2018)[1], the number of international tourists in the world continued to increase sharply (+6%), reaching 1.4 billion people. Based on the forecasts put forward by the UNWTO, this number will reach more than 1.6 billion in 2020 and 1.8 billion by 2030. It is easy then to imagine the consequences of these tourist flows on the degradation of the environment and on the host community, if

---

[1] http://www2.unwto.org/press-release/2019-01-21/international-tourist-arrivals-reach-14-billion-two-years-ahead-forecasts (Jan 2019).

© Springer Nature Switzerland AG 2019
R. Jallouli et al. (Eds.): ICDEc 2019, LNBIP 358, pp. 87–109, 2019.
https://doi.org/10.1007/978-3-030-30874-2_7

sustainable practices within the sector will not be realized. In this sense, Seguin and Rouzet (2010) underlined the necessity and urgency of integrating sustainable development (SD) issues into tourism activities.

Corporate Social Responsibility (CSR) is considered to be the corporate concept of SD. SD and CSR emphasize the goal of collective well-being, but do not propose how to implement societal concerns (ecological, social and economic). Moreover, considering the geometric variability and the blurring character of CSR, a substitutable construct to the CSR concept is adopted in this study, which's more adapted to the hospitality industry. According to some scholars, (Kang and James 2007; Dodds and Joppe 2005; Prud'homme and Raymond 2016) it is relevant to show how to proceed the implementation of the sustainability aspects or societal issues into the management of a company.

Our research draws on a societal strategic orientation (SSO) (Kang and James 2007; Koubaa 2017; Koubaa and Triki 2017). This strategic orientation integrates not only the main ecological, social and economic dimensions but also two other facets related to the physical well-being and psychological well-being of guests. Based on an integrated management system, SSO describes the real functioning of all hotel processes and presents traceability with regard to the implementation of the societal concerns in these processes.

In the academic world dealing with the marketing of sustainable tourism, a debate is emerging around the perception of guests and their behavior vis-à-vis the sustainable aspects of a hotel. Ponnapureddy et al. (2017) indicated that German tourists could be motivated to book a sustainable hotel if sustainability aspects and amenities have been communicated in a way that inspires trust in marketing materials. Sindhuri et al. (2017) highlighted the need to understand how potential customers perceive sustainability and how this affects their booking intentions. In a very recent article, Vinzenz (2019) argued that hotel SD efforts are an important additional criterion that affects guest booking behavior.

In the business world, the Accor Group (2016)[2] questioned the sensitivity of customers to SD by conducting a study in 7 countries. It turns out that SD is an important issue for all customers with differing nationalities. Germans seem to be the most concerned about SD (in ecological terms) than other nationalities. In terms of booking a hotel room, the respondents expressed that the SD is a non-priority choice criterion, but they are ready to support hoteliers in certain actions (sending invoices by mail, sorting waste, reuse of towels, etc.). Another result indicates that respondents are not willing to sacrifice comfort or location for responsible hotels and that they are interested in living a local experience during their stay (concrete social measures, visits, walks, local gastronomy, handicrafts, etc.). Finally, it seems that the Internet is the best way for them to learn about the local experiences they could benefit from.

Indeed, the tourism and hospitality sector is experiencing a digital revolution in terms of information processes, marketing decision, loyalty, positive and negative feedback, etc. To keep pace with customers who are increasingly fond of technology, new hotel and tourism activities have emerged. Social networks, artificial intelligence,

---

[2] http://www.id-tourisme.fr/etude-accorhotels-engagement-developpementdurable/ (Dec 2018).

mobile applications, geofencing allow the company to be closer to its customers. According to Kumar (2018) technological developments now enables companies to combine data across various social media platforms and generate benefits for all stakeholders.

Leung et al. (2013) pointed out the strategic role of social media in travelers' decision-making (travel planning process) and for tourism suppliers' competitiveness. The travel websites are relational platforms of web 2.0, focused essentially on reviews' experiences (travel/hotel experience) and generated content (User Generated Content- UGC/Consumer Generated content- CGC). The most popular travel sites are: Booking.com, TripAdvisor, Expedia, HolidayCheck, etc.

Recent studies outline the widespread use of social networks in tourism (Barreda and Bilgihan 2013; Neirotti et al. 2016; Sthapit 2018; Sthapit and Coudounaris 2018). Barreda and Bilgihan (2013) analyzed travelers' reviews content from the TripAdvisor site and recommend to hoteliers to improve their services and to enhance their brand image by gaining knowledge from online comments. In a similar way, Sthapit (2018) used CGC to explore the components which contribute to a memorable hotel experience.

Based on the previous discussion, we wonder about the following questions:

1. What are the societal dimensions stated in the online reviews of German guests?
2. What are the connotations generated from the guests' reviews?
3. What lessons to be learned by managers for marketing decision-making?

Our research consists of a netnographic study based on the Guests' online comments of a Tunisian hotel that has invested heavily in societal dimensions. The main objective is to explore and analyze the main facets of a societal strategic orientation in their verbatim.

2 Sustainable Development (SD) and Corporate Social Responsibility (CSR): Application to the Tourism Sector

The most notorious definition was proposed in 1987 by the World Commission on Environment and Development (WCED). This commission proposes for the first time a global definition of the SD concept: "development that meets the needs of the present, without compromising the ability of future generations to meet theirs" (Thomsen 2013).

The concept SD is a macro concept and can be applied to the company. Thus, managers are called upon to campaign for a balance between economic, social and ecological objectives that are, a priori, divergent. Improving the well-being of the community through discretionary practices (Kotler and Lee 2005); volunteerism, obligations towards stakeholders, corporate citizenship (Pasquero 2007); consideration of the positive and negative impacts of the company's activities on society (Wood 1991, Gond and Igalens 2008) are examples that define the company's societal concerns for improving human health and quality of life based on societal practices.

The angle of analysis that has the most weighting in the concepts mentioned above (sustainability, human well-being, ecological well-being, etc.) is based on an anticipatory management that really integrates all kinds of impacts.

2.1 Sustainable Tourism

Brial (2011) told that "the volume of business in the tourism sector exceeds that of the oil, food or automotive industries". This shows the dynamic of the tourism sector and the socio-economic progress it can generate.

Tourism contributes significantly to the creation of jobs and wealth for several countries. It also generates relations between different actors and stakeholders such as tourists, employees, the environment (the biosphere), tourism federations, the government, tour operators, pressure groups (Sautter and Leisen 1999; Imran et al. 2011). However, tourism is consumer of scarce resources (water) and therefore competes with the local community. It also contributes significantly to pollution (excessive energy consumption and waste management problems) and therefore represents a source of degradation of the ecosystem and biodiversity that can lead to sometimes irreversible damage (Imran et al. 2011).

Combining tourism activities with sustainability becomes unavoidable and extremely urgent, and this is not confined to a form or activity of tourism. UNWTO and UNEP (2005)[3] stressed the need to make all forms of tourism sustainable, including mass tourism and all destinations. All forms of business and leisure tourism are then concerned. In line with this reflection, sustainable tourism is expressed simply as: "Tourism that takes full account of its current and future economic, social and environmental impacts, meeting the needs of visitors, professionals, the environment and host communities" (UNEP 2005)[4]. In a similar way, Jamrozy (2007) suggested an integration of tourism into a holistic, sustainable, quality of life marketing approach of living communities.

Sustainability aspects in the hotel industry are environmental, social and economic. As part of the first aspect, waste management (reduction, sorting, recycling, recovery, etc.), water management (reduction of water consumption, reduction of the polluting load of wastewater, etc.), energy management (regular monitoring of consumption, etc.), acoustic management (acoustic comfort of buildings, etc.), air quality and landscape integration. As for the social aspect, it covers internal social processes (non-discrimination, equity between employees, gifts to employees, etc.) as well as external ones (the prosperity of the local community, cultural richness, support of local organizations, etc.). Finally, the economic aspect concerns the contribution to the wealth of stakeholders.

2.2 Societal Dimensions

Under the prism of sustainability, hotel managers need to focus on CSR concept and the integration of societal practices within their activities. Given the absence of unanimous definition of CSR construct (Combes 2005; Whitehouse 2006; Matten and Moon 2008), its contextual character (Maignan and Ralston 2002; Visser 2006) and the difficulties about the implementation of societal concerns or sustainability aspects, our research adopt a substitutable construct to CSR, which is considered more appropriate to the hospitality industry.

---

[3] http://www.unep.fr/shared/publications/pdf/dtix0592xpa-tourismpolicyen.pdf (May 2016).
[4] Ibid.

In the tourism industry, Dodds and Joppe (2005) stated that "It is difficult to make generalizations about CSR without first examining the context in which sustainable tourism operates, its demand and also assessing the numerous certification schemes, codes of conduct and best practices within the industry". In the same line, Prud'homme and Raymond (2016) showed why and how hotel managers proceeded to develop and to implement a sustainable orientation, taking into account the contextual factors.

Drawing on a qualitative study of a Tunisian hotel[5] in the MLchannel (Koubaa 2017; Koubaa and Triki 2017) and based on literature review, in particular Kang and James (2007) research, the societal strategic orientation (SSO) construct has emerged. SSO is a more adapted concept to the hotel industry. SSO was founded on the adoption of an integrated management system (labels, quality certificates, etc.), a global reflection of all the activities of the hotel on the themes of "Quality-Safety-Environment".

The SSO concept highlights the implementation of societal and sustainable practices by the hotel and thus measures the degree of orientation of the hotel in terms of deployment and implementation of these practices.

SSO is consistent with the interests of all stakeholders, but in this paper, we focus essentially on guest as an important stakeholder for the hotel. Defined as a multidimensional concept, SSO integrates within it five dimensions (Kang and James 2007; Koubaa 2017; Koubaa and Triki 2017), namely:

1- Physical well-being (PW), defined as the degree by which the hotel offers a product and/or a service that improves the physical well-being of guests, while reducing physical hazards and risks (health care, safety, food security, etc.);
2- Psychological well-being (PSW), defined as the degree by which the hotel offers a product and/or a service that generates psychological well-being to guests: hospitality, entertainment, relaxation, offers magical moments of joy and pleasure, nostalgic moments, etc.), while reducing the negative one (support and assistance in case of problems);
3- Social Relationships and Initiatives (SR), defined as the degree by which the hotel provides a product and/or a service that facilitates the development and improvement of internal social relationships and external social relationships (community and other stakeholders), while reducing negative impacts;
4- Environmental Orientation (EO), defined as the degree by which the hotel provides a product and/or a service that is beneficial to the environment while limiting its negative impacts (Environmental awareness, pollution prevention, waste management, effective energy management, etc.);
5- Economic Contribution (EC), defined as the degree to which the hotel provides a product and/or a service that is beneficial to guests and other stakeholders (employees, community, country, etc.), while reducing the losses.

Using a Netnographic approach, our exploratory study attempts to reveal these societal dimensions in the guests' online reviews.

---

[5] The hotel is an Imperial Beach 5 stars having invested in an integrated management system (ISO 9001, ISO 14001 & ISO 22000), a system that certify the implementation of a SD approach.

3 Digital Tourism Transformation

According to Bretonès (2011), many profound societal transformations have appeared. The classic B2C or B2B models are transformed into C2B (Customers to Businesses). We are seeing more dynamic and participative organizations, and will no longer be client-oriented, they will be designed for the client with the client. Internet models, such as "Facebook" or "LinkedIn", facilitate individual connections and contribute to the transformation of social relations.

Tourism industry has been deeply affected by ICT and the digital revolution, especially in the era of Big Data (Sigala et al. 2012; Gretzel et al. 2015; Del Chiappa and Baggio 2015; Koo et al. 2015; Del Vecchio et al. 2018a; Centobelli and Ndou 2019). Del Chiappa and Baggio (2015) stressed the crucial role of ICT, Internet of Things (IoT) and Cloud Computing in providing instruments and platforms that can facilitate the dissemination of information and knowledge among stakeholders. Smart tourism is "a new buzzword applied to describe the increasing reliance of tourism destinations, their industries and their tourists on emerging forms of ICT that allow for massive amounts of data to be transformed into value propositions" Gretzel et al. (2015). Similarly, Del Vecchio et al. (2018a) pointed out the role of huge social big data generated from tourists (CGC) in developing opportunities for a smart tourism destination. The aggregation of Big Data, as well as their, inter-connectivity, analysis, integration, real-time synchronization and intelligent use of data (Fuchs et al. 2015; Gretzel et al. 2015), are the main drivers of value creation. Value propositions are created for tourism stakeholders such as hoteliers and tourists. According to Buhalis and Amaranggana (2015), the objective of smart tourism destinations is to improve potentially tourism experience through personalizing offers, maximizing tourists' satisfaction and contributing to destination competitiveness.

Despite the role played by Web 2.0 technologies in the production, consumption and dissemination of information and knowledge (Sigala et al. 2012), Tavakoli and Mura (2018) have shown that Web 2.0 allows limited netnographic studies, based mainly on the analysis of texts published by tourists. New avenues with the evolution of web platforms (Web 3.0, Web 4.0 and Web 5.0) could be more innovative, more dynamic and dialogical, in particular in the field of tourism. Web 5.0 provides complex and immersive interactions between machines and humans (Tavakoli and Mura 2018).

4 Symbiotic Relationship Between ICT and Sustainability in Tourism Sector

The implementation of sustainability in an innovative way is becoming imperative for tourism stakeholders. The General Secretary of UNWTO (June 2018)[6]underlined the prominence of technology for a more universal approach to sustainable tourism "Technology helps us to better manage our social, cultural and environmental impacts.

---

[6] https://moderndiplomacy.eu/2018/06/29/use-technology-for-more-sustainable-tourism-management/ (Dec 2018).

And if well managed, tourism can act as an agent of positive change for more sustainable lifestyles, destinations, and consumption and production patterns".

Nowadays, the relationship between ICT and sustainability in tourism sector is gaining increasing attention in the scientific community (Ali and Frew 2013; Ali and Frew 2014; Del Chiappa and Baggio 2015; Gretzel et al. 2015; Lopez de Avila 2015; Gössling 2017). Ali and Frew (2013) provided insights on how ICT can play an important role in the management of sustainable tourism development. ICT is the technology that use innovative tools (integrated system of software and networked equipment) which facilitates data processing, information sharing, communication, etc. Technology is used to reduce the negative impacts of tourism from demand and supply side perspectives.

Other researchers describe the synergy between smart tourism and the development of sustainable tourism. "Smart tourism has gained momentum in research fostered by the revolution of the latest generation of information and communication technologies and has rapidly become a leading stream of literature" (Femenia-Serra and Neuhofer 2018). Lopez de Avila (2015) put the link between the use of technologies and the development of destination sustainability. He defined the smart tourism destination as: "an innovative tourist destination, built on an infrastructure of state-of-the-art technology guaranteeing the sustainable development of tourist areas, accessible to everyone, which facilitates the visitor's interaction with and integration into his or her surroundings, increases the quality of the experience at the destination, and improves residents' quality of life".

Furthermore, Del Vecchio et al. (2018b) demonstrated how big data generated by tourists on social media can be a source of open innovation supporting sustainable tourism experiences in a destination. Kim and Kim (2017) specified the status and the role of mobile technology in achieving sustainable and smart tourism.

5 Methodology

This section is structured as following: The first paragraph gives an overview on the choice of the sector. The second paragraph presents the netnographic study. Then, we will review the design of exploratory qualitative research and the content analysis of the online comments of the guests.

5.1 Choice of the Hotel Sector

The choice of the sector is not arbitrary. It is pertinent to deal with two topical trends in tourism and the hotel industry, namely: sustainability and digital transformation.

In the same vein, we will give an overview on some strategic axes of Tunisian tourism. One of the noteworthy initiatives in this area is the one known as the "Strategic Vision 3 + 1"[7]. A set of promising projects launched in 2014, spanning a

---

[7] http://www.tourisme.gov.tn/realisations-et-perspectives/vision-strategique-3-1/qualite-formation. html (May 2016).

period of 7–10 years, by the Tunisian Ministry of Tourism in collaboration with other institutions of the sector. This vision is pragmatic and focuses on multiple areas including quality, sustainability and digital tourism.

The themes that refer to sustainability projects are quality of the reception, quality of the transport, environmental quality, the training, the cultural diversification of the offer of tourist products according to the Tunisian regions and according to their specificities. Also, the implementation of a global digital strategy exploiting the web channels, mobile and social networks and involving the different parts of the Tunisian tourist ecosystem, aims both to promote and reach new customer targets. Similarly, the creation of a portal of the NOTT[8] (National Office of Tunisian Tourism) aims to improve the online visibility of the Tunisia destination and to offer rich content, up to date, accessible by the Web, mobile or tablet and in line with current technologies: geo-localization, integration of video content, photo, audio, social networks.

This sector contributes significantly to the economic development of Tunisia and deserves the attention of various institutions and tourism stakeholders. While the economic press puts a 7% (UNCTAD 2017)[9], contribution to tourism in the country's GDP, UNCTAD stated that this rate is reductive and published in its 2017 report an estimate of around 15.1% (UNCTAD 2017)[10]. This same report underlined that Tunisia has been ranked 4th in the African continent, having recorded between 2011 and 2014 the best rate of international tourist entries.

5.2 Netnographic Study

Netnography is gaining increasing attention in the scientific community, particularly in the social sciences, management and marketing (Kozinets 1998, 2012). This method of natural investigation (Lincoln and Guba 1985) is very promising and frequently used in the field of tourism (Kozinets 2015; Bartl et al. 2016; Sthapit 2018; Tavakoli and Mura 2018; Tavakoli and Wijesinghe 2019).

Netnography is also called "online ethnography", "Webnography", "cyberethnography" and "virtual ethnography" (Mkono and Markwell 2014). Kozinets (2002) defined "Netnography", or "Ethnography on the Internet" as "a new qualitative research methodology that adapts ethnographic research techniques to the study of cultures and communities emerging through computer-mediated communications. As a marketing research technique, "netnography" uses the information publicly available online to identify and understand the needs and decisions of the online consumer groups".

Kozinets (2002) noted that netnography is increasingly used by consumers and marketing researchers. By using the Internet, many forms of consumer interaction, idea sharing, and storytelling are providing more objective sources of information for product selection and branding and purchasing decision making. Online discussion

---

[8] Ibid.

[9] https://www.destinationtunisie.info/tourisme-represente-151-pib-de-tunisie-selon-cnuced/   (Dec 2018).

[10] https://unctad.org/en/PublicationsLibrary/aldcafrica2017_en.pdf (Dec 2018).

forums, the social media web, virtual communities created by consumers are also a source of information for marketing studies. It is important for marketing researchers to have rigorous and ethical methodological procedures for collecting and interpreting these data from a growing segment.

Compared to traditional methods, this method of investigation has many merits. Indeed, netnography offers geographically dispersed customers the possibility of online interaction. It also saves time and money. The investigations are processed in a natural and original context with flexibility and discretion.

Kozinets (1998, 2002, 2006) pointed out the use of netnographic studies "for participant observation in the online environment, which includes: (1) investigating possible online field sites, initiating, and making cultural entree; (2) collecting and analyzing data; (3) ensuring trustworthy interpretations; (4) conducting ethical research; and (5) providing opportunities for the feedback of culture members".

However, after an update to this approach, Kozinets (2006) described this qualitative method as flexible and "which can be used as a purely observational method or as one that incorporates a high degree of participation". In 2015, Kozinets stated that "netnography is positioned somewhere between the vast searchlights of big data analysis and the close readings of discourse analysis... Actual netnographic data itself can be rich or very thin, pro-tected or given freely... It can be generated through interactions between a real person and a researcher, or be sitting in digital archives".

5.3 Exploratory Qualitative Research

Our research proposes to study the online comments of the guests having stayed in a Tunisian hotel of the international channel ML. The objective is to explore the main facets of a societal strategic orientation in their verbatim.

The studied context is still emerging and needs to be explored. Mitchell et al. (2010) and Avci et al. (2011) emphasized the contribution of qualitative studies in tourism, leisure and hospitality activities. Netnographic studies are very promising and frequently used in the field of tourism (Kozinets 2015; Bartl et al. 2016; Sthapit 2018; Tavakoli and Mura 2018; Tavakoli and Wijesinghe 2019).

In our research, we used a netnographic study. For that, we followed some instructions recommended by Kozinets (2002), according to which a researcher must respect two preliminary stages for the realization of the netnography. First, asking himself the specific questions of his research, then identifying online forums adapted to these questions. Second, learning as much as possible about the forums, groups and individual participants he seeks to understand.

Based on these instructions, we visited at first a professional website named ReviewPro[11], which allowed us to better understand the guest's community online comments. ReviewPro provides feedbacks from customer experiences on multiple Travel and booking websites: Tripadvisor, HolidayCheck, Tophotels, Hotel.com, Facebook, Expedia, etc., each of which uses its own evaluation grid. From filters, we

---

[11] "ReviewPro is the leading provider of guest intelligence solutions to independent hotel brands worldwide" Available at: https://www.hospitalitynet.org/organization/17014180/reviewpro.html.

selected the hotel to study and the sample. We have downloaded a rather rich corpus about the guests' reviews ("Reviews/Tracking"). This corpus contains fields such as: Reviewer; Reviewer Country; Review rating; Review Title and Review Text; Rating score; Classification (positive, neutral or negative). So, guests provided both quantitative and qualitative feedback on hotel or travel experiences shared with the rest of travel and booking websites.

In line with other researches (Langer and Beckman 2005; Mkono 2012; Sthapit 2018; Tavakoli and Mura 2018), our study adopted a netnographic approach based on online reviews, in the form of non-participant observation. As we extracted archival data online (past year), there is no need to communicate the study objectives to online guests. Then we didn't obtain consent from guests, because their reviews are public and we used the corpus for a scientific purpose. Mkono (2012) indicated that "most authors agree that where data are collected from pseudonymous/anonymous public-type forums, with the researcher acting as nonparticipant observer, the requirement for informed consent of individual participants falls away". In the same direction, Heinonen and Medberg (2018) stated that: "Marketing researchers have used netnography in various ways". Indeed, they emphasize on the diversity of applying netnography in terms of the role of the researcher (active or passive), use purpose, domain of data collection, content included, analysis and combination with other methods. Furthermore, Tavakoli and Mura (2018) declared that "Since the majority of the netnographic studies were conducted on Web 1.0 or 2.0 platforms, the methods were mainly concerned on analyzing textual or video formats".

Our research is exploratory; the sample size has no statistical significance. The most important thing is to respect the principle of information saturation. According to De Ruyter and Scholl (1998), the usefulness of qualitative research does not lie in the number of respondents, but in what has been said and in the way of saying it because what matters is not the power of numbers, but the power of words and images.

In total, we analyzed 92 opinions during the year 2018. The sample was composed of German speakers mostly Germans (78%) and Austrians (20%). These guests are the main target of the hotel in question. Germans have often been the focus of research in the field of sustainable tourism (Schmücker et al. 2016; Ponnapureddy et al. 2017; Sindhuri et al. 2017). Also, the results of studies undertaken by leaders in the tourism sector such as the Accor Hotels group (2016)[12] or the tour operator TUI (2016)[13] showed that the Germans are tourists concerned about the sustainable aspects.

To further refine the qualitative analysis, we consulted HolidayCheck, a travel website dedicated to German speakers recognized for its rigor in the tourism industry. The travelers were asked to describe their experiences at the hotel in an independent review and to justify the ratings designated according to the holidayCheck rating system (from 1: poor to 6 - excellent). Using the same feedback from these guests, we were able to access other data such as their socio-demographic profile (especially the age group), the type of trip (Family, Couple, with friends, single), the duration of travel (one, two or three weeks), the reason for the trip (beach), etc. HolidayCheck also offers

---

[12] http://www.id-tourisme.fr/etude-accorhotels-engagement-developpementdurable/ (Dec 2018).

[13] https://corporate.tui.be/fr/presse/nouvelles/20170321-tourisme-durable (Dec 2018).

a wealth and variety of information (travel history and guest reviews, photos, videos, images, etc.).

The data collection corpus was the subject of a thematic content analysis (Mkono and Markwell 2014; Heinonen and Medberg 2018) from which inferences and interpretations were made.

5.4   Content Analysis

According to Bardin (2009), content analysis is "a set of increasingly refined and constantly improving methodological tools that apply to extremely diversified "discourses" (contents and containers). The common factor of these multiple techniques - from the computation of frequencies providing figures to the extraction of structure resulting in models - is a controlled hermeneutics, based on deduction: inference. As an interpretive effort, content analysis is switched between the two poles of the rigor of objectivity and the fruitfulness of subjectivity. It absolves and endorses in the researcher this attraction towards the hidden, the latent, the non-apparent, the potential of unpublished (unspoken), held by any message...".

Qualitative content analysis is a method of systematically describing the meaning of qualitative data. This analysis proceeds by assigning the successive parts of the material into categories from a coding frame (Schreier 2014).

Content to analyze can take many forms such as a speech, a document, an interview, a visual support (photo, video, film), or online comments. An analyst, particularly in the social sciences, tries to understand the cognitive activities of the speaker such as his beliefs (ideology) and his attitudes. In the marketing literature, Barreda and Bilgihan (2013) used content analysis with a twofold purpose: "to determine how travelers communicate in the cyberspace in relation to their positive and negative experiences they had when staying in a particular hotel" and "to include identifying the main themes that motivate consumers to evaluate hotel experiences in online environments and categorize the most frequently mentioned areas in the online hotel reviews".

The content analysis protocol proposed by Bardin (2009), will guide us during research. Three main stages are pursued: 1-the pre-analysis; 2-the exploitation of the material and finally 3-the treatment of the results obtained, the inference and the interpretation. Our main objective is to explore the main aspects of a societal strategic orientation based on the comments of the guests who have stayed at a ML hotel on the travel website Holiday Check.

In the first pre-analysis stage, the transcription did not take place since the content of the corpus is already online. We downloaded it in its native language. A translation was done in two languages: English and French for better assimilation. Support was provided by a multilingual person, the hotel's Assistant General Director (German-English-French-Arabic-etc. -speaking). After performing a floating reading and re-readings with identifying index and indicator, the division of the corpus (2nd stage) was carried out according to each thematic idea (key word, expression, index) referring to one of the five societal dimensions (PW, PSW, SR, EO and EC). The corpus exploitation was done manually without using a software. In order to carry out a thematic analysis and establish a thematic content analysis grid, we performed the coding in order to organize the data and the counting. According to Robert and Bouillaguet (1997), the purpose of this step is to apply, to the corpus of data, treatments allowing access to a different meaning answering the problematic but not denaturing the initial content.

In order to elaborate the analysis grid of the qualitative content, we counted the guests while opting for a classification according to the criterion of "age group". We identified 12 groups from online raw data collected. Then, we opted for an organization in five relevant classes as indicated in the Table 1. This grid allows us to find out the societal dimensions that are revealed in the online evaluations of the guests and what are the connotations of these feedbacks. A priori, this grid reveals that all the facets of the strategic societal orientation are present in the reviews of the guests of the Tunisian hotel ML, but with unequal proportions. Also, the results show that guests' reviews portrayed more positive connotations than negative ones.

6   Results and Discussion

This third and final step consists in processing the results obtained. Inference and interpretation use statistical techniques to identify the meaning and validity of results. Afterwards, the analyst can propose inferences and present interpretations. These can be used for theoretical or pragmatic purposes. A high frequency of a thematic idea, in this case societal dimension, means that it is important for the reviewer (guest).

The results displayed in the table of frequencies (Table 1) indicate the presence of the five societal dimensions in the evaluations of the societal strategic orientation of the hotel by the guests but mark, a priori, the inexistence of proximity between their frequencies of appearance.

Considering all age groups, these results are in favor of the "Psychological Well-being" (PSW) dimension. Compared to the other dimensions, this alone accounts for a percentage of around 48%. Then, the dimension of "Physical Well-being" (PW) comes with an occurrence rate of 23%. The third position is occupied by the "Social Relations and Initiatives" (SR) dimension with an occurrence frequency of 15%. The "Environmental Orientation" (EO) dimension is represented with an appearance rate of 9%. Finally, the least cited dimension concerns the "Economic Contribution" (EC) with a frequency of 5%.

The frequency table also tells us that guest ratings show the presence of positive and negative connotations in all the dimensions mentioned and for the majority of age groups. For discourses relating to positive connotations, the same trend was noted in relation to all the content generated. Indeed, the predominant dimension is "Psychological Well-being" (PSW) with an appearance rate of about 51%. The next two dimensions concern "Physical well-being"(PW) and "Social Relations and initiatives"

(SR) accounting respectively for 18% and 16%. The "Environmental Orientation" (EO) dimension appears in the positive quotes with a rate close to 10%. Finally, the "Economic Contribution" (EC) dimension is the least represented with an appearance rate close to 5%.The rather negative evaluations also affect the five dimensions with disproportionate occurrence frequencies. The "Physical Well-being" (PW) dimension is the most cited with a rate of 60%. The "Psychological Well-being" (PSW) dimension comes in second place with a frequency that is close to 25%. The dimensions of "Social Relations and Initiatives" (SR) and "Environmental Orientation" (EO) appear respectively at a rate of 6% and 5%. Finally, the last dimension similarly constitutes the lowest rate of appearance in the negative connotations of the guests.

Based on the guests' feedback, "Psychological Well-being" (PSW) refers to the main motivation for booking the hotel. Most of them stay with family (almost 60%) or in a couple (almost 35%) and rarely with friends or solo: *"Super great and many leisure activities... For teenagers, for children but also for adults "*. Some guests also seek to enjoy moments of relaxation: *"Very relaxing holiday"*, *"We felt very well and recovered properly"*; or to enjoy magical moments during animation activities, as announced in their speeches: *"The second time in this hotel. Everything perfect! Many sports. It is not worth to leave the hotel. It's Magic Life! Perfect as always"*, *"all wishes fulfilled"*, *"ABSOLUTELY SATISFIED!"*. It seems that some guests have regaled themselves in the restaurant and have had fun: *"Fruits and vegetables were delicious"*, *"A huge selection with all sorts of food"*. Some guests seem to be very affected by the care and assistance of some hotel managers in solving their problems, even external ones. Another element well received by the guests concerns the responsiveness of the staff in terms of complaints resolution: *"Complaints are dealt with quickly and an attempt is made to find a solution!"*. Negative criticisms relating to this first dimension relate in particular to the offer of beverages that are not pleasant: *"Beer is no good and otherwise there are only local alcoholic drinks (no European standard)"*. All these declarations bear witness to the preponderance of "Psychological well-being"(PSW) and evaluations with positive connotations of the guests, who are not ready to sacrifice hospitality and comfort during their stays at the expense of other societal dimensions.

With regard to "Physical Well-being" (PW), the guests agree that the factors that carry more weight are related to: the physical environment (cleanliness of the room and the hotel,) *"The rooms are functional with good facilities"*, *"The rooms were nice and very clean"*, *"the family room was large"*; the hygiene and physical comfort *"I slept well and had no back problems"*; to gastronomy *"gastronomy top"* and to safety *"But I understand that this must be for security reasons"*. Negative evaluations mainly concern the old-fashioned appearance of the furniture in the rooms: *"The rooms were already a bit older"* as well as some problems related to the installations in the bathrooms as well as the problem of the low flow of water *"The water pressure in the bathroom is a disaster "*.

The dimension "Social Relations and Initiatives" (SR) takes the third position. The positive reviews focus on the relationship between hotel staff and guests. This is particularly relevant to the guest-service, the entertainment team, the sports team, the kitchen staff and the restaurant staff: *"The staff was very friendly and accommodating!"*, *"Our waiter has always set the table for us, with the drinks we have always drunk"*, *"A big compliment to the entertainment team!!!"*. The mastery of the German language by all employees of the hotel is highly appreciated to facilitate contact and dialogue *"Everyone Speaks Perfect German"*, etc. However, the negative ratings relate to the preferential treatment given by employees to certain guests: *"The places to eat are constantly reserved by the waiters"*. Also, someones complain about the presence of other guests of different nationality: *"The only drawback and I have to say unfortunately were some guests. Especially the Russian audience was in our vacation madness"*.

"Environmental Orientation" (EO) comes in fourth place. The guests seem to be well impressed by some sub-themes of which mainly the greenery: *"The plant was very green"*, the variety of subjects and the landscape: *"horticulturally beautifully landscaped grounds, we had sea view (from the bed)"*; the cleanliness and the maintenance of the garden as well as those of the beach: *"The beach is narrow, but very well maintained"*, *"And of course a fantastic beach"*, *"hotel and grounds are nice and very clean"*, *"very nice hotel with a spacious garden area"*. However, and in relation to the environment, the guests complain about the noise (uproar):*"The only disturbing thing in the 9 days we had 7 times music until midnight"*, *"Dissatisfied, especially the balcony overlooking the washing machine room and loud noises we did not like it"*; or a moisture problem: *"it was always very humid (jungle in the middle of the hallway)"*.

Finally, the least considered dimension, the "Economic Contribution" (EC) was strongly linked to the relation quality-price: *"Value for money: very good"*, and the gratuitousness of certain activities: *"The lovers of water sports get their money's worth, from water skiing on a catamaran to banana boat everything is offered for free"*. However, some guests are unhappy because of the prices they find exorbitant: *"although the price increases"*, *"With what I paid I could prefer a holiday in Dubai"*, *"Value for money: rather bad"*.

The frequency table also informs that by uniting the five societal dimensions, positive assessments are well represented in all the age groups and in particular in the age group [36–45] at 95%. For younger guests between the ages of 14 and 25, as well as for those over 56, the appearance frequencies are equal and they are around 90%. Positive evaluations by guests from [46–55] years account for 86%. Finally, 79% refers to the percentage of positive ratings made by guests between 26 and 35 years.

Thus, we have just answered the first two objectives of our research, namely that: 1- All the five societal dimensions are revealed in the guest comments online but in a disproportionate manner. The results show that the dimension "Psychological well-being" (PSW) is higher than other societal dimensions. 2-The results highlight the existence of feed-backs with positive and negative connotations.

Some of our results are in concordance with the findings of Barreda and Bilgihan (2013) and Sthapit (2018) studies. Barreda and Bilgihan (2013) indicated that the most common concerns in traveler's expectations (positive reviews) are about "cleanliness of the hotel", "quality of service", "friendly and well trained staff", "quality of human contact". Sthapit (2018) revealed that three components which contribute to tourists' memorable hotel experiences: "a comfortable bed", "the friendly attitude of hotel staff" and "a delicious breakfast with plenty of choice as well as a good restaurant service at the hotel".

The results also show a weak presence of some very important aspects of sustainability in guest narratives. As an indication, waste management (energy saving, reduction and recovery of waste, etc.); social activities both internally (non-discrimination, integration of employees in the hotel); and externally (the community); security of the facilities; the presence of distinctions and certificates of quality are all elements of information that form the DNA of the sustainability of a hotel and therefore reflect its societal commitment.

A debate arises around the perception of guests and their behavior vis-à-vis the sustainable aspects of a hotel. For example, the studies of Ponnapureddy et al. (2017) and Sindhuri et al. (2017) highlighted the need to understand how potential tourists perceive sustainability aspects and amenities and how this affects their booking intentions.

Promising lines of research in the context of sustainable tourism have raised some questions. According to Hardeman et al. (2017), it is difficult to encourage clients to adopt a sustainable behavior (Luchs et al. 2010). In addition, these researchers asserted that tourism companies integrating sustainable practices generally have difficulty in communicating effectively their commitment to sustainable development and the resulting customer benefits (Villarino and Font 2015). Laville (2009) added that the communication on sustainability aspects in the tourism sector- "Transparent and educational communication, because a company has the customers it deserves and cannot eternally blame its customers for not appreciating its social or environmental efforts if it itself does not make the effort to communicate them honestly".

In order to face a critical view of the behavior of some companies known as Greenwashing or Socialwashing, hotel managers must be able to communicate about the social dimensions (respect of the host community; environmental protection; etc.) actually implemented within their activities and processes. The adoption of the normative tool (labels, quality certificates, etc.), the impact studies as well as the concrete results relating to their societal practices may be insufficient to constitute very powerful marketing arguments. Credible justifications for the societal commitment of hotels must be included in marketing materials (online and offline) and communicated to various influential stakeholders (tour operators, booking websites, internet users, customers, etc.). Awareness-raising and both online and offline education could positively impact the behavior of certain hotel targets (water and energy consumption, waste sorting, planting of subjects, etc.).

Brazyte et al. (2017) studied how guests respond to the sustainability efforts by discussing them in online reviews: Customers mainly discuss sustainability attributes that have direct impacts on their experience or are observable at the hotel (biodiversity, education and sustainable products). Thus, guests should be educated by hoteliers in terms of sustainability aspects measures, because higher awareness may increase customer satisfaction. In the same vein, some researchers such as Gössling (2017); Yalçinkaya et al. (2018) pointed out that it is very important that environmental awareness and sensitivity education should become widespread among managers and employees in tourism. Information technology is also known to help control environmental resources and reduce energy consumption. Indeed, as stated above, social big data could open up innovation processes that could be of support in defining sustainable tourism experience (Del Vecchio et al. 2018a).

Finally, for motivating the guest to participate in a voluntary manner to sustainable practices, hotels need to develop a persuasive message (Lee and Oh 2014).

7　Managerial Implications and Future Research

Our research has dealt with a theme that combines two major trends in tourism and hospitality: sustainability and digital transformation. This broadens our knowledge and understanding of research methodologies (netnographic study) in tourism (Tavakoli and Mura 2018).

Our research will allow ML's tourism stakeholders and hotel managers to understand how guests perceive and act regarding societal practices and guide their communication decisions. The hotel must be able to prove that its societal strategic orientation is far from the practices of Greenwashing or Social-washing.

In the face of a vertiginous development of the Web (Web 5.0) and digital transformation, the marketing communication media as well as the content (snacking content) must be more and more personalized in order to be in phase with the specific expectations of certain market segments, in this case Generation Y (digital natives).

Given the limitations of qualitative research, it would be interesting to conduct other multiple comparative spatial and temporal studies. In addition, researchers could track the guests' opinions on one or more other travel Websites, such as Booking.com or even Expedia, while maintaining the same period. It would also be of great interest to conduct a temporal research after the renovation of the Tunisian ML hotel and to revisit the HolidayCheck website in order to scrutinize the comments of German-speaking guests. Including bigger sample size and using a software solution in coding and analyzing collected data from the online guests' reviews are recommended.

As part of the recommendations of Hine (2015), it is now essential to use nethnography to be able to follow the participants through different spaces frequented. This serves both academics in the development or enrichment of knowledge as well as tourism stakeholders (tour operators, hoteliers, travel agents) in marketing decision making.

8   Conclusion

Several researches are devoted to studying the concepts of Sustainable Development, Corporate Social Responsibility and Societal Strategic Orientation. Different micro and macro perspectives were then proposed. The general orientation is to highlight the importance of balancing the different economic, social and environmental objectives of any organization over a long-term horizon. Our research retains the following societal dimensions for the analysis of the Hospitality context: Physical Well-being (PW), Psychological Well-being (PSW), Social Relations and initiatives (SR), Environmental Orientation (EO) and finally Economic Contribution (EC).

The present research consists of a netnographic study of 92 reviews of German-speaking guests who stayed at a ML Hotel and who submitted comments online in the course of 2018. These comments were reviewed with the help of a content analysis grid. The results of this exploratory study make it possible to understand to what extent the guests perceive, according to age, the effort of the hotel deployed for a societal strategic orientation. The findings identify the occurrence of the five societal dimensions. Results show the relative importance of psychological well-being which occupies the first position in terms of the frequency of appearance in the content analysis, followed by the Physical well-being, then the social relations and initiatives. The two environmental and economic dimensions were the least mentioned in the guest comments of this Hotel. The analysis concerns both occurrences in positive and negative evaluations. The discussion of these results regarding the dimensions of the strategic societal orientation, the age and the sense of the evaluation (positive or negative) shows the importance of continuing with a broader study of all the comments of the guests on several social networks. The larger volume of data allows extracting, the main trends of the most determining elements for the guests in terms of societal dimensions. The results of this exploratory research may also motivate future investigations that will incorporate other sociodemographic characteristics such as the reason for travel and length of stay. For hotel managers, the research findings can inform their future decisions in terms of communication (tools and arguments) and investment relative to each dimension with a view to maximum satisfaction of their guests.

Acknowledgments. We would like to sincerely thank the General Manager and the Assistant General Manager of the Tunisian hotel ML, who supported us during certain stages of the exploratory research carried out as part of our study.

Also, we would like to sincerely thank the anonymous reviewers of the manuscript for the inspiring and encouraging comments throughout the evaluation process.

Annex 1

Table 1. Frequency table and examples of verbatim

Guests[a] / Dim[b]		G1/13 [14-25]	G2/23 [26-35]	G3/23 [36-45]	G4/20 [46-55]	G5/13 [>56]	Abs. Freq. (n=92)	Relative freq.	Examples of verbatim
Physical Well-being (PW)	ST +	42	95	76	55	57	325	17.92% / 18%	"The rooms are functional with good facilities. I slept well and had no back problems, which I usually have after 2-3 days at the latest". "The rooms were nice and very clean", "the family room was large". "gastronomy top". "It's great how many opportunities you have to be physically active." "But I understand that this must be for security reasons", "Cleanliness is guaranteed". "Top service staff and cooks who take care of your well-being every day".
	%	13%	21%	18%	16%	21%			". But the shower does not work at all. For older people the entry and exit is almost impossible "The captain's bar would have to be renovated", « In the specialty restaurants you can not choose, but gets numerous dishes on the table (far too much, almost nothing vegetarian, hot, greasy, ...). "Room a bit old », The club is older and it's good that it's being renovated", "bathroom had only a very narrow bathtub", and "The mattress was too hard for me. « The shower is in the bath. This is very narrow. » "The water pressure in the bathroom is a disaster"
	ST -	22	75	15	30	20	162	60.22% / 60%	
	%	61%	60%	63%	55%	67%			
(Total 457)								23%	
Psychological Well-being (PSW)	ST +	197	234	203	164	129	927	51.13% / 51%	"The second time in this hotel. Everything perfect! Many sports. It is not worth to leave the hotel. It is Magic Life! Perfect as always »", "the holiday feeling has switched on immediately upon arrival and stopped until departure." "We felt very well and recovered properly." "Entertainment was good », "all wishes fulfilled », « There was everything: Banana boat, canoe, archery, quad biking and fitness program and much more!" "ABSOLUTELY SATISFIED! «We felt comfortable and would book it again in any case" "Super great and many leisure activities ... For teenagers, for children but also for adults". "Complaints are dealt with quickly and an attempt is made to find a solution", « « the water sports team of Omar does a good job and we had a lot of fun there". "Very relaxing holiday". "You will be entertained from morning until late". "There is nothing to complain ... everything to make the guests happy. Always friendly smiles and greetings or give your hand that is part of the hospitality of the country". "Fruits and vegetables were delicious"
	%	61%	51%	49%	48%	47%			« But I would have liked more cocktails at the WunderBar.", "The drinks in the bars are rather poor to not drinkable. Cocktails are not good, too sweet and bad alcohol », "Beer is not good and otherwise there are only local alcoholic drinks (no European standard)."
	ST -	8	33	5	15	6	67	24.90% / 25%	
	%	22%	27%	21%	27%	20%			
(Total 994)								48%	
Social Relationship (SR)	ST +	44	58	74	64	45	285	16.72% / 16%	"The staff was very friendly and accommodating." "Nicole from the guest service has always taken care of everything immediately. She is great". "Super friendly staff". "All the hotel staff will treat you in a friendly way." "Extremely friendly, always helpful staff - even without always tip". "Always a smile and a friendly "hello- how are you?". "Our waiter has always set the table for us, with the drinks we have always drunk". "Everyone speaks perfect German », "Also no intrusive people". "A big compliment to the entertainment team!!!!".
	%	14%	13%	18%	19%	16%			"You cannot continue without a "bribe" or permanent tip. The places to eat are constantly reserved by the waiters". "The absolute and total Nego is the "boss" of the entertainment team Orhan. This is Arrogant, rarely present and marginally unfriendly." "The only drawback and I have to say..."
	ST -	0	7	2	6	1	16		6%
	%	0%	5.6%	8%	11%	3%			
(Total 301)								15%	

Guests[20] / Dim[21]	G1/13 [14-25]	G2/23 [26-35]	G3/23 [36-45]	G4/20 [46-55]	G5/13 [+56]	Abs. Freq. (n=92)	Relative freq.		Examples of verbatim
									unfortunately were some guests. Especially the Russian audience was in our vacation a madness. Most, not all know the word consideration certainly not
Environmental Orientation (EO) ST+	22	49	43	38	27	179	10%	9.87%	*"The plant was very green", "The beach is narrow, but very well maintained"…"and of course a fantastic beach", "Hotel and grounds are nice and very clean"…"Beach and grounds are very well maintained"…"lots of green, nice beach", "the hotel's beach top", "very nice hotel with a spacious garden area", "Everywhere plants", "horticultural beautifully landscaped grounds, we had sea view (from the bed)"*
%	7%	11%	10%	11%	10%			194 9%	
ST-	6	3	2	2	2	15	6%	05.57%	*"Decomfified, especially the balcony overlooking the washing machine room and loud noises we did not like it", "it was always very humid (jungle in the middle of the hallway)», "The only disturbing thing in the 9 days we had 7 times music until midnight"*
%	17%	2%	8%	4%	7%				
Economic Contribution (EC) ST+	17	20	22	19	19	97	5%	5.35%	*"Value for money: «rather good ». "Value for money: « very good ». "An affordable dream vacation for families:". "The lovers of water sports get their money's worth, from water skiing on catamaran to banana boat everything is offered for free"*
%	5%	4%	5%	6%	7%			106 5%	
ST-	0	6	0	2	1	9	3%	03.35%	*"although the price increases », « With what I paid I could prefer a holiday in Dubai: "Value for money: rather bad"*
%	0%	5%	0%	4%	3%				
Totaux +	322	456	418	340	277	1813	87%	87.05%	
Totaux +%	90%	79%	95%	86%	90%				
Totaux -	36	124	24	55	30	269	13%	12.9%	
Totaux -%	10%	21%	5%	14%	10%				
Totaux +&-	358	580	442	395	307	2082			

[1] This line indicates the age and the number of Guests in this category. For example, G1/13 [14-25] : 13 guests aged between 14 and 25
[2] Societal Dimensions
[3] Cumulative frequencies

References

Ali, A., Frew, A.J.: Information and Communication Technologies for Sustainable Tourism. Routledge, Abingdon (2013)

Ali, A., Frew, A.J.: Technology innovation and applications in sustainable destination development. Inf. Technol. Tourism 14(4), 265–290 (2014)

Avci, U., Madanoglu, M., Okumus, F.: Strategic orientation and performance of tourism firms: evidence from a developing country. Tour. Manag. 32(1), 147–157 (2011)

Bardin: L'analyse de contenu, 2ème Edition Puf, Quadrillage Manuels (2009)

Barreda, A., Bilgihan, A.: An analysis of user-generated content for hotel experiences. J. Hosp. Tourism Technol. 4(3), 263–280 (2013)

Bartl, M., Kannan, V.K., Stockinger, H.: A review and analysis of literature on netnography research. Int. J. Technol. Mark. 11(2), 165–196 (2016)

Brazytė, K., Weber, F., Schaffner, D.: Sustainability management of hotels: how do customers respond in online reviews? J. Quality Assur. Hosp. Tourism 18(3), 282–307 (2017)

Bretonès, D.: Des transformations sociétales en profondeur. Vie & sciences de l'entreprise 1(1), 6–8 (2011)

Brial, F.: Tourisme international et prostitution féminine: le cas de Nosy-Bé (Madagascar). In: Annales de géographie, no. 3, pp. 334–347. Armand Colin (2011)

Buhalis, D., Amaranggana, A.: Smart tourism destinations enhancing tourism experience through personalisation of services. In: Tussyadiah, I., Inversini, A. (eds.) Information and Communication Technologies in Tourism 2015, pp. 377–389. Springer, Cham (2015). https://doi.org/10.1007/978-3-319-14343-9_28

Centobelli, P., Ndou, V.: Managing customer knowledge through the use of big data analytics in tourism research. Curr. Issues Tourism 22(15), 1–22 (2019)

Combes, M.: Quel avenir pour la Responsabilité Sociale des Entreprises (RSE)? Manag. Avenir 6(4), 131–145 (2005)

Del Chiappa, G., Baggio, R.: Knowledge transfer in smart tourism destinations: analyzing the effects of a network structure. J. Destin. Mark. Manag. 4(3), 145–150 (2015)

Del Vecchio, P., Mele, G., Ndou, V., Secundo, G.: Creating value from social big data: Implications for smart tourism destinations. Inf. Process. Manag. 54(5), 847–860 (2018a)

Del Vecchio, P., Mele, G., Ndou, V., Secundo, G.: Open innovation and social big data for sustainability: evidence from the tourism industry. Sustainability 10(9), 3215 (2018b)

De Ruyter, K., Scholl, N.: Positioning qualitative market research: reflections from theory and practice. Qual. Market Res. Int. J. 1(1), 7–14 (1998)

Dodds, R., Joppe, M.: CSR in the Tourism Industry?: The Status of and Potential for Certification, Codes of Conduct and Guidelines. IFC (2005)

Femenia-Serra, F., Neuhofer, B.: Smart tourism experiences: conceptualisation, key dimensions and research agenda (2018)

Fuchs, M., Höpken, W., Lexhagen, M.: Applying business intelligence for knowledge generation in tourism destinations – a case study from Sweden. In: Pechlaner, H., Smeral, E. (eds.) Tourism and Leisure, pp. 161–174. Springer, Wiesbaden (2015). https://doi.org/10.1007/978-3-658-06660-4_11

Gond, J.P., Igalens, J.: La responsabilité sociale de l'entreprise. Presses universitaires de France (2008)

Gössling, S.: Tourism, information technologies and sustainability: an exploratory review. J. Sustain. Tourism 25(7), 1024–1041 (2017)

Gretzel, U., Sigala, M., Xiang, Z., Koo, C.: Smart tourism: foundations and developments. Electron. Markets 25(3), 179–188 (2015)

Hardeman, G., Font, X., Nawijn, J.: The power of persuasive communication to influence sustainable holiday choices: appealing to self-benefits and norms. Tour. Manag. **59**, 484–493 (2017)

Heinonen, K., Medberg, G.: Netnography as a tool for understanding customers: implications for service research and practice. J. Serv. Mark. **32**(6), 657–679 (2018)

Hine, C.: Ethnography for the Internet: Embedded, Embodied and Everyday. Bloomsbury Publishing (2015)

Imran, S., Alam, K., Beaumont, N.: A holistic conceptual framework for sustainable tourism management in protected areas. In: 2011 Cambridge Business and Economics Conference Proceedings. Association for Business and Economics Research (2011)

Jamrozy, U.: Marketing of tourism: a paradigm shift toward sustainability. Int. J. Culture Tourism Hosp. Res. **1**(2), 117–130 (2007)

Kang, G.D., James, J.: Revisiting the concept of a societal orientation: conceptualization and delineation. J. Bus. Ethics **73**(3), 301–318 (2007)

Kim, D., Kim, S.: The role of mobile technology in tourism: Patents, articles, news, and mobile tour app reviews. Sustainability **9**(11), 2082 (2017)

Koo, C., Gretzel, U., Hunter, W.C., Chung, N.: The role of IT in tourism. Asia Pac. J. Inf. Syst. **25**(1), 99–104 (2015)

Kotler, P., Lee, N.: Corporate social responsibility. Hoboken (2005)

Koubaa, E.H.: Societal Strategic Orientation and Business Performance: Proposal and test of a sustainability model applied to the hotel industry. Doctoral dissertation in Marketing, Faculty of Economics and Management of Sfax (2017)

Koubaa, E.H., Triki, A.: The Societal Strategic Orientation: Development of a measurement scale in the hotel sector. In: 2nd International Congress of the Moroccan Marketing Association; Tangier, April 2017 (2017)

Kozinets, R.V.: On netnography: Initial reflections on consumer research investigations of cyberculture. ACR North American Advances (1998)

Kozinets, R.V.: The field behind the screen: Using netnography for marketing research in online communities. J. Mark. Res. **39**(1), 61–72 (2002)

Kozinets, R.V.: Click to connect: netnography and tribal advertising. J. Adv. Res. **46**(3), 279–288 (2006)

Kozinets, R.V.: Marketing netnography: Prom/ot (ulgat) ing a new research method. Methodol. Innov. Online **7**(1), 37–45 (2012)

Kozinets, R.V.: Netnography: Redefined. Sage, Thousand Oaks (2015)

Kumar, V.: Transformative marketing: the next 20 years (2018). https://journals.sagepub.com/doi/pdf/10.1509/jm.82.41

Langer, R., Beckman, S.C.: Sensitive research topics: netnography revisited. Qual. Market Res. Int. J. **8**(2), 189–203 (2005)

Laville, E.: L'entreprise verte: le développement durable change l'entreprise pour changer le monde. Pearson Education France (2009)

Lee, S., Oh, H.: Effective communication strategies for hotel guests' green behavior. Cornell Hosp. Q. **55**(1), 52–63 (2014)

Leung, D., Law, R., Van Hoof, H., Buhalis, D.: Social media in tourism and hospitality: a literature review. J. Travel Tourism Mark. **30**(1–2), 3–22 (2013)

Lincoln, Y.S., Guba, E.G.: Naturalistic Inquiry, vol. 75. Sage, Beverly Hills (1985)

Lopez de Avila, A.: Smart destinations: XXI century tourism. In: ENTER2015 Conference on Information and Communication Technologies in Tourism, Lugano, Switzerland, pp. 4–6 February 2015

Lozato-Giotart, J.P., Leroux, E., Balfet, M.: Management du tourisme: territoires, offres et stratégies. Pearson Education France (2012)

Luchs, M.G., Naylor, R.W., Irwin, J.R., Raghunathan, R.: The sustainability liability: potential negative effects of ethicality on product preference. J. Mark. **74**(5), 18–31 (2010)

Maignan, I., Ralston, D.A.: Corporate social responsibility in Europe and the US: insights from businesses' self-presentations. J. Int. Bus. Stud. **33**(3), 497–514 (2002)

Matten, D., Moon, J.: "Implicit" and "explicit" CSR: a conceptual framework for a comparative understanding of corporate social responsibility. Acad. Manag. Rev. **33**(2), 404–424 (2008)

Mitchell, R.W., Wooliscroft, B., Higham, J.: Sustainable market orientation: a new approach to managing marketing strategy. J. Macromarketing **30**(2), 160–170 (2010)

Mkono, M.: Netnographic tourist research: the internet as a virtual fieldwork site. Tourism Anal. **17**(4), 553–555 (2012)

Mkono, M., Markwell, K.: The application of netnography in tourism studies. Ann. Tourism Res. **48**, 289–291 (2014)

Neirotti, P., Raguseo, E., Paolucci, E.: Are customers' reviews creating value in the hospitality industry? Exploring the moderating effects of market positioning. Int. J. Inf. Manag. **36**(6), 1133–1143 (2016)

Pasquero, J.: Éthique des affaires, responsabilité sociale et gouvernance sociétale : démêler l'écheveau, dossier sur L'éthique en gestion : au-delà de la réglementation. Gestion **32**(1), 112–116 (2007)

Ponnapureddy, S., Priskin, J., Ohnmacht, T., Vinzenz, F., Wirth, W.: The influence of trust perceptions on German tourists' intention to book a sustainable hotel: a new approach to analysing marketing information. J. Sustain. Tourism **25**(7), 970–988 (2017)

Prud'homme, B., Raymond, L.: Implementation of sustainable development practices in the hospitality industry: a case study of five Canadian hotels. Int. J. Contemp. Hosp. Manag. **28** (3), 609–639 (2016)

Robert, A.D., Bouillaguet, A.: L'analyse de contenu. Presses universitaires de France (1997)

Sautter, E.T., Leisen, B.: Managing stakeholders a Tourism Planning Model (1999). http://www.sciencedirect.com/science/journal/01607383

Seguin, G., Rouzet, E.: Marketing du tourisme durable. Edition Dunod, Paris (2010)

Schmücker, D., Kuhn, F., Weiß, B.: Information on sustainability in tourism–Frameworks and Status Quo in the German holiday market (FINDUS 1) (No. 1-2016). NIT Working Papers (2016)

Schreier, M.: Ways of doing qualitative content analysis: disentangling terms and terminologies. In: Forum Qualitative Sozialforschung/Forum: Qualitative Social Research, vol. 15, no. 1, January 2014

Sigala, M., Christou, E., Gretzel, U. (eds.): Social Media in Travel, Tourism and Hospitality: Theory, Practice and Cases. Ashgate Publishing, Ltd (2012)

Sindhuri, P., Julianna, P., Timo, O., Friederike, V., Werner, W.: The effect of consumer scepticism on the perceived value of a sustainable hotel booking. J. Tourism Hosp. **6**(5), 312–319 (2017)

Sthapit, E.: A netnographic examination of tourists' memorable hotel experiences. Anatolia **29** (1), 108–128 (2018)

Sthapit, E., Coudounaris, D.N.: Memorable tourism experiences: Antecedents and outcomes. Scand. J. Hosp. Tourism **18**(1), 72–94 (2018)

Tavakoli, R., Mura, P.: Netnography in tourism – beyond web 2.0. Ann. Tourism Res. **73**, 190–192 (2018)

Tavakoli, R., Wijesinghe, S.N.: The evolution of the web and netnography in tourism: a systematic review. Tourism Manag. Perspect. **29**, 48–55 (2019)

Thomsen, C.: Sustainability (world commission on environment and development definition). In: Idowu, S.O., Capaldi, N., Zu, L., Gupta, A.D. (eds.) Encyclopedia of Corporate Social Responsibility. Springer, Heidelberg (2013). https://doi.org/10.1007/978-3-642-28036-8

UNEP. United Nations Environment Programme. Division of Technology, & Economics (2005). Making tourism more sustainable: A guide for policy makers. World Tourism Organization Publications. http://www.unep.fr/shared/publications/pdf/dtix0592xpa-tourismpolicyen.pdf

Villarino, J., Font, X.: Sustainability marketing myopia: the lack of persuasiveness in sustainability communication. J. Vacation Mark. 21(4), 326–335 (2015)

Vinzenz, F.: The added value of rating pictograms for sustainable hotels in classified ads. Tourism Manag. Perspect. 29, 56–65 (2019)

Visser, W.: Revisiting Carroll's CSR pyramid. Corporate citizenship in developing countries, pp. 29–56 (2006)

Whitehouse, L.: Corporate social responsibility: views from the frontline. J. Bus. Ethics 63(3), 279–296 (2006)

Wood, D.J.: Social issues on management: theory and research in corporate social performance. J. Manag. 17, 383–406 (1991)

Yalçınkaya, P., Atay, L., Korkmaz, H.: An evaluation on smart tourism. China-USA Bus. Rev. 17, 308 (2018)

Webography

http://www2.unwto.org/press-release/2019-01-21/international-tourist-arrivals-reach-14-billion-two-years-ahead-forecasts, January 2019

http://cf.cdn.unwto.org/sites/all/files/pdf/unwto_barometer_jan19_presentation_en.pdf

http://www.id-tourisme.fr/etude-accorhotels-engagement-developpementdurable/#,   December 2018

http://www.unep.fr/shared/publications/pdf/dtix0592xpa-tourismpolicyen.pdf, May 2016

https://moderndiplomacy.eu/2018/06/29/use-technology-for-more-sustainable-tourism-management/, December 2018

http://www.tourisme.gov.tn/realisations-et-perspectives/vision-strategique-3-1/qualite-formation. html (Also available at: www.beintunisia.com), May 2016

https://www.destinationtunisie.info/tourisme-represente-151-pib-de-tunisie-selon-cnuced/, December 2018

https://unctad.org/en/PublicationsLibrary/aldcafrica2017_en.pdf, December 2018

https://corporate.tui.be/fr/presse/nouvelles/20170321-tourisme-durable, December 2018

Luxury and Mass Media: How Can Brands Manage the Paradox Between Luxury Inaccessibility and Social Media Communication Tools?

Wafa Hamzaoui[✉], Nadine Tournois[✉], and Enes Hamzagic[✉]

Université Côte d'Azur, IAE, GRM, Nice, France
hamzaouiwafa2001@yahoo.fr, nadine.tournois@unice.fr,
enes.hamzagic@etu.univ-cotedazur.fr

Abstract. The world of luxury is considered as an environment in which the secular is transformed to the point of becoming sacred. This has led researchers to consider the store as a "capital" of which the luxury brand inspires its values and that's where the consumer experiences an extraordinary consumption experience. This is contradictory to the principle of the democratization of social media. From where one expresses a fear of the profanation of the luxury store. This leads us to question the legitimacy of the luxury brand's communication via social media and to try to understand how they operate in the field of luxury consumption and communication and to ask the question: can social media convey the values of luxury?

The objective of this paper is to propose new tracks for reflection in the study of the luxury consumption experience through social media that are still relevant because of the daily use of connected objects since the technology and the internet have made it possible to favor the transition from the dichotomous paradigm to the ubiquitous paradigm.

Keywords: Social media · Consumer experience · Luxury brands

1 Introduction

This work has as theoretical anchor, the consumer culture theory (CCT) which is an interdisciplinary field mobilizing interpretive and critical approaches to understand the consumer. The CCT studies social representations and cultural practices to explain consumption (Arnould and Thompson 2005).

Since the 1980s, the consumer society has experienced a new phase of upheaval, which led the philosopher Lipovetsky in 2003 to introduce the term hyper-consumption, which has a symbol of deregulation. It touched the luxury sector and made it mutate. Thus, we are now talking about a democratic luxury, popularized luxury, an open and communicative luxury through the migration towards the e-commerce and the appearance of the new trends in the social networks.

At the same time, there is the democratization of tics and the shift from traditional marketing principles to the advent of digital, which has led the luxury sector to change

© Springer Nature Switzerland AG 2019
R. Jallouli et al. (Eds.): ICDEc 2019, LNBIP 358, pp. 110–119, 2019.
https://doi.org/10.1007/978-3-030-30874-2_8

its communication strategy and to create websites and communicate via social media. As a matter of democratic luxury, we have moved from a home-grown culture to a sales culture and from an artisanal logic to an industrial logic.

In the same logic of ideas, Lipovetsky argues that the philosophers Malinowski and Mauss have shown that luxury has two functions, the first is classic and serves for statutory construction and the second presents a place to tie luxury with the sacred because that the excess of expenditure makes it possible to recompose the origin of the world. Lipovetsky also adds "religion is one of the reasons for the emergence of luxury as evidenced by the symbolic Carnival where we start to spend so that abundance is possible. Hence, luxury has the power to allow for alliance with invisible forces. In addition, the ritual is identical with the gods that must be filled with gifts and sacrifices."

Hence, alongside the religious sphere, the sacred develops in new territories: politics, culture, music ... and luxury consumption and that is what makes the store a capital in its own right (Dion 2007).

The present work is part of the perspective that sees the store as a "capital" from which the brand inspires its values and makes them universal and timeless and where the consumer experiences an extraordinary consumption experience based on the affect, story and rites (Arnould and Price 1993).

What Arnould and Price (1993) have argued is synonymous with the cultural dimensions of luxury that are the myths that give birth to the brand's history, heritage and know-how to make brand (De Barnier et al. 2012). Rituals provide a means for the luxury brand to convey its values to its consumers, with the goal of creating a strong community for it (Bonté and Izard 2016).

This is a theoretical deficiency in the analysis of consumer behavior in experiential marketing applied to digital and social media, with a focus on the three stages of the consumer experience in a luxurious context.

Before the experience: the consumer builds a general idea of the luxury consumer experience through the analysis of content perceived in the social media.

During the experience: What does the consumer experience, is it an extraordinary experience leading to immersion and emotions that lead the consumer to create content in the social media?

After: what does the consumer remember after this experience? Can we consider the communication of experience via social media as a way to immortalize the memory of the experience?

Given the various elements advanced, a general problem is emerging around the impact of the luxury consumer experience on consumer behavior in the social media while emphasizing the three phases of the experience (before, during, after).

2   The Sociology of Consumption, the Consumer Experience, the Values of Luxury in the Digital Age

According to Baudrillard (1970), "objects are no longer linked to a definite function or need. Precisely because they respond to everything else, which is either the social logic or the logic of desire, to which they serve as moving and unconscious of meaning".

Baudrillard (1970) finds that consumption is now a way of life, where man lives through the objects he consumes. Consumption has become a means of differentiation and not of satisfaction. The man of the consumer society Baudrillardienne lives in abundance, a superabundance of products and objects.

As for Lipovetsky (2015), he advances the idea of hyperconsumption: the hypermarket representing the hysteria of consumption. To reach the phase of hyperconsumption, the company has gone through two previous phases: The first phase presents an escalation of endless needs where the consumer is running tirelessly to meet the constraints of prestige and social recognition. In the second phase, this is a distinctive field of symbols where actors seek to enjoy a use value, that is used to display social rank and to outclass a hierarchy of competitive signs. At this stage, the consumer wants to access an easier and more comfortable lifestyle, freer and more hedonistic. This second phase combines two heterogeneous logic, the race to esteem and the race to pleasure.

Phase III is the time when the distracting value outweighs the horrifying value, the self-preservation over the provocative comparison, the better being on display of overt signs. Consumption at this stage becomes more and more individualistic. She is said to be hyper-individualistic.

We note that Lipovetsky's (2015) reflections are in line with Baudrillard's ideas about consumption. Holbrook and Hirschman (1982) initiated the experiential approach to consumption because, according to them, consumption is not just the value of the use of an offer or the service rendered by the use of a product.

Moreover, in terms of experiential marketing, we are talking about a shift from functional consumption to identity consumption (Carù and Cova 2003) of self-discovery and renewal (Ladwein et al. 2005). Where consumers no longer consume the product for its use value, they consume rather the meaning and the image of this product (Baudrillard 1970). Thus, the consumer is considered as a sensitive and emotional being (Maffesoli 1990) what is defined in terms of experiential marketing by hedonism. Experiential marketing considers that consumption presents a series of extraordinary immersions for the consumer (Carù and Cova 2003).

The luxury consumer experience is an extraordinary experience giving consumers the chance to immerse themselves in luxury through their consumption rather than experiencing an ordinary experience based on buying simple products and services at a high price. The extraordinary experience is a "sense of novelty in perception and process" (Privette 1983). It is triggered by unusual events that are characterized by high levels of intensity and emotional experience (Celsi et al. 1993). Through the extraordinary experience, consumers expect intense emotional results (Arnould and Price 1993). These emotions are subjective and vary according to individuals and their social situations (Denzin et al. 2001; Holbrook and Hirschman 1982). According to Arnould and Price (1993), any extraordinary consumption experience must be based on affect, narrative and rituals: this rhymes with the cultural dimensions of luxury.

2.1 The Cultural Dimensions of Luxury

Luxury identity derives its strength from the culture of its brand, which consists of rituals, myths and values that favor the social elevation of consumer status (Kapferer and Bastien 2008).

Myths:
These stories and stories reflect the tradition, heritage and know-how of the luxury brand (De Barnier, Valette-Florence et al. 2012)

Rituals:
Rituals are a way for the luxury brand to convey its values to its consumers, with the aim of creating a strong connected community for it (Bonté and Izard 2016)

Values:
Values are distinguished by a high degree of abstraction and strongly depend on customer perception (Schwartz 2007)

The values of luxury have been born in the luxury store which can be considered as an unusual world because the mythification of the places and their sacralisation proves a basic strategy adopted by the luxury stores to avoid the trivialization of the brands of luxury (Dion 2007).

Luxury can no longer be distinguished solely by the high price or the refinement of products. Rather, it is a collection of values and principles on which luxury is based and which receives its authenticity. In the luxury sector, we are no longer talking about a mere place of exhibition or sale of products. Instead, we speak of a "capital" store in which the rites and myths of luxury are born and the sacralization of the charismatic character (the founder and the artistic creator) is realized. This process of sacralization of the store comes into question when we talk about websites of luxury brands and communication through social media. One can therefore express a fear of a profanation of the sacred luxury store and ask the question in relation to the influence of the experience lived by the consumer in the luxury store or in the experiential context of his behavior in the social media.

3 Social Media and the Luxury Experience

According to Stenger and Coutant (2013), it can be concluded that identity construction is central in terms of the study of consumer behavior in social media, which has been confirmed via several researches conducted on this topic, such as the work of Belk (2013), Rolland and Parmentier (2009), and Hollenbeck et al. (2012). In addition, existing content in social media provides a reference according to which Stenger and Coutant (2013) designed the typology of social networks. Thus, through this mapping (Stenger and Coutan 2013), we can distinguish four types of social media. The digital social networks are the most "frequented" by the brands in terms of communication and this is manifested by the facebook pages associated with the brands. People behave in ways that maintain and improve their self-esteem. One way to do this is through the use of brands (Strizhakova et al. 2008; Strizhakova et al. 2011) that can be used as a means by which the consumer resorts to expressing different aspects of his self (Aaker 1997; Escalas and Bettman 2003; Torelli et al. 2011).

3.1   Digital Communication of the Luxury Brand

The Table 1 summarizes the differences between the characteristics of digital communication and traditional luxury communication.

Table 1. Traditional and digital luxury communication.

Traditional luxury communication	Communication on the internet
The impossibility of buying or interacting with the luxury brand in a place other than its prestigious distribution sites (Veg-Sala and Geerts 2012)	The close and direct accessibility of the brand with customers (Veg-Sala and Geerts 2012)
The selectivity and exclusivity of the media (Kapferer and Bastien 2008)	The visibility of the brand by a large audience (Veg-Sala and Geerts 2012)
Control of communication by the brand (Okonkwo 2010)	The loss of control of the brand and the great power of internet users (Helme-Guizon 2013)
The downward and diffusive relationship (Chevalier and Mazzalovo 2008)	The interactive and participative relationship (Chéreau 2010)

According to Table 1, traditional luxury communication is profoundly different from internet communication. The luxury brand is facing a serious challenge: it cannot do without digital technology, especially because of the constant evolution of the Internet.

The Communication of Luxury Brands on Facebook

The Table 2 clarifies how the brand's identity can communicate its image and identity on Facebook.

Table 2. Communicating brand identity on Facebook

The brand identity	The characteristics of Facebook
The aesthetic and physical elements of the brand	The Luxemosphere (Okonkwo 2010) and Visual Language (Kapferer and Bastien 2009)
The history of the brand	Storytelling (Kapferer and Bastien 2009)
The relationship with customers	The interaction between the brand and the fans and between the fans (Helme-Guizon et al. 2013)
The personality	Celebrity photos that often reflect the personality of the brand (Kapferer and Bastien 2009)
The mentalization	The promotion of the brand around social, sporting or ecological events and slogans that may reflect the brand mentalization

Facebook can be considered as a tool for communicating the identity of the brand. Yet, the luxury brand is distinguished by its culture, its values and its symbolic meanings (Kapferer and Bastien 2009). It is therefore the fans who must co-create the values and the signs according to their own senses (Carù and Cova 2003).

The Table 3 clarifies the way in which luxury identity can, through the lived experience of consumption, build the identity of its consumers.

Table 3. Brand communication on Facebook

Brand communication on Facebook		
Challenges	The risks	The solutions
Sharing and direct exchange between the brand and fans and between fans (Helme-Guizon 2013)	The loss of control (Helme-Guizon 2013)	Control the first published information (Helme-guizon 2013)
The strong interactivity between the brand and the fans and between the fans (Helme-Guizon et al. 2013) and the ease of connection between Facebook users based on friendly links (Ang 2011)	The power of fans to harm the image of the brand (Kapferer and Bastien 2009)	Always be close to fans, ask permission to create a friendly relationship, create a social environment, and limit purely commercial speech (Helmé-Guizon 2013)
The opportunity to create a brand community (Ang 2011)	The community may be negative in the case of a dissimilarity between the values of the brand and the beliefs of the fans (Tajfel and Turner 1986)	Create a positive consumer experience that allows fans to co-create brand values according to their own senses (Holbrook and Hirschman 1982)

The consumer of luxury is in search of identity through his choice to belong to an introverted community led by the principle of exclusivity and exception and via immersion in an extraordinary consumption experience in a sacred environment: the physical store of the brand. However, the consumer, once on the social media, behaves in such a way as to maintain and improve his self-esteem. One way to do this is the use of brands (Strizhakova et al. 2008; Strizhakova et al. 2011) that can serve as a tool for expressing different aspects of one's ideal self on social media like Facebook (Hollenbeck and Kaikati 2012). For example, consumers can link to luxury brands on Facebook to show their affiliation with a group of consumers with high social status, and this is reflected in huge numbers of luxury brand fans on Facebook. Thus, via this social media, the luxury brand now communicates with the mass and exposes its values and identity to all categories of consumers. It is an interaction between the brand and the fans and between the fans (Helme-Guizon et al. 2013). Kapferer and Bastien (2009) have called this "story telling". According to the mapping of social media (Stenger and Coutant 2013), we cite the category "virtual community" which reflects the principle of "story living" unlike socio-digital networks reflecting the principle of "story telling". the first category presents a social media like Facebook in which the brand tries to tell a story to the consumer. However, in the second social media called "virtual community" as Instagram, it is the consumer who lives a story with the brand that can be translated by a digital consumer experience materialized by sharing content (photo and/or video).

3.2 The Communication of Luxury Brands on Instagram

Instagram is a free application for the IOS and Android and it is unique. It is a platform for sharing photos and short videos with other users. Photos and videos can be taken directly with the app, or used from the phone's existing photo library.

A filter can be added before uploading the photo or video to a user's profile. At the same time, there is also the option to upload the photo or video to other social media sites such as Facebook and Twitter.

By deduction, based on the definition proposed by Stenger and Coutan (2013), the Instagram Photo Sharing app is a mobile social content network belonging to the "virtual community" category (Stenger and Coutan 2013).

A social media user like Instagram can be engaged with the brand in different ways, which means that there are different strategies that are employed. Firstly, brands encourage Instagram users to actively engage with the brand by participating in contests, campaigns and promotions.

User-generated content should lead to deeper and deeper relationships between brands and consumers, and more effective brand communities (Bulte et al. 2007).

We can notice the existence of videos and images of luxury hotel, which stays on Instagram. This content shared by the consumer allows others to build a general idea about the consumer experience in the luxury hotel during the "before the experience" phase.

During the experience, when the consumer is satisfied, he can create content on Instagram and share his experience which he had while staying in the luxury hotel.

Furthermore, what does the consumer remember after this experience in this luxury hotel? Can we consider the communication of experience via social media as a way to immortalize the memory of the experience?

Finally, by sharing content, the consumer will be a partner of the brand. Therefore, Being an honest partner is very important for managers. The brand must give the feeling that it speaks in a human voice (Helme-Guizon and Magnoni 2013).

4   Conclusion

The consumer experience generates pleasure and positive feelings (Carù and Cova 2003). Positive emotions are considered the first and, for some, the main response of consumers confronted with offers of experiences (Fornerino et al. 2008; Mano and Olivier 1993).

This brings us to the question whether the creation of content (photo and/or video) on Instagram can be considered as a way to express positive emotions. How can we measure the intensity of these emotions via content analysis?

The extraordinary experience is triggered by unusual events that are characterized by high levels of intensity and emotional experience (Celsi et al. 1993). By applying this to the case of Instagram, one wonders then, how the content conveyed (image and video) by Instagram can promise the consumer to live an extraordinary consumer experience in an experiential luxury context? This question arises upstream of the experience, but once the luxury consumption experience is experienced, we ask ourselves this question, how the intensity of the so-called extraordinary consumption experience can influence the behavior of the consumer in social media? Finally, downstream of the experience, how sharing the consumer experience on Instagram can impact the memory of the experience with the consumer. These three stages of experience, before, during and after. Roederer (2008) identifies three phases to a consumer experience, before experience, experience as such and after experience. This is also reminiscent of the four-phase process conceptualized by Arnould and Price (2002): the anticipation experience, the buying experience, the consumer experience, the memory experience. It is crucial to try to understand the effects of this three-phase consumer experience process lived between real and virtual on the attitudinal, behavioral and emotional reactions of the luxury consumer in search of authenticity, uniqueness and the inaccessibility offered by the world of luxury. Nevertheless, focusing solely on the subject from an experiential point of view and according to Ariely and Zauberman (2003), according to the theory of hedonic adaptation, there is a desensitization of the consumer to sensory stimuli after repeated exposure. Can we intuitively answer the question that was asked at the beginning by saying that the democratization of social media and the accessibility guaranteed by Instagram will lead to an adaptation by the consumer to consumer experiences luxury accessible via the digital world to the point of transferring the values of luxury?

References

Aaker, J.L.: Dimensions of brand personality. J. Mark. Res. **34**, 347–356 (1997)

Ang, L.: Community relationship management and social media costomerstrategy management **18**, 31–38 (2011)

Ariely, D., Zauberman, G.: Differential partitioning of extended experiences. Organ. Behav. Hum. Decis. Process. **91**, 128–139 (2003)

Arnould, E.J., Price, L., Zinkhan, G.M.: Consumers. McGraw-Hill/Irwin (2002)

Arnould, E.J., Price, L.L.: River magic: Extraordinary experience and the extended service encounter. J. Consum. Res. **20**, 24–45 (1993)

Arnould, E.J., Thompson, C.J.: Consumer culture theory (CCT): twenty years of research. J. Consum. Res. **31**, 868–882 (2005)

Baudrillard, J.: La société de consommation (The Consumer society) Denoel, Paris (1970)

Belk, R.W.: Extended self in a digital world. J. Consum. Res. **40**, 477–500 (2013)

Bonte, P.: Dictionnaire de l'ethnologie et de l'anthropologie. Presses universitaires de France, Paris (2016)

Bulte, C.V.D., Wuyts, S., Marketing Science Institute MSI: Social Networks and Marketing. MSI, Cambridge (2007)

Carù, A., Cova, B.: Approche empirique de l'immersion dans l'expérience de consommation: les opérations d'appropriation. Rech. Appl. Mark. (French Edition) **18**, 47–65 (2003)

Celsi, R.L., Rose, R.L., Leigh, T.W.: An exploration of high-risk leisure consumption through skydiving. J. Consum. Res. **20**, 1–23 (1993)

Chéreau, M.: Community management: Comment faire des communautés web les meilleures alliées des marques: Dunod (2010)

Chevalier, M., Mazzalovo, G.: Luxury Brand Management: A World of Privilege. Wiley, Boston (2008)

De Barnier, V., Falcy, S., Valette-Florence, P.: Do consumers perceive three levels of luxury? A comparison of accessible, intermediate and inaccessible luxury brands. J. Brand Manag. **19**, 623–636 (2012)

Denzin, N.K.: Interpretive Interactionism, vol. 16, 2 edn. Sage, Thousand Oaks (2001). https://doi.org/10.4135/9781412984591

Dion, D., de Paris-Gregor, I.A.E.: Processus de sacralisation des magasins de luxe. In: 12emes Journées de Recherche en Marketing de Bourgogne (2007)

Escalas, J.E., Bettman, J.R.: You are what they eat: The influence of reference groups on consumers' connections to brands. J. Consum. Psychol. **13**, 339–348 (2003)

Fornerino, M., Helme-Guizon, A., Gotteland, D.: Expériences cinématographiques en état d'immersion: effets sur la satisfaction. Rech. Appl. Mark. (French Edition) **23**, 95–113 (2008)

Helme-Guizon, A., Magnoni, F.: Les marques sont mes amies sur Facebook: Vers une typologie de fans basée sur la relation à la marque et le sentiment d'appartenance. Revue Française du Marketing, septembre **243**, 23–34 (2013)

Holbrook, M.B., Hirschman, E.C.: The experiential aspects of consumption: consumer fantasies, feelings, and fun. J. Consum. Res. **9**, 132–140 (1982)

Hollenbeck, C.R., Kaikati, A.M.: Consumers' use of brands to reflect their actual and ideal selves on Facebook. Int. J. Res. Mark. **29**, 395–405 (2012)

Hollenbeck, J.R., Beersma, B., Schouten, M.E.: Beyond team types and taxonomies: a dimensional scaling conceptualization for team description. Acad. Manag. Rev. **37**, 82–106 (2012)

Kapferer, J.-N., Bastien, V.: Luxe oblige. Groupe Eyrolles, Paris (2008)

Kapferer, J.-N., Bastien, V.: The specificity of luxury management: turning marketing upside down. J. Brand Manag. **16**, 311–322 (2009)

Ladwein, R.: L'expérience de consommation, la mise en récit de soi et la construction identitaire: le cas du trekking. Manag. Avenir **5**, 105–118 (2005)

Lipovetsky, G., Roux, E.: Le luxe éternel. De l'âge du sacré au temps des marques. Editions Gallimard, Paris (2015)

Maffesoli, M.: Au creux des apparences: pour une éthique de l'esthétique. Plon, Paris (1990)

Mano, H., Oliver, R.L.: Assessing the dimensionality and structure of the consumption experience: evaluation, feeling, and satisfaction. J. Consum. Res. **20**, 451–466 (1993)

Okonkwo, U.: Luxury Online: Style, Systems, Strategies. Palgrave Macmillan, Basingstoke (2010)

Parmentier, G., Rolland, S.: Les consommateurs des mondes virtuels: construction identitaire et expérience de consommation dans Second Life. Rech. Appl. Mark. (French Edition), **24**, 43–56 (2009). https://doi.org/10.1177/076737010902400303

Privette, G.: Peak experience, peak performance, and flow: a comparative analysis of positive human experiences. J. Pers. Soc. Psychol. **45**, 1361 (1983)

Roederer, C.: L'expérience de consommation: exploration conceptuelle, méthodologique et stratégique (2008)

Schwartz, S.H.: Value orientations: measurement, antecedents and consequences across nations. Measuring Attitudes Cross-Nationally: Lessons Eur. Soc. Surv. 161–193 (2007). London, UK: Sage

Stenger, T., Coutant, A.: Médias sociaux: clarification et cartographie Pour une approche sociotechnique. Décisions Mark. **70**, 107–117 (2013)

Strizhakova, Y., Coulter, R.A., Price, L.L.: Branded products as a passport to global citizenship: Perspectives from developed and developing countries. J. Int. Mark. **16**, 57–85 (2008)

Strizhakova, Y., Coulter, R.A., Price, L.L.: Branding in a global marketplace: the mediating effects of quality and self-identity brand signals. Int. J. Res. Mark. **28**, 342–351 (2011)

Tajfel, H., Turner, J.: The social identity theory of intergroup behaviour. u: Worchel S. i Austin WG (ur.) Psychology of intergroup relations. Nelson Hall, Chicago (1986)

Torelli, C.J., Monga, A.B., Kaikati, A.M.: Doing poorly by doing good: corporate social responsibility and brand concepts. J. Consum. Res. **38**, 948–963 (2011)

Veg-Sala, N., Geerts, A.: Gestion de la cohérence des récits des marques de luxe sur Internet: étude sémiotique et analyse comparée des secteurs de la maroquinerie et de la joaillerie. Rev. Fr. Mark. **233**, 5–26 (2012)

The Return on Investment of Professional Social Networks

Yamen Koubaa[1](✉) and Fares Medjani[2](✉)

[1] Brest Business School, Brest, France
yamen.koubaa@brest-bs.com
[2] HEC Alger, Tipaza, Algeria
famedjani@gmail.com

Abstract. The rise of social media marketing leads to questions about its return on investment (ROI). In this paper we develop a new set of metrics to evaluate both financial and non-financial ROI of social media. While most studies on social media deal with Facebook and Twitter, this is one of the rare studies that address the ROI from the perspective of one-to-one message campaigns on professional social networks. Data were collected from a French business school campaign on LinkedIn aiming to recruit new students. We used this free available data to propose a new model for calculating the ROI. This model can be easily adopted by marketers to assess the social media ROI both in monetary and non-monetary terms.

Keywords: Social media ROI · LinkedIn ROI · Return on investment · Professional social networks

1 Introduction

Calculating the return on investment (ROI) of social media (SM) campaigns is indispensable. Managers need to know how much benefits such campaigns bring to the company to decide about resources allocation to such marketing actions. This helps decision makers to make informed decisions on how to deal with SM. Despite the efforts by marketing scholars and data analysts to work out accessible solutions for this issue, it remains quite difficult for marketers to calculate the ROI of SM expenditures [15].

Facebook and Twitter are the most studied SM platforms [1]. Many studies report that the use of these platforms influences positively sales (financial outcome) and other marketing outcomes [e.g. 4, 8, 22, 26, 27, 35, 39, 43]. Although a consensus about the efficacy of the calculations leading to such conclusions is far to be reached, the works aforementioned have contributed to solving part of the ROI concerns of Facebook and Twitter's campaigns. But SM platforms are different and do not allow for achieving the same objectives [16, 30, 42]. The diversity of SM requires measurements and metrics adapted for each type [2, 44]. For instance, many academic higher institutions are using Facebook and Twitter for raising brand awareness and notoriety and using LinkedIn, which is a different platform, to recruit students by targeting potential candidates by one-to-one messages. While, most of the effects of popular SM lies in sharing and commenting the information within a group of users, most of the effects of professional

R. Jallouli et al. (Eds.): ICDEc 2019, LNBIP 358, pp. 120–130, 2019.
https://doi.org/10.1007/978-3-030-30874-2_9

social networks, like LinkedIn, lies in the sponsored one-to-one messages. From this perspective, there is a lack of research addressing the ROI measurement of professional social networks. The popular ROI measures are calculated based on the quantification of within-group influence [28, 29]. But these measures are not appropriate one-to-one messages ROI in the professional social networks where the individual response is as influential on ROI as the within-group influence.

Besides, most of the available techniques to calculate SM ROI are not accessible (high costs and lack skills) to many companies that need to calculate SM ROI while using free accessible tools and data. The objective of this paper is to respond to this need. We present a model for calculating SM ROI of professional network which uses users' easily accessible data.

2 Challenges of Measuring ROI in Social Media

It is obvious that calculating the return of invested assets is a necessary task to monitor and manage every investment. The ROI, is thus a key indicator of the performance of any project and its value is an important input to decision making. Many measures of ROI exist in the literature on finance, HR, accounting, etc. As a rule, the indicator links the expenditure value for a specific project to the value of the benefits it brings to the company. This calculation becomes challenging when the data allowing for the calculation of the expenditure and the benefits values are not easily accessible or when the benefits are not clearly known as it is the case of SM investments.

In conventional marketing, ROI is measured in terms of response rates, number of leads or profit per sale compared to the amount of invested resources [12]. In free SM marketing, marketers invest mostly time. They need time to search for users, design, diffuse, and monitor the message. What a company will get in exchange is attention and reputation which are intangible assets. Those intangible assets are supposed to generate income for the company. So, while a direct monetary impact of SM marketing is difficult to establish, SM activities have certainly indirect impacts on the company's financial performance through their effects on the company's intangible assets such as brand equity and word-of-mouth [5]. Organizations are having difficulties measuring efficiently those indirect returns using tangible metrics [29].

SM networks evolve following a structure of influence. When a network member's posted message is commented and/or forwarded by another member, it shows that the second member is influenced by the message posted by the first member. The interactions between the message creator and other members result in virality of the content. Most of the return of this interaction lies in the influence the message had on the behavior of the network members. The issue is that this influence is intangible. It results in an increased brand awareness or a higher attention towards an event for instance. Measuring the ROI of SM activities requires capturing and quantifying this influence and then measuring its effects on customer monetary value [28, 29]. These are the two main challenges of measuring ROI of SM marketing. How can we capture and quantify the influence within a social network? How can we measure the benefits of this influence in monetary terms?

3 Approaches to Social Media ROI Measurement

SM ROI measurement is discussed in both practitioner and academic literature. The debate is mainly focused on whether the ROI should be measured in financial or non-financial terms [5, 7, 34]. The pro of the non-financial approach argue that SM is about "people" not "money" [32]. Hence, relating SM activities to sales, and measuring its exact impact in financial terms is difficult [21, 32]. It should be calculated in terms of customer behavior [15].

SM marketing is about transforming attitudes and behaviors. When the impact is sufficiently strong, it may lead to concrete purchase actions which are measurable in financial terms. The non-occurrence of concrete purchase actions does not negate the occurrence of positive effects of SM activities. Nonetheless, the latter are intangibles and can't be assessed via financial measures. These can be more positive attitudes about a brand, a higher awareness about an offer, etc. It seems that reducing the measurement of SM impacts to concrete purchase rules out a plethora of intangibles effects which are as influential on the company performance as the tangible sales figures. The non-financial assessment of SM ROI seems to be inevitable.

3.1 Non-financial Social Media ROI Measurement

The advocators of the non-financial measurement approach look at SM ROI as an "umbrella concept" including different elements [33]. Measurement approaches are largely driven by "reach and frequency" [15]. For example, Moro, Rita, and Vala [36] predict reach metrics; Murdough [37] recommends a five steps SM measurement process based on three pillars, Reach, Discussions and Outcomes. Inspired from the "balance scorecard" [18, 19], Nair [38] developed the "social media scorecard". It corresponds to a set of KPIs outlining the performance of the customer, financial, internal processes and learning and growth related SM activities. Hoffman and Fodor [15] suggest estimating customer investment in SM and calculate the marketing investment the company must engage following that while calculating a set of metrics to measure the objectives of awareness, engagement and word-of-mouth.

3.2 Financial Social Media ROI Measurement

The advocators of the financial measures argue that ROI should be measured in financial terms because it is an economic concept [11]. Non-financial metrics are just intermediate because non-financial outcomes fill the gaps between the investment and the gain [5]. Financial measures are particularly important to justify future investment to senior management [12, 20, 42].

In this vain, Manchanda, et al. [31] provide evidence that joining the company's SM community lead to an economic benefit, named "social dollars", that can be quantified. However, these economic benefits are not always observable. John et al. [17] for instance found the association between SM and customer profitability is a product of selection in the sense that community membership drives buying for those predisposed to joining. The financial benefits, even when they exist, are not easily quantifiable mainly because of the difficulty to find accurate and useful data for quantification.

Many scholars have tried designing quantitative financial measures to respond to this need and this despite the considerable amount of intangibles effects SM activities have on the company performance. For example, Duboff & Wilkerson [11] and Gilfoil, Aukers, & Jobs [13] define a sales funnel which ends with estimated profits coming from the SM campaign, and then calculate the ROI based on campaign's costs and benefits. This model is easy to implement. However, it has the major drawback of taking into consideration only short-term effects (i.e. actual sales). It neglects long term effects and within-members influence that may lead in the long run to concrete purchases. Some scholars have hence presented other models to consider a long term effect using Customer Lifetime Value (CLV) [20], Customer Equity [23], or the Connected Customer Lifetime Value [41] to assess the customer return as an accumulation of reactions across a life span and not only a single immediate reaction to one campaign. Kumar & Mirchandani [28] and Kumar et al. [29] propose a model that captures within-network influence in addition to CLV. The authors propose a seven steps framework that relies on identifying influencers and incentivizing them to talk about the company/product. ROI calculation is based on four metrics namely Customer Influence Effect (CIE) and Stickiness Index (SI) for identifying the relevant influencers, and Customer Influence Value (CIV) and CLV to measure the ROI financial terms. Kumar et al's model is so far the most developed model for measuring SM ROI of word-of-mouth marketing campaign. It relies on both measures of tangible and intangibles effects. It has the merit of captivating the value inherent to within network influences in addition to the value inherent to the reactions of initial receivers. However, despite its merits, Kumar et al's model presents some limitations which make it inapplicable and irreproducible in all contexts. In fact, intentional influencing of consumer-to-consumer communications can raise questions about ethical constraints and credibility. Some countries may have laws on the disclosure of online influencers [44] and SM platforms are strengthening their privacy policies and rules rendering the collection of data allowing calculation of these metrics very challenging [28]. Besides, calculating the metrics of this model requires monitoring and tracking tools which are not accessible for everyone [44]. Finally, the model measures only the ROI of a word-of-mouth marketing campaign [25], but companies are using other strategies on SM [3], for example, interaction-satisfaction or interaction-immersion strategies increase CLV and CIV [14].

4 The Proposed ROI Measurement Model

Relying on financial or non-financial metrics is based on "the setting in which the manager operates" [34]. We argue that, "a customer's value is not always equal to how much they spend at your store. It' s far more" [12]. SM is a source of value by supporting branding, sales, customer service and support, and product development. Consequently, its value is both financial and non-financial [9] and it should be measured accordingly. We present a measurement model including both financial and non-financial SM ROI measurements while using only free available data. Our model aims at rendering the measurement of SM ROI accessible to every manager regardless of the resources available to him to manage these activities.

The model introduced here is designed to assess the efficacy of one-to-one message campaigns in a professional social network, LinkedIn. Unlike common SM networks like Facebook and Twitter, the message sharing within the group is not that important nor expected. The one-to-one messages targets the individual and not the group. To this extent, the within-network influence is not that significant on the conversion rate and hence does not play a major role in measuring the ROI. By opening the message, the customer learns about its content and may go further in seeking additional details. The content should therefore be attractive and serve as a canal to establish a strong rela-tionship with the potential customer leading to its conversion into a real consumer. It would have thus a significant impact on ROI. It's obvious that the number of targeted customers influences the ROI of the campaign. The bigger is this number, the higher would be the likelihood of opened messages and likewise of the converted customers. The reach potential of the one-to-one message should hence be considered while measuring the ROI. In communication, every message is designed to achieve a goal. The goal can be raising the awareness of customers about the brand, an event, a new product or a promotional offer. The communication campaign is effective when the goal is achieved. As in all ROI measurement, goal achievement should be considered to measure the ROI of the one-to-one message campaign.

4.1 The Measures

The financial side is measured by customer value (CV). The sales made by the target customer compared to the cost incurred during the process of conversion is the best measure to financially assess the ROI of SM activities. The non-financial side is measured through three indicators: one measuring the customer awareness of the campaign, one measuring the attractiveness of the content of the message and one measuring customer engagement (further details below). In line with Brodie et al's [6] definition, Customer engagement (CE) is seen as the predisposition of the customer to consult the message and go further in checking and/or recommending its content. Following that, we consider that the customer is engaged even if he/she will not make an effective purchase. Finally, conversion rate measures globally the power of the message to convert targeted candidates into consumers.

4.2 The Data

Data is collected from the database of a business school in France using LinkedIn to recruit students. The school has tested different campaigns on LinkedIn to raise can-didates' awareness about the school and its programs. Group campaigns, which are by nature of a general aspect, fail often to fulfil the information needs of these candidates. The communication department has thus decided to shift from group communication to one-to-one communication by using the LinkedIn inbox. First, the LinkedIn contacts of potential candidates is defined and acquired. Then, a personal message explicitly mentioning that the profile of the candidate interests the school and inviting him/her for a personal talk is sent to all the contacts (see appendix). The message includes also the weblink of the school and the link to online applications for taking an appointment for a talk. 150 candidates were contacted from November 6 to December 5th, 2018. Table 1 recapitulates the statistics of the one-to-one message campaign.

Table 1. The statistics of the one-to-one message campaign

Number of targeted candidates	Number of clicks	Number of opened messages	Number of weblink clicks	Number of individual talks	Number of converted candidates	Cost of the campaign	Cost of individual talks	Total amount of sales
150	163	63	42	15	8	1200€	900€	96000€

Four more candidates, who were not on the list of contacts of the one-to-one message are recruited. Two of them mentioned that they were informed about the program by a friend or a relative who got the inbox message.

4.3 Calculation of the Measures

Financial Measures
We divide the total payments made by the registered candidates by the total cost of the campaign. It is important to mention here that every candidate pays the totality of the fee when he/she registers.
    CV = total sales/total costs of the campaign = 96000/1200 = 8000%

Non-financial Measures
Open rate = number of opened messages/number of targeted candidates = 63/150 = 42%
This measure shows how many candidates read the message and become aware of the campaign.
    Message attractiveness is measured by two measures:
    The frequency of openings = number of opened messages/number of clicks = 63/163 = 38.6%
    This measure shows how important was the content of the message to the candidate. We assume that by clicking many times to open the same message, the candidates express an increasing interest in its content and hence the message is seen as more attractive.
    The click through rate = number of weblink clicks/number of clicks = 42/163 = 25.7%
    We assume that by reading through the message and opening the weblink included, the candidate adheres to the call-to-action issued by the school via the message. This shows that the message is convincing and attractive.
    Customer engagement (CE) is measured as the ratio of total number of individual talks requested by candidates by the total number of weblinks clicks. By asking for an individual talk, the candidate expresses a certain engagement to buy the product. He/she shows a higher predisposition to become a consumer than those who have not asked for the individual talk.

CE = number of individual talks/number of weblinks clicks = 15/42 = 35.7%.

Conversion rate = number of converted candidates/ number of targeted candidates = 8/150 = 5.33%.

Basically, the conversion rate is calculated using the total number of delivered messages. But, in LinkedIn, we consider that all the messages are delivered, and thus we use the total number of sent messages.

Table 2 recapitulates the measures of our model.

Table 2. ROI measures of one-to-one message campaign on LinkedIn of BBS

Customer value	Open rate	Frequency of openings	The click through rate	Customer engagement	Conversion rate
150	42%	38.6%	25.7%	35.7%	5.3%

The within-network influence is not that significant in measuring the ROI of one-to-one message. However, we noticed during the data analysis that 2 candidates, have joined one of the school's programs following an incitation made by a targeted candidate. The effects of the campaign go beyond the social network members. Although the recruitment of these two candidates is the result of different actions, the amount of sales earned from them can be added to the total amount of sales incurred following the campaign. In this case the CV increases up to 10000% (120000€/1200€). But because this result is the outcome of an indirect effect of the campaign, we dedicate a specific CV measure for it called the indirect CV. It is equal to the amount of sales for the two candidates divided by their cost of individual talks.

Indirect CV = 24000€/100€ = 24000%

5   Discussions and Implications

The current study describes the design and the application of new metrics to measure the ROI of one-to-one message campaign on LinkedIn. It is one of the rare studies to investigate ROI in professional social networks while referring to free accessible user data. Besides, by developing metrics to assess the ROI in LinkedIn, we provide a background for measuring the efficacy of one specific use of SM, the individual inbox messaging. In the latter case, the SM is useful not because of the connections and the within-group influence but because of the reach power and the professional image of the network. Most of the metrics developed until now have dealt with mass users SM platforms as Facebook and Twitter where most of the value created by the campaign lies in the within-group influence. In this paper, most of the value created lie in the power of the message and the conversion canal. The one-to-one message activates the information need of the candidate inciting him/her to go further in information gathering. The conversion canal plays here a pivotal role. The content of the message should be well elaborated to boost the information need already triggered by opening the message. Then, the aim is to motivate the candidate to book for an individual talk during which school's marketers try to convert the potential candidate into a consumer. The assessment of ROI of this type of SM marketing communication requires the design of metrics that tackle all of the aspects of this campaign. We argue that financial metrics are always useful and can be significant indicators of any SM campaign. However, they should be strengthened by non-financial measure to cover those qualitative aspects of the campaign. We advocated for four non-financial metrics which evaluate in quantitative terms the quality and the ROI of different pieces of the campaign. All these metrics are easy to calculate and are driven from free available data. It is however important to precise that those measures do not apply for any marketing communication campaign. Two parameters influence significantly the saliency of these metrics: the target audience and the message content. The business school launched two campaigns for two different audiences: one for young students and one targeting adults looking for higher degrees. The data used in this paper are collected from the second campaign. The campaign targeting students had no return at all. The investigation of this failure revealed that young regular students use the platform LinkedIn to look for jobs. The content of the message is influential on the success of the campaign because it is the most critical piece of information in the communication campaign to convert the potential candidate from an ordinary explorer of a received message to an information seeker about the school and its programs. This step forward measured by the click through rate is crucial because it brings the potential candidate closer to the school and gives the school the opportunity to retarget the candidate by more specific LinkedIn or other types of messages.

Our metrics enables marketers to assess both in monetary and non-monetary terms, the ROI of investing in LinkedIn one-to-one message. The monetary metrics allows for comparing the value created by LinkedIn campaigns and compare it to the value created by other types of campaign. The non-monetary terms allow marketers enhancing the content and the deployment of the LinkedIn campaign. By measuring the efficacy of every piece of the communication channel, the proposed metrics enable for detecting deficiencies and allow for corrective measures even when the campaign is going on.

6 Conclusions and Limitations

The rise of SM platforms usage among companies in different industries lead to questioning its value for the business. The marketing literature explored this question but did not give consensus, specifically from the SM financial ROI measurements perspective [24], and whether SM is profitable across business models, industries, and platforms [20]. This study is an attempt to understand of SM ROI measurement in the context of professional social networks. Our proposed model joins the body of knowledge about SM ROI measurements models and approaches. It is built on academic calculations of customer value, and customer engagement taking in consideration complexity of SM data and costs to access more sophisticated tools. Thus, the model is easy to use from marketers that are continuously asked to justify their investments to senior management. It consists of four measures calculated using free available data and allowing to capture the overall customer value (i.e. financial and non-financial value).

Despite the theoretical and practical contributions of our study, it suffers from some limitations. We acknowledge that we proposed a model only for professional social networks, and only for one-to-one message (LinkedIn sponsored InMail). We applied the proposed model in the context of a French higher education institution in the field of business. Even if we could capture within-network influence beyond SM, possible interactions with other marketing mix elements are not captured [40]. In the future, there is a need to extend the study to other SM types, other industry contexts, and other engagement behaviors. Besides, as we focused on the behavioral dimension of engagement, future studies can measure other dimensions as cognitive and affective dimensions of engagement [10]. It will be interesting to develop an econometric model relating non-financial metrics to financial ones. This can be done by attributing a monetary value of each non-financial measure. Furthermore, professional social networks metrics can be modeled with data mining approach [36]. Finally, as we aforementioned one-to-one message were more effective than other campaigns, and adults were more interested than student, there is need for a deeper analysis to assess the determinants of these differences.

Appendix: The Sponsored Message

Sponsorisé
Boostez votre carrière !

Je m'inscris

Ewen Drévès
Bonjour Damien,

Votre profil a attiré notre attention !

Vous souhaitez accélérer votre carrière, enrichir vos compétences et pratiques managériales ou valoriser votre expérience grâce à une formation reconnue ?

Brest Business School vous propose une formation de haut niveau, conçue pour les professionnels expérimentés.

Diplôme Master Grande École (Bac+5), RNCP niveau 1, L'Executive Master en Management vous permettra d'acquérir et/ou d'actualiser toutes les compétences nécessaires dans les domaines clés de la gestion et du management de l'entreprise. Ce programme unique et modulable à souhait aborde le management 2.0 : design thinking, innovation, entreprenariat, enjeux numériques... L'EMM est enseigné via des méthodes pédagogiques innovantes telles que les serious games.

J'ai le plaisir de vous inviter à participer à un webinar le **jeudi 8 novembre prochain à 18h00.** Nous vous présenterons l'Executive Master en Management et répondrons à vos interrogations à propos de cette formation à temps partagé.

Ne passez pas à côté de cette opportunité d'évolution professionnelle, inscrivez-vous !

Je m'inscris →

References

1. Alves, H., Fernandes, C., Raposo, M.: Social media marketing: a literature review and implications. Psychol. Mark. **33**(12), 1029–1038 (2016)
2. Andzulis, J., Panagopoulos, N., Rapp, A.: A review of social media and implications for the sales process. J. Pers. Selling Sales Manag. **32**(2), 305–316 (2012)
3. Ashley, C., Tuten, T.: Creative strategies in social media marketing: an exploratory study of branded social content and consumer engagement. Psychol. Mark. **32**(1), 15–27 (2015)
4. Baek, H., Oh, S., Yang, H., Ahn, J.: Electronic word-of-mouth, box office revenue and social media. Electron. Commerce Res. Appl. **22**, 13–23 (2017)
5. Blanchard, O.: Social Media ROI: Managing and Measuring Social Media Efforts in Your Organization. Pearson Education, London (2011)
6. Brodie, R., Hollebeek, L., Jurić, B., Ilić, A.: Customer engagement: conceptual domain, fundamental propositions, and implications for research. J. Serv. Res. **14**(3), 252–271 (2011)
7. Buhalis, D., Mamalakis, E.: Social media return on investment and performance evaluation in the hotel industry context. In: Tussyadiah, I., Inversini, A. (eds.) Information and Communication Technologies in Tourism 2015, pp. 241–253. Springer, Cham (2015). https://doi.org/10.1007/978-3-319-14343-9_18
8. Chevalier, J., Mayzlin, D.: The effect of word of mouth on sales: online book reviews. J. Mark. Res. **43**(3), 345–354 (2006)
9. Culnan, M.J., McHugh, P.J., Zubillaga, J.I.: How large US companies can use Twitter and other social media to gain business value. MIS Q. Executive **9**(4), 243–259 (2010)
10. Dessart, L., Veloutsou, C., Morgan-Thomas, A.: Consumer engagement in online brand communities: a social media perspective. J. Prod. Brand Manag. **24**(1), 28–42 (2015)
11. Duboff, R., Wilkerson, S.: Social media ROI marketers are seeking to answer the "greatest question". Mark. Manag. **19**(4), 32–37 (2010)
12. Fisher, T.: ROI in social media: a look at the arguments. Database Mark. Customer Strategy Manag. **16**(3), 189–195 (2009)
13. Gilfoil, D., Aukers, S., Jobs, C.: Developing and implementing a social media program while optimizing return on investment – an MBA program case study. Am. J. Bus. Educ. **8**(1), 31–48 (2015)
14. Hamilton, M., Kaltcheva, V., Rohm, A.: Social media and value creation: the role of interaction satisfaction and interaction immersion. J. Interact. Mark. **36**, 121–133 (2016)
15. Hoffman, D., Fodor, M.: Can you measure the ROI of your social media marketing? MIT Sloan Manag. Rev. **52**(1), 41–49 (2010)
16. Järvinen, J., Karjaluoto, H.: The use of Web analytics for digital marketing performance measurement. Ind. Mark. Manag. **50**, 117–127 (2015)
17. John, L., Emrich, O., Gupta, S., Norton, M.: Does "liking" lead to loving? The impact of joining a brand's social network on marketing outcomes. J. Mark. Res. **54**(1), 144–155 (2017)
18. Kaplan, R., Norton, D.: The balanced scorecard: measures that drive performance. Harvard Bus. Rev. **70**(1), 71–79 (1992)
19. Kaplan, R., Norton, D.: The Balanced Scorecard: Translating Strategy Into Action. Harvard Business Press, New York (1996)
20. Kaske, F., Kugler, M., Smolnik, S.: Return on investment in social media–does the hype pay off? Towards an assessment of the profitability of social media in organizations. In: 45th Hawaii International Conference on System Sciences, pp. 3898–3907 (2012)
21. Keegan, B., Rowley, J.: Evaluation and decision making in social media marketing. Manag. Decis. **55**(1), 15–31 (2017)

22. Kim, A., Ko, E.: Do social media marketing activities enhance customer equity? An empirical study of luxury fashion brand. J. Bus. Res. **65**(10), 1480–1486 (2012)
23. Kim, Y., Boo, S., Qu, H.: Calculating tourists' customer equity and maximizing the hotel's ROI. Tourism Manag. **69**, 408–421 (2018)
24. Kizildag, M., Altin, M., Ozdemir, O., Demirer, I.: What do we know about social media and firms' financial outcomes so far? J. Hosp. Tourism Technol. **8**(1), 39–54 (2017)
25. Kozinets, R., De Valck, K., Wojnicki, A., Wilner, S.: Networked narratives: understanding word-of-mouth marketing in online communities. J. Mark. **74**(2), 71–89 (2010)
26. Kozinets, R., Patterson, A., Ashman, R.: Networks of desire: how technology increases our passion to consume. J. Consum. Res. **43**(5), 659–682 (2016)
27. Kumar, A., Bezawada, R., Rishika, R., Janakiraman, R., Kannan, P.: From social to sale: the effects of firm-generated content in social media on customer behavior. J. Mark. **80**(1), 7–25 (2016)
28. Kumar, V., Mirchandani, R.: Increasing the ROI of social media marketing. MIT Sloan Manag. Rev. **54**(1), 55–61 (2012)
29. Kumar, V., Bhaskaran, V., Mirchandani, R., Shah, M.: Practice prize winner—creating a measurable social media marketing strategy: increasing the value and ROI of intangibles and tangibles for hokey pokey. Mark. Sci. **32**(2), 194–212 (2013)
30. Lee, I.: Social media analytics for enterprises: typology, methods, and processes. Bus. Horiz. **61**(2), 199–210 (2018)
31. Manchanda, P., Packard, G., Pattabhiramaiah, A.: Social dollars: The economic impact of customer participation in a firm-sponsored online customer community. Mark. Sci. **34**(3), 367–387 (2015)
32. McCann, M., Barlow, A.: Use and measurement of social media for SMEs. J. Small Bus. Enterprise Dev. **22**(2), 273–287 (2015)
33. Michopoulou, E., Moisa, D.: Hotel social media metrics: the ROI dilemma. Int. J. Hosp. Manag. **76**, 308–315 (2019)
34. Mintz, O., Currim, I.: What drives managerial use of marketing and financial metrics and does metric use affect performance of marketing-mix activities? J. Mark. **77**(2), 17–40 (2013)
35. Moon, S., Bergey, P., Iacobucci, D.: Dynamic effects among movie ratings, movie revenues, and viewer satisfaction. J. Mark. **74**(1), 108–121 (2010)
36. Moro, S., Rita, P., Vala, B.: Predicting social media performance metrics and evaluation of the impact on brand building: a data mining approach. J. Bus. Res. **69**(9), 3341–3351 (2016)
37. Murdough, C.: Social media measurement: It's not impossible. J. Interact. Advert. **10**(1), 94–99 (2009)
38. Nair, M.: Understanding and measuring the value of social media. J. Corp. Account. Finan. **22**(3), 45–51 (2011)
39. Sonnier, G., McAlister, L., Rutz, O.: A dynamic model of the effect of online communications on firm sales. Mark. Sci. **30**(4), 702–716 (2011)
40. Srinivasan, S., Rutz, O., Pauwels, K.: Paths to and off purchase: quantifying the impact of traditional marketing and online consumer activity. J. Acad. Mark. Sci. **44**(4), 440–453 (2016)
41. Weinberg, B., Berger, P.: Connected customer lifetime value: the impact of social media. J. Direct Data Digit. Mark. Pract. **12**(4), 328–344 (2011)
42. Weinberg, B., Pehlivan, E.: Social spending: managing the social media mix. Bus. Horiz. **54**(3), 275–282 (2011)
43. Yoshida, M., Gordon, B., Nakazawa, M., Shibuya, S., Fujiwara, N.: Bridging the gap between social media and behavioral brand loyalty. Electron. Commerce Res. Appl. **28**, 208–218 (2018)
44. Zhang, B., Vos, M.: Social media monitoring: aims, methods, and challenges for international companies. Corp. Commun. **19**(4), 371–383 (2014)

Intelligent Systems

A Trusted Group-Based Revocation Process for Intelligent Transportation System

Hamssa Hasrouny[1,4(✉)], Abed Ellatif Samhat[2], Carole Bassil[3], and Anis Laouiti[1]

[1] Telecom SudParis, CNRS Paris-Saclay SAMOVAR, UMR 5157, 91011 Evry Cedex, France
hamssa.hasrouny@liu.edu.lb,
anis.laouiti@telecom-sudparis.eu
[2] Faculty of Engineering-CRSI, Lebanese University, Hadath Campus, Hadath, Lebanon
samhat@ul.edu.lb
[3] Faculty of Science II, Lebanese University, Fanar Campus, Fanar, Lebanon
cbassil@ul.edu.lb
[4] School of Engineering, Lebanese International University, Rayak Campus, Rayak, Lebanon

Abstract. Intelligent Transportation System (ITS) aims to provide innovative services in the field of road transport and traffic management. This field includes infrastructure, vehicles and users, and interfaces with other modes of transport. Vehicles are capable of exchanging information by radio to improve road safety or allow internet access for passengers. Road safety messages exchanged between vehicles may be falsified or eliminated by malicious entities to cause accidents and endanger people life. The main concern arises how to maintain only the trustworthy participants and revoke the misbehaving ones. In this paper, we propose a new framework for the certificate revocation process within ITS. This process can be activated by Misbehavior Detection Systems (MDSs) running within vehicles and the Misbehavior Authority (MA) within the infrastructure. These MDSs rely on the trust evaluation for participating vehicles updated continuously based on their behaviors. Therefore, the revocation is done periodically through geographical Certificate Revocation List (CRL) which specifies the certificates of all revoked vehicles within a specific area. This results in a lightweight solution for CRL management and distribution within a modular and secure Public Key Infrastructure (PKI), based on group formation and trust evaluation. Simulations were carried out showing the advantages of the proposed revocation framework.

Keywords: ITS · Vehicular network · Group formation · Privacy preservation · Misbehavior detection · Revocation

1 Introduction

The vehicular network consists of vehicles equipped with Online Board Units (OBUs) communicating together or with the infrastructure and the Road Side Units (RSUs). It aims of providing safety related information and traffic management. The communication

© Springer Nature Switzerland AG 2019
R. Jallouli et al. (Eds.): ICDEc 2019, LNBIP 358, pp. 133–146, 2019.
https://doi.org/10.1007/978-3-030-30874-2_10

is either V2V (Vehicle-to-Vehicle), V2I (Vehicle-to-Infrastructure) or hybrid via DSRC (Dedicated Short Range Communication) in a single or multi-hop mode [1]. Within ITS, vehicles are able to join groups without prior knowledge of each other, but certainly after being authenticated to the Certificate Authority (CA) within the infrastructure [2]. Then, a vehicle correspondingly gets its long-term certificate that binds its public key to an identity. Afterward, it requests short-term certificates used for privacy preservation and for a set of permissions within the ITS.

Safety and traffic management entail real-time information and directly affect the lives of people traveling on the road. Without a security guarantee, some malicious vehicles may jeopardize the system by putting the users' vehicles in dangerous situations. Participants need to be trusted. If not, the network becomes more vulnerable to frequent attacks as stated in [3]. Therefore, a trust evaluation technique is required to identify the malicious vehicles and to notify the Misbehavior Authority (MA) to exclude them from the network [2]. The exclusion and revocation process can be done through a Certificate Revocation List (CRL) distribution center being part of MA. This center is required to store and distribute the CRL to participants within the network. Some solutions related to the revocation process can be found in the literature [12–27], but the appropriate way of designing an infrastructure for management, generation and publishing CRLs is still an open issue for researchers within the ITS.

In this paper we focus on the design of a framework for the revocation process within the ITS. After reviewing several solutions from the literature, we propose a novel approach for the certificates revocation process based on publishing CRL within a modular infrastructure secured by PKI [4, 5]. To provide an efficient and secure V2V communication, we rely on the formation of vehicular groups to ensure anonymity using the group signature while the privacy is provided using short-lived changing keys [2]. We also consider the usage of a Hybrid Trust Model for evaluating the trustworthiness of participating nodes [6]. Based on a Trust Model developed in [2], we use its output to generate the geographical CRLs within the MA and to distribute them amongst the vehicular network groups. This results in an efficient CRL generation within a group-based PKI in the ITS.

The rest of this paper is organized as follows: in Sect. 2 we present and investigate some existing related work. Section 3 details the proposed solution for CRL management and distribution. In Sect. 4, we evaluate the proposed solution. Finally, in Sect. 5, we conclude and mention some future works.

2   Related Work

Many researchers investigated the certificate revocation process in ITS [7–27] Some of them used CRLs; others argued about the big size of CRLs and tried to find alternatives. Both share the same objective but differ on how the certificate validity is checked. The works that adopted CRLs are divided in two categories: the standardization groups [7–11] and other proposed solutions [12–19]. The standardization groups mainly defined the basic infrastructure for CRL and the communication with specific authorities, while the other proposed solutions defined methods for managing and publishing the CRL. Meanwhile, the other alternatives tried to directly check the certificate of the participant either by contacting instantly the specified authority [16, 23, 24] or by using a hash code [25–27], or they use correspondingly specific revocation protocols [19, 22].

The CRL requires the dissemination of a blacklist of revoked certificates, while the alternatives connect to an online certificate status server/responder to check the certificate status. This latter has an overhead advantage over the CRL but presents a bottleneck within a single responder. The main drawback of the CRL solution is its length due to the enormous number of vehicles, and the short lifetime of the certificates with no infrastructure defined for CRL. In this paper, we propose a solution for the revocation process that relies on the standardization groups work [7, 8, 10] for the CRL usage and their recommendation of using geographical CRL to reduce its size and minimize the bandwidth utilization. We adopt a modular and secure CRL infrastructure with the butterfly technology [5] to assure the total privacy of the participants. We also adopt the Hybrid Trust Model in [2] to classify the behavior of the vehicles and to inform the MA about malicious ones. Based on this model a Misbehavior Detection System (MDS) acts as an input for the CRL generator.

3 Proposed Solution for CRL

3.1 System Architecture

The deployment environment is illustrated in Fig. 1 and has the following main part: The vehicular groups, the connectors, and the infrastructure. RSUs are spread out over the roads and relay information between vehicular groups and the infrastructure and vice-versa. The infrastructure is composed of many Regional Authorities (RAs) communicating together.

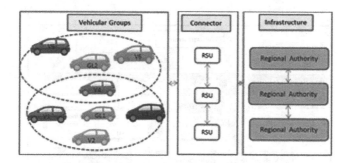

Fig. 1. Proposed framework architecture

Each Regional Authority (RA) infrastructure is similar to the infrastructure adopted in [4, 5], which provides a modular and secure PKI that assures privacy against insiders and outsiders (no possibility of tracking). Regional CAs only manage the certificates of vehicles in their region. RSUs provide a link to the Regional CA for keys revocation purposes. Infrastructure main entities are classified based on their functionalities into four groups as illustrated in Fig. 2: Policing within the Security Credential Management System (SCMS) Manager, Certificate Processing, Misbehavior Detection/ Revocation and Communication with Vehicles. Vehicular groups are formed based on the current location and speed of the vehicles on the road [2]. A group is equivalent to a geographical area of 600 m large, centered on the moving Group Leader (GL). The GL has a crucial role within the group; it is responsible for group keys generation and distribution, and group and delta CRL dissemination based on group members' activities. The group formation quickly disseminates the safety messages. Vehicles communicate together and with the infrastructure preserving a high level of security and anonymity. Nodes participating in ITS must be trusted and reliable. This issue creates a need for a mechanism to identify the validity of participating vehicles. A Hybrid Trust Model in [2, 6] is adopted for trustworthiness evaluation of participating vehicles. Based on the cooperation between vehicles and the infrastructure, this model classifies vehicles, elects GLs and deactivates others. The trust evaluation is based on different metrics to analyze vehicle behavior. When the vehicle's trust metric (within vehicles, GLs, and infrastructure) exceeds a threshold, the concerned vehicle is considered trustworthy. Otherwise, specific misbehavior detection set of rules are used to filter out the malicious ones. We consider that each vehicle (including GL) controls and sends its misbehavior report directly to MA because sometimes attacks can be directly detected by vehicles and not by GLs. A Misbehavior Detection System (MDS) within vehicles and MA is used to mitigate the effect of malicious users and exclude them from the vehicular network 2]. The Hybrid Trust Model outputs at the infrastructure level a global trust metric value for each vehicle i, a $T_{glob}(i)$, reflecting its behavior within the vehicular network. MA makes the final decision about vehicles within ITS. Within this work, we focus on Misbehavior Authority, Certificate Processing and Communication with vehicles to propose a framework for the CRL management within the Intelligent Transportation System.

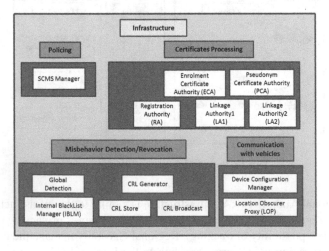

Fig. 2. Infrastructure entities

The novelty of this framework resides in the combination of a secure architecture, vehicular groups, and a hybrid Trust Model to produce and broadcast the geographical CRL.

3.2 The Revocation Work Cycle

We summarize the whole process that starts with the authentication phase and ends with the CRL management. Figure 3 respectively illustrates the mutual authentication of any vehicle i with the infrastructure and its enrolment in a specific group within the revocation framework. Each new vehicle i entering the network with a pair of pre-loaded Public (P_u) and Private (P_r) keys from the Department of Motor Vehicles (DMV) authenticates with the regional CA to get its long-term certificate and initial global Trust $T_{glob}(i)_0$ [2, 6]. $T_{glob}(i)_0$ is updated based on vehicle i behavior on the road. Vehicle i requests short-term certificates to participate in the vehicular network then try to join an existing group. The GL verifies this vehicle's certificate then gives it, the private signing key Pr_{sk} and the symmetric encryption key K_{gr} of this group. These keys are used respectively to sign the disseminated safety messages and encrypt/decrypt the confidential neighboring direct trust values [2]. The GL transfers to this vehicle the GCRL (group CRL), i.e., a list that contains all revoked certificates within this group. Vehicle i broadcasts beacons to its neighborhood. Each vehicle $j \neq i$ monitors different metrics/parameters for all its 1-hop neighbors. It calculates the related Trust metrics and transmits these values to the nearest GL. The GL, in turn, passing by the RSU transfers these values to the RA which updates the global trust value for each vehicle participating within ITS. The RA with its specific entities is responsible for maintaining the stability of the network by excluding malicious vehicles and publishing the CRL. At any misbehavior, the certificate tied to that bad V2V messages is recorded and uploaded to MA to react [2]. At *vehicle level*, each node calculates the trust metric for its neighbors and controls the behaviors of the other. This will provide a classification of these vehicles ranging from honest, intermediate to malicious ones. Notifications about malicious ones should be sent through the GL to MA. If GL is not reachable, vehicle directly notifies the MA. At the *GL level*, it concatenates all received Trust values about vehicles and does the classification. In the trust model, a simple vehicle and a GL control together because sometimes there are some attacks detected by the vehicles and not by the GLs and vice-versa. At the *infrastructure level*, it receives information from different GLs, builds a history about participating vehicles within ITS. Therefore, MA knows that a vehicle is misbehaving. It communicates with the certificate processing center and deactivates the batch of certificates related to this misbehaving vehicle by publishing a single key (seed) [4, 5, 7]. The revocation is done through geographical CRLs which specify all revoked certificates that should not be trusted within a certain group. Vehicles use CRLs to discern whether to trust the received messages or vehicles. When receiving a message, the vehicle checks the sender's certificate (seed value) against those listed in the CRL. If a match occurs, the message is ignored. Infrastructure frequently updates and disseminates *delta*CRLs containing freshly revoked certificates upon a misbehavior occurrence. Then, when new vehicles connect to the system, they are warned about specific certificates to avoid trusting. Vehicles can send misbehavior reports and receive certificate revocation lists (CRLs), and other traffic/safety updates through RSUs and GLs. Within vehicles, these misbehaviors and CRLs are recorded in the TPD of the OBU in order not to be altered by an attacker or the drivers themselves.

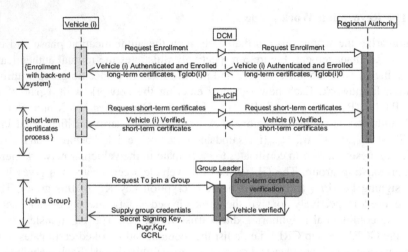

Fig. 3. Mutual authentication and group enrolment process of a vehicle within ITS

At GL and vehicles level, a local database is maintained within the Tamper-Proof Device (TPD). This database intervenes in CRL publishing within vehicles, GLs, and Infrastructure (MA). It includes the following tables:

- A Local Certificate Revocation List (LCRL): contains details about misbehaving vehicles detected *locally* by the monitoring vehicle itself after running the Misbehavior Detection Set of rules for vehicles' classification [2]. Vehicle pseudo-id and the seed value are ones of its main contents.
- A Group Certificate Revocation List (GCRL): is published by MA to RSU, then to GL and later to group members. It contains all revoked certificates of members within a specific group. It includes mainly vehicle pseudo-id, Group ID, the identity of the CA that issued the revocation information. This list is updated periodically based on *delta* and *base* CRL sent by MA.

At Infrastructure, a local database includes:

- Within the Global Detection entity, we mention two tables:
  - A table including a global trust for each vehicle i participating in a the vehicular network [2, 6], $T_{glob}(i)$ estimates the vehicle trustworthiness.
  - A table including all misbehaving details received from vehicles.
- Within the CRL Store, a table including all revoked certificates sorted by the recently revoked ones.

- Within the Internal Black List Manager, we propose three tables: white, grey and blacklists including respectively Honest, Intermediate and Malicious vehicles.

3.3 CRL Process Cycle

Certificates Updates

Privacy is a major concern in ITS security; the use of short-term certificates (pseudonyms) seemed to be a perfect solution for the traceability problem. For the certificates updates, we adopt the choice made by the NHTSA [9, 10]. To reduce privacy risks and promote security, a certificate is only valid for 5 min and completely discarded after its usage. Based on AAA (American Automobile Association) for traffic safety, an American vehicle is supposed to drive an average of 5 h weekly. So a vehicle has 60 valid certificates per week, and 3,120 certificates per year. In case a vehicle makes on average a drive greater than 5 h weekly, users can get additional short-term certificates via the short-term Certificate Issuance Proxy detailed in [2]. These batches include overlapping five-minute certificates valid for one week. "Overlapping" means that any certificate can be used at any time during the validity period. At the end of each week, OBU must replace all the certificates with 60 new certificates.

CRL Request and Distribution

When the CRL distribution center receives a CRL request, it responds by sending the requested CRL, if available. Any entity may request a CRL by generating a CRL request message via GL to the MA. To revoke a certificate, the driver within a vehicle sends a signed revocation request indicating the certificate to be revoked. MA reacts correspondingly. Revocation components generate the internal blacklist and CRLs [9, 10]. They distribute them to infrastructure components and end entities respectively via RSUs and respective GLs. If a vehicle i is on the blacklist, no certificate updates are issued. The MA sends a revocation message to the revoked vehicle i and broadcasts a *delta*CRL only to other vehicles $j \neq i$ within the group that vehicle i belongs to (geographical-group based CRL is used to reduce the CRL size). For the CRL distribution frequency within the ITS, it depends on the CRL types, on vehicle status, and different cases:

- For *FullBase* CRL: includes the list of all revoked vehicles within a specific group. We propose to distribute it on a daily basis to vehicles once they join a specific group in the vehicular network.
- For *deltaCRL*: contains only freshly revoked certificates within a certain group. We suggest that it should be incidentally broadcasted to vehicles, either when a new revocation occurs.
- For a *newly* entered vehicle, the GL checks the vehicle certificate status. After positive assurance, a *FullBase* CRL (GCRL) is downloaded to this vehicle via GL. The GCRL contains a list of revoked certificates within the geographical area of this group.

- For vehicles *leaving* the group, the identifiers of the old group should change at the same time in order not to be tracked. The identifiers are the group keys (Pu_{gr}), the group certificate ($Cert_{gr}$), the group ID (GID) and the group CRL (GCRL). If the leaving vehicle was malicious, the GCRL must be updated via *delta*CRL. Otherwise, no need to update and rebroadcast the GCRL; this vehicle authenticates with another GL, it is considered then as a newly entered car to a specific group (*case stated in the previous point*).

Update Procedure Rate

In the ITS, there is no way to accurately predict the misbehavior rate, because it depends on the intention of the participant drivers within vehicles or the attackers on the roadside. To reduce the CRL distribution communication load, we introduce the concept of downloading *FullBase* CRL once per day. The *FullBase* CRL is the GCRL (group CRL) that includes all revoked certificates within a specific group. As well, publishing the *delta*CRL that consists of the freshly revoked certificates, whenever misbehavior occurs. In this case, only cars that had not been driven for a long time will potentially have a significant update.

CRL Management and Updates

According to our proposed framework, vehicles (including GLs) monitor each other to detect the misbehavior [2]. Once misbehavior is detected, an evaluation set of misbehavior detection rules triggers within vehicles or GLs for vehicle classification and then notifies the MA to generate the specific reaction. Many circumstances take place depending on the monitoring entity: vehicles, GLs or the infrastructure. Table 1 below summarizes the CRL updates based on *Local* actions that happen within entities (vehicles and GLs) and *Global* actions that take place within the whole system.

4 Evaluation of the Proposed Solution

The certificate is a signed document of 120 bytes used mainly to authenticate vehicles within ITS. The authentication process is triggered whenever unauthenticated vehicles start communicating together. They send their certificates attached to the signed transmitted messages. When a vehicle receives a signed message, it checks the validity period of the sender's certificate then verifies it and its digital signature. This verification process induces delays as presented in Table 2 [28]. To lessen these delays, our proposed method relies on authenticating vehicles within the same group with the GL. These vehicles share common group credentials for signature and encryption which results in avoiding the need for the verification process, i.e., saves time and network resources.

Furthermore, we proposed within the revocation process to use the geographic CRL. The GCRL contains the revoked certificates of specific vehicles within a defined group area, which leads to a reduction in the CRL size and enhances the vehicular network performance.

Table 1. Summary of CRL updates and reactions within the ITS

Monitoring entity	Misbehaving vehicle status	Local action	Global action
Vehicle	'Intermediate' under inspection phase	Insert pseudo-id of misbehaving vehicle and its certificate seed in LCRL with a flag 'I'	None
	'Intermediate' inspection phase expired	1. Misbehaving continues: - Notify GL. If not reachable, notify the MA directly. If the MA is not reachable, notify the most trustworthy vehicle within the monitoring vehicle radio range. This vehicle will take hands of informing the MA - Add misbehaving vehicle identifier and certificate seed on top of LCRL - Monitoring vehicle discards messages from misbehaving vehicle until receiving deltaCRL from MA	MA analyzes the misbehaving report and takes specific action
		2. Misbehaving disappears: - Remove pseudo-id and certificate seed of misbehaving vehicle from LCRL	None
	Malicious	- Add misbehaving vehicle pseudo-id and certificate seed to LCRL. - Notify GL directly	MA analyzes the misbehaving report and takes specific action
GL	'Intermediate' under inspection phase	Insert misbehaving vehicle pseudo-id and certificate seed in LCRL with a flag 'I'	None
	'Intermediate' inspection phase expired	1. Misbehaving continues: - Investigate vehicle status and notify MA directly - Update the flag to 'M' and move misbehaving vehicle pseudo-id and certificate seed on top of LCRL - GL discards messages from misbehaving vehicle until receiving deltaCRL from MA	MA analyzes the misbehaving report and takes specific Action
		2. Misbehaving disappears: - Remove the pseudo- id of the misbehaving vehicle and its seed from LCRL	None
	Malicious	- Add misbehaving vehicle pseudo-id and its seed to LCRL. - Notify MA directly	MA analyzes the misbehaving report and takes specific Action

(*continued*)

Table 1. (*continued*)

Infrastructure	Malicious	Run Misbehavior Detection set of rules at the infrastructure, based on: - Comparison of global misbehaving Trust of vehicle i, Tglob(i) to the average global trusts of all vehicles within the Infrastructure in this region - Successive Global Trust values for the misbehaving vehicle over a certain period; if they are far away from each other - Number of notifications related to this misbehaving vehicle; if it exceeds a certain threshold of notifications - History of misbehaving records of this malicious vehicle	- MA via Internal Blacklist Manager classifies vehicles within Grey and Black lists 2 - MA via CRL Generator broadcasts deltaCRL including newly revoked vehicle to the group to which misbehaving vehicles belong. Thus the GCRL will be updated only within groups where misbehavior is detected

Table 2. Signature signing and verification times

Signature algorithm	Signing(ms)	Verification(ms)
ECDSA	0.56 ms	0.84 ms

4.1 Revoked Certificates

We used the Groovenet simulator [29] for analyzing the revoked certificates. We consider 50 circulating vehicles within a simulation area of 0.5 Km^2 around 333 7th Ave New York Location. These vehicles are equipped with DSRC for V2V or V2I communication. Initially, vehicles were positioned at 333 7th Ave New York location. Interacting vehicles are allowed to move using the Car Following Model (following GL). GL is moving based on a Uniform Speed Model varying ± 25% of the speed limit of the mentioned street. The objective of the simulation is to analyze the revoked certificates based on the MDS at different levels: the GL, the vehicles, and the infrastructure. These revoked certificates serve as inputs for *delta* and Full CRL generated by the MA to the specified groups. Then to verify if there is a probability of false negative occurrence, i.e., any malicious vehicle is detected as honest. We also investigate if any malicious is detected by a neighboring vehicle and not detected by the Group Leader or vice-versa. The simulation duration is for 5 min each.

We considered a scenario with 10% of malicious vehicles injected. 10% represents five vehicles. The malicious vehicles ($v1$, $v2$, $v3$, $v4$, and $v5$) were sending falsified emergency events as follows: at event 1, $v1$ sent a falsified emergency message. At event 2, $v2$ joined $v1$ in sending falsified messages. At event 3, $v3$ joined the group in sending falsified messages. At event 4, $v4$ joined them, and at event 5, $v5$ participated in the malicious activity. Figure 4 shows the percentage of vehicles that detected the malicious activities during the monitored period. At event 1, 72% of the fifty vehicles detected $v1$ and classified it as a malicious vehicle. 16% of the fifty vehicles classified $v1$ as intermediate and put it under inspection and the remaining 12% of the vehicles in the zone consider the malicious injected vehicle $v1$ as honest. This latter percentage reflects the false negative rate detected within the MDS. Similarly, for event 2, we notice an increase to 74% in the percentage of vehicles that classified $v1$ into the malicious vehicle, the percentage of the vehicles that put $v1$ under inspection rose to 18%, while the percentage of the ones that considered $v1$ as honest (false negative) decreased to 8%. The changes were due to the cooperation between vehicles within the Hybrid Trust Model. Additionally, 80% of the fifty vehicles classified $v2$ as malicious one, 8% of the vehicles put it under inspection, and 12% of the remaining vehicles considered it an honest one. Similarly, for event 3 we updated the detection percentage of $v1$, $v2$ and presented those of $v3$. For event 4, we updated for $v1$, $v2$, and $v3$ and added those of $v4$. Moreover, for event 5 generated by $v5$, we showed the percentage detection related to the whole malicious group.

During the simulation period, we got a maximum of 12% false negative rate which means six over 50 vehicles consider an injected malicious vehicle as an honest one. After an investigation, this is due to the indirect calculation of trust metric values. Those six vehicles judge the malicious based on other opinions; malicious vehicles are outside the direct communication range of some vehicles within the groups. Furthermore, we noticed that the percentage of false negative assumption decreased during the simulation due to the cooperation between honest vehicles within the Trust Model. It is illustrated in Fig. 4 the false negative rate of $v1$ decreased from 12% to 4%. Similarly, for $v2$, it decreased from 8% to 4%, for $v3$ from 12% to 6%...etc. Correspondingly, the vehicles that detect the malicious behaving will send misbehavior reports to the GL that investigates and informs the MA. Then the MA will take appropriate actions. Finally, the GL was among the vehicles that detected the malicious activities. The GL detected $v1$ directly after the occurrence of event 1, it detected $v2$ and $v3$ after the occurrence of event 3, it detected $v4$ after the occurrence of event 4, and lastly, it detected $v5$ after the event 5. Table 3 shows the details of the GL control process over $v2$ in term of a tenth of the minute.

Table 3. GL control results in tenth of the minute order for $v2$ during event 2

Time$_{(min.sec)}$	Vehicle (i)	Status
2.0	$v2$	Inspection
2.10	$v2$	Inspection
2.20	$v2$	Inspection
2.30	$v2$	Inspection
2.40	$v2$	Inspection
2.50	$v2$	Inspection
3.0	$v2$	Malicious

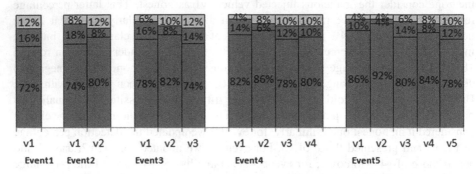

Fig. 4. Detection percentages at vehicles level with 10% malicious injected

5 Conclusion

In this paper, we propose a novel framework for certificate revocation process within the ITS. This framework is based on a secure and modular PKI infrastructure, vehicular groups and a Hybrid Trust Model. After defining the CRL infrastructure and main entities, we benefit from vehicular groups to reduce the CRL size by proposing geographical CRL published only to groups including the misbehaving members. For future work, we intend to investigate the multi-hop communication and the groups' interactions based on the revocation process.

References

1. Hasrouny, H., Samhat, A.E., Bassil, C., Laouiti, A.: VANET security challenges and solutions: a survey. Veh. Commun. **7**, 7–20 (2017)
2. Hasrouny, H., Samhat, A.E., Bassil, C., Laouiti, A.: Trust model for secure group leader-based communications in VANET. Wirel. Netw. J. 1–23 (2018). https://doi.org/10.1007/s11276-018-1756-6
3. Hasrouny, H., Bassil, C., Samhat, A.E., Laouiti, A.: Security risk analysis of a trust model for secure group leader-based communication in VANET. In: Laouiti, A., Qayyum, A., Mohamad Saad, M.N. (eds.) Vehicular Ad-Hoc Networks for Smart Cities. AISC, vol. 548, pp. 71–83. Springer, Singapore (2017). https://doi.org/10.1007/978-981-10-3503-6_6
4. Whyte, W., Weimerskirch, A., Kumar, V., Hehn, T.: A security credential management system for V2V communications. In: IEEE Vehicular Networking Conference, pp. 1–8 (2013)
5. Harding, J., et al.: Vehicle-to-vehicle communications: readiness of V2V technology for application. National Highway Traffic Safety Administration, Washington, DC, Technical report, DOT HS 812 014, August 2014
6. Hasrouny, H., Samhat, A.E., Bassil, C., Laouiti, A.: Trust model for group leader selection in VANET. In: The 4th International Conference on CSCEET, April 2017
7. IEEE Standard for Wireless Access in Vehicular Environments-Security Services for Applications and Management Messages: IEEE Std 1609.2™-2016

8. ETSI: PKI and roaming in its. In: 7th ETSI Security Workshop (2012)
9. NHTSA: Preliminary regulatory impact analysis FMVSS No. 150 vehicle-to-vehicle communication technology for light vehicles, Report no. DOT HS 812 359, December 2016
10. National Highway Traffic Safety Administration (NHTSA), Department of Transportation (DoT): Federal Motor Vehicle Safety Standards; V2V Communications, January 2016
11. EU-US ITS Task Force Standards Harmonization Working Group Harmonization Task Group 6: Cooperative-ITS Credential Management System Functional Analysis and Recommendations for Harmonization, Document HTG6-4, Version: 2015-09
12. Samara, G., Ramadas, S., Al-Salihy, W.A.H.: Design of simple and efficient revocation list distribution in urban areas for VANET's. (IJCSIS) Int. J. Comput. Sci. Inf. Secur. **8**(1) (2010)
13. Zhang, Q., Almulla, M., Ren, Y., Boukerche, A.: An efficient certificate revocation validation scheme with k-means clustering for vehicular ad hoc networks. In: IEEE Symposium on Computers and Communications (ISCC) (2012)
14. Nowatkowski, M.E., Owen, H.L.: Certificate revocation list distribution in VANETs using most pieces broadcast. In: Proceedings of the IEEE SoutheastCon, pp. 238–241 (2010)
15. Papadimitratos, P., Mezzour, Gh., Hubaux, J.-P.: Certificate revocation list distribution in vehicular communication systems. In: VANET 2008 Proceedings of the Fifth ACM International Workshop on VehiculAr Inter-NETworking, pp. 86–87 (2008)
16. Studer, A., Shi, E., Bai, F., Perrig, A.: TACKing together efficient authentication, revocation, and privacy in VANETs. In: Proceeding of SECON 2009 Proceedings of the 6th Annual IEEE Communications Society Conference on Sensor, Mesh and Ad Hoc Communications and Networks, pp. 484–492 (2009)
17. Nowatkowski, M.E., Wolfgang, J.E., McManus, Ch., Owen, H.L.: The effects of limited lifetime pseudonyms on certificate revocation list size in VANETS. In: IEEE SoutheastCon (2010)
18. Haas, J.J., Hu, Y.-C., Laberteaux, K.P.: Efficient certificate revocation list organization and distribution. IEEE J. Sel. Areas Commun. **29**(3), 594–604 (2011)
19. Samara, Gh., Al-Salihy, W.A.H., Sures, R.: Security issues and challenges of vehicular ad hoc networks (VANET). In: Second International Conference on Network Applications, Protocols and Services (2010)
20. Singh, J.R., Kumar, A., Singh, D., Dewang, R.K.: A single-hop based fast certificate revocation protocol in VANET. In: IEEE International Conference on Computational Intelligence and Networks (2016)
21. Mallissery, S., Pai, M.M.M., Ajam, N., Pai, R.M., Mouzna, J.: Transport and traffic rule violation monitoring service in ITS: a secured VANET cloud application. In: 12th Annual IEEE Consumer Communications and Networking Conference (CCNC) (2015)
22. Djamaludin, C.I., Foo, E., Camtepe, S., Corke, P.: Revocation and update of trust in autonomous delay tolerant networks. Comput. Secur. J. **60**, 15–36 (2016)
23. Rajput, U., Abbas, F., Eun, H., Oh, H.: A hybrid approach for efficient privacy preserving authentication in VANET. IEEE Access **5**, 12014–12030 (2017)
24. Caballero-Gil, C., Molina-Gil, J., Hernández-Serrano, J., León, O., Soriano-Ibañez, M.: Providing k-anonymity and revocation in ubiquitous VANETs. Ad Hoc Netw. J. **36**, 482–494 (2016)
25. Martín-Fernández, F., Caballero-Gil, P., Caballero-Gil, C.: Managing certificate revocation in VANETs using hash trees and query frequencies. In: Moreno-Díaz, R., Pichler, F., Quesada-Arencibia, A. (eds.) EUROCAST 2015. LNCS, vol. 9520, pp. 57–63. Springer, Cham (2015). https://doi.org/10.1007/978-3-319-27340-2_8

26. Gañán, C., Muñoz, J.L., Esparza, O., Mata-Díaz, J., Alins, J.: EPA: an efficient and privacy-aware revocation mechanism for vehicular ad hoc networks. Pervasive Mob. Comput. J. **21**, 75–91 (2015)
27. Wasef, A., Lu, R., Lin, X., (Sherman) Shen, X.: Complementing public key infrastructure to secure vehicular ad hoc networks. IEEE Wirel. Commun. **17**(5), 22-28 2010
28. https://www.cryptopp.com/benchmarks.html
29. GrooveNet v2.0.1, Vehicle Network Simulator. In: The Second International Workshop on Vehicle-to-Vehicle Communications (V2VCOM), San Jose, USA, July 2006. https://github.com/mlab/GrooveNet. Accessed 2012

On the Verification of Data Encryption Requirements in Internet of Things Using Event-B

Imed Abbassi[1], Layth Sliman[2]([⊠]), Mohamed Graiet[3],
and Walid Gaaloul[4]

[1] University of Tunis El Manar, Tunis, Tunisia
abbassi.imed@gmail.com
[2] EFREI Paris, 94800 Villejuif, France
layth.sliman@efrei.fr
[3] ISIMM, Monastir, Tunisia
[4] Telecom SudParis, Evry, France
walid.gaaloul@mines-telecom.fr

Abstract. In this paper, an approach for verifying data exchange requirements in the context of IoT with regard to resource constraints is described. The verification is done using Event-B method. The security requirements are defined based on the correlation concept. The capacity requirements are defined as a set of constraints on the exchanged data. The proposed approach starts by formalizing the data exchange process. Second, it extends this formalization with the data exchange security and capacity requirements. The consistency of each model and the relationship between an abstract model and its refinements are obtained by formal proofs. Finally, we use ProB model-checker to trace possible design errors.

1 Introduction

Internet of Things (IoT) [1, 2] constitutes a new paradigm, where everyday objects can be equipped with identifying, sensing, networking and processing capabilities that enable them to communicate over the Internet to accomplish some objectives. Objects can be anything that is able to provide data, while requiring other data over a network [2, 3].

There are different requirements to be considered for data exchange between objects in the context of IoT [2, 3]. In this work, we focus on security and capacity requirements. The security requirements is only studied with regard to correlation parameter [1]. Of course, other security parameters such as diffusion and confusion properties must be added for a complete verification. In this work, correlation is defined as a statistical measure which determines the capacity to predict the original data by the encrypted data using a linear relation [4]. The capacity requirements are defined as a set of constraints of two types: upper-bound and lower bound constraints. An upper-bound constraint concerns the provided data. For a given object, it defines a maximal number of data use. A lower-bound constraint concerns the required data. It defines a minimal amount of required data.

© Springer Nature Switzerland AG 2019
R. Jallouli et al. (Eds.): ICDEc 2019, LNBIP 358, pp. 147–156, 2019.
https://doi.org/10.1007/978-3-030-30874-2_11

The research problem in which we are interested in is the correctness verification of data exchange in IoT context [1, 5]. More precisely, we focus on verifying the data exchange security and capacity requirements using EventB method. To meet our objective, we first propose an Event-B formalization of the data exchange process. Then, we extend this formalization with the data exchange security and capacity requirements. The consistency of each model and the relationship between an abstract model and its refinements are obtained by formal proofs. Finally, we use ProB [6] model-checker to trace possible design errors. The rest of this paper is organized as follows: Sect. 2 presents an overview of the related work and the basic concept of the Event-B method. Section 3 describes our EventB formalization of Data exchange process and its correctness requirements in IoT context. The verification process of the consistency of such a model is described in Sect. 4. Section 5 concludes this paper and presents some future works.

2   Motivation and Background

In this section, we present an overview of the related work with an outline of their main shortcomings. Then, we describe Event-B basics.

2.1   Motivation

The data exchange problems in IoT and particularly the security issues have been gained a particular attention in the recent years. To deal with the security issues, different modern lightweight cryptosystems are designed such as Midori [7], Rectangle [8], Simeck [9, 10] and RoadRunner [11] Midori cryptosystem encrypts a 64-bit or 128-bit message with a 128-bit key. The message consists of a matrix with 4 rows and 4 columns of nybbles or bytes for 64 bits size message and 128 bits size message, respectively. Midori uses SPN structure. Midori uses involutive components. This allows to reduce cost since the same functions can be used for encryption and decryption.

RoadRunner encrypts an 80-bit message size. It is a Feistel construction with SNP as a function on 10 or 12 rounds with 80 or 128-bit key, respectively. RoadRunner uses the whitening key method to increase security. Rectangle is a bit-sliced design; it encrypts a 64-bit message with a 64 or 128-bit key. The message is carried out in the form of a matrix with 4 rows and 16 columns of bits. Rectangle uses SPN structure with 25 rounds. The bitsliced design makes the cryptosystem highly flexible for hardware implementation. Furthermore, due to columns parallelization in S-box function, the number of clock cycles is reduced.

Simeck uses only circular shifts and bitwise operations (XOR, AND) for round encryption and keySchedule function. This reduces memory and logic gate use.

The main shortcoming of the cryptanalysis done on the lightweight cryptosystems is that they not consider the correlation between encrypted and original data as it is, rightly or wrongly, considered as already covered by of the entropy analysis. However, some studies has shown that studying traditional entropy based on Shannon definition is not enough [14] and [15]. As a result, correlation should be considered independently in new designed cryptosystems. To this end, in this work we propose to use a formal method to verify this feature in cryptosystems. The approach introduced in this paper is intended to deal with data exchange security with regard to correlation issue using a formal verification method.

2.2   Event-B Formal Method

The Event-B [12] is a formal method based on the theory of sets and the first-order logic. It is a stepwise refinement approach producing a correct specification by construction since we prove the different properties of the system at each step. The Event-B is supported by the eclipse-based RODIN platform [13] on which different external tools (e.g. provers, animators, model-checkers) can be plugged in order to animate/validate an Event-B model. An Event-B model includes two types of entities to describe a system: machines and contexts. A machine represents the dynamic parts of a model. Machine may contain variables, invariants, theorems, variants and events whereas contexts represent the static parts of a model. It may contain carrier/enumerate sets, constants, axioms and theorems. Those constructs appear on Fig. 1.

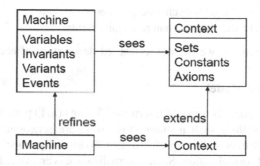

Fig. 1. Machine and context relationships

A machine is organized in different clauses: VARIABLES represents the defined variables of the model. The clause INVARIANTS represents the invariant properties of the system and must allow at least the typing of variables declared in the VARIABLES clause. EVENTS clause contains the list of events of the model. An event is modeled with a guarded substitution, is fired when its guards evaluated to true. The events occurring in an Event-B model affect the state described in VARIABLES clause.

The concept of refinement is the main feature of EventB. It allows an incremental design of systems. In any level of abstraction we introduce a detail of the modeled system. Correctness of Event-B machines are ensured by establishing proof obligations (POs); they are generated by the RODIN platform tool called proof obligations generator to check the consistency of the model. Let M be an Event-B model with v being variables. The invariants are denoted by I(v) and E is an event with an input parameter p and a guard $G(v, p)$ and a before-after predicate $R(v, p, v0)$. The initialization event is a generalized substitution of the form $v : INIT(v)$. Initial proof obligation guarantees the satisfaction of the invariants of the initialization : $INIT(v) \Rightarrow I(v)$. The second proof obligation is related to events. The event E should preserve invariants after its triggering. The Feasibility statement (FIS) and the invariants preservation (INV) are given in the following predicates:

- FIS: $I(v) \wedge G(v, p) \Rightarrow \exists v0 \cdot R(v, p, v0)$
- INV: $I(v) \wedge G(v, p) \wedge R(v, p, v0) \Rightarrow I(v0)$

An Event-B model M with invariants I is well-formed, denoted by M' I, only if M satisfies all proof obligations.

3 Formalizing Data Exchange Requirements in IoT Using Event-B

In this section, we propose an Event-B formalization for the Data Exchange Requirements in IoT. The following is the adopted formalization approach:

- Step 1: Formalizing the data exchange process.
- Step 2: Formalizing the data exchange requirements.

In the next subsections, we present a detailed description of each step.

3.1 Data Exchange Model

Object constitutes the main concept of Internet-of-Things (IoT) paradigm. An object can be any communicating thing such as smart phone, software, sensor network etc. Hence, it can provide data while eventually requiring others. To formally model the object concept, we define an event-B formalization. Such a formalization is an event-B model includes a machine "DataExchangeMachine" (see Fig. 2) and a context "DataExchangeContext" (Fig. 3).

```
MACHINE DataExchangeMachine SEES DataExchangeContext
VARIABLES
exchangedData objects sent received
INVARIANTS
type1: exchangedData ∈ P(DATA) type2: objects
∈ P(OBJECT) type3: sent ∈ objects →7
P(exchangedData) type4: received ∈ objects →7
P(exchangedData) EVENTS
...
```

Fig. 2. The DataExchangeMachine description

```
CONTEXT DataExchangeContext
SETS
DATA OBJECT
CONSTANTS
providedData requiredData
AXIOMS
axm1: providedData ∈ OBJECT → P(DATA) axm2:
requiredData ∈ OBJECT → P(DATA) END
```

Fig. 3. The DataExchangeContext description

The context "DataExchangeContext" specifies the static part of the object concept, namely the provided and required data. We define the provided and required data set using the following function:

$$providedData \in OBJECT \rightarrow P(DATA) \tag{1}$$

$$requiredData \in OBJECT \rightarrow P(DATA) \tag{2}$$

Where OBJECT represents an abstract type of objects. DATA denotes an abstract type of data. A given data can be provided/required by different objects. An object can provide or requires several data.

The event-B component DataExchangeMachine formally defines the dynamic part of objects, namely the process of data exchange. The variable's name exchangedData is a set of the exchanged Data between objects (type1). The objects that exchange data are specified using the variable objects (type2).

The variable, objects (formalized as a partial function from the set objects to P (exchangedData)), specifies the sent data set by each object. Similarly, the received data by a given object are determined by the variable received (see Fig. 4).

In addition to the previously defined variables, the machine DataExchangeMachine introduces an event named "exchangeData" to model the exchange of data between a set of objects. Such an event takes as input three parameters, namely to distinguish objects (o1 and o2) and a data to be exchanged (d). The types of these parameters are defined using the guards "grd1", "grd2" and "grd3". The guard "grd4" states that the data d must be provided by one of the two objects, while it is required by the other.

```
exchangeData = ANY d o1 o2 b
WHERE
grd1: d ∈ DATA grd2:
o1 ∈ objects grd3: o2 ∈
OBJECT
grd4: d ∈ providedData(o1) ∧ d ∈ requiredData(o2) THEN act1:
exchangedData := exchangedData ∪ {d} act2: sent := sent C− {o1
7→ (sent(o1) ∪ {d})} act3: received := received C− {o2 7→
(received(o2) ∪ {d})} END
```

Fig. 4. The formalization of the DATA exchange process between objects using Event-B notation

3.2   Extending Data Exchange Model with Security and Capacity Requirements

Different requirements shall be considered for data exchange process in context of IoT [1]. In this work, we focus on the following requirements: security and capacity requirements. The security requirements are defined based on the correlation concept. Correlation is a statistical measure which determines the capacity to predict a data d1 by another one, d2, using a linear relation [4]. More formally, we define the correlation concept as follows:

$$correlation \in (DATA \times encryptedData) \rightarrow \text{BOOL} \qquad (3)$$

The value FALSE of $correlation(d1\ 7 \rightarrow d2)$ states no linear relation between the data d1 and its encrypted one. This non linearity indicates a good encryption level of d1. However, d2 is called a bad encryption of d1 when the value of $correlation(d1\ 7 \rightarrow d2)$ is equal to TRUE.

The capacity requirements are defined as a set of constraints of two types: upper-bound and lower bound constraints. An upper-bound constraint concerns the provided data. It defines a maximal number of data use by an object. A lower-bound constraint concerns the required data. It defines a minimal number of data require by an object. We use the following functions to define the capacity constraints:

$$provideCapacity \in OBJECT \times DATA \rightarrow \text{N} \qquad (4)$$

$$requireCapacity \in OBJECT \times DATA \rightarrow \text{N} \qquad (5)$$

We formally model the capacity and security requirements, we introduce a new event-B model composed of a machine "RequirementMachine" (see Fig. 6) and a context "RequirementContext" (see Fig. 5). The context "RequirementContext" is defined by extending "DataExchangeContext" with constraints capacity requirements. The axiom "axm3" ensures that provideCapacity function can be defined only for the provided data. The axiom "axm4" states that requireCapacity function can be defined only for the required data.

The event-B machine, "RequirementMachine", refines "DataExchangeMachine" by the introduction of the security requirements. It introduces two new variables, namely encryptedData and correlation. The variable encryptedData defines a set of encrypted data. The variable correlation specifies the correlation between the encrypted data and the original one. During the refinement of DataExchangeMachine, the abstract variable exchangeData has been disappeared and replaced with encryptedData in order to specify the following need: all exchanged data are encrypted. The correctness relationship between the abstract variable and the concrete one (encryptedData) is ensured with the gluing invariant "glu1" (see Fig. 6).

In order to encrypt data before exchange process, RequirementMachine introduces a new event named "encrypt" (see Fig. 8). This event takes as input three parameters, namely a data d1 and its encrypted one d2, and a correlation level between d1 and d2. The substitution of the variable exchangedData with encryptedData systematically requires the refinement of exchangeData event. The new version of this event is described in Fig. 9.

The data exchange requirements are formalized in RequirementMachine as Event-B invariants (see Fig. 6). These invariants must be held in order to ensure a correct exchange of data between objects. In the next section, we will show how to prove such correctness (Fig. 7).

```
CONTEXT RequirementContext
EXTENDS DataExchangeContext
CONSTANTS
provideCapacity requireCapacity
AXIOMS
axm1: provideCapacity ∈ OBJECT × DATA → N axm2:
requireCapacity ∈ OBJECT × DATA → N axm3: ∀o,d·o ∈

OBJECT
            ∧d ∈ DATA
                ∧o 7→ d ∈ dom(requireCapacity) ⇒d
            ∈ requiredData(o) axm4:

∀o,d·o ∈ OBJECT
            ∧d ∈ DATA
                ∧o 7→ d ∈ dom(provideCapacity)
                ⇒d ∈ providedData(o)
END
```

Fig. 5. The RequirementContext description

```
MACHINE RequirementMachine REFINES DataExchangeMachine
SEES RequirementContext VARIABLES
objects sent received encryptedData correlation
INVARIANTS type1: encryptedData ∈ P(DATA) type2: correlation ∈ (DATA × encryptedData) → BOOL glu1:
exchangedData ⊆ encryptedData ...   EVENTS
...
```

Fig. 6. The RequirementMachine description

```
req1: ∀d1,d2·d1 ∈ encryptedData ∧ d2 ∈ DATA ∧ d1 7→ d2 ∈ dom(correlation)
⇒
correlation(d1 7→ d2) = FALSE


req2: ∀o,d·o ∈ objects ∧ d ∈ encryptedData ∩ sent(o) ∧ o 7→ d ∈ dom(provideCapacity)
⇒
provideCapacity(o 7→ d) ≤ card({o2·o2 ∈ objects ∧ d ∈ received(o2)|o2})
req3: ∀o,d·o ∈ objects ∧ d ∈ encryptedData ∩ received(o) ∧ o 7→ d ∈ dom(requireCapacity)
⇒
provideCapacity(o 7→ d) ≥ card({o2·o2 ∈ objects ∧ d ∈ sent(o2)|o2})
```

Fig. 7. The data exchange requirements formalized as Event-B invariants

```
encrypt = ANY d1 d2 corr b
          WHERE
grd1: d1 ∈ DATA
grd2: d2 ∈ DATA
grd3: corr ∈ BOOL
grd4: d1 6= d2 THEN
act1: correlation(d1 7→ d2) := corr
act2: encryptedData := encryptedData ∪ {d2} END
```

Fig. 8. The formalization of the data encryption process using Event-B

```
exchangeData = REFINES exchangeData b

ANY d o1 o2 WHERE
grd1: d ∈ DATA  grd2:
o1 ∈ objects grd3: o2 ∈

OBJECT
grd4: d ∈ providedData(o1) ∧ d ∈ requiredData(o2) grd5: d ∈
encryptedData THEN act1: sent := sent C− {o1 7→ (sent(o1) ∪
{d})} act2: received := received C− {o2 7→ (received(o2) ∪
{d})} END
```

Fig. 9. Refinement of the DATA exchange event with encryption requirements

4   Verification and Validation

In this section, we show how we proceed to ensure the correctness of the Event-B
model elaborated in the previous sections. To achieve this such goal, we propose an
approach that combines proof-based verification and model-checking.

4.1   Proof-Based Verification

The proof-based verification consists discharging a set of proof obligations (POs) It
guarantees that:

- The initialization leads to a state where the invariant is valid.
- Assuming that the machine is in a state where the invariant is valid, every enabled
  event leads to a state where the invariant is valid.

The POs define what is to be proved for an Event-B model. They are generated by a
tool, integrated in the Rodin platform celled proof obligation generator. They can be
either automatically/interactively discharged (marked with ⊘ᴬ), or undischarged
(marked with ⊘ᴬ) The symbol "A" means that the PO is automatically discharged.
Figure 10 reports an example of proof obligations where the initialization event of
the machine RequirementMachine preserves all invariants. As depicted in Fig. 10, the
encrypt event doesn't preserve the invariant req1. The reason of this non preservation is
the absence of real guarantee of a strong encryption of data. To repair this design error,
we have to add the following guard to the encrypt event: corr = FALSE.

Summarizing, the provers generate 37 POs. We notice that the work on POs is in progress: at this time, 31 of them are automatically or interactively proved. The proof of 6 POs remains to be done. That does not mean that they are false, but that the Rodin provers simply don't succeed in demonstrating the rule: it may be due to the fact that some events are not handled in an efficient manner by the provers, or due to the fact that the heuristics used for the proof are not efficient enough in this case. An effort remains to be done to manually demonstrate the unproved POs.

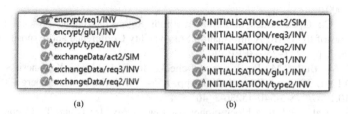

(a)   (b)

Fig. 10. Some proof obligations

4.2   Model Checking

As shown in the previous section, the provers fail to discharge automatically and interactively several POs. For this purpose, we extend the proof-based verification with a model-checking process by using ProB. This allows us to trace possible errors causing the failure of provers and then come back to improve POs. The counterexample generated by ProB that shows situations where the invariant is not satisfied was used as a guide to correct our model and then discharging some proof obligation. The constraint solving capabilities of ProB can also be used for model finding, deadlock checking and test-case generation. Depending on situations, we have made several modifications on the Event-B model related to the invariant, guard or to the action of the event.

5   Conclusion

In this paper, we proposed an approach for verifying data exchange requirements in context of IoT using Event-B method. The security requirements are defined based on the correlation concept. The capacity requirements are defined as a set of constraints on the exchanged data over Internet.

The proposed approach starts by formalizing the data exchange process. Second, it extends this formalization with the data exchange security and capacity requirements. The consistency of each model and the relationship between an abstract model and its refinements are obtained by formal proofs. Finally, we use ProB model-checker to trace possible design errors.

In the future work, many improvements will be made to this work so that it can cover the different security properties. This includes adding more requirement verifications such as diffusion level, confusion level and entropy.

References

1. Miorandi, D., Sicari, S., De Pellegrini, F., Chlamtac, I.: Internet of things: vision, applications and research challenges. Ad Hoc Netw. **10**(7), 1497–1516 (2012)
2. Whitmore, A., Agarwal, A., Da Xu, L.: The internet of thingsa survey of topics and trends. Inf. Syst. Front. **17**(2), 261–274 (2015)
3. Ma, H.-D.: Internet of things: Objectives and scientific challenges. J. Comput. Sci. Technol. **26**(6), 919–924 (2011)
4. Grasland, C.: Initiation aux methodes statistiques en sciences' sociales. Univ Paris VIIUFR GHSS (2000)
5. Meadows, C.: Open issues in formal methods for cryptographic protocol analysis. In: Proceedings of the DARPA Information Survivability Conference and Exposition, DISCEX 2000, vol. 1, pp. 237–250. IEEE (2000)
6. Leuschel, M., Butler, M.: ProB: a model checker for B. In: Araki, K., Gnesi, S., Mandrioli, D. (eds.) FME 2003. LNCS, vol. 2805, pp. 855–874. Springer, Heidelberg (2003). https://doi.org/10.1007/978-3-540-45236-2_46
7. Banik, S., et al.: Midori: a block cipher for low energy. In: Iwata, T., Cheon, J.H. (eds.) ASIACRYPT 2015. LNCS, vol. 9453, pp. 411–436. Springer, Heidelberg (2015). https://doi.org/10.1007/978-3-662-48800-3_17
8. Izadi, M., Sadeghiyan, B., Sadeghian, S.S., Khanooki, H.A.: MIBS: a new lightweight block cipher. In: Garay, Juan A., Miyaji, A., Otsuka, A. (eds.) CANS 2009. LNCS, vol. 5888, pp. 334–348. Springer, Heidelberg (2009). https://doi.org/10.1007/978-3-642-10433-6_22
9. Yang, G., Zhu, B., Suder, V., Aagaard, M.D., Gong, G.: The Simeck family of lightweight block ciphers. In: Güneysu, T., Handschuh, H. (eds.) CHES 2015. LNCS, vol. 9293, pp. 307–329. Springer, Heidelberg (2015). https://doi.org/10.1007/978-3-662-48324-4_16
10. Kolbl, S., Roy, A.: A brief comparison of simon and" simeck. IACR Cryptology ePrint Archive, vol. 2015, p. 706 (2015)
11. Baysal, A., Şahin, S.: RoadRunneR: a small and fast bitslice block cipher for low cost 8-bit processors. In: Güneysu, T., Leander, G., Moradi, A. (eds.) LightSec 2015. LNCS, vol. 9542, pp. 58–76. Springer, Cham (2016). https://doi.org/10.1007/978-3-319-29078-2_4
12. Abrial, J.: Modeling in Event-B: System and Software Engineering. Cambridge University Press, Cambridge (2010)
13. Abrial, J.-R., Butler, M., Hallerstede, S., Voisin, L.: An open extensible tool environment for Event-B. In: Liu, Z., He, J. (eds.) ICFEM 2006. LNCS, vol. 4260, pp. 588–605. Springer, Heidelberg (2006). https://doi.org/10.1007/11901433_32
14. Christiansen, M.M., Duffy, K.R., du Pin Calmon, F., Medard, M.: Brute force searching, the typical set and Guesswork. In: 2013 IEEE International Symposium on Information Theory, pp. 1257–1261 (2013)
15. Omrani, T., Rhouma, R., Sliman, L.: Lightweight cryptography for resource-constrained devices: a comparative study and rectangle cryptanalysis. In: Bach Tobji, M.A., Jallouli, R., Koubaa, Y., Nijholt, A. (eds.) ICDEc 2018. LNBIP, vol. 325, pp. 107–118. Springer, Cham (2018). https://doi.org/10.1007/978-3-319-97749-2_8

CaRT: Framework for Semantic Query Correction and Relaxation

Oumaima Mbazaia[(⊠)] and Karim Kamoun[(⊠)]

Higher School of Digital Economy, Manouba University, Manouba, Tunisia
mbazaiaoumaima@gmail.com, karim.kamoun@esen.tn

Abstract. With the emergence of the resource description framework (RDF) graphs, the SPARQL query processing on the large-scale RDF graph has become a more challenging problem. However, the efficiency of SPARQL query is difficult to reach and there are several issues that may arise. In our work, we address the problem of the no answer query. Many approaches are proposed to deal with this problem. These approaches used in generally relaxation methods to help user in finding alternative answers when their queries fail or do not return the expected answers. However, the majority of the proposed works don't detect and show to the user the cause of failure. This paper presents a Correct-and-Relax Triples (CaRT) framework designed to facilitate the exploitation of large knowledge base. Our framework proposes a new relaxation method that detects and corrects only the failed triples of a failed SPARQL query. We conducted comprehensive experiments on a benchmark RDF dataset and demonstrated the performance of our approach by improving the efficiency of the SPRQL query.

Keywords: SPARQL · RDF · No answers query · Causes of failure · Relaxation

1 Introduction

In recent years, several large ontologies have been created such as YAGO [1], or Knowledge Vault [2], which contain millions of entities and facts about them. Such information is usually stored in RDF (Resource Description Framework) or OWL (Ontology Web Language) format and queried with the SPARQL (Protocol and RDF Query Language). These ontologies are built from heterogeneous data sources. The large volume of existing data and knowledge through the web makes difficult the exploitation of the desired information. As a result, users have partial knowledge of the content and the structure of an ontology. The semantics and the supposition are not well understood by the users. A common issue encountered by users is the problem of failing queries, i.e., query results are empty also known as the problem of no answers query or do not contain the expected answers. For instance, a recent study on SPARQL endpoints [3] shows that ten percent of the submitted queries between May and July 2010 over DBpedia returned empty answers. When users build their queries, logical errors can arise from using non-existent terms or restrictions on relationships or even nonexistent relationships between entities. As an example, let us consider the ontology

R. Jallouli et al. (Eds.): ICDEc 2019, LNBIP 358, pp. 157–169, 2019.
https://doi.org/10.1007/978-3-030-30874-2_12

inspired by the LUBM[1], Benchmark depicted in Fig. 1. If a user wants to find the GraduateStudent who has undergraduateDegreeFrom the University, he may write the query Q1:

SELECT ?X ?Y
    WHERE{
        ?X rdf:type ub:Student. (t1)
        ?Yrdf:type ub:Academy. (t2)
        ?Zrdf:type ub:Department. (t3)
        ?Xub:undergraduateDegreeFrom ?Y (t4)}

Example of query Q1

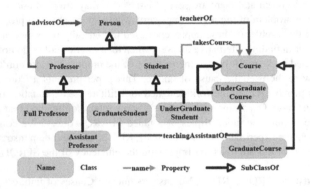

Fig. 1. Fragment of the LUBM ontology

In this query, the user makes a false assumption in the triplet pattern t1. The triplet t1 involved that the variable ?X belongs to the domain of undergraduateDegreeFrom and ?Y at his codomain. However, according to the ontology the domain of the property undergraduateDegreeFrom is GraduateStudent, thus ?X must be an instance of GraduateStudent and can't be an instance of Student as required by the triplet pattern t1. This false assumption is called an interrogation error [4]. In the same query, the user makes another false assumption in the triplet pattern t2 which is written correctly but the object "Academy" doesn't exist in the ontology. This false assumption is called a semantic error [4]. If we try to execute this SPARQL query Q1 we obtain zero answers and Q1 is considered as a failure query. Relaxation of the failing queries is one of the cooperative techniques used to retrieve alternative results. Several approaches generate multiple relaxed queries using different techniques. Among these approaches we have those who use the logical relaxation based on RDFS entailment and RDFS ontologies [5–8]. In [9] authors are based on query rewriting rules. Others relaxation techniques are also used such as statistical language models [10] or matching functions [11]. Most of these approaches using existent similarity measures to compute the similarity

---

[1] swat.cse.lehigh.edu/onto/univ-bench.owl.

between the obtained relaxed queries and the user failing query and then execute the relaxed queries in a similarity-based ranking order. These above approaches mainly propose a graphical system to build a SPARQL query and relax it using specific technique with or without the user assistance. However, its major drawback is the fact they relax the user query without knowing its failure causes. The following contributions are made in this paper:

- We provide a critical review of existing works.
- We present the CaRT framework which detect the causes of the failure SPARQL query and proposes a cooperative technique based on relaxation query to correct both *interrogation and semantic* errors.

The remainder of the paper is organized as follows: In Sect. 2, we survey existing works for the SPARQL query relaxation and a comparative table is also provided. In Sect. 3, we describe in detail the system architecture of CaRT followed by the description of its main functionalities in Sect. 4. We present a performance study in Sect. 5 and finally conclusions and future works are described in Sect. 6.

2 Related Work

Processing SPARQL query on a large-scale RDF graph has become a more challenging problem. However, the user's queries can fail by returning empty answers or answers that do not contain the expected results. To limit this issue, a number of cooperative querying approaches have been proposed in recent years to assist users in querying data. Motro [21] categorized cooperative querying approaches into two groups: Approaches that assist users in formulating their queries which using queries suggestion [22] or based on query by example [23]. Approaches that analyze the user's queries to detect anomalies in their formulation or in the expressed requirement. In this approaches there are works based on query explanation, others based on query refinement and those based on query redefinition. The query relaxation is one of the query redefinition technic. The review made by Minker [23] showed that the query redefinition is the one that considers the maximum of user's behaviors. It considers users without any knowledge about the data and the query language. As well it considers the alternative answers to guarantees the user's satisfaction. It is for this reason that we have chosen to use the query redefinition and mainly on the query relaxation in our framework CaRT.

In the following, we provide a review of the closest approaches related to our proposal for managing RDF data and/or relaxing SPARQL queries. The iSPARQL, (imprecise SPARQL) is an extension of the SPARQL language developed by Kiefer et al. [12], which allows a flexible evaluation of the query by incorporating in SPARQL similarity measures and flexibility clauses to provide approximate answers. Kiefer et al. [13], include some predicates in SPARQL to describe relaxation. The framework iSPARQL has several limitations. It forces users to specify some parameters on which the similarity is evaluated. Moreover, this extension does not really integrate relaxation techniques, it only serves to assess the similarity of imprecise answers.

The SWIP (Semantic Web Interface using Patterns) system was developed by Amarger et al. [14]. It proposes a system for translating a query from natural language to SPARQL. It consists on transmitting the natural language queries to Pivot-type queries. The pivot language is an extension of the keyword language. And then transforms the requests to SPARQL queries. Once the ontology elements have been identified, SWIP must find one or more query models that correspond to these elements. However, this step of creating query templates is done manually and therefore requires a lot of work. The mapping step leads to a set of relaxed queries. These relaxed queries are ranked to present at first those which seem most relevant. We note that SWIP does not really integrate the query relaxation approaches, it only uses the similarity measure to transform the pivot queries to SPARQL queries.

The third framework Corese (Conceptual Resource Search Engine) is a semantic search engine for the RDF language developed within the INRIA Wimmics team by Corby et al. [4]. Corese has its own query language built on the RDF model and syntactically close to SPARQL. It integrates the query approximation techniques, by providing two types of approximation: the ontological and structural approximation.

The framework Sematch (Semantic Entity Search from Knowledge Graph) is created by Ganggao et al. [15]. It's used to find semantic entities in Single Relation Typebased Queries (SRTQs) on heterogeneous KGs (Knowledge Graph) It restricts queries to others with a single relationship SRTQ. The query is first mapped to a WordNet synsets list. Then Sematch uses a semantic similarity function to optimize the precision of the WordNet synsets list. After the generation of the query graph, Sematch uses the Graph Pattern Collection (GPC) to construct the SPARQL query.

Finally, the framework QaRS (Query and Relax System) is created by Géraud et al. [16]. It has developed a cooperative technique that helps users to find alternative answers when their queries do not return the expected number of answers. The system can automatically relax the query after explaining the failure. QaRS relaxes the query with the MaXimal Succeeding Subquery XSS, i.e., the maximum subqueries that do not include the cause of failing. An assessment module is integrated in this framework to evaluate whether the query's answers meet the user needs. If not, the user can use a manual and interactive relaxation.

We note that QaRs identifies the failure of SPARQL query, then it relaxes all the query triples, thus a large number of relaxed queries is generated that build a huge search space.

The following table (Table 1) shows a comparative study between the five presented frameworks in term of the used query relaxation technique, the detection of the cause of failure of the failed query and the correction of both errors types that can lead to fail a user's SPARQL query *the semantic and the interrogation errors.*

Table 1. Comparison of the RDF data relaxation frameworks

	Query relaxation techniques	Cause of failure	Semantic errors	Interrogation errors
iSPARQL	☐	☐	☐	√
SWIP	☐	☐	☐	√
Corese	√	☐	√	√
Sematch	√	☐	☐	√
QaRs	√	√	☐	√

According to the Table 1, we note that all presented frameworks deal with the interrogation errors but only Corese treats also the semantic errors. In addition, only QaRs detects the cause of failure of the SPARQL query. Our framework CaRT described in this paper aims at filling this gap with providing a system that detects the cause of failure and helps the user to correct both semantic and interrogation errors of the failed query by using relaxation techniques and tries to decrease the number of the relaxed query.

3 CaRT's System Architecture

The architecture of CaRT is illustrated in Fig. 2. It consists of three main parts: The MFS search engine, the correction process and the relaxation process. Given a failed SPARQL query, the MFS search engine allow to identify and explain to the user the cause of the query failure. Once the failed query triplets are founded, the correction process give to the user a set of alternative answers to correct his query. This process corrects the semantic errors by using two algorithms, the WordNet algorithm and the filtering algorithm. If the query still fails even after the correction process, the third part of CaRT includes the relaxation process which based on the ontological relaxation engine the ranking engine to fix the interrogation errors. As a result, a set of alternative answers is proposed to the user. Based on these answers, the user can correct and execute his query which will not return this time an empty result.

These different process which constitute our framework CaRT will be described in detail in the next section.

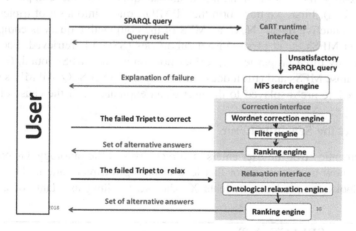

Fig. 2. CaRT architecture.

4 CaRT Functionalities

Our framework CaRT has four main functionalities: assists users to formulate complex SPARQL queries, explain the cause of failure of the SPARQL query, automatic correction to fix the semantic error using Wordnet [17] and automatic relaxation to fix the interrogation error with a relaxation process which includes the ontological relaxation and similarity measure.

4.1 Assistance in the Formulation of Complex SPARQL Query

Ontologies and the SPARQL language are still unknown or not well understood by non-expert user. In order to help user to formulate his queries, our framework propose an assistance functionality. In fact, the user can interact with an interface which contains checkbox of different operators that can be used in complex SPARQL queries for example: FILTER, OPTION, GROUP By, ORDER BY. When the user chooses one or more of these operators, a showMessageDialog appear describing these operators and the query's structure is displayed. Then, the user can complete the query's description according to his need.

4.2 Search for the Cause of Failure

The relaxation of a failed query can generate relaxed queries that continue to fail. If we identify those failed relaxed queries, we can correct them and accelerate the relaxation process. The first step of our approach defines the cause of the user query failure. Usually, only some parts of a failing SPARQL query are responsible of its failure. Finding such subqueries, named Minimal Failing Subqueries (MFSs), provides the user with an explanation of the empty answer problem. Many works have been proposed for query relaxation based on finding MFSs [15]. In our case, we adopt the Godfrey approach used for relational databases [11]. This approach defined a_mel_fast algorithm to identify the MFSs of failing relational query and the complexity of this algorithm is $O(n)$. First, we transform the SPARQL query into a set of triples patterns to form a conjunctive query. Next, an MFS of the conjunctive query is computed. To find the other MFSs, a set of significant subqueries (SSQs) is retrieved. Each SSQ is characterized by three properties: (i) it does not contain the MFSs found, (ii) it is not included in those MFSs and (iii) it does not include any other SSQ. All MFSs produced by this procedure are displayed to the user as an explanation of the cause of fail.

4.3 Correct the Semantic Error

With the semantic error the user enters incorrect terms of the ontology. Given the next example to show a semantic error that lead to failing a triplet pattern. The following query Q2 looks for graduate students X who are teaching assistants of a graduate course Y.

```
SELECT ?X ?Y
  WHERE{
    ?X rdf:type ub:GraduateStudent. (t1)
    ?X ub:teachingAssistantOf ?Y. (t2)
    ?Y rdf:type ub:GraduateCourse (t3) }
```

Example of SPARQL query Q2

If the user write the object of the first triplet as: *ub:Graduatescholar* instead of writing *ub:GraduateStudent*. This semantic error leads to failing the query. CaRT corrects the wrong object by proposing an algorithm that uses Wordnet to return a list of synonyms of the word used in the failed triplet. Then, we developed a filtering algorithm to compose the list L of existing synonyms in the ontology. In the last step, a rank-ordering of the list of selected synonyms is established according to their similarity with the elements of the failed triplet pattern. We used the Cosine similarity measure [3] to compute the similarity degree. It produces a simple summary measure that can be easily used to differentiate between similar texts, rank and order them. The similarity between the list of selected synonyms L and the word of the failed triplet pattern is described as follow:

$$sim_{tfidf}(V_{d1}.V_{d2}) = \frac{V_{d1}.V_{d2}}{\|V_{d1}\|_2.\|V_{d2}\|_2} \tag{1}$$

where V_{d1} is the list L, V_{d2} is the word of the failed triplet pattern and $\|V\|_2$ is the L^2-Vector norm. Using this measure, CaRT displays the ordered list of the correct elements of the failed triplet pattern. Then, the user can re-execute the failed query after replacing the failed triples with the new correct triples.

4.4 Relax the Interrogation Error

The Interrogation error is the second error type that leads to fail a triplet pattern. It consists of the non-existent relation in the ontology between the classes and the properties used in the user query. To deal with this type of error, we used the ontological relaxation proposed by Hurtado et al. [13] which substitute the class and the property of the failed triplet with their sub-class, super-class, sub-property and super-property respectively. With the ontological relaxation, we replace the failed triples pattern t_1 i.e. the MFSs by another triplet t_2. CaRT uses the reasoning rules 2 and 4 proposed by Hurtado et al. [13] to relax the failed triples.

$$Rule(2) = \frac{(a,sp,b)(x,a,y)}{(x,b,y)} \tag{2}$$

where the value *sp* represent *rdfs:subPropertyOf* or *rdfs:superPropertyOf*. In this rule, a is a sub/super-property of b. Then, it replaces the property a of the triplet (x,a,y) by the property b to obtain a new relaxed triplet (x,b,y).

$$Rule(4) = \frac{(a,sc,b)(x,type,a)}{(x,type,b)} \tag{3}$$

where the value *sc* and *type* represent respectively *rdfs:subClassOf* or *rdfs:superClassOf* and *rdf:type*. In this rule, a is a sub/super-class of b. Then, it replaces the class a of the triplet $(x,type,a)$ by the class b to obtain a new relaxed triplet $(x,type,b)$. When the ontological relaxation returns a list of the sub/super-classes and sub/super-properties of the relaxed triplet, we apply the Cosine similarity measure to compute the similarity degree between the returned list and the class or the property of the failed triplet pattern. The Fig. 3 shows the CaRT interface to relax failed triples.

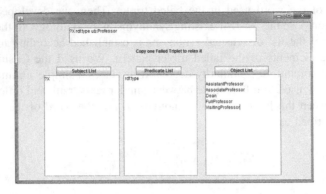

Fig. 3. CaRT interface to relax triples.

5 Experimental Environment

In order to evaluate our plugin CaRT and Due to the lack of an RDF query relaxation benchmark, we used a set of test queries proposed by Huang et al. [6] based on the LUBM benchmark. These queries are expressed in SPARQL 1.0 syntax and they have between 1 and 5 triple patterns. We chose a generated dataset LUBM1[14] to evaluate the performances of our approach on these queries. This dataset has 103,397 triples.

Table 2 shows an example of five selected queries. These queries are correct and meet the user needs.

Table 2. Test queries

Q1	SELECT ?X WHERE {?X rdf:type ub:TeachingAssistant}
Q2	SELECT ?X ?y WHERE {?Xrdf:typeub:GraduateStudent ?X ub:takesCourse ?y}
Q3	SELECT ?X ?y ?Z WHERE {?X rdf:type ub:GraduateStudent .?Z rdf:type ub: Department. ?X ub:memberOf ?Z }
Q4	SELECT ?X ?y WHERE {?X rdf:type ub:GraduateStudent. ?Y rdf:type ub:University. ?Z rdf:type ub:Department, ?X ub:undergraduateDegreeFrom ?Y}
Q5	SELECT ?X ?y ?Z WHERE {?X rdf:type ub:GraduateStudent. ?Y rdf:type ub: University.?Z rdf:type ub:Department. ?X ub:memberOf?Z,?X ub: undergraduateDegreeFrom ?Y}

We then modified these queries in order to make it fail. The Workload queries cover the range between 1 and 5 triples patterns and include 1 up to 4 MFSs..

We start this experimentation section by presenting a demo scenario and then we study the performance of our framework in term of the relevant answers given and in term of decreasing the search space of suggested queries to replace the failure.

5.1   Demo Scenario

This demo shows the interest of the MFSs as explanation of the query failure and their use for an efficient relaxation. We choose to present the execution of the failed query Q' 4 because it contains all possible errors.

```
SELECT ?X ?y ?Z
WHERE{
         ?X rdf:type ub:Student.   (t1)
         ?Y rdf:type ub:Academy. (t2)
         ?Z rdf:type ub:Department. (t3)
         ?X ub:DegreeFrom ?Y} (t4)
```

SPARQL query Q'4

The query Q'4 is about three classes and one property. Additionally, there is a binary pattern of relationships between the objects involved. It contains four triples and looks for the Student who has DegreeFrom the Academy. Q'4 is a failed query, it returns an empty result. When users execute this query, CaRT reports the existence of inconsistencies in the query.

The failed triples of Q'4 are t1: "?X rdf:type ub:Student", t2: "?Y rdf:type ub: Academy" and t4: "?X ub:DegreeFrom ?Y".

The cause of fail of t1 is the object ub:Student. The triplet pattern t4 involved that the variable ?X belongs to the domain of DegreeFrom and ?Y as this codomain. But, according to the ontology the domain of the property DegreeFrom is GraduateStudent, thus ?X must be an instance of GraduateStudent and can't be an instance of Student, as required by the triplet pattern t1. This error is an *interrogation error*. CaRT correct t1 using the relaxation process described above to relax the failed triplet by transforming the class Student by one of its sub-classes. It returns than a ranked list of the sub-classes of Student. The user re-execute the new query Q''4 with the relaxed triplet t1 "?X rdf:type ub:GraduateStudent". Though the execution will return an empty result because it contains two others MFSs t2 and t4.

The cause of fail of t2 is the object ub:Academy. This object is written correctly but not exist in the ontology. CaRT correct the wrong object using both algorithms the Wordnet-synonym and the filtering-algorithm. The first one returns a words list synonym of the word Academy and then the second give us a new ranked list of synonyms which exist in the ontology. The first ranked in this list is University. The user can re-execute his query Q'''4 with the correct triplet t2 "?Y rdf:type ub:University.". The execution will return also an empty result because it contains the MFS t4.

The cause of fail of t4 is the predicate ub:DegreeFrom. The triplet pattern t4 involved that the variable ?X belongs to the domain DegreeFrom and ?Y at his codomain. But, according to the ontology ?X is an instance of GraduateStudent and the property of the domain GraduateStudent is undergraduateDegreeFrom,. CaRT correct this *interrogation error* produced by t4 using the relaxation process. It relaxes the failed triplet by transforming the property DegreeFrom by one of its sub-properties.

After all, the user executes his new query with the relaxed triplet t4 "?X ub:under-graduateDegreeFrom ?y".

Finally, the user obtains a successful query which returns a result that meets his need because it doesn't contain any other MFS.

5.2   Performance Analysis of CaRT

We conducted this performance experiment using in all 50 failed queries divided in 5 classes. Each one contains 10 queries. The first category (Q'1) covers the queries with only one triplet, the second (Q'2) contains the queries with 2 triplets and so on. We executed all these queries to the ontology benchmark LUBM1 described above.

Performance Analysis of CaRT Returned Answers

Here, we assess of the usefulness of the returned output i.e. the performance and quality of the alternative returned answers. We compared the returned output of CaRT after correction and relaxation of the failed triples, with the output obtained through the original and correct query which meet the user's needs. We used precision, recall and F-measure as the performance measures. The precision measures how well CaRT return relevant answers that meet the user needs. The recall measures how well the system finds all relevant answers that meet the user's needs. The F-measure is the weighted average of Precision and Recall. We illustrate in the following figures the performance measures result of the workload queries returned answers according to the test query results. For all the three figures, the x-axis corresponds to the five classes of test queries.

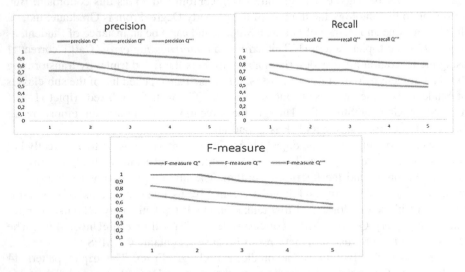

Fig. 4. Performance measures.

We have tested the answers of our workload queries according to the test queries answers. In each time we metering the performance measures of the first three suggested answers. **Q"i** of each category **i** of queries contains the first answer that have been suggested by CaRT after the correction and the relaxation of the failed triples. the queries **Q'''i** and **Q''''i**, represent respectively the second and the third ranked suggested answers.

The Fig. 4 confirm the performance of our framework CaRT in term of the quality of the returned relevant answers. All the first CaRT suggest queries has F-measure close to 1, thus F1 score reaches its best value which proves the perfection of precision and recall.

Cost Analysis of CaRT Suggested Queries

Our approach proposes a new relaxation method that corrects and relaxes only the failed triples which can considerably decrease the search space of the approximate queries that return relevant answers which meet the user needs. To assess our objective, we have compared the number of the suggested alternative output of CaRT after the correction and relaxation with the number of the suggested alternative output of the RDF data relaxation framework QaRS (Querying and relaxation system) [7]. We take the same dataset used in the previous performance analysis i.e. the 50 queries divided in five categories. The following Fig. 5. compare the number of alternative answers proposed by CaRT and those proposed by QaRS for each category of failed queries Q'i.

The results confirmed the capacity of CaRT in decreasing the search space of the approximate queries that return relevant answers which meet the user needs. Thus we showed the performance of our new relaxation method that corrects and relaxes only the failed triples of the users failed queries.

The analyses results obtained in this section illustrates the performance of CaRT returned answers in terms of quality and quantity.

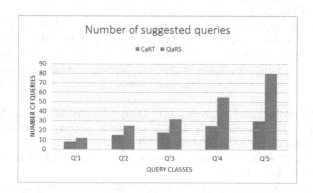

Fig. 5. Cost in number of suggested queries.

6 Conclusion and Future Work

In this paper, we propose a new framework CaRT which aims to help users when their SPARQL queries, return an empty result. Our approach aimed to answer four main questions: Why these queries are failed, which parts of a SPARQL query must be treated? how to correct failed SPARQL queries?, and how to relax SPARQL queries?.

We firstly implemented the MFS algorithm in order to extract the failed triples of the user's queries that were the cause of failure. Then we proposed new relaxation method that relaxes only the failed triples instead of relaxing all the queries triples to decrease the search space of the approximate answers that meet the user needs and facilitate to users the choice of the relaxed query to be executed. To correct the failed SPARQL queries we used the online lexical database Wordnet and for the relaxation, we used the ontological relaxation that substitutes the failed triples by their sub-classes and sub-properties.

We evaluated the performance of our approach using a real dataset generated from the LUBM benchmark. The experiments results showed the efficiency of our approach which returns all the relevant answers that were expected by users.

An interesting future work is to integrate relaxation operators to our plugin. In fact, we think it would be interesting to extend our plugin with an interactive relaxation through the integration of relaxation operators. We suppose to create new relaxation operators that take into consideration all the SPARQL features.

Finally, we look for making our framework fully automatic and do not require the user intervention. This can be by using mapping technics between the SPARQL query after transforming it in to ontology and the dataset used.

References

1. Hoffart, J., Suchanek, F.M., Berberich, K., Weikum, G.: YAGO2: a spatially and temporally enhanced knowledge base from Wikipedia. Artif. Intell. **194**, 28–61 (2013)
2. Dong, X., et al.: Knowledge vault: a web-scale approach to probabilistic knowledge fusion. In: ACM SIGKDD, (KDD 2014), pp. 601–610 (2014)
3. Saleem, M., Ali, M.I., Hogan, A., Mehmood, Q., Ngomo, A.-C.N.: LSQ: the linked SPARQL queries dataset. In: Arenas, M., et al. (eds.) ISWC 2015. LNCS, vol. 9367, pp. 261–269. Springer, Cham (2015). https://doi.org/10.1007/978-3-319-25010-6_15
4. Corby, O., Dieng-Kuntz, R., Faron-Zucker, C., Gandon, F.: Ontology-based approximate query processing for searching the semantic web with corese. Research report RR-5621 (2006)
5. Hurtado, C.A., Poulovassilis, A., Wood, P.T.: Query relaxation in RDF. In: Spaccapietra, S. (ed.) Journal on Data Semantics X. LNCS, vol. 4900, pp. 31–61. Springer, Heidelberg (2008). https://doi.org/10.1007/978-3-540-77688-8_2
6. Huang, H., Liu, C., Zhou, X.: Approximating query answering on RDF databases. J. World Wide Web **15**(1), 89–114 (2012)
7. Fokou, G., Jean, S., Hadjali, A.: Endowing semantic query languages with advanced relaxation capabilities. In: Andreasen, T., Christiansen, H., Cubero, J.-C., Raś, Zbigniew W. (eds.) ISMIS 2014. LNCS (LNAI), vol. 8502, pp. 512–517. Springer, Cham (2014). https://doi.org/10.1007/978-3-319-08326-1_53
8. Calì, A., Frosini, R., Poulovassilis, A., Wood, P.T.: Flexible querying for SPARQL. In: Meersman, R., et al. (eds.) OTM 2014. LNCS, vol. 8841, pp. 473–490. Springer, Heidelberg (2014). https://doi.org/10.1007/978-3-662-45563-0_28
9. Dolog, P., Stuckenschmidt, H., Wache, H., Diederich, J.: Relaxing RDF queries based on user and domain preferences. IJIIS **33**(3), 239–260 (2009)

10. Elbassuoni, S., Ramanath, M., Weikum, G.: Query relaxation for entity-relationship search. In: Antoniou, G., et al. (eds.) ESWC 2011. LNCS, vol. 6644, pp. 62–76. Springer, Heidelberg (2011). https://doi.org/10.1007/978-3-642-21064-8_5

11. Hogan, A., Mellotte, M., Powell, G., Stampouli, D.: Towards fuzzy query-relaxation for RDF. In: Simperl, E., Cimiano, P., Polleres, A., Corcho, O., Presutti, V. (eds.) ESWC 2012. LNCS, vol. 7295, pp. 687–702. Springer, Heidelberg (2012). https://doi.org/10.1007/978-3-642-30284-8_53

12. Kiefer, C., Bernstein, A., Stocker, M.: The fundamentals of iSPARQL: a virtual triple approach for similarity-based semantic web tasks. In: Aberer, K., et al. (eds.) ASWC/ISWC - 2007. LNCS, vol. 4825, pp. 295–309. Springer, Heidelberg (2007). https://doi.org/10.1007/978-3-540-76298-0_22

13. Kiefer, C., Bernstein, A., Lee, H.J., Klein, M., Stocker, M.: Semantic process retrieval with iSPARQL. In: Franconi, E., Kifer, M., May, W. (eds.) ESWC 2007. LNCS, vol. 4519, pp. 609–623. Springer, Heidelberg (2007). https://doi.org/10.1007/978-3-540-72667-8_43

14. Amarger, F., Haemmerlé, O., Hernandez, N., Pradel, C.: Taking SPARQL 1.1 extensions into account in the SWIP system. In: Pfeiffer, H.D., Ignatov, D.I., Poelmans, J., Gadiraju, N. (eds.) ICCS-ConceptStruct 2013. LNCS (LNAI), vol. 7735, pp. 75–89. Springer, Heidelberg (2013). https://doi.org/10.1007/978-3-642-35786-2_7

15. Ganggao, Z., Carlos, A.I.: Sematch: semantic entity search from knowledge graph. In: 1st International Workshop on Summarizing and Presenting Entities and Ontologies Co-located with the 12th Extended Semantic Web Conference, Portoroz, Slovenia (2015)

16. Géraud, F., Stéphane, J., Allel, H., Mickaël, B.: QaRS: a user-friendly graphical tool for semantic query design and relaxation. In: EDBT 2015, Brussel, Belgium, pp. 553–556 (2015)

17. George, A.M., Richard, B., Christiane, F., Derek, G., Katherine, J.M.: Introduction to WordNet: an on-line lexical database*. Int. J. Lexicogr. 3(4), 235–244 (1990)

18. Godfrey, P.: Minimization in cooperative response to failing database queries. Int. J. Coop. Inf. Syst. 06(02), 95–149 (1997)

19. Hurtado, C.A., Poulovassilis, A., Wood, P.T.: A relaxed approach to RDF querying. In: Cruz, I., et al. (eds.) ISWC 2006. LNCS, vol. 4273, pp. 314–328. Springer, Heidelberg (2006). https://doi.org/10.1007/11926078_23

20. Yuanbo, G., Zhengxiang, P., Jeff, H.: LUBM: a benchmark for owl knowledge base systems. Web Semant. Sci. Serv. Agents World Wide Web 3(2–3), 158–182 (2005)

21. Motro, A.: Cooperative database systems. Int. J. Intell. Syst. 11, 717–731 (1996)

22. Islam, M.S., Liu, C., Li, J.: Efficient answering of why-not questions in similar graph matching. IEEE Trans. Knowl. Data Eng. 27(10), 2672–2686 (2015)

23. Minker, J.: An overview of cooperative answering in databases. In: Andreasen, T., Christiansen, H., Larsen, H.L. (eds.) FQAS 1998. LNCS, vol. 1495, pp. 282–285. Springer, Heidelberg (1998). https://doi.org/10.1007/BFb0056009

E-commerce and Business Analytics

E-commerce and Business Analytics:
A Literature Review

Emrah Bilgic[1($\boxtimes$)] and Yanqing Duan[2]

[1] Mus Alparslan University, Mus, Turkey
dr.emrahbilgic@gmail.com
[2] University of Bedfordshire, Luton, UK
yanqing.duan@beds.ac.uk

Abstract. The number of users of well-known e-commerce websites such as Taobao, Jingdong, and Amazon has exceeded one billion. This means that the information provided by these and similar websites which is growing very fast, could be a valuable source of support for decision making, if discovered. All kinds of data derived from e-commerce websites must be managed and analyzed in order for them to remain competitive and to prevent reduced satisfaction or interest of customers. Business Analytics and Big Data Analytics are methodologies that can discover valuable insight hidden in data. In this paper, recent studies on e-commerce and Business Analytics or Big Data Analytics published within the last five years will be surveyed to discover what kind of business value is created with usage of analytics in these studies. This investigation also has the potential to find research gaps and direct future research.

Keywords: Business analytics · Big data analytics · E-commerce · Business value

1 Introduction

Within the last three decades business communities have gone through many changes with the rapid advent of technology and science. These fast changes have also affected consumers' attitudes, behaviors, wants and needs which created new challenges for organizations and companies. Since companies have responsibilities towards their customers, shareholders, employees and the public, they have to increase the efficiency of all business processes to create added value.

The issue of Big Data is the most important improvement that companies are facing nowadays. Data is flowing every second from different kind of sources like POS machines, Wi-Fi, RFIDs and other sensor-based internet enabled tools (Internet of Things). Just imagine the text data being generated everyday by social media, forums and other web-sites (user generated content) and also data such as web clicks, transactions and GPS data.

As previously mentioned, Big Data (BD) brings new challenges to organizations. However, it also offers many advantages as well. One can think of BD like oil, if refined it could provide useful information for the decision support processes of organizations (data driven decision making) and therefore create value. Since the data

R. Jallouli et al. (Eds.): ICDEc 2019, LNBIP 358, pp. 173–182, 2019.
https://doi.org/10.1007/978-3-030-30874-2_13

we are considering is not only big, but also complex and unstructured, new questions regarding traditional analysis methods, organizations and research are using have also emerged. For this reason, in the study [1] authors improved the traditional Knowledge Discovery and Data Mining (KDDM) model to a BD driven decision making environment.. Furthermore, the authors in [2] also criticized traditional approaches stating that these traditional approaches, used prior to Business Analytics, focused more on modelling and analysis rather than on the actual problem and the data set.

It is a well-known fact that data analytics is being applied to all areas of science nowadays: From biology to geography, chemistry to psychology, medicine to sociology etc. Perhaps the most popular and widely utilized area is business, since shopping (brick and mortar or online), finance, economy and any kind of other service offered by companies encompass our daily lives. Analytics dealing with business problems (finance, marketing, accounting, supply chain, logistics…) can be considered as BA. BA techniques support and improve managerial decisions by integrating data analytics, business processes and systems [3]. BA and Big Data Analytics (BDA) are closely related to one and other since the data companies and organizations encountering today are big (have Volume, Velocity and Variety). The relationship also lies in the definition of BDA which is the application of statistical, processing and analytical techniques for large and complex data sets that require advanced technologies for capturing, storing, managing, analyzing and visualizing advancing business [3–6]. BDA projects and BA also have the same goal: to acquire useful knowledge from the data obtained in order to have economic value and a competitive advantage [6].

The purpose of this paper is to identify the dimensions of BA usage in e-commerce research. The study will systematically survey related literature to capture how e-commerce research utilizes BA to create business value. Keywords of "Business Analytics" and "e-commerce", "Big Data Analytics and e-commerce" were searched in the database of the Web of Science in December 2018 and the most relevant papers have been included in the scope of this study.

2   Literature Review

The literature review process of this paper aims to answer the following research question: How problems of e-commerce companies can be solved with BA and what kind of value is created with BA? To achieve the research objective, we conducted an extensive literature review of "business analytics" and "big data analytics" applications in "e-commerce" studies. More than 500 papers were reviewed from the Web of Science database. 118 papers published in the last five years were found using the key words "analytics + e-commerce". 487 papers were found using the keywords "mining + e-commerce". Firstly, the abstract of the papers were inspected. If the paper was exactly related to e-commerce and BA it was downloaded and reviewed in detail. Due to the page limitation, only the most relevant ones have been included in this research.

E-commerce companies are faced with bigger data than any other companies since the data they have are constantly being generated from thousands, hundreds of thousands and even millions of customers every second. The data are both structured and unstructured which creates a challenge. While the data of the demographics and the purchasing of customers are structured, their clicks, likes, ratings and contents generated (tweets, comments, photographs, videos, sounds etc.) are unstructured [7].

Data analytic methods are divided into three types: The first ones are descriptive analytic methods such as cluster and association rule analysis used to understand the structure of data. The second ones are predictive analytical methods used to forecast future events with regression, decision trees, neural networks etc. The final ones are prescriptive analytic methods used to make decisions with mathematical programming, simulation modelling etc. [3]. In the following section recent BA applications in popular journal and conference papers will be summarized to capture what kind of data are used in the papers and what kind of value is created with the experimental results.

2.1 BA Applications in E-commerce Companies

Researches on usage of BA in e-commerce can be inspected under a few subtopics such as spam detection, web design, trustworthiness and reputation of company, service quality, pricing, product design, predicting, recommendation and logistics. These subtopics are also indicating that using BA tools, the papers are creating business value for the processes such as pricing a product/service, designing or improving a product/service and recommending a product/service, measuring service quality, etc.

2.1.1 Spam Detection

The authors in [1] proposed a novel Chinese text mining method which can automatically detect spam reviews. They first discovered the attributes evaluated in reviews (cellphone, battery etc.) and sentiments in them (beautiful, good etc.). They extract the spammers' behavior pattern and grouped them into four effective features called university degree, outlier degree, uncertainty degree and similarity degree. They use a data set from Taobao platform, totally 20 thousands reviews of ten kinds of products such as cellphone and kindle are analyzed. Logistic regression was used to classify reviews into spam or not spam and the performance of the algorithm was excellent.

In [8], authors draw attention to serious threats of transaction frauds on e-commerce web sites and propose a novel deep-learning based transaction fraud detection system. They implement the system at a Chinese e-commerce platform JD.com. They argue that users' browsing behaviors or sequence of users' click within a session are very important to be able to differentiate fraudsters from legitimate users since real users browse a lot of items. The system they propose is called CLUE which focuses on users' purchase sessions. They first model the user session and optimize it for fraud detection. The system gets a risk score at the last click of a user for each session with recurrent neural network (RNN). They conclude that CLUE performs much better than methods such as logistic regression, naive Bayes, SVM, and random forest.

2.1.2 Web Design

The paper [9] used Machine Learning and Artificial Intelligence algorithms to design interface of an e-commerce web site. They propose a framework for recommendation that takes care of user's preferences, behaviors and demographics. They call this recommendation system as demographic-content based collaborative recommendation. They also use navigation optimization through optimized prefix span algorithm, and

review summarization using Gibbs sampling based Latent Dirichlet Allocation classifier framework. All of these frameworks support making a better interface for
increased user satisfaction.

[10] emphasize that when e-commerce companies support their websites with web-
mining technology it leads to useful patterns such as both assisting the user and the
business analyst. The system they offer has five modules called page loading speed,
ease of navigation, web-content comparator, online and offline website comparison and
recommender module. This system assists customer to pay reasonable prices to genuine
products and support the company since the system can check the competitor websites.

[11] discuss that since a website is the showcase of e-commerce companies, performance of their websites are very critical. In their paper, twitter data is used for BDA
and several Twitter performance indexes are proposed to assist the website performance evaluation. They emphasize that social media plays a critical role in e-commerce
since it can promote brand awareness and generate more business by reaching a larger
group of customers online. They collected over 600K tweets which contain more than
160 Saudi e-commerce sites and proposed several Twitter performance indexes and
explained how these indexes used for performance evaluation of e-commerce websites.
In addition to Twitter data website traffic, ranking, regional related and services data for
each selected website were collected. Correlation analysis were used to evaluate the
performances.

[12] provide an effective decision support for constructing better e-commerce
websites. They improved ant colony clustering algorithm with information entropy to
segment customers' browsing path. The main purpose of the study is to depict the
specific behavior patterns of consumers in each browsing process. [13] propose a
linear-temporal logic model checking approach for analysis of structured e-commerce
web logs. The approach has been applied to a Spanish e-commerce website. The study
discovers the behaviors of users to increase the efficiency of the web-site.

2.1.3 Trustworthiness and Reputation of E-commerce Company

As known, when customers want to purchase an item from internet, most of them
review other people's opinions before purchasing decision. Trust evaluation is very
important for the success of e-commerce systems. Scores of reputation for e-commerce
companies or sellers are computed by using feedback ratings. Studies on this topic
provides insights how to assess reputation of companies and how to increase it.

[14] emphasized that reputation is very important for companies' trustworthiness
and they mined the opinions for reputation generation in the study. Their method
aggregates fused and grouped opinions to generate a reputation value by considering
the popularity and other statistics of principal opinions. They conducted a case study in
Amazon.cn on 3000 products' information and 2424 product information from
Amazon.com.

[15] also mined feedbacks on e-commerce web-sites to propose a multi-
dimensional trust evaluation model for computing reputation. They call this system
Comment-based Multi-dimensional Trust (CommTrust) which is the first work that
computes fine-grained multidimensional trust profiles automatically by mining feedback comments. In this system a recently developed natural language processing
(NLP) tool dependency relation analysis and lexicon based opinion mining techniques

are used. About 180K feedback comments were crawled for ten eBay sellers on ebay.com with five categories including camera, computers, and mobile phones. Furthermore approximately 40K comments for ten third-party sellers were crawled from amazon.com which belong to five categories such as camera, computers, and mobile phones. The authors evaluated the trustness of the companies and ranked the sellers which is strongly correlated with the ground truth rankings, their approach computes trust scores highly effective to distinguish and rank sellers.

[16] also propose a comment-based approach to compute seller trust profile for e-commerce companies. Their model has three steps: Opinionated word extraction, Sentiment classification and Trust score evaluation. The experimental results from amazon.in and flipcart.com indicates that the proposed approach is effective. [17] in their study propose an online algorithm to infer the optimal discount rate from transaction data with the aim of enhancing the e-commerce seller reputation via price discounts. The model provides optimal price discounts which will attract customers and increase the reputation scores of the seller.

2.1.4   Service Quality

[18] with the purpose of measuring service quality the authors used SERVQUAL model and text mining technique of topic modelling. Topic modelling extracts the hidden thematic structure from textual data. The study emphasizes that as textual data, online reviews provide useful information that can be used to measure the service quality as quantitative data. The data set used in the study are belong to an Italian online price comparison company and consist about 75K online reviews. They first preprocess the reviews such as removing the singleton words, stop words, numbers, and exclude short reviews. They used linear regression analysis to compare service quality dimensions between positive and negative opinions. They find that concerns about merchant responsiveness dominate negative reviews.

[19] emphasize that many of the papers focus on personalized recommendation however service quality also plays an important role in recommender systems. They also criticize the trustworthiness of user ratings. They utilize information entropy values to measure the confidence of user ratings with the idea of if users' ratings are confident their ratings must have little differences with the overall rating of services. Then, social users' contextual information are explored from spatial-temporal features and review sentimental features of ratings to constrain user rating's confidence. They fused user's confidence with contextual features to be able to calculate an overall ratings' confidence value. The authors used a unified probabilistic model to calculate overall confidence. Restaurant and Nightlife services data from Yelp and a dataset from Douban Movie were analyzed. They find that user rating's confidence is higher when a user is very far away from the rated item. Furthermore user rating's confidence is increasing over time, and increasing with review sentiment.

2.1.5   Pricing

[20] mention that the prices of internet products are changing very fast even many times within a day. Companies should always track the price change and check the price of the competitors in order to be competitive. The authors propose a novel approach (the approach uses tag path analysis) on how to automatically identify and

extract product prices. They have analyzed 50 e-shops and the case study was conducted on two e-shops web-sites from different countries. The approach first crawl e-shop websites, identifies product records and from product records it identifies product attributes.

[21] proposed a novel machine learning based model for estimating optimal prices of products in e-commerce websites. Since manually pricing is impossible for e-commerce websites with thousands of products, automatic dynamic pricing is needed. The model in this study determines optimal sales prices based on observing effects of past price changes for a given article and for related products. The algorithm used by authors is based on Bayesian inference combined with bootstrap-based confidence estimation and kernel regression. They test their model in simulated sparse and noisy data. Experiments conclude that the model can lead to increase in revenue and profit.

2.1.6   Product Design

In order to support decisions of product designers [22] proposed a framework which analyzes online product reviews. The proposed framework integrates NLP and machine learning. Machine Model is used to perform sentiment analysis on customer reviews obtained from amazon.com. As a product, a foldable chair on amazon.com and 50 reviews about it for each rating of 1 star, 2 stars…5 stars selected as a case study. The result of the Machine Model indicate that one of the positive sentiment about the chair is its comfort while a negative one is weakness of the arms.

[23] also analyzed reviews of mobile phone customers to help companies for product design. They collected customer reviews of post purchasing experiences of a specific mobile phone from Amazon.com and used text mining, cluster analysis and perceptual mapping. The positive keywords and negative keywords are separately clustered. For example positive key words are clustered into three groups, cluster one represents the dissatisfied customer service of replacement or repairs, cluster two represents the reviews about signal and connection of simcard or network cluster three is about complains to the battery and the bloatware. In the perceptual analysis authors compared and analyzed customer reviews of competitors. The research suggests that the mobile phone company they analyzed should focus following issues: improving the design of cellphone camera, battery, screen, and connection technology, reduce the bloatwares prevent the heat up.

2.1.7   Predicting

[24] emphasize that an emerging area in forecasting the sales of products is user generated contents. They used online reviews data from Amazon.com to predict sales. The scrapped real time data from Amazon.com for electronic devices pre-processed for sentiment analysis and neural network analysis. The positive and negative sentiments from 12K reviews used for neural network analysis to predict how these variables can collectively be used for predicting product sales. The neural network analysis has confirmed that all proposed predictors are influential for sales.

[25] propose a novel method for predicting sales. The model combines Bass/Norton model and sentiment analysis using product reviews. Sentiment index is computed with Naïve Bayes algorithm and it is integrated to coefficient of Bass/Norton model. For evaluating the performance of the model the authors used historical sales data and

online reviews of automotive industry data. The data belong to a specific brand and its specific model consist of about 4500 reviews.

[26] for predicting the customers purchase intention, the authors captured a real-time consumers' online search and choice scenario. The data is gathered from Amazon. com which consist of customers' real time search and reviews on a durable good, camera. Both linear and non-linear regression analysis used for predicting the purchase intention. The sentiments obtained from reviews incorporated with customers' search patterns. One of the result is sensor, display, and image stabilization of a camera pursue the customer attention. Results show that proposed models exhibit lower forecasting errors.

2.1.8 Recommendation

[9] proposes a recommendation system to a movie e-commerce company. The system takes care of user's demographic data, their preferences and their behaviors. They use machine learning and AI techniques that focus on recommender system, navigation optimization and product review mining. The data set they use belong to MovieLens and consist of 100K ratings for 1682 movie titles with 18 genres. Their study supports designing intuitive interfaces for e-commerce shopping site. This support will help human effort while shopping such as easily make purchasing decision and rate newly purchased products which will increase customer satisfaction.

[27] used a hybrid method for recommender systems (collaborative, demographic, content, utility and knowledge based techniques) to propose a more useful personalized recommendations. The reason of using hybrid method is because of continuously advancements in technology and user behavior there is a need for improving traditional RS methods and relate RS performance measures with business goals. The paper proposes a case study in a jewelry e-commerce company by analyzing search and comparison of products, user reviews, chats and forums, and performance monitoring reports/dashboards using business intelligence. [28] presents a method to explore users' preference similarities based on web browsing history data mining. [29] also uses recommender systems to satisfy customers and recommend products that best suit them.

2.1.9 Logistics

[30] emphasize that studies on e-commerce logistics are not many. The purpose of the study is to propose an unstructured data analytics for finding valuable business models of e-commerce logistics and generate beneficial strategies for e-commerce logistics management. With this purpose some logistics theories are integrated with the empirical results of big data analytics. Web crawling, data preprocessing, topic mining, and association rules mining are conducted to extract essential patterns of e-commerce logistics from massive unstructured documents in e-commerce web sites.

[31] emphasize that the success of an e-commerce company is strongly related with its logistical performance. With the purpose of development of cross border logistics service the study applied a Kansei Engineering-based approach to analyze the associations between attributes of cross border logistics service and customers perceptions which obtained by text mining. The aim of the study is to propose a Kansei Engineering based service design integrated with text mining technology. The text mining approach is applied in order to analyze the cross border logistics service user and

provider-generated online contents. The study employed a web based questionnaire to collect the data needed. The paper concluded that analysis of customer generated contents by text mining techniques can help to capture the direct feelings of customers regarding their usage experiences or usage problems.

3 Conclusion

The purpose of this paper was to identify the dimensions of BA usage in e-commerce research. The study systematically surveyed related literature to capture how e-commerce research utilizes BA to create business value. Keywords of "Business Analytics" and "e-commerce", "Big Data Analytics and e-commerce" were searched in the database of the Web of Science in December 2018 and the most relevant papers have been included in the scope of this study.

Based on the articles reviewed, the findings indicate that BA and e-commerce studies can be inspected in at least nine categories. BA when used in e-commerce companies could allow for tracking of their customers' behaviors, understanding their needs and wants with sentiment or opinion mining, have them repeat their purchases with recommendations, support decision making in marketing and sales and enhance the quality of the products and services.

Furthermore there are some studies on forecasting the purchasing, assessing optimal discount rates and ordering of products. Studies mostly used web mining, data/text mining, machine learning and advanced computing such as cloud computing.

The papers mostly used online customer reviews to create different business value since customer reviews influence the customer decisions for any product purchasing and was useful for predicting the sales. Demographic data of customers and transactions were also used for the analysis performed.

According to our knowledge and our literature survey, there are still not enough studies on e-commerce and stock management, finance, human resources management or supply chain management. These research gaps directed us to conduct a more comprehensive literature survey and a BA application on these subjects.

References

1. Li, X., Yan, X.: A novel chinese text mining method for e-commerce review spam detection. In: Cui, B., Zhang, N., Xu, J., Lian, X., Liu, D. (eds.) WAIM 2016. LNCS, vol. 9658, pp. 95–106. Springer, Cham (2016). https://doi.org/10.1007/978-3-319-39937-9_8
2. Delen, D., Zolbanin, H.M.: The analytics paradigm in business research. J. Bus. Res. **90**, 186–195 (2018)
3. Duan, L., Xiong, Y.: Big data analytics and business analytics. J. Manag. Anal. **2**, 1–21 (2015)
4. Chen, H., Chiang, R.H., Storey, V.C.: Business intelligence and analytics: from big data to big impact. MIS Q. **36**, 1165–1188 (2012)
5. Laney, D.: 3D data management: Controlling data volume, velocity and variety. META Group Res. Note **6**, 70 (2001)

6. Grover, V., Chiang, R.H., Liang, T.-P., Zhang, D.: Creating strategic business value from big data analytics: a research framework. J. Manag. Inf. Syst. **35**, 388–423 (2018)
7. Wamba, S.F., Akter, S., Edwards, A., Chopin, G., Gnanzou, D.: How 'big data'can make big impact: findings from a systematic review and a longitudinal case study. Int. J. Prod. Econ. **165**, 234–246 (2015)
8. Wang, S., Liu, C., Gao, X., Qu, H., Xu, W.: Session-based fraud detection in online e-commerce transactions using recurrent neural networks. In: Altun, Y., et al. (eds.) ECML PKDD 2017. LNCS (LNAI), vol. 10536, pp. 241–252. Springer, Cham (2017). https://doi.org/10.1007/978-3-319-71273-4_20
9. Patil, M., Rao, M.: Studying the contribution of machine learning and artificial intelligence in the interface design of e-commerce site. In: Satapathy, S.C., Bhateja, V., Das, S. (eds.) Smart Intelligent Computing and Applications. SIST, vol. 105, pp. 197–206. Springer, Singapore (2019). https://doi.org/10.1007/978-981-13-1927-3_20
10. Verma, N., Singh, J.: Improved web mining for e-commerce website restructuring. In: 2015 IEEE International Conference on Computational Intelligence & Communication Technology (CICT), pp. 155–160. IEEE (2015)
11. Makki, E., Chang, L.-C.: Leveraging social big data for performance evaluation of E-commerce websites. In: 2016 IEEE International Conference on Big Data (Big Data), pp. 2525–2534. IEEE (2016)
12. Peng, Y., Yang, X., Xu, W.: Optimization research of decision support system based on data mining algorithm. Wirel. Pers. Commun. **102**, 1–13 (2018)
13. Hernández, S., Álvarez, P., Fabra, J., Ezpeleta, J.: Analysis of users' behavior in structured e-commerce websites. IEEE Access **5**, 11941–11958 (2017)
14. Yan, Z., Jing, X., Pedrycz, W.: Fusing and mining opinions for reputation generation. Inf. Fusion **36**, 172–184 (2017)
15. Zhang, X., Cui, L., Wang, Y.: Commtrust: computing multi-dimensional trust by mining e-commerce feedback comments. IEEE Trans. Knowl. Data Eng. **26**, 1631–1643 (2014)
16. Bhargava, K., Gujral, T., Chawla, M., Gujral, T.: Comment based seller trust model for e-commerce. In: 2016 International Conference on Computational Techniques in Information and Communication Technologies (ICCTICT), pp. 387–391. IEEE (2016)
17. Xie, H., Ma, R.T., Lui, J.: Enhancing reputation via price discounts in e-commerce systems: a data-driven approach. ACM Trans. Knowl. Discov. Data (TKDD) **12**, 26 (2018)
18. Palese, B., Usai, A.: The relative importance of service quality dimensions in e-commerce experiences. Int. J. Inf. Manag. **40**, 132–140 (2018)
19. Zhao, G., Qian, X., Lei, X., Mei, T.: Service quality evaluation by exploring social users' contextual information. IEEE Trans. Knowl. Data Eng. **28**, 3382–3394 (2016)
20. Horch, A., Kett, H., Weisbecker, A.: Mining e-commerce data from e-shop websites. In: 2015 IEEE Trustcom/BigDataSE/ISPA, pp. 153–160. IEEE (2015)
21. Bauer, J., Jannach, D.: Optimal pricing in e-commerce based on sparse and noisy data. Decis. Support Syst. **106**, 53–63 (2018)
22. Ireland, R., Liu, A.: Application of data analytics for product design: sentiment analysis of online product reviews. CIRP J. Manufact. Sci. Technol. **23**, 128–144 (2018)
23. Trappey, A.J., Trappey, C.V., Chang, A.-C., Chen, L.W.: Using web mining and perceptual mapping to support customer-oriented product positions and designs. In: Transdisciplinary Engineering: Crossing Boundaries, pp. 533–542 (2016)
24. Chong, A.Y.L., Li, B., Ngai, E.W., Ch'ng, E., Lee, F.: Predicting online product sales via online reviews, sentiments, and promotion strategies: a big data architecture and neural network approach. Int. J. Oper. Prod. Manag. **36**, 358–383 (2016)

25. Fan, Z.-P., Che, Y.-J., Chen, Z.-Y.: Product sales forecasting using online reviews and historical sales data: a method combining the Bass model and sentiment analysis. J. Bus. Res. **74**, 90–100 (2017)
26. Bag, S., Tiwari, M.K., Chan, F.T.: Predicting the consumer's purchase intention of durable goods: an attribute-level analysis. J. Bus. Res. **94**, 408–419 (2019)
27. Venkatraman, S.: A proposed business intelligent framework for recommender systems. In: Informatics, pp. 40. Multidisciplinary Digital Publishing Institute (2017)
28. Li, P., Wu, C., Zhang, S., Yu, X., Zhong, H.: Mining users' preference similarities in e-commerce systems based on webpage navigation logs. Int. J. Comput. Commun. Control **12** (2017)
29. Usmani, Z., Manchekar, S., Malim, T., Mir, A.: A predictive approach for improving the sales of products in e-commerce. In: 2017 Third International Conference on Advances in Electrical, Electronics, Information, Communication and Bio-Informatics (AEEICB), pp. 188–192. IEEE (2017)
30. Wu, P.-J., Lin, K.-C.: Unstructured big data analytics for retrieving e-commerce logistics knowledge. Telematics Inform. **35**, 237–244 (2018)
31. Hsiao, Y.-H., Chen, M.-C., Liao, W.-C.: Logistics service design for cross-border E-commerce using Kansei engineering with text-mining-based online content analysis. Telematics Inform. **34**, 284–302 (2017)

Overview of E-commerce Technologies, Data Analysis Capabilities and Marketing Knowledge

Safa Kaabi[✉] and Rim Jallouli

Higher School of Digital Economy, University of Manouba, Manouba, Tunisia
safa.kaabi@esen.uma.tn, rimjallouli@esen-manouba.org

Abstract. The E-commerce trends are showing a growing rate in the last decade for both B to B and B to C trade. The e-commerce technologies enable firms to collect a huge amount of data regarding the profile of consumers, the habits of consumption, the frequency and amounts of purchases, the payment details, the level of satisfaction and also the intention to repurchase the product or equivalent products in the future. The e-commerce technologies are then helping managers to collect relevant data and orient strategic and tactical marketing decisions. The problem that faces small and medium enterprises nowadays is the lack of customer information analysis capabilities that treat the large, heterogeneous and volatile aspects of the data collected with the e-commerce tools. This paper proposes a survey of the main e-commerce technologies and tools that collect consumer data and the potential contribution of each type of data in generating relevant customer knowledge that orient the marketing decisions. This research highlights all the stages of the process from the e-commerce technologies that collect data, then the analytical phase for the extraction of knowledge and finally the marketing decision orientation.

Keywords: E-commerce technologies · Data analysis capabilities · Marketing · Customer knowledge · Analytics

1 Introduction

The e-commerce (EC) technologies have drawn a lot of attention from the research and business community as there are numerous and increasing development efforts (Kumar 2018; Roberts et al. 2014; AWS 2019).

EC is defined briefly as buying and selling on Internet. EC is based on the use of information and communication technologies. The fast growth of EC users is due to rapid advancement in the field of networking and connectivity and computer engineering. The telecommunication field provides the ease of connectivity, the relative low cost of connecting devices (smartphones, computers, tablets, objects connected, sensors nodes...) and the communication infrastructure. Computer engineering field offers applications, data analysis and approaches of processing data.

These technologies are important for enterprises in helping managers to collect relevant data and orient strategic and tactical marketing decisions.

© Springer Nature Switzerland AG 2019
R. Jallouli et al. (Eds.): ICDEc 2019, LNBIP 358, pp. 183–193, 2019.
https://doi.org/10.1007/978-3-030-30874-2_14

EC provides "anytime, anywhere, any device" commerce. For business companies, online shopping provides an additional and important channel of commerce. Nowadays, EC have been extended to social commerce, mobile commerce (m-commerce), ubiquitous and pervasive commerce. Ubiquitous commerce is described as the evolution of the e-commerce and m-commerce (Kumar et al. 2015).

The e-commerce spawns Myriad applications and tools that have the potential to customize marketing strategy in time. With EC, companies can have a competitive advantage by accomplishing just in time production and distribution. Previous research in the field of Marketing focuses on the role of technology in modern Marketing and the transformative marketing (Kumar 2018), Big data in Marketing (Amado et al. 2017) and the real time analytics for unlocking customer and driving the customer experience (Harvard Business Review Analytic Survey 2018).

This paper presents the main technologies that support the whole process of electronic commerce. We consider the development of the website, the transactional process followed by a consumer, and the customer relationship after purchasing. Then the paper identifies the range of the information analysis capabilities and the contribution of each group of EC technologies to make customer insights and orient marketing decisions.

2   E-commerce Technologies

We present the e-commerce technologies following three main stages of the e-commerce business project: The website development, the transactional process and the customer relationship especially after purchase.

2.1   EC Technologies Related to Web Development

Various technologies can be deployed to develop the website, to publish it and to promote it in the search engines. Online shopping sites can be developed by CMS (Content Management System) or other development platforms. User-friendly systems are used in the design of the front end websites. Electronic product catalogs (EPC) are one of the main components of e-commerce applications. An E-catalog is mainly structured as a set of indexed XML-based documents. It is based on a powerful search engine that operates efficient processing queries. Many solutions exist to design professional product catalogs and companies need to provide flexible product catalogs to get customer satisfaction.

Even the physical stores have been digitalized to increase traffic in the store. They are commonly called web to stores. Web stores include augmented reality and digital walls. Augmented reality mirrors enable the user to try the product before purchase. For example, a potential client can "try on" eyeglasses or clothes. This technology enables the user to upload a personal photo in a social media. In fact, studies assess that the personal experience of each shopper is of utmost importance (Barilliance 2014).

In addition to their website, many business companies provide their services through mobile platforms (app store, windows store, google play). There is a growth of mobile applications that meet customers' needs such as uber app (Uber 2018). They are called "on-demand" applications.

For managing and monitoring an online shopping site, many technologies are used. Optimizing websites involves techniques and tools with SEO, SEA and SMO. Recently, companies use cloud computing as the technology that stores and performs the collected data. Cloud computing provides the network platform, the infrastructure with high performance also as services. Moreover, collected data are stored and performed with cloud solutions.

2.2   EC Technologies Deployed in the Transactional Process

EC includes promotion, selling and distribution of products and services in an online environment. In this section, we detail first the electronic commerce transaction process in phases, then we present the technologies deployed in each phase.

The Electronic Commerce Transaction Process
Different models of electronic transaction process are defined in litterature, especially the consumer buying behavior for BtoC context and the Electronic Reference Model for Marketplace which focus on the BtoB context (Giovanoli et al. 2014).

According to these models, we describe an electronic transaction process in three phases: an information phase, an agreement phase and a settlement phase.

The Information Phase is the phase of information gathering or evaluation phase of requirements and products from various sellers. In this phase, the consumer explores many sites in order to identify what to buy and from whom. It includes all analysis done to check the suitability of a product to customer needs. From the business view, it is important to attract consumers. This phase includes marketing and catalog management. The information phase ends when the product(s) and the seller are chosen.

The agreement phase may take place when the seller enables the negotiation. In this phase the conditions, pricing and other delivery related issues are negotiated. The agreement phase ends with submitting an order or the signing of a legal contract between the customer and the supplier.

The settlement phase focuses on issues related to the order processing and fulfillment, the delivery and payment of the final goods according to the agreement. It includes also the post – purchase services that any e-seller should takes into consideration.

We depict e-commerce technologies that can be deployed in each stage of an electronic transaction process.

Technologies Deployed in the Information Phase
Companies start collecting data from the browsing and surfing through web pages. Consumer's data are also collected when filling the registration form, the cart, the stage of payment until the stage of fill in the feedback ratings. The online site presents various application forms to the surfer (Registration forms, …). Whereas, even without applying these forms the user behavior is traced via cookies. The navigation process and other information are usually traced in logs. The activities on the site are often reported on information called Key Performance Indicators (KPI). This section describes mainly cookies and solutions based on cookies.

Cookie

Cookie is a text file (piece of javascript of code) created by the web server and stored in the user's web browser either temporarily or permanently. Cookies are used (anonymously) when the visitor is surfing through the different pages of a website. Later, when the cookied visitors browse the Web, the cookie will let the retargeting provider know when to serve ads, ensuring that ads are served to only to people who have previously visited your site. There are different uses of cookies. Cookies provide a way for the website to recognize the client and keep track of his preferences. Web servers use also cookies to personalize content, serve visitors with relevant ads, and to analyze traffic. The client can block or allow cookies in its browser. There are many cookie-based technologies (for branding and conversion optimization tool). These technologies are effective when it is a part of a larger digital strategy. Retargeting tool relies on collected data. We consider it as a marketing decision based on collected data.

Software Agents

Software agents are widely deployed in ecommerce context. Since the early 1990s, cooperative multi-agent systems and intelligent agents are of increasing concern within software engineering of large scale distributed systems (Wyai et al. 2018). Agents are programs to which a user can delegate one or more tasks. They operate on behalf of a user. Agent technologies can be applied to any of these areas where a personalized, continuously running, semi-autonomous behavior is desirable. We cite agents of interest, agent of search, negotiation agent..

Technologies Associated to the Agreement Phase

To provide negotiation services, the shopping site can implement various technologies to communicate with consumers. The negotiation can be held with negotiation support systems based on software agents. In the following, we focus on technologies used to carry out communication between customers and the online shopping site.

We cite email, Chat, Forums, Chatbots, assistant robots in stores. Chat bots are increasingly deployed in order to communicate with customers in collecting requests and responding.

Technologies Associated to Settlement Phase

Payment Stage

Companies can offer to their consumers many payments options: electronic payment systems, online credit cards, electronic wallets, etc. Electronic payment system needs to be secure and fast. Digital payments are increasingly used as a tool by government to create transparency and legitimacy. Mobile payment platforms and the payments options may influence consumers on the selection of the seller.

Delivery Stage

In order to monitor product delivery, many technologies are deployed such as GPS and IoT. In plus, various web-based solutions and mobile solutions are developed for tracking and shipping (FedEx 2019).

The Internet of Things (IoT) could contribute significantly to improve product delivery services (time delivery, quality of delivery, ..) because it allows for remotely controlling the location and conditions of shipments and products. We cite as an example perishable products (Verdouw et al. 2018). Many companies call for 3rd party delivery services.

Experience Evaluation

Various Post-purchase services can be provided, for experience evaluation. E-commerce sites offer various technologies such as feedback ratings, comments and likes on social media, CRM (Customer Relationship Management) tools to communicate with the online shopping site, email, instant messaging and chat bots. Chat bots are used by the online shopping site to enable clients to chat. The answers are made by robots. They are based on Artificial Intelligence. So, the bot is learning from a knowledge base. The business company can save costs and reduce time response.

Once the client is traced in the e-commerce site, software agents can inform customers about promotions via multiple channels (social media, email address, applications such as messenger, whatsapp,..). Emails newsletters are also used. In fact, conducting email campaigns is largely deployed such as product recommendation emails. Barilliance's study shows that there is an increase of 30% in conversion rates after adding personalized product recommendations to the email newsletters (Barilliance 2018).

2.3 CRM Technologies

From a managerial perspective, EC technologies offer valuable opportunities to the firm current value chain for enhancing inter-functional collaboration and efficiency in its relationships with customers, suppliers and the main social economic and governmental partners

Applications for supply chain management SCM and the customer relationship management CRM are important for the growth of any e-commerce project. In addition, promotion management applications can help to plan and carry out promotions to attract buyers.

Following the emergence of relationship marketing and the development of EC technologies, this paper focuses on the important role of the CRM data in providing a valuable source of competitive advantage and producing knowledge that guides decision makers especially in commercial and marketing processes (Stein et al. 2013; Lindman et al. 2012).

CRM Systems

CRM can be studied as a process, a strategy or a technology. Lefebure and Venturi (2001) present CRM as *"The management of customer relations combines technologies and business strategies to provide customers with products and services that they expect. The management of customer relationships is the ability to identify, acquire and retain the best customers with the goal of increasing sales and profits."*. According to this definition, the CRM systems and technologies are implemented to support the business strategy processes.

The quality of the CRM system refers to the performance characteristics of a system including reliability, flexibility, being user-friendly and response time. The quality of the CRM system has a direct and indirect positive influence (via customer satisfaction) on profitability (Khlif and Jallouli 2014).

The CRM architecture includes three segments namely: operational CRM, collaborative CRM and analytical CRM (Teo et al. 2006). Operational CRM focuses on the daily management of a relationship with the client through the contact points (customer service, call center, sales force …). The collaborative CRM covers all the communication and interaction channels with customers and partners as well as work technology groups, such as workflow and e-mail. Finally, analytical CRM is the integration and processing of data to produce useful information for the analysis of customer relationships and project improvement (Chalmeta 2006).

As a conclusion, the CRM success is influenced by a dual value creation:

- Increasing profits with the identification of the most profitable segments, improvement of the performances of the sales force, customization of products and services.
- Increasing the visibility and the quality of the information to all stakeholders thanks to the integration of information in a single database (Krasnikov et al. 2009).

3 Data Analysis Capabilities

The previous section identifies the main EC technologies and classifies them according to the stages of the website development, the transactional process and customer relationship management. This paragraph analyses the importance of data analysis capabilities to unlock customer insights and orient in time marketing decisions based on data collected with EC technologies.

Data science in its broadest sense is defined as "a multidisciplinary field that deals with technologies, processes, and systems to extract knowledge and insight from data and supports reasoning and decision making under various sources of uncertainty" (National Academies of Sciences, Engineering, and Medicine 2017).

The data stored in companies and shared in social media is still growing at a high speed. The challenge for managers is mainly to cope with the high volume, variety and velocity of data. Core business systems such as marketing, finance and production produce structured data. However, with the increasing number of audio and video applications and the large participation of customers in social media to comment or rank a product, a brand or a company, the proportion of unstructured data has increased in a significant rate.

Structured and unstructured data have high commercial value. The challenge for companies is therefore to develop the underlying data infrastructure in order to make it more robust and agile and to extract consumer insights that enlighten the future decision in marketing area (HBR Survey 2018).

Data treatment and analysis are based on Algorithm, Visualization, machine learning or cognitive technologies as examples of tools that could help in extracting customer knowledge to orient marketing decisions (Kumar 2018).

The application characteristics include the following steps: First, Data should be queried or in some cases be moved between different platforms. Second, Data needs to be summarized, grouped and sorted. Natural language processing and video analysis are techniques that help to convert unstructured Data to structured Data. Data helps to edit business indicator statistics, predictive analysis, deep data mining and exploration reports. Finally, there are different timeliness of using such as different frequency of index statistics, Ad-hoc query, and self-service data exploration (Song et al. 2018).

Data science is a multidisciplinary field that deals with technologies, processes, and systems to extract knowledge and insight. Data Analytic techniques include exploratory analysis, predictive analysis and prescriptive analysis (Strengthening Data Science Methods Report 2017). Data sources are all types of data to support decision making under various sources of uncertainty.

The survey of Harvard Business Review (2018) on real time analytics reveals three relevant interrelated capabilities that guide consumer experience strategy:

1/Unified customer data platforms: This capability unifies mainly the company's customer data from the online and the offline channels.

2/Proactive analytics with machine learning and artificial intelligence: The purpose is to incorporate insights on customers, marketing programs and related functions.

3/Contextual interactions: This capability integrates real time insights on digital and physical costumer journeys to draw subsequent actions to pursue in the benefit of the brand or the company.

The current key tools and approaches used in companies to orient strategic and tactical decisions are the following: Segmentation tools, Survey-based choice models, Aggregate marketing mix models, Pre-test market models, Marketing metrics, New product models, Customer life time value models, Panel-based choice models, Perceptual mapping, Customer satisfaction model, Sales force allocation models, Game theory models and the Average Perceived Impact (Roberts et al. 2014).

A good example that shows the importance of developing new tools to treat the vast quantities of panel scanner data and extract customer knowledge is the large use of the logic modeling to guide responses to changes in the marketing mix (Roberts et al. 2014).

A second example of a trendy data analysis capability is data mining defined as the process allowing a search, for valuable information, in large volumes of data. This data search capability uses statistical algorithms, predictive modeling, forecasting and descriptive modelling techniques and intelligent agent systems to uncover patterns and correlations and extracts knowledge from corporate data platforms (Liao et al. 2012).

Data mining tools combined with CRM output could be an alternative to the approaches and models already on offer to improve strategic decision-making and tactical marketing activities.

The objective is orienting in time and contextual strategic decision either manually or with the help of artificial intelligence.

4 Marketing Knowledge

Scholar journals in the field of marketing research focus on advancing our knowledge by integrating new areas and exploring results confirmed in sister disciplines such as psychology, economics, finance and information systems (Shugan 2004). The role of EC technologies in the marketing research is growing significantly. Based on the Marketing Science Institutes research priorities, the recent topics in Marketing management are the understanding of mobile marketing opportunities, the role of social media and the harnessing of Big Data (Roberts et al. 2014). The study of the best sellers' textbooks of marketing shows the rise of the following topics: Digital and mobile communication in terms of access to markets and social networks, branding, customer management and integrated marketing (Roberts et al. 2014).

The key marketing decision areas are: Brand management (Developing, positioning and managing brands), New product/service management (Development, management" and diffusion of new products), Marketing strategy (Product line, multi-product and portfolio strategies), Advertising management (Spending, planning and design), Promotion management, Pricing management, Sales force management (size, allocation, and compensation), Channel management (strategy, design, and monitoring), Customer/market selection (Targeting decisions), Relationship management (Customer value assessment and maximization, acquisition, retention), Managing marketing investments (Organizing for higher returns and internal marketing) and the Service/product quality management (Roberts et al. 2014).

Based on the previous sections on EC technologies and data analysis capabilities, Fig. 1 provides an overview of the main EC technologies implemented in different stages and the contribution of these technologies to guide marketing decisions.

The first stage of website development relies mainly on CMS and Web development tools, Web services, Web design tools, Catalog design tools, Database applications, Hosting infrastructure and Cloud computing (IaaS, PaaS, SaaS). The key marketing decision areas that could be guided with these technologies are Brand management, new product/service management, marketing strategy, Advertising management, Promotion management, Pricing management, Channel management (strategy, design, and monitoring) and Customer/market selection.

The second stage concerning the electronic transaction is based mainly on the following technologies: cookies, Email campaigns, Ads channels, Email, instant messaging, chat bots, Feedback ratings, social media, Agent-mediated platforms, the shopping cart application, returns management application, contracting tools, GPS tracking, IoT and Tracking delivery applications. These technologies and applications provide valuable source of structured and unstructured data. The shopping card applications, contracting tools and GPS tracking and Tracking delivery applications are sources of high value demographic, psychological and geographical characteristics of prospects and customers. Agents, cookies and social media provide structured and unstructured data. The firm needs proactive and contextual analytics to integrate real time insights on digital and physical costumer journeys and draw subsequent actions related mainly to Brand Management, New product/service management, Promotion management, Pricing management, Sales force management, Channel management, Relationship management and the Service/product quality management.

Finally, the third group of E-commerce technologies that are studied in this paper is related to the relationship with customers via CRM technologies. Operational, collaborative and analytical CRM systems produce high potential of value creation by integrating information in a unique database used by all the stakeholders. Data mining, proactive analytics and contextual interactions are then capabilities that unify the company's data from the online and the offline channels to produce Marketing knowledge via the identification of the most profitable segments, the performance improvement of the sales force and the customization of the firm products and services.

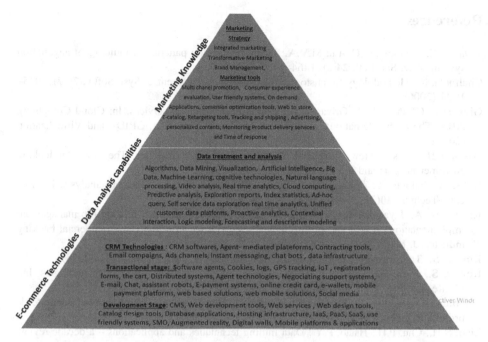

Fig. 1. Overview of e-commerce technologies, data analysis capabilities and marketing knowledge

5 Conclusion

Electronic commerce provides a great opportunity to small and medium-sized enterprises (SME) to improve their competitiveness within the global economy. With the development of information technology, consumer behavior is constantly traced and studied by researchers and developers. Business challenge is about how well it deploys technology to build Market-Winning decisions. Therefore, relying on data analysis capabilities of consumers' personal data and consumer habits, needs and preferences, it is possible to accurately grasp the needs of customers, build personalized customer service systems and lead to higher conversions and long-term customer loyalty.

This paper presents an overview of the main EC technologies implemented in different stages (Development, transactional, relational) and the contribution of these technologies to make customer insights and orient marketing decisions. The paper doesn't include security solutions and technologies deployed in e-commerce such as tokenization and blockchain.

As a final recommendation, this overview of e-commerce technologies in relationship with marketing knowledge highlights the importance of tight collaboration between researchers from Computer science and Marketing fields to develop more case studies and research papers that could be useful for a best-contextual data analysis capabilities. From a teaching perspective also, marketing students need a basic understanding of the e-commerce technologies and the analytical tools since they will need to use these approaches throughout their career as marketers.

References

Wyai, L.C., WaiShiang, C., Lu, M.V.A.: Agent negotiation patterns for multi agent negotiation system. Adv. Sci. Lett. **24**(2), 1464–1469 (2018)

Chalmeta, R.: Methodology for customer relationship management. J. Syst. Softw. **79**(7), 1015–1024 (2006)

Giovanoli, C., Pulikal, P., Grivas, S.: E-marketplace for cloud services. In: Cloud Computing 2014: The Fifth International Conference on Cloud Computing, GRIDs, and Virtualization (2014)

Harvard Business Review Analytical Services: Real Time Analytics, The key to unlocking customer insights and driving the customer experience, 12 p. (2018)

Khlif, H., Jallouli, R.: The success factors of CRM systems, an explanatory analysis. J. Glob. Bus. Technol. **10**(2), 24–41 (2014)

Krasnikov, A., Jayachandran, S., Kumar, V.: The impact of customer relationship management implementation on cost and profit efficiencies: evidence from the U.S. commercial banking industry. J. Mark. **73**(6), 61–76 (2009)

Kumar, S.: Transformative marketing: the next 20 years. J. Mark. **82**(4), 1–12 (2018)

Kumar, S., Joshi, P., Saquib, Z.: Ubiquitous commerce: the new world of technologies. Int. J. Life Sci. Eng. **1**(2), 50–55 (2015)

Lefébure, R., Ventury, G.: Gestion de la relation client Panorama des produits et conduite de projets, Eyrolles, 334 p. (2001)

Liao, S.H., Chu, P.H., Hsiao, P.Y.: Data mining techniques and applications – a decade review from 2000 to 2011. Expert Syst. Appl. **39**, 11303–11311 (2012)

National Academies of Sciences, Engineering, and Medicine: Strengthening Data Science Methods for Department of Defense Personnel and Readiness Missions. The National Academies Press, Washington, DC (2017). https://doi.org/10.17226/23670

Roberts, J.H., Kayande, U., Stremersch, S.: From academic research to marketing practice: exploring the marketing science value chain. Int. J. Res. Mark. **31**, 127–140 (2014)

Shugan, S.M.: The impact of advancing technology on marketing and academic research. Mark. Sci. **23**(4), 469–475 (2004)

Song, W., Zhang, Y., Wang, J., Li, H., Meng, Y., Cheng, R.: Research on characteristics and value analysis of power grid data asset. Procedia Comput. Sci. **139**, 158–164 (2018)

Teo, T.S.H., Devadoss, P., Pan, S.L.: Towards a holistic perspective of customer relationship management (CRM) implementation: a case study of the housing and development board, Singapore. Decis. Support Syst. **42**(3), 1613–1627 (2006)

Verdouw, C.N., Robbemond, R.M., Verwaart, T., Wolfert, J., Beulens, A.J.M.: A reference architecture for IoT-based logistic information systems in agri-food supply chains. J. Enterprise Inf. Syst. **12**(7), 755–779 (2018)

Amado, A., Cortez, P., Rita, P., Moro, S.: Research trends on big data in marketing: a text mining and topic modeling based literature analysis. Eur. Res. Manag. Bus. Econ. **24** (2017). https://doi.org/10.1016/j.iedeen.2017.06.002

Stein, A.D., Smith, M.F., Lancioni, R.A.: The development and diffusion of customer relationship management (CRM) intelligence in business-to-business environments. Ind. Mark. Manag. **42**(6), 855–861 (2013)

Lindman, M., Pennanen, K., Rothenstein, J., Scozzi, B., Vincze, Z.: The practice of customer value creation and market effectiveness among low-tech SMES. J. Glob. Bus. Technol. **8**(1), 16–35 (2012)

HBR Survey: Real Time Analytics: The key to unlocking customer insights and driving the customer experience. Harvard Business Review Analytic Services Survey, 16 p., March 2018

Webography

Uber (2018). http://www.uber.com

FedEx (2019). http://www.fedex.com

Amazon Web Services (2019). http://www.aws.com

Barilliance (2018). https://www.barilliance.com/category/email-marketing/

Barilliance (2014). https://www.barilliance.com/wp-content/uploads/2014/06/eyesdirect_n.pdf

Salesforce (2018). https://www.salesforce.com/crm/

E-commerce and Commodity Fetishism Violence in New Media Marketing

Hassan Choubassi[✉], Sahar Sharara, and Sarah Khayat

International University of Beirut – BIU, Beirut, Lebanon
{hassan.choubassi,sahar.sharara,
sarah.khayat}@liu.edu.lb

Abstract. With e-commerce advertising messages have a high reach and visibility, with the new technologies of mobile connectivity that is able to permanently track and monitor consumers and automatically observe patterns of consumed commodities it becomes easy to manipulate the consumers into psychographic commodity fetishism that will tackle individual taste and aspiration according to pre-collected profiles. It intoxicates and transforms signification into banality that renders all images to pornography-like similes. This will lead to the production of images of violence, images that violate the individual's privacy through influences, monitoring and surveillance, through panoptical shadowing of direct and indirect control that will manipulates consumption habits and political aspirations.

Keywords: E-commerce · Commodity fetishism · New media marketing · Media augmentation · Violence of information

1 Introduction

In classical political economy, a commodity is a good or service produced by human labor, and offered as product on the market. In addition to their basic function, such products inherently carry significance – a symbolism related to the identity of whoever acquires them: they are a way that helps shape a sense of self (Todd 2012). Whether through film, advertising, television or mobile phones, the media that carry those messages about the commodity are what Debord calls *spectacle* (Debord 1983). For him, it constitutes the "most glaring superficial manifestation," the "autocratic reign of the market economy;" capitalism's instrument for distracting and pacifying the masses. The "seduction of the commodity" takes place through the reduction of reality to an endless supply of commodifiable fragments, and a focus on appearances. The spectacle actively alters human interactions and relationships. Images influence our lives and beliefs on a daily basis; advertising manufacturers new desires and aspirations.

Contemporary consumer culture is forever steered towards a capitalist society of commodity fetishism, with globalization and the new technologies of E-commerce and digital advertising, the notion of commodity fetishism that Karl Marx talked about in 1867 (Marx 1992) is now taking a new higher dimension of domination.

R. Jallouli et al. (Eds.): ICDEc 2019, LNBIP 358, pp. 194–200, 2019.
https://doi.org/10.1007/978-3-030-30874-2_15

2 Commodity Fetishism

In a capitalist economy, consumers tend to assume modes of consumption that will guide them to buy any set of presumably coherent commodities. And with advertising, people are pushed into standards so they will fit into the psychographic categories of products set by the market place. To consumers, commodities seems as a reflection of their creative individuality but this commodification confines and exploits the human psyche in the service of building consumption modes that are illusionary and exemplifies human fake needs and aspirations. In creating preset individual identities that conforms to the standard of the market, people become passive consumers without them even noticing. This eventually obliterates creative act and self-determinism of individuals who become mere followers of trends or mainstream uniformities.

Literature has addressed topics associated to society's behavior related to the notion of consumption. Whether this act of buying is fulfilling a vital need or shaped by a capitalist society, which in turn is the source of manufacturing mass-produced commodities. Not only had these products concealed behind the gratifying image of commodity fetishism distorting the true nature of their origination, but their exchange-value becomes of high significance in the market place and the masses contribute by consuming the fetish of commodities, where their use-value is trivial or null.

Before "globalization" Debord speaks of the determinism of mass media and how it is instigating class alienation and cultural homogenization, when he says, "All that was once directly lived has become mere representation" (Debord 1983) he is referring to the importance of image manipulation and its reference to the market place, an image created to sell the idea of consumption itself, a link between happiness as an ultimate goal and the act of buying, thus, the image of representation becomes direct life itself. "Images, Debord says, have supplanted genuine human interaction", Where he sets the idea of image production as a spectacle, for him this "spectacle obliterates the boundaries between self and world by crushing the self besieged by the presence-absence of the world. (…) The consumer's compulsion to imitate is a truly infantile need, conditioned by all the aspects of his fundamental dispossession".

3 The Fetish of Media Augmentation

With new technologies of digital media the awe of the image is lost because of the very loss of comparison between the signifier and the signified, when one of the elements forming this duality, the signified, was nullified, or negated by the speed and the immediacy of its image. So this schizophrenic battle between the spectacle and the real, was won in advance by the realm of the illusion, the hallucinated image took over the actual, and images won over the things they are representing. The spectacle that Debord talked about in the 60s is now considered a mere "scene" although it has created a sharp split between the lived actual and the TV perfect spectacle. The spectacle manipulates the image of the actual, but simulation creates an obscene image which is itself a "reality" and actual reality becomes totally deserted. Eventually, with the mobility of virtual configurations, the actual is reoccupied again and is augmented by cybernetic devices. Digital economy is taking obscenity to the street, to actual history, so what is becoming obscene now is this combination of the actual and its image taken along instantaneously, continuously and interactively, an obscene in combo. It is not just an evil spectacle anymore, not an image manipulation nor is it a substitution of the actual by its image, not a creation of a virtual reality nor a simulacrum; but rather a combo obscenity of the actual itself along with its digital image, a process of augmenting the actual by obscenity, this is what jean Baudrillard calls "le paroxysme" the critical stage of an illness, the morbid level (Baudrillard Petit 1998).

In his magnum opus "Capital, critique of political economy" (Marx 1992) Karl Marx suggested that social relations are primarily mediated by the exchange of commodities and how those commodities are traded is depended on the costs of production and human labor involved in the production and facilitating the selling. Marx refutes all the ideas about an autonomous market that is self-regulated by fluctuating supply and demand, for him, consumers do not perceive the latent human interrelations, social activities, and power relations imbedded in all commodities which are the factual variables in the market place. For him this is where objectification takes place, this is the domination of things in the market or "reification". The product or commodity is no more a result of human labor, no more an exchanged asset between people; it is an object of fetish. This "thingification" of social relations, and all the people involved in them become expressed by the relationships between traded fetish objects, or in Marx's words: Commodity Fetishism. In "The Fetishism of Commodities and the Secret Thereof" he explains it as "the socio-economic reification of a commodity into a fetish, an object with intrinsic value and an independent economic reality" (Marx 1992). For Marx the workers, the producers, and the consumers trade their products out of their own desire and initiative without paying any attention to the market exchange. The quantities of mass-produced goods and the commercial activities involved are adjusted in relation to the variable worth of the products, and the services as they are exchanged, and in relevance to supply and demand. Therefore, social relations are always mediated and interlinked with objects, with commodities. The cost of production and the quantities of human labor determines how commodities interrelate. The psychological phenomenon of commodity fetishism attribute a self-determining value and reality to an object that has no intrinsic value but that was given to it by the producer, the advertiser, the seller, and the buyer of the commodities.

Advertising agencies study their target audience, among other segmentation criteria, in relevance to their psychological modes of buying where consumers are divided into eight categories of moods as follow: Innovators, Thinkers, Believers, Achievers, Strivers, Experiencers, Makers and Survivors, (O'Shaughnessy and O'Shaughnessy 2004), consumers in those categories are determined according to their consumption habits. "Advertising based on lifestyle differentiates a brand by depicting a lifestyle that reflects a set of values. It says, in effect, if this lifestyle or set of values resonates with you, then our product or brand is the one for you. Psychographic research can be product specific or non-specific and can be combined with demographic data for advertising purposes. The best-known system of non-specific psychographics is VALS Values, Attitude and Lifestyles", the basic idea is to link products to each other in such a way that a person who buys this or that brand will automatically buy this other psychographic linked brand, this is what is called in marketing the Mary Douglas theory: "individual purchases are ways coordinated with other purchases, as goods assembled in ownership present a set of meanings, more or less coherent, more or less intentional" (Douglas 2015). (...) "The perspective is of people continuously trying to bring about their ideal form of community life. In other words, the superordinate value for any person is his or her ideal form of community and it is the emotional attachment to this ideal which dominates as a concern in making product choices" (O'Shaughnessy and O'Shaughnessy 2004). According to Marx people tend to fit on a character mask "Charactermaske" (Marx 1992) and they tend to act and play a functional role that they can relate to in a society composed of stratified social classes, and this role-playing needs to be promoted by a set of propos and accessories that are negotiated and acquired in a market-exchange transactions. In that sense, the perception of commodities in the market place will give different values to the products, values that are more related to the role-playing psychographic modes of the consumers and the traders alike.

In their book "Dialectic of Enlightenment" in 1944 (Horkheimer and Adorno 2007), Theodor Adorno and Max Horkheimer indicate how the culture industry and the commodification of all sorts of production, and later on the commodification of humans themselves, are becoming the key factors for domination. The commercialization of human relations is alienating people out from their free-will roles to act as different and the market place economy is disturbing the development of the human psyche. They describe how creativity in all cultural fields becomes commodified when it is reduced to "natural commercial laws" of the market. Under a capitalist economy commodities appear to fulfill the initial promises of modernity, happiness and freedom. On the other hand, it seems that the market economy is capable of obliterating the sense of responsibility that some consumers have, in some cases the mere act of shopping can become an act of aggression if the consumer is aware of the manufacturing origin of commodities and the exploitative labor conditions under which the workers produce the goods and services. This act of aggression passes unnoticed and without any feeling of guilt when it is online and it is part of crowed behavior where one feels as part of big psychological crowed and thus not responsible for his acts as individual, one feels protected by the crowed (Bon 2013). The aggressiveness embedded in the act of buying is neglected and becomes trivial for the consumers when it is mediated through a system of virtual intermediaries of the online market that normalizes and polishes the product and presents it to the end customer as a normal or even necessary product, and sometimes those virtual intermediaries sweet-talk customers to convince them that they are actually doing an ethical and responsible act of charity when they associate the product to a moral, social, humanitarian or environmental cause. And to push this normalization of aggression further, e-commerce transformed the consumer into an accomplice in the act of aggression against the exploited labor forces and against other consumers too. Mass media augmentation on desktops embedded in the very personal mobile devices of the individual consumers are inescapable, and thus through this bombardment of images and the repetition of ideas even when a targeted consumer is on the move makes it impossible to avoid. E-commerce also allowed the advertiser to allocate the target audience as individuals, and to survey their movements and action, it allows for a data register of any act of buying, money transaction, and monitor the search tools of the consumers to know exactly what they need, what they want, what they love, what they hate, what they are looking for and what they are intending to buy, so it can guide them through to their needs and even worse, to persuade them to buy what they do not need. The target audience is no more a group, a collectivity or a psychological crowed, it is an individual, monitored, controlled and guided consumer.

In advertising the purpose is to sell through linking the product to an aspired prestige's status, to a higher-class category than the audience targeted. According to Alain de Botton (De Botton 2005) advertisers tackle the sensitive matter of the social status and the aspirations to prestige of the consumer. To avoid "anxiety" of not being of or belonging to the right social class, and to seek "relaxation", the consumer establishes a personal identity with the associative image that advertising had created and linked to the product when defining it as a way to belong to a higher level in society.

4 Mass Production of Obscenity

The production of sameness on the level of the market commodities was also amplified with e-commerce as it served in yet a higher level of advertising manipulation and persuasive appeal. Advertising messages also have high reach and visibility when augmented with the new technologies of mobile connectivity that is able to permanently track and monitor consumers and automatically observe patterns of consumed commodities. With media augmentation and its ability to track consumption habits and patterns of goods, it becomes easy to manipulate the consumers into psychographic commodity fetishism that will tackle individual's taste and aspiration according to pre-collected profiles. It becomes easy to set a defined and fitting social mask that the target audience longed for. In that sense the media is creating the need and the answer through persuasive appeals and psychological manipulation of human desires and aspirations, a system of information that gives the perceiver the illusion of all answers with repetitive information of the market place and the illusion of free will. Media augmentation gives a sense of reliability, as it is always there ready to answer to any demand, thus one tends to rely on it and trust its information without questioning. Individual consumers equipped with mobile smart devices have the world at their fingertips; they will not feel the need to search or question anything, but they are unaware that this quasi information is deceiving and manipulative. And the quantity of information accessible only makes them dazed and confused. This excess of information contributes mainly to the loss of knowledge: it intoxicates and transforms a scene into ob-scene, it transforms signification into banality and renders all images to pornography-like similes informing the disenchanted. For Jean Baudrillard commodity fetishism alters humane subjective feelings into consumer goods in the "realm of circulation" (Baudrillard 1981), advertising creates cultural mystifications around commodities to persuade the consumer to purchase useless products that helps to construct a cultural identity for people, in that sense, the hedonic value of the product, that is directly derived from the fetish, wins over the utilitarian value. The excess of digital commodification that filled the social space of consumerism is so much the same as all the excess of information, of images, of media, of a repetitive kind of information that leads not into knowledge. In his book the information bomb Paul Virilio wrote: "The smaller the world becomes as a result of the relativistic effect of telecommunications, the more violently situations are concertinaed, with the risk of an economic and social crash that would merely be the extension of the visual crash of this 'market of the visible', in which the virtual bubble of the inter-connected financial markets is never any other than the inevitable consequence of that visual bubble of a politics which has become both panoptical and cybernetic" (Virilio 2005), panoptical in a sense that it keeps everything and everybody under strict surveillance, a politic that gathers information from all around and amass them into a cybernetic digital database that is accessible and used in favor of the market economy in advertising, public opinion polls, political hegemony, secret service control and surveillance. Panoptical also in a sense that everybody knows that they are under the watch but yet feel safe as if this a protector's eye and in a way the excess of information gathered can also be used by end-user individuals in their quotidian lives.

5 Conclusion

With the new technologies of media augmentation the process of dumbing down reached an unprecedented level. Information at a finger tips means, in a way, no knowledge, just easy and dull information that help advertiser to reach a needle-point target audience efficiently, and thus help to increase the sales, to increase consumption with minimum of expenses. This kind of information is not of the sort of knowledge information but only a vessel to increase consumption of commodities that nobody needs, this is the symbolic violence that Bourdieu was talking about (Bourdieu 1999). Augmented media allowed advertising a high reach with a minimum cost. This media is often used and abused in a system of dumbing-down by advertising to convey information that will account for nothing on the intellectual level but on the contrary will account a lot on the level of encouraging dumb consumption. Moreover, the easiness of getting hold of information even while mobile gives the impression that the world is ready at hand and gives the individual end-user of mobile technologies the illusion of power and ultimate knowledge. Nonetheless in reality the end-user of those augmented technologies has the accessibility to only certain type of information, even when it looks like a lot but the kind of information that is allowed for the public is the kind to be used against this public, information that can help in monitoring and sug-gesting a specific desired behavior of consumption or political submission. And what really becomes dangerous is that the public enjoys the illusion of knowledge and will seek no more, search no more, and will not even think of alternative sources of information and thus neglect all conventional media and rely totally on what is at hand. This is an image of violence at its best, the sheer quantity of information it provides is an act of bombardment by itself, and this is an image that violates the individual's privacy and private space through manipulation, monitoring and surveillance, through direct and indirect control that will serve into changing consumption habits and furthers political oppression.

References

Todd, D.: You are what you buy: postmodern consumerism and the construction of the self. Hohonu: J. Acad. Writ. **10**, 48–50 (2012)

Debord, G.: Society of the Spectacle. Black & Red, Detroit (1983). Thesis 220

Marx, K.: Capital: Volume 1: A Critique of Political Economy, trans. by B. Fowkes, Reprint (Penguin Classics, 1992)

O'Shaughnessy, J., O'Shaughnessy, N.J.: Persuasion in Advertising. Routledge, London (2004)

Douglas, M.: Natural Symbols: Explorations in Cosmology, 3rd edn. Routledge, New York (2015)

Horkheimer, M., Adorno, T.W.: Dialectic of Enlightenment, ed. by G. S. Noerr, trans. by E. Jephcott, 1st edn. Stanford University Press (2007)

Bon, G.L.: The Crowd: A Study of the Popular Mind (CreateSpace Independent Publishing Platform, 2013) (2013)

De Botton, A.: Status Anxiety. Vintage International, New York (2005)

Baudrillard, J.: For a Critique of the Political Economy of the Sign. Telos Press, St. Louis (1981)

Baudrillard, J., Petit, P.: Paroxysm: Interviews with Philippe Petit. Verso, London (1998)

Bourdieu, P.: On Television, trans. New Press, The, Priscilla Parkhurst Ferguson (New York (1999)

Virilio, P.: The Information Bomb. Verso, London (2005)

E-Learning and Cloud Education

Toward Information Overload: Measuring Visual Activity in Teaching Materials Production

Kristian Dokic[1](✉), Tomislava Lauc[2], and Bojan Radisic[1]

[1] Polytechnic in Pozega, Vukovarska 17, 34000 Pozega, Croatia
{kdjokic,bradisic}@vup.hr
[2] Faculty of Humanities and Social Sciences, Ivana Lucica 3, 10000 Zagreb, Croatia
tlauc@ffzg.hr

Abstract. The paper presents information overload and visual activity of media, explaining the development of a quantitative method for measuring visual activity in video content. The measure is based on the Limited Capacity Model of Mediated Message Processing and background subtractions algorithms. The idea underlying the described method is to present the quantitative measure of media visual activity that could be useful in determining the moment when information overload could occur. The method has been applied for measuring visual activity on four groups of YouTube educational video clips. All of them are from language learning channels. The difference between these four groups is statistically significant and easily discernible.

Keywords: Information overload · Information density · Visual activity · LC4MP · Background subtraction algorithms · Gesturing

1 Introduction

Media technology has progressed rapidly in the last fifty years prompting questions about its influence on learning. In the Kaiser report [1], authors state that today no one knows about the brain activity of children as they learn to read while immersed in digital media 6–7 h a day. In order to analyze the impact of various types of television programs on the cognitive functions of pre-school children, Lillard et al. [2] used different kinds of video materials. In their research, pre-school children were divided into three groups. The first group watched a fast-paced television cartoon, the second group watched a less dynamic (slow-paced) educational film while the third group was drawing in a period of 9 min. After that, the effects on their cognitive functions were tested. The results showed that the group that watched the dynamic cartoon film solved the tests significantly worse than the other two groups. The difference concerning information overload and visual activity of video materials in both dynamic and educational cartoons has been described qualitatively.

The main idea underlying this paper is to present the quantitative measure of media visual activity that could be useful in determining the moment when information overload could occur. The measurement method does not directly include the recipient

R. Jallouli et al. (Eds.): ICDEc 2019, LNBIP 358, pp. 203–214, 2019.
https://doi.org/10.1007/978-3-030-30874-2_16

of the message, although it is founded on the Limited Capacity Model of Mediated Message Processing (LC4MP) [3–9]. The model explains how people process media content. In the context of information overload, it considers the interaction between a media user, medium and, message content and structure [3].

Therefore, the short overview of information overload and visual activity has been outlined. In addition, considering the Limited Capacity Model of Mediated Message Processing [8], the Visual Activity Index [10] and background subtraction algorithms [11], the development of a method for measuring the visual activity of video content is shortly explained. Finally, the method has been applied to four groups of YouTube video clips that contain educational material from language learning channels. The difference between these four groups is statistically significant and easily discernible.

2 Information Overload

Rogers and Agarwala-Rogers [12] defined information overload as "the state of an individual or system in which excessive communication inputs cannot be processed and utilized, leading to breakdown". Feathers [13] definition is similar and he defined information overload as a state with so much available information that they cannot be effectively utilized. Schroder [16] has described information overload graphically with inverted U-curve (see Fig. 1) whereby the increase in information load increases the accuracy in decision-making. However, at a certain point, information overload occurs and the accuracy in decision-making falls. Information overload has been the subject of scientific investigation in the fields of economy, psychology, media science, education etc. Wilson [15] defined information overload as "a perception on the part of the individual (or observers of that person) that the flow of information associated with work tasks is greater than can be managed effectively, and a perception that overload in this sense creates a degree of stress for which his or her coping strategies are ineffective". So, we can conclude that he defined information overload at the personal level. Eppler and Mengis [14] suggested a conceptual framework for information overloading investigation with five categories: information, person, task, organization and information technologies. They consider that information overload is the result of more than one factors and that they belong to previously mentioned categories. Those groups of factors have an impact on two variables, Information Processing Capacity and Information Processing Requirements. The first variable is the attribute of a person and the second one is the attribute of a task or a process.

Considering education, Pelgrum [17] quoted data from a worldwide survey where 20% of school principals and technology experts choose Information overload as a potential obstacle to the integration of ICT in education.

Information overload has been recognized by Graham et al. [18] as a problem in medical education before almost 60 years, however only on the university level.

Lang [3] introduced the Limited Capacity Model of Mediated Message Processing in order to determine the quantitative level for information overload considering video clips materials. She used Secondary task reaction time test to define the moment of information overload. Also, she explained paradox previously mentioned by Britton [19, 20], where secondary task reaction time average for the easy task was longer than that for difficult tasks.

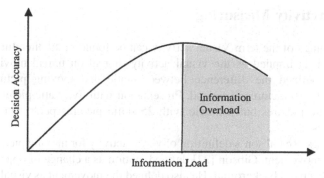

Fig. 1. Information overload [16]

The great contribution of Lang's theory is that she made a model that can be used to quantify information density. Lang [4] suggested that people have limited resources for information processing and when required resources become bigger than available resources, information overload occurs. When this happens, one part of the message has been lost. Resource allocation is complex and depends on many factors. In Lang's paper from 2006, term *Information introduced* is defined. One year later Lang et al. defined *Information density* as *information introduced* divided by elapsed time [9]. Information introduced is a number generated at every camera change that is increment for the presence of next dimensions:

1. Object change
2. Novelty
3. Relatedness
4. Distance
5. Perspective
6. Emotion
7. Form change

Information introduced can have a score ranging from 0 to 7. On Fig. 2 from Lang's paper, it can be seen that high Information introduced causes Secondary task reaction time to fall and information overload occurs. Data from Lang's paper has been used by authors to find the best method for information density measuring.

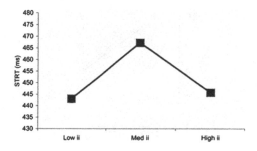

Fig. 2. Information introduced rise causes STRT fall [4]

3 Visual Activity Measuring

Different meanings of the term Visual activity can be found in the literature. However, in this paper, it is implied as the visual activity of real on unreal moving pictures. Sutcliffe [21] defined the difference between static and moving pictures as it is changing speed - 10 pictures in second. Presentation with five static pictures in minute belongs to static pictures but a movie with 25 static pictures per second belongs to moving pictures.

Some authors use Gibson's definition of visual activity for moving pictures as a sum of motion and movement. Gibson [22] defined motion as a change of objects or people in the shot with a fixed background. He also defined the movement as visual information caused by the movement of the observer or a camera in the case of the movie.

Scientists have analyzed movies and television broadcasts from their very beginnings, however, in the last decades, they have started to analyze their quantitative attributes. Salt suggested a first method and measures more than forty years ago [23]. His measure is called Average Shot Length. Sklar defines a shot as a "series of frames that runs for an uninterrupted period of time" [24]. The simplest method for calculating the average shot length is counting shots and dividing the movie time with the number of shots in the movie. Salt claimed that the films of individual authors usually had very similar average shot lengths [23]. The author analyzed fifty films and he studied the distribution of the ASL frequencies, which are the closest to the Poisson's distribution. The literature analysis related to the average shot length clearly indicates that this measure is most often used in the narrow branch of science called Cinemetrics. Baxter [25] defined it as "a statistical analysis of quantitative data, description of the structure and content of movies that one might observe as aspects of style". Brunick et al. [26] suggested later that this measure should be renamed into Average Shot Duration (ASD) because the term Average Shot Length is also used to measure the focal length of the camera.

In the Fig. 3 Cutting's chart [27] on average shot length fall in the last hundred year can be seen. Cutting analyzed almost ten thousand movies in the English language produced between 1920 and 2010. Numbers on the vertical axis are the average shot length in seconds.

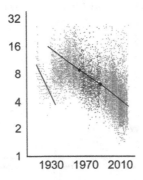

Fig. 3. ASL in the last 100 years [27]

The *Visual Activity Index* (VAI) has been introduced by Cutting in 2011. Authors declared that it "measures the amount of movement of objects in the frame, as well as the camera itself, in the entire movie". The results obtained by measuring is the number between 0 and 2, where the smaller value indicates less motion in the movie.

The *Visual Activity Index* method processes the video clips in the way that frames have to be reduced to individual images 256-pixel height and 256-pixel wide. Also, each image has to be converted to a gray JPG image file, so that each pixel can contain a value between 0 and 255. The result of the above-described preparation is approximately 165,000 individual pairs of images per movie. The authors chose Pearson's correlation to compare the neighboring images, with correlation value 1 for two identical images. In the case of larger visual activity, the images will be less similar and the correlation will, consequently, be smaller. The final value of the *Visual Activity Index* is obtained by subtracting the correlation value from number 1, giving the theoretical scope for the *Visual Activity Index* between 0 and 2. In Fig. 4 authors showed VAI in the period from 1930 to 2010. The analyzed sample included 145 movies [10].

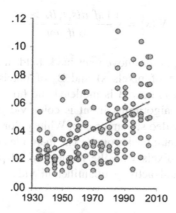

Fig. 4. VAI between 1930 and 2010 [10]

3.1 Background Subtraction Algorithm Visual Activity Index

Method for visual activity measurement, used in this paper, was developed based on background subtraction algorithms. Shaikh et al. [28] stated that "background removal is often used to detect moving objects in video content created with a static camera". Bouwmans [29] describes that algorithm for background subtraction consists of 3 activities as it can be seen in Fig. 5:

- Initialization of the background - based on a certain number of images using one of the methods defined by the model of the stationary background,
- Detection of moving objects - comparisons of current images of video clips or streams with a motionless background model moving objects are detected,

- Backing up the background - during the detection, the model of the fixed background is refreshed depending on the changes in the video clip or stream.

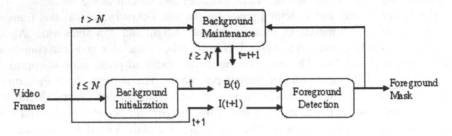

Fig. 5. How does BSA algorithm work [29]

Benezeth et al. cited a standard formula for many background removal methods:

$$Xt(s) = \begin{cases} 1 \ if \ dIs, t, Bs > \tau \\ \overline{0 \ if \ not} \end{cases} \tag{1}$$

where τ is the threshold, X_t is the movement mark field in time t, d is the difference between $I_{s,t}$ (color in time t of pixels s) and B_s of pixels background s. Between different algorithms, the key is how B is modeled and how d is calculated [30].

Background subtraction algorithms input is color video stream or clip but their output is a black and white video stream or clip. White color represents moving objects and black color represents static background. The main idea of our method is to divide the number of white color pixels with the number of all pixels in the video stream or clip. That ratio is a visual activity quantifier in video stream or clip. It can be expressed as:

$$BGSVAI = \sum n_{fg} / \sum n_{all} \tag{2}$$

where BGSVAI abbreviation for *Background Subtraction Algorithm Visual Activity Index*, n_{fg} is a number of detected moving objects pixels in one frame and n_{all} is the number of all pixels in one frame. The calculation has to be done for all frames in video clip or stream [31].

Since there are dozens of background subtraction algorithms, the question is how to choose the best. The LC4MP is appropriate because this model is empirically proven as a reliable measure of information density. The selection of the algorithm was based on the Spearman correlation between the particular Information density dimension and the particular BGS algorithm. The dataset contains 135 videos and the spreadsheet data from Lang's sample. The total correlation considering information density dimensions was the biggest for Multilayer algorithm. This algorithm is selected. The multilayer algorithm was submitted by Yao et al. [11]. In addition, BGSVAI and VAI are compared using the Spearman correlation test (r = 0,823). It was also done for 135 video clips and the spreadsheet data from Lang's sample.

4 Data, Methodology and Results

In this paper, 40 videos from four YouTube channels have been analyzed. All channels have video clips for language learning.

The first channel is called "LearnArabicwithMaha" and it is on the Internet address https://www.youtube.com/channel/UCPINCItSdAc7SBXxi6AcWpw. It has almost 350000 subscribers and more than 57 million views and it will be called Maha's channel in this paper because Maha is the main speaker on that channel. The first video clip is ten years old.

The second channel is called "Learn English with EnglishClass101.com" on the Internet address https://www.youtube.com/channel/UCeTVoczn9NOZA9blls3YgUg. It has more than 2 million subscribers and more than 82 million views and it will be called Alisha's channel in this paper because Alisha is the main speaker on that channel. The first video clip is nine years old.

The third channel is called "Eat Sleep Dream English" and it is on the Internet address https://www.youtube.com/channel/UCu4AP8qmYnXNUipUeyPQKig. It has more than 180000 subscribers and more than 10 million views and it will be called Tom's channel in this paper because Tom is the main speaker on that channel. The first video clip is two years old.

The fourth channel is called "Learn English with Emma" and it is on the Internet address https://www.youtube.com/channel/UCVBErcpqaokOf4fI5j73K_w. It has more than 2 million subscribers and more than 110 million views and it will be called Emma's channel in this paper because Emma is the main speaker on that channel. The first video clip is seven years old.

All video clips have been downloaded from youtube.com service and BGSVAI have been calculated for every video clip. In Table 1 BGSVAI results can be found in the last column for all videos. List of first ten videos are bolded and they are from Maha's channel, second ten videos are italic with a gray background and they are from Alisha's channel. List of third ten videos are italic and they are from Tom's channel. Last ten videos are bold with a gray background and they are from Emma's channel.

Table 1. Video clips data and BGSVAI values (authors)

Video clip number	Height (pixels)	Width (pixels)	Number of pixels	Number of all fore-ground pixels	Number of all pixels	BGSVAI
1	360	640	230400	401007326	2532787200	0,1583
2	360	640	230400	318661193	2627481600	0,1213
3	360	640	230400	533422161	3491020800	0,1528
4	360	640	230400	217498455	2023833600	0,1075
5	360	640	230400	248854260	1881446400	0,1323
6	360	640	230400	69348306	2184422400	0,0317
7	360	640	230400	231586102	2345932800	0,0987
8	360	640	230400	75726315	1739750400	0,0435
9	356	640	227840	79168770	1423772160	0,0556
10	356	640	227840	187317841	2336271360	0,0802
11	360	640	230400	73919014	2720332800	0,0272
12	360	640	230400	96191823	2793369600	0,0344
13	360	640	230400	104204441	3306240000	0,0315
14	360	640	230400	107092435	3419136000	0,0313
15	360	640	230400	67331418	2381414400	0,0283
16	360	640	230400	74335656	2653977600	0,0280
17	360	640	230400	76108081	3193574400	0,0238
18	360	640	230400	80249325	2806732800	0,0286
19	360	640	230400	86777883	2745446400	0,0316
20	360	640	230400	84178598	2956032000	0,0285
21	360	640	230400	102574236	3207168000	0,0320
22	360	640	230400	109964932	3070080000	0,0358
23	360	640	230400	63442133	2678400000	0,0237
24	360	640	230400	119167634	2326809600	0,0512
25	360	640	230400	90839848	2481868800	0,0366
26	360	640	230400	77614087	2318976000	0,0335
27	360	640	230400	41767768	1775462400	0,0235
28	360	640	230400	34015216	2160691200	0,0157
29	360	640	230400	120122162	3522585600	0,0341
30	360	640	230400	64594476	2583244800	0,0250
31	360	640	230400	82274804	3203251200	0,0257
32	360	640	230400	72080875	3700915200	0,0195
33	360	640	230400	152707069	3158784000	0,0483
34	360	640	230400	70238831	2167833600	0,0324
35	360	640	230400	57498241	2427724800	0,0237
36	360	640	230400	100019035	3666585600	0,0273
37	360	640	230400	64528856	2462745600	0,0262
38	360	640	230400	78863782	2343628800	0,0337
39	360	640	230400	77192604	2290406400	0,0337
40	360	640	230400	105153543	3465216000	0,0303

In the chart on Fig. 6 difference in BGSVAI values between videos can be seen.

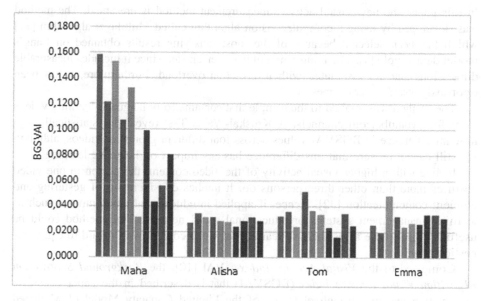

Fig. 6. BGSVAI values for all videos (authors)

Kruskal-Wallis II test was chosen to test the statistical significance of the differences between these four groups of videos and the results are shown in the figure below. GNU pspp 1.2.0-g0fb4db has been used for statistical calculations. In Table 2 mean ranks can be seen.

Table 2. Mean ranks

Group	N	Mean rank
1	10	34,20
2	10	15,10
3	10	17,50
4	10	15,20
Total	40	

A Kruskal-Wallis Test revealed a statistically significant difference in BGSVAI values across four different groups of videos. (Group 1, n = 10: Maha's videos, Group 2, n = 10: Alisha's videos, Group 3, n = 10: Tom's videos, Group 4; n = 10: Emma's videos), χ^2 (3, n = 40) = 18,58, p = .000.

It is obvious that Maha's videos are different which can be seen in videos too, because she gestures with her hands more than other three persons do. It can be quantitatively expressed by BGSVAI.

5 Discussion and Conclusion

In this paper, the new visual activity measurement method is presented. The method was developed by using a computer vision algorithm called Multilayer algorithm [11] which has been selected because of the most satisfying results obtained on Lang's model data sample [9]. The Lang's model has been chosen since it includes measurable dimensions that are associated with information overload. Furthermore, it has been rigorously tested several times.

The method was applied to the sample that contains forty language-learning videos from four youtube.com channels. A Kruskal-Wallis Test revealed a statistically significant difference in BGSVAI values across four different groups of videos, although we still cannot be sure that this difference has any impact on language learning.

In line with a higher visual activity of the video content, the person in one video gestures more than other three persons do. It implies consideration of gesturing and efficient communication [32]. Hence, if applied in educational environments such as learning management systems or educational social networks, the method could be useful to support the assessment of learning of video content with regard to e.g. over-gesticulation.

Compared to the *Visual Activity Index - VAI* [10], the *Background Subtraction Algorithm Visual Activity Index* (BGSVAI) that is described in the paper considers information density through elements of the Limited Capacity Model of Mediated Message Processing (LC4MP). However, all information density dimensions could not be included (e.g. emotions). It is important that mediated message can affect information processing dealing with the way how the message is created. Among others, it includes managing visual structural features of the message such as movement as well as scene or camera changes that are also considered in the BGSVAI. Overall, the LC4MP enables creating a message to achieve the communication purpose, one of which is learning. Thereby, the possibility of using the described method to support determining the border when the information density of an educational video begins to hinder the learning process is given into consideration for further research.

References

1. Kaiser Family Foundation: Generation M2: Media in the Lives of 8- to 18-Year-Olds. Kaiser Family Foundation, Menlo Park, California, USA (2010)
2. Lillard, A.S., Peterson, J.: The immediate impact of different types of television on young children's executive function. Pediatrics **128**, 644–649 (2011)
3. Lang, A.: The limited capacity model of mediated message processing. J. Commun. **50**(1), 46–70 (2000)
4. Lang, A.: Motivated cognition (LC4MP): the influence of appetitive and aversive activation on the processing of video games. Paper presented at the Annual Meeting of the International Communication Association, Sheraton New York, New York City, NY, 25 May 2009. http://www.allacademic.com/meta/p13157_index.html
5. Lang, A.: Using the limited capacity model of motivated mediated message processing to design effective cancer communication messages. J. Commun. **56**(1), S57–S80 (2006)

6. Lang, A.: The limited capacity model of motivated mediated message processing. In: The SAGE Handbook Of media Processes and Effects, pp. 193–204. Sage (2009)
7. Lang, A.: Discipline in crisis? The shifting paradigm of mass communication research. J. Int. Commun. Assoc. **23**(1), 10–24 (2013)
8. Lang, A.: Limited capacity model of motivated mediated message processing (LC4MP). In: The International Encyclopedia of Media Effects, pp. 1–9. Wiley, New York (2017)
9. Fox, J., Park, B., Lang, A.: When available resources become negative resources: the effects of cognitive overload on memory sensitivity and criterion bias. Commun. Res. **34**, 277–296 (2007)
10. Cutting, J., DeLong, K., Brunick, L.: Visual activity in hollywood film: 1935 to 2005 and beyond. Psychol. Aesthet. Creat. Arts **5**, 115–125 (2011)
11. Yao, J., Odobez, J.: Multi-layer background subtraction based on color and texture. In: IEEE Computer Vision and Pattern Recognition Conference, Minneapolis (2007)
12. Rogers, E.M., Agarwala-Rogers, R.: Communication in Organizations. The Free Press, New York (1976)
13. Feather, J.: The Information Society: A Study of Continuity and Change, 2nd edn. Library Association Publishing, London (1998)
14. Eppler, M., Mengis, J.: The concept of information overload: a review of literature from organization science, accounting, marketing, MIS, and related disciplines. Inform. Soc. **20**, 325–344 (2004)
15. Wilson, T.: Information overload: implications for healthcare services. Health Inform. J. **7** (2), 112–117 (2001)
16. Schroder, M., Driver, M., Streufert, S.: Human Information Processing—Individuals and Groups Functioning in Complex Social Situations. Holt, Rinehart & Winston, New York (1967)
17. Pelgrum, W.: Obstacles to the integration of ICT in education: results from a worldwide educational assessment. Comput. Educ. **37**, 163–178 (2001)
18. Graham, A., Anderson, J.: A problem in medical education: is there an information overload? Med. Educ. **14**, 4–11 (1980)
19. Britton, B., Westbrook, R., Holgredge, T.: Reading and cognitive capacity usage: effects of text difficulty. J. Exp. Psychol.: Hum. Learn. Mem. **4**, 582–591 (1978)
20. Britton, B., Tesser, A.: Effects of prior knowledge on use of cognitive capacity in three complex cognitive tasks. J. Verbal Learn. Verbal Behav. **21**, 421–436 (1982)
21. Sutcliffe, A.: Multimedia user interface design. In: The Human-Computer Interaction Handbook – Fundamentals, Evolving Technology and Emerging Applications, 2 edn. Taylor & Francis Group, New York (2008)
22. Gibson, J.: The visual perception of objective motion and subjective movement. Psychol. Rev. **61**, 304–314 (1954)
23. Salt, B.: Statistical style analysis of motion picture. Film Q. **28**(1), 13–22 (1974)
24. Sklar, R.: Film: An International History of the Medium. Thames and Hudson, London (1990)
25. Baxter, M.: Notes on Cinemetric Data Analysis (2014). http://www.cinemetrics.lv/dev/ Cinemetrics_Book_Baxter.pdf. Accessed 6 Aug 2016
26. Brunick, K., Cutting, J., DeLong, J.: Low-level features of film: what they are and why we would be lost without them. In: Psychocinematics – Exploring Cognition at the Movies. Oxford University Press (2013)
27. Cutting, J., Candan, A.: Shot durations, shot classes, and the increased pace of popular movies. Projections **9**(2), 40–62 (2015)

28. Shaikh, S.H., Saeed, K., Chaki, N.: Moving object detection using background subtraction. Moving Object Detection Using Background Subtraction. SCS, pp. 15–23. Springer, Cham (2014). https://doi.org/10.1007/978-3-319-07386-6_3
29. Bouwmans, T.: Background subtraction for visual surveillance: a fuzzy approach. In: Handbook on Soft Computing for Video Surveillance. Taylor and Francis Group (2012)
30. Benezeth, Y., Jodoin, P., Laurent, B., Rosenberger, C.: Comparative study of background subtraction algorithms. J. Electron. Imaging **19**(3), 033003 (2010)
31. Dokic, K.: Measurement of visual activity in a video content based on computer vision methods of background subtraction. In: Infusing Research and Knowledge in South-East Europe, Thessaloniki (2015)
32. Wagner, P., Malisz, Z., Kopp, S.: Gesture and speech in interaction: an overview. Speech Commun. **57**, 209–232 (2014)

A Reflection on E-learning Effectiveness in Tunisia

Rabeb Mbarek[(⊠)]

Carthage, Tunisia
rabeb_mbareke@yahoo.fr

Abstract. This research work aims to identify the determinants of E-learning Effectiveness. This effectiveness is measured through three individual variables: motivation, Individual Effectiveness, and anxiety about technology. The main objective is to enable the various parties involved to better understand the factors influencing E-learning Effectiveness.

The empirical validation of the model was carried out on a sample of 350 learners enrolled in two Tunisian institutions. Empirical validation is provided by factorial analyses and structural equation methods. Based on these analyses, we were able to partially validate the motivation effect, and the computer anxiety on learners' reactions. Furthermore, we were able to verify the important effect of motivation on learning process.

Keywords: E-learning effectiveness · Meta-analysis · Individual effectiveness · Feedback · Reactions · Learning · Transfer · Structural equations

1 Introduction

Since the end of the 1970s, there has been a recurring interest in applying Information and Communication Technology (ICT) in E-learning and online training (Bronfman 2003; Audet 2012; Cottier and Lanéelle 2016). Opportunities for using Information technologies are growing and multiplying rapidly, which contributes to the creation of a new state of mind building a culture of information sharing. These transformations have encouraged the emergence of new forms of learning such as "E-learning". Therefore, E-learning goes to the core of considerations for the renewal of learning mechanisms.

The effectiveness of E-learning concerns two main streams of research: Educational sciences and Information systems (Houze and Meisonnier 2005; Ben Romdhane 2013). Accordingly, E-learning must be effective for the main actors: who are learners. Indeed, it is crucial to point out that, as part of our research, we do not make a difference between «e-learning» and «apprentissage en ligne». Both of these two concepts designate a process of acquiring new knowledge and skills, whether individual or collective, based on information and communication technologies.

A conducted meta-analysis enabled us to explore the literature that allowed us to investigate the determinants of E-learning effectiveness. This theoretical review allowed us to identify three individual factors: motivation, individual effectiveness, and anxiety about technology.

© Springer Nature Switzerland AG 2019
R. Jallouli et al. (Eds.): ICDEc 2019, LNBIP 358, pp. 215–229, 2019.
https://doi.org/10.1007/978-3-030-30874-2_17

Based on these findings, this research has two main objectives. On the one hand, it aims to evaluate the effect of these factors on the efficiency of E-learning in the context of a university course. On the other hand, it seeks to measure the effectiveness of E-learning system.

Indeed, the research question we want to answer is: What are the factors that contribute to effective E-learning?

In terms of formulating our research question, it is most appropriate to adopt the positivist positioning, since it allows us to understand the causal links between these factors on the one hand, and E-learning on the other hand. Therefore, we adopted an exploratory quantitative approach followed by a confirmatory analysis to test the hypothetical links of our conceptual model.

In order to collect data, we chose to develop an E-learning platform: «aad-tunisie. com», which made the conduct of the experiment easier for us, in terms of assuring the management and the control of the system.

2   Theoretical Research Framework

E-learning is one of the new emerging technologies which replace or complement traditional pedagogical approaches. This practice is distinguished by certain specific aspects in that it sets up new pedagogical approaches. Thus, E-learning consists of an educational device through any electronic media (Tastlew et al. 2005). Therefore, learners acquire knowledge through an individual use of digital medias such as: computers, CD-ROMs, Internet, Intranet, wireless technologies, etc. (Homan and Macpherson 2005; Imamoglu 2007).

Several studies have studied the factors that play a key role in the effectiveness of a pedagogical platform by learners (Houze and Meizonnier 2005; Fenouillet and Dero 2006; Wang et al 2007; Lim et al. 2007a, b; Lee and Lee 2008). This research suggests that measuring E-learning effectiveness is a serious issue, whose scope has been limited in many studies using traditional learning as a benchmark (Ben Zammel et al. 2016).

The training's effectiveness reflects the study of the variables that seem to influence the results of training at different levels: before, during and after (Alvarez et al. 2004). Therefore, multiple measures of E-learning effectiveness were used: Wang et al (2007) proposed a «multi-criteria» model for the assessment of E-learning effectiveness, which is based on the six following dimensions: System Quality, Information Quality, Service Quality, System Use, User Satisfaction, System Advantages. On their behalf, Lee and Lee (2008) developed a model measuring E-learning effectiveness, through which, the authors showed that the effectiveness is determined by the learner's satisfaction.

3   Study's Context

In this research, we opted for designing an online learning platform, «aad-tunisie», based on an «open source» technology. We also chose to conduct a scheduled laboratory experiment with students having the opportunity to take an online course. In this respect, two institutions have been the subject of our experiment: The Higher Institute of Technological Studies of Nabeul and a Modern Language and IT Training Center.

In this context, we carried out a laboratory experiment based on the administration of two parts of a questionnaire: before and after navigation on the platform. The experiment took place over a period of 16 weeks during the year 2015–2016. Moreover, experimentation enabled us to measure cause-and-effect relationships (Evrard et al. 2003). To this effect, it will be used, through the questionnaire, to measure the effects on the dependent variables (reaction, E-learning and transfer) and on the independent variables (Computer anxiety and motivation) (Evrard et al. 2003).

The laboratory experiment is planned in three steps synthesized in the following table (Table 1):

Table 1. The stages of the experiment

Step 1	The student is present to participate in the study. Before starting navigation, he/she is asked to fill out the first part of a questionnaire devoted to measure the socio-demographic information of the respondent
Step 2	The respondent is invited to read the administered experiment procedure, before browsing the site to take a computer architecture course administered on the platform «aad-tunisie.com»
Step 3	Once the online course is completed, the respondent is asked to complete the second part of the questionnaire in order to measure the model variables

4 Theoretical Framework and Establishment of the Research Model

Our research work highlights two kinds of variables: four independent variables (anxiety about technology, motivation, individual effectiveness, and feedback), and a dependent variable (E-learning) which will be explained in what follows.

4.1 Influence Relationships Between the Individual Determinants and the Situational Determinant

4.1.1 The Effect of the Feedback on Motivation

Social cognitive theory considers that the feedback plays a significant role in the self-regulation of motivation. In this regard, the feedback seems to have an effect on the direction of efforts, the development of energy and the learner's challenge to fulfill their education. In this context, Zimmerman (2000) suggests that feedback influences motivation. In fact, the author considers that the feedback is one of the modalities enabling learners to develop their desires, their efforts and their perseverance in order to accomplish their actions. Several studies have shown that the feedback has an influence on the motivational processes (Zimmerman 2000). Furthermore, the feedback has a positive effect on learners' desire to follow or to repeat the learning experience.

Indeed, the more feedback the learner gets, the more efforts he will make to easily accomplish a learning behavior, and the more he will believe in his/her abilities to succeed a learning experience (Zimmerman 2000).

As part of our research, we believe that the feedback is a significant determinant of E-learning motivation. Thus, we draw upon the literature review and the social cognitive theory to put forward the following hypothesis:

H1: Positive feedback influences learners' motivation more positively and more significantly than negative feedback.

4.1.2   The Effect of Individual Computer Effectiveness on Motivation

The social cognitive theory considers that the individual effectiveness of learners plays a key role in the self-regulation of motivation. In this context, Bandura (1998) states that the individual effectiveness influences the level of effort, the perseverance, and the choice of activities. Moreover, Zimmerman (2000) suggests that the individual effectiveness has shown a convergent validity by influencing the key indicators of motivation, such as the choice of activities, the effort level, and the emotional reactions. By referring to the meta-analysis conducted by Multon et al. (1991), individual effectiveness seems to have a considerable effect on motivation according to the effort and the perseverance. Indeed, many studies have shown that individual effectiveness influences the motivational processes (Zimmerman 2000).

Thus, Zimmerman (2000) concluded that individual effectiveness is positively regarding the learner's effort to complete his apprenticeship. In fact, the more the learner believes in his/her abilities, the easier he will deal with a difficult task (Bandura 1998). Accordingly, the more the learner believes in his/her abilities to succeed his apprenticeship, the more he will have a desire to make an effort to complete that learning experience; and subsequently he/she will be motivated to learn.

Furthermore, Zimmerman (2000) considers that individual effectiveness predicts motivation in several ways. Thus, according to the author, the learners' beliefs allow them to identify their objectives. Moreover, the learners' beliefs and confidence make them more persistent to difficulties and to the assimilation of failures.

The results of the literature review and the social cognitive theory lead us to study the effect of the individual effectiveness on learners' motivation.

Thus, we formulate the following hypothesis:

H2: Individual computer effectiveness positively influences learners' motivation.

4.1.3   The Effect of Individual Computer Effectiveness on Anxiety About Technology

By referring to the social cognitive theory, Bandura (1998) considers that the fact that learners believe they have the ability to control the execution of their apprenticeship influence their emotional states, such as frustration, fear, anxiety, and stress, as well as motivation and learning results. Furthermore, the more anxious, frustrated, threatened and stressed the learner feels, the more negative cognitive representations leading to depression he/she will suffer from. Moreover, Bandura (1998) adds that the learners who believe in their abilities to accomplish successful future actions develop positive scenarios for their performance. In contrast, the learners who doubt their individual effectiveness develop negative scenarios that lead them to failure in the learning experience.

Many researchers have studied the effect of individual effectiveness on the emotional reactions of learners (Compeau and Higgins 1995; Chou 2001). In fact, Chou (2001) found that the more the learner believes in his ability to properly perform an action, the less he will be anxious or frustrated. In this respect, the individual effectiveness contributes to the regulation of learners' anxiety through the control over the person's thinking (Ozer and Bandura 1990). Individual effectiveness influences the perception of threats, as well as their cognitive processing process (Bandura 1998).

Bandura (1998) considers that social support plays a principal role in reducing learners' stress and fear. He adds that the individual effectiveness of learners reduces the anxiety through the support provided by the modalities of conduct, which turn an insecure environment into a secure one.

The results of the literature review and the social cognitive theory lead us to study the effect of individual effectiveness on learners' motivation.

Therefore, we will test the following hypothesis:

H3: Individual computer effectiveness positively influences anxiety about technology.

4.2 Influence Relationships Between Individual Determinants and E-learning

4.2.1 Motivation

Motivation can be defined as the desire, willingness, energy, effort, and intention to learn a learning content and to achieving the objectives (Meyer and Becker 2004; Guillemet 2014). In what follows, we will deal with the influence of motivation on reaction, on the one hand, and on learning, on the other.

Many researchers have found that motivation significantly and positively influences learning outcomes, such as learner's reaction (Noe and Schmitt 1986; Noe 1986; Baldwin and Ford 1988; Warr and Bunce 1995; Colquitt and Lepine 2000; Ainley et al. 2002). In this regard, the more motivated the learner is, the more he/she will positively influence the outcomes of this learning experience (Facteau et al 1995; Noe and Wilk 1993; Guillemet 2014).

Then, we can develop the following hypothesis:

H4: Motivation to learn has a positive influence on learner's learning.

4.3 Anxiety About Technology

Anxiety is considered by the literature as a negative emotional state, more precisely, a fear revealed when a person is confronted with an undesirable situation. Meanwhile, computer anxiety refers to a general feeling of nervousness, fear, anxiety, and stress anticipating negative results in relation to computer-related actions (Chang 2005).

Previous research has shown the negative influence between anxiety about technology and Learning (Warr and Bunce 1995; Brosman 1998; Chou 2001; Cybinski and

Selvanathan 2005). In fact, the more frustrated, stressed, nervous and anxious the learner is, the less he/she will provide thoughts and attention in order to acquire new knowledge and skills. Accordingly, the higher the learner's level of anxiety is, the more embarrassed and troubled he/she will be when fulfilling a learning experience.

Therefore, the anxiety is one of the most important psychological traits of the social cognitive theory incorporated into research on the effectiveness of learning.

Thus, anxious learners may show negative perceptions regarding the acquisition of knowledge and new skills in their learning experience compared to less-anxious learners (Sitzmann et al. 2008). We can then introduce the following hypothesis:

H5: Learner's anxiety about technology negatively affects E-learning effectiveness (Fig. 1).

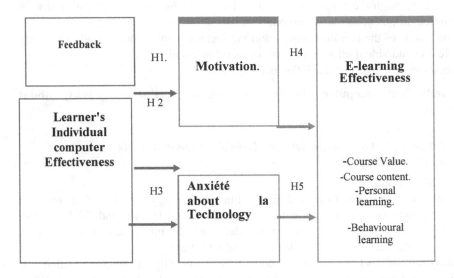

Fig. 1. Conceptual research model: the determinants of E-learning effectiveness

5   Research Methodology

In what follows, we will present a description of our sample, as well as the questionnaire administered. We will also explain the method of data analysis.

Our sample is made up of 260 learners under the age of 20, 51 learners aged 20 to 29, 38 learners aged 30 to 39, and one learner aged 40 to 49. Moreover, the sample of learners is mainly composed of men (301).

5.1   Questionnaire Development

The questionnaire of the present research was developed in the light of operationalizing the previously defined concepts and measuring the relationships set out in the theoretical model.

Hence, we assigned items drawn from information system and educational science research for each variable of the model. Consequently, these items have been adapted to the Tunisian context by the introduction of some modifications.

The average time required to complete the questionnaire is 15 to 20 min. In this context, the questionnaire is available to respondents in two stages: A first stage "T1" before starting the experiment, in which learners are required to give socio-demographic information, and a second stage T2, in which the second part of the questionnaire is communicated at the end of the experiment; that is after 16 weeks. Our final sample is made up of 350 persons.

The questionnaire was first submitted to a pre-test in order to assess the validity of its content and to check the respondents' understanding of questions. Thus, we conducted a first experiment with 105 learners, including 60 learners studying in the Higher Institute of Technological Studies of Nabeul and 45 ones from the Modern Language and IT Training Center of Nabeul.

5.2   Data Analysis Methods

In order to validate the constructs, we performed a confirmatory factor analysis, including a principal components analysis (PCA) with varimax rotation under SPSS 16.0, and a convergent validity analysis under Amos 20.0. We also calculated the Cronbach Alpha coefficient to ensure the internal consistency of our search variables.

The results are presented in the following table (Table 2):

Table 2. Syntheses of factor analyses

Variables	Analysis	PCA	Fiability	Validity
	Rating	**Explained Variance in %**	**L of cranbach > 0.6**	**P of validation > 0.5**
Motivation	Motivation	67.598	0.878	0.597
Individual Effectiveness	Individual computer Effectiveness	75.651	0.891	0.676
Anxiety about technology	Anxiety about technology la	65.659	0.824	0.545
Feedback	Positive Feedback	51.483	0.827	0.598
	Negative Feedback	67.026	0.908	
Learning	Personal Learning	20.915	0.936	0.619
	Course value	18.275	0.878	
	Course content	16.401	0.824	
	Behavioral Learning	15.783	0.824	

6 Empirical Research Results

We will deal with the statistical analyses of two partial models through a confirmatory factor analysis. Then, we will analyze the results of the different structural models in order to answer the research question.

6.1 First Partial Model Test

See Fig. 2 and Table 3.

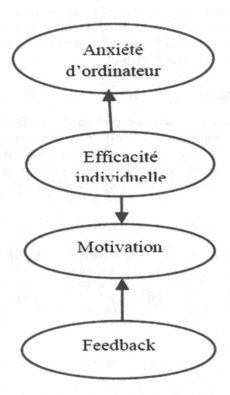

Fig. 2. The structural model regarding the links between E-learning determinants

Table 3. The results of the analysis of the first partial structural model

Liens structurels		Coefficients non standardisés	CR	P
motivation <--- Effica_indiv_ordi		1,427	3,853	0,000
Anxiété_tech <--- Effica_indiv_ordi		0,807	2,803	0,000
motivation <--- Feedback_po		0,564	6,447	0,000
motivation <--- Feedback_ne		0,676	5,886	0,000
Indices d'ajustement		Valeurs constatées		
Chi-deux		59,076		
Degré de liberté		43		
P		0,052		
Chi-deux /degrés de liberté		1,374		
GFI		0,978		
AGFI		0,954		
RMR		0,022		
RMSEA		0,030		
TLI		0,991		
CFI		0,995		
BIC du modèle/BIC du modèle saturé		347,852 /547,470		

The results of the confirmatory factor analysis regarding the partial structural model are acceptable and show the good fit of the model. Indeed, the values of GFI, AGFI and RMSEA are very satisfactory. In this respect, we can conclude that the first partial structural model is fitted to the data. Furthermore, the chi-square standardized at a value of (1.374), which respects the strictest parsimony conditions. The TLI and CFI indicators show satisfactory results (greater than 0.9). The BIC compared to the saturated model shows a good fit.

6.2 Second Partial Model Test

This step is based on testing the links between E-learning determinants (motivation and technological anxiety), and Learning dimensions (course values, course content, personal learning and behavioral learning). We used the second data collection (n = 350) and applied the structural equation method to the structural model below (Fig. 3 and Table 4).

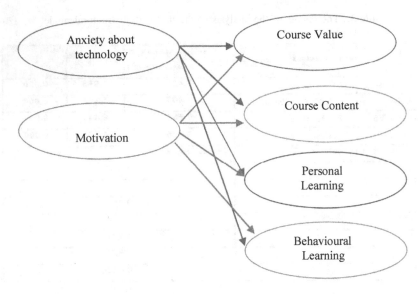

Fig. 3. The structural model regardingthe links between E-learning determinants and the Learning dimensions

Table 4. The results of the second structural model analysis

Liens structurels		Coefficients non standardisés	CR	P
Valeur_cours	<— Anxiété_ tech	0,388	3,692	0,000
contenu cours	<— Anxiété tech	0,217	6,363	0,000
Apprenti personnel	<— Anxiété tech	0,237	7,876	0,000
Apprenti comp	<— Anxiété tech	0,630	4,093	0,000
Valeur cours	<— Effica indiv ordi	0,760	4,427	0,000
Contenu cours	<— Effica indiv ordi	0,346	7,493	0,000
Apprenti personnel	<— Effica indiv ordi	1,048	7,411	0,000
Apprenti comp	<— Effica indiv ordi	0,069	3,347	0,000
Valeur cours	<— motivation	1,000	6,480	0,000
contenu cours	<— motivation	0,576	5,439	0,000
Apprenti personnel	<— motivation	1,110	6,423	0,000
Apprenti comp	<— motivation	0,588	6,666	0,000
Valeur cours	<— Feedback po	0,365	6,635	0,000
contenu cours	<— Feedback po	0,286	7,494	0,000
Apprenti personnel	<— Feedback po	0,000	6,464	0,000
Apprenti comp	<— Feedback po	0,742	8,679	0,000
Valeur cours	<— Feedback ne	0,727	6,136	0,000
Contenu cours	<— Feedback ne	0,461	3,447	0,000
Apprenti personnel	<— Feedbak ne	1,082	6,681	0,000
Apprenti comp	<— Feedback ne	0,131	7,411	0,000
Indices d'ajustement		**Valeurs constatées**		
Chi-deux		330,126		
Degré de liberté		155		
P		0,000		
Chi –deux /degrés de liberté		1,750		
GFI		0,885		
AGFI		0,887		
RMR		0,045		
RMSEA		0,04		
TLI		0,960		
CFI		0,970		
BIC du modele/BIC du modele saturé		1285,346/2367,234		

The results of the confirmatory factor analysis regarding the second structural model are acceptable, and they show the good fit of the model. In fact, the values of the GFI and AGFI are close to the appropriate standards. This gives us the opportunity to conclude on the fit of the model to the data. Our model meets parsimony standards since the standardized Chi-square has a satisfactory value (1,750), which is less than 3.

7 Discussion of the Findings

7.1 Discussion of Findings on the Causality Links Between the Determinants of E-learning Effectiveness

7.1.1 The Effect of Feedback on Learners' Motivation

The hypothesis regarding the effect of feedback on the motivation has been validated. This relationship is more significant for positive feedback than negative feedback. Therefore, the structural link is significant in the positive sense for the two dimensions of feedback, respectively ($t = 6.447 > 5.886$, with $p = 0.000$).

Our finding is in line with the social cognitive theory considering that the feedback has a significant effect on motivation (Wood and Bandura 1989). In this regard, learners can show more effort, energy and willingness to learn when they receive a feedback on their level of progress in their learning process.

7.1.2 The Effect of Individual Computer Effectiveness on Learners' Motivation

The hypothesis on the effect of the individual computer effectiveness on motivation has been equally validated. Indeed, the hypothesis states that the relationship between the individual effectiveness on the one hand, and learning motivation on the other hand, shows a positive and significant structural link ($t = 3,853$, $p = 0.000$).

Furthermore, the motivation seems to be influenced by individual computer effectiveness. This result goes along with what is proposed by the social cognitive theory, which considers that the individual effectiveness has a significant effect on the motivation (Wood and Bandura 1989). In this context, learners can show more effort, energy and willingness to learn when they believe in their abilities and skills to take a course administered online.

7.1.3 The Effect of the Individual Computer Effectiveness on Computer Anxiety

The hypothesis dealing with the effect of the individual computer effectiveness on computer anxiety is confirmed. Indeed, we found significant results regarding the influence of the individual computer effectiveness on computer anxiety. In fact, the individual computer effectiveness seems to have a significant linear link with computer anxiety ($t = 2.803$, $p = 0.000$). This result confirms the findings of previous research (Compeau and Higgins 1995; Chou 2001). This can be explained by the fact that, when using new technologies, learners associate a relationship between their fears and frustration, and their abilities and skills to use computers. The more learners believe in their abilities to use new technologies, the more their fears and anxieties diminish.

7.2   Discussion of Results on the Background of Learning and E-learning

7.2.1   The Effect of the Motivation on the Learning Process

As for the link between motivation and learning, the result obtained has been validated. This relationship is significant for the course value, the course content, the personal learning, and the behavioral learning. At this time, the structural link is significant for the four dimensions ($t = 5.480$, $p = 0.000$, $t = 5.439$, $p = 0.000$, $t = 6.423$, $p = 0.000$, $t = 6.666$, $p = 0.000$).

This confirms the results of several studies (Noe 1986; Colquitt and Lepine 2000; Tai 2006) in the field.

7.2.2   The Effect of Computer Anxiety on Learning

The hypothesis about the effect of computer anxiety on learning was rejected. Indeed, computer anxiety seems to have significant linear links to the course value, the course content, the personal learning, and the behavioral learning ($t = 3.692$, $p = 0.000$, $t = 6.353$, $p = 0.000$, $t = 7.875$, $p = 0.000$, $t = 4.093$, $p = 0.000$).

Accordingly, we can mention that computer anxiety positively influences learning. In other words, the fear and frustration of a learner motivate them to learn. This result contradicts the those found by several researchers such as Chou (2001) and Brosman (1998). Furthermore, the authors showed that the fear and frustration negatively influence learning. Finally, learning is significantly influenced, in a positive way, by the anxiety behavior that learners carry out in terms of using computers.

8   Conclusion

Throughout this research, we tried to understand the E-learning effectiveness on learners and its principal determinants. A literature review enabled us to define the explanatory of E-learning effectiveness. In the light of this theoretical approach, we proposed a conceptual model integrating the explanatory factors of E-learning effectiveness and its measures.

To test the model, we developed an E-learning platform to collect data resulting from an E-learning experience over a 16-week period. Our theoretical and empirical findings highlight the contributions and the limitations that will be mentioned hereinafter.

These choices were made while respecting the results of the literature review. Moreover, the empirical results confirmed the existence of these dimensions.

Our research work provides a better understanding of the factors influencing the effectiveness of learning. By referring to our meta-analysis, most of the research is concerned with the direct influence of these factors, through learning.

In fact, our objective is to promote the learning process to be effective, in order to minimize the failure rate, and subsequently the rejection of this new learning method. To achieve this, prior actions must be taken by the organizations through action on the determinants of E-learning effectiveness.

In other words, it would be interesting to act on the motivation and to create a favorable learning environment in order to reduce the feeling of fear that can invade the learner.

Therefore, the leaders should give more importance to the technological infrastructure to satisfy learners (clear, friendly, easy to use...), so that learners will be motivated to take an online course. Indeed, the e-learning system must be clear, understandable and user-friendly.

Thereafter, the leaders have to promote the abilities and skills of learners regarding the use of new E-learning technologies, which can be achieved through the creation of an awareness service. This will enable the learners to reveal the importance, the easiness, the friendliness of the learning platform on the one hand, and will assist them in their first learning courses, on the other hand.

The organization should also pay special attention to the communication between the learner - the tutor, in order to inform learners of their progress levels in the learning process. In this respect, the organization should ensure the quality of distance communication between the learner and the tutor.

References

Ainley, M., Hidi, S., Berndorff, D.: Interest, learning, and the psychological processes that mediate their relationship. J. Educ. Psychol. **94**, 545–561 (2002)

Alvarez, K., Salas, E., Garofan, C.M.: An integrated model of training evaluation and effectiveness. Hum. Resour. Dev. Rev. **3**(4), 385–416 (2004)

Audet, L.: Regards sur l'évolution de la formation à distance au Canada francophone. Distances et savoirs **9**(3), 313–330 (2012)

Baldwin, T.T., Ford, J.K.: Transfer of training: a review and directions for future research. Pers. Psychol. **41**(1), 63–105 (1988)

Bandura, A.: Personal and collaborative efficacy in human adaptation and change. Adv. Psychol. Sci. **1**, 52–71 (1998)

Ben Zammel, I., Chichti, F., Gharbi, J.E.: Comment favoriser le transfert d'apprentissage dans l'organisation par le biais de l'utilisation du e-learning? Réflexion à partir du contexte tunisien. @GRH **3**(20), 81–101 (2016)

Ben Romdhane, E.: La question de l'acceptation des outils de e-learning par les apprenants: quels dimensions et déterminants en milieu universitaire tunisien? Revue internationale des technologies en pédagogie universitaire **10**(1), 45–57 (2013)

Bronfman, S.V.: Facteurs de succès dans la mise en place d'un projet e-learning: une recherche action. In: Conférence de L'AIM, Grenoble (2003)

Brosman, M.J.: The impact of computer anxiety and self-efficacy upon performance. J. Comput. Assist. Learn. **14**, 223–234 (1998)

Chang, S.E.: Computer anxiety and perception of task complexity in learning programming – related skills. Comput. Hum. Behav. **21**, 713–728 (2005)

Chau, H.W., Wang, T.B.: The influence of learning style and training method on self-efficacy and learning performance in WWW homepage design training. Int. J. Inf. Manage. **20**, 455–472 (2000)

Chou, H.W.: Effects of training method and computer anxiety on learning performance and self efficacy. Comput. Hum. Behav. **17**, 51–69 (2001)

Colquitt, J.A., Lepine, J.A.: Toward an Integrative theory of training motivation: a meta – analytic path analysis of 20 years of research. J. Appl. Psychol. **85**(5), 678–707 (2000)

Compeau, D.R., Higgins, Ch.A.: Computer self-efficacy: development of a measure and initial test. MIS Q. 189–211 (1995)

Cottier, P., Laneelle, X.: Enseignement et formation en régime numérique: nouveaux rythmes, nouvelles temporalités? Distances et médiations des savoirs **16**, 1–26 (2016)

Cybinski, P., Selvanathan, S.: Learning experience and learning effectiveness in undergraduate statistics: modelling performance in traditional and flexible learning environments. Decis. Sci. J. Innov. Educ. **3**(2), 251–271 (2005)

Evrard, Y., Pras, B., Roux, E.: Market - études et recherches en marketing, Paris, 3ème éditions Dunod (2003)

Facteau, J.D., Dobbins, G.H., Russell, J.E.A., Ladd, R.T., Kudisch, J.D.: The influence of general perceptions of the training environment on pre-training motivation and perceived training transfer. J. Manag. **21**, 1–25 (1995)

Fenouillet, F., Dero, M.: Le e-learning est il efficace? Une analyse de la literature anglo-saxonnes. Savoirs **12**, 87–100 (2006)

Guillemet, P.: Les étudiants préfèrent Facebook. Distance et médiations des savoirs **6** (2014). https://doi.org/10.4000/dms.762

Homan, G., Macpherson, A.: E-learning in the corporate university. J. Eur. Ind. Training **29**(1), 75–90 (2005)

Houze, E., Meissonier, R.: Performance du e-learning: de l'amélioration des résultats de l'apprenant à la prise en compte des enjeux institutionnels. Systèmes d'Information et Management **10**(4), 1–26 (2005)

Imamoglu, Z.S.: An empirical analysis concerning the user acceptance of e-learning. J. Am. Acad. Bus. Cambrige **11**(1), 132–137 (2007)

Lee, J.-K., Lee, W.-K.: The relationship of e-learner's self-regulatory efficacy and perception of e-Learning environmental quality. Comput. Hum. Behav. **24**, 32–47 (2008)

Lim, H., Lee, S.G., Nam, K.: Validating e-learning affecting training effectiveness. Int. J. Inf. Manage. **27**, 22–35 (2007a)

Lim, J., Kim, M., Chen, S.S., Ryder, C.E.: An empirical investigation of student achievement and satisfaction in different learning environments. J. Instr. Psychol. **35**(2), 113–119 (2007b)

Meyer, J.P., Becker, T.E.: Employee commitment and motivation: a conceptual analysis and integrative model. J. Appl. Psychol. **89**(6), 991–1007 (2004)

Multon, K.D., Brown, S.D., Lent, R.W.: Relation of self-efficacy beliefs to academic outcomes: a meta-analytic investigation. J. Couns. Psychol. **18**, 30–38 (1991)

Noe, R.A.: Trainees' attributes and attitudes: neglected influences on training effectiveness. Acad. Manag. Rev. **11**(4), 736–749 (1986)

Noe, R.A., Schmitt, N.: The influence of trainee attitudes on training effectiveness: that of a model. Pers. Psychol. **39**, 497–523 (1986)

Noe, R.A., Wilk, S.L.: Investigation of the factors that influence employees' participation in development activities. J. Appl. Psychol. **78**(2), 291–302 (1993)

Ozer, E.M., Bandura, A.: Mechanisms governing empowerment effects: a self-efficacy analysis. J. Pers. Soc. Psychol. **58**, 472–486 (1990)

Sitzmann, T., Brown, K.G., Caper, W.J., Ely, K., Zimmerma, R.D.: A review and meta – analysis of nomological network of trainee reactions. J. Appl. Psychol. **93**(2), 280–295 (2008)

Tai, W.T.: Effects of training framing, general self-efficacy and training motivation on trainees' training effectiveness. Pers. Rev. **35**(1), 51–65 (2006)

Tastlew, J., White, B.A., Shackleton, P.: E-learning in higher education: the challenge, effort, and return on investment. Int. J. E-Learning **4**(2), 241–251 (2005)

Wang, Y., Wang, H., Shee, D.Y.: Measuring e-learning systems success in an organizational context: scale development and validation. Comput. Hum. Behav. **23**, 1792–1808 (2007)

Warr, P., Bunce, D.: Trainee characteristics and the outcomes of open learning. Pers. Psychol. **48**(2), 347–375 (1995)

Wood, R., Bandura, A.: Social cognitive theory of organizational management. Acad. Manag. Rev. **14**(3), 361–384 (1989)

Zimmerman, J.B.: Self-efficacy: an essential motive to learn. Contemp. Educ. Psychol. **25**, 82–91 (2000)

Deeper Learning Versus Surface Learning: The SAMR Model to Assess E-Learning Pedagogy

Dina Shouman[1,2(✉)] and Levon Momdjian[1,2]

[1] Lebanese University, Beirut, Lebanon
{Dina.shouman,Levon.momdjian}@liu.edu.lb
[2] Lebanese International University, Beirut, Lebanon

Abstract. Designing e-learning tasks that are built around emerging web-based tools and mobile technology enhance learning and truly transform the learning experience, where students experience deeper learning. The SAMR model helps assess the extent to which any instructional technology tool is used to achieve a transformative level of learning and understanding, making sure that the tool is contributing to deeper learning. The paper looks at two case studies and evaluates the depth of knowledge and learning achieved through traditional pedagogy and e-pedagogy.

Keywords: Deeper learning · E-learning pedagogy · SAMR model · EFL

1 Introduction

E-learning has been around since the 1960s; however, it wasn't until the 1990 s that traditional e-learning methods began to be widely implemented. The two main contributing factors for this change were the World Wide Web and learning management systems. These learning management systems has made it possible for educators to upload, manage and disseminate course content to their students. Students started submitting their assignments and doing assessments online. Discussion forums were being used to create more interaction in courses that incepted e-learning. By the mid-2000s, learning management systems were being widely used in tertiary educational institutions in the US and the UK [1–3], which gradually moved to other levels of the education system and eventually spread to the world.

Students now have almost continuous access to mobile devices, such as laptops, tablets and smartphones, providing them with more opportunities for e-learning. Rather than having to assign online materials for students to see in a computer lab or at home, educators are now asking students to bring their mobile devices to their classrooms. This has given students a new learning environment, a blend of traditional learning and e-learning [4].

However, educators have been somewhat slow to adopt these new technologies in a way that transforms learning, at a time when industry is challenging educational institutions to better equip students for the marketplace [5]. This delay in implementing new e-learning methods may be putting learners at a disadvantage.

© Springer Nature Switzerland AG 2019
R. Jallouli et al. (Eds.): ICDEc 2019, LNBIP 358, pp. 230–238, 2019.
https://doi.org/10.1007/978-3-030-30874-2_18

In this paper, it is argued that the need today is for more advanced e-learning strategies different from the ones widely used. The shift towards e-pedagogies that promote the transfer of sills and deeper learning is imperative. Educators need to adopt instructional methods and strategies that encourage cooperative learning, expanded web-based inquiries, apprenticeships, interdisciplinary multimedia-based projects, and other opportunities for students to discuss complex ideas, to associate academic subjects with their personal interests, and to solve open-ended, real-world problems. This is not to say that instructors can't teach for deeper learning without technology. Rather, innovative technological tools and media can be extremely conducive to students' deep learning and can be helpful to many teachers who would otherwise struggle to design such a learning opportunity. First, traditional methods and their limitations will be discussed. Then, the reasons for change, such as new emerging technologies and industry demands, are presented. Next, a model for managing the introduction of technology, SAMR model [6], and new innovative pedagogies are described.

2 Theoretical Background

2.1 Traditional Pedagogical Methods and Their Limitations

The term e-learning is mostly a recent term. In the 1980s and early 1990s, educators were using the term Computer-Based Learning or CBL [7]. Hackbarth [8] identified at least eight categories in CBL: "drill-and-practice, tutorials, problem solving, simulation, electronic performance, support system, testing, and programming" (p. 192). Based on these eight categories, teachers could design or select CBL materials that fit their educational goals or aims, in an attempt ensure an effective learning experience for their students. In most cases, the drill-and-practice and testing categories were the ones that teachers heavily relied on. Since students lacked access to computers or mobile devices in class, they had to receive instruction in traditional ways then go home and practice on their own computers or move to a computer lab to do a computer-based test.

As a result of the expansion of the World Wide Web and the innovation of learning management systems in the mid-1990s, e-learning started rising rapidly and prominently. The emergence of e-learning introduced a myriad of new possibilities and tools. Nevertheless, the shift towards these new opportunities did not always happen instantly and/or completely. In many cases, the main focus remained on drill-and-practice and testing activities. Although these activities are important for learning, they do not adequately exploit all the possibilities presented by the evolving technological software and tools to provide learners with a learning experience that equips them with 21st Century Skills.

2.2 21st Century Skills: Call for Change

The main reasons calling for change are the demands being placed on educational institutions by the industry and governments. According to the Horizon Report for Higher Education, "digital media literacy continues its rise in importance as a key skill in every discipline and profession" [5]. The marketplace is now expecting college graduates to have these skills. In addition, most of the demanded skills nowadays are skills that college graduates usually acquire in informal learning settings rather than in universities [9]. These skills, which have been referred to as 21st Century Skills, include critical thinking and problem solving, collaboration and communication, global awareness and information literacy [10, 11].

Educators have realized this, with the result that the use of new mobile technology, the Web, and Web-based tools is widely spreading through e-learning pedagogies. However, "simply capitalizing on new technology is not enough; the new pedagogical models must use these tools and services to engage students on a deeper level" [9]. Models such as the SAMR model [6] can be used to evaluate whether the use of new technology is actually achieving the desired level of learning and properly equipping learners with the demanded skills.

2.3   Puentedura's SAMR Model

Puentedura [6] has developed the SAMR model (Fig. 1) to help educators effectively infuse technology into teaching and learning, where they can enhance or transform the use of instructional technology through Bloom's higher order thinking skills. This model presents four levels of technological usage in a learning activity: substitution, augmentation, modification, and redefinition. Puentedura's model indicates that a technological tool has not helped in transforming the task until it reaches the levels of modification or redefinition. When designing e-learning tasks using all the continuously evolving online tools and mobile technology, it's important that the tasks not only enhance learning by achieving substitution and/or augmentation, but truly transform learning by modifying and/or redefining a task, which is the exact meaning of deeper learning [4]. However, it is important to understand that arriving at the level of redefining tasks with the technology being used is not an instantaneous process; it may take more time than expected. Puentedura [12] assumes that it may take up to three years for an educator to grow in using a particular technology from substitution to redefinition.

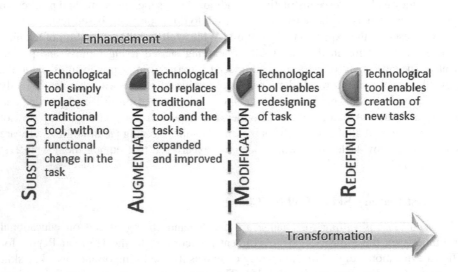

Fig. 1. SAMR model. Adapted from As We May Teach: Educational Theory, from Theory into Practice, by R. Puentedura, 2009

1. Substitution

At this level, e-learning tools simply substitute older methods and tools. Students are encouraged to complete the same tasks but online. Not much is changed in the level or scope of the required task.

2. Augmentation

Students are encouraged at this level to explore the additional new features that the online tools offer. The teaching and learning process experiences a functional change, an enhancement.

3. Modification

This third step involves changes to the task itself. Learning is not only enhanced at this stage but also transformed. The e-learning experience gives students the ability to add depth to the tasks by providing new tools.

4. Redefinition

At this stage, the potential for creativity and innovation is unleashed. Learners can venture into new online tasks that were not possible to do offline.

3 Discussion: Case Studies

Two detailed case studies will be discussed to show how the e-learning experience has contributed to the transformational change in knowledge as assessed by the SAMR model, leading to deeper learning and comparatively greater integration of 21st Century Skills. Both case studies were conducted in courses within the pre-service teacher training program in one of Lebanon's private universities. E-learning was introduced into three different courses: One course presents educational psychology and developmental theories, another course presents advanced grammar concepts to pre-service teachers and requires that they design lessons for teaching these concepts, and a third course introduces educational research and requires that the learners conduct research projects. Different sections of each course were offered during the same semester, and all sections followed the same syllabus, learning outcomes, and textbooks. However, in some of these sections, various online technological apps were used in a highly e-learning environment, and in the other sections, instruction was mainly in a traditional face-to-face classroom with occasional use of instructional technology.

3.1 Case Study 1: Learning in a Traditional Face-to-Face Classroom

The Setting

The first case study was selected from those sections of the above-mentioned courses that did not integrate e-learning in their classes. The 386 students were part of a pre-service teacher training program, some majoring in Teaching English as a Second Language and others in Childhood Education. Instructors followed the same syllabus and offered the same assessment process. Occasional instructional technology tools were used in delivering the lessons, but most instruction happened in a traditional face-to-face setting.

Applying the SAMR Model

The lessons did not achieve the level of deep learning needed as assessed by the SAMR model. Most instruction was conducted in a traditional classroom setting, with occasional use of instructional technology. The multimedia resources that instructors sometimes used helped in achieving substitution and augmentation. However, very little was done through the use of online resources to modify or redefine tasks. Therefore, while it is possible that instructors came near to the deeper learning through other instructional strategies and techniques, no technological tool was used to transform the learning process, increase transfer of knowledge, and thus achieve deeper learning.

3.2   Case Study 2: E-Learning in a Blended Classroom

The Setting

This case is selected from those sections of the same courses that fostered a blend of e-learning with traditional face-to-face instruction. The 163 students had to explore the material and learn concepts through online multimedia resources, teacher-learner and learner-learner communication happened through online platforms, and most assessments were conducted through these online tools. Students were given some control over the pace and path of the learning process. However, this e-learning mode was coupled with face-to-face interaction and teaching practices in the classroom. The e-learning experience was achieved utilizing a variety of platforms like: Coursesites, Google Classroom and Google Suite, Edmodo, Khan Academy, Study.com, and others. The activities included: Online assessments, discussion forums, collaborative writing, webquests with multiple multimedia resources, and designing lesson plans and projects.

Applying the SAMR Model

1. Substitution

Students were encouraged to use a variety of applications on their desktops or mobile devices to complete assignments, write essays, do quizzes, and gather data and information for their projects. This substitution was favored by students, especially for the benefit of ease of access. As one student explained, "Online assignments make learning easier and more interesting; we can do our assignments any time and at any place we want since we can access them from our mobile devices or tablets."

2. Augmentation

Students did not only complete assignments online, but they also had the chance to collaborate in the writing process, share ideas and opinions, post real-time comments for their classmates, explore each other's work and learn from each other, and receive instant notifications about the activity going on in their class, all through their mobile devices and regardless of time and distance. A student explained how the tools enhanced learning and "made learning easier and more interesting... made learning more interactive and collaborative, and... let us see all our classmates' points of view.

In addition, the teacher gave us meaningful feedback… assessed our understanding to see if we had any misconceptions, and… a student could correct or help another student to better understand…" When students sat for online quizzes, for example, they received instant feedback instead of having to wait for the instructor to correct and grade. Another student reflected on this saying, "Online quizzes let us be engaged in the learning process in a unique and fun way. They allow us to get immediate results, which helps us identify our gaps and improve them (Fig. 2)."

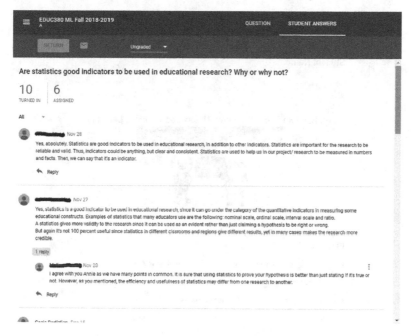

Fig. 2. Example of augmentation: discussion on Google Classroom, enabling students to share ideas, learn from each other, and correct each other's misconceptions on their mobile devices

3. Modification

Students were able to discover new ways to present assignments. They could explore the online tools at their own pace and preference. For example, students were able to explore an educational platform like Khan Academy to discover more information and navigate as deep as they could into the learning process. One student explained the benefit of using various platforms, "In comparison to my experience in other courses, using these tools helped me a lot to improve the depth of understanding in the course material." They could do online trial tests to check for the mastery of knowledge. A student reflected, "Most of the tasks given were assigned on the Khanacademy website, and honestly I learned how to calculate median, mean, mode, and standard deviation from the explanations available on the web without even opening the book. Moreover, I understood the meanings of the distributions in graphs. I acquired those skills while studying at my own pace, at the same time having the chance to repeat any explanation." Online quizzes integrated media materials, which radically transformed the process and scope of assessment (Fig. 3).

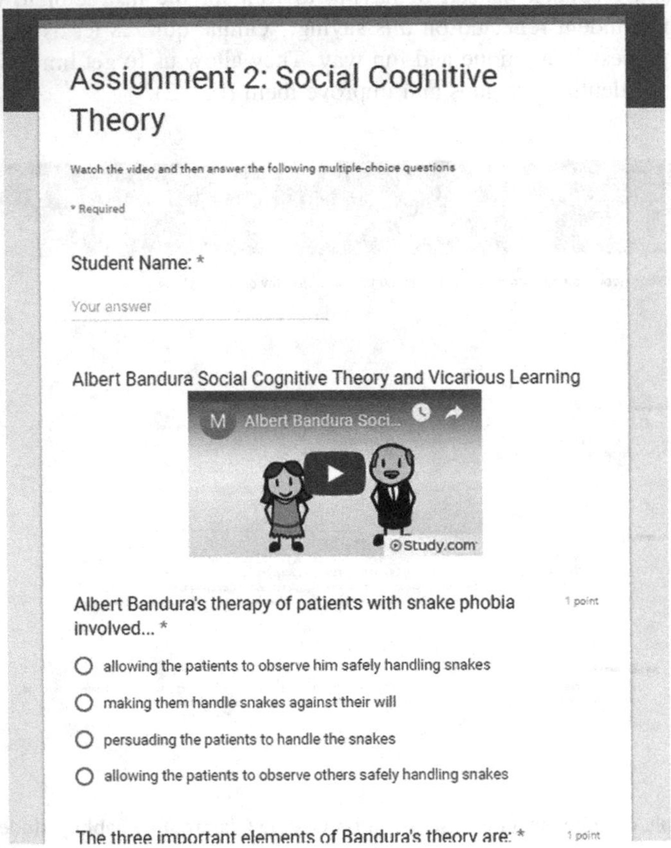

Fig. 3. Example of modification: online assignment on Google Form, enabling instructors to include multimedia in the assessment

4. Redefinition

Students brainstormed the various new ways they could use technological tools to complete tasks. For example, some designed their online surveys to gather data for their projects, others used online games to teach grammar lessons, and still others created their own Google Sheets and Docs to organize teamwork and enhance follow up in their activities. One student commented on how she could transfer her experience by saying, "the online quizzes were great because they helped us think of other ways... to test [our] students about what they've learnt in class..." At this stage, students were also able to transfer to an authentic learning experience in real world situations. When pre-service teachers applied their projects in real-life classrooms, they could video the whole process and share the video with their peers and teachers to evaluate and critique, which led to a much deeper level of learning. All these tasks would have been inconceivable without the introduced technological tools and the e-learning environment (Fig. 4).

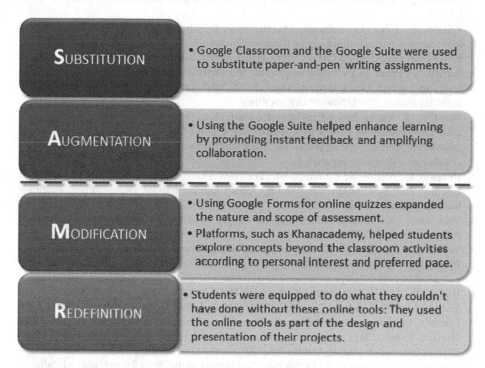

Fig. 4. Applying the SAMR model to case study 2

4   Summary

E-learning has been around since the 1960s; however, it wasn't until the 1990s that it became customary for teachers to integrate e-learning pedagogy into their lessons. For some subjects, these methods mainly included activities such as drill-and-practice and testing. However, the 2000s witnessed radical technological advancements, such as the Web 2.0 and the spreading of mobile computing devices, that have given educators more opportunities to design e-learning activities that are more collaborative and constructivist in nature. With demands from both industry and government for our students to graduate with a new skill which insures deeper learning through transfer necessary for the 21st century workplace, up-to-date e-learning activities are starting to be designed by educators [4]. One tool that is very helpful in ensuring the proper use of technology to achieve the necessary transformation of learning is Puentedura's SAMR Model [6].

References

1. Molenda, M., Bichelmeyer, B.: Issues and trends in instructional technology: slow growth as economy recovers. In: Orey, M., McClendon, J., Branch, R.M. (eds.) Educational Media and Technology Yearbook 2005, vol. 30, pp. 3–28. Libraries Unlimited, Englewood Cliffs (2005)
2. Wilson, S., Liber, O., Johnson, M., Beauvoir, P., Sharples, P., Milligan, C.: Personal learning environments: challenging the dominant design of educational systems. J. eLearning Knowl. Soc. 3(2), 27–38 (2007). http://dspace.ou.nl/bitstream/1820/727/1/sw_ectel.pdf
3. Brown, S.: From VLEs to learning webs: the implications of Web 2.0 for learning and teaching. Interact. Learn. Environ. 18(1), 1–10 (2010). http://www.tandfonline.com/doi/abs/10.1080/10494820802158983#.UrKqtxYfpfs
4. Dowling, S.: Going beyond traditional e-learning methods to create more constructivist, collaborative learning experiences, January 2014. https://www.researchgate.net/publication/268445992_Going_beyond_traditional_e-learning_methods_to_create_more_constructivist_collaborative_learning_experiences
5. Johnson, L., Adams, S., Cummins, M.: The NMC Horizon Report: 2012 Higher Education Edition. The New Media Consortium, Austin (2012). http://www.nmc.org/publications/horizon-report-2012-higher-ed-edition
6. Puentedura, R.: SAMR model (Digital image) (2009). http://hippasus.com/rrpweblog/. Accessed 10 Dec 2018
7. Williams, J., Goldberg, M.: The evolution of eLearning. In: 22nd Ascilite Conference Proceedings, Brisbane, Australia, pp. 725–728 (2005). http://www.ascilite.org.au/conferences/brisbane05/blogs/proceedings/84_Williams.pdf
8. Hackbarth, S.: The Educational Technology Handbook: A Comprehensive Guide: Process and Products for Learning. Educational Technology Publications, Englewood Cliffs (1996)
9. Johnson, L., Adams, B., Cummins, S., Estrada, V., Freeman, A., Ludgate, H.: The NMC Horizon Report: 2013 Higher Education Edition. The New Media Consortium, Austin (2013). http://www.nmc.org/publications/2013-horizon-report-higher-ed
10. Buchem, I., Hamelmann, H.: Developing 21st century skills: Web 2.0 in higher education–a case study. eLearning Papers 24, 1–4 (2011). http://openeducationeuropa.eu/en/article/Developing-21st-century-skills%3A-Web-2.0-inhigher-education.-A-Case-Study
11. Rotherham, A., Willingham, D.: "21st-century skills" – not new but a worthy challenge. American Educator, Spring (2010). http://www.aft.org/pdfs/americaneducator/spring2010/RotherhamWillingham.pdf
12. Puentedura, R.: Thinking about change in learning and technology. In: Presentation given September 25, 2012 at the 1st Global Mobile Learning Conference, Al Ain, UAE (2012). http://www.hippasus.com/rrpweblog/archives/2012/04/10/iPad_Intro.pdf

Personal Effectiveness, Commitment and Organizational Trust Impact on e-Learning Effectiveness

Arem Say[1(✉)], Ibticem Ben Zammel[2(✉)], and Tharwa Najar[1(✉)]

[1] Gafsa University, Gafsa, Tunisia
arem2say@yahoo.fr, th.najar@laposte.net
[2] Manouba University, Manouba, Tunisia
Ibticembenzammel@gmail.com

Abstract. The e-Learning gains a central position in broad and diverse methods of organizational capacities acquisition and development. However, its implementation involves a behavioral constraint. The paper discusses the factors which promote the acceptance of the use of e-learning by employees as a new learning style.

The objective of this study is to identify the determinants of the use of e-Learning as a new learning style based on a social cognitive theory, technology acceptance model, social exchange theory and organizational learning theory.

Within a human perspective, the theoretical model is built regarding to the extracted determinants from the literature. The second objective is to empirically test the developed model from a sample of employees in the Tunisian context through an exploratory qualitative study reinforced by an empirical study conducted among a sample of 318 Tunisian employees.

Keywords: e-Learning · Learning · Personal effectiveness · Commitment and organizational trust

1 Introduction

In order to meet the needs of the continuous knowledge and skills development, e-learning gains a central position in broad and diverse methods of acquisition and development of organizational capacities since it allows individuals to update their knowledge and to integrate new professional knowledge. Its implementation requires the acquisition of organizational learning. However, e-learning, may provoke the resistance of some actors who might feel themselves either threatened or incompetent to cope with this change in the way to acquiring new skills.

The major reported problems are then of human nature. It is therefore vital to ensure winning the support of human capital to the introduction of e-learning among learning methods in the enterprise. The acceptance of the use of e-learning by employees as a new learning style remains a complex phenomenon influenced by a large number of variables which are still under study. The literature review allowed us to retain the most important variables used to explain the behaviour of employee; whether to use e-learning as a new learning style or not. More accurately, this is the effect of personal

© Springer Nature Switzerland AG 2019
R. Jallouli et al. (Eds.): ICDEc 2019, LNBIP 358, pp. 239–250, 2019.
https://doi.org/10.1007/978-3-030-30874-2_19

effectiveness, commitment and organizational trust. Several Tunisian Firms, deluded by the benefits of e-learning have established this new learning style but they failed. The material challenge of e-Learning consists in the rejection of electronic applications, after their use by several firms. It is then interesting to investigate the factors influencing the implementation of e-learning as a new learning style, and to study its effectiveness in terms of learning acquisition in the Tunisian firms (Ben Zammel et al. 2016).

The foregoing raises the problematic of the factors which influence the use of this new learning style and its acceptance by employees. The problematic which constitutes the tissue of this paper can be illustrated by the following fundamental question: what are the determinants of acceptance of the use of e-Learning by employees as a new learning style? The layout of this proposal shall be as follows. We will present in the first section, the theoretical basis of our research and the definition of e-Learning. In the second section, we will introduce the conceptual framework of our research as well as the hypotheses illustrating the possible relationships between all of our variables. Eventually, the third section is devoted to the methodological aspects of our study while introducing the measurement scales of variables, as well as the incurred results.

2   The Theoretical Basis of the Research

In the present paper research, we refer to a set of theories which are; "social cognitive theory" (Bandura 1989), "the social exchange theory" (Blau 1964) and "organizational learning theory" (Argyris and Schön 1978). Based on this theoretical basis, we could partly constitute our conceptual model.

2.1   The Social Cognitive Theory (SCT)

This theory provides explanations for personal behaviour. Its psychological value is judged not only through its explanatory potential and its predictive strength, but also through its operational force in improving human functioning (Bandura 1989). It is based on the reciprocity notion because it assumes that the characteristics of the social environment (such as social pressures) or situational characteristics, cognitive factors and other personal factors (such as personality, demographics …) and individual behaviour influence each other. Thus the human behaviour in a given situation is affected by the characteristics of the environment or the situation which are, themselves, influenced by the adopted behaviour. The social cognitive theory is based then on the concept of interaction. Bandura (1989) states that it is not enough to consider the behaviour as being a function of the reciprocal effects of personal and environmental factors on each other but that the interaction must be understood as a reciprocal determinism of personal factors 'P', Environmental 'E' and 'B' behavioural.

With reference to this theory, we deduce that the human behaviour is guided by two cognitive forces; the first is linked to personal effectiveness perceptions (Bandura 1989), and the second represents the expectations compared to the results of a behaviour (Yamill and McLean 2001).

2.1.1   Personal Effectiveness Perceptions

The beliefs of an individual with regard to his own capacities to successfully perform a task or a set of tasks are to be counted among the main regulators of his behaviour (Bandura 1989). Therefore, people with a strong assurance regarding their capacities in a particular field see difficulties as opportunities to succeed rather than threats to avoid. These people set challenging goals and maintain a strong commitment in order to achieve their goals. They increase and maintain their efforts in dealing with difficulties. They quickly recover their sense of effectiveness after a failure or under-performance. They attribute failure to insufficient efforts or lack of knowledge or skills which might be acquired. As a result, they approach threatening situations with confidence because they feel control over these situations.

2.1.2   The Expectations Vis-à-Vis the Results of Behaviour

This dimension is defined as the set of beliefs established by individuals to adopt a behaviour that will lead to expected results. Thus, individuals develop behaviours which they believe result in positive results.

In this vein, these authors distinguish between two dimensions of expectations' outcome. First, the results related to job performance and the use of tools. The second dimension refers to the expectations of personal results. These are related to expectations of change in the image or the status, or even the expectations of rewards, such as promotions, etc. So the motivation of the individual to perform behaviour is influenced by the expected results following the completion of this behaviour.

2.2   Social Exchange Theory (Blau 1964)

The social exchange theory is one of the frameworks used to understand the nature of the relationship between organizational climate and employee attitudes toward this firm (trust, involvement, commitment). The working relationship can be characterized by relations of social exchange (Blau 1964). These relationships are based on a long term favors' exchange. Thus this theory captures the employment relationship as an exchange between employer and employee.

In other words, the social exchange relationship develops between two parties said exchange partners through a series of mutual exchanges. A party makes a contribution or service to the other party and thereby develops an expectation of a future return. The other part, having received something it values, develops a sense of obligation in accordance with the reciprocity norm. The obligations of both partners in the social exchange relationship is often unspecified, diffused and valued as symbol of loyalty, of mutual support and willingness and the standards for measuring the contributions of each are often vague and indeterminate, **trust** plays a central role in the establishment and maintenance of social exchange relationship. Indeed, **social exchange requires trusting others** (Blau 1964).

Previous research on social exchange in an firm environment agreed that the employee is involved in at least two social exchange relationships: one with his supervisor and the other with the firm as a system (Ben Zammel et al. 2016). This research has mobilized multiple constructs to operationalize these exchange relationships which are basically trust, perceived organizational support, the quality of exchange between leader and member, commitment and psychological contracts (Aryee et al. 2002). However among these concepts, trust and organizational commitment appear to be most used and most studied.

2.3 Organizational Learning Theory (Argyris and Schön 1978)

In literature review of organizational learning, we distinguish between three approaches: one called "holistic" which personifies the firm and understands learning starting from organizational systems such as practices, routines, procedures or even the organizational memory, the other approch is social which highlights the exchange between individuals and the firm and the last is individualist which apprehends learning from the cognitive activity of individuals in the firm (Argyris and Schön 1978).

The organizational learning theory, developed mainly by (Argyris and Schön 1978) describes the firm as "a community specialized in creation and knowledge transfer." It regards learning as primarily individual and then organizational: the individual as part of the learning system in which the individual's knowledge is exchanged and transferred, for this exchange to occur interaction is required.

Indeed, the works of Argyris and Schön (1978) place the individual at the centre of the organizational learning process. For these two authors, only individuals learn. If there is an organizational learning, it will thus never be only through individuals. This view analyzes the organizational dimension of learning based on the individual learning. Thereafter the learning shall be organizational because the knowledge brought by an individual will interest the whole organization.

This organizational learning approach which places the individual at the center of learning system somewhat transfers the responsibility of learning on the individual. Indeed, the latter is regarded as the central character of the learning device.

Our research focuses on the perspective of learning acquisition by individuals who are likely to apply their knowledge in their work. In fact, we consider that the most important factors in learning through e-learning are individuals.

3 Theoretical Model of the Determinants of Knowledge Acquisition via e-Learning

The objective of e-learning device implementation is the acquisition of new knowledge and know-how and therefore the achievement of organizational learning. The success of its implementation among the methods of continuous skills development and knowledge of the organization depends on employee's acceptance of its use as a new learning style (Ben Zammel et al. 2016). Such acceptance is facilitated by a significant number of individual variables (Fig. 1).

The literature review allowed us to retain the most important variables used to explain the organizational behaviour of individuals. More specifically, we are going to discuss in this paragraph the effects of personal effectiveness, commitment and trust.

3.1 Personal Effectiveness

Personal Effectiveness is rooted in particular in personal effectiveness theory of Bandura (1989) which postulates that the success, the performance and the motivation of an individual are subject to his level of personal effectiveness. This effectiveness is defined as the judgment which an individual carries on the use he thinks he can make his knowledge in a specific situation. It is the belief in his abilities to successfully perform a given task (Bandura 1989). It corresponds to individual judgment of the capacity to cope with the requirements of a given situation, or to achieve a goal and thus, it does not convey the real existence of skills, but the perceptions of the individual on his ability, no matter what are the skills which he have. This judgment is the result of the perception of reference group of the individual from his distinctive skills.

According to many studies, the feeling of personal effectiveness seems in any case to be an important indicator of the performance of an individual in a part of the training (Lee and Lee 2008; Ho 2009; Ben Zammel et al. 2018). Self effectiveness is supposed to positively affect the motivation of the employee to use e-learning and apply all his knowledge in the firm he works for. Thus, we suppose to integrate relevant personal effectiveness of the learner in our model as a variable which influences the achievement of learning after an e-Learning training.

Each individual tries to have an endorsement in his social group. Indeed, estimated influential members of the working environment of a person (supervisors) think it is effective that this person sees himself as such (Ben Zammel et al. 2016). Therefore, it seems relevant that the sense of personal effectiveness is strongly influenced by the group. Similarly, the beliefs of the individual with respect to the performance of behaviour are strongly influenced by the views of individuals or groups. In this respect, employees who want to undergo training believe that the use of e-learning is likely to improve their status in the firm, and they also believe that this learning style will allow them to access to useful knowledge for the performance of their jobs and the development of their skills along with having a promotion. Similarly, when members of the working environment, mainly hierarchical superiors and influential person, encourage the use of e-learning, employees will be motivated to use this new learning style to show their level of personal effectiveness. Confidence in an individual's ability to acquire knowledge and skills is strongly influenced by his surroundings. The influence of the reference group is crucial.

Hence, the following Hypothesis:

Hypothesis 1: The sense of personal effectiveness has a positive effect on the achievement of learning via e-learning.

3.2 Organizational Commitment

The earliest studies on the social exchange theory, Blau (1964), introduced the concept of commitment to illustrate the relationship which an employee builds with his firm. This theory considers the establishment of social exchange relationships requires investments which constitute a commitment towards the other party.

Meyer and Allen (1991) proposed a model of organizational commitment with three dimensions which are affective commitment, calculated commitment and normative commitment. They define them as follows: Affective commitment refers to the psychological attachment to the firm, calculated commitment refers to the costs associated with leaving the firm, and normative commitment refers to the perceived obligation to remain in the firm.

In our research we would focus on the affective commitment. Indeed, the feeling of being supported by the firm stems from the employee's belief that the firm values his contributions and cares about his well being. This belief may be formed from HRM practices established by the firm. HRM practices create an organizational climate which meets the needs of the individual to feel physically and psychologically well in the firm. The firm, through its HRM practices promotes a certain level of recognition and support for employees.

In the literature review one can see a relationship between organizational commitment and learning (Colquitt et al. 2000; Maor and Volet 2007). Some researchers consider organizational commitment as a result of participation in the training (Saks 1995). Other researchers have integrated it into their models in order to show its impact on the achievement of learning (Carlson et al. 2000; Tracey et al. 2001).

Within the framework of our research on the determinants of the use of e-Learning as a new learning style we believe that implementing e-learning project without benefit of human resources will be doomed to failure since it will be rejected. Thus, during the implementation of e-learning as a new learning style, the firm must initiate a dialogue with the staff involved in order to ensure their membership and their commitments. Such a dialogue in our opinion should not be limited only to matters of wages and profits; it should instead focus on issues concerning the acquisition of new knowledge and expertise essential to their work. Organizational commitment is supposed to positively affect the behaviour of the employee to use the e-learning as a new learning style.

Hence the following hypothesis:

Hypothesis 2: Organizational commitment has a positive effect on the achievement of learning via e-learning.

3.3   Organizational Trust

The social exchange theory suggests that social exchange requires sharing relationships based on trust with others (Blau 1964). Trust is the belief that the firm will fulfill its obligations towards the employee and will provide what they want (Aryee et al. 2002). Therefore, the employee, confident the firm's intentions towards him, would develop an emotional attachment greater than if he were not trusted. The same confidence influences the transmission of this knowledge. It gives rise therefore with a less formal approach, more cooperative and constructive where individuals are more willing to invest in a long term relationship. It constitutes the ideal location of the achievement of learning. Therefore, trust positively influences the individual's motivation to learn. Hence the following hypothesis:

Hypothesis 3: Organizational trust has a positive effect on the achievement of learning via e-learning.

The conclusion of our study consists on a theoretical model for the determinants of achievement of learning via e-learning. This model is summarized as follows (Fig. 1):

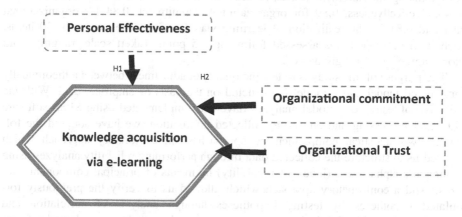

Fig. 1. Theoretical model of the determinants of knowledge acquisition via e-learning

4   Research Methodologies

The major outcome of this research study is to apprehend the following fundamental question: *what are the determinants of the acceptance of the use of e-learning by employees to acquire knowledge?*

The first part of our study has focused on developing a theoretical framework to our problem; its outcome is a theoretical model of the determinants of achievement of learning via e-learning.

In order to implement our hypotheses, we have conducted an empirical investigation in the Tunisian context.

4.1   Results of the Empirical Research

The objective of our research is to understand the effect of individual variables on the acceptance of employees to use e-learning as a new learning style. Or in other words the achievement of learning through this new system essentially based on using technology by employees. Consequently, we sought to have a large sample to ensure a higher level of objectivity in our research. The empirical validation of the theoretical model of the realization of learning via e-learning was conducted using a survey given to 560 employees, 318 questionnaires were answered i.e. a response rate of 57%. The 318 individuals who have answered our survey are composed of 128 men (40%) and 190 women (60%). This sample comprises 154 post employees (48%), 81 bank employees (25%), 83 employees belonging to private companies (27%). 113 individual have a computer at home (35%) and 85 subject have Internet access (27%). The literature review enabled us to invent a set of variables operationalizing the theoretical dimensions of our research model. We have specified each of these variables and we have developed a list of items for their measurement for further analysis. The items selected in the questionnaire measuring personal effectiveness, commitment, organizational trust and implementation of organizational learning, which have been drawn from existing measurement scales in previous research with an alpha of 0.85 for personal effectiveness, 0,89 for organizational commitment, 0.84 for organizational trust and 0.84 for the realization of learning via e-learning. The total is of 30 items. Each item developed was assessed following a 5 point 'Likert scale' ranging from "don't agree" to "strongly agree".

The purpose of this study is to test the quality of adjustment between a theoretically constructed model and a model constructed on the basis of empirical data. With the objective of testing our model analyzes have been implemented using SPSS software 17.0: and processing and analyzing collected information, we have adopted the following two statistical complementary approaches: an exploratory approach which allowed us to structure the collected data through performing reliability analyzes using Cronbach's alpha index (index of reliability) by means of principal component analyzes. And a confirmatory approach which allowed us to verify the previously formulated hypotheses by testing hypotheses through analysis of correlation and regression. For each of the adopted measurement scales, we have conducted a factor analysis to ensure the dimensional structure of the scale. Each factor analysis displays a value greater than 0.7 KMO and a significant Bartlett test. Internal consistency between the items has been guaranteed by Cronbach's alpha.

4.2   Test of Research Hypotheses and Interpretation of Results

For the aim to testing our theoretical model as well as the relationship between its variables we have analyzed correlation and regression. The correlation ratio is a significant measure of association, which assesses the relationship between an independent and a dependent variable. The most important advantage of the regression method consists on identifying the most decisive variables in the explanation of the independent variables. In this case, this method enables us to determine the importance of each variable on the behaviour of employees towards learning via e-learning. These links are expressed by regression coefficient. The less critical variables have low regression coefficient whereas those which are the most decisive have important coefficients. Besides, these coefficients facilitate understanding the direction of the influence of the explanatory variable on the variable to be explained. In the case of a coefficient less than zero, it indicates a negative effect which means that the two types of factors range in the opposite direction.

The realization of organizational learning via e-learning = f (personal effectiveness, Organizational Commitment, Organizational Trust)

Say: Y: the realization of learning via e-learning
X1, X2, X3: individual variables influencing the achievement of learning
$Y = \alpha1\ X1 + \alpha2\ X2 + \alpha3\ X3 + S + \varepsilon$
With: X1: personal effectiveness, X2: Organisational Commitment, X3 organisational Trust; S: Steady.

Regression analysis shows that the three variables which are: personal effectiveness, commitment and organizational trust account for 58% of the variance in overall perceived value (R two = 0.588; R two adjusted = 0.533). Our model is then **reliable**.

The realization of learning via e-learning = **0.650** *Organizational trust* (t = 13.218; sig = 0.000) + **0.152 Organisational commitment** *(t = 2.564; sig = 0.11)* − **0.181 personal effectiveness** *(t = −4.223; sig = 0.000)* + ε.

This regression model is written as follows: **Y = 0.650X3 + 0.152X2 − 0.181X1 + S + ε.**

This regression model shows that organizational trust constitutes the highest impact on the realization of organizational learning. It explains the realization of learning with a regression coefficient amounting to 0.650. Similarly organizational trust has a significant effect on the achievement of learning via e-learning. In contrast, personal effectiveness has a negative effect.

The sense of personal effectiveness influences in a negative way the use of e-learning as a learning style. Our model shows that the degree of correlation between these two variables is of the order of 0, 244. Similarly, the multiple regression analysis indicates that this variable has a negative impact on the realization of learning. The relationship between these two variables is determined by a regression coefficient of about −0.181. This result was surprising because at the theoretical level we stated that the individual is strongly influenced by the beliefs of the reference groups in relation to the realization of behaviour. In this regard, employees who want to undergo training believe that the use of e-learning is likely to improve their status in the enterprise, insofar as this is a learning style which can allow them to access to useful knowledge for the execution of their work and the development of their skills as well as having a promotion. Therefore, our first hypothesis is not confirmed.

Organizational trust, very significantly, the realization of learning via e-learning. Our model shows that the degree of correlation between these two variables is of the order of 0.737. Similarly, regression analysis shows that this variable has the greatest impact on the realization of learning. The relationship between these two variables is determined by a regression coefficient of about 0.650. In fact this variable can significantly affect employee's acceptance of learning via this new learning style because this practice is entirely based on the trust of the employee on his superior decisions. This result suggests that successful implementation of an e-learning project depends heavily on the level of organizational trust tools. Therefore, our third hypothesis is confirmed.

The organizational commitment influences, significantly, the realization of learning via e-learning. Our model illustrates that the degree of correlation between these two variables is of the order of 0, 491. Similarly, the multiple regression analysis shows that this variable has a significant impact on the realization of learning. The relationship between these two variables is determined by a regression coefficient of about 0.152. In fact, this result is theoretically reinforced by several authors. The feeling of being supported by the firm stems from the employee's belief that the firm values his contributions and cares about his well being. This same level of commitment will be present even if the learning is done at a distance. Organizational commitment is supposed to positively affect the motivation to learn (Carlson et al. 2000; Tracey et al. 2001, Colquitt et al. 2000). Committed individuals would be more motivated to undergo a training conducted by the firm in which they work and to transfer what they learn in the workplace (Carlson et al. 2000, Tracey et al. 2001; Facteau et al. 1995; Tannenbaum et al. 1991). However, organizational trust, insignificantly, influences the realization of learning via e-learning. Our model illustrates that the degree of correlation between these two variables is of the order of 0, 499.

5   Conclusion

Our research focuses on an acquisition perspective of knowledge by individuals who are likely to implement them in their work. For this reason we favoured to know the determinants which influence individuals to learn via e-learning.

The exploratory research allowed us to highlight the dominance of prior organizational behaviour of the employee to use e-learning as a new learning style. This behaviour is influenced by the availability of a reliable technology platform, easy to use, fast, and adapted to the characteristics and needs of each firm. However, the cultural weight of the conventional presential learning is predominant in the site. Different forms of resistance were then developed and are manifested in the refusal of the use of this new learning system. Such resistances have been eliminated by the good management practices implemented by firm.

However, since we have performed an individual approach of learning, we have considered that the success of implementation of e-learning among the modes of continuous development of skills and knowledge of the firm depends on the employee's acceptance of its use as a new learning style. This acceptance is moderated by a significant number of individual variables.

The main feature of employment in this sector is stability. The qualitative research provided us with an important explanation: the employee does not value to the opinions of his hierarchical superiors even if they are motivated to apply this new learning style.

The majority of employees are seeking to acquire an individual learning which enables them to access to a higher grade. The main objective is not the achievement of learning and knowledge acquisition but grade evolution. Therefore, the perception of personal effectiveness is influenced by the reference group within the framework of grade evolution and not learning achievement through a new mode of skills acquisition.

It follows from these results a certain number of managerial implications to take into consideration during the implementation of e-learning projects. In fact, the use of this new way of learning and especially its acceptance by employees is dependent on certain factors that the general direction of the firm which wants to implement a successful e-learning project should be considered. The study has revealed the importance of the impact of the variables like "organizational trust" and "organizational commitment" on the realization of learning via e-learning. The value of the regression coefficient relative to these two variables shows their importance. This result is consistent with previous studies on commitment on learning (Colquitt et al. 2000; Bartlett 2001; Saks 1995; Carlson et al. 2000; Tracey et al. 2001). Concerning the organizational trust which claimed a significant effect, we realized the importance of this variable after analyzing the interviews. We have claimed therefore the effect of organizational trust on the achievement of learning via eLearning. The importance of this variable for the firm is that it influences the transfer of knowledge and results therefore in a softer approach, more cooperative and constructive. For this reason we should provide great importance to this variable through enhancing the level of trust between the individuals and their firm. The best guarantee is a significant effort from the part of the General Directorate of the firm to improve communication, exchange of ideas etc. However, personal effectiveness exerts a negative effect on the achievement of learning via e-Learning. We have stated, following our reading, the significance of this variable on the behaviour of the employee. However, at the empirical level, we found that personal effectiveness exerts a negative effect on the achievement of learning via e-Learning. This link, which may seem paradoxical, may be due to the fact that the interviewed Tunisian employees, with a little and brief experience in e-Learning, do not attribute the evolution of professional status, the achievement of higher grades and the improvement of their image in the firm with the use of this learning approach. Thus, the reference group of employees, constituted by his colleagues and his superiors, appears to have no positive influence on their perceptions regarding e-learning and on its intention to use it. It should be noted here that the distribution of the sample may also explain this observation since the majority of the interviewed individuals belong to public service which is characterized by job stability regardless of the opinion of his surroundings. In order to reverse this effect, it would be interesting for HR managers to promote this learning style and to demonstrate its advantages compared to other approaches among employees and in particular by awareness raising and communication.

To conclude we can say that the main problem is not technological, but rather human and managerial. It is therefore essential to ensure winning the support of the entire human capital for the introduction of e-learning among knowledge acquisition styles in the firm. A **future research** could be considered incorporating the concept of learning transfer following an e-Learning training. The use of this new learning style should contribute to improving the employees' skills. Consequently, e-learning can be likened to a learning style which improves steadily if employees' skills contribute to the improvement of individual and organizational learning. The question then is how to consolidate various learning which will take place in the firm following the use of e-learning. Many researchers on learning (Imamoglu 2007) admit that online training is a preferred method of skill acquisition that needs to evolve. The effectiveness of this new learning style will be measured by distributed learning in the firm after its use.

Bibliography

Argyris, C., Schon, D.: Organizational Learning: A Theory of Action Perspective. Addison-Wesley, Reading (1978)

Aryee, S., Budhwar, P.S., Chen, Z.X.: Trust as a mediator of the relationship between organizational justice and work outcomes: test of social exchange model. J. Organ. Behav. **23**, 267–285 (2002)

Ben Zammel, I., Chichti, F., Gharbi, J.-E.: Comment favoriser le transfert d'apprentissage dans l'organisation par le biais de l'utilisation du e-learning? Réflexion à partir du contexte tunisien, @GRH (20), 83–103 (2016)

Ben Zammel, I., Najar, T., Belghith, A.: Determinants of e-learning effectiveness: the case of Tunisian virtual school of post office. In: Bach Tobji, M.A., Jallouli, R., Koubaa, Y., Nijholt, A. (eds.) ICDEc 2018. LNBIP, vol. 325, pp. 165–172. Springer, Cham (2018). https://doi.org/10.1007/978-3-319-97749-2_13

Bandura, A.: Social cognitive theory. In: Vasta, R. (ed.) Annals of Child Development. Six Theories of Child Development, vol. 6, pp. 1–60. JAI Press, Greenwich (1989)

Blau, P.: Exchange and Power in Social Life. Wiley, New York (1964)

Carlson, D.S., Bozeman, D.P., Kacmar, K.M., Wright, P.M., McMahan, G.C.: Training motivation in organizations: an analysis of individual-level antecedents. J. Manag. Issues 12(3), 271–287 (2000)

Colquitt, J., LePine, A., Noe, R.: Toward an integrative theory of training motivation: a meta-analytic path analysis of 20 years of research. J. Appl. Psychol. 15, 678–707 (2000)

Ho, L.A.: The antecedents of e-learning outcome: an examination of system quality, technology readiness, and learning behavior. Adolescence 44(175), 581–599 (2009)

Homan, G., Macpherson, A.: E-learning in the corporate university. J. Euro. Ind. Training, 29(1), 75–90 (2005)

Imamoglu, Z.S.: An empirical analysis concerning the user acceptance of e-learning. J. Am. Acad. Bus. Camb. 11(1), 132–137 (2007)

Lee, J.-K., Lee, W.-K.: The relationship of e-learner's self-regulatory efficacy and perception of e-learning environmental quality. Comput. Hum. Behav. 24, 32–47 (2008)

Maor, D., Volet, S.: Engagement in professional online learning: a situative analysis of media professionals who did not make it. Int. J. E-Learn. 6(1), 95–117 (2007)

Meyer, J.P., Allen, N.J.: A three component conceptualization of organizational commitment. Hum. Res. Manag. Rev. 1(1), 61–89 (1991)

Saks, A.M.: Longitudinal field investigation of the moderating and mediating effects of self-efficacy on the relationship between training and newcomer adjustment. J. Appl. Psychol. 80, 211–225 (1995)

Tracey, J.B., Hinkin, T.R., Tannenbaum, S.I., Mathieu, J.E.: The influence of individual characteristics and the work environment on varying levels of training outcomes. Hum. Res. Dev. Q. 12(1), 5–23 (2001)

Yamill, S., McLean, G.N.: Theories supporting transfer of training. Hum. Resour. Dev. Q. 12, 195–208 (2001)

E-Commerce and Digital Economy

Transparency in the E-Journals Market: Controlled Preferences and Altered Rational Choices

Rim Haidar, Nizar Hariri$^{(\boxtimes)}$ (ID), and Racquel Antoun (ID)

Faculté de Sciences économiques, Observatoire Universitaire de La Réalité
Socio-Economique, Université Saint-Joseph, Beirut, Lebanon
rimhaidar@hotmail.com,
{nizar.hariri, racquel.nakhle}@usj.edu.lb

Abstract. Studies on the transparency in the e-journals markets and its overall effect on public debates and democratic controls are scarce. This paper aims to evaluate the relevance of the microeconomic model when analyzing the systemic behavior of e-journalism. Through a simple theoretical model, where producers and consumers of information are exchanging two types of news (soft and hard news), we examine the overall effect of transparency on the market structure and how the systemic behavior impacts rational choices and decision making. We argue that e-journalism markets are imperfect, even when information seems to be perfectly transparent, as they allow individuals, communities and corporate agents to produce or share an abundant amount of information, exceeding the capacities of each single entity to filter, process, verify or debate the news. More importantly, the direct effect of revealing information has a cross-effect on others, with unpredictable retroactions on the agents' preferences and choices. Our model reveals the limits of rational choices of free individual agents, within market structures characterized by distorted choices and manipulated attitudes.

Keywords: E-Journalism · Rational choice theory · Market transparency · Market structures · Transaction costs

1 Introduction

The standard economic theory (the neoclassical model) stipulates that a transparent information system is a main feature of perfect markets' equilibrium. Yet, real markets' situations are usually subject to information asymmetries and opportunistic behaviors (Akerlof 1970). For the last fifty years, the political economy of information has been investigating the role of information in a context of asymmetrical power distribution "between those governing and those governed", showing how imperfect political markets can distort the behaviors and beliefs of rational agents (Stiglitz 2002).

However, information transparency at the era of digital news is still an emergent field of study for economic theory. Information theory at the era of digital news is an emergent field of investigation for economic theory. Compared to traditional markets, information in digital markets is highly dependent on complex interactions between

R. Jallouli et al. (Eds.): ICDEc 2019, LNBIP 358, pp. 253–265, 2019.
https://doi.org/10.1007/978-3-030-30874-2_20

various users, vendors, platforms, servers, and invisible algorithms. Digital news, also called electronic journalism, is commonly defined as new forms of media where the editorial content is distributed through the Internet. Compared to traditional media (such as printed newspapers, radio or TV broadcasting), users of online news are exposed to new sets of attitudes and behaviors, when higher levels of interactivity and hypertextuality allow any reader to comment and share news, or even to produce original content (Chung 2008; Chung et al. 2012).

According to Chung et al. (2012), interactivity includes five components that enable readers to select news in a more efficient way: controlling the frequency, searching by category, searching by keyword, personalizing the content, and saving or printing the text. Interactivity allows readers to share articles with other people in their network, therefore allowing for the selection (or omission) of the suggested news according to the level of resemblance (or dissemblance) among peers (Chung 2008). Hypertextuality is also a major feature of online news that saves a lot of time to the readers, since the jump to another article (within-site or to another web page) is reached in one click (Carpenter 2010). Thus, online media will allows consumers to experience a decrease in their "news search time cost", due to the "high search efficiency brought by new communication technologies" (Zhang and Ha 2015, p. 202)

According to microeconomic theory, this situation refers to an enhanced market transparency, opening the door for "exciting new potentials for matching up customers and suppliers" (Varian and Shapiro 1999). Nevertheless, transparency in the digital era is far from having one-sided effects on market structures, since objectivity and credibility of online news have become major issues for e-journalism (Vargo et al. 2000). In this article we claim that asymmetrical information and market imperfections seem to be persistent in e-journalism, even when the transparency is increased to perfection.

The conventional microeconomic model suggests that information transparency will increase the level of transactions in any market place, with positive effects on prices and volumes (Granados et al. 2006). This claim is also in line with the popular belief stipulating that transparent media and efficient flow of news are powerful tools in the hands of informed citizens. Yet, this Information Transparency Hypothesis (ITH) has been challenged by new complex practices in digital markets, and some scholars have claimed that the informational advantage is a double-edged sword (Zhu 2004; Brynjolfsson and Smith 2000; Wise and Morrison 2000). Similarly, many researchers have pointed out the paradoxical effects of transparency, since the increased amount of information may jeopardize the credibility and the objectivity of the delivered content, as well as the overall access to information (Johnson and Kaye 2010).

To date, transparency in the digital news markets and its overall effect on public debates and democratic controls has not been a major topic of interest for economists. This paper aims at evaluating the relevance of the microeconomic model when analyzing the systemic behavior of e-journalism. Through a simple theoretical model, where producers and consumers of information are exchanging two types of news (soft and hard news), we examine the overall effect of transparency on the market structure and show how, in return, the systemic behavior will affect rational choices and decision making process. Therefore we argue that e-journalism markets are imperfect, even when information seems to be perfectly transparent, as they allow individuals, communities and corporate agents to produce or share an abundant amount of information, exceeding the capacities of each single entity in filtering, processing, verifying or debating the news. More importantly, since the direct effect of revealing information has a cross-effect on others, with unpredictable retroactions on the agents' preferences and choices, our model reveals the limits of rational choices of free individual agents, within market structures characterized by distorted choices and manipulated attitudes.

2 Rationale

Information transparency in new media can be understood in several ways, since it refers to the content of the exchanged commodities (the edited digital news). It also involves the preferences of the agents engaged in these transactions, since both producers and consumers can decide to reveal or hide information related to their personal attitudes and behaviors. Empirical studies have focused either on the content transparency (by questioning the credibility of information), either on the preferences transparency, by analyzing the behavior of the producers of information or examining a wide range of consumers responsiveness (Boczkowski and Mitchelstein 2012). Yet little is known about the interaction between agents' attitudes and systemic behaviors (Grover et al. 1999; Carpenter 2010).

In addition to the exponential increase in the volume of shared information via online sources, each interaction between a producer and a consumer allows the former to collect significant data on the latter's preferences (information about the readers' history, tastes, personal opinions, political stances, and demographics).

Yet, knowing whether the agent freely reveals his or her preferences or whether this information is extorted by a third-party remains an open question. Indeed, the user might disclose (freely?) this information through effective choices. Alternatively, the producer obtain this valuable information through various strategies (cookies, signing in, incentives to answer surveys, etc.). Each action by which a consumer expresses a demand for a digital content is simultaneously a transaction where new information is produced regarding the consumer's preferences. The production of information (related to subjective preferences) is here a sub-product of the consumption of information (related to content). Effective choice made by consumers will reveal something about their preferences and attitudes toward the producer, and generate valuable information to unknown third parties. Therefore, our general assumptions regarding consent and freedom of choice of the economic agents are challenged by both ideological and technological features of digital news.

As stipulated by Stiglitz (2002, p. 473), "the fact that actions convey information leads people to alter their behavior, and changes how markets function". Unfortunately, scholarly debates lack a theoretical understanding of how transparency and information sharing affect the e-journals market and how in this process influences the individual behavior and alters the rational decision-making. Indeed, when taking into account how individual actions affect the economic system as a whole, and how structural constraints influence the process of decision-making process, the standard economic theory assumes a linear explanation, with the market structure being "nothing more" than the sum of its parts. Yet, in online media's interactions, the information system is always "something more" than the sum of its parts, since every new user increases the quantity of information.

Thus, stating that the abundance of information in new media market enhances transparency is one thing; stating that this transparency is socially and politically desirable for the individual agents as well as for their community is another (Zhu 2005), especially since the private desirability of transparency is divided among agents - between producers and consumers for instance, or even among producers or consumers themselves (Zhu and Weynant 2003). In an asymmetrical distribution of power, the revealed preference leaves one agent with a great leverage over the other. For instance, the revealed preferences of voters could be most welcomed for the candidates but do not systematically lead to an enhanced democratic representation. Could we claim that the enhanced transparency is socially desirable, if it enables political parties to supply customized political programs and discourses, tailored to the preferences of each sub-group or community of voters, in order to maximize votes (Buchanan 1954; Downs 1957), or even to manipulate the public opinion in order to achieve some private ends? Similarly, when the premises of the readers rational choices are altered by online news technology, can we still argue that transparency is improving public debates, especially when taking into account the ideological nature of mass media and the importance of public opinion in democratic regimes?

3 The Model

Surely, technology enhances the flow of information, so that the more a product has digital characteristics, the more its content is transparent in terms of feedbacks (Lal and Sarvary 1999). However, the agents interacting in a digital market, along with their conflicting strategies, are determinant factors that improve or degrade the information access and the overall social well-being.

In our microeconomic model, we aim to introduce a schematic representation of complex interactions between producers and consumers of digital news, in order to assess the overall effect of information transparency on the market equilibrium, and its side-effects on various types of agents within these structures. Our starting point is the same spatial competition model commonly applied to political markets and traditional journalism stipulating that a rational consumer (a reader) tries to maximize satisfaction (utility) given his time budget T, while the producer (a journal) tries to maximize profit by targeting the median reader (Downs 1957) and maximizing the number of reads. Most importantly, the marginal cost of producing additional units of information is quasi-null in information markets.

We consider a transparent market that involves e-readers and e-journals. An e-reader i's satisfaction is represented by the Utility function that depends on the quantity of articles he or she is willing to read. The consumer-reader will arbitrate between two types of news: soft news versus hard news (respectively S and H), when S_i and H_i respectively refers to the number of soft news and hard news read by the reader i. The former refers to articles of personal interest and entertainment purpose, such as cultural or historical news, sports, celebrities, or weather news, while the latter refers to public affairs and political or economic events.

The consumer's program is to maximize:

$$\begin{cases} U_i = U_i(S_i; H_i) & (1) \\ \text{Under constraint: } T = t_h * H + t_s * S & (2) \end{cases}$$

T: Number of hours allocated to search and read digital news
t_h: Unit time spent on searching and reading hard news
t_s: Unit time spent on searching and reading soft news

On the supply side, while aiming to increase their profits, e-journals focus on increasing the number of readers knowing that the marginal cost MC is null. Thus, e-journals use consumers' willingness to read (willingness of the reader i to read the article of the journal j) as a proxy to their profits, when, S_{ij} refers to the time spent by the reader i on soft news edited by the journal j, and H_{ij} the time spent by the reader i on hard news edited by the journal j.

The producer aims to maximize his profits:

$$W_{ij} = W_{ij}(S_{ij}; H_{ij}) \qquad (3)$$

Transparency is a key feature of this type of markets, since the increased number of information exchanged via online news is simultaneously the target of consumer maximizing satisfaction and producer maximizing profits.

On one hand, traditional and new media share some similarity in functioning, but with different intensities. In both cases, producers need to predict the distribution of their clients in order to reach the median reader; this target is achieved more easily by new media, due to the increased level of transparency. On the other hand, traditional media confine the consumers into a passive role, since their choice is restricted to receiving or not the information, while interactivity in online media allow consumers to be less passive vis-à-vis the information content as well as in the interaction with other users or producers.

The endogenous actions of producers and consumers could best be described within a model showing how the consumers' and the producers' programs are interrelated through a common temporal variable: the time of reading and searching for articles. Indeed, while consumers maximize their satisfaction through better allocation of their time among various type of articles (Si and Hi, soft and hard news), the producers maximize their profits by maximizing the number of articles read on their website (S_{ij} and H_{ij}). The effective choice of a reader allows the producer to customize the bundles of articles and to save time for the reader, thus engaging the customer with an extra-time to read on the website, with incentives to consume its products more frequently.

As shown by Boczkowski and Mitchelstein (2012) and Boczkowski et al. (2011), supply and demand for both soft and hard news may not be congruent in regards to the consumers and producers preferences, since is a gap exists between the topics that the readers like to consume and those that the journalists wish to produce. On one hand, journalists have a predilection for hard news and public affairs, a tendency that is consolidated through shared professional ethics and institutional norms. The journalists' community considers that informing citizens on regular basis is the major task and duty of a journalist, which explains the stickiness of supply. This general law of journalism applies to traditional as well as to new media and online sources. On the other hand, consumers' choices are more heterogeneous in nature (topic and content) and in their interests (social communication). A great proportion of readers tend to prefer soft news and topics of personal and cultural interests to hard news. In regular times, this sub-group represents the majority of readers, to the exception of periods when there is an excessive interest in public affairs, such as electoral period or economic crisis. This attitude could be understood in the light of the "monitorial citizen model", stipulating that the consumer, reader, and citizen engage in a general surveillance of the social and political framework, quickly scanning headlines rather than following all the details and gathering all information on public affairs (Schudson 1999; Graber 2004; Zaller 2003).

Thus both soft and hard news are inscribed within an imperfect market. In this context, how does the overall increased transparency affect the market structure and consequently transform the informational process? To answer this question, our starting point is a situation involving a moderate median reader, showing a tendency to mix hard and soft news, and our model will try to retrace the effect of the increased transparency on the agents' choices and attitudes.

Therefore, our population consists of moderate consumers that maximize utility by selecting various combinations of hard and soft news, with an overall preference for soft news over hard news, along with a tendency to mix goods (by avoiding extreme polarized choices, such as exclusively reading soft news or hard news).

A Convex indifference Curve therefore represents various combinations of soft news and hard news that generate the same amount of utility for a median reader, making him or her indifferent to any combination on the same indifference curve. The latter is linear, monotonous, and asymptotic to the axes.

In line with the theory of the consumer equilibrium, the reader tries to reach the highest indifference curve within the reach of the time budget, the optimal choice E_0 being a combination of S_0 a certain amount of soft news, and H_0 a certain amount of hard news that generate the maximum pleasure or utility as shown in Fig. 1.

Now Internet-based news can modify the consumer's behavior by elevating the time budget, for example from T_0 to T_1. Indeed, compared to traditional media, online news offer access to a greater number of articles for a given amount of time, by diminishing the news search time cost, and due to their higher interactivity, as well as to the enhanced responsiveness of the consumer (Zhang and Ha 2015).

When shifting from T_0 to T_1, an online based media increases the time budget without altering the preferences of the reader between soft and hard news, allowing the consumer to read more articles of both types, since the relative price (time cost) did not change when accessing the higher time budget as shown in Fig. 1.

A shift in time budget can also occur when interactivity, hypertextuality or even multimediality can privilege one type of news over the other, thus altering the relative price of both goods. For example, in electoral time, features of online media tend to lower the search time cost for hard news over soft news, in a way that hard-news consumers experience a decrease in the time-price for this type of commodity. In this case, instead of a parallel increase in the time budget, the consumer's time budget

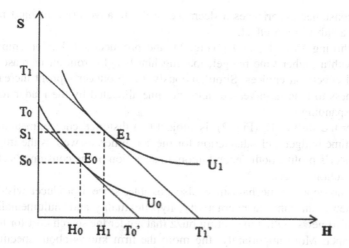

Fig. 1. The effect of an increase in time budget on a reader's indifference curve.

rotates, from T_0 to T_2 (Fig. 2). The change in the slope of the time budget indicates the modification of the relative price of the two commodities, and highlights a substitution effect by which the consumer is substituting one item to another, ceteris paribus.

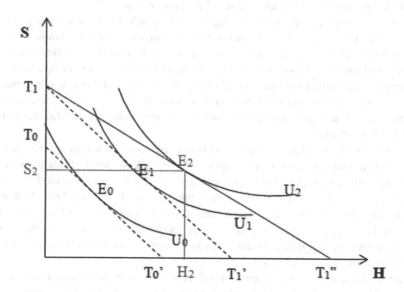

Fig. 2. The effect of a decrease in the search cost of hard news on a reader's indifference curve.

In our model, when the time budget rotates from T_0 to $T_1 T_1''$ due to the relative increase in interactivity, hypertextuality and multimediality of hard news over soft news, the consumer experiences a decrease in the relative price of hard news, thus undergoing a substitution effect.

When shifting from E_0 to E_1 (Fig. 1), the producer's behavior empowers the consumer with a higher time budget, making him benefit from an increase in utility, with neutral effects on choices. Simultaneously, the producer's profit increases, since the willingness to read is increased, and the time allocated by the reader for both H_{ij} and S_{ij} is expanding.

However the shift to E_2 (Fig. 2), is subject to a distorted choice, meaning that the increase in time budget and satisfaction for the consumer, as well as the improvement of the producer's profits, both depend upon an alteration of the consumer's choice, due to the substitution effects.

Surely, the opposite mechanism is also possible, since a producer wishing to sell more soft news can enhance interactivity, hypertextuality and multimediality of soft news over hard news, with a marketing buzz that render the search cost for this type of articles cheaper. More importantly, the more the firm knows about specific readers' profiles, the more it customizes information for the clients, increasing its control over their time budget and preferences on the long term. These shifts can be seen as an enhanced market transparency that simultaneously increases the consumers' utility and the producers' profits. Yet, the emergent market, although reaching higher levels of supply and demand, is far from perfect, since asymmetrical information and power are persistent, and the social desirability of this transparency is counterbalanced by inefficiency due to distorted choices or controlled preferences.

As shown in Fig. 2, appropriate strategies built on informational advantages for the producers can result in a greater market power. Not only the total amount of news provided increases, but the firm also has a greater control over the type of news it is providing and their corresponding bundle. Meanwhile the consumers benefiting from an increased time budget not only spends more time reading the online news, but they also tend to reveal more and more information about their subjective preferences, with each consumption and each interaction undertaken, providing the supplier with greater control over the market.

The static model of spatial competition is relevant to study traditional media, where producer's behavior and consumer's responsiveness lack the level of interactivity of e-journalism. However, it does not seem appropriate to draw from this model the same conclusions when facing information transparency in digital markets. Hence, we complete the static model by a dynamic one in order to evaluate the long term effects on the market. Applying this microeconomic model allows us to describe how the exponential increase in online media and online news sharing will modifies the consumer's behavior dynamically over time.

In an extreme (yet realistic) case, producers can exert an influence on the consumer's preferences and shift from one type of news to another. For instance, if the news search time cost for hard news (soft news) is decreased (increased) to its minimum (maximum), the reader's utility function is close to the horizontal (Fig. 3). This means that the distorted choices of the consumers are almost exclusively focused on hard news, and soft news are therefore left without any social utility. These situations are typical of times of electoral campaigns or important economic and social crisis, or periods of massive involvements in public affairs, when both journalists and public

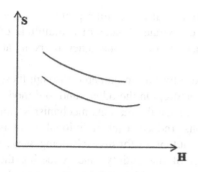

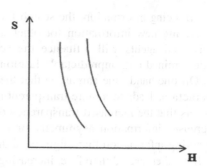

Fig. 3. Horizontal utility curves   **Fig. 4.** Vertical utility curves

opinion seems to be simultaneously shifting towards public affairs. In the opposite extreme case, some periods may be characterized by a general shift towards soft news (Fig. 4), when both journalists and the public opinion seem to neglect politics for a while, finding their common ground in entertainment, sometimes on a global effect scale, especially in sports (such as World cup or Olympic games events). As shown by Hirschman (2002) in his classical study, these cyclical "shifting involvements" of individuals and societies, back and forth from personal interests to public affairs, back and forth, are one of the main features of our modern democracies, yet they might as well serve a hidden cycle of business and economic affairs.

4 Discussion

The alteration of the individual agents' choice due to the time cost efficiency of mass media is certainly not a new phenomenon (Garhammer 1995; Mattingly and Sayer 2006). Yet, due to the increased time pressure in contemporary societies, the time allocation between new and traditional media, between soft and hard news, and between objective and biased contents has become a major topic of research in the last decade (Zhang and Ha 2015).

In this article, we suggest a model that illustrates how a competition aimed at increasing the consumer's time budget affects the market structure of new media, in a context of information abundance. The model showed that the transparency mechanism offered the producers an unprecedented leverage over the consumers' choices and behaviors, thereby questioning the autonomy and the freedom of the individual choice.

By clicking on a fitness club ad or reading an article on Obamacare, users reveal information on their preferences between soft and hard news to various media agencies. Thus, their choices of consumption are at the same time processes that produce information for other users and suppliers. As shown by Von Foerster, complexity can arise when some cybernetic interactions generate ambiguous self-referentiality, making it impossible to distinguish between the subject and the object, the end and the mean, nor between the observer and the participant (Von Foerster 2003). The observer is indeed and active part of the system, the act of consuming information become an act of producing information, the search for information is also revealing preferences and generating new information for other users, the deliberate choices of a multitude of individual agents will influence the scope of action for various other users in an undetermined and unpredictable fashion.

On one hand, one can argue that the increased information gathered through these interactions leads to a more transparent market structure. On the other hand, our model reveals that the increased transparency does not enhance the markets mechanisms, nor decreases information asymmetry or imperfections. Indeed, each individual agent is revealing information that might have unexpected outcomes for his well-being as well as for other users, therefore increasing the level of uncertainty, and rendering the market structure rather unstable. Instead of reaching a stable equilibrium, our model shows that the emergent structure could potentially lead to multiple outcomes, with possible shifts from on outcome to another.

An important side-effect of transparency was not taken into consideration by our model, yet it has major implications in concrete market situations: the manipulation of the consumers preference by the producers are not only limited to the control of news time search costs, i.e. the time budget, but new media can also control effectively the consumers preferences themselves, i.e. the shape of their indifference curves as shown in Figs. 3 and 4.

Indeed, by clicking on an ad for a fitness club, you reveal that you might be more interested by tennis shoes ads rather than cigarettes or alcohol ads. If you read an article on the benefits of the Obamacare, you reveal that you might be more interested by information on fiscal policies or social justice rather than science-fiction novels. At the age of Big Data, these revealed preferences may not lead to a stable market structure, but rather to more asymmetrical information, uncertainty, and manipulation. Firstly, the individual agent's preferences are more likely to be accurately anticipated through the revealed information in the customer history. Secondly, these higher levels of transparency and predictability can paradoxically lead to more opaque market mechanisms, since the total amount of information will allow some agents to manipulate others. Indeed, individual action can be increasingly influenced by external agents, or even controlled by alien interests, thus reducing the margins of the rational decision-making. Therefore, instead of being rationally determined by self-interest, the individual behavior may become less transparent to itself, since it is altered by various invisible and manipulated motivations. The individual rationality may then become hackable (Harari 2018), twisted by some asymmetrical information advantages, and subverted from its original motivations towards more hidden ends that individual agents are not pursuing in the first place.

For example, when the revealed preferences of various individual users searching for information on a fitness club (or Obamacare) are linked to their ethnic or religious origin, their social group, their level of education, etc., some suppliers may be able to sell targeted adds or information to other users, with similar profiles, who will have a greater chance of liking the same fitness club (or sharing the same opinion on the Obamacare). By collecting data from millions of consumers, and correlating billions of observations with the personal information of each user, the information system can predict more and more accurately the profile of new users. From the customers' history, the information system can predict their tastes, their personal opinions, as well as their intentions to vote. Those who control this information system of predictions can therefore sell customized information to each new user, according to what he or she might like.

Yet, under these conditions, when "I" read an article on the Obamacare, or on the benefit of a regular membership in a fitness club, or the latest best-seller science-fiction novel, how can I be sure that I "freely chose" to engage in these interactions. Moreover, how can I be sure that these choices truly reflect my preferences, since they were offered to me by an algorithm that predicted, more or less accurately, what I might be interested in reading? And how can these interactions reflect my personal preferences since they are more or less dictated by a systemic behavior engaging millions of other users who have revealed, in their past history, similar choices and patterns? And more importantly in which sense can we still talk here about more transparency in the market structure, since each decision or action has become more and more opaque for the individual agents themselves?

5 Conclusion

The technology underpinning E-markets allows any agent to produce or access information at the lowest cost, especially when information is extremely liquid, volatile, and instantaneous (Grover et al. 1999). However, new types of media are drastically changing the way consumers interact with online contents as well as with other users or producers of information. As a matter of fact, each individual agent is facing a plethora of web articles and news, that are usually influenced by the attitudes of peers, and manipulated by the marketing buzz or prioritized and syndicated (among thousands of other possible orders) by predefined complex algorithms such as newsfeed.

Yet, the simultaneity of the supply and demand of online news has never been yet a proper object of study, since traditional economic theory implies that the supply and demand are two autonomous behaviors, the market being nothing more than the encounter between two independent functions (two separate optimizing programs). In this article, we address this simultaneity and argue that content transparency and preferences revelation are co-dependent. In this sense, the informational interactions between producers and consumers are intertwined in such a way that render them both interdependent, endogenous, highly unstable, and subject to various strategies of distortion, manipulation and control.

In the basic model we presented, we showed that the rise of technology modifies the digital journalism market significantly and to some extent exaggerates its biases. As a matter of fact, during periods where politics matter the most such as the electoral period, consumers will subconsciously tend to read hard news, and to even prefer hard news over soft news, even though they usually prefer soft news over hard news. Hence, readers are not totally free as stated by McManus (1994): "the desires individuals bring to the market may be the products of choices the market already offers and the impacts of communities of taste, peer groups, and other external forces". This can be justified by the fact that readers lack the ability to judge the transparency and the consistency of the news content. Hence, readers ignore their own preferences in reading, and think they are freely choosing what to read.

Therefore, though each rational decision is made with perfect freedom of action, the total effect of the generative process of information may lead to controlled decisions or manipulated attitudes. Hence, analyzing the structural effects of increased transparency can have major implications for the economic theory of information, challenging some assumptions regarding free-market mechanisms and, to some extent, shaking our most common beliefs in its underlying values, such as the Liberty of individual agents, the independence and the autonomy of rational choices and the efficiency of the democratic system as a whole.

If we consider real digital markets involving millions of users simultaneously interacting with a multitude of providers, advertisers, and invisible algorithms, it is extremely difficult to draw a clear line that separates the generative process and the generated product, since the former is producing the latter while being shaped by it. Thus, it is difficult to grasp these endogenous processes of information transparency within a simple microeconomic model that reduces the total interactions to a limited number of agents operating within a pre-defined market structure, with predictable strategies and optimizing programs (such as consumers, firms, State, workers, etc.). Therefore, a precise model of behavior can only draw the general attitudes of various stakeholders, yet general conclusions regarding the efficiency of the market structures may not be easily drawn, especially if the premises of rational choices and the mental structures of rational agents are distorted, controlled, or manipulated leading to a sub-optimal equilibrium.

References

Akerlof, G.: The market for lemons: qualitative uncertainty and the market mechanism. Q. J. Econ. **84**(3), 488–500 (1970)

Boczkowski, P.J., Mitchelstein, E.: How users take advantage of different forms of interactivity on online news sites: clicking, e-mailing, and commenting. Hum. Commun. Res. **38**(1), 1–22 (2012)

Boczkowski, P.J., Mitchelstein, E., Walter, M.: Convergence across divergence: understanding the gap in the online news choices of journalists and consumers in Western Europe and Latin America. Commun. Res. **38**(3), 376–396 (2011)

Brynjolfsson, E., Smith, M.D.: Frictionless commerce? A comparison of internet and conventional retailers. Manag. Sci. **46**(4), 563–585 (2000)

Buchanan, J.M.: Individual choice in voting and the market. J. Polit. Econ. **62**(4), 334–343 (1954)

Carpenter, S.: A study of content diversity in online citizen journalism and online newspaper articles. New Media Soc. **12**(7), 1064–1084 (2010)

Chung, C.J., Nam, Y., Stefanone, M.A.: Exploring online news credibility: the relative influence of traditional and technological factors. J. Comput. Mediat. Commun. **17**(2), 171–186 (2012)

Chung, D.S.: Interactive features of online newspapers: identifying patterns and predicting use of engaged readers. J. Comput. Mediat. Commun. **13**(3), 658–679 (2008)

Downs, A.: An economic theory of political action in a democracy. J. Polit. Econ. **65**(2), 135–150 (1957)

Garhammer, M.: Changes in working hours in Germany: the resulting impact on everyday life. Time Soc. **4**(2), 167–203 (1995)

Graber, D.: Mediated politics and citizenship in the twenty-first century. Annu. Rev. Psychol. **55**, 545–571 (2004)

Granados, N.F., Gupta, A., Kauffman, R.J.: The impact of IT on market information and transparency: a unified theoretical framework. J. Assoc. Inf. Syst. **7**(3), 148–178 (2006)

Grover, V., Ramanlal, P., Segars, A.H.: Information exchange in electronic markets: implications for market structures. Int. J. Electron. Commer. **3**(4), 89–102 (1999)

Harari, Y.N.: 21 Lessons for the 21st Century. Spiegel and Grau, New York (2018)

Hirschman, A.O.: Shifting Involvements: Private Interest and Public Action. Princeton University Press, Princeton (2002)

Johnson, T.J., Kaye, B.K.: Still cruising and believing? An analysis of online credibility across three presidential campaigns. Am. Behav. Sci. **54**(1), 57–77 (2010)

Lal, R., Sarvary, M.: When and how is the Internet likely to decrease price competition? Mark. Sci. **18**(4), 485–503 (1999)

Mattingly, M.J., Sayer, L.C.: Under pressure: gender differences in the relationship between free time and feeling rushed. J. Marriage Family **68**(1), 205–221 (2006)

McManus, J.H.: Market-Driven Journalism: Let the Citizen Beware?. Sage Publications, California (1994)

Schudson, M.: The Good Citizen: A History of American Civic Life. Harvard University Press, Harvard (1999)

Shapiro, C., Varian, H.R.: Information Rules: A Strategic Guide to the Information Economy. Harvard Business School Press, Boston (1999)

Stiglitz, J.E.: Information and the change in the paradigm in economics. Am. Econ. Rev. **92**(3), 460–501 (2002)

Vargo, K., Schierhorn, C., Wearden, S.T., Schierhorn, A.B., Endres, F.F., Tabar, P.S.: How readers' respond to digital news stories in layers and links. Newsp. Res. J. **21**(2), 40–54 (2000)

Von Foerster, H.: Understanding Understanding: Essays on Cybernetics and Cognition. Springer, New York (2003)

Wise, R., Morrison, D.: Beyond the exchange: the future of B2B. Harvard Bus. Rev. **78**(6), 86–96 (2000)

Zaller, J.: A new standard of news quality: burglar alarms for the monitorial citizen. Polit. Commun. **20**(2), 109–130 (2003)

Zhang, X., Ha, L.: Time budget, news search time cost, and news media choice. Time Soc. **24**(2), 201–220 (2015)

Zhu, K.: Information transparency of business-to-business electronic markets: a game-theoretic analysis. Manag. Sci. **50**(5), 670–685 (2004)

Zhu, K.: Information transparency hypothesis: economic implications of information transparency in electronic markets. In: Tomak, K. (ed.) Advances in the Economics of Information Systems, pp. 15–42. IGI Global, Hershey (2005)

Zhu, K., Weyant, J.P.: Strategic decisions of new technology adoption under asymmetric information: a game-theoretic model. Decis. Sci. **34**(4), 643–675 (2003)

Going Viral: Elements that Lead Videos to Become Viral

Rania Abouyounes[✉] [iD]

Department of Marketing, International University of Beirut, Beirut, Lebanon
rania.abouyounes@liu.edu.lb

Abstract. Why are some video content more viral than others are? This paper takes an exploratory approach to understanding the elements of viral videos in terms of digital marketing. Using a set of data about viral videos, case studies, and observations of viral videos, this paper provides insight on what elements should be present to achieve virility and replicate the results. To overcome a noisy market full of competitor messages, the elements in this paper will allow for a better-implemented video marketing campaign. Turning a video marketing campaign into a viral video marketing campaign needs extra effort from businesses in terms of innovation and creativity.

Keywords: Viral marketing · Digital marketing · Online content · Viral video

1 Introduction

The internet has profoundly added to the lives of many to learn, to be entertained, and to build relationships (Frangoul 2019). This opportunity has allowed businesses to contribute to the noise and solve problems for customers. As time has passed, customers moved from enjoying texts, to images, to GIFs, and now to videos (Kevin Westcott 2018). Digital technology is on the rise and businesses are joining in on the benefits of digital. Communicating with customers where they spend most of their time is key for all businesses (Burke 2019). Competitors know that information and find their way online. Marketers are in the need to test out different ways to stand out from the noisy online space (Connell 2019). One way to do it is through video marketing.

Social media platforms are shifting their algorithms to push videos towards customers (Flynn 2017). Most customers prefer to save time by consuming content through video. Fast internet connections has allowed video content to win over any other type of content. Imagine now that thousands and thousands of people share this video. This will result in massive exposure for a brand. This concept is called viral video marketing (Gotter 2018).

In a world full of noise in media communication, messages barely reach customers. However, with viral videos, customers show interest and spot the video from between the noisy media. The purpose of this study is identify why some videos go viral but others do not. With that the below research questions are tackled.

1. Does the content of the video help videos go viral?
2. What elements in the content of the video make it go viral?
3. What elements surrounding the video make it go viral?

© Springer Nature Switzerland AG 2019
R. Jallouli et al. (Eds.): ICDEc 2019, LNBIP 358, pp. 266–277, 2019.
https://doi.org/10.1007/978-3-030-30874-2_21

Viral video marketing reaps many benefits but few have mastered its craft. Several information can be found about viral videos but few about what elements do all these viral videos hold. This paper outlines these elements through a qualitative approach using primary and secondary data.

2 Literature Review

It has been predicted that 80% of web traffic will be video based in 2019 (Hoben 2018). Video marketing is rapidly rising and will continue to grow in the upcoming years (Pritchard 2019). Achieving ramification for content that is high quality can provide huge value for businesses, but it requires an understanding of the perplexing human emotion, age, gender, and how it affects how humans consume and share content online, and many other factors that can be defined (Hutchinson 2016). Marketers continue to test different ways to utilize video marketing in a way that affects their business. Hence, more often than not, turning a video into a viral video in marketing is usually a campaign goal many aspire to achieve, but few are successful (Pritchard 2019).

"Viral video marketing is a marketing technique used to promote brand awareness, products, services, or to achieve other marketing objectives. This technique uses social networking and other tools to gain traction for the video" (Meyer 2015). This technique is based on one primary aspect: the viewer choosing to share the video. In other words, achieving virality occurs when the total number of shares increases with every share iteration. Hence, if 2 people share a video to their pool of virtual friends, and then they share the video, a chain reaction may occur like that shown in the graph below. This usually happens within the first hour of the video being uploaded online (Fig. 1).

Viral video marketing is helping businesses break through the noisy atmosphere that is distorting the communication message for potential and current customers (Price 2019). There are 5.3 trillion display ads shown online each year, 400 million tweets sent daily, 144,000 h of YouTube video uploaded daily, and 4.75 billion pieces of content shared on Facebook every day (Tynski 2013). Even consumers prefer video to learn about a product or service. Seventy-two percent of people prefer to use video than any other form (Hayes 2018).

Viral video marketing can enable a high engagement level in terms of shares, likes, follows, comments, and so on. The technical skills of crafting the best video marketing campaign is rarely the reason why a video goes viral. The following are some statistics collected after different companies achieved virality. A campaign created by Dove, "Dove's Real Beauty Sketches" (Dove US 2013), went viral generating nearly 30 million views in ten days, 15000 YouTube subscribers within 2 months and a general increase on other social media platforms (Tynski 2013). A common determinant in both campaigns is the feeling of sadness related directly to: human emotion. Another campaign, created by MetLife, "My dad's story" (MetLife 2015) strikes close to 16 million views on YouTube. Further, the campaign "World's Toughest Job" garnered 13.8 million views and 1.6 million social shares after 5 days of posting (Brenner 2015).

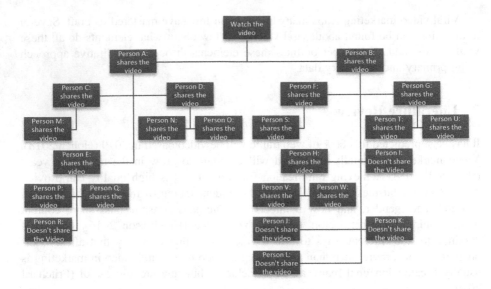

Fig. 1. Sharing viral videos

This campaign was created for the celebration of mother's day. Another campaign, the "Squatty Potty", has received 35 million views on YouTube with 101K likes and 7206 comments online. This campaign does not focus on human emotion but it does educate the viewer with a tad bit of humor that makes an embarrassing subject seem a little less embarrassing (Squatty Potty 2015). Hence, the type of video campaign may have little to do with virality.

Marketers continue to question and test out different ways to make their videos go viral. Marketers have learned the importance of video marketing, but few have been able to make content go viral let alone replicate the result (Hoben 2018). Managing Director of Harmon Brothers receives 150 million views, 13, 000% increase in web traffic and has been able to introduce new brands to the industry within days, claims that virality is unpredictable and is not repeatable (Dawson 2017). Hence, there is no defined formula to create virality. The viewer's complex reaction defines it. Another company, The Woolshed and Co, created several video marketing campaigns to master the art of viral content and was successful (Hutchinson 2016). This company believes virality can be achievable when the right elements exist.

A main indicator of a video going viral successfully is the usage of emotional triggers like happiness, surprise, anger and so on. The human emotions that are most commonly associated with viral content are curiosity, amazement, interest, astonishment, and uncertainty (Libert 2014). The reason why human emotion is a strong factor to viral video content is how easily the business can generate a quick response from viewers. Videos with such emotions allow for a higher chance for the video to go viral. Emotional triggers that have to do with happiness, surprise and admiration are the top results for viral content (Hutchinson 2016). Other element factors can also have an effect for videos going viral or not. Videos that provide value, entertain, give people an understanding of who they are, feel more connected in a relationship with others, feel like they belong and are involved in a certain community all help with setting up a video for success (Libert 2014). If the video does not go viral, the business is still able to reap benefits from a high amount of views and engagement. Other aspects that will affect the virality of a video are things like the length of the video, the length of the title, and the description or caption under the video (West 2011).

Authenticity needs to be portrayed in the video and be about the viewer rather than the brand (Brenner 2015). The message needs to be simple and told in a story format. This story format will allow the user to build an emotional connection if done right (Brenner 2015). To give the video an additional edge, strategy and creativity need to be present. After the video is online, marketers need to take action. The marketer needs to use the right media sources to push the content organically to reach millions of viewers (Brenner 2015). The words used as a description and more importantly as a headline will affect the video virality. Timing is everything to avoid noise from other media sites and still be able to convince the consumer in time for the conversion (Brenner 2015).

3   Methodology

The research design of this paper is qualitative. Both primary and secondary data collection methods have been used to come to the findings in this paper.

The purpose of this research is to determine the elements of viral video marketing to achieve success in virality. This research can allow businesses to design videos that have the elements of viral videos, increasing their chances of achieving virality.

To determine the elements and what common grounds they hold, experts in the field were surveyed, to develop a better understanding of the elements that create viral videos. Through a 10-question survey that was distributed to experts in digital marketing, primary data was obtained. The survey questions were constructed based on developing a better understanding of the elements that creates a viral video. Due to the limitation on time, 10 digital marketers were able to answer the survey on time. The majority of the digital marketers reside in Lebanon but work for clients within Lebanon, in the GCC region and some even international. The remaining digital marketers who answered the survey were abroad in Canada. These digital marketers were contact to give their opinion since they manage several clients and are frequently staying up to date on recent trends in the industry. The data collected was through SPSS.

Secondary data was collected by analyzing several articles, websites and online documents. Observation of viral videos also added to the research data. The viral videos chosen were based on Facebook, YouTube, and Google's interpretation of viral video lists.

4 Results

Viral video content has several elements that allows for a better insight on what makes videos go viral. After observing several videos of viral content, elements that contain any emotional triggers will give the company a greater chance in achieving virality (Brenner 2015). The most common emotional trigger for highly shared content is surprise. The second is happiness (Fractl n.d.). The elements of human emotions all play out with positive feeling factors, for the majority of viral videos. Using these emotional triggers in the video is not enough on its own. The majority of observed viral videos come to a resolution at the end of the video giving the customer assurance (Fractl n.d.).

A study conducted Time Magazine, taking 20 YouTube videos that had achieved virality showed elements like title length, length of the video, laughter, and element of surprise and so on (West 2011). Any element resulting with less than 25% of the sample group was ignored. Title lengths resulted in 75% of the sample population agreeing that a shorter title, 3 words, is going to receive higher engagement from the viewer. The length of the video resulted in 60% of the sample population to choose the length of the video as 3 min or less. The laughter element tested to see if there had been laughter in the first 30 s of the clip. Seventy percent had not encountered the laughter element. The element of surprise resulted in a 50/50 result from the sample population (West 2011).

Fig. 2. Percentage of people who shared an interesting video with a friend

Data collected from the surveys completed by the 10 digital marketers also yielded insight on viral video marketing. One hundred percent of the surveyed marketers claimed that they have shared a video with a friend that they found interesting (Fig. 2).

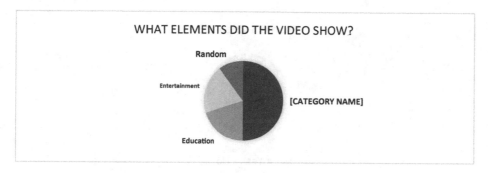

Fig. 3. Results of which elements were found in the video

Fifty percent of the surveyed claimed the video was an emotional video, twenty percent claimed it was an educational, twenty percent claimed the video was an entertainment video, and ten percent it was a random video (Fig. 3).

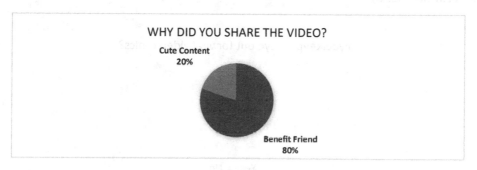

Fig. 4. The reason behind sharing the video

Eighty percent of the surveyed shared the video because they wanted their friend to benefit from the video content. Twenty percent shared the video because the content was very cute (Fig. 4).

Seventy percent of the surveyed claimed that they had shared a video ad before and thirty percent claimed that they had not (Fig. 5).

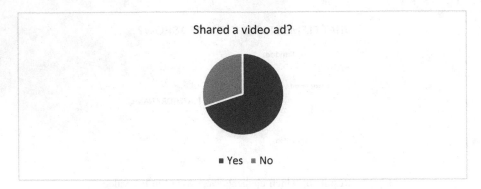

Fig. 5. Percentage of people who shared a video ad

Sixty percent of the surveyed do not look out for viral video topics while forty percent do (Fig. 6).

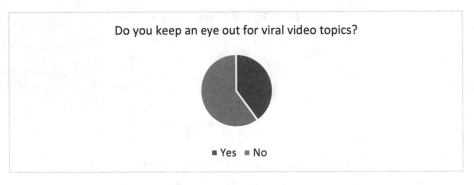

Fig. 6. Percentage of people who look out for viral video topics

Sixty percent of the surveyed believed that viral video success can be repeated while forty percent do not (Fig. 7).

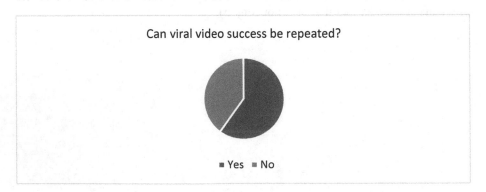

Fig. 7. Percentage of people who believe viral video success can be repeated

Eighty percent of the surveyed believed that the element of the viral video needed to be an emotional trigger. Twenty percent of the surveyed believed that the elements do not matter as much as the content of the video does (Fig. 8).

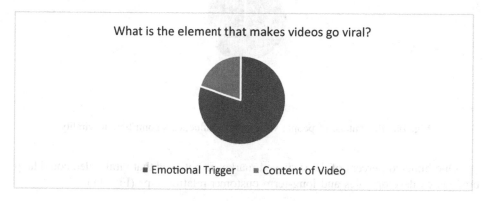

Fig. 8. Elements that make a video go viral

Ninety percent claim that users have complete control over what video goes viral while ten percent claim there is no determining factor (Fig. 9).

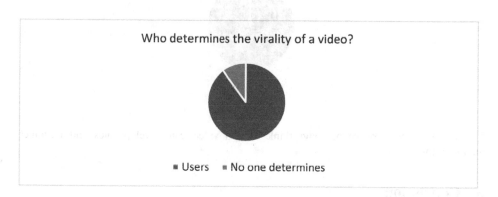

Fig. 9. Who determines the virality of a video

One hundred percent of the surveyed believe that influencers contribute to making a video go viral (Fig. 10).

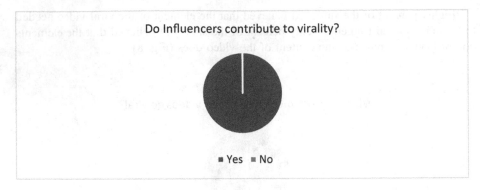

Fig. 10. Percentage of people who believe influencers contribute to virality

One hundred percent of the surveyed marketers believed that viral video could help businesses develop sales and long-term customer relationships (Fig. 11).

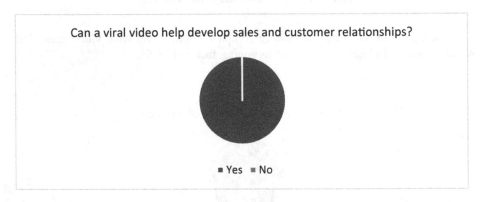

Fig. 11. Percentage of people who think a viral video can develop sales and customer relationships

5   Conclusion

Human emotions are a definite factor when it comes to viral video content. The human emotions that are most commonly associated with viral content are curiosity, amazement, interest, astonishment, and uncertainty (Libert 2014). The reason why human emotion is a strong factor to viral video content is how easily the business can generate a quick response from viewers.

Using the right elements of human emotion, title length, description, music, video quality and much more will help in succeeding with virility. If the content in the video is beneficial for the viewer or the viewer feels that this video may help someone, he or she may share it. The goal with viral marketing is not achieving fame but achieving a long-term viewer base to benefit the company's bottom line in the future.

With every research resides limitations. The research design of this paper is qualitative. This limited the amount of data collected that may have resulted in the creation of a viral video marketing model that businesses can implement. An integration of both qualitative and quantitative methods can enhance the results by conducting surveys and case studies on the subject matter. It was very difficult to find academic papers on this subject to confirm the findings and predictions.

Because the nature of this study is new and is still being tested by many, a lack of solid theoretical information was found. Time added to the limitation of being able to get more information from experts in the market, to observe more videos, and to experiment with different video elements to see which has a higher possibility of going viral.

When it comes to future research, there is a need for further examination to confirm that the elements discussed above are applicable in all industries and on all video-based platforms. To be able to develop a model that businesses can follow to achieve video virality, practical examination on the field for all industries helps create a model that can be applied by all businesses.

6 Recommendations

Chances for virility increase when marketers set the company up for success. Developing the right elements for videos and video ads will enable a higher share rate. Hence, marketers should focus on the elements that can bring forward a video. However, marketers should be aware that the video should continue to add value for customers and potential customers. Regardless of how good the video is, it will be invaluable to the viewer if it does not add value. Marketers need to be able to determine how they will apply elements to a video that will relate to their product/service.

Using human emotion is key. Having a clear understanding of who a business's customer is will enable a better outcome for the video. Determining the demographics, psychographics, geographic and even the behavior of customers will help construct a video ready to go viral. Next marketers need to create video content that will allow customers to feel the emotional element within the video.

The company website and YouTube should include the video. Social media platforms should have the video uploaded ready for sharing. Marketers need to prompt viewer to share for a benefit. This means that marketers need to inform the viewer to take an action by sharing and tell the viewer why they are sharing by speaking of the benefits. Wherever the company decides to post the video, it should consider search engine optimization and the best practices for social media.

Within an hour of uploading the video it will be determined if the video will go viral. Hence, marketers need to spend this hour engaging with influencers, press, expert sites, and customers to get the highest number of viewers for a potentially higher number of shares.

In the end, to achieve the result of a viral video, the right elements need to be present. Marketers need not focus on making the video viral, but on what value it adds for its customer.

References

Brenner, M.: Is there a science to making a viral video? (2015). Marketing Insider Group: https://marketinginsidergroup.com/content-marketing/how-to-make-a-viral-video/. Accessed 09 Jan 2019

Burke, Z.: Social media marketing: how to choose your channels and create your strategy (2019). Digital Marketing Institute: https://digitalmarketinginstitute.com/blog/social-media-marketing-choose-channels-create-strategy

Connell, A.: How to stand out online: 43 experts share their top tips (2019). Blogging Wizard: https://bloggingwizard.com/stand-out-online/

Dawson, V.: How to master a viral video campaign (2017). Forbes: https://www.forbes.com/sites/vinettaproject/2017/06/14/how-to-master-a-viral-video-campaign/#5f80398040f6. Accessed 09 Jan 2019

Dove US: Dove real beauty sketches you're more beautiful than you think (2013). Youtube: https://www.youtube.com/watch?v=XpaOjMXyJGk. Accessed 04 Jan 2019

Flynn, K.: Facebook video watch time (2017). Mashable: https://mashable.com/2017/01/26/facebook-video-watch-time/

Fractl: Why certain emotional combinations make people share (n.d.). Fractl: https://www.frac.tl/work/marketing-research/viral-content-emotions-study/. Accessed 09 Jan 2019

Frangoul, A.: 10 ways the web and internet have transformed our lives (2019). CNBC: https://www.cnbc.com/2018/02/09/10-ways-the-web-and-internet-have-transformed-our-lives.html

Gotter, A.: Viral video marketing examples (2018). Disruptive Advertising: https://www.disruptiveadvertising.com/video-advertising/viral-video-marketing-examples/

Hayes, A.: The state of video marketing in 2018 (2018). Hubspot: https://blog.hubspot.com/marketing/state-of-video-marketing-new-data. Accessed 09 Jan 2019

Hoben, N.: 10 rules for video marketing & SEO success (2018). Search Engine Journal: https://www.searchenginejournal.com/10-rules-for-video-marketing-seo-success/266405/. Accessed 04 Jan 2019

Hutchinson, A.: Cracking the code of virality: what makes a video go viral (and can you use that to advantage)? (2016). Social Media Today: https://www.socialmediatoday.com/social-networks/cracking-code-virality-what-makes-video-go-viral-and-can-you-use-advantage. Accessed 09 Jan 2019

Kevin Westcott, J.L.: Digital media segments: looking beyond generations (2018). Deliotte Insights: https://www2.deloitte.com/insights/us/en/industry/telecommunications/media-consumption-behavior-across-generations.html

Libert, K.: Age and gender matter in viral marketing (2014). Harvard Business Review: https://hbr.org/2014/08/age-and-gender-matter-in-viral-marketing. Accessed 04 Jan 2019

MetLife: "My dad's story": Dream for My Child | MetLife (2015). YouTube: https://www.youtube.com/watch?v=3bdm4NBYxII&feature=youtu.be. Accessed 04 Jan 2019

Meyer, A.: Viral video marketing: what's, why's & how's of going viral (2015). Ideal Path: https://www.idealpath.com/marketing-automation-blog/social-media-marketing/viral-video-marketing-cats-babies-and-your-company/. Accessed 04 Jan 2019

Price, S.: The power of viral marketing (2019). Super Dream: https://superdream.com/news-blog/the-power-of-viral-marketing

Pritchard, K.: 25 new video marketing statistics for 2019 (2018). Impact Bnd: https://www.impactbnd.com/blog/new-video-marketing-statistics-2019

Squatty Potty: This unicorn changed the way i poop (2015). YouTube: https://www.youtube.com/watch?v=YbYWhdLO43Q. Accessed 09 Jan 2019

Tynski, K.L.: Research: the emotions that make marketing campaigns go viral (2013). Harvard Business Review: https://hbr.org/2013/10/research-the-emotions-that-make-marketing-campaigns-go-viral. Accessed 04 Jan 2019

West, T.: Going viral: factors that lead videos to become internet phenomena. Elon J. Undergrad. Res. Commun. **2**, 1–9 (2011)

A Quantitative Model for Replacement of Medical Equipment Based on Technical and Economic Factors

Yasmine Jarikji[1], Bassam Hussein[2], and Mohamad Hajj-Hassan[1(✉)]

[1] Department of Biomedical Engineering, Lebanese International University,
Beirut, Lebanon
yasminejarikji@gmail.com,
mohamad.hajjhassan@liu.edu.lb
[2] Department of Industrial Engineering, Lebanese International University,
Beirut, Lebanon
bassam.hussein@liu.edu.lb

Abstract. Medical equipment plays a vital role in diagnosing, monitoring, and treating different kinds of medical conditions. The biomedical and clinical engineering departments within a hospital are generally responsible for inspecting and managing the maintenance of medical equipment, ensuring that the breakdown of equipment and accidents made during diagnosis and treatment are forbidden. Maintaining the efficiency of medical equipment is a challenging topic due to the fact that many factors impact it through the equipment life cycle. Traditional approaches are based on the technical factors to estimate the lifetime of medical equipment. Additional factors, such as environmental factors, can also affect medical equipments lifespan. This paper introduces a new approach for evaluating medical equipment depending on two dimensions; the standard identified technical criteria and the added environmental criteria. These factors, combined together, affect the decision making process by a clinical engineer in case of medical equipment failure.

Keywords: Medical equipment economics · Technical factors ·
Economics environmental factors · Engineering economics · Patient safety ·
Equipment lifespan

1 Introduction

Healthcare organizations deliver healthcare services to meet the health needs of target populations. Every medical organization must provide coordinated high quality healthcare delivery to patients. With the tremendous recent advances in technologies; diagnosis, treatment, and prevention of diseases, nowadays, highly depend on medical equipment. This dependency on the new and high technology, requires an efficient coordination among all specialties in healthcare organizations, to ensure a proper assessment and maintenance of medical equipment. When an equipment fails, the clinical engineer takes all the responsibility of finding a solution, either to fix or dispose that device. Since, this failure may vastly affect the main goal of a healthcare facility,

© Springer Nature Switzerland AG 2019
R. Jallouli et al. (Eds.): ICDEc 2019, LNBIP 358, pp. 278–285, 2019.
https://doi.org/10.1007/978-3-030-30874-2_22

which is patient safety; a method must be deducted to study the status of the equipment to ensure the full delivery of accurate service. Hence, it is essential to have a scientific strategy that helps the clinical engineer take a precise with an exact decision in case of this failure. Currently, the adopted method of taking these decisions in Lebanese hospitals regarding replacing/repairing process is totally based on the cost (labor and spare parts). Moreover, the engineer will repair or replace the machine, if the repair cost is less than 25% and greater than 25% of the medical equipment cost respectively. Starting from this point the problem rises, neglecting other factors that may affect highly the equipment failure and its life cycle, would put the decision under serious doubt excluding a well-studied plan with a scientific formula to depend on through the decision process.

Plenty of approaches developed to assess the lifespan of medical equipment based on technical factors that affect its status. These approaches lack the inclusion of environmental factors that impact the decision-making process. It is then necessary to establish a new risk evaluation and analytic technique, which will be introduced for healthcare equipment life time assessment study among all Lebanon focusing on two dimensions: Technical and environmental ones, in order to perform at the same level and deliver the better quality of healthcare service.

2 Literature Review

Various studies were held and implemented concerning investment decisions and replacement of equipment. A simple quantitative model for replacement of medical equipment proposed to developing countries was developed by Ouda et al. where hospitals need to take decisions on medical equipment acquisition, maintenance, use and replacement on the basis of complete and reliable information (Ouda et al. 2010). The model focuses on the replacement criteria in developing countries, where there is a lack of scientific, realistic and comprehensive assessment. In this model, they used Fault Tree Analysis (FTA) to model the replacement process using a set of indicators that impact directly or indirectly the replacement decision, by including the vendor support as a fundamental technical indicator in the analysis. The vendor support can be quantified through three indicators; (i) the availability of spare parts, (ii) the call response ratio and (iii) the repair time-to-downtime ratio. Another novel approach developed for healthcare equipment lifespan assessment by claiming that medical equipment requires five missions: (i) classify the function of the equipment into five categories, (ii) specify the mission criticality of the equipment, (iii) identify the age of the equipment, (iv) investigate risks on the equipment and (v) study the maintenance requirements of the equipment (Aridi et al. 2016). The final score for each equipment is the summation of weight multiplied by the intensity for the five criteria and arranged in descending order so that they can calculate the normalized score value that indicates the relative criticality of a device compared to other devices. So, they classified the criticality of a device into three categories: (i) should be replaced urgently, (ii) should be replaced after a year and a half, and (iii) are still functioning normally (Aridi et al. 2016; Ismail et al. 2018). Also, a survey of questions was designed for physicians, technicians, and nurses, collecting data and targeting the equipment that should be replaced directly.

According to the previous models, they have only based their assessment on technical reasons, they didn't realize that environmental factors may heavily affect this decision in many ways and this study will be implemented in Lebanon. Where Lebanese society is always altering, it is unstable economically like inflation rates, the balance of payments … (Williams 2014), always new governments and new regulations like government corruptions, interferences … (Shepherd and Rudd 2013), the security and political stability are threatened like terrorism, wars … (Goll and Rasheed 2005) and take into consideration the geography with its natural obstacles like climate changing and disasters (Giddens 1984). All the mentioned environmental factors can be taken on the level of any country not only Lebanon. Hence, the more distant the environmental factors the more difficult it is to establish proper relationships of influence.

3 Methodology

Everything in our lives has an end so do the medical equipment. This appliances' lifecycle passes through many phases: Requesting, planning, deployment, management, maintenance, and disposal to be implemented in a healthcare organization (THET n.d.). These stages might be affected by factors related to the environment that we are living in, which were explained before. So, it is important to employ these factors besides the technical ones0 by making a new risk evaluation and an analytic technique similar to the proposed technique in the Novel Approach for healthcare equipment lifespan assessment study (Aridi et al. 2016). The novel approach study (Aridi et al. 2016) proposed before, is based on the evaluation and classification of medical equipment that should be replaced according to the technical technology factors, which are function and age of a medical equipment, mission criticality, risks, and maintenance requirements which defines the technical side affecting the decision making process made by clinical engineers. Each identified criterion has a certain weight in our model and limited to a certain range of choices where every choice is assigned to certain intensity. So, for collecting regarding each criterion a survey checklist questionnaire is designed for each equipment and distributed among hospitals in Lebanon. After the filling process, by mostly clinical engineers, the scores are computed using the assigned weights and intensities and the total score is calculated. After that, for the purpose of evaluating equipment that should be replaced, the Normalized Score Value (NSV) is calculated from which the transformed score value (TSV) is calculated, where NSV indicates the relative importance of each device in comparison with other devices and TSV is the value in which the medical devices are ranked according to their importance in the replacement process. In this study, the model was applied to a Lebanese public hospital resulting in a list of equipment to be replaced after a period of time depending on the evaluation of (NSV) and (TSV) computed for each equipment, where results will be shown later on.

In our study, a new evaluation similar to this study will be proposed where environmental factors will be added and the computed NSV and TSV for each equipment will be identified depending on the factors utilizing the technical technology as mentioned in the novel approach study and the environmental factors. A survey questionnaire is constructed for our study including the name and the position of the clinical engineer, giving approximate percentages on the technical and environmental factors effect on decision-making process with rating the 4 sub-environmental criteria. After that, the classification and selection of the equipment to be replaced or repaired shall be selected depending on the computed NSV in which the total NSV will be the summation of the technical part (NSV_{TF}) and the environmental part (NSV_{EF}) from which the Total TSV can be computed and the evaluation process can be applied.

4 Results

In this part the results will be presented, at first when the similar novel approach study was implemented on a public Lebanese hospital, a list of equipment and its results are introduced in Table 1 followed by the used equations.

Table 1. (NSV) and (TSV) obtained for some equipment

Equipment name	Normalized score (NSV)	Transformed score (TSV) (%)
Defibrillator	1	100
Monitor (ICU)	0.76745621	73.400487
Pulse oximeters	0.83167396	80.721096

$$Total\ Score = \sum_{j}^{5} W_j S_{ij} \tag{1}$$

The total score of each equipment is the summation of the weights × intensity for the five defined technical criteria as shown in Eq. (1) where W is the weight of each criterion (j = 1, 2 … 5) and "i" is the intensity of each class.

$$NSV = \frac{Total\ score\ of\ Each\ device}{Maximum\ total\ score} \tag{2}$$

$$TSV = \frac{Score\ Value - Minimum}{Maximum - Minimum} \times 100 \tag{3}$$

The criticality of the device to be replaced urgently or after a specific time is classified depending on the Transformed Score Value (TSV) obtained for each medical equipment, and sorted according to their urgency as identified in Table 2.

Table 2. Criticality of a medical device according to the TSV

Criticality class	Transformed score value	Maintenance action
High	70% < TSV < 100%	To be changed urgently
Medium	30% < TSV < 70%	To be changed after a year and a half
Low	0% < TSV < 30%	To be changed after three years

The criticality of the device to be replaced urgently or after a specific time is classified depending on the Transformed Score Value (TSV) obtained for each medical equipment where the medical equipment's are sorted according to their urgency as identified in Table 2.

Second, the results for the new model in this paper when a survey questionnaire was distributed among one of the hospitals named as "Hospital C" in Beirut district are presented below in Figs. 1 and 2 as pie charts.

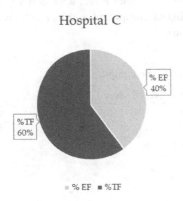

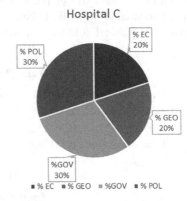

Fig. 1. Percentages of environmental & technical factors for Hospital C from survey questionnaire

Fig. 2. Percentages of the identified environmental factors for Hospital C

Overall percentages of the 44% chosen hospitals participated distributed in Beirut and Mount Lebanon are calculated, which results of Av. %EF = 21 and Av. %TF = 79 both calculated using Eqs. (4–5), with the identified environmental factors %EC = 26, %GEO = 20, %GOV = 27, %POL = 25 calculated by Eq. (6)

$$Avr\%(EF) = \frac{\sum EF\ Percentages}{Number\ of\ Repliers} \tag{4}$$

$$Avr\%(EF) = \frac{\sum EF\ Percentages}{Number\ of\ Repliers} \tag{5}$$

$$Avr\%(ENV\ Criteria) = \frac{\sum Criteria\ Percentages}{Number\ of\ Repliers} \tag{6}$$

The average % of (TF, EF & ENV criteria) indicates the average percentages identified after the filling process of the survey questionnaire depending on the responses of clinical engineers through the healthcare field in the Lebanese society.

After acquiring the weights through our survey, the parameters for classification of medical devices based on technical and environmental criteria can be computed through the Eq. (7) below:

$$Total_{NSV} = (Average \% TF) \times NSV_{TF} + (Average \% EF) \times NSV_{EF} \tag{7}$$

Our model is applied in which each environmental factor acquire an effective intensity is equal to the division of each criteria weight with the maximum weight of the four maintained environmental criteria, see Eq. (10). In the first mission, the Total Score (X) will be calculated as follows:

$$Total\ Score(X) = \sum_{j=1}^{4} W_j S_j \tag{8}$$

$$Total\ Score(X) = W_{Economics} \times I_{Economics} + W_{Geographic} \times I_{Geographic} + W_{Govermental} \times I_{Govermental} + W_{Political} \times I_{Political} \tag{9}$$

In the second mission, each of the acquired weights for the four main effecting criteria will be substituted in the given equation. Moreover, Intensity of each criterion will be calculated through the following equation:

$$Intensity = \frac{W_i}{\max(W_i)} \tag{10}$$

After the Total Score (X) is acquired, all acquired parameters will be substituted through Eq. (7), in which the Total$_{NSV}$ of each device will be acquired. Similarly, to case one, the Total$_{TSV}$ of each device will be computed.

As an example, this model will be applied on the Monitor of CCU. Starting with the calculation of the needed intensities of each of the effecting environmental criteria using Eq. (10), the intensity of the Economical factor is acquired as follows:

$$I_{Economics} = \frac{W_{Economics}}{\max(W_i)}$$

Analyzing the obtained weights through this study, the max (Wi) is equal to the highest acquired weights which is for the government regulation factor in which, max (Wi) = W_Govermental which is equal to 0.27272737. Then I_Economics can be computed as follows:

$$I_{Economics} = \frac{0.26818182}{0.27272737} = 0.98333298$$

Similarly, the intensity of each factor is computed in which the acquired parameters is substituted for the purpose of calculating the Total Score (X) where calculation is done as follows:

$$
\begin{aligned}
Total\ Score(X) &= 0.26818182 \times (0.98333298) + 0.20454555 \times (0.75) \\
&\quad + 0.27272737 \times (1) + 0.25454545 \times (0.93333298) \\
&= 0.92742421
\end{aligned}
$$

In the second mission, Eq. (7) is used in which acquired parameters is substituted and the calculation is done as follows:

$$
\begin{aligned}
Total_{NSV}(Monitor\ CCU) &= 0.79181828 \times 0.69471468 + 0.20818182 \times 0.92742421 \\
&= 0.74316064
\end{aligned}
$$

Similarly, the Total $_{NSV}$ score was computed for each medical equipment in which the defibrillator scored the maximum value, its Total$_{NSV}$ is 0.98489114. Then the Maximum Total$_{NSV}$ is 0.98489114 and the Minimum Total$_{NSV}$ is maintained as mentioned before through Case one, then the Total$_{TSV}$ is computed for each device as follows:

$$
Total_{TSV}(Monitor\ CCU) = \frac{0.74316064 - 0.19292315}{0.98489114 - 0.19292315} \times 100 = 69.477238\%
$$

So, according to Table 2, the monitor (CCU) it is considered high criticality and to be changed urgently.

5   Conclusion

The rapid advances in technology has led to the development of a broad range of medical equipment that offer the possibility of providing better healthcare services to diagnose, treat, and mitigate an illness or a disease. The proposed evaluation technique and classification process provide a new model for assessing the lifespan of medical equipment based on identified technical and environmental factors. This approach will support the precision, accuracy, and suitability of the decision making process taken by clinical engineer in case of equipment failure taking into account economic factors. The future work will focus on collecting data from more hospitals to meet the aim and the objectives of the proposed approach.

References

THET (n.d.). https://www.thet.org/wp-content/uploads/2017/07/THET_Managing_the_medical_equipment_lifecycle_LOW-RES.pdf

Aridi, M., Hussein, B., Khachfe, H.M., Hajj-Hassan, M.: A novel approach for healthcare equipment lifespan assessment. Int. J. Adv. Life Sci. 1–15 (2016)

Giddens, A.: The Constitution of Society (1984)

Goll, I., Rasheed, A.: The relationships between top management demographic characteristics, rational decision making, environmental munificence, and firm performance. Organization Studies (2005)

Ismail, S., Nehme, S., Hussein, B., Khachfe, H.M., Hajj-Hassan, M.: A holistic approach for forecasting medical equipment risks using Monte Carlo simulation (2018). Thinkmind: https://www.thinkmind.org/index.php?view=article&articleid=lifsci_v10_n12_2018_1

Ouda, B., Mohamed, A.S., Saleh, N.S.: A simple quantitative model for replacement of medical equipment proposed to developing countries. In: Biomedical Engineering Conference (CIBEC), Cairo (2010)

Shepherd, N., Rudd, J.: The influence of context on the strategic decision making process: a review of the literature. Int. J. Manag. Rev. **16**, 340–364 (2013)

Williams, L.: Factors influencing decisions of value in health care: a review of the literature (2014)

Data Science

A New Spark Based K-Means Clustering with Data Removing Strategy

Kenza Rziga(✉), Mohamed Aymen Ben HajKacem(✉), and Nadia Essoussi(✉)

Université de Tunis, Institut Supérieur de Gestion de Tunis, LARODEC,
41 Avenue de la Liberté, Cité Bouchoucha, 2000 Le Bardo, Tunisia
rzigakenza@gmail.com, medaymen.hajkacem@gmail.com,
nadia.essoussi@isg.rnu.tn

Abstract. Clustering is an important technique in machine learning, which has been used to organize data into groups of similar data points called also clusters. In fact, conventional clustering methods are not suitable when dealing with large scale data. This is explained by the high computational cost of these methods which require unrealistic time to build the grouping. We propose in this work a new Spark based K-means Clustering with Data Removing Strategy referred to as (SKMDRS). The proposed method is based on data removing strategy which aims to reduce the computational time, by removing at each iteration data points that are unlikely to change the clusters to which they belong thereafter. In addition, the clustering process is distributed through Spark framework in order to enhance the scalability. Conducted experiments show the efficiency of the proposed method compared to existing ones.

Keywords: Big data · Clustering · K-means · MapReduce · Spark

1 Introduction

Given the emergency of large amount generated data from different sources, processing and examining these data has become an important challenge also called Big data analytic. Formally, Big data analytic is generally characterized by 3 Vs which are Volume, Variety, and Velocity [1]. Volume refers to the large volume of data. Variety indicates the different data types in which data is produced. Velocity refers to the speed at which the data should be analyzed [2].

Clustering is an important technique in machine learning which aims to organize unlabeled data into groups of similar data points. The ability of clustering methods to build grouping from large scale data has become an important characteristic when designing a clustering process. For example, k-means clustering [3] one of the partitional methods, characterized by its simplicity and linear computational complexity, does not scale with large volume of data [4]. To deal with large scale data, several methods which are based on parallel frameworks [5]. MapReduce is one of the most used parallel framework for processing large

ⓒ Springer Nature Switzerland AG 2019
R. Jallouli et al. (Eds.): ICDEc 2019, LNBIP 358, pp. 289–304, 2019.
https://doi.org/10.1007/978-3-030-30874-2_23

volume of data because of its simplicity and the linear scalability [6]. Therefore, several methods of k-means clustering are based on MapReduce [7].

Despite the efficiency of these methods to build grouping from large scale data, they have some considerable shortcomings. The first shortcoming is inherit from the conventional k-means method, which requires computing every distance between all of the centroids and their data points. Many of these distance computations are redundant, because data points usually stay at the same clusters. The second shortcoming is the result of inherent conflict between MapReduce and k-means. K-means is not suitable for running within MapReduce framework since during each iteration of k-means, this framework requires reading and writing from disks, which leads to a lots of I/O operations.

To deal with these issues, we propose in this work a new **S**park based **K-**Means Clustering with **D**ata **R**emoving **S**trategy referred to as (SKMDRS). The proposed method is based on data removing strategy which aims to reduce the computational time by removing at each iteration data points that are improbable to change the clusters to which they belong thereafter. In addition, we propose fitting the clustering process through Spark in order to distribute computing over a cluster of machines rather than using a single machine.

The organization of this paper is as follows: Section 2 presents k-means method and Big data frameworks. Then, Sect. 3 presents related works which deal with Big data clustering. After that, Sect. 4 describes the proposed method while Sect. 5 presents experiments that we have performed to evaluate the efficiency of the proposed method. Finally, Sect. 6 presents conclusion and future works.

2   Background

In this section, we first present k-means method [3] followed by the presentation of MapReduce [8] and Spark framework [9].

2.1   K-Means Method

Given an input data set $X = x_1, x_2, x_3, \ldots, x_n$ containing n data points, described by r numeric attributes, the aim of k-means is to divide X into k clusters by minimizing the following objective function :

$$J = \sum_{i=1}^{n} \sum_{j=1}^{k} u_{ij} * d(x_i, c_j) \tag{1}$$

where $u_{ij} \in \{0, 1\}$ is an element of the partition matrix U_{n*k} indicating the membership of data point i in cluster j. $c_j \in C = \{c_1 \ldots c_k\}$ is the center of the cluster j and $d(x_i, c_j)$ is the dissimilarity measure which is defined as follows:

$$d(x_i, c_j) = \sum_{t=1}^{r} \sqrt{(x_{it} - c_{jt})^2}, \tag{2}$$

c_{jr} represents the mean of attribute t and cluster j, which is defined as follows:

$$c_{jt} = \frac{\sum_{i=1}^{|c_j|} x_{it}}{|c_j|}, \tag{3}$$

where $|c_j|$ the number of data points assigned to cluster j. The main steps of k-means method is shown in Algorithm 1.

Algorithm 1. K-means method

1: **Input** X: Data set, k: number of clusters
2: **Output** C: Cluster centers
3: Choose K randomly of data points as initial cluster centers
4: **While** Convergences not reached **do**
5:     **foreach** $x_i \in$ X **do**
6:         Assign x_i to the nearest cluster by computing distances using Equation (2)
7:     **end for**
8:     Update the clusters centers using Equation (3)
9: **end while**

2.2   MapReduce and Spark Frameworks

MapReduce is a parallel programming framework designed to process large data using cluster of machines [7]. It is based on two phases namely *map* and *reduce*. Each phase has ≺ key/value ≻ pairs as input and output. The map phase takes in parallel each ≺ key/value ≻ pair and generates a set of intermediate ≺ key0 /value0 ≻ pairs. Then, this framework groups all intermediate values associated with the same intermediate key as a list (known as shuffle phase). The reduce phase takes this list as input for generating final values. The inputs and outputs of MapReduce are stored in an associated distributed file system that is accessible from any machine of the used cluster. The main flowchart of MapReduce is illustrated in Fig. 1.

In spite of its efficiency, MapReduce has a significant problems with iterative algorithms [7]. Spark is an open source cluster computing framework and it is designed to overcome the limitation of MapReduce. Spark introduced a Resilient Distributed Datasets (RDDs) which are a special type of data structure, used to persist, reuse and cache results in memory. Moreover, Spark provides set of in-memory operators, beyond the MapReduce, with the aim of processing data more rapidly on distributed environments. Spark is faster up to 100x than MapReduce. However, MLlib is developed as part of the Apache Spark project. It thus gets tested and updated with each Spark release. MLlib is Apache Spark's scalable machine learning library. Also, it fits into Spark's APIs and contains many algorithms such as clustering.

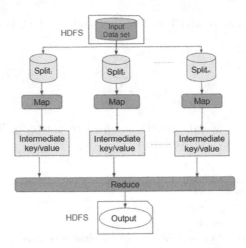

Fig. 1. Flowchart of Map Reduce [10]

3   Related Works

Several parallel clustering methods were proposed in the literature to deal with large scale data. These methods aim to distribute computing through several machines rather than using only one machine. The parallelization can be done using different frameworks such as Message Passing Interface (MPI) [11], MapReduce [7] or Graphics Processing Unit (GPU) [12]. MapReduce has become a popular framework for parallelizing algorithms due to its features such as simple programming and linear scalability. Several MapReduce based k-means methods were designed in the literature.

For example, Zaho el al. [5] implemented k-means method using MapReduce framework. This method first assigns each data point to the nearest cluster prototypes in the map phase. The reduce phase then calculates the new cluster centers. Then, this method iterates calling the two phases several times until convergence. Cui et al. [13] proposed an optimized MapReduce-based k-means method which starts by generating sample from the data set using probability sampling. Then, it executes k-means method on this sample to look for cluster centers. Ben HajKacem et al. [14] proposed a MapReduce based k-prototypes (MRKP) for clustering mixed large data. This method is based on two phases map and reduce. The map phase assigns each data point to nearest cluster using euclidean distance and simple matching. Following each assignment, the map phase computes an intermediate center for each cluster. After that, the intermediate centers produced from map phase are merged by the reduce phase, in order to update new cluster centers. Kusuma et al. [15] proposed a design intelligent kmeans based on Spark for big data clustering. It designed by using batch of data instead using original Resilient Distributed Dataset (RDD). This method is based by using batch is to change the original RDD to batch of data. It split instances from original RDD equally and put them in some batch. Batch of data still represent in RDD object but it has value as an array of value. In this case, this method based to maintain number of records in RDD which is the number of batch, and to reduce the number of array of double in 2 dimension array. After that, it apply all operation in map and reduce using this batch of data until we achieve the result. Wang et al. [16] proposed a Parallelizing K-means based Clustering on Spark. Consist of loading data into RDDs after reading into HDFS where is splitting and distributing in multiple machines. Then, it recall that computation distance between data points and k centroids of k-means which consume more time. By splitting in horizontal partition, the distance computation can be effectuated in parallel machine to minimize the volume of data to be transferred.

Despite the attested performance of these methods to offer an efficient analysis of large scale data, they have some considerable shortcomings. We observe the conventional k-means method have requires computing every distance between all of the centroids and their data points. Many of these distance computations are redundant, because data points usually stay in the same clusters. All the presented algorithms are based on the k-means algorithm using MapReduce in each iteration have problems to run with iterative algorithms. Hence, among the framework used we find that spark is more scalable and more adequate than others in terms of faster memory. Although, it is not necessary to read and write a high operations on the disk. We propose a new Spark based k-means clustering method using data removing strategy which will be presented in the following section.

4   Proposed Method: Spark Based K-Means Clustering with Data Removing Stretegy

We propose in this section new strategy which is aimed to reduce the computation time, by removing at every iteration data points that are improbable to change the clusters to which they belong thereafter. Furthermore, we propose to distribute the clustering process through Spark framework in order to enhance the scalability.

The Data Removing Strategy (DRS). We describe the different steps of data removing strategy. Starting with some definitions:

Definition 1. *Static data point means that objects are already assigned to their closest cluster.*

Definition 2. *Active data point means that object changed the cluster to another closest cluster.*

The DRS algorithm can be divided into two steps:

1. Data Removal and Recording and
2. Data Assignment and Center Update (DACU).

Data Removal and Recording. If data point is nearer to its precedent center than to any other centers, then it is defined as static data point. Otherwise it is called as active data point. The static data points are unlikely to change their membership thereafter. So, this step shows how static data points are detected and removed by the DRS algorithm. Next, we use the theorem to demonstrate, when it is close c_1 to data point x, as if cluster center and any each cluster center c_2 is far away from new cluster center c_1, then c_1 must be closer than c_2 to x.

Theorem. For the antecedent iteration Let x a data point and let c_1 center and c_2 its end of the center. Knowing that $d(c_1,c_2) \geq 2* d(x,c_1) \Rightarrow d(x,c_1) \leq d(x,c_2)$ without possess to evaluate $d(x,c_2)$.

Proof. on the basis to triangle inequality [17], we know that $d(c_1,c_2) \leq d(x,c_1) + d(x,c_1) \Rightarrow d(c_1,c_2) - d(x,c_1) \leq d(x,c_2)$.

Envisaging the left-hand side $d(c_1,c_2) - d(x,c_1) \geq 2* d(x,c_1) - d(x,c_1) = d(x,c_1) \Rightarrow d(x,c_1) \leq d(x,c_2)$.

When x_i is closer to c_1 than c_2, we can finish to c_1 than all old centers. When data point x_i is detected as static, it is important for the DRS to keep tracking the values and the number of removed data points. Once data point is removed, all information about it is lost. To this end, we record sufficient statistics for assigned cluster c_j: (1) the vector sum of the removed data points denoted by $Vsum_j$. and (2) the number of removed data points $Vnumber_j$. Following the detection of static data point x_i, the sufficient statistics of cluster c_j are recorded as follows:

$$Vsum_j = Vsum_j + x_i, \tag{4}$$

$$Vnumber_j = Vnumber_j + 1. \tag{5}$$

Data Assignment and Center Update. When data points don't satisfy the theorem, they are considered as active data points. So, this step shows how the active data points are reassigned calculating the distance to find the closest distance to the cluster centers computed at the beginning. After looking for all the data points, we update the new cluster centers. It is important to consider the sufficient statistics which are recorded in the previous step. So, we compute the new center value of each cluster j as follows:

$$c_j = \frac{Vsum_j + \sum_{x_i \in c_i}^{k} x_j}{Vnumber_j + |c_i|}, \tag{6}$$

where $|c_j|$ the number of active data points assigned to cluster c_i. Algorithm 2 describes the different steps of data removing strategy.

Algorithm 2. The main steps of Data Removing Strategy

Input X: Data set, k: number of clusters
Output C: Cluster centers
  For Each $c_i \in$ C
Compute the distance between c_i and other cluster centers.
Sort the centers in ascending order of distance to c_i.
  End For
  For Each $x_i \in$ X
Data Removal and Recording
Let c_p' the cluster center of the previous iteration of x_i.
Compute the distance between x_i and its cluster of the previous iteration c_j^{l-1}.
    If $d(c_{j1}', c_j^{l-1}) \leq 2^*d(x_i, c_j^{l-1})$
Static data point
Remove the data point x_i
Record the sum_j and $number_j$ values using Equation (3).
    Else
Data Assignment
Active data point
Reassign the data point x_i to the closet cluster center by computing distances.
  For $c_j \in$ C
Compute the distance between x_i and cluster center c_j
  End For
      End If
  End For
  Centers Update
  For Each $c_i \in$ C
Compute the new center c_i^l using Equation (4).
  End For

Application of Data Removing Strategy to K-Means. Algorithm 3 gives the new version of k-means with the proposed data removing strategy, named KMDRS. Initially, the KMDRS algorithm works exactly the same as k-means. Then, it continues to check whether it is time to start the data removing strategy. If the time to start is reached, the data removing strategy is applied.

Algorithm 3. The main steps of k-means method with data removing strategy (KMDRS algorithm)

Input X: Data set, k: number of clusters
Output C: Cluster centers
Choose k initial cluster centers randomly from X.
  While Convergences not reached
    If time to start is reached
Apply the data removing strategy.
    Else
Apply k-means iteration.
    End If
  End While

4.1   Parallel Implementation

To do the part our method is to develop a new data removing strategy in order
to be competent to process the large volume of data. Therefore, our vision is
based on a new strategy that allows us to minimize execution time and complexity compared to the old algorithm. This method gives better results in terms
of computation time compared to other algorithms. To solve the problem of scalability, the map is distributed by the mapReduce paradigm. We are interested to
use spark framework with our proposed method. That we apply in Map partition
and Reduce that are shown in Fig. 2.

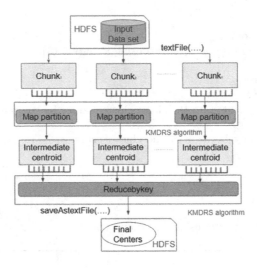

Fig. 2. Proposed approach

The map phase
At first, the data set must be stored in HDFS in the form of splits and after we
apply the map transformation, Such as the input of the map phase is the result
of splitting HDFS. We observe in which new data has been created as a data
entry key. We are assigning our Spark K-means Clustering with Data Removing
Strategy to each of the data chunks. We obtained results for each data set of
intermediate centroids.

The reduce phase
We apply again k-means with data removing strategy like in output of map
phase on intermediate centers to get a set of k final cluster centers.

5 Experiments and Results

5.1 Methodology

To evaluate the effectiveness of our proposed method we performed experiments on simulated and real data sets. We have tried in this section to determine some points.

- In the first point, we are interested to compare the existing approaches with our S-KMDRS in the case of using large data. Behind this comparison our purpose is to test the efficiency of our S-KMDRS method compared to the K-means method and MapReduce based K-means denoted by MR-KM.

- In the second point, we used different parameters in our algorithm to evaluate the clustering performance of the proposed approach with different parameters. Thus, the parameters used have a major impact on the improvement of performance in execution time.

- In a third point, we evaluate the performance of the Spark framework by analyzing the scalability of the proposed method.

5.2 Environment and Data Sets

The experiments are performed on Spark cluster running the version of Spark 1.6.0. Also, we built a cluster that consists of a master and 4 slaves in EC2 at AWS. Thus, each machine has 50 GB with CPU 4 cores and 16 GB of memory. The operating system of each machine is Ubuntu 14.10 server 64 bit. To evaluate the performance of our approach, we used on the following different data sets:

- **KDD Cup data set (KDD:**[1]**)** A real data set with normal and attack connections obtained in a military network. Treated into five connections in intrusion detection. The concerned data set contains *4, 985, 000* data points. In this case, the clustering aims to detect the attacks nature.

- **Household data set (House**[2]**)**: Household data set resulting from the measurements of electric power consumption in household. It contains *2, 075, 259* data points, where each one of the data points is described using 7 attributes. In this case, the clustering identifies the nature of electric consumption in household.

- **Poker-Hand:**[3] A normalized data set including five playing cards in a hand from a deck of 52. Every card is represented with two attributes. The data set is composed of *1,000,000* instances and 5 attributes [18].

---

[1] https://archive.ics.uci.edu/ml/machine-learning-databases/kddcup99-mld/.
[2] https://archive.ics.uci.edu/ml/machine-learning-databases/00235/.
[3] https://archive.ics.uci.edu/ml/machine-learning-databases/poker/.

– **Simulated data set:** We will note Sim10M and Sim20M, to design a simulated data set containing 10 and 20 millions data points respectively. They
represent four series of numerical large data sets that are generated. Each
data point is represented using 10 numeric attributes.

5.3   Evaluation Measures

In order to evaluate the quality of the proposed method, we use Sum Squared
Error (SSE) [19]. It is one of the most common parallel clustering criteria which
aims to measure the squared errors between each data point and the cluster
center to which the data point belongs to. SSE can be defined by:

$$SSE = \sum_{i=1}^{n} \sum_{j=1}^{k} dist(X_i, C_j) \tag{7}$$

where X_i the data point and C_j the cluster center.

In order to evaluate the ability of the proposed method to scale with large
data sets, we use in our experiments two measures to evaluate the performance in
terms of running time in Big Data: Speedup and scale-up measures. The Speed
up measure [20] the ability of the designed parallel method to scale well when
the number of machines increases and the size of data is fix. Given the execution
time using 1 node and the execution time using m nodes on the same data, the
speed up is formally described as follows:

$$Speedup = \frac{T_1}{T_m} \tag{8}$$

However, the scale up measure the capacity of the designed parallel method
to perform when we increase both the data set size and the number of machines.
The scaleup measure is given by the following formula:

$$Scaleup = \frac{T_{1s}}{T_{ms}} \tag{9}$$

Therefore, the clustering is performed with given T_{1s} the time execution in one
machines with S the size of data and T_{ms} the time execution using m machines
with mS the size of data.

5.4   Discussion

**Comparison of the Performance of S-KMDRS Versus K-Means
Method.** In this section, we studied the efficiency of the proposed methods
with different number of clusters 10 and 20 on simulated data sets and real data
sets. In the Tables 1 and 2 we show our results obtained and the best values are
boled.

The purpose of this study is to compare the computational time of our proposed approach S-KMDRS and the existing method. We assimilate the quality

Table 1. Comparison of running time and the quality of S-KMDRS versus K-means method on real data sets

Data set	K	Method	Running time (seconds)	SSE
House	10	K-means	77.867	4.4268E+07
		MR-KM	68.27	4.4268E+07
		S-KMDRS	**55.744**	1.6195E+08
	50	K-means	78.356	4.4268E+07
		MR-KM	66.24	4.4268E+07
		S-KMDRS	**51.669**	1.6119E+08
Poker	10	K-means	29.046	3.1820E+07
		MR-KM	31.24	3.1820E+07
		S-KMDRS	**16.834**	1.5947E+07
	50	K-means	27.170	3.1820E+07
		MR-KM	33.78	3.1820E+07
		S-KMDRS	**12.370**	1.5957E+07
KDD	10	K-means	576.569	6.8358E+17
		MR-KM	246.37	3.1820E+07
		S-KMDRS	**96.000**	5.5193E+17
	50	K-means	504.704	6.8350E+17
		MR-KM	280.74	3.1820E+07
		S-KMDRS	**95.920**	5.5193E+17

of our proposed method and the traditional K-means methods. In addition, the results are summarized in Table 1. We can see that our proposed method always finishes several times faster than the existing one and provides us with better results.

We can deduce that Spark framework is more suitable to cluster large scale data. Concerning the quality of clustering results, S-KMDRS converges to better results of the conventional k-means method which allows to maintain a good quality of partitioning.

This progress is induced by the efficiency of proposed methods to deal with large scale data on simulated. While k-means method takes many times before building clusters. On the other hand, obtained results show that S-KMDRS can reduce the running time of K-means method and we distinguish this method is truly executed in in-memory. This observation explains the benefits of memory computations of Spark framework when processing large scale data.

Study of the impact of Time-To-Start parametre on the performance of S-KMDRS. From these experiments, we want to follow the impact of the variation of the Time-To-Start parameter on the quality of our S-KMDRS method. The different values in Table 3 show the results of the change in *Time-To-Start (TTS)*. We notice an increase in quality using different data sets. In

Table 2. Comparison of running time and the quality of S-KMDRS versus K-means method on simulated data sets

Data set	K	Method	Running time (seconds)	SSE
Sim10M	10	K-means	1374.371	7.8592E+12
		MR-KM	380.55	7.8592E+12
		S-KMDRS	**9.280**	8.5691E+10
	50	K-means	1329.652	7.8592E+12
		MR-KM	394.11	7.8592E+12
		S-KMDRS	**9.796**	8.5969E+10
Sim20M	10	K-means	2789.751	1.5715E+13
		MR-KM	789.27	8.384+12
		S-KMDRS	**6.690**	5.3409E+10
	50	K-means	2450.656	1.5715E+13
		MR-KM	799.27	8.187+12
		S-KMDRS	**12.367**	5.3584E+10

fact the more the TTS value is small, the faster the algorithm becomes and the less the quality is.

The purpose of these tests is to study the impact and influence of the *Time-To-Start (TTS)* parameter on the performance and results of the S-KMDRS method for large scale data set. For this, we have varied the values of the parameter *TTS* knowing that k varies with time to start which the results are stored in Table 4.

Based on the array values, we can notice a considerable decrease in run time and better quality.

5.5   Scalability Analysis

To demonstrate the scalability and the ability of our method and to deal with large data sets, we evaluate the scalability of the proposed method when the machines and the size of data set are increasing at the same time. Figure 3 illustrates the scale up results on simulated and real data sets. From this Figure, we can observe that proposed methods scale very well when we execute House, KDD, Sim10M and Sim20M datasets on 1, 2, 3 and 4 machines respectively. The scale up results have almost a constant value between 0.82 and 0.86.

In addition, we measure execution time on simulated and real data sets by growing the size of the data set in terms of number of instances and the number of used nodes.

Figure 4 presents, respectively, the execution time on house, KDD, 10 millions and 20 millions of instances. We can see a down trend of running times with the rise of available machines in all experiments using at first a single machine and then we added additional machines. However, we can observe that

Table 3. The impact of time to start parameter on the quality and running time on real data sets

Data set	K	TTS	Running time (seconds)	SSE
House	10	2	**47.773**	1.6136E+08
		5	50.066	1.5785E+08
		10	55.744	1.6119E+08
	50	2	**16.856**	1.5875E+07
		5	55.993	1.5785E+08
		10	51.669	1.6119E+08
Poker	10	2	18.616	1.6112E+07
		5	18.954	1.5992E+07
		10	**16.834**	1.5947E+07
	50	2	16.634	1.6135E+08
		5	18.541	1.5807E+07
		10	**12.370**	1.5957E+07
KDD	10	2	**91.478**	5.5197E+17
		5	94.598	5.5194E+17
		10	96.000	5.5193E+17
	50	2	**94.974**	5.51941E+17
		5	95.920	5.51939E+17
		10	98.070	5.51937E+17

Table 4. The impact of time to start parameter on the quality and running time on simulated data sets

Dataset	K	TTS	Running time (seconds)	SSE
Sim10M	10	2	9.277	8.5916E+10
		5	10.686	8.5900E+10
		10	9.399	8.5691E+10
	50	2	11.019	8.5949E+10
		5	9.830	8.5921E+10
		10	6.880	8.5969E+10
Sim20M	10	2	6.503	5.3403E+10
		5	6.254	5.3444E+10
		10	6.690	5.3409E+10
	50	2	6.503	5.3403E+10
		5	5.609	5.3515E+10
		10	12.367	5.3584E+10

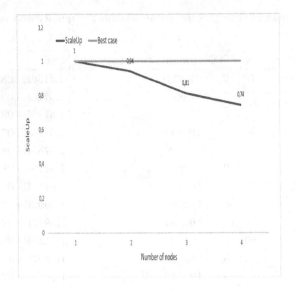

Fig. 3. Scaleup results of S-KMDRS on different data sets

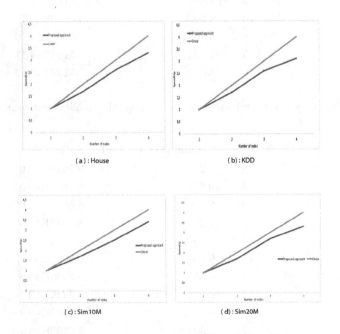

Fig. 4. Speedup results of S-KMDRS on different data sets

the speedup results showing approximately linear speedup becomes important when we increase the number of machines because it performs clustering in memory. At the same time, the decrease degree in running times differs from one data to another one.

6 Conclusion

In this paper, we have proposed a New Spark Based K-means Clustering With Data Removing Strategy to deal with large scale of data. The proposed method is based on data removing strategy which tries to reduce the number of distance computations by removing at each iteration data points that have not a chance to change the clusters thereafter. In addition, we propose to fit the clustering process using Spark framework in order to distribute computing over a cluster of machines rather than using a single machine. Although the attested performance of the proposed method, some shortcomings can be noticed. For example, S-KMDRS method performs several iterations to converge to the optimal local solution. An exciting direction of future work is to propose a scalable initialisation techniques in order to reduce the number of iterations and then may be the improvement of the scalability of S-KMDRS method.

References

1. Gorodetsky, V.: Big data: opportunities, challenges and solutions. In: Ermolayev, V., Mayr, H., Nikitchenko, M., Spivakovsky, A., Zholtkevych, G. (eds.) Information and Communication Technologies in Education, Research, and Industrial Applications. CCIS, vol. 469, pp. 3–22. Springer, Heidelberg (2014). https://doi.org/10.1007/978-3-319-13206-8_1
2. Arora, S., Chana, I.: A survey of clustering techniques for big data analysis. In: Proceedings of the 5th International Conference on Confluence 2014: The Next Generation Information Technology Summit, pp. 59–65 (2014)
3. Macqueen, J.: Some methods for classification and analysis of multivariate observations, pp. 281–297 (1967)
4. Blazquez, D., Domenech, J.: Big data sources and methods for social and economic analyses. Technol. Forecast. Soc. Chang. **130**, 99–113 (2018)
5. Zhao, W., Ma, H., He, Q.: Parallel K-means clustering based on MapReduce. In: Jaatun, M.G., Zhao, G., Rong, C. (eds.) CloudCom 2009. LNCS, vol. 5931, pp. 674–679. Springer, Heidelberg (2009). https://doi.org/10.1007/978-3-642-10665-1_71
6. Ramírez-Gallego, S., Fernández, A., García, S., Chen, M., Herrera, F.: Big data: tutorial and guidelines on information and process fusion for analytics algorithms with mapreduce. Inf. Fus. **42**, 51–61 (2018)
7. Dean, J., Ghemawat, S.: Mapreduce: simplified data processing on large clusters. Commun. ACM **51**(1), 107–113 (2008)
8. White, T.: Hadoop: The Definitive Guide (2009)
9. Zaharia, M., Chowdhury, M., Franklin, M.J., Shenker, S., Stoica, I.: Spark: cluster computing with working sets. In Proceedings of the 2nd USENIX Conference on Hot Topics in Cloud Computing, HotCloud 2010, Berkeley, CA, USA, p. 10. USENIX Association (2010)
10. Jian, L., Wang, C., Liu, Y., Liang, S., Yi, W., Shi, Y.: Parallel data mining techniques on graphics processing unit with compute unified device architecture (cuda). J. Supercomput. **64**(3), 942–967 (2013)
11. Snir, M., Otto, S., Huss-Lederman, S., Walker, D., Dongarra, J.: MPI-the complete reference, vol. 1: The MPI core (1998)

12. Owens, J.D., Houston, M., Luebke, D., Green, S., Stone, J.E., Phillips, J.C.: GPU computing, vol. 96, pp. 879–899 (2008)
13. Cui, X., Zhu, P., Yang, X., Li, K., Ji, C.: Optimized big data k-means clustering using mapreduce. J. Supercomput. **70**(3), 1249–1259 (2014)
14. HajKacem, M.A.B., N'Cir, C.-E.B., Essoussi, N.: Overview of scalable partitional methods for big data clustering. In: Nasraoui, O., Ben N'Cir, C.-E. (eds.) Clustering Methods for Big Data Analytics. USL, pp. 1–23. Springer, Cham (2019). https://doi.org/10.1007/978-3-319-97864-2_1
15. Kusuma, I., Ma'sum, M.A., Habibie, N., Jatmiko, W., Suhartanto, H.: Design of intelligent k-means based on spark for big data clustering, pp. 89–96, October 2016
16. Wang, B., Yin, J., Hua, Q., Wu, Z., Cao, J.: Parallelizing k-means-based clustering on spark, pp. 31–36 (2016)
17. Elkan, C.: Using the triangle inequality to accelerate k-means. In: Proceedings of the Twentieth International Conference on International Conference on Machine Learning, ICML2003, pp. 147–153. AAAI Press (2003)
18. Cattral, R., Oppacher, F.: Discovering rules in the poker hand dataset, p. 1870 (2007)
19. Rui, X., Wunsch, D.C.: Clustering algorithms in biomedical research: a review. IEEE Rev. Biomed. Eng. **3**, 120–154 (2010)
20. Xu, X., Jäger, J., Kriegel, H.-P.: A fast parallel clustering algorithm for large spatial databases. Data Min. Knowl. Discov. **3**(3), 263–290 (1999)

Reinforcement Learning for New Adaptive Gamified LMS

Eya Chtouka$^{(\boxtimes)}$, Wided Guezguez$^{(\boxtimes)}$, and Nahla Ben Amor$^{(\boxtimes)}$

Université de Tunis, Institut Supérieur de Gestion de Tunis, LARODEC,
Le Bardo, Tunisia
echtouka@gmail.com, widedguezguez@gmail.com, nahlabenamor@gmx.fr

Abstract. Due to the numerous advantages of the Learning Management System (LMS), such as the facility to distribute and update the course, their use has become popular not only in the education field but also in business training. In order to improve the efficiency of online courses, previous works adapted LMS to learners preferences based on their learning styles. In the other hand, Game elements had been added to LMS to increase students motivation in achieving a learning goal. In this paper, we are interested in adapting GLMS to student profiles using Q-learning algorithm to attribute an adapted gamified learning path to the user. Our work allows to deal with the users profile as a learner and player at the same time.

Keywords: Reinforcement learning · Q-learning · Learning styles ·
Gamification · Player types ·
Adaptive gamified learning management system

1 Introduction

During the last decade, the number of individuals with regular access to Internet saw an exponential growth. At the same time, technological devices become more affordable and practically essential. This contributed in making people more and more interested in on-line courses. This trend is due to the numerous advantages of the e-learning platforms such as the liberty to access the desired courses, not having to go to school to learn, spending less money than in traditional campus.

Thus, in a virtual environment the experience can be boring and not motivating since there is no human interactions. This increases the risks of easily giving up courses. Hence, the idea of using games elements in non-game systems such as e-learning in order to motivate learners, engage them and make the experience more enjoyable [1].

In our work, we aim to determine the user characteristics based on his *Learner Player Type (LPT)* by combining learning styles and player types. In this way, students preference concerns not only his learning style but also his player type at the same time which enhances the depiction of his preferences.

© Springer Nature Switzerland AG 2019
R. Jallouli et al. (Eds.): ICDEc 2019, LNBIP 358, pp. 305–314, 2019.
https://doi.org/10.1007/978-3-030-30874-2_24

In the rest of the paper, we will start by presenting the state of the art followed by the proposed course structure, the new learner player typology then the proposed algorithm for adapting gamified learning management systems.

2   State of the Art

We are interested in adapting gamified learning management system (GLMS) to users profiles. Previous works proposed several profiles models on which they base their adaptation. Among them, learning styles [2], personality traits [3], player types [4]. In our work, we are interested to learning styles and player types. Since learning styles represent student behaviour and preferences in learning environment and player types represent users behaviour and preferences in game environment as a player which concerns us since we are interested in GLMS. For this aim, we will use a reinforcement learning algorithm to adapt GLMS to the users learning styles and player types. Hence, in what follows, we will present the state of the art of adaptive GLMS more precisely learning styles, gamification, gamer types and finally the reinforcement learning.

2.1   Adaptive Gamified Learning Management System

Learning management system (LMS) is a platform allowing registration or administration for providing learning materials in all aspects of learning process, thanks to different course elements. It aims to identify and assess individual learning goals, tracks their progress while looking for achieving a goal [5].

In order to ameliorate LMS products, new concepts was proposed among them *gamified LMS (GLMS)* [6] based on gamification [7] which is the use of game design elements in on-line courses to engage participants and encourage desired behaviors. Obviously, students are generally more motivated and engaged to accomplish their tasks when the proposed curriculum is adapted to their preferences and expectations represented by their learning player types.

Learning Styles: During more than 30 years, the literature presented several definitions and interpretations. Among these definitions, [8] reported that learning styles are "Characteristic strengths and preferences in the ways they [learners] take in and process information". In this field, numerous learning styles models were proposed such as: Myers-Briggs Type Indicator (MBTI) [9], Kolbs Learning Style Model [10], The Dunn and Dunn learning style model [11] and Felder-Silverman Learning Style Model (FSLSM) in which we are interested for several reasons such as its important use in learning domain [12], its rich description of 8 learners styles based on 4 dimensions and the possibility of having more than one style at the same time based on these 4 dimensions:

- Active/Reflective: Describes the way of processing information or how to transform an information into knowledge.
- Sensing/Intuitive: Deals with the preferred source of informations.

- Visual/Verbal: Describes the perception of the information by a learner.
- Sequential/Global: Based on the difference in the way of understanding and having difficulties explaining how learners achieve their work.

Player Types: Numerous player types have been proposed such as Bartle typology [4] which is the origin of player type theory, [13] has identified 10 components for players grouped into three categories. In our case, we are interested in The BrainHex model [14], one of the most recent players typologies. This typology is an extension of the Bartle model where player types are not mutually exclusive. Four categories of players types are added:

1. Seeker: enjoys being curious about the game world.
2. Survivor: enjoys experiencing terror and flee danger.
3. Daredevil: enjoys taking risks and playing on the edge.
4. Mastermind: enjoys solving puzzle and putting strategies.
5. Conqueror: enjoys defeating difficult opponents.
6. Socializer: enjoys interacting with other users associated to the oxytocin.
7. Achiever: enjoys achieving tasks and complete them.

To develop an adaptive GLMS, we are interested in machine learning algorithms especially reinforcement learning [15] thanks to its ability to learn from mistakes and optimize results based on what he observes in his environment.

2.2 Reinforcement Learning (RL)

In RL, an agent learns by interacting with an environment [15], from the consequences of its taken actions $A = \{a_1, a_2, a_3, ...a_n\}$ given states $\in S = \{s_1, s_2, s_3, ...s_m\}$ in order to maximize numerical rewards $R = \{r_1, r_2, r_3, ...r_k\}$ of taken actions. The Agent and environment interact at discrete time steps $t = 0, 1, 2, 3...T$ where the agent observes a state s_t at time step t it produces an action, $a_t \in A(s_t)$ and gets a reward $r_{t+1} \in \mathbb{R}$, resulting next state: s_{t+1}.

In RL, the exploration-exploitation problems are the two principle possible situations: The first one consists in selecting actions to perceive their consequences on the environment and rewards. Based on the received reward, the agent builds a policy. This type of RL is also called "Trial and error learning" [15]. During exploitation, the agent will select his actions based on its past experiences. This allows the agent to improve its policy if possible.

RL can be categorized in four categories: Value-based, model-based, actor-critic and policy-based. We are interested in the last one where we distinguish two principle algorithms: SARSA algorithm [16] as an on-policy algorithm and the Q-learning as an off-policy algorithm [17]. This choice is made on the basis that the algorithm tries to learn the policy from experience sampled from the succession of a and s, a behavior policy that the agent can follow, in a way to utilize different policies at the same time, one for exploration and another for learning. The agent is then able to learn about the optimal policy during its exploratory phases, with off-policy learning [15].

Q-learning algorithm [18], is based on the Bellman updates on Q-values which allows the optimization of reward. For a state s, an action a, and a constant learning rate per episode α, for a discount factor γ, and a policy π as illustrated in Eq. 1 and Algorithm 1.

$$Q(s_t, a_t) \leftarrow Q(s_t, a_t) + \alpha[r_{t+1} + \gamma max_a Q(s_{t+1}, a) - Q(s_t, a_t)] \tag{1}$$

Algorithm 1. Q-learning off-policy algorithm

1: Initialize Q(s,a), for all $s \in S^+$, $a \in A(s)$, arbitrarily, and Q(terminal-state,.)=0
2: **Repeat**(for each episode):
3:     Initialize S
4:     **Repeat** (for each step of episode):
5:         choose a from s using policy derived from Q
6:         Take action a, observe r, s'
7:         $Q(s, a) \leftarrow Q(s, a) + \alpha[r + \gamma \max_a Q(s', a) - Q(s, a)]$
8:         $s \leftarrow s'$
9:     **Until** s is terminal

---

3   New Learner Player Typology

Since we are interested in gamified learning environments, we defined a *Learner player typology (LPT)* by merging the two typologies (learning styles [2,8] and player types [19] and [14]) in one typology. Then we propose to adapt the system based on this new learner player typology. This approach optimizes the efficiency of the adaptivity of a gamified learning platform since it allows an adaptation of the learning and gamification functionalities at the same time. We noticed that these two methods complete each others in three ways they both aim to learn on-line learning users behavior, ameliorate users experience by enhancing motivation and engagement in the learning platforms and they both use a likely description of different types (social description, self challenges, the way to achieve a goal). As a learning style model, we conclude to use the FSLSM typology [8] and the Brainhex model which are similar in two ways: they are both based on the psychological characteristics [2] and [14]. Users types are detected using questionnaires (Index of Learning Styles (ILS) for FSLSM and Brainhex questionnaire for Brainhex).

3.1   Learner Player Types Identification and Description

For each FSLSM type we cross appropriate Brainhex type based on the description of characteristics of each model [2,8,14,19]. Proposed combinations were confirmed through questionnaires results by asking 40 participants to answer ILS and Brainhex questionnaires. We obtained 77.5% of consistent results conform to proposed typology. Some participants confessed that they don't have the same behaviour of learner as player. In addition to the possibility of lack of concentration while doing the questionnaire or the lack of interest, results are hence satisfying. Based on common points between FSLSM and BrainHex model to give birth to 8 new *learner, player types* to which course elements and game elements will be adapted as follows:

1. The Sensing /seeker (denoted by SS) profile prefers a gamified learning path focusing on concrete material such as exercises and examples. Diagrams, forums and conclusions to feed their curiosity, the walker feature is the correspondent game feature to enjoy moments of wonder and represent real user advancement [8] and [1].
2. The intuitive/mastermind (denoted by IM) enjoys challenges and collecting stars, added to tasks like self-assessment tests and exercises. he prefers less number of diagrams and examples since the interest of this profile is to learn with abstract materials and solve challenges to enjoy entrancement in leaderboards [8] and [1].
3. The visual/Survivor (denoted by VSS) likes courses elements where he can use diagrams, videos, and images to understand objects. Uses diagrams and videos everytime to attract the visual memory and check leaderboards to check his rank comparing to other users and ensure the satisfaction of the survivor by making him enjoy the intensity of experiences [8] and [1].
4. The verbal/survivor (denoted by VRS) enjoys maximum of explanation, so the number of learning sections, conclusion, resumes and examples must increase. As a survivor the user has to deal with numerous written explanation, achieve QCM without training through tests and exercises. See his evolution comparing to others following a leaderboard as a game feature while [8] and [1].
5. The active/socializer (denoted by AS) prefers to learn by trying things out and doing something actively. The number of exercises should be increased after presenting few examples to try things himself. Promote tips feature to enjoy sharing and interacting with others. This profile enjoys the group working tests and forums to share experiences. [8] and [1].
6. The reflective/conqueror (denoted by RC) enjoys thinking via learning materials such as exercises and examples elements right after learning sections and content objects followed by diagrams to reflect on processes and think of learned concepts. Exercises and self assessment test are ideal steps before passing the QCM for the RC [8] and [1].
7. The sequential/achiever (denoted by SA) prefers taking time to learn materials and applies what he learned step by step he should then pass by exercises, self-assessment test and conclusion. SA enjoys being limited by a timer, encouraged and motivated by collecting stars and finally see his advancement through the walker game feature [8] and [1].
8. The global/daredevil (denoted by GD) profile prefers what resumes the course content without having to pass all steps. He prefers taking risks to skip steps and challenges himself. That is why the number of examples and diagrams have to be increased added to the QCM test directly with timer game feature which ensures a challenge in every taken step [8] and [1].

4   Reinforcement Learning for New Adaptive GLMS

We propose to model a gamified course C composed of course elements CE and game features GF:

- $C = \{Ch_0, Ch_1, Ch_2, ..., Ch_n\}$
- $Ch_i = \{ Ch_1, Ch_2, ..., Ch_m \}$
- $CE = \{ce_0, ce_1, ce_2, ..., ce_{12}\}$
- $GF = \{ce_0, ce_1, ce_2, ..., ce_5\}$

In this paper, we adopted 12 course elements (CE) and 5 game features (GF) [1]:

$CE = \{$Resume, Content object, learning section, Example, Video, Exercise, Diagram, Conclusion, Group test, Self-assessment test, Forum, QCM$\}$

$GF = \{$Walker, Leaderboard, Timer, Star, Tips$\}$

We assume that a course is gamified by adding game features to each course element to obtain a set of 12 possible gamified course elements as states s_i during the course. In the aim to have a coherent course, we proposed 10 conditions based on the general rules of a course to limit repetition and inconsistent courses without tests as follows:

- C1: A chapter should begin with a resume (s_0) followed by the content objects elements (s_1).
- C2: A chapter should end with a QCM (s_{11}).
- C3: A test element (s_8/s_9) can only have place after conclusion (s_7).
- C4: Number of occurrence of s_2, s_3, s_4, s_5, s_6 and s_{10} must be less than 3.
- C5: Learners attend at least one test (s_8/s_9).
- C6: A chapter should have one conclusion s_7.
- C7: Learner must pass by at least 6 elements before QCM (s_{11}).
- C8: Conclusion (s_7) can have place only after at least one learning section(s_1).
- C9: Chapter must contain only one test element (s_8/s_9).
- C10: Only QCM (s_{11}) and forum (s_{10}) can take place after a test (s_8/s_9).

Our main objective is to adapt a gamified on-line course to students based on their learning style and gamer type. Using Q-learning algorithm due to his numerous advantages presented previously. Q-learning is based on three sets of variables, S, A and R. For this aim, we take into consideration the set of states of gamified course elements S as the set of states of the algorithm. In addition, a set of actions A to represent the passage from a state s_i to another by taking an action a_j. Finally, a set of R to represent the reward of every chosen action a_j while state s_i.

Therefore, the considered sets of S, A and R are as follows for all the learner player types:

$S = \{$
s_0 : Reading resume,
s_1 : Reading content objects,
s_2 : Learning section,
s_3 : Reading example,
s_4 : Watching a video,
s_5 : Doing exercise and consulting the stars and timer feature,
s_6 : Checking a diagram,
s_7 : Reading conclusion and consult the walker feature,
s_8 : Attend a group test and consulting the walker and the timer feature,
s_9 : Attend a self assessment test and consulting the walker and the timer feature,
s_{10} : Checking forum and consulting the leader board feature,
s_{11} : Passing a QCM, writing tips, and consulting the walker and the timer feature,
$\}$

$A = \{$
a_0 : Load content objects,
a_1 : Load example,
a_2 : Load video,
a_3 : Load exercises,
a_4 : Load diagram,
a_5 : Load conclusion and the walker feature,
a_6 : Load exercice, the stars and timer features,
a_7 : Load the group test, the walker and the timer features,
a_8 : Load self assessment test, the walker and the timer feature,
a_9 : Load forum and the leaderboard feature,
a_{10} : Load QCM and the walker, the walker and the timer feature,
$\}$

$R = \{$
r_0 : -1,
r_1 : 0.5,
r_2 : 1,
$\}$

In our case, the Q-learning is based on three tables: S_{table}, R_{table} and Q_{table}. The S_{table} represents the corresponding state at each taken action, the R_{table} represents reward of each taken action in each state and R_{table} represents the Q_{values} of each taken action in each state.

S_{table} and Q_{table} are the same for all the profiles. R_{table} is specific for each profiles according to its preferences and corresponding course elements. The Q_{table} contains the updated Q_{value} of each possible combination of states and actions, based on the Eq. 1. Its content is first initialized by zeros in the possible combination of states and actions and updated each time the algorithm takes a new action in each episode by computing Q_{Value}. R_{table} represents the corresponding reward $R = \{r_{00}, r_{11}, r_{12}, ..., r_{i,j}\}$ where i is the number of states and j is the number of actions.

Each taken action a_i in a specific state s_j has a correspondent reward $r_{i,j}$:

$r_{i,j} = -1$ corresponds to an action which does not represent a valued results which means that does not fit with the profile preferences.
$r_{i,j} = 0.5$ corresponds to an action which fits with the profile preferences with a medium reward.
$r_{i,j} = 1$ corresponds to the most preferred action and generally represents the objective.

4.1 Algorithm Process

The algorithm unfolds on a number of episodes, in each it proposes a gamified learning chapter path. At a certain number of episodes, it converges to the best path that corresponds to the profile in concern following these steps in each single episode from the first state until the last one.

For our experimentation, we followed these steps:

1. Choose an action a_i, according to the maximum and not null value in Q_{table} or randomly from S_{table} if all the Q_{values} are null or negative.
2. Determine the corresponding reward and the next state.
3. Calculate the new Q_{value} using Q-value Eq. 1.
4. Update the Q_{table} with the new Q_{value}.
5. Update the Q_{table} and S_{table} to satisfy conditions.

4.2   Results

Q-learning algorithm proposes a gamified learning path until he converges to the optimal one based on the profile preferences and characteristics. For the 8 new learner player types we generated 20 random R_{tables} for each profile to deduce the average of convergence of the algorithm for each case to obtain results in Fig. 1. The algorithm convergence varies between 4.8 and 8.45 episodes, where the most important average of convergence is GD which can be explained by the numerous possibilities of actions with positive rewards in one state. For each random R_{table}, the Q-learning algorithm proposes an adaptive gamified learning path based on the learner player preferences in the correspondent R_{table}, by modifying the course sequencement according to the users preferences expressed in the corresponding R_{table}.

We present below examples of optimal learning paths P_c for each LPT at convergence:

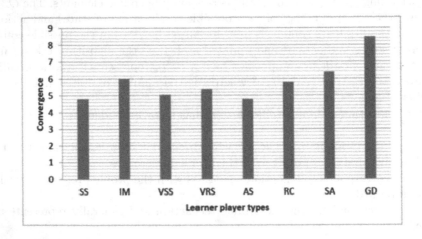

Fig. 1. Q-learning convergence for each LPT

- Sensing/seeker (SS): $P_c = s_0, s_1, s_2, s_3, s_5, s_3, s_5, s_3, s_5, s_7 s_{10}, s_{11}$.
- Intuitive/mastermind (IM): $P_c = s_0, s_1, s_2, s_2, s_2, s_2, s_7, s_8, s_{11}$.
- Visual/survivor (VSS): $P_c = s_0, s_1, s_2, s_4, s_6, s_2, s_4, s_6, s_2, s_4, s_6, s_7, s_8, s_{11}$.
- Verbal/survivor (VRS): $P_c = s_0, s_1, s_2, s_2, s_2, s_3, s_{10}, s_7, s_8, s_{11}$.

- Active/Socializer (AS): $P_c= s_0, s_1, s_2, s_3, s_5, s_5, s_5, s_7, s_8, s_{10}, s_{11}$.
- Reflective/conqueror (RC): $P_c= s_0, s_1, s_2, s_3, s_2, s_3, s_2, s_3, s_6, s_5, s_9, s_{11}$.
- Sequential/achiever (SA): $P_c= s_0, s_1, s_2, s_5, s_2, s_5, s_2, s_5, s_7, s_9, s_{11}$.
- Global/daredevil (GD): $P_c= s_0, s_1, s_2, s_6, s_6, s_6, s_7, s_9, s_{11}$.

5   Conclusion

In this work, we have proposed a new adaptive gamified learning management system using Q-learning algorithm. The adaptation was based on the proposed new learner player typology, which enhances the students characterization due to the fact that it is based on his learning styles and player type at the same time. The proposed LPT was validated through FSLSM and Brainhex questionnaires.

As future works, we can add a detection phase before the learning phase, using a machine learning algorithm to detect learner player profile of each user of a GLMS.

References

1. Monterrat, B., Lavoué, E., George, S.: Adaptation of gaming features for motivating learners. Simul. Gaming **48**, 625–656 (2017)
2. Felder, R.M., Silverman, L.K.: Learning and teaching styles in engineering education. Eng. Educ. **78**, 674–681 (1988)
3. Goldberg, L.R.: The structure of phenotypic personality traits. Am. Psychol. **48**, 26 (1993)
4. Bartle, R.: Hearts, clubs, diamonds, spades: players who suit muds. J. MUD Res. **1**, 19 (1996)
5. Szabo, M.: Cmi theory and practice: historical roots of learning managment systems. In: E-Learn: World Conference on E-Learning in Corporate, Government, Healthcare, and Higher Education, pp. 929–936 (2002)
6. Heeter, C., Lee, Y.-H., Medler, B., Magerko, B.: Beyond player types: gaming achievement goal. In: ACM SIGGRAPH 2011 Game Papers, p. 7. ACM (2011)
7. Deterding, S., Dixon, D., Khaled, R., Nacke, L.: From game design elements to gamefulness: defining gamification. In: Proceedings of the 15th International Academic MindTrek Conference: Envisioning Future Media Environments, MindTrek, pp. 9–15 (2011)
8. Richard, F.: Matters of style. ASEE Prism **6**, 11 (1996)
9. Myers, I.B.: The Myers-Briggs type indicator manual, p. 9 (1962)
10. Kolb, D.A.: The learning style inventory: Technical manual. McBer and Company, Boston, p. 11 (1976)
11. Dunn, R., Dunn, K.: Learning style as a criterion for placement in alternative programs. Phi Delta Kappan **56**, 275–278 (1974)
12. Kuljis, J., Liu, F.: A comparison of learning style theories on the suitability for elearning. In: Web Technologies, Applications, and Services, pp. 191–197 (2005)
13. Yee, N.: Motivations for play in online games. CyberPsychol. Behav. **9**, 772–775 (2006)
14. Nacke, L.E., Bateman, C., Mandryk, R.L.: Brainhex a neurobiological gamer typology survey. Entertain. Comput. **5**, 55–62 (2014)

15. Sutton, R.S., Barto, A.G.: Reinforcement Learning: An Introduction. MIT Press, Cambridge (1998)
16. Rummery, G.A., Niranjan, M.: On-line Q-learning using connectionist systems. University of Cambridge, Department of Engineering Cambridge, England (1994)
17. Watkins, C.J.C.H., Dayan, P.: Q-learning. Mach. Learn. **8**, 279–298 (1992)
18. Watkins, C.J.C.H.: Learning from Delayed Rewards. Ph.D. thesis, Cambridge University (1989)
19. Nacke, L.E., Bateman, C., Mandryk, R.L.: BrainHex: preliminary results from a neurobiological gamer typology survey. In: Anacleto, J.C., Fels, S., Graham, N., Kapralos, B., Saif El-Nasr, M., Stanley, K. (eds.) ICEC 2011. LNCS, vol. 6972, pp. 288–293. Springer, Heidelberg (2011). https://doi.org/10.1007/978-3-642-24500-8_31

A Framework for Facial Image Analytics Using Deep Learning in Social Sciences Research

Stuart J. Barnes[1(✉)] and Richard Rutter[1,2]

[1] CODA Research Centre, King's Business School, King's College London,
London, UK
stuart.barnes@kcl.ac.uk, richrutter@gmail.com
[2] School of Business, Australian College of Kuwait, Mishref, Kuwait

Abstract. Recent advances in artificial intelligence have provided exciting new tools for scientific research that have been applied in many domains, including medicine, engineering, finance, the physical sciences, and online consumer analytics. Although text analytics is now quite a mature approach, image analytics is still developing as research approach and its use is not widespread in the social sciences, particularly owing to the specialized knowledge required in visualization and machine learning. In this paper, we demonstrate how facial image analytics research can be expedited in the social sciences by introducing a simple research framework for integrating facial image classification data into studies. We explain the steps of the framework, including data collection, processing, collation, and analysis. This is accompanied by an example piece of research examining the influence of hosts' facial expressions on review scores in Airbnb.

Keywords: Faces · Classification · Data fusion · Deep learning ·
Social sciences

1 Introduction

Big data analytics and machine learning provide significant new research opportunities for social scientists focused on the digital economy, offering large volumes of rapidly accumulating data, such as text, audio, image and video, from varied sources, e.g. mobile devices, sensors (including internet of things), open or public data, online social networks, and organizational information systems (Baesens et al. 2016; Goes 2014). The majority of big data is unstructured (with estimates ranging from 80% to 95% or more; see Gandomi and Haider 2015), including much that is audio, images and video. Although big data research with text analytics has reached maturity and is being widely applied in the social sciences (e.g. see Villarroel Ordenes et al.'s 2017 paper on the examination of customer sentiment), research utilizing images seldom used, being confined to a niche of experts with knowledge of computer visualization and machine learning. A few rare examples include Zhang and Luo (2018) and Wang et al. (2018). This paper aims to provide social scientists with a simple framework to enable advanced facial analytics in new academic investigations.

Academic social science research utilizing machine learning is a very different proposition to typical business applications of the methods, which are typically

© Springer Nature Switzerland AG 2019
R. Jallouli et al. (Eds.): ICDEc 2019, LNBIP 358, pp. 315–320, 2019.
https://doi.org/10.1007/978-3-030-30874-2_25

employed to solve practical problems without mentioning theory. Such problems include predicting customer demand to enhance the efficiency of supply chains, predicting customer propensity to churn to improve approaches to customer retention, examining preferences to make customer product recommendations and increase sales, optimizing pricing to grow profits, fraud detection to lower risk, and personalization to improve customer loyalty. In the next section, we introduce steps in the research framework, illustrating its application to examine the impact of facial expressions of emotion on online reviews for Airbnb, using a freely available online data source. In the final section we draw conclusions on the opportunities and limitations for the future application of the research framework in social science research.

2   Research Framework

In this section, we examine the recommended research framework for facial image analysis in social sciences by outlining six key steps in the research process (illustrated in Fig. 1). The research framework generally fits with other generalized processes for big data analytics (e.g. Gandomi and Haider 2015). We examine each step, in turn, focusing on an example application.

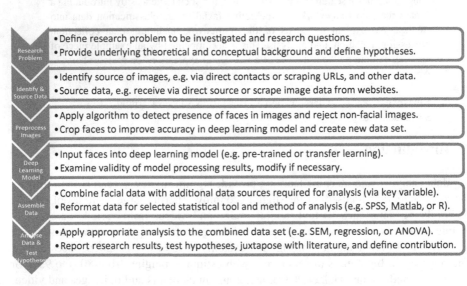

Fig. 1. Steps in the recommended process for facial image analysis

2.1   Research Problem

A key step in developing facial analytics research that makes a clear contribution to knowledge is outlining the research problem, including its motivation (both academic and practical), and articulating the research question to be answered. This should be theoretically and conceptually embedded through background literature, clear definition and justification of research hypotheses to be empirically tested, and often the development of a summary research model.

In our example application, we seek to answer the research question, "Are customers' online reviews influenced by facial expressions of emotion of accommodation hosts?" When writing an online review after experiencing accommodation, customers are typically presented with an image of the host. According to emotional contagion theory (Hatfield et al. 1993), we would expect facial expressions of emotion to provide a non-verbal form of communication that could indirectly and automatically (Hatfield et al. 1993), influence the customer in their evaluation of the accommodation. We therefore hypothesize that:

> *H1. Customers' overall review evaluations will vary according to the emotion of the accommodation host.*

2.2   Identify and Source Data

Suitable sources of data to provide the empirical basis for testing the research hypotheses should be identified – high quality data that will enable clear extraction of facial features using available algorithms. In some cases, this data may be provided by open access or via public sources, or requested from researchers or organizations, in others, the data may be commercially available or potentially scraped from websites. If the images are not easily available then it may be possible to identify images using scraping software from R, Python, MATLAB and others. Once the image URLs are found, they can be downloaded using a bulk images downloader in most browsers.

In our example piece of research, we identified Airbnb as a potential example that could be used to test our hypothesis. The website includes accommodation and host information and images, as well as reviews and ratings. From a pragmatic point of view, all of the data is provided for many cities in a processed format with additional tools on the website, insideairbnb.com. The data is available under a Creative Commons CC0 1.0 Universal (CC0 1.0) Public Domain Dedication license. We decided to focus on the city of Amsterdam (the first city listed on InsideAirbnb) and used the provided URLs to download host images for approximately half of the available properties as of 5th October 2018 (n = 8056).

2.3   Preprocess Images

All of the data used in machine learning typically needs to be examined and, if necessary, preprocessed, including numbers, text, images, and so on. Traditional numeric data can be examined via visualization and statistical analysis, and may need treatment for missing values, outliers, standardization/normalization, or reclassification. It may also be necessary to sample the data. Text analysis often requires preprocessing to improve computation, including changing to lower case, tokenizing, and removing punctuation and infrequent words. In the case of images, data that is not suitable for analysis needs to be screened out, and the images need to be formatting in a way that facilitates analysis, such as cropping the face. For faces, this procedure was facilitated by applying the Viola-Jones (Viola and Jones 2001) algorithm, which systematically examines parts of the image with a cascade of binary classifiers for the face and sub-features and rejects if facial features are not found. By applying a classification model that is based on upright and forward-facing facial features, such as Haar, with a classification and regression tree (CART) analysis, we are able to screen out images that do not contain faces or that are obscured, e.g. via lighting or objects. Other types of analysis such as local binary patterns are more forgiving and could potentially detect more detail at the expense of false positives (Ojala et al. 2002). Python and MATLAB both include implementations to allow automated image processing using the Viola-Jones algorithm and cropping. A total of 2079 images were screened out as not containing faces in this process, resulting in 5977 images. After removing listings without review ratings, this fell to 5481 images.

2.4   Deep Learning Model

A plethora of methods are available for facial image analytics, including some of the most successful methods that are appearance-based and involve statistical analysis and machine learning to find key characteristics of facial images, such as Eigenface, support vector machines, principal components analysis with Fisher's discriminant, and neural networks (Masi et al. 2018). For example, Levi and Hassner (2015a, b) develop convolutional neural networks (CNNs) for accurately classifying facial images according to gender, age and emotional expression. Although it is possible to train a CNN to identify facial emotions from an image data set entirely from scratch, numerous pretrained models are available for facial emotion classification, including network structures and pretrained weights. Many advanced CNNs for image analytics are freely available in statistical software packages (e.g. GoogLeNet, ResNet-50, VGG19, and Inception-ResNet-v2) or via internet sources such as Github or the Caffe Model Zoo. CNNs are the most advanced, accurate methods for face recognition (Masi et al. 2018).

If the images for a piece of research are similar to those used for training the original network model being used, and the classification is identical, it can often be employed successfully 'straight out of the box' as a fixed feature extractor. If the images and/or classes are different, however, then the model will need to be retrained and/or retuned using transfer learning. Results must always be checked for accuracy and it may also be necessary to test various CNNs using training and validation to identify the most accurate classifier for a data set.

As an example, we focus on one of the CNNs that is freely available via the Caffe Model Zoo for facial emotion detection (any other face detection model could be substituted). One of the most accurate networks in Levi and Hassner (2015b) was found to be the CNN with local binary patterns at a radius of 5 (LBP5) coded for cyclic codes when using the VGG_S network. The pretrained CNN consisted of 24 layers for classifying the seven facial emotions examined in this study (neutral, happy, sad, fear, disgust, anger and surprised). Color (RGB) images needed to be resized to 224 x 224 pixels for the input layer. Applying the deep classification model to our data set resulted in a large number of faces classified as neutral (4077, 74.4%), with a good number of happy faces (1103, 20.1%) and sad faces (225, 4.1%). However, the other emotional classifications had very small incidences: fear (42, 0.8%), disgust (29, 0.5%), and anger (5, 0.1%). No faces were classified as surprised.

2.5 Assemble Data

Once the deep learning data has been created it needs to be combined with other research data before the analysis can begin. If the traditional data set includes the URL or name of the image, then the name of the image can be used as a key for joining the facial emotion data set with the traditional data, e.g. host profile, review text, and review scores, in statistical packages such as SPSS, Matlab or R. In the case of our example, the Airbnb data from InsideAirbnb include the host image URL from which the image name was extracted to enable merging the data sets. Further to joining the data sets, the data may also need a further round of reformatting, depending on the intended type of statistical analysis. In our example, the variable with the strings for the dominant identified emotion in images needed to be converted to binary variables for the regression analysis.

2.6 Analyse Data and Test Hypotheses

Many forms of analysis can potentially be used to test the research hypotheses, depending on the nature of the hypotheses and the data being used. For example, testing for difference might employ ANOVA, whilst examining the significance of statistical relationships could use a suitable form of regression or structural equation modelling.

To analyze the assembled data set and test the research hypothesis regarding the impact of facial emotions on review scores, we used stepwise linear regression (probability-of-F-to-enter $<=0.05$ and probability-of-F-to-remove $>=0.10$) with the average review score as the dependent variable and each of the facial emotion binary variables as independent variables. Only a single variable was found be significant in the model (constant, $\beta = 95.454$, $p < .001$): the neutral emotion had a coefficient of -0.396 and a p-value of 0.035. This appears to suggest that host images without emotion (neutral) tended to fare less well in reviews than those with some form of emotion (positive or negative, although the issue of valence is not clear). Thus, we can state that the data supports H1. However, this finding represents a very small contribution to review scores ($R = 0.028$).

3 Conclusions

The framework for facial image analytics using deep learning discussed in this paper provides a simplified, workable process for integrating advanced image analytics into social sciences research. The research approach is not without its limitations. Deep learning can be time-consuming and computationally intensive. In addition, classification accuracy can vary significantly according to data set and network employed, suggesting that it is often prudent to use transfer learning for new data sets and to compare the performance of different networks, including new ones that may emerge.

Further, the host images were not necessarily uploaded from the beginning of the posting. To increase accuracy, the upload date could be used to filter the review date.

This research was preliminary by design and conducted on subset of data. The full study will include a more comprehensive dataset. The level of accuracy of recognition is reliant on the level of accuracy within the trained networks used. A larger scale study could therefore be used to train a new or existing network and increase accuracy. Further, this research was conducted on images only and did not take into account any lexical information. A further study is planned to analyse textual data to develop greater understanding of the relationship between facial images and text (for example, the sentiment of reviews). Further, more flexible approaches to image analytics might also provide better task accuracy, e.g. MaskRCNN could be used to conduct combined face detection and analysis. We hope that this research encourages other researchers to being exploring the potential for these new, advanced techniques in digital economy research in the social sciences.

References

Baesens, B., Bapna, R., Marsden, J.R., Vanthienen, J., Zhao, J.L.: Editorial: transformational issues of big data and analytics in networked business. MIS Q. 40(4), 807–818 (2016)

Gandomi, A., Haider, M.: Beyond the hype: big data concepts, methods, and analytics. Int. J. Inf. Manag. 35(2), 137–144 (2015)

Goes, P.: Editor's comments: big data and IS research. MIS Q. 38(3), 3–8 (2014)

Hatfield, E., Cacioppo, J.T., Rapson, R.L.: Emotional contagion. Curr. Dir. Psychol. Sci. 2(3), 96–99 (1993)

Levi, G., Hassner, T.: Age and gender classification using convolutional neural networks. In: Proceedings of the IEEE Workshop on Analysis and Modeling of Faces and Gestures (AMFG), Boston (2015a)

Levi, G., Hassner, T.: Emotion recognition in the wild via convolutional neural networks and mapped binary patterns. In: Proceedings of the ACM International Conference on Multimodal Interaction (ICMI), Seattle (2015b)

Masi, I., Wu, Y., Hassner, T., Natarajan, P.: Deep face recognition: a survey. In: Proceedings of the Conference on Graphics, Patterns and Images (SIBGRAPI), Parana, Brazil, October (2018)

Ojala, T., Pietikäinen, M., Mäenpää, T.: Multiresolution gray-scale and rotation invariant texture classification with local binary patterns. IEEE Trans. Pattern Anal. Mach. Intell. 24(7), 971–987 (2002)

Villarroel Ordenes, F., Ludwig, S., De Ruyter, K., Grewal, D., Wetzels, M.: Unveiling what is written in the stars: analyzing explicit, implicit, and discourse patterns of sentiment in social media. J. Consum. Res. 43, 875–894 (2017)

Viola, P., Jones, M.J.: Rapid object detection using a boosted cascade of simple features. In: Proceedings of the 2001 IEEE Computer Society Conference on Computer Vision and Pattern Recognition, vol. 1, pp. 511–518 (2002)

Wang, Y., Guo, Y., Song, J.: Using image-based and text-based information for sales prediction: a deep neural network model. In: Proceedings of the American Conference on Information Systems, New Orleans, August (2018)

Zhang, M., Luo, L.: Can user generated content predict restaurant survival? Deep learning of yelp photos and reviews. Available at Social Science Research Network (2018). https://ssrn.com/abstract=3108288. Accessed 23 Nov 2018

Digital Marketing

Motivations and Inhibitions Behind the Adoption and Continuous Use of IoT Wearable Devices: Exploring and Comparing Three Major Frameworks

Mourad Touzani[1] and Ahmed Anis Charfi[2(✉)]

[1] NEOMA Business School, Rouen Campus, Rouen, France
mourad.touzani@neoma-bs.fr
[2] EBS – Paris, European Business School Paris, Paris, France
anis.charfi@ebs-paris.com

Abstract. The recent growth of IoT and connected objects has given birth to a market characterized by innovative offerings and new consumer behaviors. In this framework, this paper considers the specific case of the adoption and continuous use of IoT wearable devices. The literature proposes three main theoretical models: Diffusion of Innovations theory (DOI), Theory of Planned Behavior (TPB), and Technology Acceptance Model (TAM). Through a qualitative exploratory research based on 51 in-depth interviews, we try to understand the motivations and inhibitions behind the adoption and continuous use of these new products. The findings of qualitative interviews allowed us to compare the main theoretical models available in the literature and to propose an enhanced framework adapted to the specific case of IoT wearable devices.

Keywords: Internet of Things · Connected objects · DOI · TPB · TAM · IoT acceptance

1 Introduction

Recently, a new type of IT devices has gained rapidly popularity: connected objects. Several decades of technological development going from the initial conception of connected computers to wearable devices allowing more and more connectivity and communication, Internet of Things technologies revealed to be able to integrate and extend the functions of traditional computers, smartphones and tablets to a more intimate level (Choi and Kim 2016; Rawassizadeh et al. 2014). Wearable devices and connected objects have rapidly been qualified as the 'next big thing' liable to profoundly change consumers' daily lives and habits (Cecchinato et al. 2015). Both the interest in these devices and the heavy investments made by giants like Apple, Google, and Samsung reveals the promising character of this industry. The Internet of Things (IoT) comes indeed today at the intersection between the physical and digital worlds, and makes it possible to provide a wide and diversified range of Internet services through everyday objects (Carillo et al. 2017). This research study focuses mainly on wearable IoT devices, an industry with a turnover expected to reach $3.7 billion in

© Springer Nature Switzerland AG 2019
R. Jallouli et al. (Eds.): ICDEc 2019, LNBIP 358, pp. 323–341, 2019.
https://doi.org/10.1007/978-3-030-30874-2_26

2020, and \$6.2 trillion in 2025 (Manyika et al. 2015). These devices are embedded computers and advanced electronics that users can carry and wear, while allowing for interactions not only between individuals, but also with the environment (e.g., smart home appliances and smart cities). Consumers can use these devices anytime and anywhere giving an impression of ubiquity (Piyare 2013). Our research objective is to understand the motivations and inhibitions behind the adoption and continuous use of IoT wearable devices. In this perspective, we refer to the major technology adoption, acceptance, and diffusion models. To our knowledge, the literature on connected objects does not provide an overview of the most suitable model for the adoption and continuous use of wearable IoT devices (Mital et al. 2018). However, the broader literature on IT highlights three main theoretical frameworks, namely the Diffusion of Innovations theory (DOI), the Theory of Planned Behavior (TPB), and the Technology Acceptance Model (TAM). In this research, we confront and compare these frameworks through a qualitative survey based on in-depth interviews, and propose an enhanced model better adapted to IoT wearable devices.

2 The Major Theories of Technology Acceptance

In order to better understand the adoption and continuous use of IoT wearable devices, it may be helpful to move through the major technology adoption, acceptance, and diffusion models. The literature highlights three main theoretical frameworks (Vishwanath and Barnett 2011; Zhang et al. 2012): The Diffusion of Innovations theory (DOI), the theory of planned behavior (TPB), and the Technology Acceptance Model (TAM). These theories show that an information system adoption and usage rely on users' perception of the characteristics of an innovation (DOI), their personal beliefs, and attitudes toward the technology (TAM and TPB). This section presents the three major theories and compares them, in order to move towards a more holistic approach of the IoT wearable devices.

2.1 Diffusion of Innovation Theory

Initiated in the 1960s and derived from the social sciences, Rogers' theory of diffusion of innovation (Rogers 2010) identifies several general variables finding application in various disciplines such as sociology, anthropology, communication, management, marketing, organizational studies, development studies, health sciences, education, digital commerce, and information systems. An important contribution of this theory consist in highlighting five categories of adopters of an innovation: innovators, early adopters, early majority, late majority, and laggards (Rogers 2010). These categories of adopters differ in terms of their enthusiasm to accept (or not) new products or ideas, and hold different profiles. Managers usually consider them as potential segments to target with specific positioning and offerings (Sood and Kumar 2017). These five categories of adopters are not independent: innovators and early adopters usually engage in interpersonal communication to influence the other members of the social system to adopt innovations (Rogers 2010). DOI also identifies five key characteristics of an innovation: relative advantage, compatibility, complexity, trialability, and observability (cf. Fig. 1). The definitions of these constructs are given in Appendix 1. These characteristics influence both diffusion, success and the relative speed with which users adopt innovations (Rogers 2010; Dong et al. 2017).

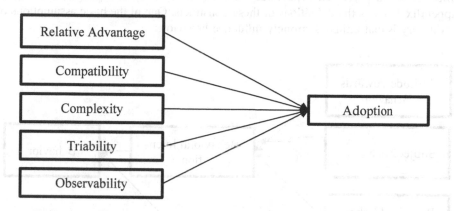

Fig. 1. The diffusion of innovation theory framework

The relative advantage of the IoT is materialized through the value it brings to users' lives, and to the whole society. Indeed, they integrate several functionalities allowing to enhance the utilitarian, hedonic, and social value of objects (Kim et al. 2017; Touzani et al. 2018). The concept of Internet of Things and the related technologies are more and more diffused all over the society, and more and more connected objects bear these technologies. This leads to increase the compatibility and to decrease the complexity of such devices (Kim et al. 2017). Technology diffusion being the result of the complex interactions and feedback occurring within the social environment, users are less and less unfamiliar with the IoT concept (Hwang et al. 2016). In the case of IoT wearable devices, trialability is very high, which facilitates the process of innovation adoption by users. Indeed, the existing products available are at the same time diverse and easily accessible, such as various wearable or mobile devices (Kim et al. 2017). The observability of IoT wearable devices is also high. Users often become familiar with their features functionalities and uses, through the media, promotional campaigns, and in-store possibilities to use the products.

Although considered the founding model, the diffusion of innovation theory is proving to be too generic for an application to the IoT wearable devices (Adhiarna et al. 2013). This model focuses on the concept of "social system" and rather locates itself at the global level of the social environment. This makes its operationalization difficult in studies that take the individual as the unit of analysis.

2.2 Theory of Planned Behavior

The second major theoretical framework is the Theory of Planned Behavior (Ajzen 1991). Resulting from the Theory of Reasoned Action (Fishbein and Ajzen 1975), this theory is widely used in information systems research. The theory of planned behavior considers behavioral intention to be a major determinant of behavior, and in particular adoption (Arpaci 2019). It highlights three determinants of the intention to adopt a new product: attitude toward act or behavior, subjective norms - with a focus on social influence - and perceived behavioral control (Ajzen 1991) as highlighted in Fig. 2. Appendix 1 shows the definitions of these constructs. One of the basic assumptions of this theory is that attitudes strongly influence behavior.

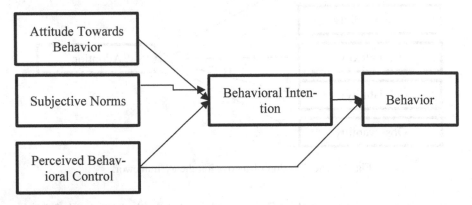

Fig. 2. The theory of planned behavior framework

Based on the assumption that the theory of planned behavior is often criticized, several authors argue that attitude cannot predict behavioral intentions (Bagozzi 1992). Moreover, even though this model revealed to be effective in predicting acceptance and use of different technologies (Harrison et al. 1997), to date little research has used this theoretical framework to explain the adoption of connected objects (Kim and Shin 2016).

However, TPB reveals to be a good theory to predict IoT wearable devices users' attitudes and behaviors, even when these rely on a set of entangled motivations. This model can integrate a wide number of factors such as quality, satisfaction, attitude, and customer intention. The TPB model provides a relevant explanation of the sequence of these factors succeed and are interrelated. Previous research studies have used TPB to predict and explain attitude formation and to predict behaviors in a wide range of products and technologies providing the framework a wide applicability and validity. TPB has been used in the fields of IoT wearables personal informatics confirming the causality between attitudes towards behavior and behavioral intentions (Li et al. 2015). Besides, as Shin (2017) puts it, the relationship between attitude and intention constitutes an interesting base to understand IoT wearables users' and especially the elements related to the quantified self.

2.3 Technology Acceptance Model

The third major theoretical framework is the Technology Acceptance Model: TAM (Davis 1989). This model relies on Ajzen's (1991) theory of planned behavior, but

attempts to improve it. This model is the most used to explain the adoption of innovations (Chau and Hu 2001). TAM indeed dominates the extant research on technology
adoption and use, and applies to many fields (Svendsen et al. 2013; Marakhimov and
Joo 2017). This model focuses on extrinsic motivational factors pertaining to the utilitarian aspects of technology (Choi and Kim 2016). According to the TAM, perceived
usefulness and perceived ease of use are the two key factors that will gradually lead the
user to adopt a technology. Perceived ease of use is also seen as directly impacting
perceived usefulness. Both factors influence behavioral intention to use technology (see
Appendix 1). Even if TAM was originally intended to predict information system use in
organization, its fields of application are varied and cover e-commerce, mobile applications, involvement in online communities, e-banking, e-health and e-learning (Wang
et al. 2012). The main strengths of this model lie in its simplicity, robustness, predictive
power and parsimonious nature (Gao and Bai 2014) (Fig. 3).

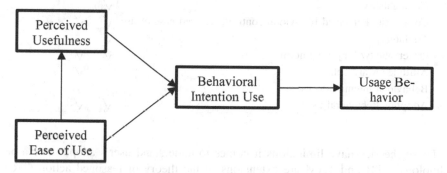

Fig. 3. The technology acceptance model framework

Extensions of TAM rely on three approaches: adding factors from other models,
adding alternative or additional belief factors, and examining moderators and predictors
of perceived ease of use and perceived usefulness (Wixom and Todd 2005). TAM 2
integrates social influence and instrumental cognitive processes (Venkatesh and Davis
2000). The Unified Theory of Acceptance and Use of Technology (UTAUT) relies on
four central constructs: performance expectancy, effort expectancy, social influence and
facilitating conditions (Venkatesh et al. 2003). TAM 3 includes trust and perceived risk
as additional determinants (Venkatesh and Bala 2008). Several authors call today for
the use of TAM in explaining the adoption of the Internet of Things (Harris et al. 2015).

TAM serves as a useful foundation for investigating users' acceptance of wearables
devices and globally IoT technologies (Gao and Bai 2014). However, there is a need of
enriching TAM to make it fit to IoT technology. Gao and Bai (2014) add trust, social
influence, perceived enjoyment, and perceived behavioral control as predictors intention to use IoT wearable devices. Park et al. (2017) add perceived enjoyment, connectedness, and control to TAM to take into account the specificities of IoT wearable
technologies. Other attempts to apply TAM (original or extended) focus on users'
intrinsic motivations, notably perceived enjoyment, vanity, need of uniqueness, and

perceived self-expressiveness. These motivations play a major role when IoT devices are hedonic and more specifically for wearables (Choi and Kim 2016).

2.4   Comparison and Limits of the Three Major Frameworks

The three theories here considered examine individuals' behaviors and their acceptance ability of a new technology through specific constructs. DOI, TPB, and TAM focus on the psychological, attitudinal and behavioral aspects of the users of the technology (Table 1).

Table 1. Comparison of the three major frameworks

Core construct	DOI	TPB	TAM
Relative advantage/Perceived usefulness	√		√
Compatibility	√		
Complexity/Perceived behavioral control/Perceived ease of use	√	√	√
Trialability	√		
Observability/Subjective norm	√	√	
Attitude toward behavior		√	
Behavioral intention to use		√	√
Adoption/Behavioral use	√	√	√

These theories have limitations it comes to understand user's adoption of a new technology. TPB and TAM are extensions of the theory of reasoned action (TRA). However, there are still areas of improvement within these theories. TPB and TAM only concern the short-term beliefs and attitude before or after the acceptance or the adoption of the technology (Wu and Chen 2017). TPB and TAM are also poor to identify dimensions that affect the behavioral intentions of users, to improve the theories ability to explain and understand users' behaviors (Venkatesh et al. 2003). For these reasons, several models enrich and extend the factors explaining the use of a technology. For example: Model of PC Utilization (MPCU) (Thompson et al. 1991); Motivational Model (MM) (Davis et al. 1992); C-TAM-TPB (Taylor and Todd 1995) a hybrid model combining constructs from TAM and TPB; Social Cognitive Theory (SCT) (Compeau and Higgins 1995); Innovation Diffusion Theory (IDT) (Moore and Benbasat 1996); Technology Acceptance Model (TAM2) (Venkatesh and Davis 2000); Expectation-confirmation model of IS continuance (Bhattacherjee 2001); and Unified Theory of Acceptance and Use of Technology (UTAUT) (Venkatesh et al. 2003).

UTAUT provides a comprehensive examination to explain better intention. It postulates that four constructs act as determinants of behavioral intentions and usage behavior: (1) performance expectancy, (2) effort expectancy, (3) social influence, (3) facilitating conditions. In addition, this model posits the role of four moderators: gender, age, experience and voluntariness of use.

DOI explains the adoption of an innovation and highlights the characteristics of an innovation predicting its adoption. However, DOI does not take into account users' perceptions and individual characteristics. Neither does it mention how the attitude affects the acceptation or the rejection of the products and the decision to use, or how innovation factors affect these decisions (Karahanna et al. 1999).

As mentioned earlier, wearable devices are today key offerings of the mobile device industry and prospectively predicted to induce significant impact on individuals' daily lives (Cecchinato et al. 2015; Choi and Kim 2016) and behaviors. It would therefore be relevant to know the determining factors of the decision to adopt or not these tools. The purpose of our empirical study is to identify the motivations and inhibitions behind the adoption and continuous use of IoT wearable devices analyzed through the lens of a comparison of the three major frameworks presented above.

3   Methodology

In order to compare the major frameworks of the adoption and continuous use of IoT wearable devices, we used an exploratory qualitative approach. Qualitative research offers indeed a good ground for advancing conceptual understanding, theory building, theory comparisons and revisions (Stiles 2010). Mobilizing a single theoretical framework limits theoretical reflection and runs into difficulties during the analysis stage (Bryman 2003). Comparing theories with a qualitative approach is a way of grounding theory development in different versions of the reality and creating stronger and more detailed theory (Pasian 2015). It also allows to broaden perspectives by going beyond the simple requirement of assigning credibility only through repeated testing (Somekh and Lewin 2005). Comparing theories with qualitative research aids to extend existing theory, offering new insights into the complex set of relationships between concepts (Denzin and Lincoln 2005; Eisenhardt and Graebner 2007). Besides, we believe that the concepts developed in the different models are not equivalent (Zhao et al. 2018). Indeed, important nuances lie in their definitions. Consequently, we have decided to adopt a face-to-face interviewing inductive methodology to go more in-depth into these nuances and distinctions. This type of study is also suitable when the phenomena are complex as it provides the most complete possible view of the problem. We have written and used an interview guide to help the researchers during the data collection. It included four themes: 1/ The opportunities related to the IoT 2/ Attitudes and perceptions about wearable IoT devices 3/ Motivations and inhibitions for the use of IoT devices in general 4/ Motivations and inhibitions for the use of IoT wearable devices. We have conducted 51 semi-directive interviews with users of IoT wearable devices. We asked informants (range 15–76 years; mean = 36 years) to participate in our study. The sample includes 21 males and 30 females with various profiles in terms of education levels (from High School to PhD), gender, age, and IoT use. Details of the participants are presented in Table 2.

We stopped gathering data when we reached the saturation threshold. The sample size complies with the standards for qualitative research: it guarantees data variability and thematic saturation (Guest et al. 2006; Boddy 2016).

We have progressively transcribed all interview recordings and imported them into Nvivo 11. The starting point for our analysis was a nodal structure drawn from the three major frameworks presented in the literature review: DOI, TPB, and TAM. We have

Table 2. Details of the participants

Number of participants	51
Gender	Female: 30, Male: 21
Age	<36: 29; >36: 22
Wearables devices	Smart balance, Smartphone, Smart Watch, Smart speakers, Smart locks; Tablet; Smart Cooker, Smart wristlet, Smart Shoes, Smart toothbrush, Drone, Smart Shutters, Connected sensor, Smart Sofa, Smart cigarette, Sleep Tracker, Smart glucose monitoring, Connected insoles, Smart Coach
Use frequency	Daily: 32 (62.75%)
	Several times per week: 16 (31.38%)
	Once per mouth: 3 (5.87%)

enriched the initial nodal structure, including the concepts presented in the three models, during the *in vivo* coding stage following the recommendations of Miles and Huberman (1994). The authors read the corpus dragged and dropped the sentences into the nodes, adding a new node each time they identified a new concept or a new relationship. The possibility in Nvivo to run coding queries per attribute allowed to implement a continuous process of comparison (Glaser and Strauss 2017). Continual discussions between the authors allowed them to settle minor disagreements related to categorization/coding, to beyond go facts and sayings and progressively highlight profound concepts and meanings. Next section compares the three retained frameworks and develops the emerging themes with detail.

4   Results and Discussion

4.1   Back to the Three Major Frameworks

The literature often presents the three major frameworks, namely the Diffusion of Innovations theory (DOI), the Theory of Planned Behavior (TPB), and the Technology Acceptance Model (TAM) as competing and not necessarily complementary (Mathieson 1991; Momani and Jamous 2017; Wixom and Todd 2005). Some comparison studies often conclude by asserting than one model is superior to the others (Gentry and Calantone 2002; Zhao et al. 2018) while some others try to propose more integrated frameworks combining two or more models (Lin 2007; Moore and Benbasat 1996; Sun et al. 2013; Wixom and Todd 2005). In this respect, some research studies draw the variables liable to better contribute to the explanation of their specific case from the dominant models (Riffai et al. 2012). Our research takes a specific approach as it adopts a qualitative approach allowing to apprehend the nuances between the key concepts of the previously proposed frameworks. Our findings that, in the specific case of wearable technologies, the key concepts of the three major frameworks are definitely not substitutable. Indeed, our informants reported situations where some of there were presented while others are not. For instance, **acceptance** was rather considered as a psychological state where potential users went through a cognitive/affective process leading to the readiness to possibly use the wearable device. This process may lead (or not) to the **behavioral intention** to buy and use the product. The factors underlying this decision are presented in the above sections. Once the product bought, here again, consumers may (or not) use it, and express the intention to use it continually. Consequently, our findings show that several stages should be crossed to reach the **adoption, i.e. the IoT wearable continuance intention** of the wearable devices as summarized in Fig. 4.

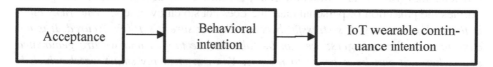

Fig. 4. Stages underlying the effective adoption of IoT wearables

4.2 Iot Wearables Characteristics

Perceived Ease of Use: According to TAM, behavioral intention can be determined especially by perceived ease of use (Davis et al. 1992). PEOU is the extent to which a person thinks that using a new system will not be and save effort (Davis 1989). It is inversely associated with the amount of effort needed to learn and use a technology as "the extent to which a person believes that using the system will be free of effort" (p. 187) (Venkatesh and Davis 2000). The analysis of the interviews shows that when sensor is intuitive, there are fewer obstacles to its use "*It's convenient and easy to use, intuitive and with a fast answer. I find easy to get this IoT device to do what I want it to do*" (M, 62 years old, Smart sensor, Sleep Tracker). In the other hand, more technology is complex, more it is tedious (Rogers 2010). PEOU seems essential for adoption and continuance to use of wearable IoT devices. Replacing this finding, in terms of the three frameworks presented above, it is important to mention that all models integrate this concept even though in DOI, it is presented differently, through "complexity", and in TPB, it is referred to as "perceived behavioral control".

Perceived Ubiquity: This characteristic refers to the possibility of using the IoT device at any time and above all, anywhere (Carillo et al. 2017). The analysis shows Perceived ubiquity as one of the most important characteristics. The ubiquitous characteristic of the wearables influence at the same time usefulness and enjoyment: "*I often use smart products and several times a day ... it is very useful and fun at the same time: when I wait for the bus thanks to the Smartphone I can know the waiting time or chat with my friends. When I play sports, I know the distance I traveled and the number of calories burned. When I'm at home, I can control my window blinds, my coffee machine, my TV, my heating from my sofa ...*" (M, 27, Master, Engineer, Smartphone, Smart Watch, Smart Sofa, Smart Heating, Smart window blinds, Smart TV). Ubiquity is generated by the continuity, immediacy, and portability developed during use. Ubiquity is a one of advantages of IoT wearable devices compared to traditional devices. It frees users from the spatial and temporal limitations and enables them to conduct ubiquitous tasks. If we want to use this result to compare the three major frameworks, we should mention that this concept is not literally mentioned as such in any of the models. However, DOI seems broad enough to encompass perceived ubiquity since it constitutes a meaningful relative advantage to potential and real users.

Privacy Features: In the interviews, several informants are concerned about threats to privacy, stemming from IoT wearable devices and the unlimited exchange of electronic information. Privacy features involves protecting the user from the risks of fraud and financial loss (Brown and Muchira 2004; Eastlick et al. 2006). Respect for privacy implies the protection of personal data and does not stolen by others: *"The tricky thing is the lack of security, It's stressful because I'm not sure it's 100% secured. It is too easy to enter for strangers; we can be followed, be tapped and we are geolocated everywhere...It can be a brake to my use. You can steal my smart watch which is synchronized with my smartphone, it can be more dangerous, if you know a little in hacking, you can access to my phone, my bank accounts ... We are sure of nothing"* (F, 21, Student, Smart cigarette, Smartphone, smart Watch). Some informants take care to not to divulge important information through smart objects in order to feel safe during the use. Similarly to perceived ubiquity, concerns about privacy are mentioned in any of the predominant frameworks we presented in the literature review. However, informants' testimonies show the privacy concerns constitute a major inhibition to feeling that the Iot wearable is consistent with users' existing values, past experience and needs. This is what Rogers (2010) call compatibility.

4.3   Individual Characteristics

Individual traits are an integral part of new technology acceptance (Agarwal and Prasad 1998; Cecchinato et al. 2015; Yang 2005; Rogers 2010; Yang et al. 2012).

Personal Innovativeness: The interviews highlight the importance of personal innovativeness in motivating the use of IoT wearable devices. Rogers and Shoemaker (1971) and Rogers (1995) explain that individuals are characterized as "innovative" if they are early to adopt an innovation. Agarwal and Prasad (1998) conceptualized the Personal innovativeness in information technology (PIIT) construct and implemented it in the original TAM (Davis 1989). In this case, it is explained by searching for information about IoT technology or by purchasing new IoT products: *"I am always the first of most other people to know of any new IoT technologies or to buy a new IoT when it appears... I am really up to technology, trying to get the last stuff. however, I can stop using these items if it doesn't work as I want or if I don't find it fun, in which case I offer or sell it and I buy a new item"* (M, 29, Executive manager, Master, Smartphone; tablet; Smart TV; Smart Fridge; Smart Activity Monitor). Interviews shows that innovative users in their social networks are most likely to perceive pleasure and usefulness when using these products. Personal innovativeness is an influencer of perceived usefulness, and perceived enjoyment. Innovative people are more likely to have risks, to accept the changes induced by connected objects, and to take advantage of their benefits (Touzani et al. 2018). Even though not present in the traditional models representing DOI, TPB and TAM, this concept is an underlying key variable in all these frameworks.

Fear of Addiction: Addiction is defined as a user's psychological state of dependence on the use of a technology. This state takes place at the expense of other important activities, ultimately infringe normal functioning, and result in a range of negative consequences (Turel and Serenko 2012). Technology addiction is assimilated to a behavioral addiction, which encapsulates a psychological dependency on the use of technology (Turel et al. 2011). The analysis shows that addiction to wearable IoT devices is manifested by absorption, to feel worry, and mood modification: *"We became quickly very dependent, we spend a lot of time there and we lose the habit of communicating directly with people. I will not be able to live without these devices, my life would be too boring and it will disturb me"* (M, 26, PhD Student in biology (Smart toothbrush; drone; Smart Shutters). Addicted users develop inflated system evaluations; they perceive technology more positively than non-addicted users (Huh and Bowman 2008). Addiction is manifested through an obsessive pattern of using and reusing the device. This state intensifies perceptions, like perceived usefulness and perceived enjoyment. The literature studying the relationship between fear of addiction and the three major acceptance theories are rather scarce. As for previous constructs, the broad character of DOI allows to integrate it easily as this aspect may be part of compatibility (Rogers 2010). Turel et al. (2011) propose the integration of addition to technologies to TAM making it more specifically adapted to wearable devices.

Anxiety-Provoking Characteristics: Anxiety is a psychological state of mind characterized by affective response, such as fear and apprehension. Anxiety when using technology specifically focuses on the user's state of mind regarding his ability and willingness to use technology-related tools (Meuter et al. 2003; Yang and Forney 2013). Several informants explain that they became anxious about using IoT wearable devices: *"Manual terms are confusing jargon and I hesitate to use IoT for fear of making mistakes. For example: I'm afraid using a connected watch, it risks to start recording intimate conversations, and sharing it on social networks. If this scenario happens, I could not fix it. These products scare me. Besides, my children gave me a smart watch that I never used for fear of doing stupid things with it. I'm afraid of being annihilated by all that"* (F, 26, Housewife, Smartphone, Smart watch). The anxiety takes form in the way users manage the Iot device and they are very sensitive to the risk to be wrong in using it. The feeling of losing control causes some respondents to minimize their use of IoT. they claim that these products can physically harm them psychologically to themselves if they become addicted: *"it was bringing me control over a part of my life. I think that there is things that we should do without these devices. And I think that Google glasses would make us stupid in a way...I am scared of becoming very lazy and not able to think by myself if I use Google glasses because it would give me access to so much information so easily"* (subject 43, F, 30 years old, unemployed, Smart Wristlet, smartphone). The fear generated by some respondents leads to a negative perception of usefulness and enjoyment during use. DOI seems the only framework where anxiety may find its place, notably through "compatibility": when wearable connected devices are compatible, they better fit consumers' background and experience, and consequently they are less liable to generate anxiety among them.

Social Norms: Social norms is the degree to which individuals have the impression that important others believe they should (be able to) use a new system, in our case IoT wearable devices (Verkasalo et al. 2010). This definition implies that consumer's behavior is influenced by they believe that others thinks that they have to be able to use the wearable. The interviews reveal that the use of IoT can respond to a need for conformity, for belonging, or adhering to a community: *"I bought my smart speaker because all my friends have one. Also this summer at the beach I was happy because I wasn't the only one who didn't have one, and it allows me to enjoy the beach. Likewise, at the gym, it's the people with who I do sport who advised me to use this model of smart wristlet... and when I forget it in my bag and see theirs, I go to get mine to put it on to know my performance"* (F, 23, Student, Smart Wristlet, Smart Speaker). Users value what the group think and the importance of its opinions belong to in forming enjoyment and usefulness. The acceptance and persistence of using IoT wearable devices depend on the behavior of the other members of people around. Even though this variable may be considered as close to Rogers' observability, in the wearable devices case it TPB and "social norm" that really fit with this construct.

4.4   Users' Perceptions

Perceived Usefulness: The analysis shows that subjects are looking for usefulness or the degree to which a person believes that using a particular system would enhance his or her job (Davis 1989). In other words, the perceived usefulness of the technology is a strong determinant of user acceptance, adoption, and usage behavior and a high predictor for the continued use of technology (e.g., Davis 1989; Bhattacherjee 2001; Limayem et al. 2007; Koo et al. 2015). The informants perceive an utilitarian advantage when they use IoT wearable devices it in everyday life associated to ease of use, convenience, organization and of time management: *"Smart devices allow you to learn cooking from distance which are more technical objects, are very useful. I think it's not only gadgets because my dishes have never been so successful ... my Smart Strips Vibes uses low level electrical pulses to stimulate or calm neural pathways through the skin. It helps me to manage my stress level by giving me a boost of energy, or inducing a sense of calm. That's a really useful stuff because I'm always stressed. There's not waste of time, especially when I'm very tired"* (F, 45, Brand manager, Master, *Smart* Headphones; tablet; Smart Strips Vibes). IoT wearable devices increase the job performance and everyday tasks. Perceived usefulness is an important determinant for continuance of use. From this point of view, following TAM researches has shown a high link between perceived usefulness and continuance of use. "Perceived usefulness" is a terminology drawn from TAM. The analyzed testimonies particularly fit with this model. However, it is important to note that this dimension is also present, even though with less acuity, in DOI (through relative advantage) and TPB (through attitude toward the behavior). It remains however, a core construct of TAM.

Perceived Enjoyment: Subjects interviewed argues that higher enjoyment associated with the use of an IoT wearable devices, leads to favorable intentions toward continuance using it. Perceived enjoyment serves as a type of fun that affects an individual's attitude and intention toward using information technology (Van Der Heijden 2004). The pleasure associated to the use of the smart object is an important motivation to intention to use it again. It refers to its design and emotions generated: *"It gives me pleasure to* *communicate with my friends and to challenge them with the watch. For the smart balance, it's fun to see the progression of my weight, which decreases, compared to that of my boyfriend. I also have smart speakers and it's too good to listen music on it"* (F, 30, Real estate agent, Smart balance, Smartphone, Smart Watch, Smart speakers, Smart Box). The pleasure factor was not part of the early work on TAM, but a few researchers explored it. Davis et al. (1992) concluded that enjoyment was one of the primary constructs through which other factors influenced usage intentions. In IoT usage, interviews appear that perceived enjoyment had effects on user's continuance intention. The hedonic dimension of the acceptance wearable devices is not directly integrated in any of the considered modeled. Nevertheless, a deeper look at the definition of the "relative advantage" show, once again, that DOI is broad enough to include such a construct.

4.5   Synthesis and Proposed Framework

As indicated earlier, the three major frameworks available in the literature, the Diffusion of Innovations theory (DOI), the Theory of Planned Behavior (TPB), and the Technology Acceptance Model (TAM) are not really competing since there are crucial nuances among them. Indeed, the analyzed interviews show that in the specific case of wearable devices, consumers go through a succession of stages moving progressively from acceptance to adoption (cf. Fig. 4). Besides, several factors may contribute to explain how consumers move from the initial to the real adoption. Below, we present a model summarizing the key concepts that emerged from our qualitative data analysis (Fig. 5):

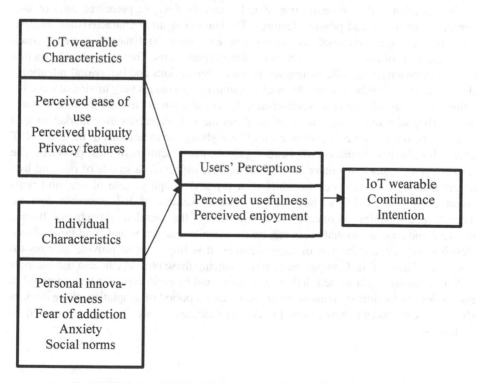

Fig. 5. Proposed framework for the wearable continuance intention

5 Contributions

From a theoretical perspective, our results include two main aspects: 1/ the comparison of three main theoretical frameworks mentioned below 2/ the proposition of a new model going beyond these three frameworks and adapted to the specific case of wearable devices. Our results show that the three considered frameworks bring interesting highlights in understanding and explaining the adoption and continuous use of IoT wearable devices. They also reveal that there is not really a more appropriate and adapted model to predict the adoption and the continuous use of IoT wearable devices, even though DOI includes broad factors liable to encompass several of our findings. However, our qualitative data highlights the importance of going beyond these three models by adding new constructs and new relationships. Our second section proposes a new model including these motivations and inhibitors related to the IoT continuance intention. The thematic analysis reveals the following motivations: users' perceived ubiquity allowing them to browse between several places at the same time, and connectedness as individuals use wearable devices as a mean of building a "social link" and connect more to their social system. The inhibitions reveal the dark side of the use of IoT wearable devices. These are the fear of addiction (as informants report that these devices stick to the body and generate absorption), anxiety-provoking characteristics, and privacy concerns taking various forms. Figure 5 shows the model resulting from these findings.

From a managerial perspective, this study first highlights the characteristics leading to the adoption and continuous use of IoT wearable devices: perceived ease of use, perceived ubiquity, and privacy features. By improving these characteristics, companies may enhance perceived usefulness and enjoyment, and therefore, better reach potential users of IoT wearables and meet their expectations. The study also shows that social norms have a significant impact on users' perceptions and behavioral intentions. By reducing the "risks" and the fears of consumers, companies may minimize negative attitudes and avoid negative word-of-mouth. Manufacturers have an interest in communicating with reassuring information about the IoT wearables they market to lead consumers to adoption and continue use. Highlighting the inhibitions of the use of IoT wearables also has significant implications for the manufacturers of these products. The results indicate that consumers may consider these objects as a source of risk and loss of control. People who seek personal data privacy, ubiquity, ease of use, and reassurance are more liable to become potential consumers of IoT wearable devices. Therefore, companies can make efforts at the level of the confidentiality charter. It must be clear and concise, so that users can easily assimilate all terms and conditions of use. Besides, to facilitate the use of these devices, it is important to provide an easy-to-understand user guide. Companies commercializing these objects can also use tutorials to help consumers get started. IoT wearables should be conceived in a way to avoid to consumers to continually parameterize them: after a period of adaptation, these devices should accommodate themselves to user preferences to significantly contribute to continuous use.

Appendix 1: The Constructs Mentioned in DOI, TPB and TAM

Theory	Factor	Definition
DOI	Relative advantage	"The degree to which an innovation is perceived as better than the idea it supersedes" (Rogers 2010, p. 15)
	Compatibility	"The degree to which an innovation is perceived as being consistent with the existing values, past experiences and needs of potential adopters" (Rogers 2010, p. 15)
	Complexity	"The degree to which an innovation is perceived as difficult to understand and use" (Rogers 2010, p. 16)
	Trialability	"The degree to which an innovation may be experimented with on a limited basis" (Rogers 2010, p. 16)
	Observability	"The degree to which the results of an innovation are visible to others" (Rogers 2010, p. 16)
	Adoption	"A decision to make full use of an innovation as the best course of action available" (Rogers 2010, p. 21)
TPB	Attitude toward behavior	"An individual's positive or negative feelings (evaluative effect) about performing the target behavior" (Fishbein and Ajzen, 1975, p. 216)
	Subjective norm	"The person's perception that most people who are important to him think he should or should not perform the behavior in question" (Fishbein and Ajzen 1975, p. 302)
	Perceived behavioral control	"The perceived ease or difficulty of performing the behavior" (Ajzen 1991, p. 188), In the context of information systems research, "Perceptions of internal and external constraints on behavior" (Taylor and Todd 1995, p 149)
	Behavioral intention to use	"The strength of one's intention to perform a specified behavior" (Fishbein and Ajzen, 1975, p. 288)
TAM	Perceived usefulness	"The degree to which a person believes that using a particular system would enhance his or her job performance" (Davis 1989, p. 320)
	Perceived ease of use	"The degree to which a person believes that using a particular system would be free of effort" (Davis 1989, p. 320)
	Behavioral intention to use	"The strength of one's intention to perform a specified behavior" (Fishbein and Ajzen, 1975, p. 288)

References

Adhiarna, N., Hwang, Y.M., Park, M.J., Rho, J.J.: An integrated framework for RFID adoption and diffusion with a stage-scale-scope cubicle model: a case of indonesia. Int. J. Inf. Manag. **33**(2), 378–389 (2013)

Agarwal, R., Prasad, J.: A conceptual and operational definition of personal innovativeness in the domain of information technology. Inf. Syst. Res. **9**(2), 204–215 (1998)

Ajzen, I.: The theory of planned behavior. Organ. Behav. Hum. Decis. Process. **50**(2), 179–211 (1991)

Arpaci, I.: A theoretical framework for IT consumerization: factors influencing the adoption of BYOD. In: Handbook of Research on Technology Integration in the Global World, pp. 114–129. IGI Global (2019)

Bagozzi, R.P.: The self-regulation of attitudes, intentions, and behavior. Soc. Psychol. Q. **55**, 178–204 (1992)

Bhattacherjee, A.: Understanding information systems continuance: an expectation-confirmation model. MIS Q. **25**(3), 351–370 (2001)

Boddy, C.R.: Sample size for qualitative research. Qual. Mark. Res.: Int. J. **19**(4), 426–432 (2016)

Brown, M., Muchira, R.: Investigating the relationship between internet privacy concerns and online purchase behavior. J. Electron. Commer. Res. **5**(1), 62–70 (2004)

Bryman, A.: Research Methods and Organization Studies. Routledge, Abingdon (2003)

Carillo, K., Scornavacca, E., Za, S.: The role of media dependency in predicting continuance intention to use ubiquitous media systems. Inf. Manag. **54**(3), 317–335 (2017)

Cecchinato, M.E., Cox, A.L., Bird, J.: Smartwatches: the good, the bad and the ugly?. In: Proceedings of the 33rd Annual ACM Conference Extended Abstracts on Human Factors in Computing Systems, April, pp. 2133–2138 (2015)

Chau, P.Y., Hu, P.J.H.: Information technology acceptance by individual professionals: a model comparison approach. Decis. Sci. **32**(4), 699–719 (2001)

Choi, J., Kim, S.: Is the smartwatch an IT product or a fashion product? A study on factors affecting the intention to use smartwatches. Comput. Hum. Behav. **63**, 777–786 (2016)

Compeau, D.R., Higgins, C.A.: Computer self-efficacy: development of a measure and initial test. MIS Q. **19**(2), 189–211 (1995)

Davis, F.D.: Perceived usefulness, perceived ease of use, and user acceptance of information technology. MIS Q. **13**(3), 319–340 (1989)

Davis, F.D., Bagozzi, R.P., Warshaw, P.R.: Extrinsic and intrinsic motivation to use computers in the workplace. J. Appl. Soc. Psychol. **22**(14), 1111–1132 (1992)

Denzin, N.K., Lincoln, Y.S.: Introduction: the Discipline and Practice of Qualitative Research the Sage Handbook of Qualitative Research, 3rd edn, pp. 1–32. Sage Publications Ltd, Thousand Oaks (2005)

Dong, X., Chang, Y., Wang, Y., Yan, J.: Understanding usage of internet of Things (IOT) systems in China: cognitive experience and affect experience as moderator. Inf. Technol. People **30**(1), 117–138 (2017)

Eastlick, M.A., Lotz, S.L., Warrington, P.: Understanding online B-to-C relationships: an integrated model of privacy concerns, trust, and commitment. J. Bus. Res. **59**(8), 877–886 (2006)

Eisenhardt, K.M., Graebner, M.E.: Theory building from cases: opportunities and challenges. Acad. Manag. J. **50**(1), 25–32 (2007)

Fishbein, M., Ajzen, I.: Belief, Attitude, Intention, and Behaviour: An Introduction to Theory and Research (1975)

Gao, L., Bai, X.: A unified perspective on the factors influencing consumer acceptance of internet of things technology. Asia Pac. J. Mark. Logist. **26**(2), 211–231 (2014)

Gentry, L., Calantone, R.: A comparison of three models to explain shop-bot use on the web. Psychol. Mark. **19**(11), 945–956 (2002)

Glaser, B.G., Strauss, A.L.: Discovery of Grounded Theory: Strategies for Qualitative Research. Routledge, Abingdon (2017)

Guest, G., Bunce, A., Johnson, L.: How many interviews are enough? An experiment with data saturation and variability. Field Methods **18**(1), 59–82 (2006)

Harris, I., Wang, Y., Wang, H.: ICT in multimodal transport and technological trends: Unleashing potential for the future. Int. J. Prod. Econ. **159**, 88–103 (2015)

Harrison, D.A., Mykytyn Jr., P.P., Riemenschneider, C.K.: Executive decisions about adoption of information technology in small business: theory and empirical tests. Inf. Syst. Res. **8**(2), 171–195 (1997)

Huh, S., Bowman, N.D.: Perception and addiction of online games as a function of personality traits. J. Media Psychol. **13**(2), 1–31 (2008)

Hwang, Y.M., Kim, M.G., Rho, J.J.: Understanding internet of things (IoT) diffusion: focusing on value configuration of rfid and sensors in business cases (2008–2012). Inf. Dev. **32**(4), 969–985 (2016)

Karahanna, E., Straub, D.W., Chervany, N.L.: Information technology adoption across time: a cross-sectional comparison of pre-adoption and post-adoption beliefs. MIS Q. **23**(2), 183–213 (1999)

Kim, J.H., Yoo, M., Lee, K.N., Seo, H.: The innovation of the internet: a semantic network analysis of the internet of things. Asian J. Technol. Innov. **25**(1), 129–139 (2017)

Kim, Y.C., Shin, E.K.: Localized use of information and communication technologies in Seoul's urban neighborhoods. Am. Behav. Sci. **60**(1), 81–100 (2016)

Koo, C., Chung, N., Nam, K.: Assessing the impact of intrinsic and extrinsic motivators on smart green IT device use: reference group perspectives. Int. J. Inf. Manag. **35**(1), 64–79 (2015)

Li, L., Rong, M., Zhang, G.: An internet of things QoE evaluation method based on multiple linear regression analysis. In: 10th International Conference on Computer Science & Education (ICCSE) July, pp. 925–928. IEEE (2015)

Limayem, M., Hirt, S.G., Cheung, C.M.K.: How habit limits the predictive power of intention: the case of information systems continuance. MIS Q. **31**(4), 705–737 (2007)

Lin, H.F.: Predicting consumer intentions to shop online: an empirical test of competing theories. Electron. Commer. Res. Appl. **6**(4), 433–442 (2007)

Manyika, J., et al.: Unlocking the Potential of the Internet of Things. McKinsey Global Institute, New York (2015)

Marakhimov, A., Joo, J.: Consumer adaptation and infusion of wearable devices for healthcare. Comput. Hum. Behav. **76**, 135–148 (2017)

Mathieson, K.: Predicting user intentions: comparing the technology acceptance model with the theory of planned behavior. Inf. Syst. Res. **2**(3), 173–191 (1991)

Meuter, M.L., Ostrom, A.L., Bitner, M.J., Roundtree, R.: The influence of technology anxiety on consumer use and experiences with self-service technologies. J. Bus. Res. **56**(11), 899–906 (2003)

Miles, M.B., Huberman, A.M.: Qualitative Data Analysis: An Expanded Sourcebook. Sage, Thousand Oaks (1994)

Mital, M., Chang, V., Choudhary, P., Papa, A., Pani, A.K.: Adoption of internet of things in India: a test of competing models using a structured equation modeling approach. Technol. Forecast. Soc. Change **136**, 339–346 (2018)

Momani, A.M., Jamous, M.: The evolution of technology acceptance theories. Int. J. Contemp. Comput. Res. **1**(1), 51–58 (2017)

Moore, G.C., Benbasat, I.: Integrating diffusion of innovations and theory of reasoned action models to predict utilization of information technology by end-users. In: Kautz, K., Pries-Heje, J. (eds.) Diffusion and Adoption of Information Technology. ITIFIP, pp. 132–146. Springer, Boston (1996). https://doi.org/10.1007/978-0-387-34982-4_10

Park, E., Cho, Y., Han, J., Kwon, S.J.: Comprehensive approaches to user acceptance of internet of things in a smart home environment. IEEE Internet Things J. **4**(6), 2342–2350 (2017)

Pasian, M.B. (ed.): Designs, Methods and Practices for Research of Project Management. Gower Publishing, Ltd., Farnham (2015)

Piyare, R.: Internet of things: ubiquitous home control and monitoring system using android based smart phone. Int. J. Internet Things **2**(1), 5–11 (2013)

Rawassizadeh, R., Price, B.A., Petre, M.: Wearables: has the age of smartwatches finally arrived? Commun. ACM **58**(1), 45–47 (2014)

Riffai, M.M.M.A., Grant, K., Edgar, D.: Big TAM in Oman: exploring the promise of on-line banking, its adoption by customers and the challenges of banking in Oman. Int. J. Inf. Manag. **32**(3), 239–250 (2012)

Rogers, E.M.: Lessons for guidelines from the diffusion of innovations. Joint Comm. J. Qual. Patient Saf. **21**(7), 324–328 (1995)

Rogers, E.M.: Diffusion of Innovations. Simon and Schuster, New York (2010)

Rogers, E.M., Shoemaker, F.F.: Communication of Innovations; A Cross-Cultural Approach (1971).

Shin, D.H.: Conceptualizing and measuring quality of experience of the internet of things: exploring how quality is perceived by users. Inf. Manag. **54**(8), 998–1011 (2017)

Somekh, B., Lewin, C. (eds.): Research Methods in the Social Sciences. Sage, Thousand Oaks (2005)

Sood, A., Kumar, V.: Analyzing client profitability across diffusion segments for a continuous innovation. J. Mark. Res. **54**(6), 932–951 (2017)

Stiles, W.B.: Theory-building case studies as practice-based evidence. In: Barkham, M., Hardy, G.E., Mellor-Clark, J. (eds.) Developing and Delivering Practice-Based Evidence, pp. 91–108. Wiley, Hoboken (2010)

Sun, Y., Wang, N., Guo, X., Peng, Z.: Understanding the acceptance of mobile health services: a comparison and integration of alternative models. J. Electron. Commer. Res. **14**(2), 183 (2013)

Svendsen, G.B., Johnsen, J.A.K., Almås-Sørensen, L., Vittersø, J.: Personality and technology acceptance: the influence of personality factors on the core constructs of the technology acceptance model. Behav. Inf. Technol. **32**(4), 323–334 (2013)

Taylor, S., Todd, P.A.: Understanding information technology usage: a test of competing models. Inf. Syst. Res. **6**(2), 144–176 (1995)

Thompson, R.L., Higgins, C.A., Howell, J.M.: Personal computing: toward a conceptual model of utilization. MIS Q. **15**(1), 125–143 (1991)

Touzani, M., Charfi, A.A., Boistel, P., Niort, M.-C.: Connecto ergo sum! An exploratory study of the motivations behind the usage of connected objects. Inf. Manag. **55**(4), 472–481 (2018)

Turel, O., Serenko, A.: The benefits and dangers of enjoyment with social networking websites. Eur. J. Inf. Syst. **21**(5), 512–528 (2012)

Turel, O., Serenko, A., Giles, P.: Integrating technology addiction and use: an empirical investigation of online auction users. MIS Q. **35**(4), 1043–1062 (2011)

Van der Heijden, H.: User acceptance of hedonic information systems. MIS Q. **28**(4), 695–704 (2004)

Venkatesh, V., Bala, H.: Technology acceptance model 3 and a research agenda on interventions. Decis. Sci. **39**(2), 273–315 (2008)

Venkatesh, V., Davis, F.D.: A theoretical extension of the technology acceptance model: four longitudinal field studies. Manag. Sci. **46**(2), 186–204 (2000)

Venkatesh, V., Morris, M.G., Davis, G.B., Davis, F.D.: User acceptance of information technology: toward a unified view. MIS Q. **27**(3), 425–478 (2003)

Verkasalo, H., López-Nicolás, C., Molina-Castillo, F.J., Bouwman, H.: Analysis of users and non-users of smartphone applications. Telemat. Inform. **27**(3), 242–255 (2010)

Vishwanath, A., Barnett, G.A.: The Diffusion of Innovations. A Communication Science Perspective. Peter Lang, New York (2011)

Wang, H., Chung, J.E., Park, N., McLaughlin, M.L., Fulk, J.: Understanding online community participation: a technology acceptance perspective. Commun. Res. **39**(6), 781–801 (2012)

Wixom, B.H., Todd, P.A.: A theoretical integration of user satisfaction and technology acceptance. Inf. Syst. Res. **16**(1), 85–102 (2005)

Wu, B., Chen, X.: Continuance intention to use MOOCs: integrating the technology acceptance model (TAM) and task technology fit (TTF) model. Comput. Hum. Behav. **67**, 221–232 (2017)

Yang, K.C.: Exploring factors affecting the adoption of mobile commerce in Singapore. Telemat. Inform. **22**(3), 257–277 (2005)

Yang, K., Forney, J.C.: The moderating role of consumer technology anxiety in mobile shopping adoption: differential effects of facilitating conditions and social influences. J. Electron. Commer. Res. **14**(4), 334 (2013)

Yang, S., Lu, Y., Gupta, S., Cao, Y., Zhang, R.: Mobile payment services adoption across time: an empirical study of the effects of behavioral beliefs, social influences, and personal traits. Comput. Hum. Behav. **28**(1), 129–142 (2012)

Zhang, L., Zhu, J., Liu, Q.: A meta-analysis of mobile commerce adoption and the moderating effect of culture. Comput. Hum. Behav. **28**(5), 1902–1911 (2012)

Zhao, Y., Ni, Q., Zhou, R.: What factors influence the mobile health service adoption? A meta-analysis and the moderating role of age. Int. J. Inf. Manag. **43**, 342–350 (2018)

Marketing Strategies in the Age of Technology

Caroline Kassabli Al Fakhry[(✉)]

Faculty of Business, Lebanese International University, Beirut, Lebanon
Caroline.kassably@liu.edu.lb

Abstract. With the rising recognition of major technology related trends, marketers are reorganizing or regenerating their strategies and practices to meet the new challenges. The aim of this paper is to highlight new strategic thinking and to accommodate the fact of such an accelerating speed of technology. The method is to analyze five selected trends and observe their possible influence on designing marketing strategies, where winning strategies in prospect will need to be receptive and adaptive rather than permanent and rigid. Close to the end of the paper is a finding and reflection section of the work. The paper concludes with two new notions discussed in literature, social customer relationship management (CRM) and Gamification that are affecting marketing strategies with related research avenues suggested. It proposes that, in today's dynamic and digitally disruptive market, it is essential to implement entrepreneurial marketing to meet the simulations of the twenty first century.

Keywords: Technology · Digitization · Marketing strategies · Green technology

1 Introduction

"A good hockey player plays where the puck is; a great hockey player plays where the puck is going to be" Wayne Gretzky. Understanding internal and external factors at a specific time and equally important anticipating future events, trends, and conditions is crucial to creating and progressing effective strategies (Mooradian et al. 2012).

Currently, both marketplace and market space transactions are taking place. Some companies operate solely in the marketplace, yet others, have begun to include the two realms. The fast growth of market space is due to the transformation power of technology. Activities that use electronic communication in inventory, exchange, advertisement, distribution, and payment is often called electronic commerce (Kerin et al. 2015). Consequently, market space is affecting the trends discussed but with varying degrees.

Although this is relatively broad, the aim of this paper is to concentrate on the context of five specific trends. After perceiving the changing environment and trends, especially with the tremendous change of technology in which marketing takes place, it is essential to develop and implement some nearly accurate marketing strategies.

Therefore, the purpose of this paper is to identify the trends that are shaping new marketing strategies; those that are creating uneasiness for companies currently and in the future, and to support those findings with examples.

© Springer Nature Switzerland AG 2019
R. Jallouli et al. (Eds.): ICDEc 2019, LNBIP 358, pp. 342–351, 2019.
https://doi.org/10.1007/978-3-030-30874-2_27

Approaching the end of the paper, the findings and reflection section is discussed followed by the conclusion section where related research avenues are suggested.

2 The Problem

Companies and marketing departments, specifically, are facing serious concerns due to the progress of technology and digitization. According to Lipiäinen (2014), many companies are struggling with the new rules and tools. This paper seeks to understand how technological pressure has created new trends and has altered marketing strategies in many ways. It intends to show how companies can use digitization and technology more efficiently to guarantee competitive advantage, supported by examples.

It is set to find the necessary role of businesses in adapting to technological improvements. What is the role of marketing specifically? Is it incorporating technology effectively and creatively?

The research methodology used is mainly desk research where sources of published information methodology are used in a conceptual framework.

3 Trend Analysis

The plan is to recognize and concentrate on the context of five specific technology related trends, in which new demanding marketing strategies are shaped. Analyzing five essential trends (1. The rise of sharing economy, 2. Globalization, 3. Digitization, 4. Accelerating technological change and 5. Green technology, ethical consumption, and sustainability aspects) will aid in answering and reviewing marketing strategies. There may be several trends affecting marketing environment; however, the process of selecting these specific trends was from in depth readings of The Consumer sector in 2030 trends and questions to consider (Benson-Armer et al. 2015) as well as scanning the marketing environment by Kerin et al. 2015 (Chapter 3). These trends are particularly chosen because they are related to technology (Hamari et al. 2016; Qadri and Bhat 2018; Newman 2017; Kerin et al. 2015; Ottman 2017). Moreover, these trends were identified in marketing literature (Kerin et al. 2015; Kelly 2015; Hamari et al. 2016; Zuhairah and Noor 2015; Benson-Armer et al. 2015; Patrutiu-Baltes 2016).

For this reason, strategies and new tactics that address technological improvement are discussed keeping in mind that marketing, like other areas of business, has a function to change business practices for successful development, and help reduce the negative effects of digitization on businesses.

3.1 The Rise of the Sharing Economy

Sharing economy is an economic model based on sharing underutilized assets from spaces to skills to stuff for monetary or non-monetary benefits (Cohen and Kietzmann 2014). In 2011, TIME nominated sharing economy as one of "10 ideas that will change the world" (Teubner 2014).

Information and communications technologies (ICTs) have facilitated the increase of Collaborative Consumption (CC) which is the peer-to-peer-based activity of obtaining, giving, or sharing the access to goods and services, synchronized through community-based online services (Hamari et al. 2016). Moreover, "the sharing economy is an emerging economic-technological phenomenon that is fueled by developments in information and communications technology (ICT), growing consumer awareness, proliferation of collaborative web communities as well as social commerce/sharing" as quoted by (Hamari et al. 2016).

Such developments started to tackle and challenge traditional (ownership-based) thinking, about how resources can and should be offered (Cohen and Kietzmann 2014). Mercedes Benz, for instance, entered the car-sharing business and adjusted its strategies to fit to the new trend. Home Depot has introduced product rental in about half of its stores. Consumers have greater interest in sharing, when the cost is minimized and the benefits are maximized, and marketers have access to consumer previous usage patterns, for example cell phone. If consumers' personal usage pattern information predicts sharing as an appeal, then marketers should be able to target customers, with a high possibility of success (Lamberton and Rose 2012). Smartphone apps allow sharers to transact wherever, to see what is being shared close by and use on the spot (Geron 2013). According to Geron (2013), at least 100 companies have sprouted up to offer owners a tiny income stream out of dozens of types of physical assets, without needing to buy anything themselves. This trend has created markets out of things that would not have been considered income-generating assets before. The share economy threatens the industrial model of companies owning and people consuming, and allows everyone to be both consumer and producer (Geron 2013). In the next section, globalization will be discussed stressing on its impact on marketing strategies.

3.2   Globalization

According to Qadri and Bhat (2018), globalization is highly correlated with technology. In addition, globalization includes a series of technological developments facilities and novelty in many forms. They include physical, human, and social capital services, and Information and Communication Technology services to bring positive changes in the economy, advance standards of living, quality of life and skills of its citizens, and develop the awareness base of the economy. Globalization, as a trend and as related to technology, has affected marketing strategies of companies; thus, it is essential to consider in this analysis. For example, more than half of Google's revenues (57%) now come from outside the United States. While some companies are very successful in growing global, others are constantly facing great effort (Kelly 2015).

Nataly Kelly, the VP of Marketing at HubSpot, observed traits that distinguish companies with increased global growth. Global companies have an innate global bias, most have a member of the executive team from a foreign country or first generation American. A second trait is that they favor the web, which makes the company more capable of entering the international markets. Working with the right partners is the third trait; cautiously choosing international partners is important at the beginning of entering markets overseas.

Businesses with global success put customers first although customers live outside their home markets. Their strategy is to attract customers, better serve them and renovate them into supporters to their brand. Taking international strategy seriously, companies assign executives who help drive strategy for international markets. In that way, companies will create a "global first" where, employees display a globally minded attitude, and engineering teams build software with international users in mind (Kelly 2015). In addition to that, understanding cultural, economic, and political-regulatory that affect global marketing practices is crucial (Kerin et al. 2015). Understanding values, customs, cultural symbols, cultural ethnocentricity, and language are significant. Mc Donald has respected the Indian values of sacred cows, and introduced chicken Maharaja Mac. Another example on cultural symbols evoke deep feelings, for example, when the white marble columns in the Parthenon that crowns the Acropolis in Athens were turned into Coca-Cola bottles, the Greeks were outraged and Coca-Cola apologized for the advertisement. Global marketers know that the best language to use in communicating with consumers is "their own". Vicks brand name common in the United States is German slang for sexual intimacy; therefore, Vicks is called Wicks in Germany. Economic consideration also affects global marketing, such as stage of economic development, economic infrastructure, consumer income and purchasing power, as well as currency exchange rate. Marketers also look at political regulatory climate, political stability, and trade regulations. In addition, the company going global should select the means of market entry from exporting, licensing, joint venture, and direct investment (Kerin et al. 2015).

Moreover, marketers are constructing product and promotion strategies based on the need of the global market. They are adapting distribution strategy based on the country's stage of economic development, as well. Pricing strategy may vary also where the company, in some cases, might sell the product at a dumping price, which is subject in many cases to severe penalties and fines (Kerin et al. 2015).

After clearly observing the changes in marketing strategies due to globalization, digitization is the third trend to be analyzed.

3.3 Digitization

Digitization is the process of converting continuous, analog information into discrete, digital and machine-readable format (De Mauro et al. 2015). According to a research of the Fletcher School at Tufts University's Institute for Business in the Global Context, digitization varies with countries. The study analyzed 50 countries, sorted into four trajectory zones. The countries that are moving the fastest include stand-out countries like Sweden, UK, USA, Korea, Canada, Singapore, and Hong Kong. With an upward trajectory today, these countries are highly innovative and seek new growth markets beyond their borders. Stall out countries have achieved high levels in the past but are losing momentum such as Finland, Demark, France, and Spain. One challenge could be the aging of stall out countries, yet, attracting talented young immigrates could help provide innovation rapidly. As for the break out countries such as Turkey, India, Brazil, and China, they have the potential, and are moving upward towards improving their digital readiness rapidly. The last is watch out countries that suffer and score low on development and improvement and institutional uncertainty and low commitment to reform. These include countries like Nigeria, Philippine, Egypt and Saudi Arabia (Chakravorti et al. 2015) (Video HBR, 2015).

Digitization has created worries on marketers. Recent research shows that social media has strong influence on purchasing decisions. So, as smart phones get smarter and networks become more sophisticated, consumer share opinions about products and services. Consequently, companies are not ignoring this fact. Actually, some invest "in ways to listen in - on and generate-social media buzz" (Benson-Armer et al. 2015).

Involving consumer in brand innovation is equally important. For instance, LEGO and Pepsi use crowdsourcing to develop and test new products. Other companies provide seamless Omni-channel experience to insure consumers have every opportunity to interact with the brand. In another case, Nordstrom customers can buy products not just in stores and on the web, but also on a mobile app, on Instagram, or via text messages. They can pick up, return, or exchange their online purchases at Nordstrom stores (Benson-Armer et al. 2015).

Digital data helps smart targeting and personalization. As in the case of Harley Davidson which was selling one or two bikes per week, and, when they applied marketing software powered by artificial intelligence (AI) and analytics, they sold 15 bikes in one weekend (Newman 2017). This was possible by using existing customer data where an analytics platform searched the company's customer relationship management (CRM) system to define the qualities of "high value" customers. AI even tested words in emails that lead to higher response rates. This is aiding marketing teams use data intelligently to map customers.

Daniel Newman explains that companies need smart application of technologies with strong analysis from a committed team to be digitally intelligent. "This is no longer an age where leaders can afford to make gut-based decisions or throw something at the wall to see what sticks. In this age, leaders are communicators at every level. They need marketing technology, data and finance with the CEO working together to take the company to the best destination" (Newman 2017).

Patrutiu-Baltes (2016), considered inbound marketing as the most important digital marketing strategy in a competitive environment such as the online environment. It is a form of marketing that connects with probable customers through materials they find useful, using media similar to blogs, social networking, search engine optimization (SEO) and viral videos and so on. The purpose of inbound marketing is to attract online customers, and it is the most advanced field nowadays when it comes to big data (Opreana and Vinerean 2015).

3.4 Accelerating Technological Change

We are in an era of dramatic technological change. Predicting technological change is difficult because it is a result of research. Yet, main changes occurring today include connectivity, internet, and computers will develop five senses to create intelligent data and green technologies. 3D technologies will alter from movie theaters and televisions to many new and useful applications (Kerin et al. 2015). Tools and strategies that were cutting-edge only some years ago are becoming obsolete (Van den Driest and Weed 2014).

Accelerating technology has a crucial impact on marketing strategy. First, customers nowadays value assessment of technology-based products, and focus on dimensions like quality, service, and relationship. Many US mobile vendors, who charge little for the phone if the purchase leads to long-term telephone service contracts, use this approach to reduce the challenge (upgrade purchases will generate revenue). Second, companies provide value through the development of new products. For example, new products expected to be available soon include injectable health monitors that send glucose, oxygen, and other clinical information to a wristwatch-like monitor and robots that use artificial intelligence to master specific task (Kerin et al. 2015). Additionally, companies are benefiting from technological development to recycle products. For example, Tomra Systems has installed more than 67,000 reverse vending machines in North America, Europe, Japan, South America, and the Middle East, facilitating the collection of more than 30 billion cans and bottles annually. Another approach marketers use is the pre recycling by reducing the amount of packaging for manufacturers and sinking the waste for consumers. Technology has also increased the marketplace, and electronic commerce. It is useful to use network technologies for monitoring daily sales, sharing information with employees as well as communicating with suppliers, distributors, and advertising agencies (Kerin et al. 2015).

Another important strategy is that companies can use technology to open labs and help "experiment with emerging technologies before they are ubiquitous" (Benson-Armer et al. 2015). The advancement in technology is so imaginable that some companies are using real-time decision-making. For example, Chico are using advanced analytics to process customer information taken from social web and stores to produce clear customer profiles for smarter marketing. This allows machines to process and make decisions faster based on real data (Newman 2017).

The financial services are making use of technology acceleration and digitization; studies show that 58% of American use their mobile devices to access their bank accounts. Major Banks have joined the "cardless ATM" field allowing customers to withdraw using a smart phone (Newman 2017). Hence, as technology continues to change, incorporated redesigned market strategies are vital.

The fifth trend analyzed shows the effects of green marketing, ethical behavior, and sustainable aspects (empowered with technology) on marketing strategies.

3.5 Green Technology, Ethical Consumption, and Sustainability Aspects

Technology is getting green. The technological progress, nowadays, is to produce greener and sustainable products whose impact is lighter on the globe than its substitutes and include a social dimension such as fair trade. Both greener and sustainable are working fine and are likely to work better and more efficiently than "brown" equivalents. In addition, over $4 billion in venture capital is being devoted in clean tech industry to maintain the development of solar and wind, bio-fuel, geothermal, and other renewable substitutes to fossil fuels. Cleantech is now the largest U.S. venture capital category representing 27% of all venture funds (Ottman 2017). Ottman (2017), adds that a particular White House office for green jobs vigorously works to instruct, train, and organize a labor force prepared for tomorrow's green technologies. Moreover, "proactive companies are inventing new greener technologies, new business models, and new designs that are capturing media attention, grabbing new customers, and establishing a competitive advantage – if not changing the rules of the game altogether." For instance, Cargill's Nature Works is showing that plastics do not have to depend on fossil fuels and can be recyclable and compostable as well (Ottman 2017).

According to Chen et al. (2006), green innovation, whether software or hardware innovation, may be separated into green products and processes. Green innovations consist of innovation in technologies, which are concerned in the design of green products; using energy saving, waste recycling, and technology to avoid pollution (Chen et al. 2006). Zuhairah and Noor (2015) state that "the literature enables to provide results on the role of green innovation and green promotion as a marketing strategy". Setting the concept of environmental protection into the design of products is green innovation, then building a green promotion, which refers as the communication that promotes the product and the services. Therefore, promoting a green advertising campaign ought to have also the distinctiveness to enhance the corporate image of social responsibility. Accordingly, "the success of the green innovation and green promotion is a success factor to influence the firms' performance" (Zuhairah and Noor 2015).

Undoubtedly, ethical consumers have influenced businesses and marketers. Consumers concern of animal welfare, fair market, and social aspects such as labor standards increased, thus, creating a trend that is probably changing the minds of businesses (Carrigan et al. 2004). According to Howie et al. (2018), marketing managers have employed a variety of strategies to differentiate their programs. Numerous companies now structure their campaigns to require active participation from the consumer. For instance, Nature Valley started their "Preserve the Parks" campaign in 2010 to benefit the National Parks Conservation Association (NPCA). By entering their Universal Product Code from their packaging on the company's website, a $1 donation will be granted in return (Cone, 2011) cited by (Howie et al. 2018). The website gave customers links to volunteer, make a personal donation, and to share program information on social media platforms. The company has used cause-related marketing (CRM) expected to benefit the company, the cause, and consumer (Howie et al. 2018). Nike is another example; it has been a leader in improving workplace conditions in Asian factories. It imposed codes of conduct to reduce unsafe, harsh, or abusive working conditions at offshore manufacturing facilities (Kerin et al. 2015).

Green technology has raised the concern of ethics and sustainable aspects as well as economic concerns, and as seen, many companies have altered their marketing strategies to meet the needs of the discussed trend. While companies cannot use the same marketing strategies in all cases and trends analyzed in the paper, they can generate synergies by treating different trends as part of a system.

4   Findings and Reflection

This paper has analyzed and explained the changes in marketing strategies due to technological influence. It stressed on the shiny end of the five basic trends; yet, there may be other perspectives to the situations. For instance, digitization that was previously explained as a revolution and innovation, might not be the gleaming end of organization. Digitization is not necessary overwhelming, it is moderately or massively disrupting some businesses (Grossman 2016). Digitization is even changing titles (Newman 2017). For example, the chief marketing officer (CMO) is becoming a central focus of digital transformation as companies look for stronger customers by understanding demands. This means that the CMO is more involved in technology purchases since he/she is responsible for achieving the next generation of customer experience.

Moreover, the positive side of technology was discussed; yet, what about its negative consequences? Actions are being tracked on the web to determine which advertisements appear on our screen. Each of the major browser makers Microsoft, Google, Mozilla, and Apple can keep a record of the web pages you visit or the topics you discuss in your e-mail, which raises the issue of privacy. The Federal Trade Commission (FTC) lately issued a report calling for better self-regulation of information collection when online, suggesting a "Do Not Track" option on the browser.

Of course, there are complex perspectives and approaches to the situations discussed in the paper consisting of many different aspects. It is important to consider that the trends discussed will not affect all customers and markets equally. For example, advanced robotics is making progress in Asia but is to take off in South America and Africa (Benson-Armer et al. 2015). Therefore, the context of the trends is not all the same.

The paper discussed the threats of five very important aspects affecting marketing strategies; yet, there may be several other technology aspects affecting the marketing strategies not covered at this point.

5 Conclusion

It was proposed that marketing, like other disciplines in business, is affected by technology and digitization. Marketing, therefore, has an important function in searching for new strategies for better successful plans. Particularly this paper suggests that marketing strategies, influenced through the rise of the sharing economy, globalization, digitization, accelerating technological change, green technology, and ethical consumption, is tackling the challenge with optimistic results of improved organizational performance.

Marketing managers are incorporating promising technologies – specifically social media applications – with existing methods to develop new means that promote stronger relationships with customers. The combination of existing CRM systems with social media technology has set way to a new concept of CRM that incorporates a network-focused approach to managing customer relationships described as social CRM (Trainor et al. 2014). This opens other research avenues where there is somewhat modest scholarly research on integrating social media and traditional media in marketing campaign (Whiting and Deshpande 2016). A secondary avenue of research, identified by Whiting and Deshpande (2016), is the motivations of social media users. A third avenue could be the various mechanisms that potentially explain earned media effects on sales (Stephen and Galak 2012).

Another interesting idea and opportunity is gamification, which particularly appeals to mobile consumers. Gamification is the use of game design elements in order to positively influence motivation, productivity, and behavior of users (Blohm and Leimeister 2013). For instance, Daily Challenge from MeYou Health drives its consumers a challenge to engage in a healthy action every 24 h, earning points for each challenge finished. They are then encouraged to share their achievement with their associations who, in turn, are encouraged to provide supportive posts. By giving social and motivational benefits by product usage rather than expenditures, gamification will possibly be notable from traditional loyalty programs. (Blohm and Leimeister 2013) as quoted by (Hofacker et al. 2016). There are several avenues with respect to gamification that may be explored. Researchers may look in more detail into the role of technology in gamification (Bui et al. 2015). Moreover, Bui et al. (2015), encourage researchers to combine the present gamification literature with the associated research areas of hedonic, persuasive, and intrinsically motivating systems.

With all these advancements and innovations, marketing is being entrepreneurial where the focus is no longer the customer and his needs as traditionally being prevalent in literature. Studies have integrated the business entrepreneur into analysis. The entrepreneur recognizes, explores opportunities, and directs strategic decisions all of which affect the dynamics of the market. Entrepreneurs start with an idea and then set out to create a market. The notion of Facebook started without market research or testing where Mark Zuckerberg used his knowledge to create a social networking site, thus, creating a new market. With an entrepreneurial mindset, firms will favor innovation, risk taking (by creating new products that they think customers want), and will be proactive (Morrish 2011).

To end, strategy gives direction, technology lights the process, and consequently, adaptive and receptive marketing strategies discussed in this paper pave a new route in the beam of technology.

References

Benson-Armer, R., Noble, S., Thiel, A.: The consumer sector in 2030: trends and questions to consider. Consumer packaged goods and retail (2015)

Blohm, I., Leimeister, J.M.: Gamification. Bus. Inf. Syst. Eng. **5**(4), 275–278 (2013)

Bui, A., Veit, D., Webster, J.: Gamification–a novel phenomenon or a new wrapping for existing concepts? (2015)

Carrigan, M., Szmigin, I., Wright, J.: Shopping for a better world? An interpretive study of the potential for ethical consumption within the older market. J. Consum. Mark. **21**(6), 401–417 (2004)

Chakravorti, B., Tunnard, C., Chaturvedi, R.S.: Where the digital economy is moving the fastest. Harvard Bus. Rev. **19**, 1–7 (2015)

Chen, Y., Lai, S., Wen, C.: The influence of green innovation performance on corporate advantage in Taiwan. J. Bus. Ethics **67**, 331–339 (2006)

Cohen, B., Kietzmann, J.: Ride on! Mobility business models for the sharing economy. Organ. Environ. **27**(3), 279–296 (2014)

De Mauro, A., Greco, M., Grimaldi, M.: What is big data? A consensual definition and a review of key research topics. In: AIP Conference Proceedings, vol. 1644, no. 1, pp. 97–104. AIP, February 2015

Geron, T.: Airbnb and the unstoppable rise of the share economy. Forbes, 23 January (2013)

Grossman, R.: The industries that are being disrupted the most by digital. Harvard Bus. Rev. **94**, 2–5 (2016)

Hamari, J., Sjöklint, M., Ukkonen, A.: The sharing economy: why people participate in collaborative consumption. J. Assoc. Inf. Sci. Technol. **67**(9), 2047–2059 (2016)

Hofacker, C.F., De Ruyter, K., Lurie, N.H., Manchanda, P., Donaldson, J.: Gamification and mobile marketing effectiveness. J. Interact. Mark. **34**, 25–36 (2016)

Howie, K.M., Yang, L., Vitell, S.J., Bush, V., Vorhies, D.: Consumer participation in cause-related marketing: an examination of effort demands and defensive denial. J. Bus. Ethics **147** (3), 679–692 (2018)

Kelly, N.: 7 traits of companies on the fast track to international growth. Harvard Bus. Rev. (2015).   https://hbr.org/2015/03/7-traits-of-companies-on-the-fast-track-to-international-growth. Accessed 20 March 2018

Kerin, R.A., Hartley, S.W., Rudelius, W.: Marketing. McGraw-Hill Education, New York (2015)

Lamberton, C.P., Rose, R.L.: When is ours better than mine? A framework for understanding and altering participation in commercial sharing systems. J. Mark. **76**(4), 109–125 (2012)

Lipiäinen, H.: Digitization of the communication and its implications for marketing. Jyväskylä Stud. Bus. Econ. **152**, 6–8 (2014)

Mooradian, T.A., Matzler, K., Ring, L.J.: Strategic Marketing. Pearson Education, New Jersey (2012)

Morrish, S.C.: Entrepreneurial marketing: a strategy for the twenty-first century? J. Res. Mark. Entrepreneurship **13**(2), 110–119 (2011)

Newman: Digital Intelligence: The Heart of Successful Digital Transformation (2017). https://www.sas.com/content/dam/SAS/en_us/doc/whitepaper2/futurum-digital-intelligence-transformation-109136.pdf. Accessed 25 March 2018

Opreana, A., Vinerean, S.: A new development in online marketing: introducing digital inbound marketing. Expert J. Mark. **3**(1), 29–34 (2015)

Ottman, J.: The New Rules of Green Marketing: Strategies, Tools, and Inspiration for Sustainable Branding. Routledge, Abingdon (2017)

Patrutiu-Baltes, L.: Inbound marketing-the most important digital marketing strategy. Bull. Transilvania Univ. Brasov Econ. Sci. Ser. V **9**(2), 61 (2016)

Qadri, B., Bhat, M.: Interface between globalization and technology. Asian J. Manag. Sci. **7**(3), 1–6 (2018)

Stephen, A.T., Galak, J.: The effects of traditional and social earned media on sales: a study of a microlending marketplace. J. Mark. Res. **49**(5), 624–639 (2012)

Teubner, T.: Thoughts on the sharing economy. In: Proceedings of the International Conference on e-Commerce, vol. 11, pp. 322–326 (2014)

Trainor, K.J., Andzulis, J.M., Rapp, A., Agnihotri, R.: Social media technology usage and customer relationship performance: a capabilities-based examination of social CRM. J. Bus. Res. **67**(6), 1201–1208 (2014)

Van den Driest, F., Weed, K.: The ultimate marketing machine. Harvard Bus. Rev. **92**, 54–63 (2014)

Video HBR, 26 August 2015. https://hbr.org/video/4443548302001/where-the-digital-economy-is-moving-the-fastest. Accessed 23 March 2018

Whiting, A., Deshpande, A.: Towards greater understanding of social media marketing: A review. J. Appl. Bus. Econ. **18**(4), 82–91 (2016)

Zuhairah, H., Noor, A.: The impact of green marketing strategy on the firm's performance in Malaysia. Procedia – Soc. Behav. Sci. **172**, 463–470 (2015)

Smart Packaging: Consumer's Perception and Diagnostic of Traceability Information

Mouna Karoui Daoud[✉] and Imene Trabelsi Trigui[✉]

Marketing Research Laboratory, Faculty of Economic Sciences
and Management of Sfax, Sfax, Tunisia
mouna_karoui@yahoo.fr, imentrigui@yahoo.fr

Abstract. The traceability enables consumers to have the history of products, leading back to knowing the food origin. In this way, the consumer can get more information to make the right decision. One of the challenges in traceability systems is means of storing and transferring data for the consumers. Smart packaging such as Barcodes, QR code and radio–frequency identification tags offer consumers additional information including production methods, promotion, links to website, videos, transport track, certification label…

This paper aims to discuss the factors influencing consumer's perception and how they evaluate the information provided by traceability, while emphasizing the role of smart packaging. An exploratory study through individual interviews develops a theoretical model for consumer behavior that integrates the perception of Tunisian consumer about smart packaging as an antecedent of information diagnosticity.

Keywords: Smart packaging · Traceability · Information diagnosticity ·
Food involvement · Knowledge about traceability

1 Introduction

In the near past, the quality and safety have been concerned all over the world. With the development of agri-food crises like the scandals of bovine spongiform encephalopathy and avian flu scares to melamine-tainted milk, consumers lose their landmarks and confidence in the supply chain. To increase safety and quality of products, food industries have made technological innovation exemplified by the Internet and the information-technology hardware (electronic data, computer processor speeds…). Parwez (2014) described information technology as a system that provides an easy solution to farmers, manufactures and even consumers in short period.

Among theses techniques, the food traceability system is an important component that used to restore consumer confidence (Kher et al. 2013) by providing them more information about products (Badia-Melis et al. 2015). In the mid 1930s, European countries emerged this system as a way to promote the authenticity (Setboonsarng et al. 2009) and assuring safety and quality of food (Bertacchini et al. 2013).

In Tunisia, with the increase of trade with Europe and the opening of the Euro-Mediterranean Free Trade Area, it is necessary to comply with their standards (Regulation EC 178/2002) in the field of traceability. This regulation defined this latter as

© Springer Nature Switzerland AG 2019
R. Jallouli et al. (Eds.): ICDEc 2019, LNBIP 358, pp. 352–370, 2019.
https://doi.org/10.1007/978-3-030-30874-2_28

"the ability to trace and follow a food, feed, food-producing animal, or substance through all stages of production and distribution". This system provides detailed information of food production such as, transfer, distribution, processing even the birthplace of animals, feeding, date of sale... (Chang et al. 2013).

Consumers research on traceability has been focused on exploring information asymmetry, the role of traceability systems (Hobbs 2004; Golan et al. 2004), consumer perception (Dickinson and Bailey 2005; Choe et al. 2009; Van Rijswijk et al. 2008) and consumers' willingness to pay for traceability systems (Dickinson and Bailey 2002; Wu et al. 2015; Jin and Zhou 2014). From the perspective of supply chain, some studies has been concentrated on analyze the economic motives and benefit of the traceability system (Hobbs et al. 2005; Aung and Chang 2014; Menozzi et al. 2015). Others focused on how to develop this technique.

One of the challenges of traceability is storing data and communicating information to consumers, which can be achieved via traditional food labels (Kehagia et al. 2007) that dominate the market but have a limited space to store the amount of information (Jin and Zhou 2014) and the increasing of modern technology (Barska and Wyrwa 2017) like: Barcodes, Radio Frequency Identification, Wireless sensor networks, Quick Response that possess the capacity to provide food quality information via traceability systems (Jin and Zhou 2014). As a result, the emerging of Smart packaging as an innovative solution that maintains, improves and monitors the food quality and safety (Ahmed et al. 2018). The terms of "smart", "intelligent" or "Active" packaging have appeared in the literature (Schaefer and Cheung 2018). In this sense, many studies have demonstrated the importance of perceived benefits for the acceptance of novel food technologies (Frewer et al. 1997, 2003). Other researches focused on these technologies as a tool that ensures food quality and safety, extends product shelf life, and reduces environmental impact specially in meat products (Quintavalla and Vicini 2002; Arvanitoyannis and Stratakos 2012; Realini and Marcos 2014). Lloyd et al. (2019) suggested that understanding consumer perception will enhance the development of products with the new technologie advancement. On the part of supply chain, Bosona and Gebresenbet (2013) identified technological innovations applied for product traceability such as product Identification, Quality and Safety Measurement, Genetic Analysis, Environmental Monitoring, Geospatial Data Capturing, Data exchange, and information integration have been identified. These authors suggest that the traceability system should improve technological aspects. However, the application and success of these techniques depend on consumer's acceptation (Siegrist 2008) and behavioral responses to the innovation (Chen et al. 2013). Ghaani et al. (2016) argued that the application of intelligent systems in the food packaging industry should take into consideration two factors such as consumers' perceptions and legislative aspects.

According to Spence et al. (2010, p. 146), there has been little studies that identifying the factors influencing consumer's perception and acceptation of technologies that provide traceability information (Chrysochou et al. 2009). Consequently, future research could provide a better understanding of the potential success of the QR code to convey traceability information to the final consumer.

Hence, the aim of this study is to understand how consumers react to the new food technologies and how such technologies may influence consumer perception and diagnostic of traceability information. The contributions of this paper are theoretical, methodological and practical. Theoretically, we aim to explain the consumer's perception on smart packaging of food products. Therefore, we explore determinants among variables from consumer behavior, such as knowledge about traceability and food involvement. In a methodological side, we applied an exploratory study allowing a deeper understanding about the factors influencing consumer's perception and the degree of helpfulness. To enrich our research, we used a materiel support: image of different smart packaging and asking the subjects to express their impressions in relation to their mental representations.

The structure of this paper is as follows. The first part provides a brief overview of the factors that influence consumer's perception toward smart packaging. In the second part, we will make a review of how this new technology can influence the diagnostic of traceability information. Then, the method and research design used in this study are described, followed by the research findings. Finally, conclusions and implications for the food industry are provided.

2 Literature Review

The concept of Smart packaging was used by Yam in 2000 to identify the role of packaging as an information source. Schaefer and Cheung (2018, p. 1023), found that smart or intelligent packaging allows "*to track and trace a product throughout its lifecycle and to analyze and control the environment inside or outside the package to inform its manufacturer, retailer or consumer on the product's condition at any given time*". In the present work, we focused on the smart packaging emerging as a novel technology that helps consumers to evaluate the product quality based on traceability information. Also, this research aimed to find what the consumers know about such packaging and how they feel about them?

2.1 Consumer's Perception of Smart Packaging

Prior Knowledge of Intelligent packaging
Prior research on consumer behavior (Bettman and Park 1980) indicated that consumers' prior knowledge and experience influence the choice process. When it is about new product, Rogers (1983) indicated that beliefs and perceptions of new product's relative advantage are one of the key determinants of innovation adoption. In line with findings reported in Siegrist's study (2008), which argue that consumer acceptance is important to the success of food product innovations. Barska and Wyrwa (2017) highlighted that the knowledge of consumer attitudes towards the modern packaging is a source of information for producers when developing marketing strategies. These authors carried out a study to investigate consumers' perception of active and intelligent packaging. Only 17% of respondents know the term of "intelligent packaging". Consumers admitted that the society needs to popularize the new generation of packaging. O'Callaghan and Kerry (2016) explored the consumer knowledge and attitudes towards the incorporation of novel packaging technologies to cheese products.

The results showed that consumers are interested and knowledgeable about the intelligent packaging and would be willing to adopt it. However, active packaging is less known for consumers of cheese. According to Yener (2015), "In Europe, legislative restrictions, a lack of knowledge regarding the consumers' preference, economic and environmental issues limit the commercial success of active and intelligent packaging technologies". Lloyd et al. (2019) concluded that consumers should have a basic knowledge into the technologies employed in smart packaging, to eliminate the anxiety about the science used to improve food packaging. Loučanová et al. (2018) admitted that the majority of respondents do not know what intelligent and active packaging is. By increasing awareness of these innovations, customers' perception can be improved. Stand on the theory of reasoned action (Ajzen and Fishbein 1980) and theory of planned behavior (Ajzen 1985), Davis (1989) developed the technology acceptance model (TAM), that explain the way consumers develop perceptions toward smart packaging. Indeed, TAM suggests that people beliefs about technology's pros and cons influence his attitudes and, as a result, his intention and behavior toward it. In this technology adoption model, individual beliefs present his perceptions toward the technology usefulness and ease of use. As a matter of fact and based on theory of reasoned action, individual beliefs are based on his knowledge. Accordingly, consumers' prior knowledge toward new technologies related to food packaging influence his perception toward the smart packaging. Therefore, the following hypothesis is proposed:

H1: Prior knowledge of food technology is likely to influence consumer's perception of smart packaging

Credibility of Product Information

The source credibility is an important element that ensures, on the one hand, the authenticity and reliability of the information displayed on the products. And on the other hand, a guarantee in case of a security incident has occurred. As a result, a certification authority provided consumer with authentic and understandable information that enhance their trust in the product information.

Based on the theories of Cue Utilization Theory (Olson and Jacoby 1972) and Signaling theory (Spence 1973), the consumer count on intrinsic and extrinsic indication to evaluate the product quality (Richardson et al. 1994). The theories explain how consumers use product information to distinguish between better and less products quality when they have no direct experience with the products. The credibility of product information such as government, retailers and manufacturers might act as signals of quality for consumers.

Also, the consumers perceive that a smart packaging and traceability as a signal of higher product quality. However, people can rely on signals and making the purchase decisions (Richardson et al. 1994).

Chrysochou et al. (2009) pointed out that Consumers' perception of traceability depends on its ability to enhance consumer confidence in the product information given by the retailer. To accept labels, the reliability and credibility of product information is an important element (Salaün and Flores 2001). These authors concluded that consumer's show a higher level of confidence toward the technologies provided information traceability such as RFID and the barcode system, if they believe it has less chances of being counterfeited. These systems give consumers a sense of reassurance about the credibility of information offered.

Ghaani et al. (2016) concluded European consumer desire a clear regulatory framework which led to know the new packaging solutions into the market. In the same vein, O'Callaghan and Kerry (2016) identified several Barrier in the application of such technologies like: unclear regulatory guidelines, and acceptance by retailers and consumers (Coles and Frewer 2013). Consumer attitudes towards food technologies are critical as they can lead to market success or failure. However, to increase consumer confidence about the safety of packaging, the government should implement regulations that assure the public safety and the reliability of information (Chen et al. 2013). Accordingly, we hypothesize:

H2: The credibility of product information will positively influence consumer's perception of smart packaging

2.2 Information Diagnosticity

Food crises are steadily increasing and the consumer has become aware of food quality and safety. He only wants to consume products that meet his demands and preserve his health (Henriëtta and Gerrie 2012, p. 210). Traceability is the tool that gives consumers a sense of reassurance and control. Therefore, the diagnostic of information is meant to help consumers to assess the quality of the products. It also obliges the seller to provide the buyer with more relevant information (Choe et al. 2009), which mitigates the quality of products and reduces the asymmetry of the information. In fact, diagnostic has become one of the most important criteria that motivate consumer's behavior (Beemer and Gregg 2013).

Kempf and Smith (1998, p. 328) indicate that perceived diagnosticity is defined "*as the degree to which the consumer believes the trial is useful in evaluating the brand's attribute*". Jiang and Benbasat (2004, p. 117) defined it as "*consumers' perceptions of the ability of a website to convey relevant product information that can assist them in understanding and evaluating the quality and performance of products sold online*". In the context of traceability, the term was developed by Choe et al. (2008), Chen and Huang (2013) and Buaprommee and Polyorat (2016). These authors describe diagnosticity as "*the degree to which the traceability system is believed to be helpful in the evaluation of a product*" (Choe et al. 2009, p. 171). The main purpose of product's evaluation is to help consumers to make the proper decisions. The present research focuses on the diagnosticity of external information such as the information provided by traceability. The latter, in fact, helps consumers to evaluate or get a real feel of product for its quality and performance.

Filieri (2015, p. 2) found that diagnosticity is determined by the perceived correlation between the information available to a consumer and the decision-making process and is often conceptualised as the degree of helpfulness of information (Dick et al.

1990; Qiu et al. 2012; Skowronski and Carlston 1987). Moreover, consumers counted on informational cues to judge product's quality. However, when the information is not diagnostic, people rely more on inferences and intuitive reasoning (Tsai and McGill 2011). The more retailers provide signals that help consumers, the more that the information provided will be perceived as diagnostic because it enables an adequate evaluation of the quality of the products. In this sense, we conclude that traceability represents a good means that aids consumer to evaluate information by different technologies such as radio frequency tags (RFID), barcodes and QR codes. In the same respect, Spence et al. (2010) described that the quick response (QR) code as a traceability label helps consumers easily to access to traceability information through their smart phones. Huang (2016) showed that the consumers build the cognitive structure from their consumptive needs, before searching for products information. To create their attitudes and knowledge, they should collect product information before making purchase decision. Regattieri et al. (2013) focused on the radio frequency identification as a system that can identify people or objects tracked in the system and collects data in order to communicate information to the final customer. Majid et al. (2016) proved that the new generation brings knowledge about food characteristics and helps in providing basic idea to the retailer, customer and manufacturer (Restuccia et al. 2010). Based on the European Commission (2004), "consumers and food packaging companies must be informed on how to use the active and intelligent materials and articles safely and appropriately". To boost consumer's perception of food safety and quality, the connection of traceability system with the whole documentation and control system represents an effective means. Such technologies could be successful if, consumers' perceive its functional qualities (Cantwell 2002). Consumers having an idea about the intelligent packaging are more likely to find the traceability system helpful for the evaluation of product quality and safety. Based on this, the following hypothesis is proposed:

H3: Consumer's perception of smart packaging is likely to influence the diagnosticity of information provided by traceability.

3 Description of the Qualitative Study

Our research focuses on smart packaging and traceability which has not been sufficiently explored in Tunisia by the Marketers. An exploratory methodology was employed to investigate a new concept for consumers and the study of perception. According to Mack (2005, p. 1), *"Qualitative methods provides information about the "human" side of an issue that is, the often contradictory behaviors, beliefs, opinions, emotions, and relationships of individual"*. Following these criteria, we chose to adopt a qualitative research using the semi-structured interview and the analysis phase was limited to a thematic treatment by the NVIVO 11 software. The interview guide was prepared following the four phases suggested by Giannelloni and Vernette (1995,

p. 78): introduction phase, central phase, in-depth phase, and conclusion phase (Appendix 1). The first theme is focuses on food crises especially the awareness about food change and the importance of health to the consumer. Second theme is the risk reduction strategies such as research information (reading labels, detailed information …). The third is the traceability of food product and lastly consumer's perception toward smart packaging.

3.1   Population and Sample

The purpose of this research step is to explore some specific behaviors in the context of the diagnostic of traced products. Qualitative approaches bring detail to explore view points in early stages of the research allowing the researcher to gain a better initial understanding of issues (Healy and Perry 2000). Semi-structured interview is a good tool for generating proposals and interpreting consumer's way of thinking, aimed at understanding consumers' perceptions of the concept of smart packaging, and how they evaluate the traceability information through this new generation.

The sampling unit was people above 18 years old who are responsible for food purchases. These individuals are supposed to provide us with useful answers relative to our context whose characteristics are summarized in Table 1. The selected sample, which was not representative of the whole population, satisfied the diversity and saturation conditions (Pires 1997) (Table 1).

Table 1. Sample characteristics of semi-structured interviews

Criteria		Number of interviews
Gender	Female	9
	Male	6
Age	<30	6
	30–50	6
	More then 50	3
Number of children	1 child	4
	2 children	4
	3 and more children	1

3.2   Data Collection

We collected data through interviews of fifteen people, lasting from 30 to 45 min. There was a guide to facilitate the communication. It included four themes to be discussed. We approached our analysis thematically by following the steps recommended by Bardin (1977). To achieve this thematic analysis, we assigned to the program called NVIVO.11 in order to facilitate categorizing and coding the data. This software helps us to make a link between the themes and sub themes. Also, we put a vertical and horizontal grid summarizing the emerging theme and sub-theme, some of the interview's verbatim transcription (Gavard-Perret and Helme-Guizon 2008) and we calculated the occurrences of appearance for each theme in the aim of interpreting its level of importance in the interviewees' speech (Appendix 2).

4 Results

The participants identified intelligent packaging as the main factors in their diagnostic among this; were Qr code, barecode, and RFID. These innovative technologies were seen as important by most participants. They help them to do the diagnostic of information due to traceability. In the following discussion, we examine in details these elements and the impact of moderating variables like food involvement and knowledge about traceability.

4.1 Smart Packaging: Knowledge and Tool to Evaluate the Information

With the rapid development of food production, a considerable attention in recent years has been devoted to the nature and types of information desired by consumers on food product labels. We found that consumer want to know more about the food, including manufacturing, ingredients, and freshness.

> "We should have a clear idea about the product: by reading ingredients, geographical origin... it's also a useful element that can help us to identify the quality of the product. For example for us as a Tunisian consumer we know the quality of oranges of cape bon, or the olive oil..."

In this research we aimed to examine consumer knowledge about the intelligent packaging and his perception. The conducted research shows that there are two levels of knowledge of the term "intelligent packaging": lack and good knowledge of the concept. The term was known by 47% of respondents.

> "Yes of course, I am an active technology adopter; I think that I'm familiar with scanning QR codes located on magazines or products. It's useful and it informs me about product's history and conditions"

> "Yes for example, In Tunisia, I see the RFID only on clothes but I think the information is not accessible. In Europe, there are many functions of this technology, for example: one of the largest European amusement parks, where approximately 1,600 children are separated from their parents each season, this park rents child RFID location tags".

> "Yes I know it. It gives us the possibility of easy access to information or additional content. I know the QR code or barcodes...the intelligent packaging is a good tool, I like it..."

Then, after defining the term, we found that the consumers have a positive perception about the new technology. They liked the idea of being able to use intelligent packaging systems easily and immediately to determine the condition of the food. These results are suited with the study of O' Callaghan and Kerry (2016) who found that intelligent packaging is functional and give the consumers an easy access to the information of food.

In addition to investigating consumer's preferences for information availability, participants were further asked about some tools that help them to evaluate the information provided by the traceability. As a result consumers want easy and accessible information. They don't have plenty of time for shopping. Therefore, they need more detailed information but in a very limited time.

"As the consumer does not have much time, it is better to have information labeled on the product's package. For example today, all people have a smart phone, so the diagnostic of detailed information will be easier. I speak here about the QR code as tools to have information which is a very simple as new technology"

"The QR code can be used to read the instructions on how to use a pharmaceutical product without the necessity to open the box and flip through the leaflet. Or if we want to know about the date, place of production, the harmful additive... of a food product. This system can also save costs for the manufacturing: less paper to print and stick for the description of their product"

A number of participants also indicated that barcode scanners would be useful tools for providing additional information on products like information regarding food packaging date, lot number, package weight, nutritional profile, cooking instructions, and the address of manufacturer's websites can be encoded in the barcodes, but they think that it's not accessible for consumers.

"I know the barcodes "the black-and-white" but I think we don't have access to the database where additional information is stored"

"We are now more concerned than ever with the provenance and nutritional value of our food with this technology... We are more familiar with the barcode but this technique has a limited amount of data that needs to be stored in the code"

As far as one can see, the majority of respondents request the Quick Response Code as a tool that helps them to do the diagnostic of information. This smart packaging is the best solution to communicate the food conditions. Particularly, it provided useful information for consumers and helps them to make their decision. Intelligent packaging can play an important role in facilitating the flow information between the supply chain and the consumer. Such information is helpful in assessing the quality and performance of products. As a conclusion, smart packaging allows to track and trace a product lifecycle. It also analyses and controls the environment inside or outside the package to inform its retailer, manufacturer, or consumer on the product's condition at any time.

4.2 Knowledge About Traceability

Consumer knowledge is an important factor in the consumer decision-making (Pieniak et al. 2013). It influences the consumers' choice and the organization of the information to purchase products (Alba and Hutchinson 1987).

Consumers with a higher level of knowledge about traceability are more frequently to consume healthier food and to look for information. In our study, we speak about the subjective knowledge that is defined as people's perceptions of what or how much they know about a product, based on their subjective interpretation making (Pieniak et al. 2013, p. 26). We asked the interviewees about the definition of the traceability.

"The role of traceability is to give the maximum of information to the consumer. It's really interesting as a tool..."

"I think that it's a technique to know from where the product comes, and if he follows the modes of hygiene..."

"Yes, I know it because I'm an engineer in agricultural and agri-food management and traceability is a part of my training. So, that it means the history of the product from the farm to the table"

The present statements show that, the interviewees had a quite knowledge of what is traceability. They define it as "ability to trace", "history", "give information about the food product". Our results are different from those which state that traceability is a hard notion for consumers and they were not able to define or to describe it (Chryssochoidis et al. 2006, Van Rijswijk et al. 2008, Van Rijswijk and Frewer 2008). Barcellos et al. (2012) indicated that consumers had insufficient knowledge on traceability, as its concept is directly associated with health issues (Fig. 1).

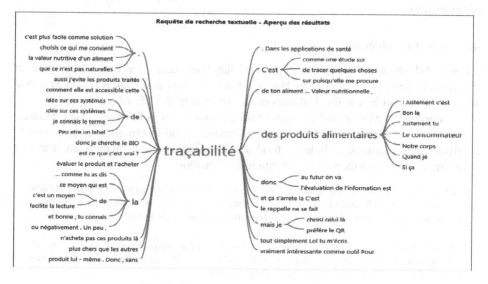

Fig. 1. Text search query (Traceability)

Also, participants want to have information about the composition like ingredients or healthiness. Others are attached to the sensory factors of the food product (freshness, taste) as is shown by the following statements collected in the interviews:

"Before I don't understand what it is written on the labels. But based on my studies, I realized that it is very important to know the nutritional value of the product whether there is more magnesium or less fat..."

"If I find unknown additives, I will not buy the product"

"I am not a simple consumer I always try to find information. I think that this system provide us with more information that help me to evaluate my product."

We achieve also, that consumers with high level of knowledge about traceability may rely on smart packaging in information evaluations. More explicitly, the knowledge about this system makes easier to consumers to use the smart packaging.

"If I have an idea about traceability, I'm going to explore the technological development. It's easy, an app is downloading, and the code is scanned with my smartphone to call up additional information about the product, for example information for allergy sufferers"

"If you do not have an idea about this system, you will not use it. So, the role of campanies is to create a connection with consumers. Today is the age of technologie, you should make people aware about the importance of the traceability and how they can get the information? Seriously, it's very important"

This allows us to state the following proposition:

P1: A higher level of knowledge about traceability will significantly influence the relationship between consumer's perception of smart packaging and information diagnosticity.

4.3   Food Involvement

Chen (2007) showed that food-related personality traits, defined as food involvement or the level of importance that food has in a person's. Bell and Marshall (2003) define food involvement as the level of importance of food in the life of a person.

According to Mollet and Rowland (2002), consumers believe that food products influence their health, so they are more interested in the information on ingredients, nutrition, fats, calories… Indeed, food involvement and information are the key determinants of consumers to make purchase decisions.

"I love food and I like speaking about it, but I want a safeguard food quality. I find that the new technologies like QR code and Near Filed Communication are materials that monitor the state of the product and provide me a lot of information that helps me to make my decision"

"Food is usually an enjoyable and necessary part of life. I talk too much about food, my friends get angry at a certain time … but I want a healthier food with more information. I think that traceability provide us with more detailed information"

The study found that food involvement plays a moderating function in the relationship between smart packaging and information diagnosticity. Therefore, the higher a person's degree of involvement, the greater they find the smart packaging is useful for the traceability system. Accordingly, the proposition is proposed as follows:

P2: A higher level of food involvement will significantly influence the relationship between consumer's perception of smart packaging and information diagnosticity.

Finally, from the literature review and the qualitative research, we propose the following preliminary conceptual model (Fig. 2):

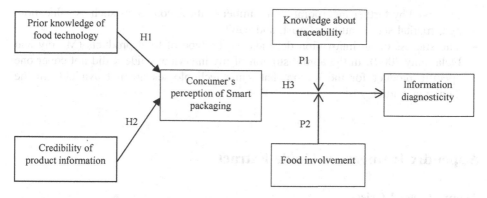

Fig. 2. The proposed research model

5 Managerial Implications

The results of this study may have practical implications for e-marketers and business practitioners. As the findings suggest that consumers consider smart packaging to provide helpful information about foods. It recommends that companies must focus on the application of technologies on product packages and think outside the box by using nontraditional packaging to meet new challenges. What's more is that this study takes into account consumers' personality traits (food involvement) and cognitive psychology (Knowledge about traceability) factors, to explain what could affect individuals' evaluations regarding traceability information. Food marketers should encourage consumers to accept food traceability system to enforce and protect their rights. Also, the findings of this work contribute to a better understanding the reasons of why consumers would perceive positively the new generation technologies. To clarify and popularize the packaging innovation, the society should adopt a commercial success to include and accept this technology with their current information infrastructures.

6 Conclusion

This paper can be considered as an exploration of consumer behavior toward traced product. A particular attention is given to the need for additional information for the consumer by the novel technologies such as intelligent packaging. We proposed a conceptual model combining the results of a qualitative study and a literature review. In this model, the smart packaging such as QR code, barcodes and RFID appears as a principal guide for consumers to evaluate the traceability information. In spite of its theoretical and managerial contributions, this study has some limits, notably:

- The semi structured interview generates a number of proposals that cannot be quantitatively validated because of their exploratory effects. Therefore, It will be more appropriate to tested and validate the relations during a quantitative survey.
- Socio demographic and psychosocial factors (Menozzi et al. 2013) are not included in the interpretation of consumer' behaviors. Our exploratory model can be

improved by further incorporating a number of these constructs such as: education, age, marital status, attitude, trust, and habits.

- The success of an innovation depends on the type of food products (Murray and Delahunty 2000). In the administration of my interview guide, I did not cover one specific product for the reason that some technologies are not available in the Tunisian market.

Appendix 1: Interview Guide Extract

Theme 1: Food Crises

- For you, which apple is more captivating than the other?

- Do you think that food can affect your health?
- What do you think when we say food and crises?
- Can you give me some examples of crises that you heard about?
- Do you control the products you eat? What exactly you do?
- Which of the following criteria are the most important to choose a product? (Information about the place of production, information on the origin, price, labels, brand, address and telephone number of the producer).

Theme 2: Information Research

- What kind of information do you prefer in the product? (simple information or detailed?)
- Do you often read the label on the packaging when you buy a food product? Did you find this information is sufficient and useful?
- In your opinion, what are the tools that provide you with detailed information on the products?

- Where do you want the information to appear? (on the packaging, at the shop next to the product, a scanner, or with the internet)
- Is information about geographical indication, ingredients, production method (organic or farmer's milk) are buying criteria for you as a consumer? if yes, why?

Theme 3: Traceability of Food Products

- Can you describe this photo? What do you see?

- What does traceability mean to you?
- In your opinion, what extent do you think that detailed information helps you evaluate the product?
- Have you an idea about a system able to trace food products?
- What do you think of this labeling system?

Theme 4: Smart Packaging: Consumer's Perception

- What is the first thing to get your attention in food packaging?
- Have you ever heard of the word smart packaging in the context of food production? What does it mean to you?
- Can you give me some examples of smart packaging?
- Why you choose products with smart packaging over traditional packaging?
- Do you consider smart packaging to be a way of communicating information about food traceability?
- What should be done in order to increase public acceptability of innovative packaging?

Appendix 2: Vertical and Horizontal Analysis: An Extract from the Grid

Theme	Interview number															Occur-rency	Statements
	1	2	3	4	5	6	7	8	9	10	11	12	13	14	15	Abso-lute	
Food crises																	I9: These problems related to food crises are a big danger because eating contaminated food can destroy our health.
Awareness of food change	3	2	5	4	1	1	1	1	3	1	3	1	2	3	1	32	
Consumption of organic products	1	1	0	0	4	3	1	0	0	0	0	0	1	1	0	12	I9: Really it's horrible, the question here is: where is the control or the government, are they aware that these crises affects the human being?
Total	4	3	5	4	5	4	2	1	3	1	3	1	3	4	1	44	
Information research																	I2: yes I read the label ... I trust information communicate on the packaging, I believe they are sincere and sufficient whatever be a Tunisian or foreign product.
Word of mouth	1	2	4	0	1	3	2	0	6	1	1	0	0	1	2	23	
Information on the packaging	0	5	1	1	2	1	1	0	0	0	1	0	0	0	2	14	I11: the label or the word of mouth. If I hear that it is a good product I buy it.
Total	1	7	5	1	3	4	3	0	6	1	2	0	0	1	4	38	I15: I check everything that is written on the packaging
Traceability of food products																	I4: Yes I know it, following or have the trace of a product
Knowledge about traceability	1	0	1	1	0	1	1	1	1	0	0	1	0	1	1	10	I4: Very important tool yes, a good and clear information influences the evaluation and the diagnostic especially for fresh products.
Information diagnosticity	2	0	1	1	0	2	3	2	1	0	1	0	0	2	2	16	
Smart packaging	2	0	1	1	0	1	1	1	0	0	0	1	0	0	0	7	I1: In health applications when we click on the QR code we get the detailed information about the cheese for example.
Total	5	0	3	3	0	4	5	4	2	0	1	2	0	3	3	34	
Smart Packaging : consumer's perception																	I6: the future belongs to intelligent packaging
																	I8: the Smart packaging has an informative role and is intended to supplement information indicated on the label, for example the preservation of the product.
Prior Knowledge	1	0	1	1	0	1	1	1	0	1	0	0	1	0	1	9	
Credibility of product information	3	2	2	2	3	1	1	1	0	2	0	1	3	0	1	21	I7: It allows authenticating the origin of the product and reassuring the consumer about his purchase.
Total	4	2	3	3	3	2	2	2	0	3	0	1	4	0	1	30	I3: I do not trust the information provided by the producer himself.... Well, I would like to have information from experts aggregated by the State or by non-governmental organizations that defend the right of the consumer.

References

Ahmed, I., et al.: An overview of smart packaging technologies for monitoring safety and quality of meat and meat products. Packag. Technol. Sci. **31**(7), 449–471 (2018)

Alba, J.W., Hutchinson, J.W.: Dimensions of consumer expertise. J. Consum. Res. **13**, 411–454 (1987)

Ajzen, I., Fishbein, M.: Understanding attitudes and predicting social behavior. Prentice Hall, Englewood Cliffs (1980)

Ajzen, I.: From intentions to actions: a theory of planned behavior. In: Kuhl, J., Beckmann, J. (eds.) Action Control, pp. 11–39. Springer, Berlin (1985). https://doi.org/10.1007/978-3-642-69746-3_2

Bettman, J.R., Park, C.W.: Effects of prior knowledge and experience and phase of the choice process on consumer decision processes: a protocol analysis. J. Consum. Res. **7**(3), 234–248 (1980)

Bertacchini, L., et al.: The impact of chemometrics on food traceability. In: Data Handling in Science and Technology, vol. 28, pp. 371–410. Elsevier (2013)

Badia-Melis, R., Mishra, P., Ruiz-García, L.: Food traceability: new trends and recent advances. A review. Food Control **57**, 393–401 (2015)

Beemer, B.A., Gregg, D.G.: Dynamic interaction in decision support: effects on perceived diagnosticity and confidence in unstructured domains. IEEE Trans. Syst. Man Cybern.: Syst. **43**(1), 74–84 (2013)

Bardin, L.: L'analyse de contenu, vol. 69. Presses universitaires de France, Paris (1977)

Barcellos, J.O.J., Abicht, A.D.M., Brandão, F.S., Canozzi, M.E.A., Collares, F.C.: Consumer perception of Brazilian traced beef. Revista Brasileira de Zootecnia **41**(3), 771–774 (2012)

Buaprommee, N., Polyorat, K.: The antecedents of purchase intention of meat with traceability in Thai consumers. Asia Pacific Manag. Rev. **21**(3), 161–169 (2016)

Chen, M.F.: Consumer attitudes and purchase intentions in relation to organic foods in Taiwan: moderating effects of food-related personality traits. Food Qual. Prefer. **18**(7), 1008–1021 (2007)

Chryssochoidis, G.M., Kehagia, O.C., Chrysochou, P.E.: Traceability: European consumers' perceptions regarding its definition, expectations and differences by product types and importance of label schemes. In: Comunicaciónpresentada al 98th EAAE Seminar, Chania, Crete, June 2006

Chrysochou, P., Chryssochoidis, G., Kehagia, O.: Traceability information carriers. The technology backgrounds and consumers' perceptions of the technological solutions. Appetite **53**(3), 322–331 (2009)

Chen, M.F., Huang, C.H.: The impacts of the food traceability system and consumer involvement on consumers' purchase intentions toward fast foods. Food Control **33**(2), 313–319 (2013)

Choe, Y.C., Park, J., Chung, M., Moon, J.: Effect of the food traceability system for building trust: price premium and buying behavior. Inf. Syst. Front. **11**(2), 167–179 (2009)

Dick, A., Chakravarti, D., Biehal, G.: Memory-based inferences during consumer choice. J. Consum. Res. **17**(1), 82–93 (1990)

Davis, F.D.: Perceived usefulness, perceived ease of use, and user acceptance of information technology. MIS Q. **13**, 319–340 (1989)

Filieri, R.: What makes online reviews helpful? A diagnosticity-adoption framework to explain informational and normative influences in e-WOM. J. Bus. Res. **68**(6), 1261–1270 (2015)

Jiang, Z., Benbasat, I.: Virtual product experience: effects of visual and functional control of products on perceived diagnosticity and flow in (2004)

Healy, M., Perry, C.: Comprehensive criteria to judge validity and reliability of qualitative research within the realism paradigm. Qual. Market Res. Int. J. **3**(3), 118–126 (2000)

Gavard-Perret, M.L., Helme-Guizon, A.: Choisir parmi les techniques spécifiques d'analyse qualitative (No. halshs-00325144) (2008)

Kempf, D.S., Smith, R.E.: Consumer processing of product trial and the influence of prior advertising: a structural modeling approach. J. Mark. Res. **35**, 325–338 (1998)

Lloyd, K., Mirosa, M., Birch, J.: Active and Intelligent Packaging. Encyclopedia of Food Chemistry, pp. 177–182. Elsevier, Amsterdam (2019)

Mollet, B., Rowland, I.: Functional foods: at the frontier between food and pharma. Curr. Opin. Biotechnol. **5**(13), 483–485 (2002)

Majid, I., Nayik, G.A., Dar, S.M., Nanda, V.: Novel food packaging technologies: innovations and future prospective. J. Saudi Soc. Agric. Sci. **17**, 454–462 (2016)

Mack, N.: Qualitative research methods: a data collector's field guide (2005)

O'Callaghan, K.A., Kerry, J.P.: Consumer attitudes towards the application of smart packaging technologies to cheese products. Food Packag. Shelf Life **9**, 1–9 (2016)

Pieniak, Z., Vanhonacker, F., Verbeke, W.: Consumer knowledge and use of information about fish and aquaculture. Food Policy **40**, 25–30 (2013)

Pires, A.P.: Échantillonnage et recherche qualitative: essai théorique et méthodologique. La recherche qualitative. Enjeux épistémologiques et méthodologiques, pp. 113–169. Electronic Shopping. J. Manag. Inf. Syst. **21**(3), 111–147 (1997)

Qiu, L., Pang, J., Lim, K.H.: Effects of conflicting aggregated rating on e-WOM review credibility and diagnosticity: the moderating role of review valence. Decis. Support Syst. **54** (1), 631–643 (2012)

Rogers, E.M.: Diffusion of Innovations, 3rd edn. Free Press, New York (1983)

Setboonsarng, S., Sakai, J., Vancura, L.: Food safety and ICT traceability systems: lessons from Japan for developing countries, no. 139. ADBI working paper series (2009)

Skowronski, J.J., Carlston, D.E.: Social judgment and social memory: the role of cue diagnosticity in negativity, positivity, and extremity biases. J. Pers. Soc. Psychol. **52**(4), 689–699 (1987)

Salaün, Y., Flores, K.: Information quality: meeting the needs of the consumer. Int. J. Inf. Manag. **21**, 21–37 (2001)

Schaefer, D., Cheung, W.M.: Smart packaging: opportunities and challenges. Procedia CIRP **72**, 1022–1027 (2018)

Spence, M.: Job market signaling. Q. J. Econ. **87**, 355–374 (1973)

Tsai, C.I., McGill, A.L.: No pain, no gain? How fluency and construal level affect consumer confidence. J. Consum. Res. **37**(5), 807–821 (2011)

Van Rijswijk, W., Frewer, L.J.: Consumer perceptions of food quality and safety and their relation to traceability. Br. Food J. **110**(10), 1034–1046 (2008)

Van Rijswijk, W., Frewer, L.J., Menozzi, D., Faioli, G.: Consumer perceptions of traceability: a cross-national comparison of the associated benefits. Food Qual. Prefer. **19**(5), 452–464 (2008)

Wu, L., Wang, S., Zhu, D., Hu, W., Wang, H.: Chinese consumers' preferences and willingness to pay for traceable food quality and safety attributes: the case of pork. China Econ. Rev. **35**, 121–136 (2015)

Parwez, S.: Food supply chain management in Indian agriculture: issues,opportunities and further research. African J. Bus. Manag. **8**(14) (2014)

Richardson, P.S., Dick, A.S., Jain, A.K.: Extrinsic and intrinsic cue effects on perceptions of store brand quality. J. Mark. **58**(4), 28–36 (1994)

Ghaani, M., Cozzolino, C.A., Castelli, G., Farris, S.: An overview of the intelligent packaging technologies in the food sector. Trends Food Sci. Technol. **51**, 1–11 (2016)

Frewer, L.J., Howard, C., Hedderley, D., Shepherd, R.: Consumer attitudes towards different food-processing technologies used in cheese production—the influence of consumer benefit. Food Qual. Prefer. **8**(4), 271–280 (1997)

Erika, L., Martina, N., Ján, P., Dopico, A.: The Kano model use to evaluate the perception of intelligent and active packaging of Slovak customers. Studia Universitatis "Vasile Goldis" Arad–Econ. Series **28**(1), 35–45 (2018)

Huang, L.T.: Exploring utilitarian and hedonic antecedents for adopting information from a recommendation agent and unplanned purchase behaviour. New Rev. Hypermedia Multimedia **22**(1–2), 139–165 (2016)

Frewer, L.J., Scholderer, J., Bredahl, L.: Communicating about the risks and benefits of genetically modified foods: the mediating role of trust. Risk Anal.: Int. J. **23**(6), 1117–1133 (2003)

Coles, D., Frewer, L.J.: Nanotechnology applied to European food production–A review of ethical and regulatory issues. Trends Food Sci. Technol. **34**(1), 32–43 (2013)

Krystallis, A., Frewer, L., Rowe, G., Houghton, J., Kehagia, O., Perrea, T.: A perceptual divide? Consumer and expert attitudes to food risk management in Europe. Health Risk Soci. **9**(4), 407–424 (2007)

Yener, D.: Factors that affect the attitudes of consumers toward halal-certified products in Turkey. J. Food Prod. Mark. **21**(2), 160–178 (2015)

Restuccia, D., et al.: New EU regulation aspects and global market of active and intelligent packaging for food industry applications. Food Control **21**(11), 1425–1435 (2010)

Spence, M., Stancu, V., Elliott, C.T., Dean, M.: Exploring consumer purchase intentions towards traceable minced beef and beef steak using the theory of planned behavior. Food Control **91**, 138–147 (2010)

Olson, J.C., Jacoby, J.: Cue utilization in the quality perception process. ACR Special Volumes (1972)

Hobbs, J.E., Bailey, D., Dickinson, D.L., Haghiri, M.: Traceability in the Canadian red meat sector: do consumers care? Can. J. Agric. Econ. Rev. Can. D'agroeconomie, 53(1), 47–65 (2005)

Golan, E.H., Krissoff, B., Kuchler, F., Calvin, L., Nelson, K.E., Price, G.K.: Traceability in the US food supply: economic theory and industry studies (No. 1473-2016-120760) (2004)

Chang, A., Tseng, C.H., Chu, M.Y.: Value creation from a food traceability system based on a hierarchical model of consumer personality traits. Br. Food J. **115**(9), 1361–1380 (2013)

Hobbs, J.E.: Information asymmetry and the role of traceability systems. Agribus.: Int. J. **20**(4), 397–415 (2004)

Kher, S.V., et al.: Consumer perceptions of risks of chemical and microbiological contaminants associated with food chains: a cross-national study. Int. J. Consum. Stud. **37**(1), 73–83 (2013)

Siegrist, M.: Factors influencing public acceptance of innovative food technologies and products. Trends Food Sci. Technol. **19**(11), 603–608 (2008)

Quintavalla, S., Vicini, L.: Antimicrobial food packaging in meat industry. Meat Sci. **62**(3), 373–380 (2002)

Aung, M.M., Chang, Y.S.: Traceability in a food supply chain: safety and quality perspectives. Food Control **39**, 172–184 (2014)

Menozzi, D., Halawany-Darson, R., Mora, C., Giraud, G.: Motives towards traceable food choice: a comparison between French and Italian consumers. Food Control **49**, 40–48 (2015)

Wyrwa, J., Barska, A.: Innovations in the food packaging market: active packaging. Eur. Food Res. Technol. **243**(10), 1681–1692 (2017)

Jin, S., Zhou, L.: Consumer interest in information provided by food traceability systems in Japan. Food Qual. Prefer. **36**, 144–152 (2014)

Arvanitoyannis, I.S., Stratakos, A.C.: Application of modified atmosphere packaging and active/smart technologies to red meat and poultry: a review. Food Bioprocess Technol. **5**(5), 1423–1446 (2012). ISO 690

Realini, C.E., Marcos, B.: Active and intelligent packaging systems for a modern society. Meat Sci. **98**(3), 404–419 (2014)

du Plessis, H.J., Gerrie, E.: The significance of traceability in consumer decision making towards Karoo lamb. Food Res. Intcr. **47**(2), 210–217 (2012)

Dickinson, D.L. Bailey D.: Meat traceability: are U.S. Consumers willing to pay for it? J. Agric. Res. Econ. **27**, 348–364 (2002)

Dickinson, D.L., Bailey, D.V.: Experimental evidence on willingness to pay for red meat traceability in the United States, Canada, the United Kingdom, and Japan. J. Agric. Appl. Econ. **37**(3) 537 (2005)

Gavard-Perret, M.L., Gotteland, D., Haon, C., Jolibert, A.: Méthodologie de la recherche. Editions Pearson Education France (2008)

Giannelloni, J.L. Vernette E.: Études de marché, Vuibert, Paris (1995)

Cantwell, B.: Introduction to Symmetry Analysis Paperback with CD-ROM, vol. 29. Cambridge University Press. Cambridge (2002)

Bosona, T., Gebresenbet, G.: Food traceability as an integral part of logistics management in food and agricultural supply chain. Food Control **33**(1), 32–48 (2013)

Digital Business Models

Multi-sided Platforms in the Sharing Economy – A Case Study Analysis for the Development of a Generic Platform

Claudia Vienken$^{(\boxtimes)}$ (ID), Nizar Abdelkafi, and Cyrine Tangour (ID)

Fraunhofer Center for International Management and Knowledge Economy
IMW, Leipzig, Germany
{claudia.vienken, nizar.abdelkafi,
cyrine.tangour}@imw.fraunhofer.de

Abstract. In the digitization era, multi-sided platforms (MSPs) have evolved to powerful business models. Companies from the Sharing Economy (SE) use such business models to act as intermediaries between suppliers and customers through implementing specific functionalities on their platforms. This paper uses a case study methodology and analyzes the platform functionalities of five companies: Airbnb, Uber, Couchsurfing, BlaBlaCar and TaskRabbit. The analysis shows that these companies exhibit similarities and differences in the design of their platform functionalities. Subsequently, the results obtained here are used to elaborate a generic concept for the design of digital platforms in this field. The identified functional areas are: tendering, search for offers, booking of services and associated fees, rating systems and safety, as well as trust functions. As such, the paper contributes to the scientific discussion in the field of platform-based business model design in the SE.

Keywords: Sharing economy · Multi-sided platform · Platform functionalities · Case study analysis · Generic concept · Platform design

1 Introduction

Advances in digital technologies, changes in consumer behavior, reduced need for ownership, and easier access to digital data and information are all factors that have led to changes in traditional market structures [1, 2].

As a result, companies are increasingly using digital platforms, which are integrated in websites and apps, as a 'backbone' for their business models [3, p. 50]. These platforms connect two or multiple independent groups for the purpose of direct interactions [4]. Platform rules and functionalities support these direct interactions. They allow for an efficient exchange of information, products, services and currencies between user groups [5]. Basically, a multi-sided platform (MSP) can be considered as a physical or virtual marketplace [6].

Indirect network effects and asymmetric pricing structures are key characteristics of MSPs. Indirect network effects imply that the platform value for one user group increases with the number of participants of a complementary user group. The credit

© Springer Nature Switzerland AG 2019
R. Jallouli et al. (Eds.): ICDEc 2019, LNBIP 358, pp. 373–386, 2019.
https://doi.org/10.1007/978-3-030-30874-2_29

card market is a prominent example that illustrates these indirect network effects. Cardholders only benefit from the advantages of credit card payment, if there are enough merchants that accept this kind of payment. Merchants, however, only benefit from this service, if enough customers use credit cards for their payment [7]. Platforms are thus able to increase their overall value by fulfilling the demands of different user groups [7–10]. In addition, MSPs implement asymmetric pricing structures to control the level of transaction and interaction over the platform. Different subscription and transaction fees influence the overall market outcome. For instance, platforms can subsidize price-sensitive user groups by charging them low or even no fees. This may lead to higher prices or more participation on the side of the complementary user group [11]. In contrast, the market outcome of one-sided markets is only determined by the price level [7, 12].

In the Sharing Economy (SE), companies use such platform-based business models. In recent years, SE has gained increasing attention in the scientific and public discussion. However, the scientific community has not yet agreed on a single definition of the term [1]. In this paper, SE describes digital networks, in which users share, exchange, or sell resources, products, and services with the help of internet-based digital and functional platforms [13, 14]. The SE has further contributed to the emergence of new organizational structures: consumer-to-consumer or peer-to-peer (P2P) interaction models [15]. These models enable an efficient internet-based exchange between strangers in a peer group [16]. Thus, SE companies especially need to deal with asymmetric distribution of information and endow their platforms with functionalities to support trust during digital interactions. Rating and feedback systems or specific certifications, such as brand, platform or profile certifications, are all useful functionalities to establish trust between the individual platform users [1].

Users of SE platforms only receive rights of usage, but no rights of ownership after the execution of the transaction process. In contrast to companies in traditional markets such as car rental companies or taxi companies, with their own car fleets, SE companies do not own the objects that are shared, given that they are bought by users [17]. When operating platforms, SE companies must acquire enough users. This objective is difficult to achieve due to the chicken-egg problem.

In general, the scientific literature is lacking research on platform design. This paper contributes to filling this gap by answering the following question: 'What are the platform functionalities that make SE companies successful in the market?' This leads to the following theses:

1. SE companies follow a similar concept in the design of their platform functionalities. New SE companies may consider these common functionalities when designing their platforms.
2. A generic concept can be developed by using best practices of successful SE companies.

These theses will be verified based on a descriptive case study analysis of five successful SE companies with platform-based business models. The platforms are examined with regard to their functionalities. A cross case analysis is then used to identify the similarities and differences among the platform functionalities. The results of the cross case analysis are leveraged to develop a generic concept that summarizes the main functionalities of the MSP concept applied in the SE.

2 Literature Review

MSPs have been an important business model concept in many industries such as telecommunication, finance and computer game industries since several decades. Platforms, such as the 'yellow pages', facilitate direct interactions between specific groups by providing a way to match buyers and sellers [18]. The concept of MSPs is therefore closely related to the concept of marketplaces [19]. Platforms leverage two-sided network effects, leading to an increased value of the platform for any user, as the number of users on the opposite user side increases [7–10]. Consequently, the overall value of the platform highly depends on the efficiency of matching supply and demand.

Digital platforms have become prevalent [10]. They allow companies to offer their services by means of user-friendly apps or websites that are time- and location-independent. Furthermore, they enable customers to have access to a variety of offers and services [20]. Transactions can be executed easily and at low costs (in particular search costs) [21]. Additionally, strong indirect network effects enable company's growth through a constant increase in the number of users. Asymmetric pricing structures make it possible to adapt to different needs of the user sides. The SE success can, therefore, be mainly attributed to the use of digital platforms as part of the business model. SE companies consider the changes in consumer behavior by implementing novel platform features that create added value for the actors involved [22]. Depending on the design of these platforms, several new SE business models such as P2P-interaction models have emerged. They compete with established companies on the market. Digital platforms, MSPs in particular, are changing the structures of entire industry sectors [3, 23]. This confirms the importance of platform-based business models and carefully designed platform functionalities.

3 Research Design

A case study analysis will allow for identifying SE platform functionalities. Conducting a case study analysis is always appropriate, if three basic conditions are met: if a 'how' or 'why' research question should be answered, if a current phenomenon is addressed, which is not clearly distinguishable from external conditions due to its novelty, and if the external researcher has little or no influence on the subject of investigation [24, 25]. These requirements apply to the present research design.

In the following case study analysis, the companies, and both their service expansion and functionalities are described by means of specific criteria. The functionalities can be categorized according to five areas: tendering, search for offers, booking process, fees and rating, security and trust functions. These areas and the corresponding platform functionalities have been identified on the websites of the companies. Moreover, the investigations of Sundararajan [1], Parker et al. [5] and Täuscher et al. [26] are considered in proposing and validating the developed set of criteria. For instance, Sundararajan [1] developed a method for the categorization of platform-based companies by means of 22 dimensions. These dimensions describe platform features, such as 'provider chooses pricing' or 'platform assigns provider to customer' [1, p. 78-79], which enables the categorization of platforms in the range between hierarchy and market-like companies. On the other hand, Parker et al. [5] developed principles for the design of successful platforms. The authors outline in detail how to carefully design a platform with regard to core interaction and pull, facilitate and match functions. The design of the features need to facilitate the exchange of information, goods or services and traditional or intangible forms of currency for consumers and producers. Täuscher et al. [26] developed a framework for design and analysis of business models for digital service market places. The authors identified 23 business model elements for digital service market places such as confidence building, pricing mechanisms, and selection of transaction partners. They applied them to the special case of Airbnb's business model. Elements and dimensions used in these scientific papers have been carefully selected by their relevance for the design of platform functionalities for SE companies and have been compared to the findings on the websites of the companies analyzed in this paper. They have then been considered in the set of criteria (Appendix 1).

The websites, apps, and blogs of the companies constitute the data sources for the data collection. These data sources provide the most recent information. When available, this data basis was extended by further findings from the scientific literature. Subsequently, a comparison of the results shall identify the similarities and differences among platform companies.

Companies selected here are: Airbnb, Uber, Couchsurfing, Blablacar, and TaskRabbit. These companies emerged during the time period between 2004 and 2009 and allow for a P2P-based exchange, either partly or exclusively. The selection of the platform companies for this paper is justified by their strong disruptive market potential. In recent years, they could achieve a high user reach, while extending their services to numerous cities and countries worldwide (Table 1).

Table 1. Selected Sharing Economy Companies

Companies	Founded in	Sector	Coverage	Availability
Airbnb	2008	Accommodation	300 million guests	81 000 cities, 191 countries
Uber	2009	Short-distance mobility	78 million members	632 cities, 78 countries
Couchsurfing	2004	Accommodation	14 million members	200 000 cities
BlaBlaCar	2006	Long-distance mobility	60 million members, 54 million travelers per year	22 countries
TaskRabbit	2008	Home services	50 000 providers	40 cities, 2 countries

4 Empirical Analysis

4.1 Case Studies

In the following, all five selected companies are analyzed according to the same set of criteria. First, the company is presented. Subsequently, the extended range of services, as well as special platform functionalities in the functional areas of tendering, search of offer, booking process, fees, rating, security and trust functions are discussed in more detail. Unless otherwise stated, data used for this analysis is based on the information available on the websites and apps of the companies.

Airbnb. Airbnb describes itself on its website as a trustworthy community marketplace, on which people can advertise, discover and book unique accommodations all over the world. Thus, Airbnb is a two-sided online platform that connects peers, who want to rent out their space to others who are looking for affordable accommodations [27].

Airbnb is constantly developing its existing range of services through complementary offers. For example, the platform recently introduced new accommodation options for business trips as well as the possibility to book local 'experiences', such as sightseeing tours or cooking classes. Moreover, Airbnb has recently expanded the product category to Airbnb Plus, which includes hotel-like luxury accommodations with quality certifications issued by the platform itself.

Airbnb offers several platform functionalities to ensure an efficient transaction between hosts and guests. It provides a website and an app for this service. First, hosts are required to create an Airbnb profile in order to be able to offer a listing on the platform [28]. In this case, hosts can make use of selection criteria and add informative pictures and descriptions to further individualize their listings. Additional functionalities such as a calendar function efficiently assist hosts when creating listings. Hosts are then required to propose an appropriate price for their listings [29]. The platform also offers a smart pricing tool for hosts, which automatically adapts the price of a listing to the actual market demands [30]. Moreover, hosts can choose among three standardized cancellation fees for guests. However, this platform charges higher cancellation fees for platform hosts.

The search function constitutes the core function of the platform, because it connects hosts and guests. Guests can further customize search requests with the help of additional filter functions. A smart algorithm then lists appropriate accommodations and experiences with regard to individual search requests. Guests can choose a transaction partner according to their preferences, given that they have created a profile in advance. Following a successful booking process, the platform itself executes the payment process and charges hosts and guests with transaction fees at varying levels.

To reduce information asymmetries between users, the platform offers several additional functionalities such as e.g., a messaging service. Moreover, users need to verify their profile, e.g. with a telephone number, in order to interact on the platform. Additional community standards define the desirable code of conduct for interaction. Further the platform offers hosts a warranty for possible damages or losses. A mutual and public rating system and a special distinction of superhosts shall guarantee a high level of transaction quality. Superhosts are those hosts with an excellent overall rating and a high level of activity on the platform. The platform also performs risk analyses for every transaction and provides a customer service with non-stop operation.

Uber. Uber is a global intermediary platform for transport and logistics services. The platform's core competence is to provide a market place for arranging car rides. It connects private drivers and potential passengers for short distance rides through a mobile app. The platform does not own car fleets, but creates a significant benefit for customers by reducing transaction and search costs [31]. Due to regulatory issues and the competition with traditional taxi companies over recent years, Uber constantly adapted its own business model in numerous countries to local conditions [32].

The platform's range of services includes various levels of service, which mainly differ in the qualification of the driver, as well as the type, size and equipment of the vehicle used. The platform has recently established new service options in selected countries, such as business trips and logistics services (Uber Freights) as well a delivery service (Uber Eats and Uber Rush).

Interested parties can register directly as drivers in the Uber app or website and create a profile. To complete the registration process, drivers must go through country-specific screening and identity checks [32]. After a successful registration process, drivers are entitled to log in to the system and are then automatically assigned to passengers' booking requests in the surrounding area [32]. Potential passengers must also create a profile in order to use the platform and search for a ride. Uber offers a search function for this purpose, in which users can enter information on the desired route and choose from different vehicle options and drivers. The platform determines a price range for each selection option based on a fare estimation tool. Uber uses a surge pricing method to adjust the price range to a final fare. It uses several criteria such as e.g., the actual level of demand for this method. Moreover, the platform uses a central matching algorithm to connect drivers and passengers: if a user makes a booking request via the platform, this request is directly forwarded to a driver selected by Uber [33]. Recently, Uber started providing an additional option to book rides in the Google Maps service app. Nevertheless, the payment process takes place over the Uber platform itself. Uber then charges transaction fees on drivers and retains about 20% of the fare for its profit [32], whereas possible cancellation fees are paid by passengers.

To protect its users, Uber offers a detailed code of conduct ensuring that users act in accordance with the platform rules. Moreover, drivers' driving status and GPS data can be shared in real time by using additional platform functionalities. GPS data and customer information for each trip are stored for safety reasons. This procedure shall prevent unnecessary detours or inappropriate behavior by the platform users. Uber further provides a mutual and anonymous rating system and a customer service with non-stop operation.

Couchsurfing. Couchsurfing is a global travel community platform. It provides, similar to Airbnb, an app and a website in order to connect providers of private accommodations and travelers. The platform aims to build a global network that allows users to share their accommodations and experiences with other travelers based on social incentives. Incurred costs are borne by advertising revenues. Furthermore, the platform offers the possibility to organize community events and a 'friend function', through which users can communicate and stay in contact.

In order to interact over the platform, users need to create a Couchsurfing profile in advance. Hosts can then create listings interdependently and with the help of additional functions such as standardized selection criteria and calendar functions. Potential guests can search for accommodations by using the search function. Additional filter functions further allow for an individualized search query. Guests can then select potential hosts based on their profile information or the description of the potential accommodation. Guests can further personalize booking requests. A message function enables communication among users. The platform generally does not charge for intermediation between travelers and hosts due to its non-for-profit orientation. For this reason, there are no cancellation fees. However, since 2017, there is the possibility to verify user profiles for a one-time contribution. This intends to increase the overall brokerage rate, as the authenticity of the users can be guaranteed. Moreover, the platform subsidizes hosts. They receive a free verification for a period of three months for every guest they accept.

The Couchsurfing platform also offers many security and trust functions to reduce information asymmetries. Among other functions, users have access to a public rating system that allows mutual evaluation within 14 days of a stay. This shall enable users to benefit from the experience of other members in the network. The Couchsurfing platform continues to select the most active and well-rated users to award them with a participation possibility in an Ambassador Program. These ambassadors serve as moderators of the platform. A community guideline ensures compliant behavior of the user groups. A user profile must also be complete to a certain percentage to take advantage of the offered functions.

BlaBlaCar. BlaBlaCar is a platform-based carpooling company that provides direct contact between drivers and potential passengers. The offered services on the platform are –in contrast to Uber in the area of long-distance mobility. The platform provides a website and an app to deliver the services as an intermediary without having a fleet of cars [34]. Its own range of services has not yet been extended with complementary services. Nevertheless, BlaBlaCar embarked on a cooperation with Google in 2017, so that the rides offered on the platform are also proposed in the Google maps service app.

Drivers can submit offers via BlaBlaCar using a standardized application, provided that they have a user account. Drivers need to propose a price per passenger. This price must be based on a price range that has been specified in advance by the platform. The search function enables potential riders with a user account to search for suitable offers. The search can also be personalized by using filter applications. A message function enables communication among users. Riders can search for rides via the app or website. In Germany, the platform offered its services free of charge until 2016. BlablaCar then introduced a transaction fee paid by passengers, depending on the traveled distance and the price of the journey [34]. Since March 2018, BlaBlaCar uses a new pricing model. This corresponds to a contribution fee and is intended to increase customer loyalty. Payment is possible in cash and electronically via the platform. Both user groups are allowed to cancel the trips, whereas cancellation fees are only incurred for passengers.

BlaBlaCar also offers its users the possibility to evaluate each other. Thus, the problems of asymmetric information distribution are solved. Ratings can be provided up to 14 days after the ride. BlaBlaCar additionally rewards active platform users that got sufficient positive reviews with special awards. A code of conduct for platform users should allow for a smooth ride. Furthermore, BlaBlaCar drivers are protected by an insurance for the duration of the ride. In case of problems, a member service supports both sides of the platform.

TaskRabbit. TaskRabbit is a communication platform that connects customers and so-called Taskers. Taskers constitute the supply side of the platform. They can offer any kind of household work or smaller services that do not require a professional license on the platform. TaskRabbit is currently available as a website and as an app in the U.S. and the UK and was taken over by the global furniture company IKEA. It can be assumed that the platform's offering will expand globally in the future [35]. Since the takeover of the platform in 2017, the service offering has been expanded to include an official IKEA TaskRabbit Assembly Portal. Customers can have their furniture purchased and delivered by IKEA. The assembly service of the furniture can be booked directly via IKEA or via the TaskRabbit's platform [36].

To create an offer on the TaskRabbit platform, a Tasker must be registered. This registration process underlies a comprehensive review process involving identity and criminal background checks. Taskers can then place individual offers on the platform and independently set the hourly rate of the service offered. Specific additional functions such as a Work Area Map make it easier for Taskers to submit their offers. In order for potential customers to book a Tasker, they also need a profile account. By means of a standardized search application and filtering functions, users can then find a suitable service provider. For time-critical searches such as tasks that have to be carried out on the same day, the platform offers the 'Quick Assign' capability in some cities. In this case, the next possible Tasker can be automatically assigned by the platform for a set price. The involved parties can communicate via a messaging system as well as via an in-app call function of the platform after a terminated booking process. Service providers can cancel a booking, if a customer has not responded to a message. However, the platform charges cancellation fees for customers under certain conditions. A payment process is handled exclusively over the platform.

TaskRabbit charges Taskers a one-time fee for registration. For customers, registration on the platform is free of charge. Customers pay a service fee as well as a trust and safety fee to the platform. TaskRabbit also provides many features on the platform to reduce problems of asymmetric distribution of information and ensures smooth service delivery. Users of the platform have access to a customer support team when it is necessary. The platform also has limited liability for any damage or loss that occurs or may occur to a customer or service during the execution of the order. TaskRabbit also offers the function of mutual evaluation within 30 days after completion of the order.

4.2   Cross Case Analysis

In the following, the results of the individual case study analyses are used to examine, whether the SE companies show similarities or differences in their type of company and service expansion as well as in the design of their platform functionalities.

Company. The analyses of the five companies from the SE show that all of them, except for Couchsurfing, are commercially-oriented. All companies offer intermediary services through their platforms. They use the resources of others to match between both sides of the platform. The platforms also enable transactions in a simple way and with transparent offer overviews.

Service Expansion. The prerequisite for companies to deliver intermediary services by matching at least two sides of a market is the establishment of a website and an app. The creation of a user account, as well as the assessment of the interaction risk for the customers is an additional condition. Apps and websites enable companies to scale up their businesses and to provide their services in different countries. Uber is the only platform that offers its services exclusively via an app. The website is only used as a source of information, for instance to display the prices of a ride. To submit offers and take advantage of the services, all users have to create an account. A verification of the user account confirms the user identity, which in turn guarantees security for the platform user. Further testing procedures by the platform additionally support security issues. By comparing the developments of the range of services offered by the platforms over the past years, it has turned out that, except for BlaBlaCar, four of the companies have expanded their ranges of services to complementary ones. Platforms expand their service as a strategy to provide added value to customers, while staying competitive and, ideally, forcing competitors out of the market. A larger access to users can also be achieved through collaboration with other companies outside the industry. For this reason, BlaBlaCar and Uber cooperate with Google (GoogleMaps). The acquisition of TaskRabbit by IKEA will probably increase the acceptance and utilization of this platform. Cooperation and acquisitions are thus considered to be effective measures to strengthen the market position of platforms.

Platform functionalities play a central role in transaction brokerage and can be divided into five areas: tendering, search for offers, booking process, fees and contributions, as well as rating, security and trust functions. In these areas, successful interactions lay the foundations for positive network effects.

Tendering. The submission of offers over the platforms takes place by the provider of the service for all companies, except for Uber. These companies offer a standardized application for this purpose. The service providers active on the platforms of Airbnb, BlaBlaCar and TaskRabbit can also set the price for the service on their own, whereas specific features such as 'smart pricing' are only provided by Airbnb and BlaBlaCar. Reference prices can be displayed by the platform to the user to optimize the pricing of the offerings. One exception is Uber, over which offer submissions by providers automatically take place. Moreover, the price for a ride is always adjusted by the platform according to the current state of the demand in order to motivate the profit-oriented service providers to continue working with Uber. The use of automatic bid submissions and demand-based pricing are important for time-critical services. Furthermore, platforms generally provide additional functions to make it easier for the service providers to submit their offers.

Search for Offers. Search functions enable platforms to match supply and demand efficiently and are used by all platforms. The search functions can be adapted to individual customer needs by using filter options. The efficiency of a search function depends on the number of filters and varies among the platforms studied. Following a search request, apart from Uber, potential customers will receive a list of suitable listings. On platforms such as Uber and TaskRabbit, time-critical customer requests are automatically assigned to providers. In general, search functions require the use of service-related filters that can be personalized by the customer. The higher the number of possible filters, the better the service for the customers to find optimal transaction partners according to their specific needs.

Booking Process. After a successful matching of vendors and customers, all platforms allow for further communication possibilities between users through in-platform messaging. Messaging systems simplify the exchange of service-related information and support the execution of the transaction. In effect, the communication between the involved transaction partners is of special importance to guarantee the success of a transaction. The processing of payment modalities is a fundamental function of platforms and enables a trouble-free and secure payment process on four out of five platforms. Couchsurfing mainly offers non-commercial services on its platform. Therefore, payment functions are only provided for the process of account verification. Online payment modalities are generally among the special service tasks. This also allows the platform to charge for the brokerage service.

Fees and Contributions. Fees contribute significantly to the turnover of the SE companies. These include transaction, subscription, membership, cancellation and service fees. However, platforms do not charge the same rates. Note that Couchsurfing charges no fees for the use of the brokerage service due to the community nature and the non-for-profit orientation of the platform. Nevertheless, Couchsurfing users can make use of a temporary fee-based account verification option, which shall guarantee a supposedly better brokerage rate. Thus, platforms charge vendors and customers differently. In general, platforms subsidize more price-sensitive user groups by charging lower fees. Another strategy constitutes charging lower fees for user groups that are crucial to provide the service offered by the platform. For instance, Airbnb charges hosts lower transaction fees than guests. All platforms further use cancellation fees and predominantly charge customers for cancellation.

Ratings, Security and Trust Functions. Security and trust functions are essential platform features to overcome the problem of anonymity between service vendors and customers and to minimize mutual risks associated with the transactions. All platforms use a mutual rating system. Airbnb, BlaBlaCar and Couchsurfing also use the award feature such as superhosts to reward the most active users of the platform. Platforms also define code of conducts to guarantee compliant behavior of the users on the platform. This function is available on all platforms except for TaskRabbit. The platforms also offer customer services and, with the exception of Couchsurfing, offer compensations to users in the case of accidents or damage.

5   Results and Discussion

The cross case analysis shows that platforms have similarities as well as differences in their functionalities. Consequently, specific requirements for the design of platform functionalities in the SE and design recommendations can be derived. This provides the basis of the following generic concept.

The fundamental element of a successful service is the provision of location-independent apps and websites. They constitute the basis for the digital business model. The design of the platform functions has a large impact on the transaction process and on the communication options among users. Standardized offers with predefined selection criteria and additional personalization options is the prerequisite for fast and efficient transaction processing. Such a functionality combined with the possibility that vendors set their own prices, is particularly suitable for such platform services. Smart pricing algorithms and a predetermined price range by the platform serve as help for vendors on the platform and can improve the rate of successful transactions. The more time-critical the individual service request, the more should a platform automate these functions. The use of additional service-related functions such as card and calendar functions supports and facilitates bidding for the provider. If possible, such additional services should always be used when it comes to improving the planning basis for service providers. Search features should include a sufficient number of services and personal filters. Automated algorithms can also support the search process, thus improving the success rate of transactions. The automatic assignment of transaction partners by means of algorithms is advantageous for services that have to be fastly executed.

Moreover, the integration of execution and communication features reduces user efforts, thereby increasing the level of customer loyalty. Additionally, an integrated message system optimizes the exchange of information between vendors and customers before and after the transaction. Functional platforms must also offer an integrated payment function. This allows the company to act as a payment intermediate, thus ensuring secure and low-effort payment processing. Furthermore, integrated payment functions enable the company to monetize their services by the use of fees. The fees should be lower for that user group of the platform from which the platform benefits the most. Additional cancellation fees have a signaling effect on potential users, leading to higher planning accuracy. Platforms predominantly charge customers for cancellation, but the amount of fees charged by the platform should be proportionate to the total price of the service. Customer reviews as well as security and trust functions increase the willingness to interact over the platform. A rating system to evaluate vendors and customers strengthens the trust among users on the platform. The submission of a rating, however, must be limited to a certain period after the completion of the respective service. Additional functions, such as the award of particularly active users, also improve the quality of the offered services. Prescribed codes of conduct also boost users' trust in the platform. Furthermore, individual and service-related insurances can reduce the perceived risk of a transaction. A risk assessment function before the execution of the transaction further has a positive effect on users. A user account that enables access to the platform reduces the risk of undesired user behavior. Thus, the quality of the service and trust in the transaction process can be increased. Consequently, the general willingness to use a platform is improved.

6   Conclusions and Directions for Future Research

Due to a dynamic and rapidly evolving market environment, SE platforms constantly need to adapt their functionalities, technology and coverage. The platform functions identified in this paper define a generic concept for the design of a multi-sided platform in the Sharing Economy. However, this concept should solely be considered as a guideline for this purpose. Companies investigated in this study only represent a selection of best practices and should not be considered representative. Moreover, the identified criteria only represent a selection out of a larger range of platform functionalities. Further criteria could be considered for future extensive investigations.

Appendix

Appendix 1. Criteria used for the case study analysis

Functional Areas	Criteria
Company	- Type and characteristics
	- Range of services
Service expansion	- Type of expansion
Tendering	- Prerequisities of tendering
	- Process of offer creation
	- Price determination
	- Additional service-related functionalities
Offer search	- Search prerequisities
	- Search function design
	- Filter function design
	- Aditional service-related functionalities
Booking process	- Selection of transaction partners
	- Booking function design
	- Communication systems
	- Payment process
	- Cancellation process
	- Additional service-related functionalities
Fees	- Pricing structures
Rating, security and trust functions	- Rating system
	- Customer service
	- Warranties
	- Code of conduct
	- Additional service-related functionalities

References

1. Sundararajan, A.: The Sharing Economy: The End of Employment and the Rise of Crowd-Based Capitalism. The MIT Press, Cambridge (2016)
2. Heinrichs, H., Grunenberg, H.: Sharing Economy - Auf dem Weg in eine neue Konsumkultur? (2012). https://nbn-resolving.org/urn:nbn:de:0168-ssoar-427486
3. Jaekel, M.: Die Macht der digitalen Plattformen. Springer, Wiesbaden (2017). https://doi.org/10.1007/978-3-658-19178-8
4. Hagiu, A., Wright, J.: Multi-sided platforms. Int. J. Ind. Organ. **43**, 162–174 (2015). https://doi.org/10.1016/j.ijindorg.2015.03.003
5. Parker, G., van Alstyne, M., Choudary, S.P.: Platform Revolution: How Networked Markets are Transforming the Economy - And How to Make them Work for You. W.W. Norton & Company, New York (2016)
6. Evans, D.S., Schmalensee, R.: Matchmakers: The New Economics of Multisided Platforms. Harvard Business Review Press, Boston (2016)
7. Rochet, J.-C., Tirole, J.: Platform competition in two-sided markets. J. Eur. Econ. Assoc. **1**(4), 990–1029 (2003). https://doi.org/10.1162/154247603322493212
8. Caillaud, B., Jullien, B.: Chicken & egg: competition among intermediation service providers. RAND J. Econ. **34**(2), 309–328 (2003)
9. Armstrong, M.: Competition in two-sided markets. RAND J. Econ. **37**(3), 668–691 (2006). https://doi.org/10.1111/j.1756-2171.2006.tb00037.x
10. Eisenmann, T.R., Parker, G., van Alstyne, M.W.: Strategies for two-sided markets. Harv. Bus. Rev. **84**(10), 92–101 (2006)
11. Rysman, M.: The Economics of two-sided markets. J. Econ. Perspect. **23**(3), 125–143 (2009). https://doi.org/10.1257/jep.23.3.125
12. Peitz, M.: Marktplätze und indirekte Netzwerkeffekte. Persp. Wirtschaftspol **7**(3), 317–333 (2006). https://doi.org/10.1111/j.1468-2516.2006.00214.x
13. Gansky, L.: The Mesh: Why the Future of Business is Sharing. Portfolio Penguin, New York (2010)
14. Botsman, R., Rogers, R.: What's mine is yours: How collaborative consumption is changing the way we live. Collins, London (2011)
15. Puschmann, T., Alt, R.: Sharing economy. Bus. Inf. Syst. Eng. **58**(1), 93–99 (2016). https://doi.org/10.1007/s12599-015-0420-2
16. Andersson, M., Hjalmarsson, A., Avital, M.: Peer-to-peer service sharing platforms: driving share and share alike on a mass-scale. In: Proceedings of the 34th International Conference on Information Systems, ICIS 2013 (2013)
17. Schwalbe, U., Peitz, M.: Kollaboratives Wirtschaften oder Turbokapitalismus? Zur Ökonomie der Sharing Economy. Persp. Wirtschaftspol **17**(3), 232–252 (2016). https://doi.org/10.1515/pwp-2016-0018
18. Evans, D.S.: Some empirical aspects of multi-sided platform industries. Rev. Netw. Econ. **2**(3), 191–209 (2003)
19. Hagiu, A., Wright, J.: Marketplace or reseller? Manag. Sci. **61**, 184–203 (2015). https://doi.org/10.1287/mnsc.2014.2042
20. Engelhardt, S., Wangler, L., Wischmann, S.: Eigenschaften und Erfolgsfaktoren digitaler Plattformen. Eine Studie im Rahmen der Begleitforschung zum Technologieprogramm AUTONOMIK für Industrie 4.0 des Bundesministeriums für Wirtschaft und Energie (2017)

21. Haucap, J.: Die Chancen der Sharing Economy und ihre möglichen Risiken und Nebenwirkungen. Wirtschaftsdienst: Zeitschrift für Wirtschaftspolitik **95**(2), 91–94 (2015). https://doi.org/10.1007/s10273-015-1785-z
22. van Alstyne, M.W., Schrage, M.: The best platforms are more than matchmakers. Harv. Bus. Rev. **94**(7/8), 2–6 (2016)
23. Theurl, T.: Ökonomie des Teilens: Governance konsequent zu Ende gedacht. Wirtschaftsdienst: Zeitschrift für Wirtschaftspolitik **95**(2), 87–91 (2015). https://doi.org/10.1007/s10273-015-1785-z
24. Eisenhardt, K.M.: Building theories from case study research. AMR **14**(4), 532–550 (1989). https://doi.org/10.5465/amr.1989.4308385
25. Yin, R.K.: Case Study Research: Design and Methods. SAGE, Los Angeles (2003)
26. Täuscher, K., Hilbig, R., Abdelkafi, N.: Geschäftsmodellelemente mehrseitiger Plattformen. In: Schallmo, D., Rusnjak, A., Anzengruber, J., Werani, T., Jünger, M. (eds.) Digitale Transformation von Geschäftsmodellen. SBMI, pp. 179–211. Springer, Wiesbaden (2017). https://doi.org/10.1007/978-3-658-12388-8_7
27. Overgoor, J.: Experiments at Airbnb (2014). https://medium.com/airbnb-engineering/experiments-at-airbnb-e2db3abf39e7
28. Airbnb Blog: Getting started as a host (2018). https://blog.atairbnb.com/getting-started-host/
29. Zervas, G., Proserpio, D., Byers, J.W.: The rise of the sharing economy: estimating the impact of Airbnb on the hotel industry. J. Mark. Res. **54**(5), 687–705 (2017). https://doi.org/10.1509/jmr.15.0204
30. Airbnb Blog: Smart pricing (2017). https://blog.atairbnb.com/smart-pricing-locale-de/
31. Henten, A.H., Windekilde, I.M.: Transaction costs and the sharing economy. INFO **18**(1), 1–15 (2016). https://doi.org/10.1108/info-09-2015-0044
32. Schneider, H.: Creative Destruction and the Sharing Economy: Uber as Disruptive Innovation. Edward Elgar Publishing, Cheltenham (2017)
33. Petropoulos, G.: Collaborative economy: market design and basic regulatory principles. Inter. Econ. **52**(6), 340–345 (2017). https://doi.org/10.1007/s10272-017-0701-8
34. Krämer, A.: Die Mobilisierung von preissensibler Nachfrage in einer digitalisierten Welt. Die Entstehung von vier Quasi-Monopolen im deutschen Fernverkehrsmarkt. Internationales Verkehrswesen **70**(1), 2–6 (2018)
35. Hsu, T.: Ikea enters 'Gig Economy' by acquiring TaskRabbit (2017). https://www.nytimes.com/2017/09/28/business/ikeataskrabbit.html
36. TaskRabbit Blog: TaskRabbit + IKEA (2017). https://blog.taskrabbit.com/2017/09/28/taskrabbit-ikea/

So You Want to Be a Platform: Where to Start?

Lino Markfort[✉], Sebastian Haugk, and Cyrine Tangour

Fraunhofer Center for International Management and Knowledge
Economy - IMW, Leipzig, Germany
{lino.markfort, sebastian.haugk,
cyrine.tangour}@imw.fraunhofer.de

Abstract. Platforms change numerous industries in a very short time. Many companies therefore want to become platforms themselves. Our paper gives a brief overview of the most important concepts in the area of platform-based business models and business ecosystems. In addition, from three approaches to transforming traditional business models into platform companies, we derive recommendations on how companies should position themselves to become platform companies.

Keywords: Platform business model · Ecosystem ·
Business model transformation

1 Introduction

For years and decades, product-oriented companies have transformed themselves into service-oriented companies. Customers do not want to buy a product anymore; they rather want a solution for their problem. This transformation has been widely described as Servitization (e.g. [1–4]).

The breakthrough of digital technologies and the internet economy is now bringing about a further fundamental transformation. Value chains are becoming increasingly complex and are thus transforming into value creation networks. Companies have to analyze their position in such a network and adapt their business model so that they are in an advantageous position in the value creation process.

In recent years, some of the most successful companies are involved in platform businesses. They operate platforms in different industries that bring together various players and simplify or facilitate transactions or interactions. As platform operators, they earn a small part of each transaction or finance their platform in other ways, such as advertising or subscription revenues.

Google's revenue model, for example, is primarily based on content-targeted advertising or contextual mobile advertising. In addition, Google uses electronic auctions to allocate key words to advertisers web pages for the highest bidder [5]. Another example is eBay, which built a platform in the form of a digital market place, where buyer and seller meet and negotiate the sale of a physical good. It is a digital form of brokerage where the key process is the price discovery and the profits are generated based on commission fees for transactions [5].

R. Jallouli et al. (Eds.): ICDEc 2019, LNBIP 358, pp. 387–396, 2019.
https://doi.org/10.1007/978-3-030-30874-2_30

Many platform companies have radically changed their respective industries and, in the process, have driven some established companies out of the market or weakened them significantly. It is therefore important for companies to evaluate their own position in the value creation process. Operating a platform can be an attractive option.

As [6] explain, there are three main reasons why companies should consider to transform their business from a linear value chain based business model to a platform-based business model. In the following, we want to describe possibilities how companies can develop towards platform companies.

2   Literature Review

2.1   Defining a Business Model

The concepts of business models have become increasingly popular to explain differences in companies' successes and design new value propositions to sustain their competitiveness.

Business model research suggests that appropriate business models can enable a business organisation to create more value than its competitors, which results in a sustainable competitive advantage [7, 8]. Even though the importance of design and innovation of business models is obvious, researchers still did not agree on a common definition of the concept itself. An unclear distinction remains between the concepts of business models, strategies, and operations. While all three concepts address similar problems such as how to increase market share, they address different levels with different timeframes.

Strategy focuses on the planning level where a company's long-term vision, goals, and objectives are set and devised into action plans [9]. Operations are at the implementation level, concerned with the organization and workflow of day-to-day tasks and activities. Consequently, a business model is what connects strategy and operations, since it is shaped by the company's strategy and serves as a dashboard that guides the operational tasks.

Essentially, business models can be understood either according to the value-based view or according to an activity-based view. The activity-based view considers a business model as a system of interdependent activities spanning the boundaries of a company. With this view, business model innovation occurs by adding new activities or linking already existing ones in a new way or by relocating any activity to one or more new parties [10]. The value-based view describes how a company generates revenues and profits by creating and delivering value to its customers [11, 12]. This view emphasizes the importance of creating value for the customer first, and then building the model around delivering the product to them [9]. The following definition outlines our understanding of the concept in the scope of this paper: "A business model describes how a company communicates, creates, delivers and captures value out of a value proposition." [11].

2.2   Defining a Platform

The term platform is often used differently depending on the context it is used in. One common definition for "platforms" is that they are technologies, products, or services, which serve as a foundation for external stakeholders to interact, perform transactions, or create and commercialize complementary innovations [13, 14]. In recent years, the term platform has gained popularity, which lead some scholars to declare, that "we are living in the age of the platforms" [15, 16].

However, platforms have long been known from the physical world. For instance in the 1970s companies, such Intel or AMD, started to offer computer chips to software developers as a possibility to build an operating system upon this technological basis. The video game industry provides other examples. Consoles from Sony (Playstation) or Microsoft (XBox) became the basis for external developers to build video games for the different systems. Thus, in this example the console is a platform. The console producers capture value by charging third-party game developers a fee to release their games for the console.

The term platform is also commonly used to describe a marketplace, where supply and demand of stakeholders are brought together (Following [17–19]). Currently numerous classifications for platforms exist, for instance based on the type of service they are offering such as *matchmaking* or *exchange* ([20, 21]) or as *retail platforms* ([22]). Moreover, [21] outlined further types of platforms, e.g. *collaborative innovation platforms* for companies or *investment platforms*. All platforms seem to have in common that they facilitate transactions or interactions between different participators of a multi-sided market.

2.3   Business Ecosystem

Todays' firms have supply chains that are more complex and more dispersed. For this reason, scholars have started using the terms "supply chain networks" or just "supply networks" (e.g. [23, 24]) to describe the chain of activities from the extraction of raw materials to selling the final product to consumers [25]. Other terms can also be found in the literature, such as "value network", to describe the transactions between enterprises, customers, suppliers, and other strategic partners [26]. Whereas supply chain network and value network perspectives describe operational exchanges between various types of stakeholders (activities, currencies), they fail to include the strategic layer that drives the interactions of the system. Consequently, scholars rather use the term business ecosystem than the value chain or supply chain perspectives because it encompasses the strategic layer of a network and captures further concepts such as competition, mental models, or shared vision.

According to [27] a business ecosystem is "an economic community supported by a foundation of interacting organizations and individuals - the organisms of the business world. This economic community produces goods and services of value to customers, who are themselves members of the ecosystem." [28] stress the importance of describing the members of the ecosystem as "loosely interconnected" while they need one another to evolve. Also, [29] describe an ecosystem as a community of loosely connected participants, which depend on each other for their effectiveness and mutual survival.

Although companies usually focus on their own manufacturing plants and distribution systems to succeed in a turbulent business environment, the design of a network of external partners is critical for companies in global competition [30]. In fact, in the future competition might not only exist between companies but between business ecosystems, because more and more companies could join forces to benefit from network effects as well as economies of scale and scope.

In addition, [27] outlined that a central company, which provides leadership and a shared vision amongst ecosystem participants, characterizes a business ecosystem. Thus, in platform-based ecosystems, this central firm is called platform leader and provides a technological foundation upon which companies from the outside can develop complementary products, services, or technologies [14, 31].

[6] present their understanding of the players in a platform ecosystem, where a platform is maintained by *providers*, who develop the technological interfaces for the platform as well as *owners*, who control the intellectual property of the platform and function as an arbiter to decide who and in which way a company participates in the platform. Moreover, they speak of *producers*, who create the offerings for the platform and *consumers*, who buy or use those offerings. Both, producers and users, exchange value and data through the platform and give feedback to the platform providers and owner.

3 Methodology

This paper builds on literature to develop a framework to support companies in transforming their traditional business model towards a platform business model. While numerous concepts exist that explain how a company can evolve from a linear value chain to platform-based business model, the authors consider specifically the three concepts by [6, 32, 33], worth analyzing, as they are explicitly specific according the elements needed to establish a platform. The main recommendations of these three approaches are structured, compared, and integrated into a higher-level framework. The authors analyse the concepts based on the framework of [34], which supports the business model innovation process. The meta-level of analysis comprises four phases, namely, Initiation, Ideation, Integration, and Implementation (see Table 1). For the integration of the approaches into a higher-level framework, recommendations that appear in different approaches are consolidated and gaps that exist in the approaches are filled on the basis of additional literature and the experiences of the authors from various interviews and workshops on platform business models. The results are presented in the next section.

4 Framework for Building a Platform-Based Business Model

First, [6, 32, 33] recommend that the platform based business model should be added to the existing portfolio of offerings a company and can substitute those offerings only when the platform becomes profitable.

As shown in Table 1, only the steps of [32, 33] can be matched to the meta-levels of the business model innovation process by [34]. The work of [6] offers valuable recommendations with respect to the design of a platform, which are presented below in Table 1. However, it does not provide practical steps that guide companies to change into platform companies. Interestingly, all three sources do not provide any steps to initiate the transformation of linear business models into platform business models.

Table 1. Comparison of the concepts from Choudary (2015) and Reillier & Reillier (2017)

Meta-level	Choudary (2015) [32]	Reillier & Reillier (2017) [33]
Initiation	—	—
Ideation	1. Re-imagine your (linear) business model allocation of resources and labour for a platform scale	
Integration	2. Leverage interaction-first design 3. Build cumulative value, Facilitate incentives for participating, Improve the platform in iterative steps and minimize interaction failure	1. Attract (incentivize) potential participants to join the platform until it reaches a tipping point
	4. Solve chicken and egg problems. Use the network effects of a platform to reach a critical mass of users. Only a sufficient number of transactions will enable a platform to persist	2. Match the needs of both suppliers and demanders to facilitate a transaction
	5. Design viral engines that will become more and more indispensable for the platform's current and potential participants	3. Combine the information about participants to improve the platform service and minimize the risk for a transactions happening outside of the platform
Implementation	6. Account for reverse network effects from, for example, a receding exclusivity with an accompanying growth of participants	4. Maximize the number of value adding transactions as well as core interactions to guarantee a direct or indirect monetization
		5. Optimize the platform in iterative steps to build or maintain your market share

In addition to these steps, the recommendations of [6] are taken into consideration as described above to create an integrated framework. These recommendations include (1) enabling a fluid, safe and reliable transaction of value streams between the participants, (2) matching the needs of different participants, (3) making the platform an inevitable tool for its participants, (4) exploiting possible value-adding business opportunities that accompany the core business, (5) applying the end-to-end principle,

(6) designing the platform in a modular way, (7) adapting the platform to changing circumstances, and (8) improving the platform iteratively.

In the following, the authors build on the three concepts to propose an integrated framework for the transformation toward platform business model (see Table 2). Based on the four stages of [34] and the recommendations of [6, 32, 33], six steps are derived with which companies can transform their business model. The gap in the initiation stage is filled based on additional literature. For the Ideation and Integration stage, two steps are identified from the existing approaches as well as one step for the Implementation stage. The steps are explained below, together with the rationale for their inclusion in the framework.

Table 2. Framework for transformation toward a platform-based business model

Initiation	1. Analyze the core business
Ideation	2. Ideate services that serve the core business
	3. Evaluate the possibilities for monetization
Integration	4. Do not play an All-In-Game
	5. Think global, act local
Implementation	6. Fast realization

1. Analyze the core business

As [33] note, it is important to attract multiple sides of a platform to make sure that the platform can monetize its value-adding offer. Therefore, a company should analyze its core business to highlight the current key value proposition that is offered to its customers. With re-inventing or implementing a new business model, most executives think of disruptive change, which necessitates a different strategy. In contrast to this, [35] explain that analyzing the core business and understanding the underlying principles is important to re-invent a business model, which fits to the company's structure. Disregarding existing structures of a company also means neglecting advantages that a pre-existing company setting offered. Moreover, the core business is often the main revenue driver. By adding a service based on the key value proposition, the "critical mass" [33] and a possible monetization can be reached as soon as possible. For example, Amazon build upon their pre-existing platform the Amazon FBA program to incentivize third party sellers to offer their products through the online store of the company as well.

2. Ideate services that serve the core business

The platform should be as close as possible to the core business of the company. Nonetheless, the ideas for adding value with a platform business model can be innovative. One way to accomplish outside-of-the-box ideas would be to initialize workshops with customers, experts, and company internals – the participants of the ecosystem of a company [6]. Apple already practices such a process with its WWDC congress that invites software developers to not only improve the current products, but also come up with new ideas for potential business fields that could be explored.

3. Evaluate the possibilities for monetization

In addition to a creative idea for a platform business model, the possibilities of monetization must also be evaluated. As [32] shows, it is not always possible to monetize the services provided by a platform from the outset. However, in order to be profitable in the long term, there should be a strong link to the core business. A "platform-as-a-service" will generally increase a company's value proposition, generating a competitive advantage.

4. Do not play an All-In-Game

As a platform company, patience is required [33] to minimize the risk of playing a short-handed game. The platform business model should initially be seen as a powerful tool to use in difficult situations. As [9] explain through the example of Xerox, new business opportunities with an underlying business model differing from the former should be tested first and then integrated into the broader firm context. Step by step, a company can then replace the linear value chain-based business model with a platform. Netflix followed this rule, which led it from a video rental service to an on-demand streaming service.

5. Think global, act local

When companies rebuild their business model, local establishment is initially helpful. A local, supportive community for a platform business shortens time and distances to receive feedback from participants. This follows the idea of [36], who described this as Uppsala Internationalization Model. The model proposes focusing on markets that are well known for a company first and then expanding to foreign markets that are near geographically and psychologically. After some early errors and failures have been erased, expansion can take place, supported by a trusted and reliable user base [33]. This principle was implemented, for example, by the German music retailer Thomann, who first established its platform on the German market and then expanded throughout Europe and the United States of America.

6. First come, first serve

More than ever, the era of platforms requires action sooner rather than later [32]. Being a first mover as a company minimizes the possibility of becoming marginalized or even obsolete. In the past few years a lot of industries seem to be consolidated, which is according to [37] an extensive change. Thus, business model innovation is necessary to keep a firm successful, adapt to costumers needs, and evolve the value proposition [38]. The example of Amazon shows that within a decade an entire economic sector such as the retail sector was disrupted, mostly by a single company, leading to the closure of several stationary retail stores in Europe and America.

5   Conclusion

The digital transformation is massively changing many industries in a very short period of time. In order not to become obsolete, it can be a promising strategy to introduce a platform-based business model. Literature shows that this should be done step by step and that the core business should be retained until a certain time. However, companies must analyze their position in the value chain in order to not find themselves in an unfavourable position or even become obsolete.

Our short overview explains the main concepts in the context of platforms and business ecosystems. Based on the literature, we propose six steps for companies to develop their business model towards a platform. We tried to combine existing approaches from the literature and to close gaps that we believe still exist. However, further research is necessary to test this framework in practice. This could be done through a comprehensive analysis of corresponding case studies or a series of expert interviews.

References

1. Vandermerwe, S., Rada, J.: Servitization of business: adding value by adding services. Eur. Manag. J. **6**(4), 314–324 (1988). https://doi.org/10.1016/0263-2373(88)90033-3
2. Neely, A.D. (ed.): Business Performance Measurement: Unifying Theories and Integrating Practice, 2nd edn. Cambridge University Press, Cambridge (2007)
3. Baines, T.W., Lightfoot, H.: Servitization of the manufacturing firm: exploring the operations practices and technologies that deliver advanced services. IJOPM **34**(1), 2–35 (2013). https://doi.org/10.1108/IJOPM-02-2012-0086
4. Baines, T.S., Lightfoot, H.W., Benedettini, O., et al.: The servitization of manufacturing. J. Manuf. Tech. Manag. **20**(5), 547–567 (2009). https://doi.org/10.1108/17410380910960984
5. Remane, G., Hanelt, A., Tesch, J.F., et al.: The business model pattern database —: a tool for systematic business model innovation. IJIM **21**(01), 1750004 (2017). https://doi.org/10.1142/s1363919617500049. (61 pages)
6. Parker, G., van Alstyne, M., Choudary, S.P.: Platform Revolution: How Networked Markets are Transforming the Economy - and How to Make them Work for You. W.W. Norton & Company, New York (2017). First published as a Norton paperback
7. Zott, C., Amit, R.: The fit between product market strategy and business model: implications for firm performance. SMJ **29**(1), 1–26 (2008). https://doi.org/10.1002/smj.642
8. Magretta, J.: Why business models Matter. HBR **80**(5), 86–92 (2002)
9. Chesbrough, H., Rosenbloom, R.S.: The role of business model in capturing value from innovation: evidence from Xerox Corporation's technology spinn-off companies. Ind. Corp. Change **11**(3), 529–555 (2002). https://doi.org/10.1515/9783110887242.3
10. Amit, R., Zott, C.: Creating value through business model innovation. MIT SMR **53**(3), 41–49 (2012)
11. Abdelkafi, N., Makhotin, S., Posselt, T.: Business model innovations for electric mobility: what can be learned from existing business model patterns? Int. J. Innov. Manag. **17**(01), 1340003 (2013). https://doi.org/10.1142/S1363919613400033
12. Osterwalder, A., Pigneur, Y.: Business Model Generation: A Handbook for Visionaries, Game Changers, and Challengers. Wiley, Hoboken (2010)
13. Frattini, F., Bianchi, M., de Massis, A., et al.: The role of early adopters in the diffusion of new products: differences between platform and nonplatform innovations. J. Prod. Innov. Manag. **31**(3), 466–488 (2014). https://doi.org/10.1111/jpim.12108
14. Gawer, A., Cusumano, M.A.: Industry platforms and ecosystem innovation. J. Prod. Innov. Manag. **31**(3), 417–433 (2014). https://doi.org/10.1111/jpim.12105

15. Simon, P.: The Age of the Platform: How Amazon, Apple, Facebook, and Google Have Redefined Business, Revised edition (2013)
16. van Alstyne, M.W., Parker, G.G., Choudary, S.P.: Pipelines, platforms, and the new rules of strategy. HBR **94**, 54–62 (2016)
17. Casadesus-Masanell, R., Hałaburda, H.: When does a platform create value by limiting choice? JEMS **23**(2), 259–293 (2014). https://doi.org/10.1111/jems.12052
18. Hagiu, A., Spulber, D.: First-party content and coordination in two-sided markets. Manag. Sci. **59**(4), 933–949 (2013). https://doi.org/10.1287/mnsc.1120.1577
19. Rysman, M.: The Economics of Two-Sided Markets. JEP **23**(3), 125–143 (2009). https://doi. org/10.1257/jep.23.3.125
20. Ardolino, M., Saccani, N., Perona, M.: The analysis of multisided platforms: results from a literature review (2016)
21. Evans, P.C., Gawer, A.: The rise of the platform enterprise: a global survey, the center for global enterprise. The emerging platform economy series No. 1 (2016)
22. Kenney, M., Zysman, J.: The rise of the platform economy. Issues Sci. Technol. **32**, 61 (2016)
23. Choi, T.Y., Dooley, K.J., Rungtusanatham, M.: Supply networks and complex adaptive systems: control versus emergence. J. Oper. Manag. **19**(3), 351–366 (2001). https://doi.org/ 10.1016/S0272-6963(00)00068-1
24. Bode, C., Wagner, S.M.: Structural drivers of upstream supply chain complexity and the frequency of supply chain disruptions. J. Oper. Manag. **36**(3), 215–228 (2015). https://doi. org/10.1016/j.jom.2014.12.004
25. Sturgeon, T.J.: How do we define value chains and production networks?*. IDS Bull. **32**(3), 9–18 (2001). https://doi.org/10.1111/j.1759-5436.2001.mp32003002.x
26. Allee, V.: Reconfiguring the value network. J. Bus. Strat. **21**(4), 36–39 (2000). https://doi. org/10.1108/cb040103
27. Moore, J.F.: The Death of Competition: Leadership and Strategy in the Age of Business Ecosystems, 1st edn. HarperBusiness, New York (1996)
28. Shang, T., Chen, Y., Shi, Y.: Orchestrating ecosystem co-opetition: case studies on the business models of the EV demonstration programme in China. In: Beeton, D., Meyer, G. (eds.) Electric Vehicle Business Models. LNM, pp. 215–227. Springer, Cham (2015). https:// doi.org/10.1007/978-3-319-12244-1_13
29. Iansiti, M., Levien, R.: The Keystone Advantage: What the New Dynamics of Business Ecosystems Mean for Strategy, Innovation, and Sustainability. Harvard Business School Press, Boston (2004)
30. Slamanig, M., Winkler, H.: Management of product change projects: a supply chain perspective. IJSOM **11**(4), 481–500 (2012)
31. Gawer, A.: Platforms, Markets and Innovation. Edward Elgar, Cheltenham (2009)
32. Choudary, S.P.: Platform scale: How an emerging business model helps startups build large empires with minimum investment, 1st edn. Platform Thinking Labs Pte. Ltd., Boston (2015)
33. Reillier, L.C., Reillier, B.: Platform Strategy: How to Unlock the Power of Communities and Networks to Grow Your Business. Routledge Taylor & Francis Group, London (2017)
34. Frankenberger, K., Weiblen, T., Csik, M., et al.: The 4I-framework of business model innovation: a structured view on process phases and challenges. IJPD **18**(3/4), 249 (2013). https://doi.org/10.1504/IJPD.2013.055012
35. Johnson, M.W., Christensen, C.M., Kagermann, H.: Reinventing your business model. HBR **86**(12), 57–68 (2008)

36. Johanson, J., Vahlne, J.-E.: The internationalization process of the firm—A model of knowledge development and increasing foreign market commitments. JIBS **8**(1), 23–32 (1977). https://doi.org/10.1057/palgrave.jibs.8490676
37. Whittington, R., Johnson, G., Scholes, K.: Exploring Corporate Strategy. Prentice Hall, Harlow (2005)
38. Demil, B., Lecocq, X.: Business model evolution: in search of dynamic consistency. LRP **43**(2–3), 227–246 (2010)

Digital Business Model Patterns of Big Pharmaceutical Companies - A Cluster Analysis

Cyrine Tangour[1]([⊠]) [iD], Marc Gebauer[2], Luise Fischer[1] [iD],
and Herwig Winkler[2]

[1] Fraunhofer Center for International Management and Knowledge
Economy – IMW, Leipzig, Germany
{cyrine.tangour, luise.fischer}@imw.fraunhofer.de
[2] Brandenburg University of Technology Cottbus - Senftenberg – BTU,
Cottbus, Germany
marc.gebauer@b-tu.de

Abstract. Digital technologies are changing numerous industries in a very short time, especially the healthcare sector. Many established companies want to become digital themselves. Our paper gives a brief overview of patterns of digital business model observed in the big pharmaceutical companies. The patterns vary in the degree of digitalization of the products and services, the value creating activities that can be in collaboration with technology firms or even competitors and the target of the product with regard to main milestones of the patient's medical journey. The results of the study are not limited to big pharmaceutical companies. The authors recommend the application of the results to other types of companies in the pharmaceutical industry and in other industries.

Keywords: Digital technologies · Digital business model patterns · Big pharmaceutical companies · Cluster analysis

1 Introduction

Digital technologies, such as artificial intelligence, sensor technology and mobile technology have already changed our society in many aspects. Providers of accommodation, mobility and communication services do not necessarily need to own hotels, taxis or telecommunication network infrastructures to be successful [1]. The examples of Airbnb, Uber and Skype have shown that digital technologies enable companies to provide best services without needing to own any assets [1]. Successful digital companies were able to develop innovative models to unlock and exploit the latent potential of the new digital technology and create a unique value proposition for the society. Because technology *per se* does not hold the sole power to create commercial success, it needs to be incorporated in valuable offers, and included in the design of so called business models [2]. A business model is a company's mental model that describes how it communicates, creates, delivers and captures value out of a value proposition

---

The original version of this chapter was revised: The name of the fourth author has been corrected. The correction to this chapter is available at https://doi.org/10.1007/978-3-030-30874-2_32

© Springer Nature Switzerland AG 2019
R. Jallouli et al. (Eds.): ICDEc 2019, LNBIP 358, pp. 397–412, 2019.
https://doi.org/10.1007/978-3-030-30874-2_31

[3]. Thus, a digital business model makes use of digital technologies in at least one of the business model's value dimensions.

Many scholars agree that companies in the digital economy are brandishing formidable new business models. The business model pattern called multi-sided platforms is one of the dominant designs of digital companies (e.g. [2, 4, 5]). However, life sciences companies have penetrated the digital economy with other business model patterns. The authors aim at creating valuable business model patterns, which could provide big pharma companies with new knowledge to enable them to secure their role in the digital health industry and serve as role models for other types of companies. The existing business model pattern literature (e.g. [3–5]) describes business model patterns from a large range of sectors. However this literature is neither easily adaptable for the specificities of e-health sector [6] nor is sufficient for the design of e-health business models [7]. Despite the fact that the research stream of business models have experienced a recent increase of interest [8], literature remains limited with regard to the business model innovation of life sciences companies [6]. A knowledge gap has been identified regarding the existence of sufficient knowledge to support health care companies such as big pharmaceutical companies, to create, deliver and capture new values from the digital technologies. In addition, the authors address a methodological shortcoming in the literature, especially regarding the methodologies and tools of the development of industry specific business model patterns.

The authors choose to focus on big pharmaceutical companies because of the higher challenge they face in transitioning to digital business models as well as the important role they play in the industry. While new entrants in the industry have more flexibility to develop innovative business models, established companies are more constrained by their prevailing business practices or so called path dependent behaviours [9]. The path dependent behaviours of established big pharmaceutical companies hinder their ability to unlock the latent value associated with digital technologies. Consequently, by identifying digital business model patterns for big pharmaceutical companies, one can understand how established firms are currently bringing innovative digital products to the market.

This paper is guided by a main research question: What are the patterns of digital business models observed for the big pharma companies? The authors conduct a cluster analysis of digital pharmaceutical products to identify new digital business models patterns. Based on the results of the cluster analysis pharmaceutical companies should have a more comprehensive understanding of what business model patterns they should pursue in the digital economy. The observed digital business model pattern can serve as guidance to other pharmaceutical companies wishing to venture on the path of digitalization.

The next section presents a review of the literature regarding the pharmaceutical business environment, applications of digital technologies in the pharmaceutical industry and the concept of business model innovation. Section 3 describes the paper's research design, the conceptual framework and the cluster analysis methodology. In Sect. 4, the authors present the main findings and discuss them in Sect. 5. Finally, the authors conclude the paper by discussing practical applications, indicating study limitations and suggesting further research possibilities.

2 Literature Review

2.1 Pharmaceutical Business Environment

The pharmaceutical industry consists of a network of companies that ensure the discovery, development, production, distribution and marketing of different types of medicines [10]. This industry is highly regulated (e.g. patenting, clinical trials, marketing authorization), it shows a long time lag between investment and revenues, and high financial risks attributed to research and development (R&D) [11]. In fact, health care payers - agencies or organizations that are responsible for paying for medical treatments- have a policy of reimbursement of medicines based on performance by comparing the relative (clinical) effectiveness, safety, and cost of two or more therapies used to treat the same condition [12]. The pharmaceutical industry is heavily dependent on innovation and the rapid adoption of new technologies to remain competitive in the healthcare sector [11, 13] and get high reimbursement rates for its products.

Nowadays, key actors of the pharmaceutical environment are large branded products multinationals, large generic multinationals, local pharmaceutical companies and biotechnology companies. Large generic multinationals develop and manufacture pharmaceutical products after the expiration of their patents. Local pharmaceutical companies manufacture both generic and branded products under license or contract basis. Biotechnology companies are the new entrants in the industry since they have a focus on biotechnology research and drug discovery with limited to absent manufacturing capabilities. Finally, large branded products multinationals, also called big pharma companies, are companies with necessary capabilities and assets for discovering, patenting, developing, manufacturing, and distributing innovative products [10]. Big pharmaceutical companies are investing highly in R&D activities. This type of company represents 30% of the world top 50 companies in the fiscal year 2017/2018 with a total amount of 84007.9 million euros in R&D investment. The commercial success of the big pharmaceutical companies is underpinned by the so-called blockbuster business model [13]. It is a business model pattern, which builds on the ability of a company to make the large share of its turnovers based only on one, or few products form her portfolio. The blockbuster drugs have an annual global revenue greater than $1 billion [13]. The blockbuster product is more profitable (relatively higher returns) than lower value drugs while a valid drug patent guarantees a monopoly for the firm.

In the case of the diffusion of biotechnology in the pharmaceutical industry, business model portfolios of big pharma companies evolved, from only in-house innovation that builds on secrecy to include open innovation practices that span outside of the firm's boundaries [14]. Similarly, the introduction of digital technologies requires new types of business models of the big pharmaceutical companies.

2.2 Digital Technologies in the Pharmaceutical Industry

The bourgeoning literature stream on the impact of digital technologies on the pharmaceutical industry has just started to takeoff. In fact these new technologies, such as artificial intelligence or augmented reality, provide new possibilities to improve the treatment of diseases that traditional approaches fall short of [15] and are also one of the most important factors for growth in health technologies [16]. Especially with the increasing costs of modern drug development (average \$US 2.56B per new medicine) [17], big pharma companies need to turn to digital technologies to innovate in their products and keep their competitiveness. For instance, digital therapeutics are a new type of therapy that either complements traditional treatment, or even offers alternative treatments to drugs, such as sensory stimuli delivered through mobile devices to treat psychiatric diseases [7, 16, 17]. So far, recent scientific literature has not yet establish a precise definition of what digital pharmaceutical products are. Terms like digital therapeutics and digital combined products are timidly surfacing in the literature. According to [17 p. 72] "Digital therapeutics represent a new treatment modality in which digital systems such as smartphone apps are used as regulatory-approved, prescribed therapeutic interventions to treat medical conditions". For instance, Proteus Digital Health is a technology firm or so-called digital therapeutics company that developed a smart pill (Abilify MyCite®) - in collaboration with Otsuka Pharmaceutical (pharmaceutical company)- that is the first FDA approved digital therapeutic on the market [18].

Digital technologies can for example facilitate personalized healthcare as well as dosing and treatment duration. With sensor technology blood pressure, mobility, posture, skin conductance, oxygen levels, respiration, temperature, sleep, heart rate can be monitored and medical treatment adjusted accordingly [19]. Monitoring health conditions can result in "...increased accuracy, reduced need for clinical site visits, shift from treatment to prevention [...] streamlined clinical decision-making..." [20 p. 9].

Also purely pharmaceutical processes, like the delivery of drugs, can be made more efficient by using digital technologies such as deep leaning [16]. According to [16, 21] 43,000 health related apps were found in the iTunes repository in 2013. The apps focus on treatments for hypertension, obesity, asthma or diabetes as well as supporting behavioral changes considering smoking, sports and nutrition [16]. Thus digital technologies are enabling companies to transform from a product focused to more service oriented business models [19, 22].

Big pharmaceutical companies need to deliver new digitally enabled solutions for the highly unmet medical needs to remain compatible and to overcome the competitive threat of new entrants such as technology firms. Therefore, in this paper, the authors look for new digital business model patterns that can support patients improve in disease awareness, diagnosis or self-management of their condition across a wide range of therapy areas.

2.3   Business Model Innovation

Scholars and practitioners attribute the success of companies driven by digital technologies like Apple, Uber and Amazon to well-designed and executed business models e.g. [23]. According to [24] "a mediocre technology pursued with a great business model may be more valuable than a great technology exploited via a mediocre business model" [24 p. 354]. New technologies like the digital ones need to be commercialized with a suitable or innovative business model [25]. So far, there is no agreement upon the definition of the term business model. Existing and frequently cited definitions reach from "...stories that explain how enterprises work..." [26 p. 87] to "...a conceptual tool that contains a set of elements and their relationships…" [27 p. 10]. For the purpose of this article a business model is "…a representation of a firm's underlying logic and strategic choices for creating and capturing value within a value network" [28 p. 202]. The logic of value creation and value capture can be defined, not only for companies, but also for business fields or even singular products [29]. Generic frameworks with a set of business model dimensions are used to analyze and describe business models. For this article we use the business model dimensions value proposition, value creation, value delivery and value capture [3, 4]. Each value dimension can be described in terms of one or more elements. For instance, customer segments and distribution channels are the elements of the value delivery [3, 4]. In a specific business model an elements can have more than one attribute. For instance in the framework of [4] customer segments has three attributes, namely: specific new customer segment, lock-in existing customers and other companies (B2B). Furthermore, the authors consider that a business model innovation is any modification or novelty of at least one the value dimensions' elements [5, 27].

In spite of the high interest of researchers and practitioners and the acceleration of publication rate, the fields of business models and business model innovation remains under-researched and need more scrutiny from the research community (e.g. [8]). More specific methodologies and tools for the process of business model innovation need to be developed [30]. According to [4], business model patterns are a powerful tool which help conducting systematic business model innovation. Business model patterns are defined in a different way by several authors. In this paper they are defined according to [2] as "…business models with similar characteristics, similar arrangements of business model building blocks…" [2 p. 55]. One of the most well-known set of business model patterns is the one by [5]. They provide 55 patterns of innovative business models like razors/blades or freemium, which provide orientation and source of inspiration when designing a business model innovation. Previous research shows that using business model pattern to innovate in specific e-health service increase their viability [7]. Consequently, business model patterns allow researchers and practitioners to capture the essence of successful business models and to have possibilities for reuse and combinations [3, 4, 6]. Managers in the pharmaceutical industry can benefit highly from business model patterns that are specific to their industry. In the next section, the authors present a conceptual framework of business model attributes used to assess, empirically, the digital business models of the big pharmaceutical companies. By using cluster analysis, the authors structure the data collected and deduce new digital business model patterns.

3 Methods and Designs

3.1 Conceptual Framework

The conceptual framework is developed based on the existing research of [3, 4, 8] on business model dimensions and on industry specific elements identified from the practitioners' web pages and journals. The authors found that certain elements, which are essential for pharmaceutical companies, such as the aim of the product along the patient journey - Prevention, diagnostic, Treatment- are not included in generic business model frameworks. Adding industry specific attributes for the business model elements is in line with [4, 31]. As shown in Table 1, the conceptual framework has four so called value dimensions, i.e. value proposition, value delivery, value creation and value capture as described in the business model elements of [3, 4]. The elements *customer segments*, *key partnerships* and *revenue streams* are based on [2–4] and the element *degree of digitalization* was only mentioned in [4]. Because the element *aim of the product* does not figure in the literature but is highly relevant for the pharmaceutical industry it was added to the framework.

Table 1. Conceptual framework for the business model patterns

Dimension	Elements	Attributes	Description
Value proposition	Degree of digitalization	Purely digital	Only digital software and digital hardware
		Combined products	Bundle of a physical product (e.g. pill), digital hardware (e.g. sensor) and digital software
		Digitally enabled	Bundle of physical product (e.g. medical device) and digital software
	Aim of the product	Prevention	Any manoeuvre intended to minimise the incidence or effects of disease
		Diagnostic	Action serving to identify a particular disease; characteristic
		Treatment	Combating of a disease or disorder; called also therapy
Value delivery	Customer segments	Patient/potential Patient	A person who is/might be ill or is/might be undergoing treatment for disease
		Health professional	One who treat patients and promote wellness in a clinic environment
Value creation	Key partnerships	None	
		Cooperation	Collaboration with other companies except for competitors
		Coopetition	Cooperation between competitors
Value capture	Revenue stream	Sell	To exchange or deliver for money
		Free	To exchange or deliver for no money

3.2 Data Collection and Analysis

Nine pharmaceutical companies (see Appendix 2, Table 3) were selected among the top 20 companies with revenue greater than $10 billion [32], on highest global market-based sales in 2017 [33] and having a market capitalization (NASDAQ Market Cap) higher than 1billion dollars [34].

The authors used secondary data sources to collect information regarding the name and description of the pharmaceutical companies' digital products and the business models used or planned to commercialize them (based on the framework in Table 1). Data were collected from companies' websites, practitioner magazines such as MobilHealthNews that is a publication of the Healthcare Information and Management Systems Society and both digital stores for smartphone application (app), i.e. Google Play Store (Android apps) and Apple App Store (iOS apps). A total of 90 sources were analysed based on the methodology of qualitative content analysis using the conceptual framework as coding system. The qualitative content analysis is a research method used to examine qualitative data, such as in documents and communication artefacts, in a replicable and systematic manner [35]. The sources were coded manually using the MAXQDA 12 software based on the approach of Directed Content Analysis [36].

The qualitative content analysis led to the creation of a data set of 53 digital products each described according to the presence or absence of the attributes of the conceptual framework. Then the method of cluster analysis where used to design the digital business model patterns in a systematic way.

3.3 Cluster Analysis

Cluster analysis is a multivariate method, which were used to classify the sample of objects in this case 53 digital pharmaceutical products identified, into relatively homogenous groups or clusters. Objects in our case are the pharmaceutical products and classification characteristics are the attributes of conceptual framework. As proposed by [31] a hierarchical cluster analysis is an appropriate method that can be used to find business model patterns. Cluster analysis is the only quantitative empirical method used for the identification of business model patterns [31, 37]. Similarly, to [31] the authors gave N characteristics to each object. The characteristics were attributed a binary coding (1 for presence of the characteristic in the object and 0 for its absence). The Euclidian distance was used to measure the homogeneity of the objects. The ward method was used for creating groups of the objects, which were then depicted in a dendrogram to discuss sets of suitable patterns. Thus, the business models are compared concerning their similarities in their industry specific business model elements.

4 Empirical Findings

The cluster analysis resulted in a dendrogram (see Fig. 1 in the Appendix 1) that shows the different steps of the grouping process of 53 digital products according to the similarity index (Euclidian distance). The clustering process resulted in six different cluster that are described in Table 2. The list of the pharmaceutical products and the pharmaceutical firms for each cluster is presented in Table 3 (appendix).

Table 2. Descriptive table of the clusters

Cluster number	1	2	3	4	5	6
Number of firms	4	5	5	3	4	6
Number of pharmaceutical products	10	7	11	7	7	11

The authors decided that at least four clusters out of six were suitable to constitute business model patterns considering the similarity of the groups's elements. The authors decided that similarity showed in the clusters number 3 and 6 are not enough to devise clear business model patterns. The clusters number 1, 2, 4 and 5 are described in more details in the following.

4.1   Cluster N° 1: Sell Digital Products to Health Professional for Diagnostic

The cluster appear relatively heterogeneous and consists of a total of ten products owned by Abbott, Bayer, MSD and GSK. The range of products include all three degrees of digitalization from intelligent contrast injectors for radiology use (Bayer's MEDRAD® MRXperion) to an app for dentists to update their knowledge (GSK discovery).

The cluster includes products that target only health professionals with the aim to support them improving their diagnostics abilities. For example, the CTEPH Pattern Recognition Artificial Intelligence Software of Bayer and MSD is an excellent example of purely digital product. The chronic thromboembolic pulmonary hypertension (CTEPH) is a rare form of pulmonary hypertension and a life-threatening condition (5 individuals per million per year globally) that is difficult to diagnose because of the similarity of its symptoms to other condition such as Asthma [38]. Radiologists may have the first opportunity to diagnose the disease. That is why the software uses deep learning technology that identifies signs of the disease in scans and images to better support decision-making processes of radiologists.

In addition, in this cluster the products are developed mostly by one big pharmaceutical company alone or in collaboration with a competitor (in one object) and the revenue model is simply to sell it (except for one object). The GSK discovery, an educational app for dentists is given free of charge.

4.2   Cluster N° 2: Free Disease Management Platforms Developed with Partners

The cluster appear relatively homogeneous in terms of business model attributes and display apps or mobile-based platforms owned by Novartis, Pfizer, Novo Nordisk, MSD and GSK. The value proposition consists of products that are purely digital such as Novartis's Galaxies of Hope, a digital storytelling app that supports neuroendocrine tumour cancer patient in coping with their condition through a multimodal approach. Interestingly, the big pharmaceutical companies have all cooperated with non-competing companies to create the value though their apps. For instance, Novartis teamed up with the video game company Numinous Games to develop Galaxies of Hope and Pfizer's Quitter's Circle app was developed in partnership with the American Lung Association. Another examples is the one of Merck and Healthy Interactions, who have launched map4health™, a platform for diabetes management. Map4health™ is designed to support patients monitor personal health goals and engage them in taking a more active role in managing their health. The app uses in-person counselling programs developed by Healthy Interactions that is a health company offering programs for chronic disease management and education in digital and in-person format.

This cluster regroups health products that aim at treating patients as well as preventing the occurrence of a disease or complications of health conditions. All apps are provided to patients or health professionals free of charge.

4.3   Cluster N° 4: Free Apps for the Prevention of Diseases

In this cluster, firms are Pfizer, Novartis and GSK, and they developed only digital products in the form of apps. For instance, Pfizer's LivingWith™ is a cancer support app and HemMobile™ is a app for people living with hemophilia. HemMobile™ allow logging of events such as bleeds, transfusions and activities either manually or automatically by using HealthKit. Healthkit is a new Health app introduced by Apple in 2014 alongside iOS 8 for storing, managing, and sharing health data [18]. By using the app, patients can better monitor their condition, easily share new status with doctors and reduce the occurrence of complications. All apps are provided free of charge to patients only.

4.4   Cluster N° 5: Free Apps to Support Patient's Treatment

In the following cluster, Johnson & Johnson, Pfizer, Bayer and Abbvie developed only digitally enabled products in the form of apps. Interestingly all the digital products of Abbvie are included in this cluster. For instance, Ori for Me™ is an app that manage the treatment of patient that are being prescribed Orilissa™ (elagolix). Orilissa™ is an FDA-approved oral pill that is sold by Abbvie for women with moderate to severe endometriosis pain [39]. The app is designed to treat a medical condition by creating value in combination with the intake of the drug. Companies in this cluster have developed the apps internally with no collaboration with key actors cited. All apps are provided free of charge to patients only.

5   Discussion

The findings of this study clearly show that the process of analyzing and classifying the 53 digital pharmaceutical products has yielded new insights into the general attributes of digital business models for big pharmaceutical companies. The four patterns identified provide a first perception of the underlying differences of the various ways of creating, delivering and capturing value from digital health related value proposition. The results show that pharmaceutical companies are providers of health products of all ranges of digitalization, from a simple app for locating the next store that sells Robitussin products (Pfizer's Robitussin Relief Finder 2.0) to artificial intelligence software capable of interpreting images and scans as good as a radiologist (Bayer and MSD's CTEPH Pattern Recognition Artificial Intelligence Software). Moreover, even though big pharmaceutical companies have integrated the development of these digital software (mainly apps) into their core activities, they are still building connections to exiting platforms such as Apple health app suite (ResearchKit, HealthKit and CareKit)

[34] and Google's Fitbit [35]. For instance, in 2019, Merck launched a new Fitbit-powered study in collaboration with National Sleep Foundation to investigate whether wearable sleep trackers could play a role in the treatment of insomnia by equipping patients and their doctors with data from Fitbit devices.

In addition, new products are targeting both patients and healthcare professionals. This denotes of a tendency of companies towards disintermediation – the creation of channels of direct value delivery to the final customers. The disintermediation is a general business model pattern that has been attributed to the success of Dell, which succeeded in delivering its products directly to its end-customers without going through retailers [3, 5]. However, such business model pattern is not possible in the pharmaceutical industry, because of regulatory constraints on the matter of direct interaction with patients. Consequently, digital technologies are offering big pharmaceutical company a direct channel to interact with their end-customers.

Interestingly there is rather a low variety regarding the revenue streams pursued by the pharmaceutical companies. It was observed often that the selected firms either give apps free of charge or sell medical devices or drugs together with their enabling digital technology. Finally, the combination of medical devices, sensors and digital software is found often in the area of diagnostics, while apps are mostly aiming at preventive medicine or enhancing outcomes of established treatments. This is in line with recent literature. According to [17], deep learning and artificial intelligence are a natural fit for analyzing medical images. They see that artificial intelligence will assist radiologists because of its ability to teach computers to recognize objects in pictures and to build patterns [17]. This could make diagnosis faster, cheaper and thus more accessible [17]. However, healthcare professionals have mixed feelings about the technology, because of the threat of substitution that the machines might constitute. Interestingly, [17] argue that far from replacing radiologists, artificial intelligence enables machines to see nuances that humans cannot and thus radiologists will be able to create a unique value based on their intuition and expertise [17].

Because the pharmaceutical industry is highly regulated, new guidelines might emerge that potentially reduce the attractiveness of the recommended digital business model patterns. In fact, regulatory authorities such as US Food and Drug Administration (FDA) are facing challenges in defining the appropriate frameworks to guaranty the efficiency, safety and quality of digital products such as smart pills [37] without hindering the innovative momentum of the industry. In 2017, Abilify MyCite® (Proteus Digital Health and Otsuka Pharmaceutical) was the first FDA approved, smart pill on the market [38]. The pill (aripiprazole), that has an ingestible sensor, is prescribed for the treatment of schizophrenia [38]. Consequently, the smart pill can record if patients have been observant of their treatments thanks to its embedded sensor that records when the medication was taken. Recently, the FDA has started granting digital medical products, such as the CTEPH pattern recognition software from Bayer and MSD, with the breakthrough device designation [31]. In fact, the FDA is taking significant steps to uncover the appropriate regulatory framework for the approval of drugs and medical devices that are combined with digital products. However, pharmaceutical professionals fear that the measures taken would decelerate the rate of digital innovation in the industry [40].

6 Conclusion

Patients are different because of their genetic constitution and social environment, which is why the one-size-fits-all solution cannot be the most adequate for all human beings. The ability to define precisely the specificities of individuals in sickness and health has been revolutionized by the emergence of digital technologies. The aim of this study was to develop digital business model patterns to support big pharmaceutical companies in devising digital innovation in the healthcare sector. The identification of the patterns is based on a cluster analysis of pharmaceutical products with various degrees of digitalization. As a result, the authors found four cluster describing new digital business model patterns that can support patients improve in disease awareness, diagnosis or self-management of their condition across a wide range of therapy areas. Thus, the patterns vary in terms of value proposition, value creation, value delivery and value capture, i.e., the degree of digitalization of the products or services, the collaboration with technology firms or even competitors and by the target of the product with regard to the patient's medical journey and the revenue stream.

The methodology of cluster analysis have been already used in business model literature to create industry specific business model patterns. Nonetheless, there are limitations to our procedure. First, the project of clustering the whole business model portfolio of an entire pharmaceutical company is very ambitious. Consequently, insights related to how a company's business model portfolio is evolving to integrate identified digital products among other innovative products, such as new biological drugs, could not be derived from the data. Second, the choice of companies and products might be enriched in number. In addition, the attributes used to describe the business model elements are chosen with a degree of subjectivity. Finally, the authors applied only the ward algorithm in combination with the Euclidian distance for identifying business model patterns. Other algorithms of hierarchical cluster analysis as well as other measures of quality of the clustering might be suitable as well and could provide different groupings of business models.

This paper enriches business model literature by providing a systematic method (cluster analysis) to capture empirical data and transform them into business model patterns that play an important role in the process of business model innovation. Furthermore, the paper contributes to the scholarly debate about digital technologies adoption and diffusion in the pharmaceutical industry by providing new ways for companies to capture a share of the value they create.

The results of the study and the four business model patterns are not limited to big pharmaceutical companies and the authors encourage possible application of the patterns for other types of companies in the pharmaceutical industry as well as in other industries. The authors suggest that future research topic in the stream of business model design and innovation could deal further with developing methods and tools to support companies in managing the transition toward new digital business models. In fact, the transformation of business model portfolios of entire pharmaceutical companies would be very interesting for future research.

Appendix 1

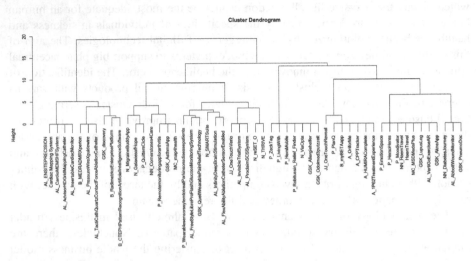

Fig. 1. Dendrogram of a cluster analysis of 53 digital business models of pharmaceutical products from nine top pharmaceutical companies.

Appendix 2

Table 3. Descriptive table of the clusters including firms and products names

	Firms	Digital products
Cluster 1	Abbott Laboratories	ENSITE PRECISION™ Cardiac Mapping System
		CardioMEMS™ HF System
		Advisor™ HD Grid Mapping Catheter
		Insertable Cardiac Monitor
		PressureWire™ X guidewire
		TactiCath Quartz™ Contact Force Ablation Catheter
	GlaxoSmithKline	GSK discovery
	Bayer	MEDRAD® MRXperion
		Radimetrics™ Enterprise Platform
	Bayer and MSD*	CTEPH Pattern Recognition Artificial Intelligence Software
Cluster 2	Novartis	Migraine Buddy app
		Galaxies of Hope
	Pfizer	Quitter's Cicle
		Remote monitoring app for arthritis (in clinical trial)
	Novo Nordisk	Cornerstones4Care®
	GlaxoSmithKline	AsthmaApp
	MSD *	map4health™

(continued)

Table 3. (*continued*)

	Firms	Digital products
Cluster 3	Pfizer	Wearable sensors system to treat Parkinson's disease patients
	Abbott Laboratories	FreeStyle Libre Pro Flash Glucose Monitoring System
		ProclaimTM SCS System
		Infinity™ Deep Brain Stimulation
		FlexAbility™ Ablation Catheter, Sensor Enabled™
		Invisible Trial System™
	GlaxoSmithKline	Quell Wearable Pain Relief Technology
	Johnson & Johnson	OneTouch® Verio®
	Novartis	SMART Suite
		reSET-O™
		THRIVE™
Cluster 4	Pfizer	ZeckTag
		LivingWith™
		HemMobile
		Robitussin Relief Finder 2.0
	Novartis	ViaOpta
	GlaxoSmithKline	Allergiehelfer
		Odol-med3 putzzeit
Cluster 5	Johnson & Johnson	OneTouch Reveal®
	Pfizer	Plan Q
	Bayer	myBETAapp™
	Abbvie	HUMIRA Complete
		1.62% Treatment Experience™
		CPP Tracker
		Ori for Me
Cluster 6	Pfizer	Emotion Space
		HemoHeres!
		Moodivator
	Novo Nordisk	Diabetes Journey
		HaemTravel
	MSD *	MSD MedsPlus
	Abbott Laboratories	VertiGo Exercise (AR)
		Abbott Wound Monitor (AWM)
	GlaxoSmithKline	Akne App
		LupusLog
		PneumoDoc

*Merck & Co. is called MSD in the USA.

References

1. Gassmann, O., Frankenberger, K., Sauer, R.: Exploring the Field of Business Model Innovation: New Theoretical Perspectives. Palgrave Pivot. Palgrave Macmillan, Cham (2016)
2. Osterwalder, A., Pigneur, Y.: Business Model Generation: A Handbook for Visionaries, Game Changers, and Challengers. Wiley, Hoboken (2010)
3. Abdelkafi, N., Makhotin, S., Posselt, T.: Business model innovations for electric mobility: what can be learned from existing business model patterns? Int. J. Innov. Manag. 17(01), 1340003 (2013). https://doi.org/10.1142/s1363919613400033
4. Remane, G., Hanelt, A., Tesch, J.F., et al.: The business model pattern database—: a tool for systematic business model innovation. Int. J. Innov. Manag. 21(01), 1750004 (2017). https://doi.org/10.1142/s1363919617500049. (61 Pages)
5. Gassmann, O., Frankenberger, K., Csik, M.: The Business Model Navigator: 55 Models that Will Revolutionise Your Business. Pearson, Harlow (2014)
6. Sprenger, M., Mettler, T.: On the utility of e-health business model design patterns. In: 24th European Conference on Information Systems (ECIS) 2016. Bogaziçi University, Istanbul, Turkey, pp. 1–16 (2016)
7. Sprenger, M.: Supporting the viability of e-health services with pattern-based business model design. In: Li, H., Nykänen, P., Suomi, R., Wickramasinghe, N., Widén, G., Zhan, M. (eds.) WIS 2016. CCIS, vol. 636, pp. 161–175. Springer, Cham (2016). https://doi.org/10.1007/978-3-319-44672-1_14
8. Foss, N.J., Saebi, T.: Fifteen years of research on business model innovation. JOM 43(1), 200–227 (2017). https://doi.org/10.1177/0149206316675927
9. Bohnsack, R., Pinkse, J., Kolk, A.: Business models for sustainable technologies: exploring business model evolution in the case of electric vehicles. Res. Policy 43(2), 284–300 (2014). https://doi.org/10.1016/j.respol.2013.10.014
10. Mehralian, G., Rajabzadeh Gatari, A., Morakabati, M., et al.: Developing a suitable model for supplier selection based on supply chain risks: an empirical study from Iranian pharmaceutical companies. Iran J. Pharm. Res. 11(1), 209–219 (2012)
11. Sabatier, V., Mangematin, V., Rousselle, T.: From recipe to dinner: business model portfolios in the European biopharmaceutical industry. Long Range Plan. 43(2–3), 431–447 (2010). https://doi.org/10.1016/j.lrp.2010.02.001
12. Chalkidou, K., Tunis, S., Lopert, R., et al.: Comparative effectiveness research and evidence-based health policy: experience from four countries. Milbank Q. 87(2), 339–367 (2009). https://doi.org/10.1111/j.1468-0009.2009.00560.x
13. Gassmann, O., Reepmeyer, G., Zedtwitz, M.: Leading pharmaceutical innovation: trends and drivers for growth in the pharmaceutical industry, 2nd edn. Springer, Heidelberg (2008). https://doi.org/10.1007/978-3-540-77636-9
14. Schuhmacher, A., Gassmann, O., Hinder, M.: Changing R&D models in research-based pharmaceutical companies. J. Transl. Med. 14(1), 105 (2016). https://doi.org/10.1186/s12967-016-0838-4
15. Lee, M., Ly, H., Möller, C.C., et al.: Innovation in regulatory science is meeting evolution of clinical evidence generation. Clin. Pharmacol. Ther. 105, 886–898 (2019). https://doi.org/10.1002/cpt.1354
16. Pinto, M.D., Greenblatt, A.M., Hickman, R.L., et al.: Assessing the critical parameters of eSMART-MH: a promising avatar-based digital therapeutic intervention to reduce depressive symptoms. Perspect. Psychiatr. Care 52(3), 157–168 (2016). https://doi.org/10.1111/ppc.12112

17. Sverdlov, O., van Dam, J., Hannesdottir, K., et al.: Digital therapeutics: an integral component of digital innovation in drug development. Clin. Pharmacol. Ther. **104**(1), 72–80 (2018)

18. Inc A HealthKit - Apple Developer. https://developer.apple.com/healthkit/. Accessed 15 Feb 2019

19. Rodarte, C.: Pharmaceutical perspective: how digital biomarkers and contextual data will enable therapeutic environments. Digit Biomark. **1**, 73–81 (2017). https://doi.org/10.1159/000479951

20. Smith, B., Sverdlov, A.: Digital technology: the future is bright. Clin. Pharmacol. Ther. **104**(1), 9–11 (2018)

21. Robert Wood Johnson Foundation: Assessment Report (2013). https://www.rwjf.org/en/library/research/2013/12/2013-assessment-report.html. Accessed 15 Feb 2019

22. Ernst & Young Global Limited: How to manage disruptions to gain competitive advantage (2017). https://www.ey.com/en_gl/life-sciences/how-to-manage-disruptions-to-gain-compe titive-advantage. Accessed 15 Feb 2019

23. Koen, P.A., Bertels, H.M.J., Elsum, I.R.: The three faces of business model innovation: challenges for established firms. Res. Technol. Manag. **54**(3), 52–59 (2011). https://doi.org/10.5437/08953608x5403009

24. Chesbrough, H.: Business model innovation: opportunities and barriers. Long Range Plan. **43**(2–3), 354–363 (2010). https://doi.org/10.1016/j.lrp.2009.07.010

25. Chesbrough, H., Rosenbloom, R.S.: The role of business model in capturing value from innovation: evidence from Xerox Corporation's technology spinn-off companies, **11**(3), 529–555 (2002)

26. Magretta, J.: Why business models Matter. Harv. Bus. Rev. **80**(5), 86–92 (2002)

27. Osterwalder, A., Pigneur, Y., Tucci, C.L.: Clarifying business models: origins, present, and future of the concept. Commun. Assoc. Inf. Syst. (15), 1–43 (2005)

28. Shafer, S.M., Smith, H.J., Linder, J.C.: The power of business models. Bus. Horiz. **48**(3), 199–207 (2005). https://doi.org/10.1016/j.bushor.2004.10.014

29. Schallmo, D., Brecht, L.: Business model innovation in business-to-business markets -: procedure and examples. Paper presented at the 3rd ISPIM Innovation Symposium: "Managing the Art of Innovation: Turning Concepts into Reality", Quebec City, Canada (2010)

30. Spieth, P., Schneckenberg, D., Ricart, J.E.: Business model innovation - state of the art and future challenges for the field. R&D Manag. **44**(3), 237–247 (2014). https://doi.org/10.1111/radm.12071

31. Morris, M.H., Shirokova, G., Shatalov, A.: The business model and firm performance: the case of russian food service ventures. JSBM **51**(1), 46–65 (2013)

32. Wikipedia: List of largest pharmaceutical companies by revenue – Wikipedia (2019). https://en.wikipedia.org/w/index.php?oldid=883348703. Accessed 14 Feb 2019

33. Top 50 Global Pharma Companies - 2018 (Pharmaceutical Executive)—Ranking The Brands. https://www.rankingthebrands.com/The-Brand-Rankings.aspx?rankingID=370. Accessed 14 Feb 2019

34. Health Care Companies. https://www.nasdaq.com/screening/companies-by-industry.aspx?industry=Health+Care. Accessed 14 Feb 2019

35. Bryman, A., Bell, E.: Business Research Methods, 3rd edn. Oxford University Press, Oxford (2011)

36. Hsieh, H.-F., Shannon, S.E.: Three approaches to qualitative content analysis. Qual. Health Res. **15**(9), 1277–1288 (2005). https://doi.org/10.1177/1049732305276687

37. Camisón, C., Villar-López, A.: Business models in Spanish industry: a taxonomy-based efficacy analysis. M@n@gement **13**(4), 298 (2010). https://doi.org/10.3917/mana.134.0298

38. Communications BAG FDA grants breakthrough device designation to artificial intelligence software for CTEPH pattern recognition from Bayer and MSD - Bayer News. https://media. bayer.com/baynews/baynews.nsf/id/FDA-grants-breakthrough-device-designation-artificial-intelligence-software-CTEPH-pattern. Accessed 14 Feb 2019
39. ORILISSA™ (elagolix) 150 mg or 200 mg Tablets (2019). https://www.orilissa.com/about/what-is-orilissa. Accessed 15 Feb 2019
40. Mobihealthnews: FDA's new draft guidance could hinder applications for digital combination products (2019). https://www.mobihealthnews.com/content/fdas-new-draft-guidance-could-hinder-applications-digital-combination-products. Accessed 15 Feb 2019

Correction to: Digital Business Model Patterns of Big Pharmaceutical Companies - A Cluster Analysis

Cyrine Tangour(iD), Marc Gebauer, Luise Fischer(iD),
and Herwig Winkler

Correction to:
Chapter "Digital Business Model Patterns of Big
Pharmaceutical Companies - A Cluster Analysis"
in: R. Jallouli et al. (Eds.): *Digital Economy*, LNBIP 358,
https://doi.org/10.1007/978-3-030-30874-2_31

In the originally published version of this chapter, the name of the fourth author Herwig Winkler was incorrect. The name of the author has been corrected.

The updated version of this chapter can be found at
https://doi.org/10.1007/978-3-030-30874-2_31

Author Index

Abbassi, Imed   147
Abdallah, Farid   15
Abdallah, Mira   43
Abdelkafi, Nizar   373
Abouyounes, Rania   266
Al-Sabri, Rami   66
Amor, Nahla Ben   305
Antoun, Racquel   253

Barnes, Stuart J.   315
Bassil, Carole   133
Ben HajKacem, Mohamed Aymen   289
Ben Zammel, Ibticem   239
Bilgic, Emrah   173

Charfi, Ahmed Anis   323
Choubassi, Hassan   194
Chtouka, Eya   305

Daoud, Mouna Karoui   352
Dokic, Kristian   203
Duan, Yanqing   173

Elhoss, Walid   15
Essoussi, Nadia   289

Fischer, Luise   397

Gaaloul, Walid   147
Gadasina, Lyudmila   3
Gebauer, Marc   397
Gopane, Thabo J.   53
Graiet, Mohamed   147
Guezguez, Wided   305

Haidar, Rim   253
Hajj-Hassan, Mohamad   278
Hamzagic, Enes   110
Hamzaoui, Wafa   110
Hariri, Nizar   253
Hasrouny, Hamssa   133
Haugk, Sebastian   387
Hussein, Bassam   278

Ivanova, Victoriia   3

Jallouli, Rim   87, 183
Jarikji, Yasmine   278

Kaabi, Safa   183
Kamoun, Karim   157
Kassabli Al Fakhry, Caroline   342
Khayat, Sarah   194
Koubaa, Hasna   87
Koubaa, Yamen   120

Laouiti, Anis   133
Lauc, Tomislava   203
Lezina, Tatiana   3

Makki, Mohammad   43
Markfort, Lino   387
Mbarek, Rabeb   215
Mbazaia, Oumaima   157
Medjani, Fares   120
Momdjian, Levon   230

Najar, Tharwa   239

Radisic, Bojan   203
Rutter, Richard   315
Rziga, Kenza   289

Samhat, Abed Ellatif   133
Say, Arem   239
Sharara, Sahar   194
Shouman, Dina   230
Sinno, Nadine   29
Sliman, Layth   147
Stoianova, Olga   3

Tangour, Cyrine   373, 387, 397
Tournois, Nadine   110
Touzani, Mourad   323
Trigui, Imene Trabelsi   352

Vienken, Claudia   373

Winkler, Herwig   397